OBJECTI
(Num

For Competitive Examinations
conducted by
Banks, L.I.C., G.I.C., Excise, Income Tax, Railways, Hotels, U.P.S.C.,
Forest Services, Defence Services, S.S.C. & other departments

R.S. AGGARWAL
M.Sc., Ph.D.

Dear Students,
  Do not buy pirated editions. Many of our best selling titles have been unlawfully printed by unscrupulous persons. Your sincere effort in this direction may stop piracy and save intellectuals' rights.
  For authentication of this book check the 3-D hologram.

S. CHAND
AN ISO 9001 : 2000 COMPANY

S. CHAND & COMPANY LTD.
RAM NAGAR, NEW DELHI-110 055

S. CHAND & COMPANY LTD.
(An ISO 9001 : 2000 Company)
Head Office : 7361, RAM NAGAR, NEW DELHI - 110 055
Phones : 23672080-81-82, 9899107446, 9911310888;
Fax : 91-11-23677446
Shop at: **schandgroup.com**; E-mail: **schand@vsnl.com**

Branches :
- 1st Floor, Heritage, Near Gujarat Vidhyapeeth, Ashram Road, **Ahmedabad**-380 014. Ph. 27541965, 27542369.
- No. 6, Ahuja Chambers, 1st Cross, Kumara Krupa Road, **Bangalore**-560 001. Ph : 22268048, 22354008
- 238-A M.P. Nagar, Zone 1, **Bhopal** - 462 011. Ph : 4274723
- 152, Anna Salai, **Chennai**-600 002. Ph : 28460026
- S.C.O. 6, 7 & 8, Sector 9D, **Chandigarh**-160017, Ph-2749376, 2749377
- 1st Floor, Bhartia Tower, Badambadi, **Cuttack**-753 009, Ph-2332580; 2332581
- 1st Floor, 52-A, Rajpur Road, **Dehradun**-248 001. Ph : 2740889, 2740861
- Pan Bazar, **Guwahati**-781 001. Ph : 2514155
- Sultan Bazar, **Hyderabad**-500 195. Ph : 24651135, 24744815
- Mai Hiran Gate, **Jalandhar** - 144008 . Ph. 2401630
- A-14 Janta Store Shopping Complex, University Marg, Bapu Nagar, **Jaipur** - 302 015, Phone : 2709153
- 613-7, M.G. Road, Ernakulam, **Kochi**-682 035. Ph : 2381740
- 285/J, Bipin Bihari Ganguli Street, **Kolkata**-700 012. Ph : 22367459, 22373914
- Mahabeer Market, 25 Gwynne Road, Aminabad, **Lucknow**-226 018. Ph : 2626801, 2284815
- Blackie House, 103/5, Walchand Hirachand Marg , Opp. G.P.O., **Mumbai**-400 001. Ph : 22690881, 22610885
- Karnal Bag, Model Mill **Chowk**, Umrer Road, Nagpur-440 032 Ph : 2723901, 2777666
- 104, Citicentre Ashok, Govind Mitra Road, **Patna**-800 004. Ph : 2300489, 2302100

© 1990, R.S. Aggarwal

All rights reserved. No part of this publication may be reproduced, stored in a retrieval system or transmitted, in any form or by any means, electronic, mechanical, photocopying, recording or otherwise, without the prior permission of the Publishers.

S. CHAND'S Seal of Trust

In our endeavour to protect you against counterfeit/fake books we have put a Hologram Sticker on the cover of some of our fast moving titles. The hologram displays a unique 3D multi-level, multi-colour effect of our logo from different angles when tilted or properly illuminated under a single source of light.

Background artwork seems to be "under" or "behind" the logo, giving the illusion of depth. **A fake hologram does not give any illusion of depth.**

First Edition 1990
Subsequent Editions and Reprints 1991, 92, 93 (Twice), 94, 95 (Twice), 96, 97, 98, 99, 2000, 2001, 2002, 2003, 2004 (Twice), 2005, 2006
Reprints 2007

ISBN : 81-219-0741-1
Code : 06 029

PRINTED IN INDIA

By Rajendra Ravindra Printers (Pvt.) Ltd., 7361, Ram Nagar, New Delhi-110 055 and published by S. Chand & Company Ltd., 7361, Ram Nagar, New Delhi-110 055

Preface

The tremendous response from the readers prompted me to bring out this thoroughly revised new edition. This book on objective Arithmetic is really an asset to those who plan to appear in a competitive examination for an executive post or as an assistant.

This book caters the needs of students appearing for *Railways, Banks, Insurance; Excise & Income Tax; Hotel Managers; Police Services; Defence Services; Forest Services* and all other competitive examinations.

Most of the books in the market carry objective type questions with their answers. But, how to get these answers is not given therein. Moreover, to solve a question is not significant in such examinations.

The most important aspect is to solve each question in a fraction of a minute, using short cut methods.

This book contains a huge accumulation of objective type questions with their solutions by short cut methods. The reference of questions asked in various examinations, collected from various examinees on their memory basis, have been given.

It is very much hoped that the subject matter will create a confidence among the candidates and the book will help them like an ideal teacher.

I convey my gratitude to Shri R.K. Gupta, Director and Shri T.N. Goel, Manager, S. Chand & Co., Delhi for taking all pains and interest in the publication of this revised manuscript.

For good typesetting, I am thankful to Mr. Mukesh Maheshwari of *Brillient Computers*, Meerut.

R.S. Aggarwal
Veenalaya
11/146 (Sector 3)
Rajender Nagar
Sahibabad-201005 (INDIA)

Contents

Chapters	Pages
1. Numbers	1 – 21
2. H.C.F. & L.C.M. of Numbers	22 – 36
3. Decimal Fractions	37 – 57
4. Simplification	58 – 75
5. Square Root and Cube Root	76 – 95
6. Percentage	96 – 123
7. Average	124 – 138
8. Ratio & Proportion	139 – 162
9. Partnership	163 – 172
10. Profit & Loss	173 – 205
11. Time & Work	206 – 222
12. Pipes & Cisterns	223 – 230
13. Time & Distance	231 – 243
14. Trains	244 – 257
15. Boats & Streams	258 – 266
16. Problems on Numbers	267 – 278
17. Problems on Ages	279 – 285
18. Simple Interest	286 – 298
19. Compound Interest	299 – 312
20. Area	313 – 344
21. Volume & Surface Areas	345 – 368
22. Chain Rule	369 – 383
23. Alligation or Mixture	384 – 395
24. Races & Games of Skill	396 – 405
25. Calendar	406 – 411
26. Clock	412 – 419
27. Stock & Shares	420 – 431
28. True Discount	432 – 440
29. Banker's Discount	441 – 448
30. Tabulation	449 – 460
31. Data Analysis	461 – 485
32. Odd man out & Series	486 – 496
33. Miscellaneous Exercises	497 – 536
34. Model Test Papers	537 – 561
Latest Questions	563 – 594

S. CHAND'S SENSATIONAL OFFERS FOR 2002

SUBSCRIPTION FORM

S. Chand's
COMPETITION WORLD

Period	Total Amount	You Pay	Your Saving	*Additional Gift of books
1 year (12 issues)	360.00	250.00	110.00	Rs. 100.00
2 years (24 issues)	720.00	460.00	260.00	Rs. 150.00
3 years (36 issues)	1080.00	650.00	430.00	Rs. 250.00

* The list of books is given next page.

------------ ✂ ------------ Cut Here ------------ ✂ ------------

I want to subscribe............................... Name ....
Age................ Address ....
....
DD No. .... Dated .... for Rs..
1 year ☐   2 years ☐   3 years ☐
Note : Please send all payments through D.D. in favour of S. Chand Print Media payable at New Delhi.

S. CHAND PRINT MEDIA
7361, Ram Nagar, Qutab Road, New Delhi-55
Phones : 3672080-81-82
Fax : 91-11-3677446
Shop at : schandgroup.com
E-mail : schand@vsnl.com

LIST OF BOOKS FOR FREE GIFTS
COMPETITION BOOKS

R.S. AGGARWAL
06068 Advanced Objective General Knowledge 185.00

K. MOHAN
06001 Mani Ram Aggarwal's General Knowledge Digest & General Studies with Latest G.K. (Rev. Edn. 2002) 250.00

A.N. KAPUR
06093 General English for Competitions 175.00

R.S. AGGARWAL & VIKAS AGGARWAL
06082 Objective General English 240.00

आर.एस. अग्रवाल
06095 वस्तुनिष्ठ सामान्य हिन्दी 140.00

T. SARAN
11103 Precis Writing & Drafting 60.00

T. SARAN
06014 सारांश लेखन और आलेखन 60.00
06053 A Modern Approach to Verbal Reasoning 240.00

R.S. AGGARWAL
06054 A Modern Approach to Non-Verbal Reasoning 150.00
14101 Arithmetic for Competitive Examinations 155.00
14200 अंकगणित: प्रतियोगी परीक्षाओं के लिए (वस्तुनिष्ठ प्रश्नों सहित) 155.00

K.L. KUMAR
06091 Your Interview 110.00

G.D. MAHESHWARI
06101 Complete Guide to Career Planning 75.00

PRAKASH & SUMAN KANT
06108 BCA Entrance Guide 175.00
06109 BBA/BBM/BBS Entrance Guide 175.00

ESSAYS

H.C. MAHAJAN
06106 Modern Essays for Competitive Exams. 110.00

DICTIONARIES
11157 Compact English Dictionary 60.00
11158 Small School Dictionary 50.00

Martin
11740 English Dictionary 150.00

Father Camil Bulcke
11159 English-Hindi Dictionary 190.00

डा. द्वारका प्रसाद
21549 एस.चन्द हिन्दी-हिन्दी शब्दकोश 170.00
21559 S. Chand's Hindi-English-Hindi Dictionary in Roman Alphabetical Order 250.00

A.N. KAPUR
11739 Chand's Dictionary of English & Hindi Usage for Competitive Exams. 95.00

M.A. PINK & S.E. THOMAS
11171 English Grammar Composition & Effective Business Communication 100.00

1

NUMBERS

(Four Fundamental Rules)
$\{+, -, \times, \div\}$

NUMBERS : In Hindu Arabic System, we use ten symbols 0, 1, 2, 3, 4, 5, 6, 7, 8 & 9, called *digits* to represent any number.

Numeral : *A group of figures, representing a number is called a numeral.*

Representation of a number in figures is called *notation* and expressing a number in words is called *numeration*.

We use place value system to represent a number. For a given numeral, we start from the extreme right as *'Unit's place; Ten's place; Hundred's place* etc.

Solved Examples

Ex. 1. We represent the number **'689074632'** as :

Ten crores	Crores	Ten Lacs (millions)	Lacs	Ten Thousands	Thousands	Hundreds	Tens	Units
10^8	10^7	10^6	10^5	10^4	10^3	10^2	10^1	10^0
6	8	9	0	7	4	6	3	2

We read it as :

'Sixty eight crores, ninety lacs, seventy four thousands, six hundred and thirty two'.

We may write :

$$689074632 = 6 \times 10^8 + 8 \times 10^7 + 9 \times 10^6 + 0 \times 10^5 + 7 \times 10^4$$
$$+ 4 \times 10^3 + 6 \times 10^2 + 3 \times 10^1 + 2 \times 10^0.$$

In this number :

The place value *or* local value of 2 is 2 units = 2;

The place value of 3 is 3 tens = 30;

The place value of 6 is 6 hundreds = 600;

The place value of 4 is 4 thousands = 4000

and so on.

Face Value : *The face value of a digit is the value of the digit itself, wherever it may be.*

The face value of 4 in the above numeral is 4;
The face value of 6 in the above numeral is 6.

Even Numbers : *A number divisible by 2 is called an even number,* such as 2, 4, 6, 8, 10, 124, 536 etc.

Odd Numbers : *A number not divisible by 2 is called an odd number,* such as 1, 3, 5, 7, 9, 11, 123 etc.

Prime Numbers : *A number, other than 1 is called a prime number, if it is divisible by 1 and itself only.*

Composite Numbers : *A number, other than 1, which is not prime is called a composite number.*

Ex. 2. The prime numbers upto 100 are :
2, 3, 5, 7, 11, 13, 17, 19, 23, 29, 31, 37, 41, 43, 47, 53, 59, 61, 67, 71, 73, 79, 83, 89, 97.

Test, whether a given number is prime :

If we want to test any number more than 100, whether it is prime or not, take an integer larger than the approximate square root of that number. Let it be a. Test the divisibility of the given number by every prime number less than a. If it is not divisible by any of them, then it is prime; otherwise it is composite.

Ex. 3. Which of the following numbers are prime ?
     (i) 331   (ii) 481

Sol. (i) The square root of 331 is nearly 19.

Prime numbers less than 19 are 2, 3, 5, 7, 11, 13, 17.

Clearly, 331 is not divisible by any of them.

So, 331 is a prime number.

(ii) The square root of 481 is nearly 22.

Prime numbers less than 22 are 2, 3, 5, 7, 11, 13, 17, 19.

Out of these, 481 is divisible by 13.

So, 481 is not a prime number.

ADDITION & SUBTRACTION (Short Cut Method)

Ex. 4. $86324 - (698 + 4366 + 32517 + 10651) = ?$

     Method (*Explanation*) :

     1st *Column* : $8 + 6 + 7 + 1 = 22.$

     To obtain 4 at unit's place add 2 to make 24.

     In the answer, write 2 at the unit place and carry over 2.

     2nd *Column* : $2 + 5 + 1 + 6 + 9 = 23.$

     To obtain 2 at the ten's place add 9 to make 32.

     In the answer, write 9 at the ten's place and carry over 3.

     3rd *Column* : $3 + 6 + 5 + 3 + 6 = 23.$

```
  86324
    698 ⎤
   4366 ⎥
  32517 ⎥
  10651 ⎦
  -----
  38092
```

In the answer, write 8 at the thousand's place and carry over 1.
5th Column : $1 + 1 + 3 = 5$.
To obtain 8 at the ten thousand's place add 3 to it to make 8.
In the answer, write 3 at the ten-thousand's place.
$\therefore 86324 - (698 + 4366 + 32517 + 10651) = 38092$.

Ex. 5. $78341 - (567 + 2356 + 53172 + 10741) = ?$

Sol.
```
  78341
    567 ⎤
   2356 ⎥
  53172 ⎥
  10741 ⎦
  ─────
  11505
```

LINEAR EQUATIONS : *An equality containing an unknown number is called a linear equation, such as* $x + 3 = 5, 2x - 7 = 9$ *etc.*

In a linear equation, we can :
(*i*) add same number on both sides;
(*ii*) subtract same number from both sides;
(*iii*) multiply both sides by a same non-zero number;
(*iv*) divide both sides by a same non-zero number.

Clearly, $5x = 15 \Rightarrow x = \dfrac{15}{5} = 3$.

Transposition : *In a linear equation, we can take any number on the other side with its sign changed from + to − and from − to +.*

Thus, $x + 5 = 7$ is the same as $x = 7 - 5$.
and $x - 3 = 10$ is the same as $x = 10 + 3$.
This process is called transposition.

Ex. 6. $9873 + ? = 13200$.

Sol. Let $9873 + x = 13200$. Then,
$x = (13200 - 9873) = 3327$.

Ex. 7. $7048 - ? = 3999$

Sol. Let $7048 - x = 3999$.
Then, $x = (7048 - 3999) = 3049$.

Ex. 8. $? - 1398 = 2133$

Sol. Let $x - 1398 = 2133$.
Then, $x = (2133 + 1398) = 3531$.

MULTIPLICATION (Short cut Methods)

Multiplication of a Given Number by 9, 99, 999 etc.

Rule : *Place as many zeros to the right of the multiplicand as is the number of nines and from the number so formed, subtract the multiplicand to get the answer.*

Ex. 9. Multiply :

(i) **5874 by 99**   (ii) **9626 by 999**
(iii) **3618 by 9999**   (iv) **8986 by 99999**

Sol. (i) $5874 \times 99 = 5874 \times (100 - 1)$
$= 587400 - 5874 = 581526.$

(ii) $9626 \times 999 = 9626 \times (1000 - 1)$
$= 9626000 - 9626 = 9616374.$

(iii) $3618 \times 9999 = 3618 \times (10000 - 1)$
$= 36180000 - 3618 = 36176382.$

(iv) $8986 \times 99999 = 8986 \times (100000 - 1)$
$= 898600000 - 8986 = 898591014.$

Multiplication of a Given Number by a Power of 5

Rule : *Put as many zeros to the right of the multiplicand as is the number of power of 5. Divide the number so formed by 2 to the same power as is the number of power of 5.*

Ex. 10. Multiply :

(i) **65798 by 125**   (ii) **43986 by 625.**

Sol. (i) $65798 \times 125 = (65798 \times 5^3) = \dfrac{65798000}{2^3}$

$= \dfrac{65798000}{8} = 8224750.$

(ii) $43986 \times 625 = 43986 \times 5^4 = \dfrac{439860000}{2^4}$

$= \dfrac{439860000}{16} = 27491250.$

Distributive Laws : *For any three numbers a, b, c we have*
(i) $a \times b + a \times c = a \times (b + c)$ (ii) $a \times b - a \times c = a \times (b - c).$

Ex. 11. Simplify :

(i) $869 \times 746 + 869 \times 254 = ?$
(ii) $931 \times 497 - 931 \times 397 = ?$

Sol. (i) $869 \times 746 + 869 \times 254 = 869 \times (746 + 254)$
$= 869 \times 1000 = 869000.$

(ii) $931 \times 497 - 931 \times 397 = 931 \times (497 - 397)$
$= 931 \times 100 = 93100.$

Numbers

Multiplication (by using formulae)

The formulae given below are quite useful for quick multiplication:

(i) $(a+b)^2 = a^2 + b^2 + 2ab$;
(ii) $(a-b)^2 = a^2 + b^2 - 2ab$;
(iii) $(a+b)^2 - (a-b)^2 = 4ab$;
(iv) $(a+b)^2 + (a-b)^2 = 2(a^2 + b^2)$;
(v) $(a^2 - b^2) = (a+b)(a-b)$;
(vi) $(a+b)^3 = a^3 + b^3 + 3ab(a+b)$;
(vii) $(a-b)^3 = a^3 - b^3 - 3ab(a-b)$;
(viii) $(a^3 + b^3) = (a+b)(a^2 - ab + b^2)$;
(ix) $(a^3 - b^3) = (a-b)(a^2 + ab + b^2)$.

Ex. 12. Simplify :

(i) $1405 \times 1405 = ?$ (ii) $1298 \times 1298 = ?$

Sol.   (i) $1405 \times 1405 = (1405)^2 = (1400 + 5)^2$
$= (1400)^2 + 5^2 + 2 \times 1400 \times 5$
$= 1960000 + 25 + 14000$
$= 1974025.$

(ii) $1298 \times 1298 = (1298)^2 = (1300 - 2)^2$
$= (1300)^2 + 2^2 - 2 \times 1300 \times 2$
$= 1690000 + 4 - 5200$
$= 1684804.$

Ex. 13. Simplify :

(i) $596 \times 596 - 104 \times 104 = ?$
(ii) $47 \times 47 + 53 \times 53 + 2 \times 47 \times 53 = ?$
(iii) $91 \times 91 + 78 \times 78 - 2 \times 91 \times 78 = ?$

Sol.   (i) $596 \times 596 - 104 \times 104 = (596)^2 - (104)^2$
$= (596 + 104) \times (596 - 104)$
$= 700 \times 492 = 344400.$

(ii) $47 \times 47 + 53 \times 53 + 2 \times 47 \times 53$
$= (47)^2 + (53)^2 + 2 \times 47 \times 53$
$= (47 + 53)^2 = (100)^2 = 10000.$

(iii) $91 \times 91 + 78 \times 78 - 2 \times 91 \times 78$
$= (91)^2 + (78)^2 - 2 \times 91 \times 78$
$= (91 - 78)^2 = (13)^2 = 13 \times 13 = 169.$

Ex. 14. Simplify :

(i) $\dfrac{463 \times 463 \times 463 + 337 \times 337 \times 337}{463 \times 463 - 463 \times 337 + 337 \times 337} = ?$

(ii) $\dfrac{131 \times 131 \times 131 - 67 \times 67 \times 67}{131 \times 131 + 131 \times 67 + 67 \times 67} = ?$

Sol. (i) Given Expression $= \dfrac{(a^3 + b^3)}{(a^2 - ab + b^2)}$, where $a = 463, b = 337$

$= \dfrac{(a+b)(a^2 - ab + b^2)}{(a^2 - ab + b^2)} = (a+b)$

$= (463 + 337) = 800.$

(ii) Given Expression $= \dfrac{(a^3 - b^3)}{(a^2 + ab + b^2)}$, where $a = 131, b = 67$

$= \dfrac{(a-b)(a^2 + ab + b^2)}{(a^2 + ab + b^2)} = (a-b)$

$= (131 - 67) = 64.$

Ex. 15. The sum of two numbers is 25 and the difference of their squares is 75. Find the difference between the numbers.

Sol. Let the numbers be a and b. Then,

$a + b = 25$ and $a^2 - b^2 = 75.$

$\therefore (a - b) = \dfrac{(a^2 - b^2)}{(a + b)} = \dfrac{75}{25} = 3.$

Ex. 16. Evaluate : $213 \times 213 + 187 \times 187.$

Sol. $2 \times (a^2 + b^2) = (a+b)^2 + (a-b)^2$

$\Rightarrow 2 \times [(213 \times 213) + (187 \times 187)] = (213 + 187)^2 + (213 - 187)^2$

$= (400)^2 + (26)^2$

$= 160000 + 676 = 160676$

$\Rightarrow (213 \times 213) + (187 \times 187) = \dfrac{160676}{2} = 80338.$

DIVISION

If we divide a given number by another number, then

Dividend = (Divisor × quotient) + Remainder

Let us divide 163 by 17,

Numbers

$$17 \overline{\smash{\big)}\, 163} \, (\, 9$$
$$\underline{153}$$
$$\underline{10}$$

Thus, whewe divide 163 by 17, we get.
9 as quotient and 10 as remainder.
Here, dividend = 163 and divisor = 17.

Ex. 17. On dividing **59761** by a certain number, the quotient is **189** and the remainder is **37**. Find the divisor.

Sol. Divisor = $\dfrac{\text{(Dividend - Remainder)}}{\text{(Quotient)}} = \dfrac{(59761-37)}{189} = 316.$

Ex. 18. What least number must be subtracted from **1000** to get a number exactly divisible by **17** ?

Sol. On dividing 1000 by 17, the remainder obtained is 14.
∴ The required number is 14.

Ex. 19. What least number must be added to **2000** to get a number exactly divisible by **19** ?

Sol. On dividing 2000 by 19, the remainder is 5.
∴ The required number to be added = (19 − 5) = 14.

Ex. 20. Find the number which is nearest to **3006** and exactly divisible by **21**.

Sol. On dividing 3006 by 29, the remainder is 19, which is more than half of 29.
So, we have to add (29 − 19) = 10 to the number.
∴ Required number = (3006 + 10) = 3016.

Ex. 21. A number when divided by **779** gives a remainder **47**. By dividing the same number by **19**, what would be the remainder ?

Sol. Number = $(779 \times k) + 47$, where k is the quotient.
= $(19 \times 41 \times k) + (19 \times 2) + 9$
= $19 \times (41k + 2) + 9$
= $19 \times$ (new quotient) + 9
∴ Required remainder = 9.

EXERCISE 1

1. The local value of 7 in the numeral 5679032 is :
   (a) 7   □   (b) 70000   □

(c) 10000 ☐   (d) 5070000 ☐

2. The face value of 8 in the numeral 458926 is :
   (a) 8000 ☐ (b) 8 ☐
   (c) 1000 ☐ (d) 458000 ☐

3. 66066 + 6606 + 66 + 6 = ?
   (a) 258126 ☐ (b) 72744 ☐
   (c) 72798 ☐ (d) none of these ☐

4. 9501 − ? = 3697
   (a) 13198 ☐ (b) 5814 ☐
   (c) 5804 ☐ (d) 4894 ☐

5. ? − 4799 = 1714
   (a) 6513 ☐ (b) 7403 ☐
   (c) 3085 ☐ (d) none of these ☐

6. 36800 − 9999 − 3333 − 66 = ?
   (a) 30200 ☐ (b) 27912 ☐
   (c) 23402 ☐ (d) 24102 ☐

7. 3571 + ? − 6086 = 115
   (a) 2400 ☐ (b) 2630 ☐
   (c) 2515 ☐ (d) none of these ☐

8. ? + 6207 − 9038 = 107
   (a) 2724 ☐ (b) 2938 ☐
   (c) 2814 ☐ (d) none of these ☐

9. ? − 1046 − 398 − 69 = 999
   (a) 2502 ☐ (b) 2512 ☐
   (c) 2472 ☐ (d) 514 ☐

10. 36000 − 888 = 37000 − ?
    (a) 2018 ☐ (b) 1848 ☐
    (c) 1888 ☐ (d) 1978 ☐

11. 4003 − ? − 1599 = 716
    (a) 1598 ☐ (b) 1688 ☐
    (c) 3120 ☐ (d) none of these ☐

12. 8888 + 7777 + 666 + ? = 19000
    (a) 2719 ☐ (b) 2679 ☐
    (c) 1669 ☐ (d) none of these ☐

13. 9998 × 999 = ?
    (a) 9997001 ☐ (b) 9988002 ☐
    (c) 9987012 ☐ (d) 9898012 ☐

Numbers

14. 6674 × 625 = ?
    (a) 4170160
    (b) 4072360
    (c) 4171050
    (d) 4171250

15. 9856 × 156 + 9856 × 844
    (a) 9856000
    (b) 9836500
    (c) 9794560
    (d) 9698350

16. 356 × 936 − 356 × 836 = ?
    (a) 35600
    (b) 34500
    (c) 49630
    (d) 93600

17. ? × 147 = 6909
    (a) 37
    (b) 47
    (c) 27
    (d) 67

18. 87 × ? = 3393
    (a) 39
    (b) 49
    (c) 29
    (d) 109

19. ? × 11 = 555555
    (a) 505
    (b) 5050
    (c) 50505
    (d) 5005

20. 777777 ÷ 11 = ?
    (a) 7077
    (b) 70707
    (c) 7707
    (d) 7007

21. 2013 × ? 1 = 62403
    (a) 1
    (b) 2
    (c) 3
    (d) 4

22. 2 ? 63 ÷ 11 = 233
    (a) 4
    (b) 3
    (c) 6
    (d) 5

23. 469157 × 9999 = ?
    (a) 4586970843
    (b) 4686970743
    (c) 4691100843
    (d) 4586870843

24. 387 × 387 + 114 × 114 + 2 × 387 × 114 = ?
    (a) 250001
    (b) 251001
    (c) 260101
    (d) 261001

25. 1014 × 986 = ?
    (a) 998904
    (b) 999804
    (c) 998814
    (d) 998804

26. 1299 × 1299 = ?
    (a) 1585301
    (b) 1684701

       (c) 1685401 ☐   (d) 1687401 ☐

27. $1307 \times 1307 = ?$
       (a) 1601249 ☐   (b) 1607249 ☐
       (c) 1701249 ☐   (d) 1708249 ☐

28. $5358 \times 51 = ?$
       (a) 273358 ☐   (b) 273258 ☐
       (c) 273348 ☐   (d) 273268 ☐

29. $106 \times 106 + 94 \times 94 = ?$
       (a) 21032 ☐   (b) 20032 ☐
       (c) 23032 ☐   (d) 20072 ☐

30. $? \times 48 = 173 \times 240$ **(Bank P.O. 1988)**
       (a) 545 ☐   (b) 685 ☐
       (c) 865 ☐   (d) 495 ☐

31. $\dfrac{80}{?} = \dfrac{?}{20}$
       (Bank P.O. 1988)
       (a) 40 ☐   (b) 400 ☐
       (c) 800 ☐   (d) 1600 ☐

32. $\dfrac{4050}{\sqrt{?}} = 450$
       (a) 49 ☐   (b) 100 ☐
       (c) 81 ☐   (d) 9 ☐

33. $\dfrac{\sqrt{?}}{19} = 4$
       (a) 76 ☐   (b) 5776 ☐
       (c) 304 ☐   (d) 1296 ☐

34. $\dfrac{?}{54} = \dfrac{96}{?}$
       (a) 72 ☐   (b) 27 ☐
       (c) 36 ☐   (d) 63 ☐

35. $42060 \div 15 + 5 = ?$ **(Bank Clerical 1992)**
       (a) 2804 ☐   (b) 2809 ☐
       (c) 2103 ☐   (d) 289 ☐

36. $\dfrac{343 \times 343 \times 343 + 257 \times 257 \times 257}{343 \times 343 - 343 \times 257 + 257 \times 257} = ?$
       (a) 8600 ☐   (b) 800 ☐
       (c) 600 ☐   (d) 2600 ☐

37. $\dfrac{117 \times 117 \times 117 - 98 \times 98 \times 98}{117 \times 117 + 117 \times 98 + 98 \times 98} = ?$

Numbers

(a) 215 ☐ (b) 311 ☐
(c) 19 ☐ (d) 29 ☐

38. $\dfrac{137 \times 137 + 137 \times 133 + 133 \times 133}{137 \times 137 \times 137 - 133 \times 133 \times 133} = ?$

(a) 4 ☐ (b) 270 ☐
(c) $\dfrac{1}{4}$ ☐ (d) $\dfrac{1}{270}$ ☐

39. $\left(1-\dfrac{1}{3}\right)\left(1-\dfrac{1}{4}\right)\left(1-\dfrac{1}{5}\right)\ldots\ldots\left(1-\dfrac{1}{n}\right) = ?$

(Excise 1988)

(a) $\dfrac{1}{n}$ ☐ (b) $\dfrac{2}{n}$ ☐
(c) $\dfrac{2(n-1)}{n}$ ☐ (d) $\dfrac{2}{n(n+1)}$ ☐

40. When simplified, the product (C.P.I. 1990)

$\left(2-\dfrac{1}{3}\right)\left(2-\dfrac{3}{5}\right)\left(2-\dfrac{5}{7}\right)\ldots\ldots\left(2-\dfrac{997}{999}\right)$ is equal to :

(a) $\dfrac{5}{999}$ ☐ (b) $\dfrac{1001}{999}$ ☐
(c) $\dfrac{1001}{3}$ ☐ (d) none of these ☐

41. If $\dfrac{a}{b} = \dfrac{4}{3}$, then $\dfrac{3a+2b}{3a-2b} = ?$

(C.B.I. 1990)

(a) 6 ☐ (b) 3 ☐
(c) 5 ☐ (d) −1 ☐

42. If $\sqrt{3^n} = 81$, then $n = ?$ (Assistant Grade 1990)

(a) 2 ☐ (b) 4 ☐
(c) 6 ☐ (d) 8 ☐

43. If $\dfrac{x}{y} = \dfrac{4}{5}$, then the value of $\left(\dfrac{4}{7} + \dfrac{2y-x}{2y+x}\right)$ is :

(a) $\dfrac{3}{7}$ ☐ (b) $1\dfrac{1}{7}$ ☐
(c) 1 ☐ (d) 2 ☐

44. $\sqrt{\dfrac{?}{196}} = \dfrac{72}{56}$

(Bank P.O. 1991)

(a) 18 ☐ (b) 14 ☐
(c) 324 ☐ (d) 212 ☐

45. $\dfrac{24}{18} = \dfrac{?}{6}$
 (Bank P.O. 1991)
 (a) 12 □ (b) 10 □
 (c) 9 □ (d) 8 □

46. $\dfrac{10}{11} = \dfrac{110}{?}$
 (Bank P.O. 1991)
 (a) 111 □ (b) 1100 □
 (c) 121 □ (d) 100 □

47. The first prime number is :
 (a) 0 □ (b) 1 □
 (c) 2 □ (d) 3 □

48. The sum of first four prime numbers is (C.D.S. 1991)
 (a) 10 □ (b) 11 □
 (c) 16 □ (d) 17 □

49. Which of the following numbers is prime ?
 (a) 119 □ (b) 187 □
 (c) 247 □ (d) 551 □
 (e) none of these □

50. The number $(10^n - 1)$ is divisible by 11 for :
 (a) all values of n □ (b) odd values of n □
 (c) even values of n □ (d) n = multiples of 11 □

51. $\dfrac{392}{\sqrt{?}} = 28$
 (a) 144 □ (b) 196 □
 (c) 24 □ (d) 48 □

52. The largest number of four digits exactly divisible by 88 is :
 (a) 9768 □ (b) 8888 □
 (c) 9988 □ (d) 9944 □

53. The least number of five digits exactly divisible by 456 is
 (a) 10142 □ (b) 10232 □
 (c) 10032 □ (d) 10012 □

54. What least number must be subtracted from 13601 to get a number exactly divisible by 87 :
 (a) 49 □ (b) 23 □
 (c) 29 □ (d) 31 □

55. What least number must be added to 1056 to get a number exactly divisible by 23 :
 (a) 21 □ (b) 25 □

Numbers

(c) 3   (d) 2

56. What least value must be given to * so that the number 6135 * 2 is exactly divisible by 9 :
 (a) 0   (b) 1
 (c) 2   (d) 3

57. What least value must be given to * so that the number 97215 * 6 is divisible by 11 :
 (a) 1   (b) 2
 (c) 3   (d) 5

58. What least value must be given to * so that the number 91876 * 2 is divisible by 8 :
 (a) 1   (b) 2
 (c) 3   (d) 4

59. Which of the following numbers is exactly divisible by 99 :
 (a) 3572404   (b) 135792
 (c) 913464   (d) 114345

60. Which number should replace both the asterisisics in $\left(\dfrac{*}{21}\right) \times \left(\dfrac{*}{189}\right) = 1$? (C.B.I. 1991)
 (a) 21   (b) 63
 (c) 3969   (d) 147

61. If in a long division sum, the dividend is 380606 and the successive remainders from the first to the last are 434, 125 and 413, then the divisor is : (Delhi Police 1991)
 (a) 451   (b) 843
 (c) 4215   (d) 3372

62. In a divison sum, the divisor is 12 times the quotient and 5 times the remainder. If the remainder be 48, then the dividend is :
 (a) 240   (b) 576
 (c) 4800   (d) 4848
 (C.B.I. 1991)

63. What least number must be subtracted from 1294 so that the remainder when divided by 9, 11, 13 will leave in each case the same remainder 6 ? (C.B.I. 1991)
 (a) 0   (b) 1
 (c) 2   (d) 3

64. When a certain number is multiplied by 13, the product consists entirely of fives. The smallest such number is :
 (a) 41625   (b) 42515

(c) 42735   (d) 42135

65. Which of the following numbers is prime :
(a) 119   (b) 187
(c) 247   (d) 551
(e) None of these

66. If $a = 16$ and $b = 5$, the value of $\left(\dfrac{a^2 + b^2 + ab}{a^3 - b^3}\right)$ is :

(a) $\dfrac{1}{11}$ (b) $\dfrac{1}{19}$

(c) $\dfrac{121}{3971}$ (d) None of these

67. The largest natural number by which the product of three consecutive even natural numbers is always divisible, is
(a) 16   (b) 24
(c) 48   (d) 96

(Central Excise & I. Tax 1988)

68. If $\dfrac{x}{y} = \dfrac{3}{4}$, then the value of $\left(\dfrac{6}{7} + \dfrac{y-x}{y+x}\right)$ equals : (B.S.R.B. Exam 1989)

(a) $\dfrac{5}{7}$ (b) $1\dfrac{1}{7}$

(c) 1   (d) 2

69. $62976 \div ? = 123$
(a) 412   (b) 502
(c) 512   (d) 522

70. If $\sqrt{\left(1 + \dfrac{27}{169}\right)} = \left(1 + \dfrac{x}{13}\right)$, then the value of x is :

(a) 1   (b) 3
(c) 5   (d) 7

(Central Excise and I.Tax 1989)

ANSWERS (EXERCISE 1)

1. (b) 2. (b) 3. (b) 4. (c) 5. (a) 6. (c) 7. (b) 8. (b) 9. (b)
10. (c) 11. (b) 12. (c) 13. (b) 14. (d) 15. (a) 16. (a) 17. (b) 18. (a)
19. (b) 20. (b) 21. (c) 22. (d) 23. (c) 24. (b) 25. (b) 26. (d) 27. (d)
28. (b) 29. (d) 30. (c) 31. (a) 32. (c) 33. (b) 34. (a) 35. (b) 36. (c)
37. (c) 38. (c) 39. (b) 40. (c) 41. (b) 42. (d) 43. (c) 44. (c) 45. (d)
46. (c) 47. (c) 48. (d) 49. (e) 50. (c) 51. (b) 52. (d) 53. (c) 54. (c)

Numbers
15

55. (d) 56. (b) 57. (c) 58. (c) 59. (d) 60. (b) 61. (b) 62. (d) 63. (b)
64. (c) 65. (e) 66. (a) 67. (c) 68. (c) 69. (c) 70. (a)

SOLUTIONS (Exercise 1)

1. The local value of 7 in 5679032 is 70000.

2. The face value of 8 in 458926 is 8.

3.
```
  66066
   6606
     66
+     6
───────
  72744
```

4. Let $9501 - x = 3697$
Then, $x = 9501 - 3697$
```
  9501
- 3697
──────
  5804
```

5. Let $x - 4799 = 1714$
Then, $x = 4799 + 1714 = 6513$.

6.
```
   9999              36800
   3333            - 13398
+    66            ───────
──────               23402
  13398
```

7. Let $3571 + x - 6086 = 115$
Then, $x = (6086 + 115) - 3571$
$= (6201 - 3571) = 2630$.

8. Let $x + 6207 - 9038 = 107$
Then, $x = (107 + 9038) - (6207) = 2938$.

9. Let $x - 1046 - 398 - 69 = 999$
Then, $x = 999 + 1046 + 398 + 69 = 2512$.

10. Let $37000 - x = 36000 - 888$
Then, $x = 37000 - 36000 + 888 = 1888$.

11. Let $4003 - x - 1599 = 716$

Then, $x = 4003 - 1599 - 716$
$= 4003 - (1599 + 716) = (4003 - 2315) = 1688.$

12. Let $8888 + 7777 + 666 + x = 19000$
Then, $17331 + x = 19000$ or $x = (19000 - 17331) = 1669.$

13. $9998 \times 999 = 9998 \times (1000 - 1)$
$= 9998 \times 1000 - 9998 \times 1$
$= 9998000 - 9998 = 9988002.$

14. $6674 \times 625 = 6674 \times (5)^4 = \dfrac{6674 \times (10)^4}{2^4} = \dfrac{66740000}{16} = 4171250.$

15. $9856 \times 156 + 9856 \times 844 = 9856 \times (156 + 844)$
$= 9856 \times 1000 = 9856000.$

16. $356 \times 936 - 356 \times 836 = 356 \times (936 - 836) = 356 \times 100 = 35600.$

17. Let $x \times 147 = 6909$. Then, $x = \dfrac{6909}{147} = 47.$

18. Let $87 \times x = 3393$. Then, $x = \dfrac{3393}{87} = 39.$

19. Let $x \times 11 = 555555$. Then, $x = \dfrac{555555}{11} = 50505.$

20. $\dfrac{777777}{11} = 70707.$

21. Let $2013 \times x = 62403$. Then, $x = \dfrac{62403}{2013} = 31.$
$\therefore$ Missing digit is 3.

22. Let $\dfrac{x}{11} = 233$. Then, $x = 233 \times 11 = 2563.$
$\therefore$ Missing digit is 5.

23. $469157 \times 9999 = 469157 \times (10000 - 1)$
$= 4691570000 - 469157 = 4691100843.$

24. Given Expression $= a^2 + b^2 + 2ab$
$= (a + b)^2 = (387 + 114)^2 = (501)^2$
$= (500 + 1)^2 = (500)^2 + (1)^2 + 2 \times 500 \times 1$
$= 250000 + 1 + 1000 = 251001.$

25. $1014 \times 986 = (1000 + 14) \times (1000 - 14)$
$= (1000)^2 - (14)^2 = (1000000 - 196) = 999804.$

26. $1299 \times 1299 = (1299)^2$

Numbers 17

$= (1300-1)^2 = (1300)^2 + (1)^2 - 2 \times 1300 \times 1$
$= 1690000 + 1 - 2600 = 1687401.$

27. $1307 \times 1307 = (1307)^2$
    $= (1300 + 7)^2$
    $= (1300)^2 + (7)^2 + 2 \times 1300 \times 7$
    $= 1690000 + 49 + 18200 = 1708249.$

28. $5358 \times 51 = 5358 \times (50 + 1)$
    $= 5358 \times 50 + 5358 \times 1 = 267900 + 5358 = 273258.$

29. $106 \times 106 + 94 \times 94 = (106)^2 + (94)^2$
    $= \frac{1}{2}\left[2(a^2 + b^2)\right] = \frac{1}{2}\left[(a+b)^2 + (a-b)^2\right]$
    $= \frac{1}{2}\left[(106 + 94)^2 + (106 - 94)^2\right]$
    $= \frac{1}{2}\left[(200)^2 + (12)^2\right]$
    $= \frac{1}{2} \times [40000 + 144] = \frac{40144}{2} = 20072.$

30. Let $x \times 48 = 173 \times 240.$
    Then, $x = \frac{173 \times 240}{48} = (173 \times 5) = 865.$

31. Let $\frac{80}{x} = \frac{x}{20}$. Then, $x^2 = 80 \times 20 = 1600.$
    $\therefore x = \sqrt{1600} = 40.$

32. Let $\frac{4050}{\sqrt{x}} = 450.$ Then, $\sqrt{x} = \frac{4050}{450} = 9$
    $\therefore x = (9 \times 9) = 81.$

33. Let $\frac{\sqrt{x}}{19} = 4.$ Then, $\sqrt{x} = 19 \times 4 = 76.$
    $\therefore x = (76 \times 76 = 5776).$

34. Let $\frac{x}{54} = \frac{94}{x}$. Then, $x^2 = 54 \times 96.$
    $\therefore x = \sqrt{54 \times 96} = \sqrt{6 \times 9 \times 6 \times 16} = 6 \times 3 \times 4 = 72.$

35. Given Expression $= \frac{42060}{15} + 5 = 2804 + 5 = 2809.$

36. Given Expression $= \frac{a^3 + b^3}{a^2 - ab + b^2}$, where $a = 343, b = 257$

$$= \frac{(a+b)(a^2-ab+b^2)}{(a^2-ab+b^2)} = (a+b)$$
$$= (343 + 257) = 600.$$

37. Given Expression $= \dfrac{(a^3-b^3)}{(a^2+ab+b^2)}$, where $a = 117$, $b = 98$

$$= \frac{(a-b)(a^2+ab+b^2)}{(a^2+ab+b^2)} = (a-b)$$
$$= (117 - 98) = 19.$$

38. Given Expression $= \dfrac{a^2+ab+b^2}{a^3-b^3}$, where $a = 137$, $b = 133$

$$= \frac{(a^2+ab+b^2)}{(a-b)(a^2+ab+b^2)} = \frac{1}{(a-b)}$$
$$= \frac{1}{137-133} = \frac{1}{4}.$$

39. $\left(1-\dfrac{1}{3}\right)\left(1-\dfrac{1}{4}\right)\left(1-\dfrac{1}{5}\right)\ldots\left(1-\dfrac{1}{n}\right)$
$= \dfrac{2}{3} \times \dfrac{3}{4} \times \dfrac{4}{5} \times \ldots \times \dfrac{(n-1)}{n} = \dfrac{2}{n}.$

40. $\left(2-\dfrac{1}{3}\right)\left(2-\dfrac{3}{5}\right)\left(2-\dfrac{5}{7}\right)\ldots\left(2-\dfrac{997}{999}\right)$
$= \dfrac{5}{3} \times \dfrac{7}{5} \times \dfrac{9}{7} \times \ldots \times \dfrac{1001}{999} = \dfrac{1001}{3}.$

41. Dividing numerator as well as denominator by b, we get :

$$\frac{3a+2b}{3a-2b} = \frac{3 \cdot \dfrac{a}{b}+2}{3 \cdot \dfrac{a}{b}-2} = \frac{3 \times \dfrac{4}{3}+2}{3 \times \dfrac{4}{3}-2} = \frac{4+2}{4-2} = 3.$$

42. $\sqrt{3^n} = 81 \Rightarrow 3^{n/2} = 3^4 \Rightarrow \dfrac{n}{2} = 4 \Rightarrow n = 8.$

43. Dividing numerator as well as denominator by y, we get

$$\frac{4}{7} + \frac{2y-x}{2y+x} = \frac{4}{7} + \frac{2-\dfrac{x}{y}}{2+\dfrac{x}{y}} = \frac{4}{7} + \frac{2-\dfrac{4}{5}}{2+\dfrac{4}{5}}$$
$$= \frac{4}{7} + \frac{6}{14} = \frac{4}{7} + \frac{3}{7} = \frac{7}{7} = 1.$$

Numbers

44. Let $\sqrt{\dfrac{x}{196}} = \dfrac{72}{56} = \dfrac{9}{7}$.

    Then, $\dfrac{x}{196} = \dfrac{9}{7} \times \dfrac{9}{7} = \dfrac{81}{49}$. So, $x = \dfrac{81 \times 196}{49} = 324$.

45. Let $\dfrac{24}{18} = \dfrac{x}{6}$. Then, $18x = 24 \times 6$.

    $\therefore\ x = \dfrac{24 \times 6}{18} = 8$.

46. Let $\dfrac{10}{11} = \dfrac{110}{x}$. Then, $10x = 11 \times 110$.

    $\therefore\ x = \dfrac{11 \times 110}{10} = 121$.

47. The first prime number is 2.

48. First four prime numbers are 2, 3, 5, 7.
    Their sum = (2 + 3 + 5 + 7) = 17.

49. 119 is divisible by 7; 187 is divisible by 11; 247 is divisible by 13 and 551 is divisible by 19. So, none of the given numbers is prime.

50. For even values of n, the number $(10^n - 1)$ consists of even numbers of nines and hence it will be divisible by 11.

51. Let $\dfrac{392}{\sqrt{x}} = 28$. Then, $\sqrt{x} = \dfrac{392}{28} = 14$.

    $\therefore\ x = 14 \times 14 = 196$.

52. Largest number of four digits = 9999.

    ```
        88 ) 9999 ( 113
             88
             ───
             119
              88
             ───
             319
             264
             ───
              55
    ```

    $\therefore$ Required number = (9999 − 55) = 9944.

53. Least number of five digits = 10000.

```
       456 ) 10000 ( 21
             912
             ———
             880
             456
             ———
             424
```

∴ Required number = 10000 + (456 − 424) = 10032.

54.
```
       87 ) 13601 ( 156
            87
            ———
            490
            435
            ———
            551
            552
            ———
             29
```

∴ Required number = 29.

55. On dividing 1056 by 23, we get 21 as remainder.
∴ Required number to be added = (23 − 21) = 2.

56. $6 + 1 + 3 + 5 + x + 2 = 17 + x$ must be divisible by 9. So, $x = 1$.

57. $(9 + 2 + 5 + 6 +) − (7 + 1 + x) = 14 − x$
must be divisible by 11. so, $x = 3$.

58. By hit and trial we find that 632 is divisble by 8. So, * must be replaced by 3.

59. Clearly 114345 is divisble by 9 as well as 11. So, it is divisible by 99.

60. Let $\dfrac{x}{21} \times \dfrac{x}{189} = 1$. Then, $x^2 = 21 \times 189 = 21 \times 21 \times 9$
∴ $x = (21 \times 3) = 63$.

62. Let quotient = Q and remainder = R.
Then, divisor = $12Q = 5R$.
Now $R = 48 \Rightarrow 12Q = 5 \times 48 \Rightarrow Q = 20$.
∴ Dividend = $(20 \times 240 + 48) = 4848$.

63. The number when divided by 9, 11, 13 leaving remainder 6 = (l.c.m. of 9, 11, 13) + 6 = 1293.
∴ Required number = (1294 − 1293) = 1.

64. By trial, we find that the smallest number consisting entirely of fives

Numbers   21

and exactly divisible by 13 is 555555. On dividing 555555 by 13, we get 42735 as quotient.

65. Clearly, 119 is divisible by 17, 187 is divisible by 11 ; 247 is divisible by 13 and 551 is divisible by 19.

So none of the given numbers is prime.

66. $\left(\dfrac{a^2 + b^2 + ab}{a^3 - b^3}\right) = \dfrac{1}{(a-b)} = \dfrac{1}{(16-5)} = \dfrac{1}{11}$.

67. It is $2 \times 4 \times 6 = 48$.

68. $\dfrac{6}{7} + \dfrac{y-x}{y+x} = \dfrac{6}{7} + \dfrac{1 - \dfrac{x}{y}}{1 + \dfrac{x}{y}}$

$= \dfrac{6}{7} + \dfrac{1 - \dfrac{3}{4}}{1 + \dfrac{3}{4}} = \dfrac{6}{7} + \dfrac{1}{7} = 1$

69. Let $\dfrac{62976}{x} = 123$. Then, $x = \dfrac{62976}{123} = 512$.

70. $\sqrt{\dfrac{196}{169}} = 1 + \dfrac{x}{13} \Rightarrow \dfrac{14}{13} - 1 = \dfrac{x}{13}$

$\Rightarrow \dfrac{1}{13} = \dfrac{x}{13}$ i.e. $x = 1$.

2
H.C.F. & L.C.M. OF NUMBERS

Factors And Multiples : *If a number x divides another number y exactly, we say that x is a factor of y. Also, in this case, y is called a multiple of x.*

Highest Common Factor (H.C.F. or G.C.D. or G.C.M.) : *The H.C.F. of two or more than two numbers is the greatest number that divides each one of them exactly.*

The Highest Common Factor is also known as *Greatest Common divisor* or *Greatest Common Measure.*

H.C.F. By Factorization : *Express each one of the given numbers as the product of prime factors. Now, choose common factors and take the product of these factors to obtain the required H.C.F.*

Ex. 1. Find the H.C.F. of 96, 528, 1584 and 2016.

Sol. $96 = 2^5 \times 3$; $528 = 2^4 \times 3 \times 11$; $1584 = 2^4 \times 3^2 \times 11$
and $2016 = 2^5 \times 3^2 \times 7$.
$\therefore$ H.C.F. $= (2^4 \times 3) = (16 \times 3) = 48$.

H.C.F. By Division Method : *Suppose we have to find the H.C.F. of two given numbers. Divide the larger number by the smaller one. Now, divide the divisor by the remainder. Repeat the process of dividing the preceding divisor by the remainder last obtained, till a remainder zero is obtained. The last divisor is the H.C.F. of given numbers.*

Suppose we have to find the H.C.F. of three numbers. Then, H.C.F. of (H.C.F. of any two and the third number) gives the H.C.F. of given three numbers.

Similarly, the H.C.F. of more than three numbers may be obtained.

Ex. 2. Find the H.C.F. of 1026, 1215 and 2349.

H.C.F. & L.C.M. of Numbers

Sol.
```
    1215 ) 2349 ( 1
           1215
           ────
           1134 ) 1215 ( 1
                  1134
                  ────
                    81 ) 1134 ( 14
                          81
                         ────
                          324
                          324
                         ────
                           ×
```

Thus, the H.C.F. of 1215 and 2349 is 81.

Now, we find the H.C.F. of 81 and 1026.

```
81 ) 1026 ( 12
     81
     ──
     216
     162
     ───
      54 ) 81 ( 1
           54
           ──
           27 ) 54 ( 2
                54
                ──
                ×
```

∴ Required H.C.F. = 27.

Lowest Common Multiple (L.C.M.) : *The least number which is exactly divisible by each one of the given numbers, is called their L.C.M.*

FORMULA :

Product of Two Numbers = (Their H.C.F.) × (Their L.C.M.).

L.C.M. By Factorization : *Resolve each one of the given numbers into prime factors. Then, L.C.M. is the product of highest powers of all the factors.*

Ex. 3. Find the L.C.M. of **48, 108 and 280.**

Sol. $48 = 2^4 \times 3; \ 108 = 2^2 \times 3^3 \ \& \ 280 = 2^3 \times 5 \times 7.$

∴ L.C.M. = $2^4 \times 3^3 \times 5 \times 7 = 15120$.

Ex. 4. Find L.C.M. of **852 and 1491.**

Sol. H.C.F. of 852 and 1491 is 213.

∴ L.C.M. = $\dfrac{\text{Product of Numbers}}{\text{H.C.F.}} = \dfrac{852 \times 1491}{213} = 5964$.

Remark : *L.C.M. of three numbers*

= L.C.M. of (L.C.M. of any two & third).

Similarly, the L.C.M. of more than three numbers can be obtained.

Ex. 5. *(Shortcut Method)* : Find the L.C.M. of **15, 18, 24, 27, 36 and 56.**

Sol.

```
3 | 15 - 18 - 24 - 27 - 36 - 56
2 |  5 -  6 -  8 -  9 - 12 - 56
2 |  5 -  3 -  4 -  9 -  6 - 28
2 |  5 -  3 -  2 -  9 -  3 - 14
3 |  5 -  3 -  1 -  9 -  3 -  7
  |  5 -  1 -  1 -  3 -  1 -  7
```

∴ L.C.M. = $(3 \times 2 \times 2 \times 2 \times 3 \times 5 \times 3 \times 7) = 7560$.

H.C.F. and L.C.M. of Fractions :

(i) H.C.F. of Fractions = $\dfrac{\text{H.C.F. of Numerators}}{\text{L.C.M. of Denominators}}$.

(ii) L.C.M. of Fractions = $\dfrac{\text{L.C.M. of Numerators}}{\text{H.C.F. of Denominators}}$.

Ex. 6. Find the H.C.F. and L.C.M. of $\dfrac{2}{3}, \dfrac{8}{9}, \dfrac{32}{81}, \dfrac{10}{27}$.

Sol. H.C.F. of given fractions = $\dfrac{\text{H.C.F. of 2, 8, 32, 10}}{\text{L.C.M. of 3, 9, 81, 27}} = \dfrac{2}{81}$.

L.C.M. of given fractions = $\dfrac{\text{L.C.M. of 2, 8, 32, 10}}{\text{H.C.F. of 3, 9, 81, 27}} = \dfrac{160}{3}$.

SOLVED EXAMPLES

Ex. 1. Reduce $\dfrac{777}{1147}$ to lowest terms.

H.C.F. & L.C.M. of Numbers

Sol. H.C.F. of 777 and 1147 is 37.

On dividing the numerator and denominator by 37, we get :

$$\frac{777}{1147} = \frac{21}{31}.$$

Ex. 2. Arrange the following fractions into ascending order :

$$\frac{2}{3}, \frac{5}{9}, \frac{7}{11}, \frac{3}{7}, \frac{9}{13} \text{ and } \frac{15}{19}.$$

Sol. Express each one of the given fractions in decimal form.

Thus, $\frac{2}{3} = 0.666$, $\frac{5}{9} = 0.555$, $\frac{7}{11} = 0.636$, $\frac{3}{7} = 0.428$,

$\frac{9}{13} = 0.692$ and $\frac{15}{19} = 0.789$.

Clearly $0.428 < 0.555 < 0.636 < 0.666 < 0.692 < 0.789$.

$\therefore \frac{3}{7} < \frac{5}{9} < \frac{7}{11} < \frac{2}{3} < \frac{9}{13} < \frac{15}{19}.$

Ex. 3. The H.C.F. of two numbers is 4 and their L.C.M. is 576. If one of the numbers is 64, find the other number.

Sol. The other number $= \frac{\text{H.C.F.} \times \text{L.C.M.}}{\text{Given Number}} = \frac{4 \times 576}{64} = 36.$

Ex. 4. Three drums contain 36 litres, 45 litres and 72 litres of oil. What biggest measure can measure all the different quantities exactly ?

Sol. Biggest Measure = (H.C.F. of 36, 45, 72) litres = 9 litres.

Ex. 5. Find the largest number which can exactly divide 513, 783 and 1107.

Sol. Required number = H.C.F. of 513, 783 and 1107 = 27.

Ex. 6. Find the smallest number exactly divisible by 12, 15, 20 and 27.

Sol. Required number = L.C.M. of 12, 15, 20 and 27 = 540.

Ex. 7. Find the least number which when divided by 6, 7, 8, 9 and 12 leaves the same remainder 2 in each case.

Sol. Required number = (L.C.M. of 6, 7, 8, 9, 12) + 2
= (504 + 2) = 506.

Exercise 2

1. $\frac{561}{748}$ when reduced to lowest terms is :

(a) $\dfrac{13}{14}$ ☐ (b) $\dfrac{3}{4}$ ☐

(c) $\dfrac{11}{14}$ ☐ (d) $\dfrac{23}{24}$ ☐

2. $\dfrac{1095}{1168}$ in simplest form is :

(a) $\dfrac{13}{16}$ ☐ (b) $\dfrac{15}{16}$ ☐

(c) $\dfrac{17}{26}$ ☐ (d) $\dfrac{25}{26}$ ☐

3. H.C.F. of 1485 and 4356 is :
   (a) 189 ☐ (b) 89 ☐
   (c) 99 ☐ (d) 83 ☐

4. H.C.F. of 42, 63 and 140 is :
   (a) 14 ☐ (b) 9 ☐
   (c) 21 ☐ (d) 7 ☐

5. H.C.F. of 2^3, 3^2, 4 and 15 is :
   (a) 2^3 ☐ (b) 3^2 ☐
   (c) 1 ☐ (d) 360 ☐

6. Which of the following is a pair of co-primes ?
   (a) (14, 35) ☐ (b) (18, 25) ☐
   (c) (31, 93) ☐ (d) (32, 62) ☐

7. L.C.M. of 87 and 145 is :
   (a) 870 ☐ (b) 1305 ☐
   (c) 435 ☐ (d) 1740 ☐

8. L.C.M. of 22, 54, 108, 135 and 198 is :
   (a) 330 ☐ (b) 1980 ☐
   (c) 5940 ☐ (d) 11880 ☐

9. L.C.M. of 3^3, 4 , 4^2 and 3 is :
   (a) 12 ☐ (b) 48 ☐
   (c) 432 ☐ (d) none of these ☐

10. H.C.F. of $\dfrac{1}{2}, \dfrac{2}{3}, \dfrac{3}{4}, \dfrac{4}{5}$ is :
    (a) 1 ☐ (b) 12 ☐
    (c) $\dfrac{4}{5}$ ☐ (d) $\dfrac{1}{60}$ ☐

H.C.F. & L.C.M. of Numbers   27

11. H.C.F. of $\dfrac{1}{2}, \dfrac{3}{4}, \dfrac{5}{6}, \dfrac{7}{8}, \dfrac{9}{10}$ is :

   (a) $\dfrac{1}{2}$ ☐   (b) $\dfrac{1}{10}$ ☐

   (c) $\dfrac{9}{120}$ ☐   (d) $\dfrac{1}{120}$ ☐

12. L.C.M. of $\dfrac{3}{4}, \dfrac{6}{7}, \dfrac{9}{8}$ is :

   (a) 18 ☐   (b) 3 ☐

   (c) $\dfrac{3}{56}$ ☐   (d) $\dfrac{9}{28}$ ☐

13. L.C.M. of $\dfrac{2}{3}, \dfrac{4}{9}, \dfrac{5}{6}$ and $\dfrac{7}{12}$ is :

   (a) $\dfrac{1}{18}$ ☐   (b) $\dfrac{1}{36}$ ☐

   (c) $\dfrac{35}{9}$ ☐   (d) $\dfrac{140}{3}$ ☐

14. Which of the following fractions is the greatest of all ?
   $\dfrac{7}{8}, \dfrac{6}{7}, \dfrac{4}{5}, \dfrac{5}{6}$:   (Railway Recruitment, 1991)

   (a) $\dfrac{6}{7}$ ☐   (b) $\dfrac{4}{5}$ ☐

   (c) $\dfrac{5}{6}$ ☐   (d) $\dfrac{7}{8}$ ☐

15. Which of the following is in ascending order ?   (Bank P.O. 1988)

   (a) $\dfrac{5}{7}, \dfrac{7}{8}, \dfrac{9}{11}$ ☐   (b) $\dfrac{5}{7}, \dfrac{9}{11}, \dfrac{7}{8}$ ☐

   (c) $\dfrac{7}{8}, \dfrac{5}{7}, \dfrac{9}{11}$ ☐   (d) $\dfrac{9}{11}, \dfrac{7}{8}, \dfrac{5}{7}$ ☐

16. Which of the following is in descending order ?

   (a) $\dfrac{3}{5}, \dfrac{5}{7}, \dfrac{7}{9}$ ☐   (b) $\dfrac{7}{9}, \dfrac{5}{7}, \dfrac{3}{5}$ ☐

   (c) $\dfrac{5}{7}, \dfrac{7}{9}, \dfrac{3}{5}$ ☐   (d) $\dfrac{7}{9}, \dfrac{3}{5}, \dfrac{5}{7}$ ☐

17. Which of the fractions $\dfrac{1}{2}, \dfrac{3}{7}, \dfrac{3}{5}, \dfrac{4}{9}$ is the smallest ?

   (a) $\dfrac{4}{9}$ ☐   (b) $\dfrac{3}{5}$ ☐

Objective Arithmetic

    (c) $\frac{3}{7}$ (d) $\frac{1}{2}$

                                                                (Railway Recruitment, 1991)

18. L.C.M. of $\frac{2}{7}, \frac{3}{14}$ and $\frac{5}{3}$ is ?

                                                                                    (C.B.I. 1991)

    (a) 45   (b) 35

    (c) 30   (d) 25

19. About the number of pairs which have 16 as their H.C.F. and 136 as their L.C.M., we can definitely say that :   **(C.B.I. 1990)**

    (a) Only one such pair exists

    (b) Only two such pairs exist

    (c) Many such pairs exist

    (d) No such pair exists

20. H.C.F. of three numbers is 12. If they be in the ratio 1 : 2 : 3, the numbers are :   **(C.B.I. 1991)**

    (a) 12, 24, 36   (b) 10, 20, 30

    (c) 5, 10, 15   (d) 4, 8, 12

21. The product of two numbers is 1600 and their H.C.F. is 5. The L.C.M. of the numbers is :

    (a) 320   (b) 1605

    (c) 1595   (d) 8000

22. The H.C.F. of two numbers is 16 and their L.C.M. is 160. If one of the numbers is 32, then the other number is :

    (a) 48   (b) 80

    (c) 96   (d) 112

                                                             (Hotel Management, 1991)

23. The product of two two-digit numbers is 2160 and their G.C.M. is 12. The numbers are :

    (a) 72, 30   (b) 36, 60

    (c) 96, 25   (d) none of these

24. The H.C.F. of two numbers is 12 and their diffrence is also 12. The numbers are :   **(Central Excise & I. Tax 1988)**

    (a) 66, 78   (b) 70, 82

    (c) 94, 106   (d) 84, 96

25. The sum of two numbers is 216 and their H.C.F. is 27. The numbers are :

    (a) 54, 162   (b) 108, 108

    (c) 27, 189   (d) none of these

H.C.F. & L.C.M. of Numbers

26. The largest number which exactly divides 210, 315, 147 and 161 is :
    (a) 3 (b) 7
    (c) 21 (d) 4410

27. Three pieces of timber 42 m, 49 m and 63 m long have to be divided into planks of the same length. What is the greatest possible length of each plank ?
    (a) 7 m (b) 14 m
    (c) 42 m (d) 63 m

28. Three different containers contain different qualities of mixtures of milk and water, whose measurements are 403 kg, 434 kg and 465 kg. What biggest measure must be there to measure all the different quantities exactly :
    (a) 1 kg (b) 7 kg
    (c) 31 kg (d) 41 kg

29. The greatest possible length which can be used to measure exactly the lengths 7 m, 3 m 85 cm, 12 m 95 cm, is :
    (a) 15 cm (b) 25 cm
    (c) 35 cm (d) 42 cm

30. The least perfect square number which is divisible by 3, 4, 5, 6 and 8, is : (Central Excise & I. Tax 1989)
    (a) 900 (b) 1200
    (c) 2500 (d) 3600

31. The smallest number which is divisible by 12, 15, 20 and is a perfect square, is : (C.B.I. 1991)
    (a) 400 (b) 900
    (c) 1600 (d) 3600

32. The least number of square tiles required to pave the ceiling of a room 15 m 17 cm long and 9 m 2 cm broad, is :
    (a) 656 (b) 738
    (c) 814 (d) 902

33. The largest number which divides 77, 147 and 252 to leave the same remainder in each case, is :
    (a) 9 (b) 15
    (c) 25 (d) 35

34. The greatest number which can divide 1354, 1866 and 2762 leaving the same remainder 10 in each case, is :
    (a) 64 (b) 124
    (c) 156 (d) 260

35. The largest natural number which exactly divides the product of any four consecutive natural numbers, is : (C.B.I. 1991)
(a) 6 (b) 12
(c) 24 (d) 120

36. The least number which when divided by 15, 27, 35 and 42, leaves in each case, a remainder 7, is :
(a) 1883 (b) 1897
(c) 1987 (d) 2007

37. The least multiple of 7, which leaves a remainder of 4, when divided by 6, 9, 15 and 18, is :
(a) 74 (b) 94
(c) 184 (d) 364

38. The greatest number of four digits which is divisible by each one of the numbers 12, 18, 21 and 28, is :
(a) 9848 (b) 9864
(c) 9828 (d) 9636

39. Six bells commence tolling together and toll at intervals of 2, 4, 6, 8, 10 and 12 seconds respectively. In 30 minutes, how many times do they toll together ? (C.B.I. 1991)
(a) 4 (b) 10
(c) 15 (d) 16

40. The least number which when divided by 16, 18 and 21 leaves the remainders 3, 5 and 8 respectively, is :
(a) 893 (b) 992
(c) 995 (d) 1024

41. The smallest number which when diminished by 3, is divisible by 21, 28, 36 and 45, is :
(a) 420 (b) 1257
(c) 1260 (d) 1263

42. The least number, which when divided by 35, 45 and 55 leaves the remainder 18, 28 and 38 respectively, is :
(a) 2468 (b) 3448
(c) 3265 (d) 3482

43. The smallest number, which when divided by 20, 25, 35 and 40 leaves the remainder 14, 19, 29 and 34 respectively, is :
(a) 1394 (b) 1404
(c) 1406 (d) 1664

H.C.F. & L.C.M. of Numbers

44. The traffic lights at three different road crossings change after every 48 sec., 72 sec. and 108 sec. respectively. If they all change simultaneously at 8 : 20 : 00 hrs; then they will again change simultaneously at : (C.B.I. 1991)
  (a) 8 : 27 : 12 hrs   (b) 8 : 27 : 24 hrs
  (c) 8 : 27 : 36 hrs   (d) 8 : 27 : 48 hrs

45. The greatest number by which if 1657 and 2037 are divided the remainders will be 6 and 5 respectively, is :
  (a) 127   (b) 235
  (c) 260   (d) 305

46. The least number which when divided by 5, 6, 7 and 8 leaves a remainder 3, but when divided by 9 leaves no remainder, is :
  (a) 1677   (b) 1683
  (c) 2523   (d) 3363

47. The H.C.F. and L.C.M. of two numbers are 44 and 264 respectively. If the first number is divided by 2, the quotient is 44. The other number is : (Astt. Grade 1987)
  (a) 33   (b) 66
  (c) 132   (d) 264

48. What least number must be subtracted from 1294 so that the remainder when divided by 9, 11, 13 will leave in each case the same remainder 6 ? (C.B.I. 1991)
  (a) 0   (b) 1
  (c) 2   (d) 3

49. The number of prime factors in the expression $(6)^{10} \times (7)^{17} \times (11)^{27}$ is : (Central Excise & I. Tax 1988)
  (a) 54   (b) 64
  (c) 71   (d) 81

50. The total number of prime factors of the product $(8)^{20} (15)^{24} (7)^{15}$ is :
  (a) 59   (b) 98
  (c) 123   (d) 138

  (C.B.I. 1991)

51. The number of prime factors in $2^{222} \times 3^{333} \times 5^{555}$ is :
  (a) 3   (b) 1107
  (c) 1110   (d) 1272

  (Astt. Grade 1987)

52. Three measuring rods are 64 cm, 80 cm and 96 cm in length. The least length of cloth that can be measured exact number of times using any

one of the above rods is : (Central Excise & I. Tax 1989)
(a) 0.96 m (b) 19.20 m
(c) 9.60 m (d) 96.00 m

Answers

1. (b) 2. (b) 3. (c) 4. (d) 5. (c) 6. (b) 7. (c) 8. (c) 9. (c)
10. (d) 11. (d) 12. (a) 13. (d) 14. (d) 15. (b) 16. (b) 17. (c) 18. (c)
19. (d) 20. (a) 21. (a) 22. (b) 23. (b) 24. (d) 25. (c) 26. (b) 27. (a)
28. (c) 29. (c) 30. (d) 31. (d) 32. (c) 33. (d) 34. (a) 35. (c) 36. (b)
37. (d) 38. (c) 39. (d) 40. (c) 41. (d) 42. (b) 43. (a) 44. (a) 45. (a)
46. (b) 47. (c) 48. (b) 49. (b) 50. (c) 51. (c) 52. (c).

Solution (Exercise 2)

1. H.C.F. of 561, 748 is 187.

   Dividing Nume. and Denom. by 187, we get, $\frac{561}{748} = \frac{3}{4}$.

2. H.C.F. of 1095 and 1168 is 73.

   Dividing Nume. & Denom. by 73, we get, $\frac{1095}{1168} = \frac{15}{16}$.

3. H.C.F. of 1485 and 4356 is 99.
4. H.C.F. of 42 and 63 is 21.
   H.C.F. of 21 and 140 is 7.
   ∴ H.C.F. of 42, 63 and 140 is 7.
5. Clearly, 1 is the highest common factor of $2^3, 3^2$, 4 and 15.
6. H.C.F. of 18 and 25 is 1.
   So, 18 and 25 are Co-primes.
7. H.C.F. of 87 and 145 is 29.
   ∴ L.C.M. = $\frac{87 \times 145}{29}$ = 435.

H.C.F. & L.C.M. of Numbers

8.
```
2 | 22 - 54 - 108 - 135 - 198
3 | 11 - 27 - 54 - 135 - 99
3 | 11 -  9 - 18 -  45 - 33
3 | 11 -  3 -  6 -  15 - 11
11| 11 -  1 -  2 -   5 - 11
  |  1 -  1 -  2 -   5 -  1
```

∴ L.C.M. = $2 \times 3 \times 3 \times 3 \times 11 \times 2 \times 5 = 5940$.

9. L.C.M. = $3^3 \times 2^4 = 27 \times 16 = 432$.

10. H.C.F. = $\dfrac{\text{H.C.F. of } 1, 2, 3, 4}{\text{L.C.M. of } 2, 3, 4, 5} = \dfrac{1}{60}$.

11. H.C.F. = $\dfrac{\text{H.C.F. of } 1, 3, 5, 7, 9}{\text{L.C.M. of } 2, 4, 6, 8, 10} = \dfrac{1}{120}$.

12. L.C.M. = $\dfrac{\text{L.C.M. of } 3, 6, 9}{\text{H.C.F. of } 4, 7, 8} = \dfrac{18}{1} = 18$.

13. L.C.M. = $\dfrac{\text{L.C.M. of } 2, 4, 5, 7}{\text{H.C.F. of } 3, 9, 6, 12} = \dfrac{140}{3}$.

14. $\dfrac{7}{8} = 0.875,\ \dfrac{6}{7} = 0.857,\ \dfrac{4}{5} = 0.8$ and $\dfrac{5}{6} = 0.833$

   Now, $0.875 > 0.875 > 0.833 > 0.8$.

   So, $\dfrac{7}{8}$ is the greatest.

15. $\dfrac{5}{7} = 0.714,\ \dfrac{7}{8} = 0.875$ and $\dfrac{9}{11} = 0.818$.

   Now, $0.714 < 0.818 < 0.875$ *i.e.* $\dfrac{5}{7} < \dfrac{9}{11} < \dfrac{7}{8}$.

16. $\dfrac{3}{5} = 0.6,\ \dfrac{5}{7} = 0.714$ and $\dfrac{7}{9} = 0.777$

   Clearly $0.777 > 0.714 > 0.6$ *i.e.* $\dfrac{7}{9} > \dfrac{5}{7} > \dfrac{3}{5}$.

17. $\dfrac{1}{2} = 0.5,\ \dfrac{3}{7} = 0.428,\ \dfrac{3}{5} = 0.6$ & $\dfrac{4}{9} = 0.444$.

   Clearly, $\dfrac{3}{7}$ is the smallest.

18. L.C.M. = $\dfrac{\text{L.C.M. of } 2, 3, 5}{\text{H.C.F. of } 7, 14, 3} = \dfrac{30}{1} = 30.$

19. H.C.F. is always a factor of L.C.M.
    SO, no two numbers exist with H.C.F. = 16 and L.C.M. = 136.

20. Let the numbers be $x, 2x$ and $3x$.
    Then, their H.C.F. = x. So, $x = 12$.
    $\therefore$ The numbers are 12, 24, 36.

21. L.C.M. = $\dfrac{\text{Product}}{\text{H.C.F.}} = \dfrac{1600}{5} = 320.$

22. The other number = $\dfrac{\text{H.C.F.} \times \text{L.C.M.}}{\text{Given number}} = \dfrac{16 \times 160}{32} = 80.$

23. Let the numbers be $12a$ and $12b$.
    Then, $12a \times 12b = 2160$ or $ab = 15$.
    $\therefore$ Values of co-primes a and b are $(1, 15), (3, 5)$.
    So, the two digit numbers are 12×3 & 12×5. i.e. 36 and 60.

24. The difference of requisite numbers must be 12 and each one must be divisible by 12. So, the numbers are 84, 96.

25. Let the numbers be $27a$ and $27b$.
    Then, $27a + 27b = 216$ or $27(a + b) = 216$ or $a + b = \dfrac{216}{27} = 8.$
    $\therefore$ Values of Co-primes (with sum 8) are $(1, 7)$ & $(3, 5)$.
    So, the numbers are $(27 \times 1, 27 \times 7)$ i.e. $(27, 189)$.

26. The largest number is the H.C.F. of 210, 315, 147 and 168, which is 21.

27. Greatest possible length of each plank
    = (H.C.F. of 42, 49, 63) m = 7 m.

28. Biggest measure = (H.C.F. of 403, 434 and 465) kg = 31 kg.

29. Required length = (H.C.F. of 700, 385, 1295) cm = 35 cn

30.
    $\begin{array}{r|l}
    3 & 3 - 4 - 5 - 6 - 8 \\
    \hline
    2 & 1 - 4 - 5 - 2 - 8 \\
    \hline
    2 & 1 - 2 - 5 - 1 - 4 \\
    \hline
      & 1 - 1 - 5 - 1 - 2
    \end{array}$

    L.C.M. of 3, 4, 5, 6, 8 = $3 \times 2 \times 2 \times 5 \times 2$.
    Required number = $(3 \times 3 \times 2 \times 2 \times 5 \times 5 \times 2 \times 2) = 3600.$

H.C.F. & L.C.M. of Numbers

31.
```
5 | 12 - 15 - 20
  |---------------
3 | 12 -  3 -  4
  |---------------
4 |  4 -  1 -  4
  |---------------
  |  1 -  1 -  1
```
∴ L.C.M. of 12, 15, 20 is $5 \times 3 \times 4 = 60$.
Required number = $(60 \times 60) = 3600$.

32. Side of each tile = (H.C.F. of 1517 and 902) cm = 41 cm.

∴ Number of tiles = $\dfrac{1517 \times 902}{41 \times 41} = 814$.

33. Required number is the H.C.F. of $(147 - 77)$, $(252 - 147)$ and $(252 - 77)$ i.e. H.C.F. of 70, 105 and 175. This is 35.

34. Required number = H.C.F. of 1344, 1856 & 2752 = 64.

35. $1 \times 2 \times 3 \times 4 = 24$.
∴ Required number = 24.

36. Required number = (L.C.M. of 15, 27, 35, 42) + 7
    = $(1890 + 7) = 1897$.

37. L.C.M. of 6, 9, 15 and 18 is 90.
Let the least multiple of 7 be x, which when divided by 90 leaves the remainder 4. Then, x is of the form $90 k + 4$.
Now, the minimum value of k for which $90 k + 4$ is divisible by 7 is 4.
∴ $x = 90 \times 4 + 4 = 364$.

38. Required number is divisible by the L.C.M. of 12, 18, 21, 28 i.e., 252.
Now, greatest number of four digits = 9999.
On dividing 9999 by 252, the remainder is 171.
∴ Required number = $(9999 - 171) = 9828$.

39. L.C.M. of 2, 4, 6, 8, 10 and 12 is 120.
So, the bells will toll together after 120 seconds, i.e. 2 minutes.

In 30 min. they will toll together in $\left(\dfrac{30}{2}\right) + 1$ times, i.e. 16 times.

40. Here $(16 - 3) = 13$, $(18 - 5) = 13$ and $(21 - 8) = 13$.
So, required number = (L.C.M. of 16, 18, 21) − 13
    = $(1008 - 13) = 995$.

41. Required number = (L.C.M. of 21, 28, 36, 45) + 3
    = $(1260 + 3) = 1263$.

42. Here $(35 - 18) = 17$, $(45 - 28) = 17$ and $(55 - 38) = 17$.
∴ Required number = (L.C.M. of 35, 45, 55) − 17
= (3465 − 17) = 3448.

43. Here $(20 - 14) = (25 - 19) = (35 - 29) = (40 - 34) = 6$.
∴ Required number = (L.C.M. of 20, 25, 35, 40) − 6
= (1400 − 6) = 1394.

44. Interval of change = (L.C.M. of 48, 72, 108) sec. = 432.
So, the lights will change after every 432 seconds *i.e.* 7 min. 12 sec.
So, the next simultaneous change will take place at 8 : 27 : 12 hrs.

45. Required number = H.C.F. of $(1657 - 6)$ and $(2037 - 5)$
= H.C.F. of 1651 and 2032 = 127.

46. L.C.M. of 5, 6, 7, 8 is 840.
So, the number is of the form $840k + 3$
Least value of k for which $(840k + 3)$ is divisible by 9 is $k = 2$.
∴ Required number = $(840 \times 2 + 3) = 1683$.

47. First number = $2 \times 44 = 88$.
Second number = $\dfrac{44 \times 264}{88} = 132$.

48. L.C.M. of 9, 11, 13 is 1287.
On dividing 1294 by 1287, the remainder is 7.
∴ 1 must be subtracted from 1294 so that 1293 when divided by 9, 11, 13 leaves in each case the same remainder 6.

49. Since 2, 3, 7, 11 are prime numbers and the given expression is $2^{10} \times 3^{10} \times 7^{17} \times 11^{27}$, so the number of prime factors in the given expression is $(10 + 10 + 17 + 27) = 64$.

50. Since 2, 3, 5, 17 are prime numbers and the given expression is $(2^3)^{20} \times (3 \times 5)^{24} \times (17)^{15}$ *i.e.* $2^{60} \times 3^{24} \times 5^{24} \times 17^{15}$, so the number of prime factors in the given expression is $(60 + 24 + 24 + 15) = 123$.

51. The number of prime factors in the given product
= $(222 + 333 + 555) = 1110$.

52. Required length = (L.C.M. of 64, 80, 96) cm = 960 cm = 9.60 m.

3

DECIMAL FRACTIONS

DECIMAL FRACTIONS : *Fractions in which denominators are powers of 10 are called decimal fractions.*

$\frac{1}{10}, \frac{1}{100}, \frac{1}{1000}$ etc. are respectively the *tenth*, the *hundredth* and the *thousandth* part of 1.

$\frac{7}{10}$ is 7 tenths, written as .7 (called *decimal seven*);

$\frac{13}{100}$ is 13 hundredths, written as .13 (called *decimal one-three*)

$\frac{9}{100}$ is 9 hundredths, written as .09 (called *decimal zero-nine*)

$\frac{4}{1000}$ is 4 thousandths, written as .004 (called *decimal zero-zero-four*)

and so on.

53.678 = 50 + 3 + .6 + .07 + .008.

CONVERTING A DECIMAL INTO A VULGAR FRACTION

Rule : *Put 1 in the denominator, under the decimal point and anex with it as many zeros as is the number of digits after the decimal point. Now, remove the decimal point and reduce the fraction to its lowest terms.*

Ex. 1. (i) $0.54 = \frac{54}{100} = \frac{27}{50}$.

(ii) $2.005 = \frac{2005}{1000} = \frac{401}{200} = 2\frac{1}{200}$.

Remark 1 : Annexing zeros to the extreme right of a decimal fraction does not change its value.

Thus, 0.7 = 0.70 = 0.700 etc.

Remark 2 : If numerator and denominator of a fraction contain the same number of decimal places, then we may remove the decimal sign.

Ex. 2. (i) $\frac{5.63}{7.91} = \frac{563}{791}$.

(ii) $\frac{9.0341}{17.8632} = \frac{90341}{178632}$.

ADDITION & SUBTRACTION OF DECIMAL FRACTIONS

RULE : *The given numbers are so placed under each. Other that the decimal point lies in one column. The numbers so arranged can now be added or subtracted in a usual way.*

Ex. 3. (i) $213 + 2.013 + .213 + 2.0013 = ?$ (L.I.C. 1991)
(ii) $3.045 + 3.28 + .039 + 7.6 + .2 + 2 = ?$

Sol. (i) 213
2.013
.213
+ 2.0013
———
217.2273

(ii) 3.045
3.28
.039
7.6
.2
+ 2
———
16.164

Ex. 4. Subtract :
(i) **16.3629 from 21.003.**
(ii) **8.2967 from 11.**

Sol. (i) 21.003
− 16.3629
———
4.6401

(ii) 11.0000
− 8.2967
———
2.7033

Ex. 5. $32.52 + ? = 452.345.$ (G.I.C. 1991)
Sol. Let $32.53 + x = 452.345.$

$\therefore x = (452.345 - 32.52) = 419.825$

452.345
− 32.52
———
419.825

Multiplication of A Decimal Fraction by A Power of 10 :
Rule : *Shift the decimal point to the right by as many places of decimal, as is the power of 10.*

Ex. 6. Multiply :
(i) **4.7209 by 100**   (ii) **0.3456 by 1000**
(iii) **.034 by 10000**   (iv) **.11 by 100000.**

Sol. (i) $4.7209 \times 100 = 472.09.$
(ii) $0.3456 \times 1000 = 345.6.$
(iii) $.034 \times 10000 = .0340 \times 10000 = 340.$

Decimal Fractions

(iv) $.11 \times 100000 = .11000 \times 100000 = 11000.$

Multiplication Of Two Or More Decimal Fractions

Rule : *Multiply the given numbers considering them without the decimal point. Now, in the product, the decimal point is marked off to obtain as many places of decimal as is the sum of the number of decimal places in the given numbers.*

Ex. 7. Find the products :

(i) 1.71×1.2 (ii) 3.746×11.4

Sol. (i) $171 \times 12 = 2052.$

The sum of decimal places of given numbers $= (2 + 1) = 3.$

∴ $1.71 \times 1.2 = 2.052.$

(ii)   3746
      × 114
      ─────
      14984
      3746×
      3746××
      ─────
      427044

Thus, $3746 \times 114 = 427044.$

Sum of decimal places of given numbers $= (3 + 1) = 4.$

∴ $3.746 \times 11.4 = 42.7044.$

Ex. 8. $.5 \times .05 \times .005 \times 50 = ?$

Sol. $5 \times 5 \times 5 \times 50 = 6250.$

The sum of decimal places of given numbers = six.

∴ $.5 \times .05 \times .005 \times 50 = .006250.$

Ex. 9. Given that $172 \times 38 = 6536$, find $1.72 \times .38.$

Sol. Sum of decimal places $= (2 + 2) = 4.$

∴ $1.72 \times .38 = .6536.$

Dividing A Decimal Fraction By A Counting Number :

Rule : *Divide the given decimal numeral without considering the decimal point, by the given counting number. Now, in the quotient, put the decimal point to give as many places of decimal as are there in the dividend.*

Ex. 10. Divide :

(i) **0.49 by 7**   (ii) **0.0182 by 14.**

Sol. (i) $49 \div 7 = 7$.

Dividend contains two places of decimal.

$\therefore 0.49 \div 7 = 0.07$.

(ii) $182 \div 14 = 13$.

Dividend contains four places of decimal.

$\therefore 0.0182 \div 14 = .0013$.

Dividing A Decimal Fraction By A Decimal Fraction

Rule : *Multiply both the dividend and the divisor by a suitable multiple of 10 to make divisor a whole number. Now, proceed as above.*

Ex. 11. Divide :

(i) 25 by .05   (ii) **0.00044 by 0.11**

(iii) **40.40 by 0.0008**   (iv) **4.2 by 0.006**

Sol. (i) $\dfrac{25}{.05} = \dfrac{25 \times 100}{.05 \times 100} = \dfrac{2500}{5} = 500$.

(ii) $\dfrac{0.00044}{0.11} = \dfrac{0.00044}{0.11} \times \dfrac{100}{100} = \dfrac{.044}{11} = .004$.

(iii) $\dfrac{40.40}{0.0008} = \dfrac{40.40}{0.0008} \times \dfrac{10000}{10000} = \dfrac{404000}{8} = 50500$.

(iv) $\dfrac{4.2}{0.006} = \dfrac{4.2}{0.006} \times \dfrac{1000}{1000} = \dfrac{4200}{6} = 700$.

Ex. 12. (i) $0.001 \div ? = 0.1$.   (ii) $? \div .025 = 40$.

Sol. (i) Let $\dfrac{0.001}{x} = 0.1$. Then, $x = \dfrac{0.001}{0.100} = \dfrac{1}{100} = .01$.

(ii) Let $\dfrac{x}{.025} = 40$. Then, $x = 40 \times .025 = 1$.

H.C.F. & L.C.M. of Decimal Fractions

Rule : *In given numbers, make the same number of decimal places by annexing zeros in some numbers, if necessary. Considering these numbers without decimal point, find H.C.F. or L.C.M., as the case may be. Now, in the result, mark off as many decimal places as are there in each of the given numbers.*

Ex. 13. Find the H.C.F. and L.C.M. of 1.75, 5.6 and 7.

Sol. Making the same number of decimal places, the numbers may be written as 1.75, 5.60 and 7.00.

Without decimal point, these numbers are 175, 560 and 700.

Now, H.C.F. of 175, 560 and 700 is 35.

∴ H.C.F. of 1.75, 5.6 and 7 is 0.35.
L.C.M. of 175, 560 and 700 is 2800.
∴ L.C.M. of 1.75, 5.6 and 7 is 28.00 i.e. 28.

Comparison of Fractions

Rule : *Convert each one of the given fractions in the decimal form. Now, arrange them in ascending or descending order, as per requirement.*

Ex. 14. Arrange the fractions $\frac{3}{8}, \frac{7}{12}, \frac{2}{3}, \frac{14}{19}, \frac{16}{25}$ and $\frac{1}{2}$ in ascending order of magnitude.

Sol. Converting each of the given fractions into decimal form, we get :

$$\frac{3}{8} = 0.375, \frac{7}{12} = 0.583, \frac{2}{3} = 0.666, \frac{14}{19} = 0.736,$$

$$\frac{16}{25} = 0.64 \text{ and } \frac{1}{2} = 0.5.$$

Clearly, $0.375 < 0.5 < 0.583 < 0.64 < 0.666 < 0.736$.

$$\therefore \frac{3}{8} < \frac{1}{2} < \frac{7}{12} < \frac{16}{25} < \frac{2}{3} < \frac{14}{19}.$$

Recurring Decimal : *If in a decimal fraction, a figure or set of figures is repeated continuously, then such a number is called a recurring decimal.*

If a single figure is repeated, then it is expressed by putting a dot on it. If a set of figures is repeated, it is expressed by putting a bar on the set.

Ex. 15. (i) $\frac{2}{3} = 0.6666\ldots\ldots = 0.\dot{6}$.

(ii) $\frac{1}{7} = 0.142857\ 142857\ \ldots\ldots = \overline{0.142857}$.

Pure Recurring Decimal : *A decimal fraction in which all the figures after the decimal point are repeated, is called a pure recurring decimal.*

Rule : *For converting a pure recurring decimal into a vulgar fraction, write the repeated figures only once in the numerator and take as many nines in the denominator as is the number of repeating figures.*

Ex. 16. Express the following as vulgar fractions :

(i) $0.\overline{7}$ (ii) $0.\overline{41}$ (iii) $0.\overline{057}$

Sol. (i) $0.\overline{7} = \dfrac{7}{9}$ (ii) $0.\overline{41} = \dfrac{41}{99}$

(iii) $0.\overline{057} = \dfrac{57}{999}$.

Mixed Recurring Decimal : *A decimal fraction in which some figures do not repeat and some of them repeat, is called a mixed recurring decimal.*

Rule : *For converting a mixed recurring decimal into a vulgar fraction, in the numerator, take the difference between the number formed by all the digits after decimal point (taking the repeated digits only once) and that formed by non-repeating digits. In the denominator, take the number formed by as many nines as there are repeating digits, followed by as many zeros as is the number of non-repeating digits.*

Ex. 17. Express each of the following as a vulgar fraction :

(i) $0.1\dot{7}$ (ii) $0.12\overline{54}$ (iii) $2.53\overline{6}$

Sol. (i) $0.1\dot{7} = \dfrac{17-1}{90} = \dfrac{16}{90} = \dfrac{8}{45}$.

(ii) $0.12\overline{54} = \dfrac{1254-12}{9900} = \dfrac{1242}{9900} = \dfrac{69}{550}$.

(iii) $2.54\overline{6} = 2 + 0.53\overline{6} = 2 + \dfrac{536-53}{900} = 2 + \dfrac{483}{900}$

$= 2 + \dfrac{161}{300} = 2\dfrac{161}{300}$.

EXERCISE 3

1. $0.6 + 0.66 + 0.066 + 6.606 = ?$
   - (a) 6.744
   - (b) 6.738
   - (c) 7.932
   - (d) 7.388

2. $16.7 + 12.38 - ? = 10.09$
   - (a) 17.89
   - (b) 18.99
   - (c) 16.98
   - (d) 20.09

3. $3 \times 0.3 \times 0.03 \times 0.003 \times 30 = ?$
   - (a) .0000243
   - (b) .000243
   - (c) .00243
   - (d) .0243

4. $15.60 \times 0.30 = ?$ **(Bank P.O. 1991)**
   - (a) 4.68
   - (b) 0.458

Decimal Fractions

    (c) 0.468   (d) 0.0468

5.   0.0169 ÷ 0.013 = ?
    (a) .13   (b) .013
    (c) 1.3   (d) 13

6.   50.8 ÷ 2540 = ?
    (a) 2   (b) .2
    (c) 0.002   (d) 0.02

7.   12 ÷ 0.09 of 0.3 × 2 = ?
    (a) 0.8   (b) 0.08
    (c) 8   (d) none of these

8.   25 ÷ .0005 = ?
    (a) 50   (b) 500
    (c) 5000   (d) none of these

9.   0.000033 ÷ 0.11 = ?
    (a) .003   (b) .03
    (c) .0003   (d) .3

10.   0.001 ÷ ? = 0.01
    (a) 10   (b) .1
    (c) .01   (d) .001

11.   ? ÷ .0025 = 800
    (a) .2   (b) .02
    (c) 2000   (d) 2

12.   ?% of 10.8 = 32.4
    (a) 3   (b) 30
    (c) 300   (d) 0.3

13.   0.09 × 0.008 = ?
    (a) 0.072   (b) 0.0072
    (c) 0.00072   (d) 0.72

14.   0.8 × ? = 0.0004
    (a) .0005   (b) .005
    (c) .5   (d) .00005

15. $\dfrac{3420}{19} = \dfrac{?}{0.01} \times 7$

                                                                                                                          (Bank P.O. 1988)

    (a) $\dfrac{35}{9}$ (b) $\dfrac{18}{7}$

(c) $\frac{63}{5}$　　　　(d) none of these

16. $\frac{17.28 + ?}{3.6 \times 0.2} = 200$

　　　　　　　　　　　　　　　　(Bank P.O. 1988)
(a) 120　　　　(b) 1.20
(c) 12　　　　(d) 0.12

17. $\frac{20 + 8 \times 0.5}{20 - ?} = 12$

　　　　　　　　　　　　　　　　(Bank Clerical, 1990)
(a) 8　　　　(b) 18
(c) 2　　　　(d) none of these

18. $0.15 \div \frac{0.5}{15} = ?$

　　　　　　　　　　　　　　　　(Bank Clerical, 1990)
(a) 4.5　　　　(b) 45
(c) 0.03　　　　(d) 0.45

19. If $\frac{1}{3.718} = .2689$, then the value of $\frac{1}{.0003718}$ is :
(a) 2689　　　　(b) 2.689
(c) 26890　　　　(d) .2689

20. If $12276 \div 155 = 79.2$, the value of $122.76 \div 15.5$ is :　(C.D.S. 1991)
(a) 7.092　　　　(b) 7.92
(c) 79.02　　　　(d) 79.2

21. If $\sqrt{5} = 2.24$, then the value of $\frac{3\sqrt{5}}{2\sqrt{5} - 0.48}$ is :
(a) 0.168　　　　(b) 1.68
(c) 16.8　　　　(d) 168

　　　　　　　　　　(Central Excise & I. Tax 1988)

22. If $\sqrt{15} = 3.88$, the value of $\sqrt{\frac{5}{3}}$ is :

　　　　　　　　　　　　　　　　(Bank P.O. 1987)
(a) 0.43　　　　(b) 1.89
(c) 1.29　　　　(d) 1.63

23. If $\sqrt{4096} = 64$, then the value of
$\sqrt{40.96} + \sqrt{0.4096} + \sqrt{0.004096} + \sqrt{0.00004096}$ is :
(a) 7.09　　　　(b) 7.1014
(c) 7.1104　　　　(d) 7.12

24. $\sqrt{\frac{0.289}{0.00121}} = ?$

　　　　　　　　　　　(Railway Recruitment, 1991)

Decimal Fractions

(a) $\dfrac{170}{11}$ (b) $\dfrac{17}{110}$

(c) $\dfrac{17}{1100}$ (d) $\dfrac{17}{11}$

25. The square root of $\dfrac{0.324 \times 0.081 \times 4.624}{1.5625 \times 0.0289 \times 72.9 \times 64}$ is :

(a) 24   (b) 2.4
(c) 0.024   (d) none of these

(Assistant Grade, 1990)

26. If 2805 ÷ 2.55 = 1100, then 280.5 ÷ 25.5 is equal to : **(Bank P.O. 1987)**

(a) 1.01   (b) 1.1
(c) 0.11   (d) 11

27. $\dfrac{.35 \times .0015}{.25 \times .07}$ written as a percentage, is :

(a) 0.3%   (b) 3%
(c) 30%   (d) none of these

28. $\dfrac{.24 \times .35}{.14 \times .15 \times .02}$ is equal to :

(a) 2   (b) 20
(c) 200   (d) 2000

29. Which of the following fractions are in ascending order :

(a) $\dfrac{16}{19}, \dfrac{11}{14}, \dfrac{17}{22}$ (b) $\dfrac{11}{14}, \dfrac{16}{19}, \dfrac{17}{22}$

(c) $\dfrac{17}{22}, \dfrac{11}{14}, \dfrac{16}{19}$ (d) $\dfrac{16}{19}, \dfrac{17}{22}, \dfrac{11}{14}$

(Bank P.O. 1987)

30. Which of the following fractions is the smallest ?   **(C.B.I. 1990)**

(a) $\dfrac{11}{13}$ (b) $\dfrac{9}{11}$

(c) $\dfrac{3}{4}$ (d) $\dfrac{5}{7}$

31. What decimal of an hour is a second ?

(a) .0025   (b) .0256
(c) .00027   (d) .000126

32. The H.C.F. of 0.54, 1.8 and 7.2 is :

(a) 1.8   (b) .18
(c) .018   (d) 18

33. G.C.D. of 1.08, .36 and .9 is :
  (a) .03   (b) .9
  (c) .18   (d) .108

34. The L.C.M. of 3, 0.09 and 2.7 is :
  (a) 2.7   (b) .27
  (c) .027   (d) 27

35. $\left\{\dfrac{(0.1)^2 - (0.01)^2}{0.0001} + 1\right\}$ is equal to :
  (C.B.I. 1989)
  (a) 100   (b) 101
  (c) 1010   (d) 1101

36. $\dfrac{3}{3 + \dfrac{0.3 - 3.03}{3 \times 0.91}} = ?$
  (a) 1.5   (b) 15
  (c) .75   (d) 1.75

37. The value of $\dfrac{47}{10000}$ is :
  (a) .0047   (b) .0470
  (c) .00047   (d) .000047

38. $(0.04)^3 = ?$
  (a) 0.064   (b) 0.0064
  (c) 0.00064   (d) 0.000064

39. $\dfrac{(0.87)^3 + (0.13)^3}{(0.87)^2 + (0.13)^2 - 0.87 \times 0.13} = ?$
  (Central Excise & I. Tax 1988)
  (a) 0.13   (b) 0.74
  (c) 0.87   (d) 1

40. $\left(\dfrac{1.04 \times 1.04 + 1.04 \times 0.04 + 0.04 \times 0.04}{1.04 \times 1.04 \times 1.04 - 0.04 \times 0.04 \times 0.04}\right) = ?$
  (Assistant Grade, 1987)
  (a) 0.10   (b) 0.1
  (c) 1   (d) 0.01

41. $\left(\dfrac{0.47 \times 0.47 \times 0.47 - 0.33 \times 0.33 \times 0.33}{0.47 \times 0.47 + 0.47 \times 0.33 + 0.33 \times 0.33}\right) = ?$
  (a) 0.14   (b) 0.8
  (c) 15.51   (d) 1

Decimal Fractions

42. $\dfrac{.125 + .027}{.5 \times .5 - .15 + .09} = ?$

    (a) .08 (b) 1
    (c) .2   (d) .8

43. $\dfrac{0.5 \times 0.5 \times 0.5 + 0.6 \times 0.6 \times 0.6}{0.5 \times 0.5 - 0.3 + 0.6 \times 0.6} = ?$

    (Hotel Management, 1991)

    (a) 0.3 (b) 1.1
    (c) 0.1 (d) 0.61

44. $\dfrac{3.65 \times 3.65 + 2.35 \times 2.35 - 2 \times 2.35 \times 3.65}{1.69} = ?$

    (a) 1.69 (b) 2.35
    (c) 3.65 (d) 1

45. $\dfrac{.356 \times .356 - 2 \times .356 \times .106 + .106 \times .106}{.632 \times .632 + 2 \times .632 \times .368 + .368 \times .368} = ?$

    (a) .25   (b) .0765
    (c) .0345 (d) .0625

46. $\dfrac{.896 \times .752 + .896 \times .248}{.7 \times .034 + .7 \times .966} = ?$

    (a) 1.28 (b) 0.976
    (c) 12.8 (d) 9.76

47. $13.065 \times 13.065 - 3.065 \times 3.065 = ?$

    (a) 161.3 (b) 159.5
    (c) 141.6 (d) 100

48. $(9.75 \times 9.75 - 2 \times 9.75 \times 5.75 + 5.75 \times 5.75) = ?$

    (a) 13.25 (b) 3.625
    (c) 4   (d) 16

49. $8.32 \times 0.999 = ?$

    (a) 0.831168 (b) 8.31618
    (c) 8.31168   (d) 8.31668

50. $\dfrac{(0.05)^2 + (0.41)^2 + (0.073)^2}{(0.005)^2 + (0.041)^2 + (0.0073)^2} = ?$

    (a) 0.1 (b) 10
    (c) 100 (d) 1000

51. $\dfrac{.538 \times .538 - .462 \times .462}{1 - .924} = ?$

    (a) .076 (b) 1.042

(c) 1 (d) 2

52. $\dfrac{6.5 \times 4.7 + 6.5 \times 5.3}{1.3 \times 7.9 - 1.3 \times 6.9} = ?$

(a) 3.9 (b) 39
(c) 34.45 (d) 50

53. $(.803 \times .647 + .803 \times .353) = ?$

(a) .803 (b) 1
(c) .45 (d) 1.450

54. $\dfrac{(3.537 - .948)^2 + (3.537 + .948)^2}{(3.537)^2 + (.948)^2} = ?$

(a) 4.485 (b) 2.589
(c) 4 (d) 2

55. $\dfrac{.23 - .023}{.0023 \div 23} = ?$

(L.I.C. 1991)

(a) .207 (b) 207
(c) 2070 (d) .0207

56. $\dfrac{? - 0.11}{1.6} = 1.6$

(L.I.C. 1991)

(a) 2.56 (b) 1.76
(c) .267 (d) none of these

57. $2.53 \times .154$ is the same as : (L.I.C. 1991)

(a) $253 \times .00154$ (b) 25.3×1.54
(c) $253 \times .0154$ (d) $253 \times .0154$

58. If $\sqrt{.05 \times .5 \times a} = .5 \times .05 \times \sqrt{b}$, then $\dfrac{a}{b} = ?$

(a) .0025 (b) .025
(c) .25 (d) none of these

59. If $1.5x = 0.04y$, then the value of $\dfrac{y-x}{y+x}$ is :

(L. I.C. 1991)

(a) $\dfrac{730}{77}$ (b) $\dfrac{73}{77}$

(c) $\dfrac{7.3}{77}$ (d) none of these

60. $(.\overline{6} + .\overline{7} + .\overline{8} + .\overline{3}) = ?$ (Central Excise & I. Tax 1988)

(a) $2\dfrac{3}{10}$ (b) $2\dfrac{33}{100}$

(c) $2\frac{2}{3}$ (d) $2.\overline{35}$

61. $0.\overline{53} = ?$

(a) $\frac{53}{100}$ (b) $\frac{53}{90}$

(c) $\frac{53}{99}$ (d) $\frac{26}{45}$

62. What should be less by the multiplication of 0.527 and 2.013 to get 1 ?

(a) 0.060851   (b) 2.060851

(c) 0.939085   (d) 1.939085

63. 1 litre of water weighs 1 kg. How many cubic millimetres of water will weigh 0.1 gm ?

(a) 0.1   (b) 1

(c) 10   (d) 100

64. The value of $4.\dot{1}\dot{2}$ is :

(a) $4\frac{11}{99}$ (b) $5\frac{2}{9}$

(c) $4\frac{11}{90}$ (d) none of these

65. $(2.\overline{47} + 3.\overline{53} + 0.\overline{05}) = ?$

(a) 6   (b) $0.\overline{06}$

(c) $0.\overline{66}$ (d) $6.\overline{01}$

66. $(3.\overline{57} - 2.\overline{14}) = ?$

(a) 1.43   (b) $1.43\overline{01}$

(c) $1.\overline{43}$ (d) 1.43

67. $(0.3\overline{467} + 0.1\overline{333}) = ?$

(a) 0.48   (b) $0.48\overline{01}$

(c) $0.\overline{48}$ (d) 0.48

68. $(0.\overline{63} + 0.\overline{37}) = ?$

(a) 1   (b) $1.\overline{01}$

(c) $.\overline{101}$ (d) 1.01

69. $0.1\overline{36} = ?$

(a) $\dfrac{136}{1000}$ ☐ (b) $\dfrac{136}{999}$ ☐

(c) $\dfrac{136}{990}$ ☐ (d) $\dfrac{3}{22}$ ☐

70. What decimal fraction is 40 ml of a litre ?
  (a) .4 ☐ (b) .04 ☐
  (c) .05 ☐ (d) none of these ☐

71. 3.5 + 21 × 1.3 = ?
  (a) 7.28 ☐ (b) 6.13 ☐
  (c) 72.8 ☐ (d) none of these ☐

72. By how much is 12% of 24.2 more than 10% of 14.2 ?
  (a) 0.1484 ☐ (b) 14.84 ☐
  (c) 1.484 ☐ (d) 2.762 ☐
  (Bank P.O. 1991)

73. (.58 × .58 × .58 − .42 × .42 × .42 − 3 × .58 × .42 × .16) = ?
  (a) 0.004096 ☐ (b) 1.3976 ☐
  (c) 0.16 ☐ (d) 1 ☐

74. (.6 × .6 × .6 + .4 × .4 × .4 + 3 × .6 × .4) = ?
  (a) 21.736 ☐ (b) 2.1736 ☐
  (c) .21736 ☐ (d) 1 ☐

75. The place value of 3 in 0.07359 is :
  (a) 3 ☐ (b) $\dfrac{3}{100}$ ☐
  (c) $\dfrac{3}{1000}$ ☐ (d) $\dfrac{3}{10000}$ ☐

76. The greatest fraction out of $\dfrac{2}{5}, \dfrac{5}{6}, \dfrac{11}{12}$ and $\dfrac{7}{8}$ is :
  (Bank P.O. 1989)
  (a) $\dfrac{7}{8}$ ☐ (b) $\dfrac{11}{12}$ ☐
  (c) $\dfrac{5}{6}$ ☐ (d) $\dfrac{2}{5}$ ☐

ANSWERS (Exercise 3)

1. (c) 2. (b) 3. (c) 4. (a) 5. (c) 6. (d) 7. (d) 8. (d) 9. (c)
10. (b) 11. (d) 12. (c) 13. (c) 14. (a) 15. (d) 16. (d) 17. (b) 18. (a)
19. (a) 20. (b) 21. (b) 22. (c) 23. (c) 24. (a) 25. (c) 26. (d) 27. (b)
28. (c) 29. (c) 30. (d) 31. (c) 32. (b) 33. (c) 34. (d) 35. (a) 36. (a)
37. (a) 38. (d) 39. (d) 40. (c) 41. (a) 42. (d) 43. (b) 44. (d) 45. (d)

Decimal Fractions

46. (a) 47. (a) 48. (d) 49. (c) 50. (c) 51. (c) 52. (d) 53. (a) 54. (d)
55. (c) 56. (d) 57. (a) 58. (b) 59. (b) 60. (c) 61. (c) 62. (a) 63. (d)
64. (c) 65. (d) 66. (c) 67. (b) 68. (b) 69. (d) 70. (b) 71. (d) 72. (c)
73. (a) 74. (d) 75. (c) 76. (b).

SOLUTION (Exercise 3)

1.   0.6
      0.66
      0.066
      6.606

      7.932
      -----

2. Let $16.7 + 12.38 - x = 10.09$.
      $\therefore x = (16.7 + 12.38 - 10.09) = 18.99$.

3. $3 \times 3 \times 3 \times 3 \times 30 = 2430$
      $\therefore 3 \times 0.3 \times 0.03 \times 0.003 \times 30 = 0.002430$ (Six places of decimal)

4. $1560 \times 30 = 46800$.
      $\therefore 15.60 \times 0.30 = 4.6800 = 4.68$ (Four places of decimal)

5. $\dfrac{0.0169}{0.0130} = \dfrac{169}{130} = \dfrac{13}{10} = 1.3$.

6. $\dfrac{50.8}{2540} = \dfrac{508}{25400} = \dfrac{2}{100} = .02$.

7. Given Expression = $12 + 0.027 \times 2$
      $= \dfrac{12}{0.027} \times 2 = \dfrac{24000}{27} = \dfrac{8000}{9}$.

8. $\dfrac{25}{.0005} = \dfrac{250000}{5} = 50000$.

9. $\dfrac{0.000033}{0.11} = \dfrac{0.0033}{11} = .0003$.

10. Let $\dfrac{0.001}{x} = 0.01$. Then, $x = \dfrac{0.001}{0.01} = \dfrac{0.001}{0.010} = \dfrac{1}{10} = 0.1$.

11. Let $\dfrac{x}{.0025} = 800$. Then, $x = 800 \times .0025 = \dfrac{800 \times 25}{10000} = 2$.

12. Let $x\%$ of $10.8 = 32.4$.
      Then, $\dfrac{x}{100} \times 10.8 = 32.4$ or $x = \dfrac{32.4 \times 100}{10.8} = 300$.

13. $9 \times 8 = 72$.
    $\therefore 0.09 \times 0.008 = 0.00072$ (Five places of decimal)

14. Let $0.8 \times x = 0.0004$.
    Then, $x = \dfrac{0.0004}{0.8} = \dfrac{0.004}{8} = .0005$.

15. Let $\dfrac{3420}{19} = \dfrac{x}{0.01} \times 7$.
    Then, $x = \dfrac{3420}{19} \times \dfrac{0.01}{7} = \dfrac{180}{700} = \dfrac{9}{35}$.

16. Let $\dfrac{17.28 + x}{3.6 \times 0.2} = 200$.
    Then, $\dfrac{17.28}{x} = 200 \times 3.6 \times 0.2$
    $\therefore x = \dfrac{17.28}{200 \times 3.6 \times 0.2} = \dfrac{1728}{200 \times 36 \times 2} = 0.12$.

17. Let $\dfrac{20 + 8 \times 0.5}{20 - x} = 12$. Then, $24 = 12(20 - x)$
    $\therefore 12x = 216$ or $x = 18$.

18. $0.15 \div \dfrac{0.5}{15} = \dfrac{15}{100} \div \dfrac{5}{150} = \dfrac{15}{100} \times \dfrac{150}{5} = 4.5$.

19. $\dfrac{1}{.0003718} = \dfrac{10000}{3.718} = \left(10000 \times \dfrac{1}{3.718}\right) = 10000 \times 0.2689 = 2689$.

20. $\dfrac{122.76}{15.50} = \dfrac{12276}{1550} = \dfrac{12276}{155} \times \dfrac{1}{10} = \dfrac{79.2}{10} = 7.92$.

21. $\dfrac{3\sqrt{5}}{2\sqrt{5} - 0.48} = \dfrac{3 \times 2.24}{2 \times 2.24 - 0.48} = \dfrac{6.72}{4.48 - 0.48} = \dfrac{6.72}{4} = 1.68$.

22. $\sqrt{\dfrac{5}{3}} = \dfrac{\sqrt{5}}{\sqrt{3}} \times \dfrac{\sqrt{3}}{\sqrt{3}} = \dfrac{\sqrt{15}}{3} = \dfrac{3.88}{3} = 1.29$.

23. Given Expression
    $= \sqrt{\dfrac{4096}{100}} + \sqrt{\dfrac{4096}{10000}} + \sqrt{\dfrac{4096}{1000000}} + \sqrt{\dfrac{4096}{100000000}}$
    $= \dfrac{\sqrt{4096}}{10} + \dfrac{\sqrt{4096}}{100} + \dfrac{\sqrt{4096}}{1000} + \dfrac{\sqrt{4096}}{10000}$
    $= \dfrac{64}{10} + \dfrac{64}{100} + \dfrac{64}{1000} + \dfrac{64}{10000}$
    $= 6.4 + .64 + .064 + .0064 = 7.1104$.

Decimal Fractions

24. $\sqrt{\dfrac{0.289}{0.00121}} = \sqrt{\dfrac{0.28900}{0.00121}} = \sqrt{\dfrac{28900}{121}} = \dfrac{\sqrt{28900}}{\sqrt{121}} = \dfrac{170}{11}$.

25. Given Expression = $\dfrac{324 \times 81 \times 4624}{15625 \times 289 \times 729 \times 64} = \dfrac{9}{15625}$.

    $\therefore$ Its square root = $\dfrac{3}{125} = .024$.

26. $\dfrac{280.5}{25.5} = \dfrac{2805}{255} = \dfrac{2805}{2.55 \times 100} = \dfrac{1100}{100} = 11$.

27. $\dfrac{.35 \times .0015}{.25 \times .07} = \dfrac{35 \times 15}{25 \times 700} = \left(\dfrac{3}{100} \times 100\right)\% = 3\%$.

28. $\dfrac{.24 \times .35}{.14 \times .15 \times .02} = \dfrac{24 \times 35 \times 100}{14 \times 15 \times 2} = 200$.

29. $\dfrac{16}{19} = 0.842, \dfrac{11}{14} = 0.785$ and $\dfrac{17}{22} = 0.772$.

    $\therefore \ 0.772 < 0.785 < 0.842$ or $\dfrac{17}{22} < \dfrac{11}{14} < \dfrac{16}{19}$.

30. $\dfrac{11}{13} = 0.846, \dfrac{9}{11} = 0.818, \dfrac{3}{4} = 0.75$ and $\dfrac{5}{7} = 0.714$.

    Clearly, 0.714 is the smallest and hence $\dfrac{5}{7}$ is smallest.

31. Required decimal = $\dfrac{1}{60 \times 60} = .00027$.

32. The given numbers are 0.54, 1.80 and 7.20.
    H.C.F. of 54, 180 and 720 is 18.
    $\therefore$ H.C.F. of given numbers = 0.18.

33. The given numbers are 1.08, .36 and .90.
    G.C.D. of 108, 36 and 90 is 18.
    $\therefore$ Required G.C.D. = 0.18.

34. The given numbers are 3.00, 0.09 and 2.70.
    L.C.M. of 300, 9 and 270 is 2700.
    $\therefore$ Required L.C.M. = 27.00 = 27.

35. Given Expression = $\left(\dfrac{0.01 - 0.0001}{0.0001} + 1\right)$

    = $\left(\dfrac{.0099}{.0001} + 1\right) = (99 + 1) = 100$.

36. Given Expression $= \cfrac{3}{3-\cfrac{2.73}{3\times 0.91}} = \cfrac{3}{3-\cfrac{273}{3\times 91}} = \cfrac{3}{3-1} = \cfrac{3}{2} = 1.5$.

37. $\cfrac{47}{10000} = .0047$.

38. $(0.04)^3 = 0.04 \times 0.04 \times 0.04 = .000064$.

39. Given Expression $= \cfrac{a^3 + b^3}{a^2 + b^2 - ab}$, where $a = 0.87$ & $b = 0.13$

$= \cfrac{(a+b)(a^2 + b^2 - ab)}{(a^2 + b^2 - ab)} = (a+b) = (0.87 + 0.13) = 1$

40. Given Expression $= \cfrac{(1.04)^2 + 1.4 \times 0.04 + (0.04)^2}{(1.04)^3 - (0.04)^3}$

$= \cfrac{a^2 + ab + b^2}{a^3 - b^3} = \cfrac{(a^2 + ab + b^2)}{(a-b)(a^2 + ab + b^2)}$

$= \cfrac{1}{a-b} = \cfrac{1}{1.04 - 0.04} = 1$.

41. Given Expression $= \cfrac{(0.47)^3 - (0.33)^3}{(0.47)^2 + 0.47 \times 0.33 + (0.33)^2}$

$= \cfrac{(a^3 - b^3)}{(a^2 + ab + b^2)} = \cfrac{(a-b)(a^2 + ab + b^2)}{(a^2 + ab + b^2)}$

$= (a - b) = (0.47 - 0.33) = 0.14$.

42. Given Expression $= \cfrac{(0.5)^3 + (0.3)^3}{(0.5)^2 - 0.5 \times 0.3 + (0.3)^2}$

$= \left(\cfrac{a^3 + b^3}{a^2 - ab + b^2}\right) = \cfrac{(a+b)(a^2 - ab + b^2)}{(a^2 - ab + b^2)}$

$= (a + b) = (0.5 + 0.3) = 0.8$.

43. Given Expression $= \cfrac{(0.5)^3 + (0.6)^3}{(0.5)^2 - 0.5 \times 0.6 + (0.6)^2}$

$= \left(\cfrac{a^3 + b^3}{a^2 - ab + b^2}\right)$

$= (a + b) = (0.5 + 0.6) = 1.1$.

44. Given Expression $= \cfrac{(3.65)^2 + (2.35)^2 - 2 \times 3.65 \times 2.35}{1.69}$

Decimal Fractions

$$= \frac{a^2 + b^2 - 2ab}{1.69}, \text{ where } a = 3.65 \text{ and } b = 2.35$$

$$= \frac{(a-b)^2}{1.69} = \frac{(3.65 - 2.35)^2}{1.69} = \frac{(1.3)^2}{1.69} = \frac{1.69}{1.69} = 1.$$

45. Given Expression $= \frac{(.356)^2 - 2 \times .356 \times .106 + (.106)^2}{(.632)^2 + 2 \times .632 \times .368 + (.368)^2}$

$$= \left(\frac{a^2 - 2ab + b^2}{c^2 + 2cd + d^2}\right) = \frac{(a-b)^2}{(c+d)^2} = \frac{(.356 - .106)^2}{(.632 + .368)^2}$$

$$= (.25)^2 = .0625.$$

46. Given Expression $= \frac{.896 \times (.752 + .248)}{.7 \times (.034 + .966)} = \frac{.896 \times 1}{.700 \times 1} = \frac{896}{700} = 1.28.$

47. Given Expression $= (13.065)^2 - (3.065)^2$

$$= (13.065 + 3.065) \times (13.065 - 3.065)$$

$$= (16.13 \times 10) = 161.3.$$

48. Given Expression $= (a^2 - 2ab + b^2)$, where $a = 9.75$ and $b = 5.75$

$$= (a - b)^2 = (9.75 - 5.75)^2 = (4)^2 = 16.$$

49. $8.32 \times 0.999 = 8.32 \times (1 - 0.001) = 8.32 - 8.32 \times 0.001$

$$= 8.32 - .00832 = 8.31168.$$

50. Given Expression

$$= \frac{(a^2 + b^2 + c^2)}{\left(\frac{a}{10}\right)^2 + \left(\frac{b}{10}\right)^2 + \left(\frac{c}{10}\right)^2} = \frac{100 \times (a^2 + b^2 + c^2)}{(a^2 + b^2 + c^2)} = 100.$$

51. Given Expression

$$= \frac{(.538)^2 - (.462)^2}{.076} = \frac{(.538 + .462)(.538 - .462)}{.076} = \frac{.076}{.076} = 1.$$

52. Given Expression $= \frac{6.5 \times (4.7 + 5.3)}{13 \times (7.9 - 6.9)} = \frac{6.5 \times 10}{1.3 \times 1} = 50.$

53. Given Expression $= .803 \times (.647 + .353) = .803 \times 1 = .803.$

54. Given Expression $= \frac{(a-b)^2 + (a+b)^2}{(a^2 + b^2)} = \frac{2(a^2 + b^2)}{(a^2 + b^2)} = 2.$

55. Given Expression $= \frac{.207}{\frac{.0023}{23}} = \frac{.207}{.0001} = \frac{.2070}{.0001} = 2070.$

56. Let $\dfrac{x-0.11}{1.6} = 1.6$. Then, $x - 0.11 = 1.6 \times 1.6 = 2.56$.

$\therefore x = 2.56 + 0.11 = 2.67$.

57. Clearly $2.53 \times .154$ is the same as $253 \times .00154$ as both contain same number of decimal places.

58. $\sqrt{.05 \times .5 \times a} = .5 \times .05 \times \sqrt{b} \Rightarrow \sqrt{.025 \times a} = 0.25 \times \sqrt{b}$

$\therefore .025\, a = .025 \times .025 \times b$ or $\dfrac{a}{b} = \dfrac{.025 \times .025}{.025} = .025$.

59. $\dfrac{x}{y} = \dfrac{0.04}{1.5} = \dfrac{4}{150} = \dfrac{2}{75}$.

$\therefore \dfrac{y-x}{y+x} = \dfrac{1 - \dfrac{x}{y}}{1 + \dfrac{x}{y}} = \dfrac{1 - \dfrac{2}{75}}{1 + \dfrac{2}{75}} = \left(\dfrac{73}{75} \times \dfrac{75}{77}\right) = \dfrac{73}{77}$.

60. $.\overline{6} + .\overline{7} + .\overline{8} + .\overline{3} = \left(\dfrac{6}{9} + \dfrac{7}{9} + \dfrac{8}{9} + \dfrac{3}{9}\right) = \dfrac{24}{9} = \dfrac{8}{3} = 2\dfrac{2}{3}$.

61. $0.\overline{53} = \dfrac{53}{99}$.

62. $0.527 \times 2.013 = 1.060851$.

Hence, the required number $= .060851$.

63. 1000 gm is the weight of 1000 cu. cm.

1 gm is the weight of 1 cu. cm = 1000 cu.mm.

$\dfrac{1}{10}$ gm is the weight of $\left(\dfrac{1000}{10}\right)$ Cu.mm = 100 Cu.mm.

64. $4.\overline{12} = 4 + 0.\overline{12} = 4 + \dfrac{12-1}{90} = 4\dfrac{11}{90}$.

65. $2.\overline{47} + 3.\overline{53} + 0.\overline{05} = 5 + \dfrac{47}{99} + \dfrac{53}{99} = 5 + \dfrac{100}{99} = 5 + 1\dfrac{1}{99}$

$= 6\dfrac{1}{99} = 6.\overline{01}$.

66. $3.\overline{57} - 2.\overline{14} = 3 + \dfrac{57}{99} - 2 - \dfrac{14}{99} = 1 + \dfrac{57}{99} - \dfrac{14}{99}$

$= 1 + \dfrac{43}{99} = 1.\overline{43}$.

67. $0.3\overline{467} + 0.1\overline{333} = \dfrac{3467 - 34}{9900} + \dfrac{1333 - 13}{9900}$

$$= \frac{3433 + 1320}{9900} = \frac{4753}{9900} = \frac{4801 - 48}{9900} = 0.4\overline{801}.$$

68. $0.\overline{63} + 0.\overline{37} = \frac{63}{99} + \frac{37}{99} = \frac{100}{99} = 1\frac{1}{99} = 1.\overline{01}.$

69. $0.1\overline{36} = \frac{136 - 1}{990} = \frac{135}{990} = \frac{3}{22}.$

70. Required fraction $= \frac{40}{1000} = \frac{4}{100} = .04.$

71. Given Expression = 3.5 + 27.3 = 30.8.

72. It is more by $\left(\frac{12}{100} \times 24.2 - \frac{10}{100} \times 14.2\right) = 2.904 - 1.42 = 1.484.$

73. Given Expression $= a^3 - b^3 - 3\,ab\,(a - b) = (a - b)^3$
$= (.58 - .42)^3 = .16 \times .16 \times .16 = .004096.$

74. Given Expression $= (.6)^3 + (.4)^3 + 3 \times .6 \times .4 \times (.6 + .4)$
$= a^3 + b^3 + 3\,ab\,(a + b) = (a + b)^3$
$= (.6 + .4)^3 = 1^3 = 1.$

75. The place value of 3 in the given decimal fraction is .003 *i.e.* $\frac{3}{1000}.$

76. $\frac{2}{5} = 0.4, \frac{5}{6} = 0.833, \frac{11}{12} = 0.916$ and $\frac{7}{8} = 0.875.$

Clearly, the greatest number is 0.916 *i.e.* $\frac{11}{12}.$

4
SIMPLIFICATION

In simplifying an expression, first of all vinculum or bar must be removed.

Ex. We know that $-6-8 = -14$.

But, $\overline{-6-8} = -(-2) = 2$.

After removing the bar, the brackets must be removed, strictly in the order ( ), { } and [ ].

After removing the brackets, we must use the following operations, strictly in the order, given below.

(*i*) **of** (*ii*) **Division** (*iii*) **Multiplication** (*iv*) **Addition** and (*v*) **Subtraction**.

Remark : Remember the word, 'BODMAS', where B, O, D, M, A and S stand for *Bracket, of, Division, Multiplication, Addition* and *Subtraction* respectively.

Strictly follow the above order of operations.

SOLVED EXAMPLES

Ex. 1. Simplify : $2 - [3 - \{6 - (5 - \overline{4-3})\}]$.

Sol. Given Expression $= 2 - [3 - \{6 - (5-1)\}]$
$= 2 - [3 - \{6-4\}]$
$= 2 - [3-2] = (2-1) = 1$.

Ex. 2. Simplify : $1 + [1 + 1 \div \{1 + 1 \div (1 + 1 \div 3)\}]$.

Sol. Given Expression $= 1 + \left[1 + 1 \div \left\{1 + 1 \div \left(1 + \frac{1}{3}\right)\right\}\right]$

$= 1 + \left[1 + 1 \div \left\{1 + 1 \div \frac{4}{3}\right\}\right]$

$= 1 + \left[1 + 1 \div \frac{7}{4}\right]$

$= 1 + \left[1 + \frac{4}{7}\right] = 1 + \frac{11}{7} = \left(1 \times \frac{7}{11}\right) = \frac{7}{11}$.

Ex. 3. Simplify : $1 + \frac{3}{7}$ of $\left(2\frac{3}{10} + 2\frac{3}{5}\right) + \frac{1}{5} \div 1\frac{2}{5} - \frac{2}{7}$.

Simplification

Sol. Given Expression $= 1 \div \dfrac{3}{7}$ of $\left(\dfrac{23}{10} + \dfrac{13}{5}\right) + \dfrac{1}{5} \div \dfrac{7}{5} - \dfrac{2}{7}$

$= 1 \div \dfrac{3}{7}$ of $\dfrac{49}{10} + \dfrac{1}{5} \times \dfrac{5}{7} - \dfrac{2}{7}$

$= 1 \div \dfrac{21}{10} + \dfrac{1}{7} - \dfrac{2}{7}$

$= 1 \times \dfrac{10}{21} + \dfrac{1}{7} - \dfrac{2}{7} = \dfrac{10}{21} + \dfrac{1}{7} - \dfrac{2}{7}$

$= \left(\dfrac{10 + 3 - 6}{21}\right) = \dfrac{7}{21} = \dfrac{1}{3}$.

Ex. 4. Simplify : $3.5 \div .7$ of $7 + .5 \times .3 - .1$.

Sol. Given Expression $= 3.5 \div 4.9 + .15 - .1$

$= \dfrac{3.5}{4.9} + .15 - .1 = \dfrac{5}{7} + \dfrac{3}{20} - \dfrac{1}{10}$

$= \left(\dfrac{100 + 21 - 14}{140}\right) = \dfrac{107}{140}$.

Ex. 5. Evaluate : $\left(\dfrac{0.47 \times 0.47 + 0.35 \times 0.35 - 2 \times 0.47 \times 0.35}{0.12}\right)$.

Sol. Given Expression $= \dfrac{(0.47)^2 + (0.35)^2 - 2 \times 0.47 \times 0.35}{0.12}$

$= \dfrac{(0.47 - 0.35)^2}{0.12} = \dfrac{0.12 \times 0.12}{0.12} = 0.12$.

Ex. 6. Simplify : $\dfrac{4\dfrac{1}{7} - 2\dfrac{1}{4}}{3\dfrac{1}{2} + 1\dfrac{1}{7}} \div \dfrac{1}{2 + \dfrac{1}{2 + \dfrac{1}{5 - \dfrac{1}{5}}}}$

Sol. Given Expression $= \dfrac{\dfrac{29}{7} - \dfrac{9}{4}}{\dfrac{7}{2} + \dfrac{8}{7}} \div \dfrac{1}{2 + \dfrac{1}{2 + \dfrac{5}{24}}}$

$= \left(\dfrac{53}{28} \times \dfrac{14}{65}\right) \div \dfrac{1}{2 + \dfrac{24}{53}}$

$= \dfrac{53}{130} \div \dfrac{53}{130} = \left(\dfrac{53}{130} \times \dfrac{130}{53}\right) = 1$.

Ex. 7. Evaluate : $\dfrac{.7541 \times .7541 \times .7541 - .2459 \times .2459 \times .2459}{.7541 \times .7541 + .7541 \times .2459 + .2459 \times .2459}$.

Sol. Given Expression $= \dfrac{a^3 - b^3}{a^2 + ab + b^2}$, where $a = .7541$, & $b = .2459$

$= \dfrac{(a-b)(a^2 + ab + b^2)}{(a^2 + ab + b^2)} = (a - b)$

$= (.7541 - .2459) = .5082.$

Ex. 8. Evaluate : $\dfrac{0.125 + 0.027}{0.25 - .15 + .09}.$

Sol. Given Expression $= \dfrac{(0.5)^3 + (0.3)^3}{(0.5)^2 - 0.5 \times 0.3 + (0.3)^2}$

$= \dfrac{a^3 + b^3}{a^2 - ab + b^2}$, where $a = 0.5$ and $b = 0.3$

$= (a + b) = (0.5 + 0.3) = 0.8.$

Exercise 4

1. $171 \div 19 \times 9 = ?$ **(S.B.I. P.O. Exam, 1987)**
   - (a) 0
   - (b) 1
   - (c) 18
   - (d) 81

2. $5005 - 5000 \div 10.00 = ?$ **(Bank P.O. 1988)**
   - (a) 0.5
   - (b) 50
   - (c) 5000
   - (d) 4505

3. $7 + 7 \div 7 \times 7 = ?$
   - (a) $\dfrac{2}{7}$
   - (b) 14
   - (c) $7\dfrac{1}{7}$
   - (d) 42

4. $3120 \div 26 + 13 \times 30 = ?$ **(S.B.I. P.O. Exam, 1991)**
   - (a) 2400
   - (b) 3900
   - (c) 536
   - (d) none of these

5. $(20 \div 5) \div 2 + (16 \div 8) \times 2 + (10 \div 5) \times (3 \div 2) = ?$
   - (a) 9
   - (b) 12
   - (c) 15
   - (d) 18

    (Clerical Grade, 1991)

6. $8 \div 4 (3 - 2) \times 4 + 3 - 7 = ?$ **(Railway Recruitment, 1991)**
   - (a) −3
   - (b) −4
   - (c) 4
   - (d) 5

7. $0.5 \times 0.5 + 0.5 \div 5 = ?$
   - (a) 0.15
   - (b) 0.25
   - (c) 0.35
   - (d) 0.45

8. $4 - 3.6 \div 4 + 0.2 \times 0.5 = ?$

Simplification

  (a) 3.2 (b) .2
  (c) 1.65 (d) .15

9. .05 × 5 − .005 × 5 = ?
  (a) 2.25 (b) .225
  (c) 2.025 (d) .29875

10. .01 × .3 ÷ .4 × .5 = ?
  (a) .015 (b) .0375
  (c) .00375 (d) .1

11. $\dfrac{48 - 12 \times 3 + 9}{12 - 9 \div 3} = ?$

  (Railway Recruitment, 1991)
  (a) 3 (b) 21
  (c) $\dfrac{7}{3}$ (d) $\dfrac{1}{3}$

12. $\dfrac{69 - 14 \times 3 + 2}{9 \times 5 - (5)^2} = ?$

  (Railway Recruitment, 1991)
  (a) 1.45 (b) 2.75
  (c) 26.5 (d) 265

13. $\dfrac{(272 - 32)(124 + 176)}{17 \times 15 - 15} = ?$

  (Bank P.O. 1991)
  (a) 0 (b) 2.25
  (c) 300 (d) none of these

14. $\dfrac{(7 + 7 + 7) \div 7}{5 + 5 + 5 \div 5} = ?$

  (a) 1 (b) $\dfrac{1}{5}$
  (c) $\dfrac{15}{11}$ (d) $\dfrac{3}{11}$

15. $\dfrac{17.28 \div ?}{3.6 \times 0.2} = 2$

  (S.B.I. P.O. Exam, 1988)
  (a) 120 (b) 1.20
  (c) 12 (d) 0.12

16. $\dfrac{1}{2} + \dfrac{1}{2} \div \dfrac{1}{2} = ?$

  (a) 2 (b) $\dfrac{1}{2}$
  (c) $\dfrac{3}{2}$ (d) $\dfrac{3}{4}$

17. 2 of $\dfrac{3}{4} + \dfrac{3}{4} + \dfrac{1}{4} = ?$

(a) $\dfrac{3}{2}$ ☐ (b) $\dfrac{5}{2}$ ☐

(c) $\dfrac{8}{3}$ ☐ (d) $\dfrac{9}{4}$ ☐

18. $1 + 1 \div \left\{1 + 1 \div \left(1 + \dfrac{1}{3}\right)\right\} = ?$

(a) $1\dfrac{1}{3}$ ☐ (b) $1\dfrac{4}{7}$ ☐

(c) $1\dfrac{1}{8}$ ☐ (d) $1\dfrac{2}{3}$ ☐

19. $3 \div \left[(8 - 5) \div \left\{(4 - 2) \div \left(2 + \dfrac{8}{13}\right)\right\}\right] = ?$

(Hotel Management, 1991)

(a) $\dfrac{13}{17}$ ☐ (b) $\dfrac{68}{13}$ ☐

(c) $\dfrac{17}{13}$ ☐ (d) $\dfrac{13}{68}$ ☐

20. $10 - [9 - \{8 - (7 - 6)\}] - 5$ is equal to (C.B.I. Exam, 1991)

(a) -5 ☐ (b) 1 ☐
(c) 3 ☐ (d) 9 ☐

21. The value of

$48 \div 12 \times \left(\dfrac{9}{8} \text{ of } \dfrac{4}{3} \div \dfrac{3}{4} \text{ of } \dfrac{2}{3}\right)$ is

(C.B.I. Exam, 1991)

(a) $1\dfrac{1}{3}$ ☐ (b) $5\dfrac{1}{3}$ ☐

(c) 3 ☐ (d) 12 ☐

22. $3\dfrac{1}{4} + 4\dfrac{1}{6} + ? + \dfrac{1}{4} = 10$

(a) $2\dfrac{1}{6}$ ☐ (b) $4\dfrac{1}{3}$ ☐

(c) $1\dfrac{1}{3}$ ☐ (d) $2\dfrac{1}{3}$ ☐

23. $\left(1\dfrac{3}{5} - \dfrac{2}{3} \div \dfrac{12}{13} + \dfrac{7}{5} \times \dfrac{1}{3}\right)$ is equal to

(Clerical Grade, 1991)

(a) $1\dfrac{31}{90}$ ☐ (b) $\dfrac{19}{30}$ ☐

(c) $\dfrac{11}{30}$ ☐ (d) 30 ☐

24. $108 \div 36 \text{ of } \dfrac{1}{3} + \dfrac{2}{5} \times 3\dfrac{3}{4} = ?$

Simplification

(a) $8\frac{3}{4}$ □ (b) $6\frac{1}{4}$ □

(c) $2\frac{1}{2}$ □ (d) $10\frac{1}{2}$ □

25. $\frac{31}{10} \times \frac{3}{10} + \frac{7}{5} \div 20 = ?$ **(Bank P.O. 1988)**

(a) 0 □ (b) 1 □

(c) 100 □ (d) $\frac{107}{200}$ □

26. $4\frac{2}{17} \div 1\frac{2}{5} \times 2\frac{2}{33} = ?$

(a) $4\frac{2}{33}$ □ (b) $6\frac{2}{33}$ □

(c) $6\frac{1}{11}$ □ (d) $8\frac{1}{11}$ □

27. $\left(4.59 \times 1.8 \div 3.6 + 5.4 \text{ of } \frac{1}{9} - \frac{1}{5}\right) = ?$

(a) 3.015 □ (b) 2.705 □

(c) 2.695 □ (d) none of these □

28. $15\frac{2}{3} \times 3\frac{1}{6} + 6\frac{1}{3} = 11\frac{7}{18} + ?$ **(G.I.C. A.A.O. Exam, 1988)**

(a) $39\frac{5}{9}$ □ (b) $137\frac{4}{9}$ □

(c) $29\frac{7}{9}$ □ (d) none of these □

29. $\frac{5}{6} \div \frac{6}{7} \times ? - \frac{8}{9} \div 1\frac{3}{5} + \frac{3}{4} \times 3\frac{1}{3} = 2\frac{7}{9}$.

(a) $\frac{7}{6}$ □ (b) $\frac{6}{7}$ □

(c) 1 □ (d) none of these □

30. $\frac{3}{4} \div 2\frac{1}{4} \text{ of } \frac{2}{3} - \dfrac{\frac{1}{2} - \frac{1}{3}}{\frac{1}{2} + \frac{1}{3}} \times 3\frac{1}{3} + \frac{5}{6} = ?$

(a) $\frac{7}{18}$ □ (b) $\frac{49}{54}$ □

(c) $\frac{2}{3}$ □ (d) $\frac{1}{6}$ □

31. $\left\{7\frac{1}{2} + \frac{1}{2} \div \frac{1}{2} \text{ of } \frac{1}{4} - \frac{2}{5} \times 2\frac{1}{3} \div 1\frac{7}{8} \text{ of } \left(1\frac{2}{5} - 1\frac{1}{3}\right)\right\} = ?$

(a) $3\frac{1}{5}$ (b) $2\frac{1}{24}$

(c) $4\frac{1}{30}$ (d) none of these

32. $\dfrac{\frac{1}{4} + \frac{1}{4} \div 1\frac{1}{4}}{\frac{1}{4} \times \frac{1}{4} + 2\frac{1}{4}} = ?$

(a) $\dfrac{16}{25}$ (b) $\dfrac{32}{185}$

(c) $\dfrac{36}{185}$ (d) none of these

33. $\dfrac{\frac{1}{5} \div \frac{1}{5} \text{ of } \frac{1}{5}}{\frac{1}{5} \text{ of } \frac{1}{5} \div \frac{1}{5}} = ?$

(Railway Recruitment, 1991)

(a) 1   (b) 5

(c) $\dfrac{1}{5}$ (d) 25

34. $\dfrac{50}{?} = \dfrac{?}{12\frac{1}{2}}$

(Railway Recruitment, 1991)

(a) $\dfrac{25}{2}$ (b) $\dfrac{4}{25}$

(c) 4   (d) 25

35. $7\frac{1}{2} - \left[2\frac{1}{4} \div \left\{1\frac{1}{4} - \frac{1}{2}\left(1\frac{1}{2} - \frac{1}{3} - \frac{1}{6}\right)\right\}\right]$ is equal to :

(a) $\dfrac{2}{9}$ (b) 1

(c) $4\dfrac{1}{2}$ (d) $1\dfrac{77}{288}$

36. The value of $1 + \dfrac{1}{1 + \dfrac{1}{1 + \dfrac{1}{9}}}$ is :

(Hotel Management, 1991)

(a) $\dfrac{29}{19}$ (b) $\dfrac{10}{19}$

(c) $\dfrac{29}{10}$ (d) $\dfrac{10}{9}$

Simplification

37. The simplification of $1 + \dfrac{1}{2 + \dfrac{1}{1 - \dfrac{1}{3}}}$ yields the result :

(I. Tax & Central Excise, 1989)

(a) $\dfrac{2}{7}$ ☐ (b) $\dfrac{7}{9}$ ☐

(c) $\dfrac{9}{7}$ ☐ (d) $\dfrac{13}{7}$ ☐

38. The value of $1 + \dfrac{1}{4 \times 3} + \dfrac{1}{4 \times 3^2} + \dfrac{1}{4 \times 3^3}$ upto four places of decimals is :

(a) 1.1202 ☐ (b) 1.1203 ☐
(c) 1.1204 ☐ (d) none of these ☐

(I. Tax & Central Excise, 1989)

39. $\dfrac{1}{1.2.3} + \dfrac{1}{2.3.4} + \dfrac{1}{3.4.5} + \dfrac{1}{4.5.6}$ is equal to :

(C.B.I. Exam, 1991)

(a) $\dfrac{7}{30}$ ☐ (b) $\dfrac{11}{30}$ ☐

(c) $\dfrac{13}{30}$ ☐ (d) $\dfrac{17}{30}$ ☐

40. The value of $\dfrac{9^2 \times 18^4}{3^{16}}$ is :

(C.B.I. Exam, 1991)

(a) $\dfrac{2}{3}$ ☐ (b) $\dfrac{4}{9}$ ☐

(c) $\dfrac{16}{81}$ ☐ (d) $\dfrac{32}{243}$ ☐

41. $\dfrac{\dfrac{1}{2} \div 4 + 20}{\dfrac{1}{2} \times 4 + 20} = ?$

(Bank P.O. 1990)

(a) $\dfrac{81}{88}$ ☐ (b) $2\dfrac{3}{11}$ ☐

(c) $\dfrac{161}{176}$ ☐ (d) 1 ☐

42. $\dfrac{69842 \times 69842 - 30158 \times 30158}{69842 - 30158} = ?$

(Clerical Grade, 1991)

(a) 100000 ☐ (b) 69842 ☐
(c) 39684 ☐ (d) 30158 ☐

43. $\frac{3}{48}$ is what part of $\frac{1}{12}$? (Railway Recruitment, 1991)
    (a) $\frac{3}{7}$ (b) $\frac{1}{12}$
    (c) $\frac{4}{3}$ (d) none of these

44. How many $\frac{1}{8}$'s are there in $37\frac{1}{2}$? (S.B.I. P.O. Exam, 1988)
    (a) 300 (b) 400
    (c) 500 (d) cannot be determined

45. $\dfrac{885 \times 885 \times 885 + 115 \times 115 \times 115}{885 \times 885 + 115 \times 115 - 885 \times 115}$ is equal to : (Clerical Grade, 1991)
    (a) 115 (b) 770
    (c) 885 (d) 1000

46. When simplified, the product
    $\left(2-\frac{1}{3}\right)\left(2-\frac{3}{5}\right)\left(2-\frac{5}{7}\right).....\left(2-\frac{999}{1001}\right)$ is equal to : (C.B.I. Exam, 1990)
    (a) $\frac{991}{1001}$ (b) $\frac{1001}{13}$
    (c) $\frac{1003}{3}$ (d) none of these

47. If $\frac{x}{2y} = \frac{3}{2}$, then the value of $\frac{2x+y}{x-2y}$ equals :
    (a) $\frac{1}{7}$ (b) 7
    (c) 7.1 (d) none of these

48. If $\frac{a}{b} = \frac{1}{3}$, then $\frac{3a+2b}{3a-2b}$ is equal to : (Delhi Police, 1990)
    (a) 3 (b) -3
    (c) -5 (d) -1

49. If $\frac{x}{y} = \frac{4}{5}$, then the value of $\left(\frac{4}{7} + \frac{2y-x}{2y+x}\right)$ is :
    (a) $\frac{3}{7}$ (b) 1
    (c) $1\frac{1}{7}$ (d) 2

50. A boy was asked to multiply a given number by (8/17). Instead, he divided the given number by (8/17) and got the result 225 more than what he should have got if he had multiplied the number by (8/17). The given number was : (I. Tax & Central Excise, 1989)

Simplification

(a) 8 ☐ (b) 17 ☐
(c) 64 ☐ (d) 136 ☐

51. In an examination, a student was asked to find (3/14) of a certain number. By mistake he found (3/4) of it. His answer was 150 more than the correct answer. The given number is : (Assistant Grade, 1990)

(a) 180 ☐ (b) 240 ☐
(c) 280 ☐ (d) 290 ☐

52. If we multiply a fraction by itself and divide the product by its reciprocal, the fraction thus obtained is $18\frac{26}{27}$. The original fraction is :

(a) $\frac{8}{27}$ ☐ (b) $2\frac{2}{3}$ ☐
(c) $1\frac{1}{3}$ ☐ (d) none of these ☐

(L.I.C. A.A.O. Exam, 1988)

53. In a college, $\frac{1}{5}$ th of the girls and $\frac{1}{8}$ th of the boys took part in a social camp. What of the total number of students in the college took part in the camp ? (S.B.I. P.O. Exam, 1988)

(a) $\frac{13}{40}$ ☐ (b) $\frac{13}{80}$ ☐
(c) $\frac{2}{13}$ ☐ (d) Data inadequate ☐

54. The value of $\dfrac{1}{3+\dfrac{2}{2+\dfrac{1}{2}}}$ is :

(S.S.C. Exam, 1987)

(a) $\frac{5}{19}$ ☐ (b) $\frac{19}{5}$ ☐
(c) $\frac{4}{5}$ ☐ (d) $\frac{5}{4}$ ☐

55. The highest score in an inning was $\frac{3}{11}$ of the total and the next highest was $\frac{3}{11}$ of the remainder. If the scores differed by 9, then the total score is :

(a) 99 ☐ (b) 110 ☐
(c) 121 ☐ (d) 132 ☐

56. Gopal was asked to find $\frac{7}{9}$ of a fraction. But he made a mistake of dividing the given fraction by $\frac{7}{9}$ and got an answer which exceeded the correct answer by $\frac{8}{21}$. The correct answer is :

   (a) $\frac{3}{7}$ ☐ (b) $\frac{7}{12}$ ☐
   (c) $\frac{2}{21}$ ☐ (d) $\frac{1}{3}$ ☐

57. In a certain office, (1/3) of the workers are women, (1/2) of the women are married and (1/3) of the married women have children. If (3/4) of the men are married and $\frac{2}{3}$ of the married men have children, what part of workers are without children ? (S.B.I. P.O. Exam, 1987)

   (a) $\frac{5}{18}$ ☐ (b) $\frac{4}{9}$ ☐
   (c) $\frac{11}{18}$ ☐ (d) $\frac{17}{36}$ ☐

58. Ravi earns twice as much in January as in each of the other months. What part of his annual earnings he earns in that month ?

   (a) $\frac{2}{13}$ ☐ (b) $\frac{1}{10}$ ☐
   (c) $\frac{5}{7}$ ☐ (d) $\frac{1}{5}$ ☐

   (Railway Recruitment, 1991)

59. In a family, the father took $\frac{1}{4}$ of the cake and he had 3 times as much as others had. The total number of family members is :

   (a) 3 ☐ (b) 7 ☐
   (c) 10 ☐ (d) 12 ☐

   (Railway Recruitment, 1991)

60. The smallest fraction which should be substracted from the sum of $1\frac{3}{4}, 2\frac{1}{2}, 5\frac{7}{12}, 3\frac{1}{3}$ and $2\frac{1}{4}$ to make the result a whole number is

   (a) $\frac{5}{12}$ ☐ (b) $\frac{7}{12}$ ☐
   (c) $\frac{1}{2}$ ☐ (d) 7 ☐

   (C.B.I. Exam, 1991)

Simplification 69

Answers (Exercise 4)

1. (d) 2. (d) 3. (b) 4. (d) 5. (a) 6. (c) 7. (c) 8. (a) 9. (b)
10. (c) 11. (c) 12. (a) 13. (c) 14. (d) 15. (c) 16. (c) 17. (d) 18. (d)
19. (a) 20. (c) 21. (d) 22. (d) 23. (a) 24. (d) 25. (b) 26. (b) 27. (c)
28. (d) 29. (b) 30. (c) 31. (c) 32. (c) 33. (d) 34. (d) 35. (c) 36. (a)
37. (c) 38. (b) 39. (a) 40. (c) 41. (c) 42. (a) 43. (d) 44. (a) 45. (d)
46. (c) 47. (b) 48. (b) 49. (b) 50. (d) 51. (c) 52. (b) 53. (c) 54. (a)
55. (c) 56. (b) 57. (c) 58. (a) 59. (c) 60. (a).

Solution (Exercise 4)

1. $171 \div 19 \times 9 = 171 \times \frac{1}{19} \times 9 = 81.$

2. Given expression $= 5005 - \frac{5000}{10} = 5005 - 500 = 4505.$

3. $7 + 7 \div 7 \times 7 = 7 + 7 \times \frac{1}{7} \times 7 = 7 + 7 = 14.$

4. $3120 \div 26 + 13 \times 30 = 120 + 13 \times 30 = 120 + 390 = 510.$

5. Given Expression $= \frac{4}{2} + 2 \times 2 + 2 \times \frac{3}{2} = 2 + 4 + 3 = 9.$

6. Given Expression $= 8 \div 4 \times 1 \times 4 + 3 - 7$
   $= 8 \times \frac{1}{4} \times 1 \times 4 + 3 - 7 = 8 + 3 - 7 = 4.$

7. $0.5 \times 0.5 + 0.5 \div 5 = 0.5 \times 0.5 + \frac{0.5}{5}$
   $= 0.25 + 0.1 = 0.35.$

8. Given Expression $= 4 - \frac{3.6}{4} + 0.2 \times 0.5$
   $= 4 - 0.9 + 0.1 = 3.2.$

9. Given Expression $= .25 - .025 = 0.225.$

10. Given Expression $= .01 \times \frac{.3}{.4} \times .5 = \frac{.0015}{.4} = .00375.$

11. Given Expression $= \frac{48 - 36 + 9}{12 - 3} = \frac{21}{9} = \frac{7}{3}.$

12. Given Expression $= \frac{69 - 42 + 2}{45 - 25} = \frac{29}{20} = 1.45.$

13. Given Expression $= \frac{240 \times 300}{240} = 300.$

14. Given Expression $= \dfrac{21 \div 7}{5 + 5 + \dfrac{5}{5}} = \dfrac{3}{11}$.

15. Let $\dfrac{17.28 \div x}{3.6 \times 0.2} = 2$.

    Then, $\dfrac{17.28}{x} = 1.44$ or $x = \dfrac{17.28}{1.44} = 12$.

16. Given Expression $= \dfrac{1}{2} + 1 = \dfrac{3}{2}$.

17. Given Expression $= \dfrac{3}{2} \times \dfrac{4}{3} + \dfrac{1}{4} = 2 + \dfrac{1}{4} = \dfrac{9}{4}$.

18. Given Expression $= 1 + 1 \div \left\{1 + 1 \div \dfrac{4}{3}\right\}$
    $= 1 + 1 \div \left\{1 + \dfrac{3}{4}\right\}$
    $= 1 + 1 \div \dfrac{7}{4} = 1 + 1 \times \dfrac{4}{7}$
    $= 1 + \dfrac{4}{7} = 1\dfrac{4}{7}$.

19. Given Expression $= 3 \div \left[3 \div \left\{2 \div \dfrac{34}{13}\right\}\right]$
    $= 3 \div \left[3 \div \left\{2 \times \dfrac{13}{34}\right\}\right]$
    $= 3 \div \left[3 \div \dfrac{13}{17}\right] = 3 \div \left[3 \times \dfrac{17}{13}\right]$
    $= 3 \times \dfrac{13}{51} = \dfrac{13}{17}$.

20. Given Expression $= 10 - [9 - \{8 - 1\}] - 5$
    $= 10 - [9 - 7] - 5 = 10 - 2 - 5 = 3$.

21. Given Expression $= \dfrac{48}{12} \times \left(\dfrac{3}{2} \div \dfrac{1}{2}\right) = 4 \times \left(\dfrac{3}{2} \times 2\right) = 12$.

22. Let $\dfrac{13}{4} + \dfrac{25}{6} + x + \dfrac{1}{4} = 10$. Then,

    $x = 10 - \left(\dfrac{13}{4} + \dfrac{25}{6} + \dfrac{1}{4}\right) = 10 - \left(\dfrac{39 + 50 + 3}{12}\right) = \left(10 - \dfrac{92}{12}\right) = \dfrac{7}{3} = 2\dfrac{1}{3}$.

23. Given Expression $= \dfrac{8}{5} - \dfrac{2}{3} \times \dfrac{13}{12} + \dfrac{7}{5} \times \dfrac{1}{3} = \dfrac{8}{5} - \dfrac{13}{18} + \dfrac{7}{15}$
    $= \dfrac{144 - 65 + 42}{90} = \dfrac{121}{90} = 1\dfrac{31}{90}$.

Simplification

24. Given Expression $= 108 \div 12 + \dfrac{2}{5} \times \dfrac{15}{4}$

    $= 9 + \dfrac{3}{2} = \dfrac{21}{2} = 10\dfrac{1}{2}.$

25. Given Expression $= \dfrac{93}{100} + \dfrac{7}{5} \times \dfrac{1}{20} = \dfrac{93}{100} + \dfrac{7}{100} = 1.$

26. Given Expression $= \dfrac{70}{17} \div \dfrac{7}{5} \times \dfrac{68}{33}$

    $= \dfrac{70}{17} \times \dfrac{5}{7} \times \dfrac{68}{33} = \dfrac{200}{33} = 6\dfrac{2}{33}.$

27. Given Expression $= 4.59 \times \dfrac{1.8}{3.6} + 0.6 - 0.2$

    $= 2.295 + 0.6 - 0.2 = 2.695.$

28. Let $\dfrac{47}{3} \times \dfrac{19}{6} + \dfrac{19}{3} = \dfrac{205}{18} + x.$

    Then, $x = \dfrac{893}{18} + \dfrac{19}{3} - \dfrac{205}{18} = \dfrac{893 + 114 - 205}{18} = \dfrac{802}{18} = 44\dfrac{5}{9}.$

29. Let $\dfrac{5}{6} \div \dfrac{6}{7} \times x - \dfrac{8}{9} \div \dfrac{8}{5} + \dfrac{3}{4} \times \dfrac{10}{3} = \dfrac{25}{9}.$

    Then, $\dfrac{5}{6} \times \dfrac{7}{6} \times x - \dfrac{8}{9} \times \dfrac{5}{8} + \dfrac{5}{2} = \dfrac{25}{9}$

    or $\dfrac{35}{36} x = \dfrac{25}{9} + \dfrac{5}{9} - \dfrac{5}{2} = \left(\dfrac{50 + 10 - 45}{18}\right) = \dfrac{5}{6}.$

    $\therefore x = \left(\dfrac{5}{6} \times \dfrac{36}{35}\right) = \dfrac{6}{7}.$

30. Given Expression

    $= \dfrac{3}{4} \div \dfrac{9}{4} \text{ of } \dfrac{2}{3} - \dfrac{(1/6)}{(5/6)} \times \dfrac{10}{3} + \dfrac{5}{6}$

    $= \dfrac{3}{4} \times \dfrac{2}{3} - \dfrac{1}{6} \times \dfrac{6}{5} \times \dfrac{10}{3} + \dfrac{5}{6} = \dfrac{1}{2} - \dfrac{2}{3} + \dfrac{5}{6} = \dfrac{3 - 4 + 5}{6} = \dfrac{4}{6} = \dfrac{2}{3}.$

31. Given Expression

    $= \dfrac{15}{2} + \dfrac{1}{2} + \dfrac{1}{8} - \dfrac{2}{5} \times \dfrac{7}{3} \div \dfrac{15}{8} \text{ of } \left(\dfrac{7}{5} - \dfrac{4}{3}\right)$

    $= \dfrac{15}{2} + 4 - \dfrac{2}{5} \times \dfrac{7}{3} \div \dfrac{15}{8} \text{ of } \dfrac{1}{15}$

    $= \dfrac{15}{2} + 4 - \dfrac{2}{5} \times \dfrac{7}{3} \div \dfrac{1}{8} = \dfrac{15}{2} + 4 - \dfrac{2}{5} \times \dfrac{7}{3} \times \dfrac{8}{1}$

    $= \dfrac{15}{2} + 4 - \dfrac{112}{15} = \dfrac{23}{2} - \dfrac{112}{15} = \dfrac{121}{30} = 4\dfrac{1}{30}.$

32. Given Expression $\dfrac{\frac{1}{4}+\frac{1}{4}\times\frac{4}{5}}{\frac{1}{16}+\frac{9}{4}} = \dfrac{\frac{1}{4}+\frac{1}{5}}{\frac{37}{16}} = \dfrac{9}{20}\times\dfrac{16}{37} = \dfrac{36}{185}$.

33. Given Expression $= \dfrac{\frac{1}{5}\div\frac{1}{25}}{\frac{1}{25}\div\frac{1}{5}} = \dfrac{\frac{1}{5}\times 25}{\frac{1}{25}\times 5} = (5\times 5) = 25.$

34. Let $\dfrac{50}{x} = \dfrac{x}{\left(\frac{25}{2}\right)}$ or $x^2 = 50\times\dfrac{25}{2} = 625.$

    $\therefore\ x = \sqrt{625} = 25.$

35. Given Expression $= \dfrac{15}{2} - \left[\dfrac{9}{4} \div \left\{\dfrac{5}{4} - \dfrac{1}{2}\left(\dfrac{3}{2} - \dfrac{1}{3} - \dfrac{1}{6}\right)\right\}\right]$

    $= \dfrac{15}{2} - \left[\dfrac{9}{4} \div \left\{\dfrac{5}{4} - \dfrac{1}{2}\times 1\right\}\right]$

    $= \dfrac{15}{2} - \left[\dfrac{9}{4} \div \left\{\dfrac{5}{4} - \dfrac{1}{2}\right\}\right]$

    $= \dfrac{15}{2} - \left[\dfrac{9}{4} \div \dfrac{3}{4}\right] = \dfrac{15}{2} - \left[\dfrac{9}{4}\times\dfrac{4}{3}\right]$

    $= \left(\dfrac{15}{2} - 3\right) = \dfrac{9}{2} = 4\dfrac{1}{2}.$

36. Given Expression $= 1 + \dfrac{1}{1+\dfrac{1}{\left(\frac{10}{9}\right)}} = 1 + \dfrac{1}{1+\dfrac{9}{10}} = 1 + \dfrac{1}{\frac{19}{10}}$

    $= 1 + \dfrac{10}{19} = \dfrac{29}{19}.$

37. Given Expression $= 1 + \dfrac{1}{2+\dfrac{1}{\frac{2}{3}}} = 1 + \dfrac{1}{2+\dfrac{3}{2}}$

    $= 1 + \dfrac{1}{\frac{7}{2}} = 1 + \dfrac{2}{7} = \dfrac{9}{7}.$

38. Given Expression $= \dfrac{108+9+3+1}{108} = \dfrac{121}{108} = 1.1203.$

39. Given Expression $= \dfrac{4\times 5\times 6 + 5\times 6 + 2\times 6 + 2\times 3}{2\times 3\times 4\times 5\times 6} = \dfrac{168}{24\times 30} = \dfrac{7}{30}.$

Simplification   73

40. Given Expression $= \dfrac{(3^2)^2 \times (3 \times 3 \times 2)^4}{3^{16}} = \dfrac{3^4 \times 3^8 \times 2^4}{3^{16}}$

$= \dfrac{2^4}{3^4} = \dfrac{16}{81}.$

41. Given Expression $= \dfrac{\dfrac{1}{2} \times \dfrac{1}{4} + 20}{2 + 20} = \dfrac{161}{8} \times \dfrac{1}{22} = \dfrac{161}{176}.$

42. Given Expression $= \dfrac{(69842)^2 - (30158)^2}{(69842 - 30158)}$

$= \dfrac{(69842 - 30158)(69842 + 30158)}{(60842 - 30158)} = 100000.$

43. Let x of $\dfrac{1}{12} = \dfrac{3}{48}$. Then, $x = \dfrac{3}{48} \times 12 = \dfrac{3}{4}.$

44. Number of $\dfrac{1}{8}$ s $= \dfrac{75}{2} \div \dfrac{1}{8} = \dfrac{75}{2} \times 8 = 300.$

45. Given Expression $= \left(\dfrac{a^3 + b^3}{a^2 + b^2 - ab}\right) = \dfrac{(a+b)(a^2 + b^2 - ab)}{(a^2 + b^2 - ab)} = (a+b)$

$= (885 + 115) = 1000.$

46. Given Expression $= \dfrac{5}{3} \times \dfrac{7}{5} \times \dfrac{9}{7} \times \ldots \times \dfrac{1003}{1001} = \dfrac{1003}{3}.$

47. Dividing Num and Denom by y, we get :

$\dfrac{2x + y}{x - 2y} = \dfrac{2\left(\dfrac{x}{y}\right) + 1}{\left(\dfrac{x}{y}\right) - 2} = \dfrac{2 \times 3 + 1}{3 - 2} = \dfrac{7}{1} = 7.$

$\left[\because \dfrac{x}{2y} = \dfrac{3}{2} \Rightarrow \dfrac{x}{y} = \left(\dfrac{3}{2} \times 2\right) = 3\right]$

48. $\dfrac{3a + 2b}{3a - 2b} = \dfrac{3\left(\dfrac{a}{b}\right) + 2}{3\left(\dfrac{a}{b}\right) - 2} = \dfrac{3 \times \dfrac{1}{3} + 2}{3 \times \dfrac{1}{3} - 2} = \dfrac{3}{-1} = -3.$

49. $\dfrac{4}{7} + \dfrac{2y - x}{2y + x} = \dfrac{4}{7} + \dfrac{2 - \left(\dfrac{x}{y}\right)}{2 + \left(\dfrac{x}{y}\right)} = \dfrac{4}{7} + \dfrac{2 - \dfrac{4}{5}}{2 + \dfrac{4}{5}}$

$= \dfrac{4}{7} + \dfrac{6}{5} \times \dfrac{5}{14} = \dfrac{4}{7} + \dfrac{3}{7} = 1.$

50. $x \times \dfrac{17}{8} - x \times \dfrac{8}{17} = 225$ or $\dfrac{225}{136} x = 225$.

$\therefore x = \left(225 \times \dfrac{136}{225}\right) = 136$.

51. $\dfrac{3}{4} x - \dfrac{3}{14} x = 150$ or $\dfrac{15}{28} x = 150$.

$\therefore x = \left(150 \times \dfrac{28}{15}\right) = 280$.

52. $x \times x \div \dfrac{1}{x} = 18 \dfrac{26}{27}$ or $x^3 = \dfrac{512}{27}$.

$\therefore x^3 = \left(\dfrac{8}{3}\right)^3$ and so $x = \dfrac{8}{3} = 2\dfrac{2}{3}$.

53. Out of the 5 girls, 1 took part in the camp.
Out of the 8 boys, 1 took part in the camp.
Out of 13 students, 2 took part in the camp.

$\therefore \dfrac{2}{13}$ of total number of students took part in the camp.

54. Given Expression $= \dfrac{1}{3 + \dfrac{2}{\left(\dfrac{5}{2}\right)}} = \dfrac{1}{3 + 2 \times \dfrac{2}{5}} = \dfrac{1}{\left(\dfrac{19}{5}\right)} = \dfrac{5}{19}$.

55. Let total score be x.

Then, highest score $= \dfrac{3}{11} x$.

Remainder $= \left(x - \dfrac{3x}{11}\right) = \dfrac{8}{11} x$.

Next highest score $= \dfrac{3}{11}$ of $\dfrac{8}{11} x = \dfrac{24}{121} x$.

Now, $\dfrac{3x}{11} - \dfrac{24x}{121} = 9 \Rightarrow \dfrac{9x}{121} = 9$ or $x = 121$.

56. $\dfrac{9}{7} x - \dfrac{7}{9} x = \dfrac{8}{21} \Rightarrow \dfrac{32}{63} x = \dfrac{8}{21}$ or $x = \dfrac{8}{21} \times \dfrac{63}{32} = \dfrac{3}{4}$.

$\therefore$ Correct Answer $= \dfrac{7}{9} x = \dfrac{7}{9} \times \dfrac{3}{4} = \dfrac{7}{12}$.

57. Let, total number of workers be x.

Then, number of women $= \dfrac{x}{3}$.

Simplification 75

Number of men = $\frac{2x}{3}$.

Number of women having children = $\frac{1}{3}$ of $\frac{1}{2}$ of $\frac{1}{3}x = \frac{x}{18}$.

Number of men having children = $\frac{2}{3}$ of $\frac{3}{4}$ of $\frac{2x}{3} = \frac{x}{3}$.

Number of workers having children = $\frac{x}{18} + \frac{x}{3} = \frac{7}{18}x$.

Number of workers having no children = $\left(x - \frac{7}{18}x\right) = \frac{11x}{18}$

$= \left(\frac{11}{18} \text{ of all workers}\right)$.

58. Suppose he earns Rs. x in each of the 11 months.
Then, earning in January = Rs. $2x$.
∴ Total annual income = $(11x + 2x)$ = Rs. $13x$.
So, earning in January = $\frac{2x}{13x} = \frac{2}{13}$.

59. Let there be x members, other than father.
Father's share = $\frac{1}{4}$, other's share = $\frac{3}{4}$.

Each other's share = $\frac{3}{4x}$.

∴ $3 \times \frac{3}{4x} = \frac{1}{4}$ or $x = 9$.

Hence, the total number of members = 10.

60. $\frac{7}{4} + \frac{5}{2} + \frac{67}{12} + \frac{10}{3} + \frac{9}{4} = \left(\frac{21 + 30 + 67 + 40 + 27}{12}\right) = \frac{185}{12}$.

This is nearly greater than 15.

Let $\frac{185}{12} - x = 15$. Then, $x = \left(\frac{185}{12} - 15\right) = \frac{5}{12}$.

5
SQUARE ROOT & CUBE ROOT

Square Root of A Number : *The square root of a number is that number, the product of which by itself, is equal to the given number.*

The square root of x is denoted by $\sqrt{x}$.

Thus, $\sqrt{9} = 3$, $\sqrt{16} = 4$, $\sqrt{10000} = 100$ etc.

Square Root by Factorization : *When a given number is a perfect square, we resolve it into prime factors and take the product of prime factors, choosing one out of every pair.*

Ex. 1. Find the square root of 23409.

Sol. Resolving 23409 into prime factors, we get :

$23409 = 3 \times 3 \times 3 \times 3 \times 17 \times 17$.

3	23409
3	7803
3	2601
3	867
17	289
	17

$\therefore \sqrt{23409} = 3 \times 3 \times 17 = 153$.

General Method

Ex. 2. Find the square root of 1734489.

```
        1 | 1 73 44 89 ( 1317
          | 1
          |------
       23 |  73
          |  69
          |------
      261 |   444
          |   261
          |------
     2627 |   18389
          |   18389
          |------
          |     ×
```

$\therefore \sqrt{1734489} = 1317$.

Square Root & Cube Root

Square Root of Quotient & Product

We have $\sqrt{\dfrac{a}{b}} = \dfrac{\sqrt{a}}{\sqrt{b}}$ and $\sqrt{ab} = \sqrt{a} \times \sqrt{b}$.

Ex. 3. Evaluate :

(i) $\sqrt{486} \times \sqrt{6}$

(ii) $\dfrac{\sqrt{1323}}{\sqrt{75}}$.

Sol. (i) $\sqrt{486} \times \sqrt{6} = \sqrt{486 \times 6}$
$= \sqrt{6 \times 81 \times 6} = \sqrt{6 \times 6 \times 9 \times 9}$
$= (6 \times 9) = 54.$

(ii) $\dfrac{\sqrt{1323}}{\sqrt{75}} = \sqrt{\dfrac{1323}{75}} = \sqrt{\dfrac{441}{25}} = \dfrac{\sqrt{441}}{\sqrt{25}} = \dfrac{21}{5}.$

Ex. 4. If $\sqrt{21} = 4.582$, find the value of $\sqrt{\dfrac{3}{7}}$.

Sol. $\sqrt{\dfrac{3}{7}} = \dfrac{\sqrt{3}}{\sqrt{7}} = \dfrac{\sqrt{3}}{\sqrt{7}} \times \dfrac{\sqrt{7}}{\sqrt{7}} = \dfrac{\sqrt{3} \times \sqrt{7}}{7} = \dfrac{\sqrt{21}}{7}$

$= \dfrac{4.582}{7} = 0.6546.$

Ex. 5. If $\sqrt{1369} = 37$, find the value of :
$\sqrt{13.69} + \sqrt{.1369} + \sqrt{.001369}.$

Sol. Given Expression $= \sqrt{\dfrac{1369}{100}} + \sqrt{\dfrac{1369}{10000}} + \sqrt{\dfrac{1369}{1000000}}$

$= \dfrac{\sqrt{1369}}{\sqrt{100}} + \dfrac{\sqrt{1369}}{\sqrt{10000}} + \dfrac{\sqrt{1369}}{\sqrt{1000000}}$

$= \left(\dfrac{37}{10} + \dfrac{37}{100} + \dfrac{37}{1000}\right)$

$= (3.7 + 0.37 + 0.037) = 4.107.$

Ex. 6. Given that $\sqrt{15} = 3.8729$, evaluate $\left(\dfrac{\sqrt{5} + \sqrt{3}}{\sqrt{5} - \sqrt{3}}\right)$.

Sol. $\dfrac{(\sqrt{5} + \sqrt{3})}{(\sqrt{5} - \sqrt{3})} = \dfrac{(\sqrt{5} + \sqrt{3})}{(\sqrt{5} - \sqrt{3})} \times \dfrac{(\sqrt{5} + \sqrt{3})}{(\sqrt{5} + \sqrt{3})} = \dfrac{(\sqrt{5} + \sqrt{3})^2}{(5 - 3)}$

$= \left(\dfrac{5 + 3 + 2 \times \sqrt{5} \times \sqrt{3}}{2}\right) = (4 + \sqrt{15})$

$= (4 + 3.8729) = 7.8729.$

Square Root of Decimal Fractions

Rule : *Make an even number of decimal places by affixing a zero, if necessary. Now, mark off periods and extract the square root as shown below.*

Ex. 7. Evaluate $\sqrt{176.252176}$.

Sol. The given number contains even number of decimal places. So, mark off periods and proceed.

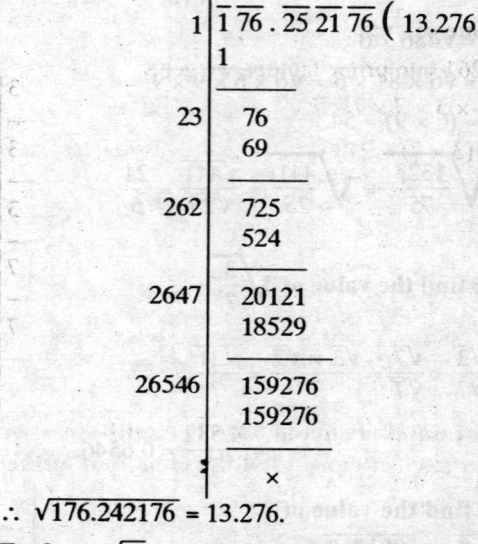

```
     1  | 1̄ 7̄6̄ . 2̄5̄ 2̄1̄ 7̄6̄ ( 13.276
        | 1
    23  | 76
        | 69
   262  | 725
        | 524
  2647  | 20121
        | 18529
 26546  | 159276
        | 159276
        | ×
```

$\therefore \sqrt{176.242176} = 13.276$.

Ex. 8. Evaluate $\sqrt{.4}$ **upto four places of decimal.**

Sol. Making even number of decimal places, we have $\sqrt{.4} = \sqrt{.40}$.

```
     6  | .40 ( .6324
        |  36
   123  | 400
        | 369
  1262  | 3100
        | 2524
 12644  | 57600
        | 50576
```

$\therefore \sqrt{.4} = .6324$.

Square Root & Cube Root

Cube Root : *The cube root of a number x is the number whose cube is x.*
We denote the cube root of x by $\sqrt[3]{x}$.

Cube Root by Factorization : *Resolve the given number into prime factors and take the product of prime numbers, choosing one out of three of each type.*

Thus, $\sqrt[3]{8} = \sqrt[3]{2 \times 2 \times 2} = 2$ and $\sqrt[3]{343} = \sqrt[3]{7 \times 7 \times 7} = 7$.

Ex. 9. Find the value of $\sqrt[3]{9261}$.

Sol. Resolving 9261 into prime factors, we get :
$9261 = 3 \times 3 \times 3 \times 7 \times 7 \times 7$.
$\therefore \sqrt[3]{9261} = (3 \times 7) = 21$.

3	9261
3	3087
3	1029
7	343
7	49
	7

Ex. 10. By what least number should 9720 be multiplied to get a perfect cube. Find the cube root of the number so obtained.

Sol. We have :
$9720 = 2 \times 2 \times 2 \times 3 \times 3 \times 3 \times 5 \times 3 \times 3$.
To make it a perfect cube, the given number must be multiplied by $5 \times 5 \times 3$ i.e. 75.
Cube root of the new number
$= 2 \times 3 \times 5 \times 3 = 90$.

2	9720
2	4860
2	2430
3	1215
3	405
3	135
5	45
3	9
	3

Exercise 5

1. $\sqrt{64009} = ?$
   - (a) 803
   - (b) 363
   - (c) 253
   - (d) 347

2. $\dfrac{\sqrt{4375}}{\sqrt{7}} = ?$
   - (a) 24.75
   - (b) 27.25
   - (c) 25
   - (d) 35

3. $\sqrt{10} \times \sqrt{250} = ?$
   - (a) 46.95
   - (b) 43.75
   - (c) 50.25
   - (d) 50

4. $\dfrac{250}{\sqrt{?}} = 10$
   - (a) 25
   - (b) 250
   - (c) 625
   - (d) 2500

5. $\dfrac{\sqrt{?}}{200} = 0.02$

   (Bank Clerical 1990)
   - (a) 0.4
   - (b) 4
   - (c) 16
   - (d) 1.6

6. $\sqrt{10} \times \sqrt{15} = ?$

   (Clerical Grade 1991)
   - (a) $5\sqrt{6}$
   - (b) $6\sqrt{5}$
   - (c) 5
   - (d) $\sqrt{30}$

7. $\dfrac{\sqrt{288}}{\sqrt{128}} = ?$
   - (a) $\dfrac{\sqrt{3}}{2}$
   - (b) $\dfrac{3}{\sqrt{2}}$
   - (c) $\dfrac{3}{2}$
   - (d) $\sqrt{\dfrac{3}{2}}$

8. If $\sqrt{256} \div \sqrt{x} = 2$, then x is equal to : (C.B.I. 1990)
   - (a) 64
   - (b) 128
   - (c) 512
   - (d) 1024

9. $\sqrt{.04} = ?$ (Railway Recruitment 1991)
   - (a) .02
   - (b) .2
   - (c) .002
   - (d) none of these

10. Given that $\sqrt{4096} = 64$, the value of $\sqrt{4096} + \sqrt{40.96} + \sqrt{.004096}$ is : (C.B.I. 1991)

Square Root & Cube Root

(a) 70.4   (b) 70.464
(c) 71.104   (d) 71.4

11. $\sqrt{176 + \sqrt{2401}} = ?$ (Clerical Grade 1991)

    (a) 14   (b) 15
    (c) 18   (d) 24

12. $\sqrt{248 + \sqrt{52 + \sqrt{144}}}$

    (a) 14   (b) 16
    (c) 16.6   (d) 18.8

13. $\dfrac{112}{\sqrt{196}} \times \dfrac{\sqrt{576}}{12} \times \dfrac{\sqrt{256}}{8} = ?$ (Bank P.O. 1988)

    (a) 8   (b) 12
    (c) 16   (d) 32

14. If $\sqrt{\dfrac{x}{169}} = \dfrac{54}{39}$, then x is equal to: (Railway Recruitment, 1991)

    (a) 108   (b) 324
    (c) 2916   (d) 4800

15. If $\sqrt{\left(1 + \dfrac{27}{169}\right)} = \left(1 + \dfrac{x}{13}\right)$, then x equals: (Central Excise 1988)

    (a) 1   (b) 3
    (c) 5   (d) 7

16. $\dfrac{\sqrt{1296}}{?} = \dfrac{?}{2.25}$ (Railway Recruitment 1990)

    (a) 6   (b) 7
    (c) 8   (d) 9

17. If $\sqrt{15625} = 125$, then the value of $\sqrt{15625} + \sqrt{156.25} + \sqrt{1.5625}$ is: (Assistant Grade, 1990)

    (a) 1.3875   (b) 13.875
    (c) 138.75   (d) 156.25

18. $\sqrt{\dfrac{0.324 \times 0.081 \times 4.624}{1.5625 \times 0.0289 \times 72.9 \times 64}} = ?$ (Assistant Grade 1990)

    (a) 24   (b) 2.40
    (c) 0.024   (d) none of these

19. $\sqrt{\dfrac{1.21 \times 0.9}{1.1 \times 0.11}} = ?$

(C.D.S. 1991)

(a) 2   (b) 3
(c) 9   (d) 11

20. $\dfrac{\sqrt{324}}{1.5} = \dfrac{?}{\sqrt{256}}$

(Bank P.O. 1991)

(a) 192   (b) 432
(c) 288   (d) 122

21. $\dfrac{1872}{\sqrt{?}} = 234$

(a) 324   (b) 64
(c) 8   (d) 256

22. $\sqrt{1\dfrac{9}{16}} = ?$

(a) $1\dfrac{3}{4}$ (b) $1\dfrac{1}{4}$
(c) 1.125   (d) none of these

23. $\sqrt{\dfrac{25}{15625}} = \sqrt{\dfrac{?}{30625}}$

(a) 2   (b) 35
(c) 49   (d) 1225

24. If $\sqrt{2^n} = 64$, then the value of n is :

(Assistant Grade 1990)

(a) 2   (b) 4
(c) 6   (d) 12

25. If $\sqrt{6} = 2.55$, then the value of $\sqrt{\dfrac{2}{3}} + 3 \cdot \sqrt{\dfrac{3}{2}}$ is :

(a) 4.48   (b) 4.49
(c) 4.50   (d) none of these

26. If $\sqrt{3} = 1.732$ and $\sqrt{2} = 1.414$, the value of $\dfrac{1}{\sqrt{3} + \sqrt{2}}$ is :

(C.B.I. 1991)

(a) 0.064   (b) 0.308
(c) 0.318   (d) 2.146

27. $\sqrt{\dfrac{.289}{.00121}} = ?$

(a) $\dfrac{1.7}{11}$ □ (b) $\dfrac{17}{11}$ □

(c) $\dfrac{170}{11}$ □ (d) $\dfrac{17}{110}$ □

28. $\sqrt{\dfrac{36.1}{102.4}} = ?$

(a) $\dfrac{29}{32}$ □ (b) $\dfrac{19}{72}$ □

(c) $\dfrac{19}{32}$ □ (d) $\dfrac{29}{62}$ □

29. If $\sqrt{(75.24 + x)} = 8.71$, then the value of x is : **(L.I.C. A.A.O. 1988)**

(a) .6241 □ (b) 6.241 □
(c) 62.41 □ (d) none of these □

30. $\dfrac{?}{\sqrt{2.25}} = 550$

(Bank P.O. 1987)

(a) 825 □ (b) 82.5 □
(c) 3666.66 □ (d) 2 □

31. $\dfrac{\sqrt{32} + \sqrt{48}}{\sqrt{8} + \sqrt{12}} = ?$

(Bank P.O. 1988)

(a) $\sqrt{2}$ □ (b) 2 □
(c) 4 □ (d) 8 □

32. If $\sqrt{24} = 4.899$, then the value of $\sqrt{\dfrac{8}{3}}$ is :

(Bank P.O. 1989)

(a) 0.544 □ (b) 2.666 □
(c) 1.633 □ (d) 1.333 □

33. If $\sqrt{3} = 1.732$, then the approximate value of $\dfrac{1}{\sqrt{3}}$ is :

(a) 0.617 □ (b) 0.313 □
(c) 0.577 □ (d) 0.173 □

34. If $\sqrt{2} = 1.4142$, then the approximate value of $\sqrt{\dfrac{2}{9}}$ is :

(a) 0.2321 □ (b) 0.4714 □
(c) 0.3174 □ (d) 0.4174 □

35. $\sqrt{\dfrac{4}{3}} - \sqrt{\dfrac{3}{4}} = ?$

(Central Excise & I. Tax 1988)

(a) $\dfrac{1}{2\sqrt{3}}$ (b) $-\dfrac{1}{2\sqrt{3}}$

(c) 1   (d) $\dfrac{5\sqrt{3}}{6}$

36. The least perfect square number divisible by 3, 4, 5, 6, 8 is :
(a) 900   (b) 1200
(c) 2500   (d) 3600

(Central Excise & I. Tax 1989)

37. $\dfrac{\sqrt{5}-\sqrt{3}}{\sqrt{5}+\sqrt{3}}$ is equal to :

(Clerk's Grade 1991)

(a) $4+\sqrt{15}$ (b) $4-\sqrt{15}$

(c) $\dfrac{1}{2}$ (d) 1

38. $\dfrac{1}{\sqrt{9}-\sqrt{8}} = ?$

(Delhi Police 1990)

(a) $\dfrac{1}{2}(3-2\sqrt{2})$ (b) $\dfrac{1}{3+2\sqrt{2}}$

(c) $(3-2\sqrt{2})$ (d) $(3+2\sqrt{2})$

39. If $a = \dfrac{\sqrt{5}+1}{\sqrt{5}-1}$ and $b = \dfrac{\sqrt{5}-1}{\sqrt{5}+1}$, then the value of $\dfrac{a^2+ab+b^2}{a^2-ab+b^2}$ is :

(a) $\dfrac{3}{4}$ (b) $\dfrac{4}{3}$

(c) $\dfrac{3}{5}$ (d) $\dfrac{5}{3}$

(Delhi Police & C.B.I. 1990)

40. $\left[3+\dfrac{1}{\sqrt{3}}+\dfrac{1}{3+\sqrt{3}}+\dfrac{1}{\sqrt{3}-3}\right]$ equals :

(a) 0   (b) 1
(c) 3   (d) $3+\sqrt{3}$

41. If $\sqrt{0.04 \times 0.4 \times a} = 0.4 \times 0.04 \times \sqrt{b}$, then the value of $\dfrac{a}{b}$ is :

(a) 0.016   (b) 1.60
(c) 0.16   (d) none of these

(G.I.C. A.A.O. 1988)

42. $\sqrt{\left(12+\sqrt{12+\sqrt{12+\ldots\ldots}}\right)} = ?$

(Delhi Police, 1990)

(a) 3   (b) 4
(c) 6   (d) greater than 6

Square Root & Cube Root

43. Which of the following numbers, wherein some of the digits have been suppressed by symbols, can possibly be the perfect square of a 3 digit odd number? (Bank P.O. 1987)

(a) 65 × × × 1 ☐ (b) 9 × × 1 ☐
(c) 10 × × × 4 ☐ (d) 9 × × × × × × 5 ☐

44. $\sqrt{0.0009} \div \sqrt{0.01} = ?$ (Clerical Grade, 1991)

(a) 3 ☐ (b) 0.3 ☐
(c) $\frac{1}{3}$ ☐ (d) none of these ☐

45. $\sqrt{0.01} + \sqrt{0.0064} = ?$ (Bank Clerical, 1991)

(a) 0.3 ☐ (b) 0.03 ☐
(c) $\sqrt{0.18}$ ☐ (d) none of these ☐

46. $\sqrt{.00059049} = ?$ (Railway Recruitment, 1988)

(a) .243 ☐ (b) .0243 ☐
(c) .00243 ☐ (d) .000243 ☐

47. If $\sqrt{2} = 1.4142$, the value of $\dfrac{7}{3+\sqrt{2}}$ is :

(a) 1.5858 ☐ (b) 4.4142 ☐
(c) 3.4852 ☐ (d) 3.5858 ☐

48. If $\sqrt{2401} = \sqrt{7^x}$, then the value of x is :

(a) 3 ☐ (b) 4 ☐
(c) 5 ☐ (d) 6 ☐

49. $\sqrt{2\sqrt{2\sqrt{2\sqrt{2\sqrt{2}}}}} = ?$

(a) 0 ☐ (b) 1 ☐
(c) 2 ☐ (d) $2^{31/32}$ ☐

50. The value of $\sqrt{0.9}$ is :

(a) 0.3 ☐ (b) 0.03 ☐
(c) 0.33 ☐ (d) 0.94 ☐

51. The value of $\sqrt{0.121}$ is :

(a) 0.11 ☐ (b) 1.1 ☐
(c) 0.347 ☐ (d) 0.011 ☐

52. The value of $\sqrt{0.064}$ is :

(a) 0.8 ☐ (b) 0.08 ☐
(c) 0.008 ☐ (d) 0.252 ☐

53. The value of $\sqrt{\dfrac{0.16}{0.4}}$ is :
    - (a) 0.2
    - (b) 0.02
    - (c) 0.63
    - (d) $\dfrac{2\sqrt{5}}{5}$

54. The largest number of 5 digits, which is a perfect square is :
    - (a) 99999
    - (b) 99764
    - (c) 99976
    - (d) 99856

55. The smallest number of 4 digits, which is a perfect square, is :
    - (a) 1000
    - (b) 1016
    - (c) 1024
    - (d) 1036

56. What smallest number must be added to 269 to make it a perfect square :
    - (a) 31
    - (b) 16
    - (c) 7
    - (d) 20

57. The least number by which 176 be multiplied to make the result a perfect square, is :
    - (a) 8
    - (b) 9
    - (c) 10
    - (d) 11

58. The least number by which 216 must be divided to make the result a perfect square, is :
    - (a) 3
    - (b) 4
    - (c) 6
    - (d) 9

59. The least number to be subtracted from 16800 to make it a perfect square, is :
    - (a) 249
    - (b) 159
    - (c) 169
    - (d) 219

60. $\dfrac{\sqrt{24} + \sqrt{216}}{\sqrt{96}} = ?$

    (Railway Recruitment 1991)
    - (a) $2\sqrt{6}$
    - (b) $6\sqrt{2}$
    - (c) 2
    - (d) $\dfrac{2}{\sqrt{6}}$

61. A gardner wants to plant 17956 trees and arranges them in such a way that there are as many rows as there are trees in a row. The number of trees in a row is :
    - (a) 144
    - (b) 136
    - (c) 154
    - (d) 134

Square Root & Cube Root

62. A group of students decided to collect as many paise from each member of the group as is the number of members. If the total collection amounts to Rs. 22.09, the number of members in the group is :
    (a) 37 (b) 47
    (c) 107 (d) 43

63. A general wishes to draw up his 36562 soldiers in the form of a solid square. After arranging them, he found that some of them are left over. How many are left ?
    (a) 36 (b) 65
    (c) 81 (d) 97

64. The length of diagonal of a square is 8 cm. The length of the side of the square is :
    (a) 2 cm (b) 2.8 cm
    (c) 1.414 cm (d) 5.64 cm

65. The cube root of .000027 is :
    (a) .3 (b) .03
    (c) .003 (d) none of these

66. $\sqrt[3]{4\frac{12}{125}} = ?$
    (a) $1\frac{3}{5}$ (b) $1\frac{2}{5}$
    (c) $2\frac{2}{5}$ (d) $1\frac{4}{5}$

67. $\sqrt[3]{1 - \frac{91}{216}} = ?$
    (a) $1 - \frac{5}{6}$ (b) $\frac{5}{6}$
    (c) $1 - \frac{\sqrt[3]{91}}{6}$ (d) none of these

68. By what least number must 21600 be multiplied to make it a perfect cube ?
    (a) 6 (b) 10
    (c) 30 (d) 60

69. What is the smallest number by which 3600 be divided to make it a perfect cube ?
    (a) 9 (b) 50
    (c) 300 (d) 450

Answers

1. (c) 2. (c) 3. (d) 4. (c) 5. (c) 6. (a) 7. (c) 8. (a) 9. (b)
10. (b) 11. (b) 12. (b) 13. (d) 14. (b) 15. (a) 16. (d) 17. (c) 18. (c)
19. (b) 20. (a) 21. (b) 22. (b) 23. (c) 24. (d) 25. (d) 26. (c) 27. (c)
28. (c) 29. (a) 30. (a) 31. (b) 32. (c) 33. (c) 34. (b) 35. (a) 36. (d)
37. (b) 38. (d) 39. (b) 40. (c) 41. (a) 42. (b) 43. (a) 44. (b) 45. (a)
46. (b) 47. (a) 48. (b) 49. (d) 50. (d) 51. (c) 52. (d) 53. (c) 54. (d)
55. (c) 56. (d) 57. (d) 58. (c) 59. (b) 60. (c) 61. (d) 62. (b) 63. (c)
64. (d) 65. (b) 66. (a) 67. (b) 68. (b) 69. (d)

Solution (Exercise 5)

1.
```
    2 | 6 40 09  ( 253
        4
       ---  ---
    45 | 240
         225
       ---  ---
   503 | 1509
         1509
         -----
            ×
```
$\therefore \sqrt{64009} = 253$.

2. $\dfrac{\sqrt{4375}}{\sqrt{7}} = \sqrt{\dfrac{4375}{7}} = \sqrt{625} = 25$.

3. $\sqrt{10} \times \sqrt{250} = \sqrt{10 \times 250} = \sqrt{2500} = 50$.

4. Let $\dfrac{250}{\sqrt{x}} = 10$. Then, $\sqrt{x} = \dfrac{250}{10} = 25$.

   $\therefore x = (25)^2 = 625$.

5. Let $\dfrac{\sqrt{x}}{200} = 0.02$. Then, $\sqrt{x} = 200 \times 0.02 = 4$. So, $x = 16$.

6. $\sqrt{10} \times \sqrt{15} = \sqrt{10 \times 15} = \sqrt{150} = \sqrt{25 \times 6} = \sqrt{25} \times \sqrt{6} = 5\sqrt{6}$.

7. $\dfrac{\sqrt{288}}{\sqrt{128}} = \sqrt{\dfrac{288}{128}} = \sqrt{\dfrac{9}{4}} = \dfrac{\sqrt{9}}{\sqrt{4}} = \dfrac{3}{2}$.

8. $\dfrac{\sqrt{256}}{\sqrt{x}} = 2$ or $16 = 2\sqrt{x}$ or $\sqrt{x} = 8$ or $x = 64$.

Square Root & Cube Root

9. $\sqrt{.04} = \sqrt{\dfrac{4}{100}} = \dfrac{\sqrt{4}}{\sqrt{100}} = \dfrac{2}{10} = .2.$

10. $\sqrt{4096} + \sqrt{40.96} + \sqrt{.004096}$

$= \sqrt{4096} + \sqrt{\dfrac{4096}{100}} + \sqrt{\dfrac{4096}{1000000}}$

$= \sqrt{4096} + \dfrac{\sqrt{4096}}{\sqrt{100}} + \dfrac{\sqrt{4096}}{\sqrt{1000000}}$

$= 64 + \dfrac{64}{10} + \dfrac{64}{1000} = 64 + 6.4 + .064 = 70.464.$

11. $\sqrt{176 + \sqrt{2401}} = \sqrt{176 + 49} = \sqrt{225} = 15.$

12. $\sqrt{248 + \sqrt{52 + \sqrt{144}}} = \sqrt{248 + \sqrt{52 + 12}} = \sqrt{248 + \sqrt{64}}$

$\qquad = \sqrt{248 + 8} = \sqrt{256} = 16.$

13. Given Expression $= \left(\dfrac{112}{14} \times \dfrac{24}{12} \times \dfrac{16}{8}\right) = 32.$

14. $\sqrt{\dfrac{x}{169}} = \dfrac{54}{39} \Rightarrow \dfrac{x}{169} = \dfrac{54}{39} \times \dfrac{54}{39}.$

$\therefore x = \left(\dfrac{54}{39} \times \dfrac{54}{39} \times 169\right) = 324.$

15. $\sqrt{\left(1 + \dfrac{27}{169}\right)} = \left(1 + \dfrac{x}{13}\right)$

$\therefore \sqrt{\dfrac{196}{169}} = \left(1 + \dfrac{x}{13}\right)$ or $\dfrac{14}{13} = \left(1 + \dfrac{x}{13}\right)$

or $\dfrac{x}{13} = \left(\dfrac{14}{13} - 1\right) = \dfrac{1}{13}$ or $x = \left(13 \times \dfrac{1}{13}\right) = 1.$

16. Let $\dfrac{\sqrt{1296}}{x} = \dfrac{x}{2.25}.$

Then, $\dfrac{36}{x} = \dfrac{x}{2.25}$ or $x^2 = \left(36 \times \dfrac{225}{100}\right)$

$\therefore x = \sqrt{\dfrac{36 \times 225}{100}} = \dfrac{6 \times 15}{10} = 9.$

17. Given Expression $= \sqrt{15625} + \sqrt{\dfrac{15625}{100}} + \sqrt{\dfrac{15625}{10000}}$

$= \left(125 + \dfrac{125}{10} + \dfrac{125}{100}\right) = (125 + 12.5 + 1.25) = 138.75.$

18. Given Expression $= \sqrt{\dfrac{324 \times 81 \times 4624}{15625 \times 289 \times 729 \times 64}}$

(*Sum of decimal places being equal in Nume and Denom.*)

$= \dfrac{18 \times 9 \times 68}{125 \times 17 \times 27 \times 8} = \dfrac{3}{125} = 0.024.$

19. Given Expression $= \sqrt{\dfrac{121 \times 9}{11 \times 11}} = \sqrt{9} = 3.$

(*Sum of decimal places being equal in Nume and Denom*)

20. $\dfrac{\sqrt{324}}{1.5} = \dfrac{x}{\sqrt{256}}$ or $\dfrac{18}{1.5} = \dfrac{x}{16}.$

$\therefore x = \dfrac{18 \times 16}{1.5} = \left(\dfrac{18 \times 16 \times 10}{15}\right) = 192.$

21. Let $\dfrac{1872}{\sqrt{x}} = 234.$ Then, $\sqrt{x} = \dfrac{1872}{234} = 8.$

$\therefore x = (8 \times 8) = 64.$

22. $\sqrt{1\dfrac{9}{16}} = \sqrt{\dfrac{25}{16}} = \dfrac{\sqrt{25}}{\sqrt{16}} = \dfrac{5}{4} = 1\dfrac{1}{4}.$

23. Let $\sqrt{\dfrac{25}{15625}} = \sqrt{\dfrac{x}{30625}}$.

Then, $\dfrac{25}{15625} = \dfrac{x}{30625}$ or $\dfrac{1}{625} = \dfrac{x}{30625}$

$\therefore x = \dfrac{30625}{625} = 49.$

24. $\sqrt{2^n} = 64 = 2^6 \Rightarrow 2^{n/2} = 2^6.$

So, $\dfrac{n}{2} = 6$ or $n = 12.$

25. $\sqrt{\dfrac{2}{3}} + 3 \cdot \sqrt{\dfrac{3}{2}} = \dfrac{\sqrt{2}}{\sqrt{3}} \times \dfrac{\sqrt{3}}{\sqrt{3}} + 3 \times \dfrac{\sqrt{3}}{\sqrt{2}} \times \dfrac{\sqrt{2}}{\sqrt{2}}$

$= \dfrac{\sqrt{6}}{3} + \dfrac{3\sqrt{6}}{2} = \dfrac{2.55}{3} + \dfrac{3 \times 2.55}{2}$

$= \dfrac{2.55}{3} + \dfrac{7.65}{2} = \dfrac{5.10 + 22.95}{6}$

$= \dfrac{28.05}{6} = 4.675.$

Square Root & Cube Root 91

26. $\dfrac{1}{\sqrt{3}+\sqrt{2}} = \dfrac{1}{(\sqrt{3}+\sqrt{2})} \times \dfrac{(\sqrt{3}-\sqrt{2})}{(\sqrt{3}-\sqrt{2})} = \left(\dfrac{\sqrt{3}-\sqrt{2}}{3-2}\right)$
    $= (\sqrt{3}-\sqrt{2}) = (1.732 - 1.414) = 0.318.$

27. $\sqrt{\dfrac{.289}{.00121}} = \sqrt{\dfrac{.28900}{.00121}} = \sqrt{\dfrac{28900}{121}} = \dfrac{\sqrt{28900}}{\sqrt{121}} = \dfrac{170}{11}.$

28. $\sqrt{\dfrac{36.1}{102.4}} = \sqrt{\dfrac{361}{1024}} = \dfrac{\sqrt{361}}{\sqrt{1024}} = \dfrac{19}{32}.$

29. $75.24 + x = 8.71 \times 8.71 \ \text{or} \ x = .6241.$

30. Let $\dfrac{x}{\sqrt{2.25}} = 550.$ Then, $\dfrac{x}{1.5} = 550$
    $\therefore x = (550 \times 1.5) = \left(\dfrac{550 \times 15}{10}\right) = 825.$

31. $\dfrac{\sqrt{32}+\sqrt{48}}{\sqrt{8}+\sqrt{12}} = \dfrac{\sqrt{16 \times 2}+\sqrt{16 \times 3}}{\sqrt{4 \times 2}+\sqrt{4 \times 3}} = \dfrac{4\sqrt{2}+4\sqrt{3}}{2\sqrt{2}+2\sqrt{3}}$
    $= \dfrac{4(\sqrt{2}+\sqrt{3})}{2(\sqrt{2}+\sqrt{3})} = 2.$

32. $\sqrt{\dfrac{8}{3}} = \dfrac{\sqrt{8}}{\sqrt{3}} \times \dfrac{\sqrt{3}}{\sqrt{3}} = \dfrac{\sqrt{24}}{3} = \dfrac{4.899}{3} = 1.633.$

33. $\dfrac{1}{\sqrt{3}} = \dfrac{1}{\sqrt{3}} \times \dfrac{\sqrt{3}}{\sqrt{3}} = \dfrac{\sqrt{3}}{3} = \dfrac{1.732}{3} = 0.577.$

34. $\sqrt{\dfrac{2}{9}} = \dfrac{\sqrt{2}}{\sqrt{9}} = \dfrac{\sqrt{2}}{3} = \dfrac{1.4142}{3} = 0.4714.$

35. $\dfrac{\sqrt{4}}{\sqrt{3}} - \dfrac{\sqrt{3}}{\sqrt{4}} = \dfrac{2}{\sqrt{3}} - \dfrac{\sqrt{3}}{2} = \dfrac{4-3}{2\sqrt{3}} = \dfrac{1}{2\sqrt{3}}.$

36. L.C.M. of 3, 4, 5, 6, 8 is 120.
    Now, $120 = 2 \times 2 \times 2 \times 3 \times 5.$
    $\therefore$ Required number $= 2 \times 2 \times 2 \times 3 \times 5 \times 2 \times 3 \times 5 = 3600.$

37. $\dfrac{(\sqrt{5}-\sqrt{3})}{(\sqrt{5}+\sqrt{3})} = \dfrac{(\sqrt{5}-\sqrt{3})}{(\sqrt{5}+\sqrt{3})} \times \dfrac{(\sqrt{5}-\sqrt{3})}{(\sqrt{5}-\sqrt{3})} = \dfrac{(\sqrt{5}-\sqrt{3})^2}{(5-3)}$
    $= \dfrac{5+3-2\sqrt{15}}{2} = \dfrac{2(4-\sqrt{15})}{2} = (4-\sqrt{15}).$

38. $\dfrac{1}{\sqrt{9}-\sqrt{8}} = \dfrac{1}{\sqrt{9}-\sqrt{8}} \times \dfrac{\sqrt{9}+\sqrt{8}}{\sqrt{9}+\sqrt{8}} = \dfrac{3+2\sqrt{2}}{9-8} = (3+2\sqrt{2}).$

39. $a = \dfrac{\sqrt{5}+1}{\sqrt{5}-1} \times \dfrac{\sqrt{5}+1}{\sqrt{5}+1} = \dfrac{(\sqrt{5}+1)^2}{(5-1)} = \dfrac{5+1+2\sqrt{5}}{4} = \left(\dfrac{3+\sqrt{5}}{2}\right),$

$$b = \frac{\sqrt{5}-1}{\sqrt{5}+1} \times \frac{\sqrt{5}-1}{\sqrt{5}-1} = \frac{(\sqrt{5}-1)^2}{(5-1)} = \frac{5+1-2\sqrt{5}}{4} = \left(\frac{3-\sqrt{5}}{2}\right),$$

$$a^2 + b^2 = \frac{(3+\sqrt{5})^2 + (3-\sqrt{5})^2}{4} = \frac{2(9+5)}{4} = 7 \text{ and } ab = 1.$$

$$\therefore \frac{a^2 + ab + b^2}{a^2 - ab + b^2} = \frac{7+1}{7-1} = \frac{8}{6} = \frac{4}{3}.$$

40. $3 + \dfrac{1}{\sqrt{3}} + \dfrac{1}{3+\sqrt{3}} + \dfrac{1}{\sqrt{3}-3}$

$= 3 + \dfrac{1}{\sqrt{3}} \times \dfrac{\sqrt{3}}{\sqrt{3}} + \dfrac{1}{3+\sqrt{3}} \times \dfrac{3-\sqrt{3}}{3-\sqrt{3}} + \dfrac{1}{\sqrt{3}-3} \times \dfrac{\sqrt{3}+3}{\sqrt{3}+3}$

$= 3 + \dfrac{\sqrt{3}}{3} + \dfrac{3-\sqrt{3}}{6} + \dfrac{\sqrt{3}+3}{-6}$

$= \dfrac{18 + 2\sqrt{3} + 3 - \sqrt{3} - \sqrt{3} - 3}{6} = \dfrac{18}{6} = 3.$

41. $\sqrt{0.016\, a} = 0.016 \times \sqrt{b} \Rightarrow \dfrac{\sqrt{a}}{\sqrt{b}} = \dfrac{0.016}{\sqrt{0.016}} = \sqrt{0.016}.$

Thus, $\sqrt{\dfrac{a}{b}} = \sqrt{0.016}$ and so $\dfrac{a}{b} = 0.016.$

42. Let, given expression $= x.$
Then, $\sqrt{12+x} = x \Rightarrow 12 + x = x^2.$
$\therefore x^2 - x - 12 = 0$ or $(x-4)(x+3) = 0$
So, $x = 4$ (neglecting $x = -3$).

43. The square of an odd number can not have 4 as the unit digit. The square of a 3 digit number will have at least 5 digits and at the most 6 digits. So, answer (a) is correct.

44. Given Expression $= \dfrac{\sqrt{0.0009}}{\sqrt{0.01}} = \sqrt{\dfrac{0.0009}{0.0100}} = \sqrt{\dfrac{9}{100}} = \dfrac{\sqrt{9}}{\sqrt{100}}$

$= \dfrac{3}{10} = 0.3.$

45. Given Expression $= \sqrt{0.01 + 0.08} = \sqrt{0.09} = 0.3.$

46. $\sqrt{.00059049} = \sqrt{\dfrac{59049}{100000000}} = \dfrac{\sqrt{59049}}{10000} = \dfrac{243}{10000} = .0243.$

47. $\dfrac{7}{3+\sqrt{2}} = \dfrac{7}{(3+\sqrt{2})} \times \dfrac{(3-\sqrt{2})}{(3-\sqrt{2})} = \dfrac{7(3-\sqrt{2})}{7} = (3-\sqrt{2}) = (3-1.4142)$

$= 1.5858.$

48. $\sqrt{2401} = \sqrt{7^x} \Rightarrow 7^x = 2401 = 7^4 \Rightarrow x = 4.$

Square Root & Cube Root

49. Given Expression

$$= \sqrt{2 \times \sqrt{2 \times \sqrt{2 \sqrt{(2 \times 2^{1/2})}}}} = \sqrt{2 \times \sqrt{2 \times \sqrt{(2 \times 2^{3/4})}}}$$

$$= \sqrt{2 \times \sqrt{2 \times 2^{7/8}}} = \sqrt{2 \times 2^{15/16}} = 2^{31/32}.$$

50. $\sqrt{0.9} = \sqrt{0.90} = \sqrt{\dfrac{90}{100}} = \dfrac{\sqrt{90}}{10} = \dfrac{9.4}{10} = 0.94.$

51. $\sqrt{0.121} = \sqrt{0.1210} = \sqrt{\dfrac{1210}{10000}} = \dfrac{\sqrt{1210}}{100} = \dfrac{34.7}{100} = 0.347.$

52. $\sqrt{0.064} = \sqrt{0.0640} = \sqrt{\dfrac{640}{10000}} = \dfrac{\sqrt{640}}{100} = \dfrac{25.2}{10} = 0.252.$

53. $\sqrt{\dfrac{0.16}{0.4}} = \sqrt{\dfrac{0.16}{0.40}} = \sqrt{\dfrac{16}{40}} = \sqrt{\dfrac{4}{10}} = \sqrt{0.4} = \sqrt{0.40} = \sqrt{\dfrac{40}{100}}$

$$= \dfrac{\sqrt{40}}{10} = \dfrac{6.3}{10} = 0.63.$$

54. The largest number of 5 digits = 99999.

```
 3 | 9 99 99 ( 316
   | 9
   |------
61 | 99
   | 61
   |------
626| 3899
   | 3756
   |------
   | 143
```

∴ Required number = (99999 − 143) = (99856).

55. The smallest number of 4 digits = 1000.

```
 3 | 10 00 ( 31
   | 9
   |------
61 | 100
   | 61
   |------
   | 39
```

∴ Required number = $(32)^2$ = 1024.

56.
```
    1 | 2̄ 6̄9̄ ( 16
      |  1
      | ----
   26 | 169
      | 156
      | ----
      |  13
```
∴ Required number to be added = $(17)^2 - 269 = 20$.

57. $176 = 2 \times 2 \times 2 \times 2 \times 11$.

So, in order to make it a perfect square, it must be multiplied by 11.

58. $216 = 2 \times 2 \times 2 \times 3 \times 3 \times 3$.

Clearly, in order to make it a perfect square, it must be divided by 2×3 i.e. 6.

59.
```
    1 | 1̄ 6̄8̄ 0̄0̄ ( 129
      |  1
      | -----
   22 |  68
      |  44
      | -----
  249 | 2400
      | 2241
      | -----
      |  159
      | -----
```
∴ Required number to be subtracted = 159.

60. $\dfrac{\sqrt{24} + \sqrt{216}}{\sqrt{96}} = \dfrac{\sqrt{4 \times 6} + \sqrt{36 \times 6}}{\sqrt{16 \times 6}} = \dfrac{2\sqrt{6} + 6\sqrt{6}}{4\sqrt{6}} = \dfrac{8\sqrt{6}}{4\sqrt{6}} = 2$.

61.
```
    1 | 1̄ 7̄9̄ 5̄6̄ ( 134
      |  1
      | -----
   23 |  79
      |  69
      | -----
  264 | 1056
      | 1056
      | -----
      |   ×
```
∴ Number of trees in a row = 134.

62. Number of members = $\sqrt{2209} = 47$.

Square Root & Cube Root

63.

```
    1  | 3 65 62 ( 191
       | 1
   ----|------
    29 | 265
       | 261
   ----|------
   381 | 462
       | 381
   ----|------
       |  81
```

∴ Number of men left over = 81.

64. $a^2 + a^2 = (8)^2 \Rightarrow 2a^2 = 64$ or $a^2 = 32$.

∴ $a = \sqrt{32} = 4\sqrt{2} = (4 \times 1.41) = 5.64$ cm.

65. $(.000027)^{1/3} = \left(\dfrac{27}{1000000}\right)^{1/3} = \dfrac{(27)^{1/3}}{(10^6)^{1/3}} = \dfrac{3}{100} = .03$.

66. $\left(4\dfrac{12}{125}\right)^{1/3} = \left(\dfrac{512}{125}\right)^{1/3} = \dfrac{(8 \times 8 \times 8)^{1/3}}{(5 \times 5 \times 5)^{1/3}} = \dfrac{8}{5} = 1\dfrac{3}{5}$.

67. $\left(1 - \dfrac{91}{216}\right)^{1/3} = \left(\dfrac{125}{216}\right)^{1/3} = \left(\dfrac{5 \times 5 \times 5}{6 \times 6 \times 6}\right)^{1/3} = \dfrac{5}{6}$.

68. $21600 = 6 \times 6 \times 6 \times 10 \times 10$.

To make the given number a perfect cube, it must be multiplied by 10.

69. $3600 = 2 \times 2 \times 2 \times 2 \times 3 \times 3 \times 5 \times 5$.

To make it a perfect cube, the given number must be divided by $2 \times 3 \times 3 \times 5 \times 5 = 450$.

6
PERCENTAGE

By a certain **per cent**, we mean that many hundredths. Thus x per cent means x hundredths, written as $x\%$.

Ex. 1. (i) $9\% = \dfrac{9}{100}$ (ii) $16\% = \dfrac{16}{100} = \dfrac{4}{25}$.

Ex. 2. (i) $\dfrac{3}{4} = \left(\dfrac{3}{4} \times 100\right)\% = 75\%$. (ii) $\dfrac{7}{4} = \left(\dfrac{7}{4} \times 100\right)\% = 175\%$.

Ex. 3. (i) $0.2 = \dfrac{2}{10} = \left(\dfrac{2}{10} \times 100\right)\% = 20\%$.

(ii) $0.05 = \dfrac{5}{100} = \left(\dfrac{5}{100} \times 100\right)\% = 5\%$.

SOLVED EXAMPLES

Ex. 1. Express each of the following as a fraction :
  (i) **64%** (ii) **6%** (iii) **0.5%**

Sol. (i) $64\% = \dfrac{64}{100} = \dfrac{16}{25}$.

(ii) $6\% = \dfrac{6}{100} = \dfrac{3}{50}$.

(iii) $0.5\% = \dfrac{0.5}{100} = \dfrac{5}{1000} = \dfrac{1}{200}$.

Ex. 2. Express each of the following as a decimal :
  (i) **36%** (ii) **8%** (iii) **0.3%**

Sol. (i) $36\% = \dfrac{36}{100} = 0.36$.

(ii) $8\% = \dfrac{8}{100} = 0.08$.

(iii) $0.3\% = \dfrac{0.3}{100} = 0.003$.

Ex. 3. Express each of the following as rate per cent :

Percentage

(i) $\frac{2}{3}$ (ii) $\frac{1}{12}$ (iii) 0.002

Sol. (i) $\frac{2}{3} = \left(\frac{2}{3} \times 100\right)\% = 66\frac{2}{3}\%$.

(ii) $\frac{1}{12} = \left(\frac{1}{12} \times 100\right)\% = 8\frac{1}{3}\%$.

(iii) $0.002 = \left(\frac{2}{1000} \times 100\right)\% = 0.2\%$.

Ex. 4. Find :

(i) **70% of 70** (ii) **90% of 9** (iii) **3% of 6**

Sol. (i) 70% of 70 $= \left(\frac{70}{100} \times 70\right) = 49$.

(ii) 90% of 9 $= \left(\frac{90}{100} \times 9\right) = 8.1$.

(iii) 3% of 6 $= \left(\frac{3}{100} \times 6\right) = 0.18$.

Ex. 5. Fill in the blanks :

(i) (...?...) % of 64 = 8

(ii) (?) % of 36 = 144

(iii) (?) % of 24 = .72

Sol. (i) Let x% of 64 = 8.

Then, $\frac{x}{100} \times 64 = 8$ or $x = \frac{8 \times 100}{64} = 12.5$.

(ii) Let x% of 36 = 144.

Then, $\frac{x}{100} \times 36 = 144$ or $x = \frac{144 \times 100}{36} = 400$.

(iii) Let x% of 24 = .72.

Then, $\frac{x}{100} \times 24 = .72$ or $x = \frac{.72 \times 100}{24} = 3$.

Ex. 6. (i) What per cent is 120 of 90 ?

(ii) What per cent is 5 gms of 1 kg ?

(iii) What per cent is 150 ml of 3.5 litres ?

Sol. (i) It is $\left(\frac{120}{90} \times 100\right)\% = 133\frac{1}{3}\%$.

(ii) It is $\left(\frac{5}{1000} \times 100\right)\% = 0.5\%$.

(iii) It is $\left(\dfrac{150}{3500} \times 100\right)\% = 4\dfrac{2}{7}\%$.

Rule 1. (Shortcut Method):

(i) If A's income is r% more than B's income, then B's income is less than A's income by $\left[\dfrac{r}{(100+r)} \times 100\right]\%$.

(ii) If A's income is r% less than B's income, then B's income is more than A's income by $\left[\dfrac{r}{(100-r)} \times 100\right]\%$.

Ex. 7. If A's salary is 50% more than that of B, then how much per cent is B's salary less than that of A ?

Sol. B's salary is less than that of A by $\left[\dfrac{r}{(100+r)} \times 100\right]\%$

$= \left(\dfrac{50}{150} \times 100\right)\% = 33\dfrac{1}{3}\%$.

Ex. 8. If A's salary is 30% less than that of B, then how much per cent is B's salary more than that of A ?

Sol. B's salary is more than that of A by $\left[\dfrac{r}{(100-r)} \times 100\right]\%$

$= \left(\dfrac{30}{70} \times 100\right)\% = 42\dfrac{6}{7}\%$.

Ex. 9. The tax on a commodity is diminished by 20% and its consumption increases by 15%. Find the effect on the revenue.

Sol. New Revenue = (Consumption × Tax)

$= (115\% \times 80\%)$ of the original

$= \left(\dfrac{115}{100} \times \dfrac{80}{100}\right)$ of the orignal

$= \left(\dfrac{115}{100} \times \dfrac{80}{100} \times 100\right)\%$ of original = 92% of original.

Thus, the revenue is decreased by 8%.

Rule 2. (shortcut Method) : *If the price of a commodity increases by r%, then reduction in consumption so as not to increase the expenditure, is* $\left[\dfrac{r}{(100+r)} \times 100\right]\%$.

Ex. 10. If the price of tea is increased by 20%, find by how much per cent a householder must reduce her consumption of tea so as not to increase the expenditure ?

Percentage

Sol. Reduction in consumption $= \left[\dfrac{r}{(100+r)} \times 100\right]\%$

$= \left(\dfrac{20}{120} \times 100\right)\% = 16\dfrac{2}{3}\%.$

Rule 3. (Shortcut Method) : *If the price of a commodity decreases by r%, then increase in consumption, so as not to decrease the expenditure, is $\left[\dfrac{r}{(100-r)} \times 100\right]\%.$*

Ex. 11. If the price of sugar falls down by 10%, by how much per cent must a householder increase its consumption, so as not to decrease expenditure on this item ?

Sol. Increase in consumption $= \left[\dfrac{10}{(100-10)} \times 100\right]\%$

$= \left(\dfrac{10}{90} \times 100\right)\% = 11\dfrac{1}{9}\%.$

PROBLEMS ON POPULATION

Formulae :

I. If the population of a town (or the length of a tree) is P and its annual increase is r%, then :

(i) Population (or length of tree) after n years $= P\left(1 + \dfrac{r}{100}\right)^n.$

(ii) Population (or length of tree) n years ago $= \dfrac{P}{\left(1 + \dfrac{r}{100}\right)^n}.$

II. If the population (or value of a machine in rupees) is P and annual decrease (or depreciation) is r%, then

(i) Population (or value of machine) after n years $= P\left(1 - \dfrac{r}{100}\right)^n.$

(ii) Population (or value of machine) n years ago $= \dfrac{P}{\left(1 - \dfrac{r}{100}\right)^n}.$

Ex. 12. The population of a town is **176400**. It increases annually at the rate of 5% per annum. What will be its population after 2 years ?

What it was 2 years ago ?

Sol. Population after 2 years $= \left[176400 \times \left(1 + \dfrac{5}{100}\right)^2\right]$

$= \left(176400 \times \dfrac{21}{20} \times \dfrac{21}{20}\right) = 194481.$

Population 2 years ago $= \dfrac{176400}{\left(1 + \dfrac{5}{100}\right)^2} = \left(176400 \times \dfrac{20}{21} \times \dfrac{20}{21}\right)$

$= 160000.$

Ex. 13. The value of a machine depreciates at the rate of 10% per annum. If its present value is Rs. 81000, what will be its worth after 3 years?

What was the value of the machine 2 years ago?

Sol. Value of the machine after 3 years

$= \text{Rs.} \left[81000 \times \left(1 - \dfrac{10}{100}\right)^3\right] = \text{Rs. } 59049.$

Value of the machine 2 years ago $= \text{Rs.} \left[\dfrac{81000}{\left(1 - \dfrac{10}{100}\right)^2}\right]$

$= \text{Rs.} \left(81000 \times \dfrac{10}{9} \times \dfrac{10}{9}\right) = \text{Rs. } 100000.$

Exercise 6

1. $8\dfrac{1}{3}$ % expressed as a fraction is :

 (C.B.I. 1990)

 (a) $\dfrac{25}{3}$ ☐ (b) $\dfrac{3}{25}$ ☐

 (c) $\dfrac{1}{12}$ ☐ (d) $\dfrac{1}{4}$ ☐

2. .025 in terms of rate per cent is :

 (a) 25% ☐ (b) 2.5% ☐

 (c) 0.25% ☐ (d) $37\dfrac{1}{2}$% ☐

3. .02 = (...?...) %

 (Bank P.O. 1986)

 (a) 20 ☐ (b) 2 ☐

 (c) .02 ☐ (d) .2 ☐

Percentage

4. What per cent of $\frac{2}{7}$ is $\frac{1}{35}$?
   (a) 2.5%
   (b) 10%
   (c) 25%
   (d) 20%

5. What per cent of 7.2 kg is 18 gms?
   (a) .025%
   (b) .25%
   (c) 2.5%
   (d) 25%

   (Bank P.O. 1987)

6. ?% of 130 = 10.4
   (a) 80
   (b) 8
   (c) 0.8
   (d) 0.08

7. The fraction equivalent to $\frac{2}{5}$% is:
   (a) $\frac{1}{40}$
   (b) $\frac{1}{125}$
   (c) $\frac{1}{250}$
   (d) $\frac{1}{500}$

   (A.O. Exam, 1990)

8. 30% of 140 = ?% or 840
   (a) 5
   (b) 15
   (c) 24
   (d) 60

   (Bank P.O. 1990)

9. ?% of 250 + 25% of 68 = 67
   (a) 10
   (b) 15
   (c) 20
   (d) 25

   (Central Excise & I. Tax 1989)

10. 5% of [50% of Rs. 300] is:
    (a) Rs. 5
    (b) Rs. 7.50
    (c) Rs. 8.50
    (d) Rs. 10

    (Assistant Grade 1987)

11. What is 25% of 25% equal to:
    (a) 6.25
    (b) .625
    (c) .0625
    (d) .00625

12. The number .05 is how many per cent of 20: **(Assistant Grade 1990)**
    (a) 25
    (b) .025
    (c) .25
    (d) 2.5

    (Bank P.O. 1988)

13. ? × 15 = 37.5% of 220
    (a) 82.5
    (b) 8250
    (c) 11
    (d) 5.5

14. $\left(0.756 \times \frac{3}{4}\right) = 24$ is equivalent to:

(a) 18.9 % (b) 37.8 %
(c) 56.7 % (d) 75 %

15. $\dfrac{30\% \text{ of } 80}{?} = 24$

(Delhi Police 1989)

(a) $\dfrac{3}{10}$ (b) $\dfrac{3}{17}$
(c) 1 (d) 2

16. 8% of 96 = ? of $\dfrac{1}{25}$

(L.I.C. 1991)

(a) 19.2 (b) 7.68
(c) 1.92 (d) none of these

17. If 8% of x = 4% of y, then 20% of x is :

(G.I.C. 1991)

(a) 10% of y (b) 16% of y
(c) 80% of y (d) none of these

18. If x is 90% of y, then what per cent of x is y :

(a) 90 (b) 190
(c) 101.1 (d) 111.1

(Hotel Management 1991)

19. (x% of y + y% of x) is equal to :

(Delhi Police 1991)

(a) x% of y (b) y% of x
(c) 2% of xy (d) xy% of 3

20. If 31% of a number is 46.5, the number is :

(Clerk's Grade 1991)

(a) 150 (b) 155
(c) 160 (d) 165

21. Which number is 60% less than 80 ?

(Assistant Grade 1990)

(a) 48 (b) 42
(c) 32 (d) 12

22. A number exceeds 20% of itself by 40. The number is :

(a) 50 (b) 60
(c) 80 (d) 320

(Assistant Grade 1990)

23. If 90% of A = 30% of B and B = x% of A, then the value of x is :

(a) 900 (b) 800
(c) 600 (d) 300

(Assistant Grade 1987)

24. Which is greatest $33\dfrac{1}{3}$ %, $\dfrac{4}{15}$ or .35 ?

Percentage 103

    (a) $33\frac{1}{3}\%$ (b) $\frac{4}{15}$

    (c) .35   (d) can not be compared

                                                                                               (Bank P.O. 1990)

25. 200 = ?% of 300

    (a) $33\frac{1}{3}$ (b) 85

    (c) $66\frac{2}{3}$ (d) 150

                                                                                               (Bank P.O. 1991)

26. 45 × ? = 25% of 900

    (a) 16.20   (b) 4

    (c) 5   (d) 500

27. If 0.5% of x = 85 paise, then the value of x is :

    (a) Rs. 170   (b) Rs. 17

    (c) Rs. 1.70   (d) Rs. 4.25

28. What per cent is 3% of 5% ?

    (a) 15%   (b) 1.5%

    (c) 0.15%   (d) none of these

                                                                                               (Bank P.O. 1987)

29. 75% of 480 = (?) × 15

    (a) 32   (b) 18

    (c) 360   (d) none of these

30. 30 quintals is what per cent of 2 metric tonnes :

    (a) 15%   (b) 1.5%

    (c) 150%   (d) 30%

31. $x\%$ of y is $y\%$ of ?

    (a) x (b) $100 x$

    (c) $\frac{x}{100}$ (d) $\frac{y}{100}$

                                                                          (Bank P.O. 1991)

32. 12.5% of 192 = 50% of ?

    (a) 48   (b) 96

    (c) 24   (d) none of these

33. If $37\frac{1}{2}\%$ of a number is 900, then $62\frac{1}{2}\%$ of the number is :

    (a) 1200   (b) 1350

    (c) 1500   (d) 540

34. Subtracting 6% of x from x is equivalent to multiplying x by how much ?

    (a) 0.94   (b) 9.4

(c) 0.094 □ (d) 94 □

35. By how much is 30% of 80 greater than $\frac{4}{5}$ th of 25 ?
 (a) 2 □ (b) 4 □
 (c) 10 □ (d) 15 □
               (Bank P.O. 1990)

36. The price of an article is cut by 10%. To restore it to the former value, the new price must be increased by : **(Delhi Police & C.B.I. 1990)**
 (a) 10% □ (b) $9\frac{1}{11}$% □
 (c) $11\frac{1}{9}$% □ (d) 11% □

37. The income of a broker remains unchanged though the rate of commission is increased from 4% to 5%. The percentage of slump in business is : **(Assistant Grade 1990)**
 (a) 8% □ (b) 1% □
 (c) 20% □ (d) 80% □

38. One-third of 1206 is what per cent of 134 :
 (a) 3 □ (b) 30 □
 (c) 300 □ (d) none of these □

39. Rakesh credits 15% of his salary in his fixed deposit account and spends 30% of the remaining amount on groceries. If the cash in hand is Rs. 2380, what is his salary ? **(Assistant Grade 1990)**
 (a) Rs. 3500 □ (b) Rs. 4000 □
 (c) Rs. 4500 □ (d) Rs. 5000 □

40. A man donated 5% of his income to a charitable organisation and deposited 20% of the remainder in a bank. If he now has Rs. 1919 left, what is his income ? **(Assistant Grade 1990)**
 (a) Rs. 2558.60 □ (b) Rs. 2525 □
 (c) Rs. 2500 □ (d) Rs. 2300 □

41. After spending 40% in machinery, 25% in building, 15% in raw material and 5% on furniture, Harilal had a balance of Rs. 1305. The money with him was : **(Bank P.O. 1987)**
 (a) Rs. 6500 □ (b) Rs. 7225 □
 (c) Rs. 8700 □ (d) Rs. 1390 □

42. A number increased by $37\frac{1}{2}$% gives 33. The number is :
 (a) 22 □ (b) 24 □

Percentage

      (c) 25   (d) 27

43. A number decreased by $27\frac{1}{2}$% gives 87. The number is :

    (a) 58   (b) 110
    (c) 120   (d) 135

44. 25% of a number is more than 18% of 650 by 19. The number is :

    (a) 380.8   (b) 450
    (c) 544   (d) none of these

45. 96% of the population of a village is 23040. The total population of the village is :

    (a) 32256   (b) 24000
    (c) 24936   (d) 25640

46. After deducting a commission of 5% a T.V. set costs Rs 9595. Its gross value is :

    (a) Rs. 10000   (b) Rs. 10074.75
    (c) Rs. 10100   (d) none of these

47. A man spends Rs. 3500 per month and saves $12\frac{1}{2}$% of his income. His monthly income is :

    (a) Rs. 4400   (b) Rs. 4270
    (c) Rs. 4000   (d) Rs. 3937.50

48. If 70% of the students in a school are boys and the number of girls be 504, the number of boys is :

    (a) 1176   (b) 1008
    (c) 1208   (d) 3024

49. An ore contains 12% copper. How many kg of ore are required to get 69 kg of copper ?

    (a) 424 kg   (b) 575 kg
    (c) 828 kg   (d) $1736\frac{2}{3}$ kg

50. A fruit seller had some apples. He sells 40% and still has 420 apples. Originally, he had :

    (a) 588 apples   (b) 600 apples
    (c) 672 apples   (d) 700 appies

51. In an examination, 65% of the total examinees passed. If the number of failures is 420, the total number of examinees is :

    (a) 567   (b) 693

(c) 1000
(d) 1200

52. $\sqrt{(3.6\% \text{ of } 40)}$ is equal to :
   (a) 2.8
   (b) 1.8
   (c) 1.2
   (d) none of these

53. 75% of a number when added to 75 is equal to the number. The number is :
   (Railway Recruitment 1991)
   (a) 150
   (b) 200
   (c) 225
   (d) 300

54. In mathematics exam. a student scored 30% marks in the first paper, out of a total of 180. How much should he score in second paper out of a total of 150, if he is to get an overall average of at least 50% :
   (a) 74%
   (b) 76%
   (c) 70%
   (d) 80%

   (Railway Recruitment 1991)

55. 5% income of A is equal to 15% income of B and 10% income of B is equal to 20% income of C. If income of C is Rs. 2000, then total income of A, B and C is :
   (Bank P.O. 1990)
   (a) Rs. 6000
   (b) Rs. 18000
   (c) Rs. 20000
   (d) Rs. 14000

56. From the salary of an officer, 10% is deducted as house rent, 15% of the rest he spends on children's education and 10% of the balance, he spends on clothes. After this expenditure, he is left with Rs. 1377. His salary is :
   (a) Rs. 2000
   (b) Rs. 2040
   (c) Rs. 2100
   (d) Rs. 2200

57. In an examination, it is required to get 36% of maximum marks to pass. A student got 113 marks and declared failed by 85 marks. The maximum marks are :
   (a) 500
   (b) 550
   (c) 640
   (d) 1008

58. Two numbers are less than a third number by 30% and 37% respectively. How much per cent is the second number less than the first ?
   (a) 3%
   (b) 4%
   (c) 7%
   (d) 10%

59. In an examination, 42% students failed in Hindi and 52% failed in English. If 17% failed in both the subjects, the percentage of those who passed in both the subjects, is :
   (a) 23%
   (b) 27%

Percentage 107

    (c) 34% ☐   (d) 40% ☐

60. In an examination, there were 2000 candidates, out of which 900 candidates were boys and rest were girls. If 32% of the boys and 38% of the girls passed, then the total percentage of failed candidates is :
    (a) 35.3% ☐   (b) 64.7% ☐
    (c) 68.5% ☐   (d) 70% ☐

61. A student who secures 20% marks in an examination fails by 30 marks. Another student who secures 32% marks gets 42 marks more than those required to pass. The percentage of marks required to pass is :
    (a) 20 ☐   (b) 25 ☐
    (c) 28 ☐   (d) 30 ☐
    (Clerk's Grade, 1991)

62. There were 600 students in a school. Each offered either English or Hindi or both. If 75% offered English and 45% Hindi, how many offered both ?
    (a) 48 ☐   (b) 60 ☐
    (c) 80 ☐   (d) 120 ☐

63. In a college election, a candidate secured 62% of the votes and is elected by a majority of 144 votes. The total number of votes polled is :   (Astt. Grade, 1990)
    (a) 600 ☐   (b) 800 ☐
    (c) 925 ☐   (d) 1200 ☐

64. In an election between two candidates, the candidate who gets 30% of the votes polled is defeated by 15000 votes. The number of votes polled by the winning candidate is :   (Central Excise & I. Tax, 1988)
    (a) 11250 ☐   (b) 15000 ☐
    (c) 26250 ☐   (d) 37500 ☐

65. In an election between two candidates, one got 55% of the total valid votes. 20% of the votes were invalid. If the total number of votes was 7500, the number of valid votes that the other candidate got was :
    (a) 2700 ☐   (b) 2900 ☐
    (c) 3000 ☐   (d) 3100 ☐

66. What will be 80 per cent of a number whose 200 per cent is 90 ?
    (a) 144 ☐   (b) 72 ☐
    (c) 36 ☐   (d) none of these ☐
    (Bank P.O. 1989)

67. The price of cooking oil has increased by 25%. The per centage of reduction that a family should effect in the use of cooking oil so as not to increase the expenditure on this account is :

(a) 15% □ (b) 20% □
(c) 25% □ (d) 30% □
(Central Excise & I. Tax, 1988)

68. The price of sugar is increased by 20%. If the expenditure is not allowed to increase, the ratio between the reduction in consumption and the original consumption is : (Assistant Grade, 1987)

(a) 1 : 3 □ (b) 1 : 4 □
(c) 1 : 6 □ (d) 1 : 5 □

69. 3 litres of water is added to 15 litres of a mixture of a 20% solution of alcohol in water. The strength of alcohol is now :

(a) $12\frac{1}{2}\%$ □ (b) $16\frac{2}{3}\%$ □
(c) 24 % □ (d) 16% □

70. Water tax is increased by 20% but its consumption is decreased by 20%. Then, the increase or decrease in the expenditure of the money is :

(a) No change □ (b) 5% decrease □
(c) 4% increase □ (d) 4% decrease □
(C.B.I. Exam, 1991)

71. On decreasing the price of T.V. sets by 30%, its sale is increased by 20%. What is the effect on the revenue received by the shopkeeper ?

(a) 10% increase □ (b) 10% decrease □
(c) 16% increase □ (d) 16% decrease □
(Bank P.O., 1988)

72. The population of a town is 8000. It increases by 10% during first year and by 20% during the second year. The population after 2 years will be :

(a) 10400 □ (b) 10560 □
(c) 10620 □ (d) none of these □

73. In a vocational course in a college, 15% seats increase annually. If there were 800 students in 1992, how many students will be there in 1994 ?

(a) 920 □ (b) 1040 □
(c) 1058 □ (d) 1178 □

74. The value of a machine depreciates 10% annually. If its pre sent value is Rs. 4000, its value 2 years hence will be :

(a) Rs. 3200 □ (b) Rs. 3240 □
(c) Rs. 3260 □ (d) Rs. 3280 □

Percentage

75. The population of a town increases by 5% annually. If it is 15435 now, its population 2 years ago was :
(a) 13700 (b) 14000
(c) 14800 (d) 15000

76. A papaya tree was planted 2 years ago. It increases at the rate of 20% every year. If at present, the height of the tree is 540 cm, what was it when the tree was planted ?
(a) 324 cms (b) 375 cms
(c) 400 cms (d) 432 cms

77. The value of a machine depreciates at the rate of 10% every year. It was purchased 3 years ago. If its present value is Rs. 8748, its purchase price was :
(a) Rs. 10000 (b) Rs. 11372.40
(c) Rs. 12000 (d) none of these

78. The current birth rate per thousand is 32 whereas corresponding death rate is 11 per thousand. The net growth rate in terms of population increase in per cent is given by :
(a) 0.021% (b) 0.0021%
(c) 21% (d) 2.1%

79. A man's basic pay for a 40 hour week is Rs. 20. Overtime is paid for at 25% above the basic rate. In a certain week he worked overtime and his total wage was Rs. 25. He therefore worked for a total of :
(a) 45 hours (b) 47 hours
(c) 48 hours (d) 50 hours
(C.B.I. Exam, 1991)

80. The population of a town increases 4% annually but is decreased by emigration annually to the extent of (1/2) %. What will be the increase per cent in three years ? (C.B.I. Exam, 1991)
(a) 9.8 (b) 10
(c) 10.5 (d) 10.8

81. Sameer spends 40% of his salary on food articles, and $\frac{1}{3}$rd of the remaining on transport. If he saves Rs. 450 per month, which is half of the balance after spending on food items and transport, what is his monthly salary ? (S.B.I. P.O. Exam, 1991)
(a) Rs. 1125 (b) Rs. 2250
(c) Rs. 2500 (d) Rs. 4500

82. A man's wages were decreased by 50%. Again the reduced wages were increased by 50%. He has a loss of :
    (a) 0%
    (b) 0.25%
    (c) 2.5%
    (d) 25%

83. A man spends 75% of his income. His income is increased by 20% and he increased his expenditure by 10%. His savings are increased by :
    (a) 10%
    (b) 25%
    (c) $37\frac{1}{2}$%
    (d) 50%

84. p is six times as large as q. The percent that q is less than p, is :
    (a) $83\frac{1}{3}$
    (b) $16\frac{2}{3}$
    (c) 90
    (d) 60

    (C.B.I. Exam, 1990)

85. The price of an article has been reduced by 25%. In order to restore the original price, the new price must be increased by :
    (a) $33\frac{1}{3}$%
    (b) $11\frac{1}{9}$%
    (c) $9\frac{1}{11}$%
    (d) $66\frac{2}{3}$%

    (Hotel Management, 1991)

86. If A's salary is 30% more than B's, then how much per cent is B's salary less than A's ?
    (a) 30%
    (b) 25%
    (c) $23\frac{1}{13}$%
    (d) $33\frac{1}{3}$%

87. If the numerator of a fraction is increased by 20% and the denominator be diminished by 10%, the value of the fraction is $\frac{16}{21}$. The original fraction is :
    (a) $\frac{3}{5}$
    (b) $\frac{4}{7}$
    (c) $\frac{2}{3}$
    (d) $\frac{5}{7}$

88. The boys and girls in a college are in ratio 3 : 2. If 20% of the boys and 25% of the girls are adults, the percentage of students who are not adults is :
    (a) 58%
    (b) 67.5%

(c) 78% (d) 82.5%

89. A mixture of 40 litres of milk and water contains 10% water. How much water should be added to this so that water may be 20% in the new mixture ?
    (a) 4 litres   (b) 5 litres
    (c) 6.5 litres   (d) 7.5 litres

90. One litre of water is evaporated from 6 litres of a solution containing 5% salt. The percentage of salt in the remaining solution is :
    (a) $4\frac{4}{9}\%$ (b) $5\frac{5}{7}\%$
    (c) 5%   (d) 6%

91. The price of rice has increased by 60%. In order to restore to the original price, the new price must be reduced by :
    (a) $33\frac{1}{3}\%$ (b) $37\frac{1}{2}\%$
    (c) 40%   (d) 45%

92. 72% of the students of a certain class took Biology and 44% took Mathematics. If each student took Biology or Mathematics and 40 took both, the total number of students in the class was :
    (a) 200   (b) 240
    (c) 250   (d) 320

93. If the side of a square is increased by 30%, its area is increased by :
    (a) 9%   (b) 30%
    (c) 60%   (d) 69%
    (S.S.C. Exam, 1986)

94. In measuring the side of a square, an error of 5% in excess is made. The error per cent in the calculated area is :
    (a) 10%   (b) 10.25%
    (c) 10.5%   (d) 25%

95. The length and breadth of a square are increased by 30% and 20% respectively. The area of the rectangle so formed exceeds the area of the square by :
    (a) 20%   (b) 36%
    (c) 50%   (d) 56%

96. The length of a rectangle is increased by 10% and breadth decreased by 10%. Then, the area of new rectangle is :
    (a) neither decreased nor increased
    (b) increased by 1%

    (c) decreased by 1%

    (d) decreased by 2%

97. The length of a rectangle is increased by 60%. By what per cent would the width have to be decreased to maintain the same area ?

    (a) $37\frac{1}{2}\%$ (b) 60%

    (c) 75%   (d) none of these

                                                (S.B.I. P.O. Exam, 1988)

98. The radius of a circle is increased by 1%. What is the increased per cent in its area ?

    (a) 1%   (b) 1.1%

    (c) 2%   (d) 2.01%

99. For a sphere of radius 10 cms, the numerical value of the surface area is how many percent of the numerical value of its volume ?

    (a) 24%   (b) 26.5%

    (c) 30%   (d) 45%

100. A reduction of 21% in the price of wheat enables a person to buy 10.5 kg more for Rs. 100. What is the reduced price per kg ?

    (a) Rs. 2   (b) Rs. 2.25

    (c) Rs. 2.30   (d) Rs. 2.50

Answers (Exercise 6)

1. (c) 2. (b) 3. (b) 4. (b) 5. (b) 6. (b) 7. (c) 8. (a) 9. (c)
10. (b) 11. (c) 12. (c) 13. (d) 14. (c) 15. (c) 16. (d) 17. (a) 18. (d)
19. (c) 20. (a) 21. (c) 22. (a) 23. (d) 24. (c) 25. (c) 26. (c) 27. (a)
28. (d) 29. (d) 30. (c) 31. (a) 32. (a) 33. (c) 34. (a) 35. (b) 36. (c)
37. (c) 38. (c) 39. (b) 40. (b) 41. (a) 42. (b) 43. (c) 44. (c) 45. (b)
46. (c) 47. (c) 48. (a) 49. (b) 50. (d) 51. (d) 52. (c) 53. (d) 54. (a)
55. (b) 56. (a) 57. (b) 58. (d) 59. (a) 60. (b) 61. (b) 62. (d) 63. (a)
64. (c) 65. (a) 66. (c) 67. (b) 68. (c) 69. (b) 70. (d) 71. (d) 72. (b)
73. (c) 74. (b) 75. (b) 76. (b) 77. (c) 78. (d) 79. (c) 80. (d) 81. (b)
82. (d) 83. (d) 84. (a) 85. (a) 86. (c) 87. (b) 88. (c) 89. (b) 90. (d)
91. (b) 92. (c) 93. (d) 94. (b) 95. (d) 96. (c) 97. (a) 98. (d) 99. (c)
100. (a).

Percentage

Solution (Exercise 6)

1. $8\frac{1}{3}\% = \left(\frac{25}{3} \times \frac{1}{100}\right) = \frac{1}{12}$.

2. $.025 = \left(\frac{25}{1000} \times 100\right)\% = 2.5\%$.

3. $.02 = \left(\frac{2}{100} \times 100\right)\% = 2\%$.

4. Required percentage $= \left[\frac{(1/35)}{(2/7)} \times 100\right]\%$
   $= \left(\frac{1}{35} \times \frac{7}{2} \times 100\right)\% = 10\%$.

5. Required percentage $= \left(\frac{18}{7.2 \times 1000} \times 100\right)\% = 0.25\%$.

6. Let $x\%$ of $130 = 10.4$.
   Then, $\frac{x}{100} \times 130 = 10.4$ or $x = \frac{10.4 \times 100}{130} = 8$.

7. $\frac{2}{5}\% = \left(\frac{2}{5} \times \frac{1}{100}\right) = \frac{1}{250}$.

8. Let $x\%$ of $840 = 30\%$ of 140.
   Then, $\frac{x}{100} \times 840 = \frac{30}{100} \times 140$ or $x = \left(\frac{30}{100} \times 140 \times \frac{100}{840}\right) = 5$.

9. Let $x\%$ of $250 + 25\%$ of $68 = 67$.
   Then, $\frac{x}{100} \times 250 + \frac{25}{100} \times 68 = 67$ or $\frac{5x}{2} = 50$
   $\therefore x = \left(\frac{50 \times 2}{5}\right) = 20$.

10. 5% of (50% of Rs. 300) = Rs. $\left(\frac{5}{100} \times \frac{50}{100} \times 300\right)$ = Rs. 7.50.

11. 25% of $25\% = \frac{25}{100} \times \frac{25}{100} = \frac{625}{10000} = .0625$.

12. Let $x\%$ of $20 = .05$.
    Then, $\frac{x}{100} \times 20 = .05$ or $x = .25$.

13. Let $x \times 15 = 37.5\%$ of 220.
    Then, $15x = \left(\frac{37.5}{100} \times 220\right)$ or $x = \frac{37.5 \times 220}{100 \times 15} = 5.5$.

14. $\left(0.756 \times \dfrac{3}{4}\right) = \left(\dfrac{756}{1000} \times \dfrac{3}{4} \times 100\right)\% = 56.7\%$.

15. Let $\dfrac{30\% \text{ of } 80}{x} = 24$.

    Then, $24x = \left(\dfrac{30}{100} \times 80\right)$ or $x = \left(\dfrac{30 \times 80}{24 \times 100}\right) = 1$.

16. Let 8% of $96 = x$ of $\dfrac{1}{25}$. Then,

    $\dfrac{8}{100} \times 96 = \dfrac{x}{25}$ or $x = \dfrac{8}{100} \times 96 \times 25 = 192$.

17. 8% of $x = 4\%$ of y

    $\therefore \dfrac{8}{100} x = \dfrac{4}{100} y$ or $x = \left(\dfrac{4}{100} \times \dfrac{100}{8}\right) y = \dfrac{y}{2}$.

    $\therefore 20\%$ of $x = \left(\dfrac{20}{100} \times x\right) = \left(\dfrac{1}{5} \times \dfrac{y}{2}\right) = \dfrac{1}{10} y = \left(\dfrac{1}{10} \times 100\right)\%$ of y
    $= 10\%$ of y.

18. $x = 90\%$ of $y \Rightarrow x = \dfrac{90}{100} y$.

    Let $z\%$ of $x = y$. Then, $\dfrac{z}{100} \times x = y$

    or $\dfrac{z}{100} \times \dfrac{90}{100} y = y$ or $z = \dfrac{100 \times 100}{90} = 111.1$.

19. $x\%$ of $y + y\%$ of $x = \left(\dfrac{x}{100} \times y\right) + \left(\dfrac{y}{100} \times x\right)$

    $= \dfrac{2}{100} xy = 2\%$ of xy.

20. Let 31% of $x = 46.5$.

    Then, $\dfrac{31}{100} x = 46.5$ or $x = \dfrac{46.5 \times 100}{31} = 150$.

21. Required number $= (80 - 60\%$ of $80) = \left(80 - \dfrac{60}{100} \times 80\right) = 32$.

22. $x - 20\%$ of $x = 40$ or $x - \dfrac{x}{5} = 40$ or $\dfrac{4x}{5} = 40$.

    $\therefore x = \dfrac{40 \times 5}{4} = 50$.

23. $\dfrac{90}{100} A = \dfrac{30}{100} B = \dfrac{30}{100} \times \dfrac{x}{100} A$

$\therefore x = \left(100 \times \dfrac{100}{30} \times \dfrac{90}{100}\right) = 300.$

24. $33\dfrac{1}{3}\% = \left(\dfrac{100}{3} \times \dfrac{1}{100}\right) = \dfrac{1}{3} = 0.33;\ \dfrac{4}{15} = 0.26.$
Clearly $0.35 > 0.33 > 0.26.$
$\therefore 0.35$ is greatest.

25. Let $200 = x\%$ of 300. Then, $\dfrac{x}{100} \times 300 = 200.$

or $x = \dfrac{200}{3} = 66\dfrac{2}{3}.$

26. Let $45 \times x = \dfrac{25}{100} \times 900$ or $x = \dfrac{25 \times 9}{45} = 5.$

27. $\dfrac{0.5}{100}$ of $x = \dfrac{85}{100}$ or $x = $ Rs. $\left(\dfrac{85}{0.5}\right) = $ Rs. $170.$

28. Required percent $= \left[\dfrac{(3/100)}{(5/100)} \times 100\right]\%$

$= \left(\dfrac{3}{100} \times \dfrac{100}{5} \times 100\right)\% = 60\%.$

29. Let 75% of $480 = x \times 15$. Then,

$\dfrac{75}{100} \times 480 = 15x$ or $x = \dfrac{75 \times 480}{100 \times 15} = 24.$

30. Required per cent $= \left(\dfrac{30}{2 \times 10} \times 100\right)\% = 150\%.$

31. Let $x\%$ of $y = y\%$ of z.
Then, $\dfrac{x}{100} \times y = \dfrac{y}{100} \times z$ or $z = \left(\dfrac{xy}{100} \times \dfrac{100}{y}\right) = x.$

32. Let 12.5% of $192 = 50\%$ of x. Then,

$\dfrac{12.5}{100} \times 192 = \dfrac{50}{100} \times x.$ Then, $x = \dfrac{12.5 \times 192}{50} = 48.$

33. Let $37\dfrac{1}{2}\%$ of $x = 900$. Then, $\dfrac{75x}{2 \times 100} = 900$

$\therefore x = \dfrac{900 \times 2 \times 100}{75} = 2400.$

So, $62\dfrac{1}{2}\%$ of $x = \left(\dfrac{125}{2} \times \dfrac{1}{100} \times 2400\right) = 1500.$

34. Let $x - 6\%$ of $x = xz$. Then, $\dfrac{94}{100} x \times \dfrac{1}{x} = z$ or $z = 0.94.$

35. It is $\left(\dfrac{30}{100} \times 80 - \dfrac{4}{5} \times 25\right) = (24 - 20) = 4$.

36. Let original price = Rs. 100. Then, new price = Rs. 90.
    Increase on Rs. 90 = Rs. 10
    Increase % = $\left(\dfrac{10}{90} \times 100\right)\% = 11\dfrac{1}{9}\%$.

37. Let the business value changes from x to y. Then
    4% of x = 5% of y or $\dfrac{4}{100} \times x = \dfrac{5}{100} \times y$ or $y = \dfrac{4}{5}x$.
    $\therefore$ Change in business = $\left(x - \dfrac{4}{5}x\right) = \dfrac{1}{5}x$.
    Percentage slump in business = $\left(\dfrac{1}{5}x \times \dfrac{1}{x} \times 100\right)\% = 20\%$.

38. $\dfrac{1}{3} \times 1206 = \dfrac{x}{100} \times 134$ or $x = \dfrac{402 \times 100}{134} = 300$.

39. Let salary be Rs. x. Then,
    $x - 15\%$ of $x - 30\%$ of 85% of $x = 2380$
    or $x - \dfrac{15x}{100} - \dfrac{30 \times 85 \times x}{100 \times 100} = 2380$
    or $200x - 30x - 51x = 2380 \times 200$
    or $119x = 2380 \times 200$ or $x = \dfrac{2380 \times 200}{119} = 4000$.

40. Let his income be Rs. x. Then,
    $x - 5\%$ of $x - 20\%$ of 95% of $x = 1919$
    or $x - \dfrac{x}{20} - \dfrac{20 \times 95 \times x}{100 \times 100} = 1919$
    or $x - \dfrac{x}{20} - \dfrac{19x}{100} = 1919$ or $100x - 5x - 19x = 191900$
    $\therefore x = \dfrac{191900}{76} = 2525$.

41. $x - [40\%$ of $x + 25\%$ of $x + 15\%$ of $x + 5\%$ of $x] = 1305$
    or $x - 85\%$ of $x = 1305$ or 15% of $x = 1305$
    $\therefore x = \dfrac{1305 \times 100}{15} = 8700$.

42. $137\dfrac{1}{2}\%$ of $x = 33$.
    $\therefore \dfrac{275}{2} \times \dfrac{1}{100} x = 33$ or $x = \dfrac{33 \times 2 \times 100}{275} = 24$.

Percentage 117

43. $72\frac{1}{2}\%$ of $x = 87$.

∴ $\frac{145}{2} \times \frac{1}{100} x = 87$ or $x = \frac{87 \times 2 \times 100}{145} = 120$.

44. $(25\%$ of $x) - (18\%$ of $650) = 19$

or $\frac{x}{4} = \left(19 + \frac{18}{100} \times 650\right) = 136$

∴ $x = (136 \times 4) = 544$.

45. 96% of $x = 23040$.

∴ $x = \frac{23040 \times 100}{96} = 24000$.

46. 95% of $x = 9595$ or $x = \frac{9595 \times 100}{95} = 10100$.

47. $87\frac{1}{2}\%$ of $x = 3500$

or $\frac{175}{2} \times \frac{1}{100} \times x = 3500$ or $x = \frac{3500 \times 2 \times 100}{175} = 4000$.

48. Let total number of students be x.

Then, 30% of $x = 504$ or $x = \frac{504 \times 100}{30} = 1680$.

∴ Number of boys $= (1680 - 504) = 1176$.

49. 12% of $x = 69 \Rightarrow x = \frac{69 \times 100}{12} = 575$ kg.

50. 60% of $x = 420$ or $x = \frac{420 \times 100}{60} = 700$.

51. 35% of $x = 420$ or $x = \frac{420 \times 100}{35} = 1200$.

52. $\sqrt{\frac{3.6}{100} \times 40} = \sqrt{1.44} = 1.2$.

53. $75 + 75\%$ of $x = x$ or $x - \frac{3}{4}x = 75$ or $\frac{1}{4}x = 75$

∴ $x = (75 \times 4) = 300$.

54. 30% of $180 + x\%$ of $150 = 50\%$ of $(180 + 150)$

or $54 + \frac{x}{100} \times 150 = 165$ or $\frac{3x}{2} = 111$ or $x = \frac{111}{3} \cdot \frac{2}{3} = 74$.

55. $5\% A = 15\% B$ and $10\% B = 20\% C$.

$$\therefore \frac{A}{20} = \frac{3B}{20} \text{ and } \frac{B}{10} = \frac{C}{5} \text{ or } B = 2C.$$

$$\therefore \frac{A}{20} = \frac{3}{20} \times 2C = \frac{3}{10} C = \frac{3}{10} \times 2000 = 600$$

$$\therefore A = (600 \times 20) = 12000, B = (2 \times 2000) = 4000.$$

$$\therefore A + B + C = (12000 + 4000 + 2000) = 18000.$$

56. Suppose that his salary = Rs. 100.

House Rent = Rs. 10. So, balance = Rs. 90.

Expenditure on education = Rs. $\left(\frac{15}{100} \times 90\right)$ = Rs. 13.50.

Balance = Rs. 76.50

Expenditure on clothes = Rs. $\left(\frac{10}{100} \times 76.50\right)$ = Rs. 7.65.

Balance now = Rs. 68.85

If balance is Rs. 68.85, salary = Rs. 100

If balance is Rs. 1377, salary = Rs. $\left(\frac{100}{68.85} \times 1377\right)$ = Rs. 2000.

57. 36% of $x = (113 + 85)$ or $x = \frac{100 \times 198}{36} = 550.$

58. Let third number be x.

Then, first number = 70% of $x = \frac{7x}{10}$.

And, second number = 63% of $x = \frac{63x}{100}$.

Difference = $\frac{7x}{10} - \frac{63x}{100} = \frac{7x}{100}$.

$\therefore$ Required percentage = $\left(\frac{7x}{100} \times \frac{10}{7x} \times 100\right)\% = 10\%.$

59. Failed in Hindi only = $(42 - 17) = 25.$

Failed in English only = $(52 - 17) = 35.$

Failed in both = 17.

$\therefore$ Passed in both = $100 - (25 + 35 + 17) = 23\%.$

60. Boys = 900, Girls = 1100.

Passed = (32% of 900) + (38% of 1100) = (288 + 418) = 706.

Failed = (2000 - 706) = 1294.

Failed % = $\left(\frac{1294}{2000} \times 100\right)\% = 64.7\%.$

61. 20% of $x + 30 = 32\%$ of $x - 42$

or 12% of $x = 72$. So, $x = \dfrac{72 \times 100}{12} = 600$.

Pass marks = 20% of 600 + 30 = 150.

Pass percentage = $\left(\dfrac{150}{600} \times 100\right)\% = 25\%$.

62. $n(A) = 75\%$ of $600 = 450$, $n(B) = 45\%$ of $600 = 270$ and $n(A \cup B) = 600$.
∴ $n(A \cap B) = n(A) + n(B) - n(A \cup B) = (450 + 270 - 600) = 120$.

63. (62% of x – 38% of x) = 144 or 24% of x = 144
∴ $x = \dfrac{144 \times 100}{24} = 600$.

64. Let the votes polled by the winning candidate be x.
Then, $(x - 15000) = 30\%$ of $[x + (x - 15000)]$ or $x = 26250$.

65. Valid votes = $\left(\dfrac{80}{100} \times 7500\right) = 6000$.

Votes polled by the other candidate = $\left(\dfrac{45}{100} \times 6000\right) = 2700$.

66. 200% of $x = 90 \Rightarrow x = \dfrac{90 \times 100}{200} = 45$.
∴ 80% of $x = \left(\dfrac{80}{100} \times 45\right) = 36$.

67. Reduction in consumption = $\left(\dfrac{25}{125} \times 100\right)\% = 20\%$.

68. Reduction in consumption = $\left(\dfrac{20}{120} \times 100\right)\% = \dfrac{50}{3}\%$
∴ $\dfrac{\text{Reduction in Consumption}}{\text{Original Consumption}} = \left(\dfrac{50}{3} \times \dfrac{1}{100}\right) = \dfrac{1}{6} = 1 : 6$.

69. Alcohol in 15 litres = $\left(\dfrac{20}{100} \times 15\right)$ litres = 3 litres.
Now, alcohol in 18 litres = 3 litres
∴ Strength of alcohol = $\left(\dfrac{3}{18} \times 100\right)\% = 16\dfrac{2}{3}\%$.

70. Let Tax = Rs. 100 and Consumption = 100 units.
Original Expenditure = Rs. (100×100) = Rs. 10000.
New Expenditure = Rs. (120×80) = Rs. 9600.
∴ Decrease in expenditure = $\left(\dfrac{400}{10000} \times 100\right)\% = 4\%$.

71. Let, price = Rs. 100, sale = 100.

Then, sale value = Rs. (100 × 100) = Rs. 10000.
New sale value = Rs. (70 × 120) = Rs. 8400.

Decrease % = $\left(\dfrac{1600}{10000} \times 100\right)$ % = 16%.

72. Population after 2 years = $8000\left(1+\dfrac{10}{100}\right)\left(1+\dfrac{20}{100}\right)$

$= \left(8000 \times \dfrac{11}{10} \times \dfrac{6}{5}\right) = 10560.$

73. Required number = $800 \times \left(1+\dfrac{15}{100}\right)^2 = \left(800 \times \dfrac{23}{20} \times \dfrac{23}{20}\right) = 1058.$

74. Value of the machine 2 years hence = Rs. $\left[4000 \times \left(1-\dfrac{10}{100}\right)^2\right]$

$= \text{Rs. } \left(4000 \times \dfrac{9}{10} \times \dfrac{9}{10}\right) = \text{Rs. } 3240.$

75. Population 2 years ago = $\dfrac{15435}{\left(1+\dfrac{5}{100}\right)^2} = \left(15435 \times \dfrac{20}{21} \times \dfrac{20}{21}\right) = 14000.$

76. $540 = x\left(1+\dfrac{20}{100}\right)^2$ or $x = \left(540 \times \dfrac{5}{6} \times \dfrac{5}{6}\right) = 375.$

77. $x\left(1-\dfrac{10}{100}\right)^3 = 8748$ or $x = \left(8748 \times \dfrac{10}{9} \times \dfrac{10}{9} \times \dfrac{10}{9}\right) = 12000.$

78. Net growth on 1000 = 21

Net growth on 100 = $\left(\dfrac{21}{1000} \times 100\right) = 2.1\%.$

79. Basic rate per hour = Re. $\left(\dfrac{20}{40}\right)$ = Re. $\dfrac{1}{2}$.

Overtime per hour = 125% of Re. $\dfrac{1}{2}$ = Re. $\dfrac{5}{8}$.

Suppose he worked x hours overtime.

Then, $20 + \dfrac{5}{8}x = 25$ or $\dfrac{5}{8}x = 5$

$\therefore x = \dfrac{5 \times 8}{5} = 8$ hours.

So, he worked in all for (40 + 8) hours = 48 hours.

80. Increase in 3 years over 100 = $100 \times \left(1+\dfrac{7}{2 \times 100}\right)^3$

Percentage

$$= \left(100 \times \frac{207}{200} \times \frac{207}{200} \times \frac{207}{200}\right)$$

$$= \frac{(200+7)^3}{80000} = \frac{(200)^3 + (7)^3 + 4200(200+7)}{80000}$$

$$= \frac{8869743}{80000} = 110.8718$$

∴ Increase % = 10.8%.

81. Suppose, salary = Rs. 100.
   Expenditure on food = Rs. 40; Balance = Rs. 60.
   Expenditure on transport = $\frac{1}{3}$ × Rs. 60 = Rs. 20.
   Now, balance = Rs. 40.
   Saving = Rs. 20.
   If saving is Rs. 20, salary = Rs. 100
   If saving is Rs. 450, salary = Rs. $\left(\frac{100}{20} \times 450\right)$ = Rs. 2250.

82. Let original wages = Rs. 100.
   Reduced wages = Rs. 50.
   Increased wages = 150% of Rs. 50 = $\left(\frac{150}{100} \times 50\right)$ = Rs. 75.
   ∴ Loss = 25%.

83. Let, income = Rs. 100.
   Then, expenditure = Rs. 75 and saving = Rs. 25.
   New income = Rs. 120,
   New expenditure = 110% of Rs. 75 = Rs. $\frac{165}{2}$.
   Now, saving = Rs. $\left(120 - \frac{165}{2}\right)$ = Rs. $\frac{75}{2}$.
   Increase in saving = Rs. $\left(\frac{75}{2} - 25\right)$ = Rs. $\frac{25}{2}$.
   ∴ Increase% = $\left(\frac{25}{2} \times \frac{1}{25} \times 100\right)$% = 50%.

84. $p = 6q$. Thus, q is less than p by $5q$.
   ∴ q is less than p by $\left(\frac{5q}{6q} \times 100\right)$% = $83\frac{1}{3}$%.

85. Let original price = Rs. 100.
   Reduced price = Rs. 75.
   Increase on Rs. 75 = Rs. 25
   Increase on Rs. 100 = $\left(\frac{25}{75} \times 100\right)$% = $33\frac{1}{3}$%.

86. B's salary is less than A's by $\left(\dfrac{30}{130} \times 100\right)\% = 23\dfrac{1}{13}\%$.

87. Let the fraction be $\dfrac{x}{y}$.

    Now, $\dfrac{120\% \text{ of } x}{90\% \text{ of } y} = \dfrac{16}{21}$ or $\dfrac{4}{3} \times \dfrac{x}{y} = \dfrac{16}{21}$ or $\dfrac{x}{y} = \left(\dfrac{16}{21} \times \dfrac{3}{4}\right) = \dfrac{4}{7}$.

88. Suppose boys = $3x$ and girls = $2x$.

    Not adults = (80% of $3x$) + (75% of $2x$) = $\left(\dfrac{12x}{5} + \dfrac{3x}{2}\right) = \dfrac{39x}{10}$.

    ∴ Required percentage = $\left(\dfrac{39x}{10} \times \dfrac{1}{5x} \times 100\right)\% = 78\%$.

89. Milk = 90% of 40 = 36 litres, water = 4 litres.

    ∴ $\dfrac{4+x}{40+x} \times 100 = 20$ or $20(40+x) = 100(4+x)$

    So, $80x = 400$ or $x = 5$.

90. Salt in 6 litres = 5% of 6 = 0.30.

    Salt in new solution = $\left(\dfrac{0.30}{5} \times 100\right)\% = 6\%$.

91. Let, original price = Rs. 100.
    Increased price = Rs. 160.
    Decrease on Rs. 160 = Rs. 60
    Decrease on Rs. 100 = $\left(\dfrac{60}{160} \times 100\right)\% = 37\dfrac{1}{2}\%$.

92. Let the total number of students be 100.
    Then, $n(A \cap B) = n(A) + n(B) - n(A \cup B) = (72 + 44 - 100)\% = 16\%$.
    Now, 16% of $x = 40$ or $\dfrac{16}{100} \times x = 40$ or $x = \dfrac{100 \times 40}{16} = 250$.

93. Let, side = 100 cm.
    Area = (100×100) cm^2 = 10000 cm^2
    New Area = (130×130) cm^2 = 16900 cm^2.
    Increase in area = $\left(\dfrac{6900}{10000} \times 100\right)\% = 69\%$.

94. Let actual side = 100 cm
    Measured length = 105 cm.
    Error in area = $(105)^2 - (100)^2 = (105+100)(105-100) = 1025$.
    Error % = $\left(\dfrac{1025}{10000} \times 100\right)\% = 10.25\%$.

95. Let length = 100 m and breadth = 100 m.

Area = (100×100) m^2 = 10000 m^2.
New length = 130 m & new breadth = 120 m.
New area = (130×120) m^2 = 15600 m^2.
Increase % = $\left(\dfrac{5600}{10000} \times 100\right)$ % = 56%.

96. Let length = 100 m and breadth = 100 m.
Area = (100×100) m^2 = 10000 m^2.
New length = 110 m & new breadth = 90 m.
New area = (110×90) m^2 = 9900 m^2.
Decrease % = $\left(\dfrac{100}{10000} \times 100\right)$ % = 1%.

97. Let length = 100 m, breadth = 100 m.
New length = 160 m, new breadth = x metres.
Then, $160 \times x = 100 \times 100$ or $x = \dfrac{100 \times 100}{160} = \dfrac{125}{2}$.
Decrease in breadth = $\left(100 - \dfrac{125}{2}\right)$ % = $37\dfrac{1}{2}$ %.

98. Let radius = 100 m. New radius = 101 m.
Original area = $\left[\pi \times (100)^2\right]$ m^2.
New area = $\left[\pi \times (101)^2\right]$ m^2.
Increase % = $\left[\dfrac{\pi \times \{(101)^2 - (100)^2\}}{\pi \times 100 \times 100} \times 100\right]$ % = $\dfrac{201}{100}$ % = 2.01%.

99. Surface area = $4\pi \times (10)^2 = (400\pi)$ cm^2.
Volume = $\dfrac{4}{3}\pi \times (10)^3 = \left(\dfrac{4000\pi}{3}\right)$ cm^3.
∴ Required percentage = $\left(400\pi \times \dfrac{3}{4000\pi} \times 100\right)$ % = 30%.

100. Let original rate = Rs. x per kg.
New rate = 79% of Rs. x per kg = Rs. $\left(\dfrac{79x}{100}\right)$ per kg.
$\dfrac{100}{\frac{79x}{100}} - \dfrac{100}{x} = 10.5$ or $\dfrac{10000}{79x} - \dfrac{100}{x} = 10.5$
or $10000 - 7900 = 10.5 \times 79 x$
∴ $x = \left(\dfrac{2100}{10.5 \times 79}\right)$
Reduced rate = Rs. $\left(\dfrac{79}{100} \times \dfrac{2100}{10.5 \times 79}\right)$ per kg = Rs. 2 per kg.

7

AVERAGE

Formula :

$$\text{Average} = \left(\frac{\text{Sum of observations}}{\text{Number of observations}}\right).$$

SOLVED EXAMPLES

Ex. 1. A cricketer makes 72, 59, 18, 101 and 7 runs respectively in five matches played by him. Find his average score.

Sol. Average score $= \left(\dfrac{72+59+18+101+7}{5}\right) = \dfrac{257}{5} = 51.4.$

Ex. 2. Find the average of first five multiples of 3.

(Central Excise & I. Tax 1988)

Sol. Average $= \dfrac{3(1+2+3+4+5)}{5} = \left(\dfrac{3 \times 15}{5}\right) = 9.$

Ex. 3. The average weight of a class of 24 students is 35 kg. If the weight of the teacher be included, the average rises by 400 gms. Find the weight of the teacher.

Sol. Total weight of 24 students $= (24 \times 35)$ kg $= 840$ kg.

Total weight of 24 students and the teacher
$= (25 \times 35.4)$ kg $= 885$ kg.

$\therefore$ Weight of teacher $= (885 - 840)$ kg $= 45$ kg.

Ex. 4. A batsman makes a score of 87 runs in the 17th inning and thus increased his average by 3. Find his average after 17th inning.

Sol. Let the average after 17th inning $= x.$

Then, average after 16th inning $= (x - 3).$

$\therefore$ $16(x - 3) + 87 = 17x$ or $x = (87 - 48) = 39.$

Hence, the average after 17th inning $= 39.$

Ex. 5. The average monthly expenditure of a family was Rs. 4050 during first 3 months, Rs. 4260 during next 4 months and Rs. 4346 during last 5 months of the year. If the total saving during the year be Rs. 8720, find average monthly income.

Sol. Total income during the year

Average 125

$$= Rs [4050 \times 3 + 4260 \times 4 + 4346 \times 5 + 8720]$$
$$= Rs. 59640$$

∴ Average monthly income = Rs. $\left(\dfrac{59640}{12}\right)$ = Rs. 4970.

Ex. 6. The average of 11 results is 50. If the average of first six results is 49 and that of last six is 52, find the sixth result.

Sol. Sum of 11 results = (11 × 50) = 550.

Sum of first 6 results = (6 × 49) = 294.

Sum of last 6 results = (6 × 52) = 312.

∴ 6th result = (294 + 312 − 550) = 56.

Ex. 7. The average temperature for Monday, Tuesday and Wednesday was 40°C. The average for Tuesday, Wednesday and Thursday was 41°C. If the temperature on Thursday be 42°C, find the temperature on Monday.

Sol. (M + T + W) = (3 × 40) = 120 .... (i)

(T + W + Th) = (3 × 41) = 123 .... (ii)

Substracting (i) from (ii), we get

(Th − M) = 3 or 42 − M = 3

∴ M = (42 − 3) = 39.

Hence, the temperature on Monday was = 39°C.

Ex. 8. The average age of a family of 6 members is 22 years. If the age of the youngest member be 7 years, find the average age of the family at the birth of the youngest member.

Sol. Sum of ages of all members = (22 × 6) years
= 132 years.

Sum of their ages 7 years ago = (132 − 7 × 6)
= 90 years.

At that time there were 5 members.

∴ Average age at that time = $\left(\dfrac{90}{5}\right)$ years = 18 years.

Ex. 9. The average weight of 10 oarsmen in a boat is increased by 1.5 kg when one of the crew, who weighs 58 kg is replaced by a new man. Find the weight of the new man.

Sol. Total weight increased = (10 × 1.5) kg = 15 kg.

Weight of new man = (58 + 15) kg = 73 kg.

Ex. 10. 10 sheep and 5 pigs were bought for Rs. 6000. If the average price of a sheep be Rs. 450, find the average price of a pig.

Sol. Total price of 5 pigs = Rs. [6000 − (10 × 450)]
= Rs. 1500.

∴ Average price of a pig = Rs. $\left(\dfrac{1500}{5}\right)$ = Rs. 300.

Ex. 11. Sandeep covers a journey from Meerut to Delhi by car at an average speed of 40 km/hr. He returns back by scooter with an average speed of 24 km/hr. Find his average speed during the whole journey.

Sol. Average speed = $\left(\dfrac{2xy}{x+y}\right)$ km/hr = $\left(\dfrac{2 \times 40 \times 24}{40 + 24}\right)$ km/hr
= 30 km/hr.

Exercise 7

1. The average of numbers 0.64204, 0.64203, 0.64202 and 0.64201 is :
   - (a) 0.642020 ☐
   - (b) 0.642021 ☐
   - (c) 0.642022 ☐
   - (d) 0.642025 ☐

2. The average of 30 results is 20 and the average of other 20 results is 30. What is the average of all the results ?
   - (a) 24 ☐
   - (b) 25 ☐
   - (c) 48 ☐
   - (d) 50 ☐

3. The average of five results is 46 and that of the first four is 45. The fifth result is : **(Clerical Grade, 1991)**
   - (a) 1 ☐
   - (b) 10 ☐
   - (c) 12.5 ☐
   - (d) 50 ☐

4. The average of odd numbers upto 100 is :
   - (a) 51 ☐
   - (b) 50 ☐
   - (c) 49.5 ☐
   - (d) 49 ☐

5. The average of first nine multiples of 3 is :
   - (a) 12.0 ☐
   - (b) 12.5 ☐
   - (c) 15.0 ☐
   - (d) 18.5 ☐

   (I. Tax & Central Excise, 1989)

6. Out of three numbers, the first is twice the second and is half of the third. If the average of the three numbers is 56, the three numbers in order are :
   (I. Tax & Central Excise, 1988)

Average 127

  (a) 48, 96, 24   (b) 48, 24, 96
  (c) 96, 24, 48   (d) 96, 48, 24

7. The average of three numbers is 42. The first is twice the second and the second is twice the third. The difference between the largest and the smallest number is :   (I. Tax & Central Excise, 1989)
  (a) 18   (b) 36
  (c) 54   (d) 72

8. The average age of three boys is 15 years. If their ages are in the ratio 3 : 5 : 7, the age of the youngest boy is :   (S.B.I. P.O. Exam, 1987)
  (a) 9 years   (b) 15 years
  (c) 18 years   (d) 21 years

9. If a, b, c, d, e are five consecutive odd numbers, their average is :
  (a) $5(a+4)$ (b) $\dfrac{abcde}{5}$
  (c) $5(a+b+c+d+e)$ (d) none of these
                      (Bank P.O. Exam, 1989)

10. The average height of 30 girls out of a class of 40 is 160 cms. and that of the remaining girls is 156 cms. The average height of the whole class is :   (I. Tax & Central Excise, 1988)
  (a) 158 cms   (b) 158.5 cms.
  (c) 159 cms   (d) 159.5 cms.

11. The average score of a cricketer in 2 matches is 27 and that in 3 others is 32. Then his average score in 5 matches is :
  (a) 11.8   (b) 25
  (c) 29.5   (d) 30

12. The average score of a cricketer for 10 matches is 43.9 runs. If the average for the first six matches is 53, the average for the last four matches is :
  (a) 17.15   (b) 29.75
  (c) 30.25   (d) 31

13. The average of 50 numbers is 38. If two numbers, namely 45 and 55 are discarded, the average of the remaining numbers is :
  (a) 36.5   (b) 37.0
  (c) 37.5   (d) 37.52
                      (C.B.I. Exam, 1990)

14. The average of 8 numbers is 21. If each of the numbers is multiplied by 8, the average of the new set of numbers is :
                  (I. Tax & Central Excise, 1989)
  (a) 8   (b) 21

(c) 29   (d) 168

15. The average age of 30 students in a class is 12 years. The average age of a group of 5 of the students is 10 years and that of another group of 5 of them is 14 years. The average age of the remaining students is :   (Bank P.O. Exam, 1990)
   (a) 8 years   (b) 10 years
   (c) 12 years   (d) 14 years

16. The average consumption of petrol for a car for seven months is 110 litres and for next five months it is 86 litres. The average monthly consumption is :
   (a) 96 litres   (b) 98 litres
   (c) 100 litres   (d) 102 litres

17. A ship sails out to a mark at the rate of 15 km/ph and sails back at the rate of 10 kmph. The average rate of sailing is :
   (a) 5 km/hr   (b) 12 km/hr
   (c) 12.5 km/hr   (d) 25 km/hr

18. The average temperature of the first three days is 27° C and that of the next three is 29°C. If the average of the whole week is 28.5°C, the temperature of the last day of the week is :   (R.R.B. Exam, 1991)
   (a) 10.5°C   (b) 21°C
   (c) 31.5°C   (d) 42°C

19. A man goes to a place at the rate of 4 kmph. He comes back on a bicycle at 16 kmph. His average speed for the entire journey is :
   (a) 5 km/hr   (b) 6.4 km/hr
   (c) 8.5 km/hr   (d) 10 km/hr
   (Clerical Grade, 1991)

20. The average of 25 results is 18; that of first twelve is 14 and of last twelve is 17. Thirteenth result is :   (C.B.I. Exam, 1991)
   (a) 28   (b) 72
   (c) 78   (d) 85

21. The average of 13 results is 68. The average of first seven is 63 and that of the last seven is 70, the seventh result is :
   (a) 47   (b) 65.5
   (c) 73.5   (d) 94

22. The average of 10 numbers is calculated as 15. It is discovered later on that while calculating the average one number, namely 36 was wrongly read as 26. The correct average is :   (C.B.I. Exam, 1990)
   (a) 12.4   (b) 14

Average 129

    (c) 16   ☐   (d) 18.6   ☐

23. Out of four numbers, the average of first three is 15 and that of the last three is 16. If the last number is 19, the first is :
    (a) 15   ☐   (b) 16   ☐
    (c) 18   ☐   (d) 19   ☐
                                              (C.B.I. Exam, 1991)

24. The average of 6 observations is 12. A new seventh observation is included and the new average is decreased by 1. The seventh observation is :   (C.B.I. Exam, 1990)
    (a) 1   ☐   (b) 3   ☐
    (c) 5   ☐   (d) 6   ☐

25. The average age of an adult class is 40 years. 12 new students with an average age of 32 years join the class, thereby decreasing the average by 4 years. The original strength of the class was :
    (a) 10   ☐   (b) 11   ☐
    (c) 12   ☐   (d) 15   ☐
                            (I. Tax & Central Excise, 1989)

26. In a class, there are 20 boys whose average age is decreased by 2 months, when one boy aged 18 years is replaced by a new boy. The age of the new boy is :
    (a) 14 years 8 months   ☐   (b) 15 years   ☐
    (c) 16 years 4 months   ☐   (d) 17 years 10 months   ☐

27. The average weight of 19 students is 15 kg. By the admission of a new student the average weight is reduced to 14.8 kg. The weight of the new student is :
    (a) 10.6 kg   ☐   (b) 10.8 kg   ☐
    (c) 11 kg   ☐   (d) 14.9 kg   ☐

28. The average weight of 8 persons is increased by 2.5 kg when one of them whose weight is 56 kg is replaced by a new man. The weight of the new man is :   (I. Tax & Central Excise, 1988)
    (a) 66 kg   ☐   (b) 75 kg   ☐
    (c) 76 kg   ☐   (d) 86 kg   ☐

29. The average weight of 8 men is increased by 2 kg when one of the men, whose weight is 50 kg is replaced by a new man. The weight of the new man is :   (Delhi Police, 1991)
    (a) 52 kg   ☐   (b) 58 kg   ☐
    (c) 66 kg   ☐   (d) 68 kg   ☐

30. The average of the daily income of A, B and C is Rs. 60. If B earns Rs. 20 more than C and A earns double of what C earns; what is the

daily income of C ?

(a) Rs. 75 □   (b) Rs. 60 □
(c) Rs. 40 □   (d) none of these □

31. The average weight of a class of 40 students is 40 kg. If the weight of the teacher be included, the average weight increases by 500 gms. The weight of the teacher is :   (Rajasthan Lok Seva Ayog, 1986)

(a) 40.5 kg □   (b) 60 kg □
(c) 60.5 kg □   (d) 62 kg □

32. The average age of four players is 18.5 years. If the age of the coach is also included, the average age increases by 20%. The age of the coach is :

(a) 28 years □   (b) 31 years □
(c) 34 years □   (d) 37 years □

33. The average age of four children in a family is 12 years. If the spacing between their ages is 4 years, the age of the youngest child is :

(a) 6 years □   (b) 7 years □
(c) 8 years □   (d) 9 years □

34. In a TV factory, an average of 60 TVs are produced per day for the first 25 days of the month. A few workers fell ill for the next five days, reducing the daily average for the month to 58 sets per day. The average production per day for the last 5 days is :

(a) 45 □   (b) 48 □
(c) 52 □   (d) 58 □

35. The average salary of 20 workers in an office is Rs. 1900 per month. If the manager's salary is added, the average salary becomes Rs. 2000 p.m. What is the manager's annual salary ?   (S.B.I. P.O. Exam, 1988)

(a) Rs. 24000 □   (b) Rs. 25200 □
(c) Rs. 45600 □   (d) none of these □

36. With an average speed of 40 km/hr a train reaches its destination in time. If it goes with an average speed of 35 km/hr, it is late by 15 minutes. The total journey is :

(a) 30 km □   (b) 40 km □
(c) 70 km □   (d) 80 km □

37. The average expenditure of a man for the first five months is Rs. 120 and for the next seven months it is Rs. 130. If he saves Rs. 290 in that year, his monthly average income is :   (R.R.B. Exam, 1991)

(a) Rs. 140 □   (b) Rs. 150 □
(c) Rs. 160 □   (d) Rs. 170 □

Average

38. The average of marks obtained by 120 candidates was 35. If the average of marks of passed candidates was 39 and that of failed candidates was 15, the number of candidates who passed the examination is : **(Clerical Grade, 1991)**
(a) 100   (b) 110
(c) 120   (d) 150

39. The average age of 24 students in a class is 10. If the teacher's age is included, the average increases by one. The age of the teacher is :
(a) 25 years   (b) 30 years
(c) 35 years   (d) 40 years
(A.A.O. Exam, 1990)

40. Average monthly income of a family of 4 earning members was Rs. 735. One of the earning members died and therefore the average income came down to Rs. 650. The income of the deceased was :
(a) Rs. 692.80   (b) Rs. 820
(c) Rs. 990   (d) Rs. 1385

41. On a journey across Delhi, a taxi averages 30 kmph for 60% of the distance, 20 kmph for 20% of it and 10 kmph for the remainder. The average speed for the whole journey is :
(a) 20 km/hr   (b) 22.5 km/hr
(c) 24.625 km/hr   (d) 25 km/hr

42. The average weight of A, B, C is 45 kg. If the average weight of A and B be 40 kg and that of B and C be 43 kg, then the weight of B is :
(a) 17 kg   (b) 20 kg
(c) 26 kg   (d) 31 kg

43. The average salary per head of all the workers in a workshop is Rs. 850. If the average salary per head of 7 technicians is Rs. 1000 and the average salary per head of the rest is Rs. 780, the total number of workers in the workshop is :
(a) 18   (b) 20
(c) 22   (d) 24

44. The average earning of a mechanic for the first four days of a week is Rs. 18 and for the last four days is Rs. 22. If he earns Rs. 20 on the fourth day, his average earning for the whole week is :
(a) Rs. 18.95   (b) Rs. 16
(c) Rs. 20   (d) Rs. 25.71

45. The average age of 11 players of a cricket team is decreased by 2 months when two of them aged 17 years and 20 years are replaced by two reserves. The average age of the reserves is :

(a) 17 years 1 month ☐ (b) 17 years 7 months ☐
(c) 17 years 11 months ☐ (d) 18 years 3 months ☐

46. The average age of A, B, C, D five years ago was 45 years. By including X, the present average age of all the five is 49 years. The present age of X is : (Bank P.O., 1988)

(a) 64 years ☐ (b) 48 years ☐
(c) 45 years ☐ (d) 40 years ☐

47. The average age of 5 members of a committee is the same as it was 3 years ago, because an old member has been replaced by a new member. The difference between the ages of old and new member is :

(a) 2 years ☐ (b) 4 years ☐
(c) 8 years ☐ (d) 15 years ☐

48. Average temperature of first 4 days of a week is 38.6°C and that of the last 4 days is 40.3°C. If the average temperature of the week be 39.1°C, the temperature on 4th day is :

(a) 36.7°C ☐ (b) 38.6°C ☐
(c) 39.8°C ☐ (d) 41.9°C ☐

49. The mean temperature of Monday to Wednesday was 37°C and of Tuesday to Thursday was 34°C. If the temperature on Thursday was $\frac{4}{5}$ th that of Monday, what was the temperature on Thursday ?

(a) 34°C ☐ (b) 35.5°C ☐
(c) 36°C ☐ (d) 36.5°C ☐

50. Ten years ago, the average age of a family of 4 members was 24 years. Two children having been born, the average age of the family is same today. What is the present age of the youngtest child if they differ in age by 2 years ?

(a) 1 years ☐ (b) 2 years ☐
(c) 3 years ☐ (d) 5 years ☐

51. The average age of a husband and a wife was 23 years when they were married 5 years ago. The average age of the husband, the wife and a child, who was born during the interval, is 20 years now. How old is the child now ?

(a) less than 1 year ☐ (b) 1 year ☐
(c) 3 years ☐ (d) 4 years ☐

52. A batsman has a certain average runs for 11 innings. In the 12th inning

Average   133

he made a score of 90 runs and thereby decreased his average by 5. His average after 12th inning is :

(a) 127   (b) 145
(c) 150   (d) 217

53. There were 35 students in a hostel. If the number of students increased by 7, the expenses of the mess were increased by Rs. 42 per day while the average expenditure per head diminished by Re. 1. The original expenditure of the mess was :

(a) Rs. 400   (b) Rs. 420
(c) Rs. 432   (d) Rs. 442

54. The average weight of three men A, B and C is 84 kg. Another man D joins the group and the average now becomes 80 kg. If another man E, whose weight is 3 kg more than that of D, replaces A, then the average weight of B, C, D and E becomes 79 kg. The weight of A is :   (Bank P.O. 1989)

(a) 70 kg   (b) 72 kg
(c) 75 kg   (d) 80 kg

55. A man whose bowling average is 12.4 takes 5 wickets for 26 runs and thereby decreases his average by 0.4. The number of wickets, taken by him, before his last match, is :   (C.B.I. Exam. 1991)

(a) 85   (b) 78
(c) 72   (d) 64

56. The average of 5 consecutive numbers is n. If the next two numbers are also included, the average of 7 numbers will :

(a) increase by 2   (b) increase by 1
(c) remains the same   (d) increase by 1.4

57. A shopkeeper earned Rs. 504 in 12 days. His average income for the first four days was Rs. 40 a day. His average income for the remaining days is :   (Clerk's Grade 1991)

(a) Rs. 40   (b) Rs. 42
(c) Rs. 43   (d) Rs. 45

58. The average temperature of Monday, Tuesday, Wednesday and Thursday was 38° and that of Tuesday, Wednesday, Thursday and Friday was 40°. If the temperature on Monday was 30°, the temperature of Friday was :   (Clerk's Grade 1991)

(a) 40°   (b) 39°
(C) 38°   (d) 30°

Answers (Exercise 7)

1. (d) 2. (a) 3. (d) 4. (b) 5. (c) 6. (b) 7. (c) 8. (a) 9. (d)
10. (c) 11. (d) 12. (c) 13. (c) 14. (d) 15. (c) 16. (c) 17. (b) 18. (c)
19. (b) 20. (c) 21. (a) 22. (c) 23. (b) 24. (c) 25. (c) 26. (a) 27. (c)
28. (c) 29. (c) 30. (c) 31. (c) 32. (d) 33. (a) 34. (b) 35. (d) 36. (c)
37. (b) 38. (a) 39. (c) 40. (c) 41. (a) 42. (d) 43. (c) 44. (c) 45. (b)
46. (c) 47. (d) 48. (d) 49. (c) 50. (c) 51. (d) 52. (b) 53. (b) 54. (c)
55. (a) 56. (b) 57. (c) 58. (c).

Solutions (Exercise 7)

1. Average $= \left(\dfrac{0.64204 + 0.64203 + 0.64202 + 0.64201}{4}\right) = \left(\dfrac{2.5681}{4}\right)$
   $= 0.642025.$

2. Total of 50 results $= (30 \times 20 + 20 \times 30) = 1200.$
   $\therefore$ Average $= \dfrac{1200}{50} = 24.$

3. Fifth result $= (5 \times 46 - 4 \times 45) = (230 - 180) = 50.$

4. Sum of odd numbers upto 100
   $= 1 + 3 + 5 + 7 + \ldots + 95 + 97 + 99$
   $= (1 + 99) + (3 + 97) + (5 + 95) + \ldots$ upto 25 terms
   $= 100 + 100 + 100 + \ldots$ upto 25 terms
   $= 2500.$
   $\therefore$ Average $= \left(\dfrac{2500}{50}\right) = 50.$

5. Average $= \dfrac{3 + 6 + 9 + 12 + 15 + 18 + 21 + 24 + 27}{9}$
   $= \dfrac{3(1 + 2 + 3 + 4 + 5 + 6 + 7 + 8 + 9)}{9} = \left(\dfrac{45}{3}\right) = 15.$

6. Let second number $= x.$ Then, first one $= 2x$ and third number $= 4x.$
   $\therefore \dfrac{x + 2x + 4x}{3} = 56 \Rightarrow 7x = 168$ or $x = 24.$
   So, the number are 48, 24, 96.

7. Let third number $= x.$ Then, second number $= 2x$ and first number $= 4x.$
   $\therefore \dfrac{x + 2x + 4x}{3} = 42 \Rightarrow 7x = 42 \times 3$ or $x = 18.$
   So, (largest) $-$ (smallest) $= (4x - x) = 3x = 54.$

Average 135

8. $\dfrac{3x + 5x + 7x}{3} = 15 \Rightarrow 15x = 15 \times 3$ or $x = 3$.

   $\therefore$ Age of youngest = $3x = 9$ years.

9. Average = $\dfrac{a + (a+2) + (a+4) + (a+6) + (a+8)}{5} = (a+4)$.

10. Average height of the whole class = $\left(\dfrac{30 \times 160 + 10 \times 156}{40}\right) = 159$ cms.

11. Average = $\left(\dfrac{2 \times 27 + 3 \times 32}{5}\right) = \dfrac{150}{5} = 30$.

12. $53 \times 6 + x \times 4 = 10 \times 43.9$

    $\therefore 4x = 439 - 318$ or $4x = 121$ or $x = 30.25$.

13. Total of 50 numbers = $(50 \times 38) = 1900$.

    Total of 48 numbers = $[1900 - (45 + 55)] = 1800$.

    $\therefore$ Required average = $\dfrac{1800}{48} = \dfrac{225}{6} = 37.5$.

14. Average of new numbers = $(21 \times 8) = 168$.

15. Let it be x. Then :

    $5 \times 10 + 5 \times 14 + 20 \times x = 30 \times 12$

    $\therefore 20x = 360 - 120$ or $20x = 240$ or $x = 12$.

16. Average = $\left(\dfrac{110 \times 7 + 86 \times 5}{12}\right) = \left(\dfrac{1200}{12}\right) = 100$ litres.

17. Average = $\left(\dfrac{2xy}{x+y}\right)$ km/hr = $\left(\dfrac{2 \times 15 \times 10}{15 + 10}\right)$ km/hr = 12 km/hr.

18. $3 \times 27 + 3 \times 29 + x = 7 \times 28.5$

    $\therefore x = 31.5$.

19. Average speed = $\left(\dfrac{2xy}{x+y}\right)$ km/hr = $\left(\dfrac{2 \times 4 \times 16}{4 + 16}\right)$ km/hr = 6.4 km/hr.

20. Thirteenth Result = $(25 \times 18 - 12 \times 14 + 12 \times 17) = 78$.

21. Seventh Result = $(7 \times 63 + 7 \times 70 - 13 \times 68) = 47$.

22. Sum of numbers = $(10 \times 15 - 26 + 36) = 160$.

    $\therefore$ Correct average = $\dfrac{160}{10} = 16$.

23. Sum of four numbers = $(15 \times 3 + 19) = 64$.

    Sum of last three numbers = $(16 \times 3) = 48$.

    $\therefore$ First number = $(64 - 48) = 16$.

24. Seventh observation = $(7 \times 11 - 6 \times 12) = 5$.

25. Let original strength = x. Then,
 $40x + 12 \times 32 = (x + 12) \times 36$
 or $40x + 384 = 36x + 432$ or $4x = 48$ or $x = 12$.
26. Total decrease = (20×2) months = 3 years 4 months.
 $\therefore$ Age of the new boy = (18 years) − (3 years 4 months)
 = 14 years 8 months.
27. Weight of new student = $(20 \times 14.8 - 19 \times 15)$ kg = 11 kg.
28. Total increase = (8×2.5) kg = 20 kg.
 Weight of new man = $(56 + 20)$ kg = 76 kg.
29. Weight increased = (8×2) kg = 16 kg.
 Weight of new man = $(50 + 16)$ kg = 66 kg.
30. Let C's earning = Rs. x. Then, B's earning = Rs. $(x + 20)$ and A's earning = Rs. $2x$.
 $\therefore 2x + x + 20 + x = 3 \times 60$ or $4x = 160$ or $x = 40$.
 Hence, the daily earning of C = Rs. 40.
31. Weight of the teacher = $(41 \times 40.5 - 40 \times 40)$ kg = 60.5 kg.
32. New average = (120% of 18.5) = $\left(\dfrac{120}{100} \times 18.5\right) = 22.2$.
 Age of coach = $(5 \times 22.2 - 4 \times 18.5) = 37$ years.
33. $x + (x + 4) + (x + 8) + (x + 12) = 4 \times 12$.
 $\therefore 4x = (48 - 24) = 24$ or $x = 6$.
 Hence, the age of the youngest child = 6 years.
34. Production during these 5 days = $(30 \times 58 - 25 \times 60) = 240$.
 $\therefore$ Average for 5 days = $\dfrac{240}{5} = 48$.
35. Manager's salary per month = Rs. $(21 \times 2000 - 20 \times 1900)$ = Rs. 4000.
 $\therefore$ Manager's annual salary = Rs. (4000×12) = Rs. 48000.
36. $\dfrac{x}{35} - \dfrac{x}{40} = \dfrac{15}{60}$ or $\dfrac{5x}{35 \times 40} = \dfrac{1}{4}$ or $x = \left(\dfrac{35 \times 40}{4 \times 5}\right) = 70$.
 $\therefore$ Total journey = 70 km.
37. Total income = Rs. $(120 \times 5 + 130 \times 7 + 290)$ = Rs. 1800.
 Average monthly income = Rs. $\left(\dfrac{1800}{12}\right)$ = Rs. 150.
38. Let the number of candidates who passed = x. Then,
 $39 \times x + 15 \times (120 - x) = 120 \times 35$

Average

$\therefore 24x = 4200 - 1800$ or $x = \left(\dfrac{2400}{24}\right) = 100$.

39. Age of the teacher $= (25 \times 11 - 24 \times 10)$ years $= 35$ years.
40. Income of the deceased $=$ Rs. $(735 \times 4 - 650 \times 3) =$ Rs. 990.
41. Let total journey $= x$ km.

    Total time taken $= \left(\dfrac{60}{100} x \times \dfrac{1}{30} + \dfrac{20}{100} x \times \dfrac{1}{20} + \dfrac{20}{100} x \times \dfrac{1}{10}\right)$ hrs.

    $= \left(\dfrac{x}{50} + \dfrac{x}{100} + \dfrac{x}{50}\right)$ hrs. $= \left(\dfrac{x}{20}\right)$ hrs.

    $\therefore$ Average speed $= \left(x \times \dfrac{20}{x}\right)$ km/hr $= 20$ km/hr.

42. Weight of $(A + B) = (2 \times 40)$ kg $= 80$ kg.
    Weight of $(B + C) = (2 \times 43)$ kg $= 86$ kg.
    Weight of $(A + 2B + C) = (80 + 86)$ kg $= 166$ kg.
    Weight of $(A + B + C) = (3 \times 45)$ kg $= 135$ kg.
    $\therefore$ Weight of $B = (166 - 135)$ kg $= 31$ kg.

43. $7 \times 1000 + x \times 780 = (x + 7) \times 850$
    $\therefore (850 - 780) x = (7000 - 5950)$ or $70 x = 1050$ or $x = 15$.
    Hence, the total number of workers $= (7 + 15) = 22$.

44. Total earning for the week $=$ Rs. $(4 \times 18 + 4 \times 22 - 20) =$ Rs. 140
    $\therefore$ Average earning $=$ Rs. $\left(\dfrac{140}{7}\right) =$ Rs. 20.

45. Decrease $= (11 \times 2)$ months $= 1$ year 10 months.
    Total age of reserves $= (17 + 20)$ years $- (1$ year 10 months$)$
    $= 35$ years 2 months.
    Average age of reserves $= 17$ years 7 months.

46. Present age of X $= [(49 \times 5) - (4 \times 45 + 4 \times 5)]$ years $= 45$ years.
47. Increase during 3 years $= (3 \times 5)$ years $= 15$ years.
    So, the difference between ages of old and new member is 15 years.
48. $4 \times 38.6 + 4 \times 40.3 - x = 7 \times 39.1$ or $x = 41.9$.
    $\therefore$ Temperature on 4th day $= 41.9°$C.

49. $(M + T + W) = (3 \times 37) = 111.$ ...... (i)
    $(T + W + Th) = (3 \times 34) = 102.$ ...... (ii)
    Let $M = x$. Then, $Th = \dfrac{4}{5} x$.
    Subtracting (ii) from (i), we get :

M − Th = 9 or $x - \frac{4}{5}x = 9$ or $x = 45$.

∴ Temperature on Thursday = $\left(\frac{4}{5} \times 45\right) = 36°C$.

50. $x + x + 2 = (24 \times 6 - 24 \times 4 + 4 \times 10) \Rightarrow 2x + 2 = 8$ or $x = 3$.
51. Age of child = $[(20 \times 3) - (23 \times 2 + 5 \times 2)]$ years = 4 years.
52. $11x + 90 = (x - 5) \times 12$ or $x = 150$.

∴ Average after 12th inning = $(150 - 5) = 145$.

53. Let the original expenditure be Rs. x. Then,

$$\frac{x}{35} - \frac{x + 42}{42} = 1 \Rightarrow 42x - 35(x + 42) = 35 \times 42$$

∴ $7x = 35 \times 42 + 35 \times 42 \Rightarrow x = \frac{2 \times 35 \times 42}{7} = 420$.

Hence, the original expenditure = Rs. 420.

54. $A + B + C = 3 \times 84 = 252$, $A + B + C + D = (4 \times 80) = 320$.

∴ $D = (320 - 252) = 68$ and so $E = (68 + 3) = 71$.
Now, $B + C + D + E = (4 \times 79) = 316$
∴ $B + C + D = (316 - 71) = 245$
So, $A = (320 - 245) = 75$ kg.

55. Let the number of wickets taken before the last match = x.

Then, $\frac{12.4x + 26}{x + 5} = 12 \Rightarrow x = 85$.

56. $x + (x + 1) + (x + 2) + (x + 3) + (x + 4) = 5n$
$\Rightarrow 5x + 10 = 5n \Rightarrow x = (n - 2)$.

Average of 7 consecutive integers

$= \frac{(5x + 10) + (x + 5) + (x + 6)}{7} = \frac{7x + 21}{7} = x + 3$.

∴ New average = $(n - 2 + 3) = n + 1$.
So, the average increases by 1.

57. Let the average for remaining 8 days be Rs. x a day.
Then, $4 \times 40 + 8 \times x = 504$ or $8x = 344$ or $x = 43$.

∴ Required average = Rs. 43.

58. $M + T + W + Th = (4 \times 38) = 152$.
∴ $T + W + Th = (152 - 30) = 122$.
$T + W + Th + F = (4 \times 40) = 160$
∴ $F = (160 - 122) = 38°$.

8
RATIO & PROPORTION

Ratio : *The ratio of two quantities in the same units is a fraction that one quantity is of the other.*

Thus, a to b is a ratio $\left(\dfrac{a}{b}\right)$, written as $a : b$.

The first term of a ratio is called *antecedent,* while the second term is known as *consequent.*

Thus, the ratio $4 : 7$ represents $\dfrac{4}{7}$ with antecedent 4 and consequent 7.

Rule : *The multiplication or division of each term of a ratio by a same non-zero number does not effect the ratio.*

Thus, $3 : 5$ is the same as $6 : 10$ or $9 : 15$ or $12 : 20$ etc.

Proportion : *The equality of two ratios is called proportion.*

Thus, $2 : 3 = 8 : 12$ is written as $2 : 3 :: 8 : 12$ and we say that 2, 3, 8 and 12 are in proportion.

In a proportion, the first and fourth terms are known as *extremes,* while second and third terms are known as *means.*

In a proportion, we always have :

Product of Means = Product of Extremes.

SOLVED PROBLEMS

Ex. 1. A stick 1.4 m long casts a shadow 1.3 m long at the same time when a pole casts a shadow 5.2 m long. Find the length of the pole.

Sol. Clearly, more is the length of shadow, more is the length of the object. Let the length of the pole be x metres.

Then, $1.3 : 5.2 :: 1.4 : x.$

$\therefore\ 1.3 \times x = 5.2 \times 1.4$ or $x = \dfrac{5.2 \times 1.4}{1.3} = 5.6.$

Hence, the length of the pole is 5.6 m.

Ex. 2. If $a : b = 2 : 3$ and $b : c = 5 : 7$, find $a : c$ and $a : b : c$.

Sol. $\dfrac{a}{b} = \dfrac{2}{3}$ and $\dfrac{b}{c} = \dfrac{5}{7}$.

$\therefore \dfrac{a}{c} = \left(\dfrac{a}{b} \times \dfrac{b}{c}\right) = \left(\dfrac{2}{3} \times \dfrac{5}{7}\right) = \dfrac{10}{21}$.

Hence, $a : c = 10 : 21$.

Now, L.C.M. of 3 and 5 is 15.

$\therefore\ a : b = 2 : 3 = 10 : 15$ and $b : c = 5 : 7 = 15 : 21$.

Hence, $a : b : c = 10 : 15 : 21$.

Ex. 3. Divide Rs. 455 in the ratio 4 : 3.

Sol. Sum of the terms of the ratio = $(4 + 3) = 7$.

$\therefore$ First part = Rs. $\left(455 \times \dfrac{4}{7}\right)$ = Rs. 260.

Second part = Rs. $\left(455 \times \dfrac{3}{7}\right)$ = Rs. 195.

Ex. 4. A bag contains rupee, 50 paise and 25 paise coins in the ratio 5 : 6 : 8. If the total amount is Rs. 420, find the number of coins of each type.

Sol. Ratio of values = $5 : \dfrac{6}{2} : \dfrac{8}{4} = 5 : 3 : 2$.

Divide Rs. 420 in the ratio 5 : 3 : 2.

1st part = Rs. $\left(420 \times \dfrac{5}{10}\right)$ = Rs. 210.

2nd part = Rs. $\left(420 \times \dfrac{3}{10}\right)$ = Rs. 126.

3rd part = Rs. $\left(420 \times \dfrac{2}{10}\right)$ = Rs. 84.

$\therefore$ Number of one-rupee coins = 210.

Number of 50 paise coins = $(126 \times 2) = 252$.

Number of 25 paise coins = $(84 \times 4) = 336$.

Ex. 5. Find three numbers in the ratio 2 : 3 : 5, the sum of whose squares is 608.

Sol. Let the numbers be $2x, 3x$ and $5x$.

Then, $4x^2 + 9x^2 + 25x^2 = 608$ or $38x^2 = 608$.

$\therefore x^2 = \dfrac{608}{38} = 16$ or $x = 4$.

So, the numbers are 8, 12 and 20.

Ratio & Proportion

Ex. 6. In a mixture of 35 litres, the ratio of milk and water is 4 : 1. Now, 7 litres of water is added to the mixture. Find the ratio of milk and water in the new mixture.

Sol. Milk in 35 litres of mix. = $\left(35 \times \dfrac{4}{5}\right)$ = 28 litres.

Water in this mix. = (35 − 28) = 7 litres.

New mixture contains milk = 28 litres.

Water in new mixture = (7 + 7) litres = 14 litres.

∴ Ratio of milk and water in new mix. = 28 : 14 = 2 : 1.

Ex. 7. A mixture contains alcohol and water in the ratio 4 : 3. If 7 litres of water is added to the mixture, the ratio of alcohol and water becomes 3 : 4. Find the quantity of alcohol in the mixture.

Sol. Let the quantity of alcohol and water be $4x$ and $3x$ litres respectively. Then,

$$\dfrac{4x}{3x+7} = \dfrac{3}{4} \text{ or } x = 3.$$

∴ Quantity of alcohol in the mix. = 12 litres.

Ex. 8. Three utensils contain equal mixtures of milk and water in the ratio 6 : 1, 5 : 2, and 3 : 1 respectively. If all the solutions are mixed together, find the ratio of milk and water in the final mixture.

Sol. In final mixture, we have :

quantity of milk = $\left(\dfrac{6}{7} + \dfrac{5}{7} + \dfrac{3}{4}\right) = \dfrac{65}{28}$,

quantity of water = $\left(\dfrac{1}{7} + \dfrac{2}{7} + \dfrac{1}{4}\right) = \dfrac{19}{28}$.

∴ Milk : water = $\dfrac{65}{28} : \dfrac{19}{28}$ = 65 : 19.

Ex. 9. Find the fourth proportional to 4, 5 and 12.

Sol. Let 4 : 5 :: 12 : x.

Then, $4 \times x = 5 \times 12$ or $x = \left(\dfrac{5 \times 12}{4}\right) = 15$.

Hence, the fourth proportional to 4, 5 and 12 is 15.

Ex. 10. Find the third proportional to 9 and 12.

Sol. Third proportional to 9 and 12 is the same as the fourth proportional to 9, 12 and 12.

Let $9 : 12 :: 12 : x$.

Then, $9 \times x = 12 \times 12$ or $x = \left(\dfrac{12 \times 12}{9}\right) = 16$.

Hence, the third proportional to 9 and 12 is 16.

Ex. 11. Find the mean proportional between 49 and 64.

Sol. The mean proportional between a and b is $\sqrt{ab}$.

∴ Man proportional between 49 and 64 $= \sqrt{49 \times 64}$

$= (7 \times 8) = 56$.

Ex. 12. Divide 1162 into three parts such that 4 times the first part, 5 times the second part and 7 times the third part are equal.

Sol. Let $4A = 5B = 7C = x$.

Then, $A = \dfrac{x}{4}, B = \dfrac{x}{5}$ and $C = \dfrac{x}{7}$.

∴ $A : B : C = \dfrac{x}{4} : \dfrac{x}{5} : \dfrac{x}{7} = 35 : 28 : 20$.

Sum of the terms of the ratio = 83.

∴ $A = \left(\dfrac{1162 \times 35}{83}\right) = 490, B = \left(\dfrac{1162 \times 28}{83}\right) = 392$

and $C = \left(\dfrac{1162 \times 20}{83}\right) = 280$.

Ex. 13. Compare the ratio 2 : 3 and 4 : 7.

Sol. 2 : 3 represents $\dfrac{2}{3} = 0.66$;

4 : 7 represents $\dfrac{4}{7} = 0.57$.

Clearly, $0.66 > 0.57$

Hence $(2 : 3) > (4 : 7)$.

Exercise 8

1. If $A : B = 2 : 3$ and $B : C = 4 : 5$, then $C : A$ is equal to :
   - (a) 15 : 8 ☐
   - (b) 12 : 10 ☐
   - (c) 8 : 5 ☐
   - (d) 8 : 15 ☐

   (Railway Recruitment 1991)

2. If 10% of x is the same as 20% of y, then $x : y$ is equal to :
   - (a) 1 : 2 ☐
   - (b) 2 : 1 ☐

Ratio & Proportion 143

  (c) 5 : 1   □   (d) 10 : 1   □
                    (C.B.I. 1990)
3. 0.6 of a number equals 0.09 of another number. The ratio of the numbers is :
  (a) 2 : 3   □   (b) 1 : 15   □
  (c) 20 : 3   □   (d) 3 : 20   □
4. If $A : B = 7 : 9$ and $B : C = 3 : 5$, then $A : B : C$ is :
  (a) 7 : 9 : 5   □   (b) 21 : 35 : 45   □
  (c) 7 : 9 : 15   □   (d) 7 : 3 : 15   □
              (Assistant Grade 1990)
5. If $A : B = 5 : 7$ and $B : C = 6 : 11$, then $A : B : C$ is :
  (a) 55 : 77 : 66   □   (b) 30 : 42 : 77   □
  (c) 35 : 49 : 42   □   (d) none of these   □
6. If $A = \frac{1}{3}B$ and $B = \frac{1}{2}C$, then $A : B : C$ is :
                (Delhi Police 1988)
  (a) 1 : 3 : 6   □   (b) 2 : 3 : 6   □
  (c) 3 : 2 : 6   □   (d) 3 : 1 : 2   □
7. If $A : B = 2 : 3, B : C = 4 : 5$ and $C : D = 6 : 7$, then $A : D$ is equal to :
  (a) 2 : 7   □   (b) 7 : 8   □
  (c) 16 : 35   □   (d) 4 : 13   □
              (Clerk's Grade 1991)
8. If $2A = 3B = 4C$ then $A : B : C$ is :
  (a) 2 : 3 : 4   □   (b) 4 : 3 : 2   □
  (c) 6 : 4 : 3   □   (d) 3 : 4 : 6   □
9. If $2A = 3B$ and $4B = 5C$, then $A : C$ is :
  (a) 3 : 4   □   (b) 8 : 15   □
  (c) 15 : 8   □   (d) 4 : 3   □
10. If $x : y = 2 : 3$ and $2 : x = 1 : 2$, then the value of y is :
  (a) 4   □   (b) 6   □
  (c) $\frac{1}{3}$ □   (d) $\frac{3}{2}$ □
11. Two numbers are in the ratio 3 : 5. If each number is increased by 10, the ratio becomes 5 : 7. The numbers are : **(R.R.B. Exam. 1989)**
  (a) 3, 5   □   (b) 7, 9   □
  (c) 13, 22   □   (d) 15, 25   □
12. The ratio which $\left(\frac{1}{3} \text{ of Rs. } 9.30\right)$ bears to (0.6 of Rs. 1.55) is :
  (a) 1 : 3   □   (b) 10 : 3   □

(c) 3 : 10   (d) 3 : 1

13. If one-third of A, one-fourth of B and one-fifth of C are equal, then A : B : C is :
    (a) 3 : 4 : 5
    (b) 4 : 3 : 5
    (c) 5 : 4 : 3
    (d) $\frac{1}{3} : \frac{1}{4} : \frac{1}{5}$

14. If $\frac{1}{5} : \frac{1}{x} = \frac{1}{x} : \frac{1}{1.25}$, then the value of x is :
    (a) 1.25
    (b) 1.5
    (c) 2.5
    (d) 2.25

15. Out of the ratios 7 : 15, 15 : 23, 17 : 25 and 21 : 29, the smallest one is :
    (a) 17 : 25
    (b) 7 : 15
    (c) 15 : 23
    (d) 21 : 29

16. In a ratio which is equal to 5 : 8, if the antecedent is 40, then consequent is :
    (a) 25
    (b) 64
    (c) 48
    (d) none of these

17. What must be added to each term of the ratio 7 : 13 so that the ratio becomes 2 : 3 ?
    (a) 1
    (b) 2
    (c) 3
    (d) 5

18. A fraction bears the same ratio to $\frac{1}{27}$ as $\frac{3}{7}$ does to $\frac{5}{9}$. The fraction is :
    (a) $\frac{7}{45}$
    (b) $\frac{1}{35}$
    (c) $\frac{45}{7}$
    (d) $\frac{5}{21}$

19. What number should be added to each one of 6, 14, 18, 38 to make it equally proportionate :
    (a) 1
    (b) 2
    (c) 3
    (d) 4

20. What number should be subtracted from each of the numbers 54, 71, 75 and 99 so that the remainders may be proportional :
    (a) 1
    (b) 2
    (c) 3
    (d) 6

21. The fourth proportional to 0.2, 0.12 and 0.3 is :

(a) 0.13   (b) 0.15
(c) 0.18   (d) 0.8

22. The third proportional to 0.8 and 0.2 is :
    (a) 0.4   (b) 0.8
    (c) 0.05   (d) 0.032

23. The mean proportional between 0.32 and 0.02 is :
    (a) 0.34   (b) 0.3
    (c) 0.16   (d) 0.08
    (Central Excise & I. Tax 1988)

24. The weight of a 13 m long iron rod is 23.4 kg. The weight of 6 m long of such rod will be : (Bank P.O. 1986)
    (a) 7.2 kg   (b) 12.4 kg
    (c) 10.8 kg   (d) 18 kg

25. Two whole numbers whose sum is 64, cannot be in the ratio :
    (a) 5 : 3   (b) 7 : 1
    (c) 3 : 4   (d) 9 : 7

26. If a carton containing a dozen mirrors is dropped, which of the following cannot be the ratio of broken mirrors to unbroken mirrors ?
    (Bank P.O. 1987)
    (a) 2 : 1   (b) 3 : 1
    (c) 3 : 2   (d) 7 : 5

27. The ratio of two numbers is 3 : 4 and their sum is 420. The greater of the two numbers is : (Railway Recruitment 1991)
    (a) 175   (b) 200
    (c) 240   (d) 315

28. A bag contains 25 paise, 10 paise and 5 paise coins in the ratio 1 : 2 : 3. If their total value is Rs. 30, the number of 5 paise coins is :
    (a) 50   (b) 100
    (c) 150   (d) 200
    (Clerk's Grade 1991)

29. The monthly salary of A, B, C is in the proportion of 2 : 3 : 5. If C's monthly salary is Rs. 1200 more than that of A, then B's annual salary is : (Bank P.O. 1991)
    (a) Rs. 14400   (b) Rs. 24000
    (c) Rs. 1200   (d) Rs. 2000

30. Three friends divide Rs. 624 among themselves in the ratio $\frac{1}{2} : \frac{1}{3} : \frac{1}{4}$.
    The share of the third friend is : (Clerk's Grade 1991)

    (a) Rs. 288   ☐   (b) Rs. 192   ☐
    (c) Rs. 148   ☐   (d) Rs. 144   ☐

31. A, B and C can do a work in 20, 25 and 30 days respectively. They undertook to finish the work together for Rs. 2220, then the share of A exceeds that of B by :   (Central Excise & I. Tax 1989)
    (a) Rs. 120   ☐   (b) Rs. 180   ☐
    (c) Rs. 300   ☐   (d) Rs. 600   ☐

32. In a class, the number of boys is more than the number of girls by 12% of the total strength. The ratio of boys to girls is : (C.D.S. 1991)
    (a) 11 : 14   ☐   (b) 14 : 11   ☐
    (c) 25 : 28   ☐   (d) 28 : 25   ☐

33. A circle and a square have same area. Therefore, the ratio of the side of the square and the radius of the circle is :   (C.D.S. 1991)
    (a) $\sqrt{\pi} : 1$ ☐   (b) $1 : \sqrt{\pi}$ ☐
    (c) $1 : \pi$ ☐   (d) $\pi : 1$ ☐

34. A right cylinder and a right circular cone have the same radius and the same volume. The ratio of the height of the cylinder to that of the cone is :   (C.D.S. 1991)
    (a) 3 : 5   ☐   (b) 2 : 5   ☐
    (c) 3 : 1   ☐   (d) 1 : 3   ☐

35. The areas of two spheres are in the ratio 1 : 4. The ratio of their volumes is :
    (a) 1 : 2   ☐   (b) 1 : 4   ☐
    (c) 1 : 8   ☐   (d) 1 : 6   ☐

36. If $18 : x = x : 8$, then x is equal to :   (Clerk's Grade 1991)
    (a) 144   ☐   (b) 72   ☐
    (c) 26   ☐   (d) 12   ☐

37. The prices of a scooter and a television set are in the ratio 3 : 2. If a scooter costs Rs. 6000 more than the television set, the price of the television set is :   (Bank P.O. 1989)
    (a) Rs. 6000   ☐   (b) Rs. 10000   ☐
    (c) Rs. 12000   ☐   (d) Rs. 18000   ☐

38. A certain amount was divided between Kavita and Reena in the ratio 4 : 3. If Reena's share was Rs. 2400, the amount is : (Bank P.O. 1988)
    (a) Rs. 5600   ☐   (b) Rs. 3200   ☐
    (c) Rs. 9600   ☐   (d) none of these   ☐

39. Rs. 5625 is divided among A, B and C so that A may receive $\frac{1}{2}$ as much as B and C together receive and B receives $\frac{1}{4}$ of what A and C together receive. The share of A is more than that of B by :
   (a) Rs. 750 ☐   (b) Rs. 775 ☐
   (c) Rs. 1500 ☐   (d) Rs. 1600 ☐
                                         (Excise & I. Tax 1988)

40. The ratio of money with Ram and Gopal is 7 : 17 and that with Gopal and Krishan is 7 : 17. If Ram has Rs. 490, Krishan has :
   (a) Rs. 2890 ☐   (b) Rs. 2330 ☐
   (c) Rs. 1190 ☐   (d) Rs. 2680 ☐
                                         (Assistant Grade 1987)

41. The cost of making an article is divided between materials, labour and overheads in the ratio of 3 : 4 : 1. If the materials cost Rs. 67.50, the cost of article is :
   (a) Rs. 180 ☐   (b) Rs. 122.50 ☐
   (c) Rs. 380 ☐   (d) Rs. 540 ☐

42. The students in three classes are in the ratio 2 : 3 : 5. If 20 students are increased in each class, the ratio changes to 4 : 5 : 7. The total number of students before the increase were :   (L.I.C. A.A.O. 1988)
   (a) 10 ☐   (b) 90 ☐
   (c) 100 ☐   (d) none of these ☐

43. The ratio of the first and second class fares between two stations is 4 : 1 and that of the number of passengers travelling by first and second class is 1 : 40. If Rs. 1100 is collected as fare, the amount collected from first class passengers is :
   (a) Rs. 275 ☐   (b) Rs. 315 ☐
   (c) Rs. 137.50 ☐   (d) Rs. 100 ☐

44. The incomes of A and B are in the ratio 3 : 2 and their expenditures in the ratio 5 : 3. If each saves Rs. 1000, A's income is :
   (a) Rs. 3000 ☐   (b) Rs. 4000 ☐
   (c) Rs. 6000 ☐   (d) Rs. 9000 ☐

45. A sum of money is divided among A, B, C so that to each rupee A gets, B gets 65 paise and C gets 35 paise. If C's share is Rs. 28, the sum is :
   (a) Rs. 120 ☐   (b) Rs. 140 ☐
   (c) Rs. 160 ☐   (d) Rs. 180 ☐

46. Rs. 53 is divided among A, B and C in such a way that B gets Rs. 7

more than what B gets and B gets Rs. 8 more than what C gets. The ratio of their shares is :

(a) 16 : 9 : 18 □ (b) 25 : 18 : 10 □
(c) 18 : 25 : 10 □ (d) 15 : 8 : 30 □

47. The speeds of three cars are in the ratio 3 : 4 : 5. The ratio between times taken by them to travel the same distance is :

(a) 3 : 4 : 5 □ (b) 5 : 4 : 3 □
(c) 12 : 15 : 20 □ (d) 20 : 15 : 12 □

48. The sides of a triangle are in the ratio $\frac{1}{3} : \frac{1}{4} : \frac{1}{5}$ and its perimeter is 94 cm, the length of smallest side is :

(a) 18.8 cm □ (b) 23.5 cm □
(c) 24 cm □ (d) 31.3 cm □

49. Rs. 2430 has been divided among A, B, C in such a way that if their shares be diminished by Rs. 5, Rs. 10 and Rs. 15 respectively, the remainders are in the ratio 3 : 4 : 5. Then A's share is :

(a) Rs. 800 □ (b) Rs. 600 □
(c) Rs. 595 □ (d) Rs. 605 □

50. Rs. 680 has been divided among A, B, C such that A gets $\frac{2}{3}$ of what B gets and B gets $\frac{1}{4}$ of what C gets. Then, B's share is :

(a) Rs. 60 □ (b) Rs. 80 □
(c) Rs. 120 □ (d) Rs. 160 □

51. 94 is divided into two parts in such a way that fifth part of the first and eighth part of the second are in the ratio 3 : 4. The first part is :

(a) 27 □ (b) 30 □
(c) 36 □ (d) 48 □

52. Some money is divided among A, B and C in such a way that 5 times A's share, 3 times B's share and 2 times C's share are all equal. The ratio between the shares of A, B, C is :

(a) 5 : 3 : 2 □ (b) 2 : 2 : 5 □
(c) 15 : 10 : 6 □ (d) 6 : 10 : 15 □

53. Rs. 385 has been divided among A, B, C in such a way that A receives $\frac{2}{9}$ th of what B and C together receive. Then, A's share is :

(a) Rs. 70 □ (b) Rs. 77 □
(c) Rs. 82.50 □ (d) Rs. 85 □

Ratio & Proportion 149

54. Rs. 1870 has been divided into three parts in such a way that half of the first part, one-third of the second part and one-sixth of the third part are equal. The third part is :

(a) Rs. 510 ☐ (b) Rs. 680 ☐
(c) Rs. 850 ☐ (d) Rs. 1020 ☐

55. A and B are two alloys of gold and copper prepared by mixing metals in proportions 7 : 2 and 7 : 11 respectively. If equal quantities of the alloys are melted to form a third alloy C, the proportion of gold and copper in C will be : **(C.D.S. 1989)**

(a) 5 : 9 ☐ (b) 5 : 7 ☐
(c) 7 : 5 ☐ (d) 9 : 5 ☐

56. 729 ml of a mixture contains milk and water in the ratio 7 : 2. How much more water is to be added to get a new mixture containing milk and water in the ratio of 7 : 3 ? **(Railway Recruitment 1991)**

(a) 60 ml ☐ (b) 70 ml ☐
(c) 81 ml ☐ (d) 90 ml ☐

57. Divide Rs. 600 among A, B and C so that Rs. 40 more than $\frac{2}{5}$ th of A's share, Rs. 20 more than $\frac{2}{7}$ th of B's share and Rs. 10 more than $\frac{9}{17}$ th of C's share may all be equal. What is A's share ?

(a) Rs. 280 ☐ (b) Rs. 150 ☐
(c) Rs. 170 ☐ (d) Rs. 200 ☐
(Railway Recruitment 1991)

58. Rs. 1050 is divided among P, Q and R. The share of P is $\frac{2}{5}$ of the combined share of Q and R. Thus, P gets : **(C.B.I. 1990)**

(a) Rs. 200 ☐ (b) Rs. 300 ☐
(c) Rs. 320 ☐ (d) Rs. 420 ☐

59. If $a : b = c : d$, then $\frac{ma + nc}{mb + nd}$ is equal to : **(C.B.I. 1990)**

(a) $m : n$ ☐ (b) $na : mb$ ☐
(c) $a : b$ ☐ (d) $md : nc$ ☐

60. Gold is 19 times as heavy as water and copper 9 times as heavy as water. The ratio in which these two metals be mixed so that the mixture is 15 times as heavy as water, is : **(Delhi Police 1990)**

(a) 1 : 2 ☐ (b) 2 : 3 ☐
(c) 3 : 2 ☐ (d) 19 : 135 ☐

61. One-fourth of the boys and three-eighth of the girls in a school participated in the annual sports. What fractional part of the total student population of the school participated in the annual sports ?

   (a) $\dfrac{4}{12}$ (b) $\dfrac{5}{8}$

   (c) $\dfrac{8}{12}$ (d) data inadequate

   (Bank P.O. 1990)

62. Vinay got thrice as many marks in Maths as in English. The proportion of his marks in Maths and History is 4 : 3. If his total marks in Maths, English and History are 250, what are his marks in English ?

   (a) 120 (b) 90
   (c) 40   (d) 80

   (Bank P.O. 1990)

63. 15 litres of a mixture contains 20% alcohol and the rest water. If 3 litres of water be mixed in it, the percentage of alcohol in the new mixture will be : **(Clerk's Grade 1991)**

   (a) 17 (b) $16\dfrac{2}{3}$
   (c) $18\dfrac{1}{2}$ (d) 15

64. A's money is to B's money as 4 : 5 and B's money is to C's money as 2 : 3. If A has Rs. 800, C has : **(C.B.I. 1991)**

   (a) Rs. 1000 (b) Rs. 1200
   (c) Rs. 1500 (d) Rs. 2000

65. The proportion of zinc and copper in a brass piece is 13 : 7. How much zinc will be there in 100 kg of such a piece ?

   (a) 20 kg (b) 35 kg
   (c) 55 kg (d) 65 kg

66. A mixture contains milk and water in the ratio 5 : 1. On adding 5 litres of water, the ratio of milk and water becomes 5 : 2. The quantity of milk in the mixture is :

   (a) 16 litres (b) 25 litres
   (c) 32.5 litres (d) 22.75 litres

67. The ratio of milk and water in 85 kg of adulterated milk is 27 : 7. The amount of water which must be added to make the ratio 3 : 1 is :

   (a) 5 kg (b) 6.5 kg
   (c) 7.25 kg (d) 8 kg

68. Two equal glasses are respectively $\frac{1}{3}$ and $\frac{1}{4}$ full of milk. They are then filled up with water and the contents mixed in a tumbler. The ratio of milk and water in the tumbler is :
    (a) 7 : 5
    (b) 7 : 17
    (c) 3 : 7
    (d) 11 : 23

69. A sum of Rs. 1300 is divided between A, B, C and D such that $\frac{A\text{'s share}}{B\text{'s share}} = \frac{B\text{'s share}}{C\text{'s share}} = \frac{C\text{'s share}}{D\text{'s share}} = \frac{2}{3}.$
    Then, A's share is :
    (a) Rs. 140
    (b) Rs. 160
    (c) Rs. 240
    (d) Rs. 320

70. In a mixture of 60 litres, the ratio of milk and water is 2 : 1. What amount of water must be added to make the ratio 1 : 2 ?
    (a) 42 litres
    (b) 56 litres
    (c) 60 litres
    (d) 77 litres

    (N.D.A. 1990)

71. The ratio between two numbers is 3 : 4 and their L.C.M. is 180. The first number is :
    (a) 15
    (b) 20
    (c) 45
    (d) 60

72. 6 men, 8 women and 6 children complete a job for a sum of Rs. 950. If their individual wages are in ratio 4 : 3 : 2, the total money earned by the children is :
    (a) Rs. 190
    (b) Rs. 195
    (c) Rs. 215
    (d) Rs. 230

73. A man has some hens and cows. If the number of heads be 48 and number of feet equals 140, the number of hens will be :
    (a) 22
    (b) 23
    (c) 24
    (d) 26

74. The average age of 3 girls is 20 years and their ages are in the proportion 3 : 5 : 7. The age of youngest girl is :
    (a) 4 years
    (b) 6 years 8 months
    (c) 8 years 3 months
    (d) 12 years

75. A father's age was 5 times his son's age 5 years ago and will be 3 times son's age after 2 years. the ratio of their present ages is :
    (a) 5 : 2
    (b) 5 : 3
    (c) 10 : 3
    (d) 11 : 5

76. The ratio between the ages of Kamla and Savitri is 6 : 5 and the sum of their ages is 44 years. The ratio of their ages after 8 years will be :

    (a) 5 : 6 ☐   (b) 7 : 8 ☐
    (c) 8 : 7 ☐   (d) 14 : 13 ☐

    (Bank P.O. 1987)

77. The ratio of father's age to son's age is 4 : 1. The product of their ages is 196. The ratio of their ages after 5 years will be :

    (a) 3 : 1 ☐   (b) 10 : 3 ☐
    (c) 11 : 4 ☐   (d) 14 : 5 ☐

78. The ages of Vivek and Sumit are in the ratio 2 : 3. After 12 years, their ages will be in the ratio 11 : 15. The age of Sumit is :

    (a) 32 years ☐   (b) 42 years ☐
    (c) 48 years ☐   (d) 56 years ☐

79. The ratio between Sumit's and Prakash's age at present is 2 : 3. Sumit is 6 years younger than Prakash. The ratio of Sumit's age to Prakash's age after 6 years will be :   (Railway Recruitment, 1991)

    (a) 1 : 2 ☐   (b) 2 : 3 ☐
    (c) 3 : 4 ☐   (d) 3 : 8 ☐

80. One year ago the ratio between Laxman's and Gopal's salary was 3 : 4. The ratios of their individual salaries between last year's and this year's salaries are 4 : 5 and 2 : 3 respectively. At present the total of their salary is Rs. 4160. The salary of Laxman now, is :

    (a) Rs. 1040 ☐   (b) Rs. 1600 ☐
    (c) Rs. 2560 ☐   (d) Rs. 3120 ☐

    (S.B.I. P.O. Exam, 1987)

ANSWERS (Exercise 8)

1. (a)   2. (b)   3. (d)   4. (c)   5. (b)   6. (a)   7. (c)   8. (c)   9. (c)
10. (b)   11. (d)   12. (b)   13. (a)   14. (c)   15. (b)   16. (b)   17. (d)   18. (b)
19. (b)   20. (c)   21. (c)   22. (c)   23. (d)   24. (c)   25. (c)   26. (c)   27. (c)
28. (c)   29. (a)   30. (d)   31. (b)   32. (b)   33. (a)   34. (d)   35. (c)   36. (d)
37. (c)   38. (a)   39. (a)   40. (a)   41. (a)   42. (c)   43. (d)   44. (c)   45. (c)
46. (b)   47. (d)   48. (c)   49. (d)   50. (c)   51. (b)   52. (d)   53. (a)   54. (d)
55. (c)   56. (c)   57. (b)   58. (b)   59. (c)   60. (c)   61. (d)   62. (c)   63. (b)
64. (c)   65. (d)   66. (b)   67. (a)   68. (b)   69. (b)   70. (c)   71. (c)   72. (a)
73. (d)   74. (d)   75. (c)   76. (c)   77. (c)   78. (c)   79. (c)   80. (b)

SOLUTION (Exercise 8)

1. $\dfrac{A}{B} = \dfrac{2}{3}$ and $\dfrac{B}{C} = \dfrac{4}{5}$.

   $\therefore \dfrac{A}{C} = \left(\dfrac{A}{B} \times \dfrac{B}{C}\right) = \left(\dfrac{2}{3} \times \dfrac{4}{5}\right) = \left(\dfrac{8}{15}\right)$.

   So, $\dfrac{C}{A} = \dfrac{15}{8}$ and hence $C : A = 15 : 8$.

2. 10% of x = 20% of $y \Rightarrow \dfrac{10}{100} x = \dfrac{20}{100} y$

   $\therefore \dfrac{x}{10} = \dfrac{y}{5}$ or $\dfrac{x}{y} = \dfrac{10}{5} = \dfrac{2}{1}$.

   Hence, $x : y = 2 : 1$.

3. $0.6 x = 0.09 y \Rightarrow \dfrac{x}{y} = \dfrac{0.09}{0.60} = \dfrac{9}{60} = \dfrac{3}{20}$.

4. $A : B = 7 : 9$ and $B : C = 3 : 5 = 9 : 15$.

   $\therefore A : B : C = 7 : 9 : 15$.

5. L.C.M. of 7 and 6 is 42.

   $\therefore A : B = 5 : 7 = 30 : 42$ and $B : C = 6 : 11 = 42 : 77$

   Hence, $A : B : C = 30 : 42 : 77$.

6. Let $A = x$. Then, $B = 3x$, $C = 2B = 6x$.

   $\therefore A : B : C = x : 3x : 6x = 1 : 3 : 6$.

7. $\dfrac{A}{D} = \left(\dfrac{A}{B} \times \dfrac{B}{C} \times \dfrac{C}{D}\right) = \left(\dfrac{2}{3} \times \dfrac{4}{5} \times \dfrac{6}{7}\right) = \dfrac{16}{35}$.

   $\therefore A : D = 16 : 35$.

8. Let $2A = 3B = 4C = x$.

   Then, $A = \dfrac{x}{2}$, $B = \dfrac{x}{3}$ and $C = \dfrac{x}{4}$.

   $\therefore A : B : C = \dfrac{x}{2} : \dfrac{x}{3} : \dfrac{x}{4} = 6 : 4 : 3$.

   Hence, $A : B : C = 6 : 4 : 3$.

9. $2A = 3B$ and $4B = 5C$.

   $\therefore 8A = 12B$ and $12B = 15C$

   So, $8A = 12B = 15C = x$

   $\therefore A = \dfrac{x}{8}$, $B = \dfrac{x}{12}$, $C = \dfrac{x}{15}$.

   So, $A : C = \dfrac{x}{8} : \dfrac{x}{15} = 15 : 8$.

10. $\frac{x}{y} = \frac{2}{3}$ and $\frac{2}{x} = \frac{1}{2}$.

$\therefore \frac{x}{y} \times \frac{2}{x} = \frac{2}{3} \times \frac{1}{2}$ or $\frac{2}{y} = \frac{1}{3}$ or $y = 6$.

11. Let the numbers be $3x$ and $5x$.

Then, $\frac{3x+10}{5x+10} = \frac{5}{7}$ or $7(3x+10) = 5(5x+10)$.

$\therefore 4x = 20$ or $x = 5$.

So, the numbers are 15, 25.

12. $\frac{\frac{1}{3} \text{ of Rs. } 9.30}{0.6 \text{ of Rs. } 1.55} = \frac{3.10}{.93} = \frac{310}{93} = \frac{10}{3}$.

13. $\frac{1}{3}A = \frac{1}{4}B = \frac{1}{5}C = x$.

Then, $A = 3x, B = 4x$ and $C = 5x$.

$\therefore A : B : C = 3x : 4x : 5x = 3 : 4 : 5$.

14. $\frac{1}{x} \times \frac{1}{x} = \frac{1}{5} \times \frac{1}{1.25}$ or $\frac{1}{x^2} = \frac{4}{25}$ or $x^2 = \frac{25}{4}$

$\therefore x = \frac{5}{2} = 2.5$.

15. $7 : 15 = \frac{7}{15} = 0.466$; $15 : 23 = \frac{15}{23} = 0.652$;

$17 : 25 = \frac{17}{25} = 0.68$ & $21 : 29 = \frac{21}{29} = 0.724$.

$\therefore$ The smallest one is $7 : 15$.

16. $\frac{5}{8} = \frac{5 \times 8}{8 \times 8} = \frac{40}{64}$.

$\therefore$ Consequent = 64.

17. $\frac{7+x}{13+x} = \frac{2}{3} \Rightarrow 3(7+x) = 2(13+x)$ or $x = 5$.

18. $x : \frac{1}{27} = \frac{3}{7} : \frac{5}{9} \Rightarrow \frac{5}{9}x = \frac{1}{27} \times \frac{3}{7}$.

$\therefore \frac{5}{9}x = \frac{1}{63}$ or $x = \left(\frac{1}{63} \times \frac{9}{5}\right) = \frac{1}{35}$.

19. $\frac{6+x}{14+x} = \frac{18+x}{38+x} \Rightarrow (6+x)(38+x) = (18+x)(14+x)$.

or $x^2 + 44x + 228 = x^2 + 32x + 252$

or $12x = 24$ or $x = 2$.

20. $\dfrac{54-x}{71-x} = \dfrac{75-x}{99-x} \Rightarrow (54-x)(99-x) = (75-x)(71-x)$.

or $x^2 - 153x + 5346 = x^2 - 146x + 5325$ or $x = 3$.

21. Let $0.2 : 0.12 :: 0.3 : x$.

Then, $0.2x = 0.12 \times 0.3$ or $x = \dfrac{0.12 \times 0.3}{0.2} = 0.18$.

22. Let $0.8 : 0.2 :: 0.2 : x$.

Then, $0.8x = 0.2 \times 0.2$ or $x = \dfrac{0.2 \times 0.2}{0.8} = \dfrac{0.04}{0.80} = \dfrac{4}{80} = 0.05$.

23. Mean proportional $= \sqrt{0.32 \times 0.02} = \sqrt{0.0064} = 0.08$.

24. Less length, less weight.

$\therefore 13 : 6 :: 23.4 : x$.

So, $13x = 6 \times 23.4$ or $x = \dfrac{6 \times 23.4}{13} = 10.8$.

25. For dividing 64 into two whole numbers, the sum of the terms of the ratio must be a factor of 64.

$\therefore$ So, they can not be in the ratio $3 : 4$.

26. For dividing 12 into two whole numbers, the sum of the terms of the ratio must be a factor of 12.

So, they can not be in the ratio $3 : 2$.

27. Greater number $= \left(420 \times \dfrac{4}{7}\right) = 240$.

28. Ratio of their values $= \dfrac{1}{4} : \dfrac{2}{10} : \dfrac{3}{20} = 5 : 4 : 3$.

$\therefore$ Value of 5-paise coins = Rs. $\left(30 \times \dfrac{3}{12}\right)$ = Rs. 7.50.

$\therefore$ Number of 5-paise coins $= \dfrac{750}{5} = 150$.

29. Let the monthly salary of A, B, C be $2x$, $3x$ & $5x$.

Then, $5x - 2x = 1200$ or $x = 400$.

$\therefore$ B's monthly salary $= 3x$ = Rs. 1200.

Hence, B's annual salary = Rs. (12×1200) = Rs. 14400.

30. Ratio $= \dfrac{1}{2} : \dfrac{1}{3} : \dfrac{1}{4} = 6 : 4 : 3$.

$\therefore$ Share of third friend = Rs. $\left(624 \times \dfrac{3}{13}\right)$ = Rs. 144.

31. Ratio of shares of A, B & $C = \dfrac{1}{20} : \dfrac{1}{25} : \dfrac{1}{30} = 15 : 12 : 10$.

$\therefore$ A's share = Rs. $\left(2220 \times \dfrac{15}{37}\right)$ = Rs. 900.

B's share = Rs. $\left(2220 \times \dfrac{12}{37}\right)$ = Rs. 720.

Thus, the share of A exceeds that of B by Rs. $(900 - 720)$ = Rs. 180.

32. Let the number of boys and girls be x and y respectively. Then,

$(x - y) = 12\%$ of $(x + y)$ or $x - y = \dfrac{3}{25}(x + y)$

$\therefore$ $25x - 25y = 3x + 3y$ or $22x = 28y$ or $\dfrac{x}{y} = \dfrac{28}{22} = \dfrac{14}{11}$.

33. Let the side of the square be x and let the radius of the circle be y.

Then, $x^2 = \pi y^2 \Rightarrow \dfrac{x^2}{y^2} = \pi$ or $\dfrac{x}{y} = \sqrt{\pi}$.

$\therefore$ $x : y = \sqrt{\pi} : 1$.

34. Let the heights of the cylinder and cone be h and H respectively. Then,

$\pi r^2 h = \dfrac{1}{3} \pi r^2 H$ or $\dfrac{h}{H} = \dfrac{1}{3}$.

So, their heights are in the ratio $1 : 3$.

35. $\dfrac{4 \pi r^2}{4 \pi R^2} = \dfrac{1}{4} \Rightarrow \dfrac{r^2}{R^2} = \dfrac{1}{4}$ and so $\dfrac{r}{R} = \dfrac{1}{2}$.

$\therefore$ $\dfrac{r^3}{R^3} = \dfrac{1}{8}$. Hence, $\dfrac{\dfrac{4}{3} \pi r^3}{\dfrac{4}{3} \pi R^3} = \dfrac{1}{8}$.

Thus, their volumes are in the ratio $1 : 8$.

36. $18 \times 8 = x^2$ or $x = \sqrt{144} = 12$.

37. Let the price of a scooter be Rs. $3x$ and that of a television set be Rs. $2x$.

Then, $3x - 2x = 6000$ or $x = 6000$.

$\therefore$ Cost of a television set = $2x$ = Rs. 12000.

38. Let their shares be Rs. $4x$ and Rs. $3x$.

Then, $3x = 2400 \Rightarrow x = 800$.

$\therefore$ Total amount = $7x$ = Rs. 5600.

39. $A = \dfrac{1}{2}(B + C)$ or $B + C = 2A \Rightarrow A + B + C = 3A$.

Thus, $3A = 5625$ or $A = 1875$.

Again, $B = \dfrac{1}{4}(A + C) \Rightarrow A + C = 4B \Rightarrow A + B + C = 5B$.

$\therefore\ 5B = 5625$ or $B = 1125$.

Thus, A's share is more than that of B by Rs. $(1875 - 1125)$ i.e. Rs. 750.

40. Ram : Gopal = 7 : 17 = 49 : 119

Gopal : Krishan = 7 : 17 = 119 : 289

$\therefore$ Ram : Gopal : Krishan = 49 : 119 : 289

or Ram : Krishan = 49 : 289

Thus, $49 : 289 = 490 : x$

$\therefore\ x = \dfrac{289 \times 490}{49} = 2890$.

41. If materials cost Rs. 3, the cost of the article is $(3 + 4 + 1)$.

If materials cost Rs. 67.50, the cost of the article

$= \text{Rs.} \left(\dfrac{8}{3} \times 67.50\right) = \text{Rs. } 180$.

42. Let the number of students be $2x$, $3x$ and $5x$.

Then, $(2x + 20) : (3x + 20) : (5x + 20) = 4 : 5 : 7$

So, $\dfrac{2x+20}{4} = \dfrac{3x+20}{5} = \dfrac{5x+20}{7}$

$\therefore\ 5(2x+20) = 4(3x+20)$ or $x = 10$.

Hence, total number of students before increase $= 10x = 100$.

43. Ratio of amounts collected from 1st and 2nd class

$= (4 \times 1 : 1 \times 40) = (1 : 10)$.

$\therefore$ Amount collected as 1st class fare $= \text{Rs.} \left(1100 \times \dfrac{1}{11}\right) = \text{Rs. } 100$.

44. Let their incomes be $3x, 2x$ and expenditures $5y, 3y$ respectively.

Then,

$3x - 5y = 1000$ and $2x - 3y = 1000$.

Solving these equations, we get $x = 2000$, $y = 1000$

$\therefore\ A$'s income $= 3x = \text{Rs. } 6000$.

45. $A : B : C = 100 : 65 : 35 = 20 : 13 : 7$.

If C's share is Rs. 7, the sum is Rs. 40.

If C's share is Rs. 28, the sum is Rs. $\left(\dfrac{40}{7} \times 28\right) = \text{Rs. } 160$.

46. Suppose C gets Rs. x.

Then, B gets Rs. $(x + 8)$ and A gets Rs. $(x + 15)$.
$\therefore x + x + 8 + x + 15 = 53$ or $x = 10$.
So, A gets Rs. 25, B gets Rs. 18 and C gets Rs. 10.
$\therefore A : B : C = 25 : 18 : 10$.

47. Ratio of time taken $= \dfrac{1}{3} : \dfrac{1}{4} : \dfrac{1}{5} = 20 : 15 : 12$.

48. Ratio of sides $= \dfrac{1}{3} : \dfrac{1}{4} : \dfrac{1}{5} = 20 : 15 : 12$.

    Length of smallest side $= \left(94 \times \dfrac{12}{47}\right)$ cm $= 24$ cm.

49. Remainder = Rs. $[2430 - (5 + 10 + 15)]$ = Rs. 2400.

    $\therefore A$'s share = Rs. $\left[\left(2400 \times \dfrac{3}{12}\right) + 5\right]$ = Rs. 605.

50. Suppose C gets Re. 1. Then, B gets Re. $\left(\dfrac{1}{4}\right)$

    $\therefore A$ gets = Re. $\left(\dfrac{2}{3} \times \dfrac{1}{4}\right)$ = Re. $\dfrac{1}{6}$.

    $\therefore A : B : C = \dfrac{1}{6} : \dfrac{1}{4} : 1 = 2 : 3 : 12$.

    Hence, B's share = Rs. $\left(680 \times \dfrac{3}{17}\right)$ = Rs. 120.

51. $\dfrac{1}{5}A : \dfrac{1}{8}B = 3 : 4$

    or $\dfrac{8A}{5B} = \dfrac{120}{160}$ or $\dfrac{A}{B} = \dfrac{120}{160} \times \dfrac{5}{8} = \dfrac{15}{32}$.

    $\therefore$ First part = Rs. $\left(94 \times \dfrac{15}{47}\right)$ = Rs. 30.

52. $5A = 3B = 2C = x \Rightarrow A = \dfrac{x}{5}, B = \dfrac{x}{3}$ and $C = \dfrac{x}{2}$.

    $\therefore A : B : C = \dfrac{x}{5} : \dfrac{x}{3} : \dfrac{x}{2} = 6 : 10 : 15$.

53. $A : (B + C) = 2 : 9$.

    $\therefore A$'s share = Rs. $\left(385 \times \dfrac{2}{11}\right)$ = Rs. 70.

54. $\dfrac{1}{2}A = \dfrac{1}{3}B = \dfrac{1}{6}C = x \Rightarrow A = 2x, B = 3x, C = 6x$.

    $\therefore A : B : C = 2 : 3 : 6$.

Ratio & Proportion   159

$\therefore$ Third part = Rs. $\left(1870 \times \dfrac{6}{11}\right)$ = Rs. 1020.

55. Gold in $C = \left(\dfrac{7}{9} + \dfrac{7}{18}\right) = \dfrac{21}{18} = \dfrac{7}{6}$.

   Copper in $C = \left(\dfrac{2}{9} + \dfrac{11}{18}\right) = \dfrac{15}{18} = \dfrac{5}{6}$.

   $\therefore$ Gold : Copper $= \dfrac{7}{6} : \dfrac{5}{6} = 7 : 5$.

56. Milk $= \left(729 \times \dfrac{7}{9}\right) = 567$ ml.

   Water $= \left(729 \times \dfrac{2}{9}\right) = 162$ ml.

   $\therefore \dfrac{567}{162 + x} = \dfrac{7}{3} \Rightarrow 7(162 + x) = 3 \times 567$.

   $\therefore 7x = 1701 - 1134$ or $x = \dfrac{567}{7} = 81$ ml.

57. $\dfrac{2}{5}A + 40 = \dfrac{2}{7}B + 20 = \dfrac{9}{17}C + 10 = x$

   $\therefore A = \dfrac{5}{2}(x - 40), B = \dfrac{7}{2}(x - 20)$ and $C = \dfrac{17}{9}(x - 10)$.

   $\therefore \dfrac{5}{2}(x - 40) + \dfrac{7}{2}(x - 20) + \dfrac{17}{9}(x - 10) = 600$.

   $45x - 1800 + 63x - 1260 + 34x - 340 = 10800$

   $142x = 14200$ or $x = \dfrac{14200}{142} = 100$.

   Hence, A's share $= \dfrac{5}{2}(100 - 40) =$ Rs. 150.

58. $P : (Q + R) = 2 : 5$

   $\therefore P$'s share = Rs. $\left(1050 \times \dfrac{2}{7}\right)$ = Rs. 300.

59. Let $\dfrac{a}{b} = \dfrac{c}{d} = k$. Then, $a = bk$ and $c = dk$.

   $\therefore \dfrac{ma + nc}{mb + nd} = \dfrac{mbk + ndk}{mb + nd} = k\left(\dfrac{mb + nd}{mb + nd}\right) = k = \dfrac{a}{b}$.

60. Let __ gm of gold be mixed with x gm of copper to given $(1 + x)$ gm of mixture.

   Now $1G = 19W$ and $1c = 9W$ & mixture $= 15W$.

   Now, 1 gm gold + x gm copper = $(1 + x)$ gm mixture

$\therefore$ $19W + 9W \times x = (1 + x) \times 15W$

Thus $4W = 6Wx$ or $x = \dfrac{4W}{6W} = \dfrac{4}{6} = \dfrac{2}{3}$.

So, the ratio is $1 : \dfrac{2}{3}$ i.e. $3 : 2$.

61. Data is inadequate.

62. $M = 3E$ and $\dfrac{M}{H} = \dfrac{4}{3}$.

$\therefore H = \dfrac{3}{4} M = \dfrac{3}{4} \times 3E = \dfrac{9}{4} E$.

Now, $M + E + H = 250 \Rightarrow 3E + E + \dfrac{9}{4} E = 250$

$\therefore 25E = 1000$ or $E = 40$.

63. Alcohol $= \left(\dfrac{20}{100} \times 15\right)$ litres $= 3$ litres, Water $= 12$ litres.

New mix. contains alcohol $= 3$ litres, water $= 15$ litres.

$\therefore$ Percentage of alcohol in new mix. $= \left(\dfrac{3}{18} \times 100\right) \%$

$= 16\dfrac{2}{3} \%$.

64. $A : B = 4 : 5 = 8 : 10$ & $B : C = 2 : 3 = 10 : 15$.

$\therefore A : B : C = 8 : 10 : 15$.

If A has Rs. 8, C has Rs. 15

If A has Rs. 800, C has Rs. $\left(\dfrac{15}{8} \times 800\right) =$ Rs. 1500.

65. 20 kg of brass contains Zinc $= 13$ kg

100 kg of brass contains Zinc $= \left(\dfrac{13}{20} \times 100\right)$ kg $= 65$ kg.

66. Let quantity of milk and water be $5x$ and x litres.

Then, $\dfrac{5x}{x+5} = \dfrac{5}{2}$ or $10x = 5x + 25$ or $x = 5$.

$\therefore$ Quantity of milk $= 5x = 25$ litres.

67. Milk $= \left(85 \times \dfrac{27}{34}\right)$ kg $= \left(\dfrac{135}{2}\right)$ kg $= 67.5$ kg.

Water $= \left(85 \times \dfrac{7}{34}\right)$ kg $= \left(\dfrac{35}{2}\right)$ kg $= 17.5$ kg.

$\dfrac{67.5}{17.5 + x} = \dfrac{3}{1} \Rightarrow 3(17.5 + x) = 67.5$ or $x = 5$.

∴ Water to be added = 5 kg.

68. First glass contains milk = $\frac{1}{3}$ and water = $\frac{2}{3}$.

   Second glass contains milk = $\frac{1}{4}$ and water = $\frac{3}{4}$.

   ∴ New tumbler contains, milk = $\left(\frac{1}{3} + \frac{1}{4}\right) = \frac{7}{12}$.

   New tumber contains, water = $\left(\frac{2}{3} + \frac{3}{4}\right) = \frac{17}{12}$.

   ∴ Ratio of milk and water = $\frac{7}{12} : \frac{17}{12} = 7 : 17$.

69. $A : B = 2 : 3, B : C = 2 : 3$ and $C : D = 2 : 3$
    $A : B = 8 : 12, B : C = 12 : 18$ and $C : D = 18 : 27$
    ∴ $A : B : C : D = 8 : 12 : 18 : 27$.
    So, A's share = Rs. $\left(1300 \times \frac{8}{65}\right)$ = Rs. 160.

70. Milk = $\left(60 \times \frac{2}{3}\right)$ litres = 40 litres.
    Water = (60 – 40) litres = 20 litres.
    ∴ $\frac{40}{20 + x} = \frac{1}{2} \Rightarrow 20 + x = 80$ or $x = 60$.
    Hence, water to be added = 60 litres.

71. Let the numbers be $3x$ and $4x$.
    Then, their L.C.M. = $12x$.
    ∴ $12x = 180$ or $x = 15$.
    Hence, the first number = 45.

72. Ratio of wages of 6 men, 8 women and 6 children
    $= 6 \times 4 : 8 \times 3 : 6 \times 2 = 24 : 24 : 12 = 2 : 2 : 1$.
    ∴ Money earned by children = Rs. $\left(950 \times \frac{1}{5}\right)$ = Rs. 190.

73. Let the number of hens = x & number of cows = y.
    Then, $x + y = 48$ and $2x + 4y = 140$.
    Solving these equations, we get, $2y = 44$ or $y = 22$.
    So, $x = (48 - 22) = 26$.
    ∴ Number of hens = 26.

74. Their total age = (3×20) years = 60 years.
    Let their ages be $3x, 5x$ and $7x$ years. Then,

$3x + 5x + 7x = 60$ or $x = 4$.

∴ Youngest girl is $= 3x = 12$ years old.

75. Let son's age 5 years ago $= x$ years.

Then, father's age at that time $= (5x)$ years.

After 2 years, son's age $= (x + 7)$ years

After 2 years, father's age $= (5x + 7)$ years.

∴ $3(x + 7) = 5x + 7$ or $x = 7$.

Father's age now $= (5x + 5) = 40$ years.

Son's age now $= (x + 5) = 12$ years.

∴ Ratio of their present ages $= 40 : 12 = 10 : 3$.

76. Let their ages be $6x$ and $5x$ years.

∴ $6x + 5x = 44$ or $x = 4$.

So, their present ages are 24 years & 20 years.

Ratio of their ages after 8 years $= 32 : 28 = 8 : 7$.

77. Let their ages be $4x$ and x years. Then,

$4x \times x = 196$ or $x^2 = 49$ or $x = 7$.

Their ages are 28 years and 7 years.

Ratio of their ages after 5 years $= 33 : 12 = 11 : 4$.

78. Let their ages be $2x$ and $3x$ years.

$\dfrac{2x + 12}{3x + 12} = \dfrac{11}{15}$ or $15(2x + 12) = 11(3x + 12)$

or $3x = 48$ or $x = 16$

∴ Age of Sumit $= 3x = 48$ years.

79. Let their ages be $2x$ and $3x$ years.

$3x - 2x = 6$ or $x = 6$.

Sumit's age $= 12$ years, Prakash's age $= 18$ years.

After 6 years, Sumit's age $= 18$ years.

After 6 years, Prakash's age $= 24$ years.

∴ Ratio of their ages $= 18 : 24 = 3 : 4$.

80. Let the salaries of Laxman and Gopal one year before be x_1, y_1 respectively and now x_2, y_2 respectively. Then,

$\dfrac{x_1}{y_1} = \dfrac{3}{4}, \dfrac{x_1}{x_2} = \dfrac{4}{5}, \dfrac{y_1}{y_2} = \dfrac{2}{3}$ and $x_2 + y_2 = 4160$.

Solving these equations, we get $x_2 = 1600$.

9

PARTNERSHIP

Results on Partnership

(i) When two or more than two persons run a business jointly, they are called *partners* and the deal is known as *partnership*.

(ii) When investments of all the partners are for the same time, the profits or losses are divided among them in the ratio of their investments.

(iii) When investments are for different time, then equivalent capitals are calculated for a unit of time by multiplying the capital with the number of units. Gains or losses are divided in the ratio of these capitals.

(iv) A partner who manages the business is called a *working partner* while the one who simply invests money but does not look after the business is called a *sleeping partner*.

SOLVED EXAMPLES

Ex. 1. Dilip and Manohar started a business by investing Rs. 100000 and Rs. 150000 respectively. Find the share of each out of a profit of Rs. 24000.

Sol. Ratio of shares of Dilip and Manohar
$$= 100000 : 150000 = 2 : 3.$$
$\therefore$ Dilip's share = Rs. $\left(24000 \times \dfrac{2}{5}\right)$ = Rs. 9600.

Manohar's share = Rs. $\left(24000 \times \dfrac{3}{5}\right)$ = Rs. 14400.

Ex. 2. Sanjay and Raju started a business and invested Rs. 20000 and Rs. 25000 respectively. After 4 months, Raju left and Naresh joined by investing Rs. 15000. At the end of the year, there was a profit of Rs. 4600. What is the share of Naresh?

Sol. Ratio of shares of Sanjay, Raju and Naresh
$$= 20000 \times 12 : 25000 \times 4 : 15000 \times 8$$
$$= 12 : 5 : 6.$$
$\therefore$ Share of Naresh = Rs. $\left(4600 \times \dfrac{6}{23}\right)$ = Rs. 1200.

Ex. 3. Three partners A, B, C start a business. Twice the investment of A is equal to thrice the capital of B and the capital of B is four times the capital of C. Find the share of each out of a profit of Rs. 297000.

Sol. Let C's capital = Rs. x. Then, B's capital = Rs. $4x$

Now, $2 (A\text{'s capital}) = 3 (B\text{'s capital}) = (3 \times 4x)$

$\therefore A\text{'s capital} = \left(\dfrac{3 \times 4x}{2}\right) = 6x.$

So, Ratio of shares of A, B & $C = 6x : 4x : x = 6 : 4 : 1$.

$\therefore A\text{'s share} = \text{Rs.} \left(297000 \times \dfrac{6}{11}\right) = \text{Rs. } 162000;$

$B\text{'s share} = \text{Rs.} \left(297000 \times \dfrac{4}{11}\right) = \text{Rs. } 108000$

and $C\text{'s share} = \text{Rs.} \left(297000 \times \dfrac{1}{11}\right) = \text{Rs. } 27000.$

Ex. 4. A, B, C hire a meadow for Rs. 2934.60. A puts in 10 oxen for 20 days; B 30 oxen for 8 days and C 16 oxen for 9 days. Find the rent paid by each.

Sol. Ratio of rents to be paid by A, B and C

$= (10 \times 20 : 30 \times 8 : 16 \times 9) = 25 : 30 : 18.$

$\therefore$ Rent to be paid by $A = \text{Rs.} \left(2934.60 \times \dfrac{25}{73}\right)$

$= \text{Rs. } 1005.$

Rent o be paid by $B = \text{Rs.} \left(2934.60 \times \dfrac{30}{73}\right)$

$= \text{Rs. } 1206.$

Rent to be paid by $C = \text{Rs. } [2934.60 - (1005 + 1206)]$

$= \text{Rs. } 723.60.$

Ex. 5. A began a business with Rs. 2100 and is joined afterwards by B with Rs. 3600. After how many months did B join, if the profits at the end of the year are divided equally?

Sol. Suppose B joined after x months. Then, B's money remained invested for $(12 - x)$ months.

$\therefore 2100 \times 12 = 3600 \times (12 - x)$

or $3600x = 43200 - 25200$ or $x = \dfrac{18000}{3600} = 5.$

So, B joined after 5 months.

Partnership

Exercise 9

1. Three partners A, B, C invest Rs. 26000, Rs. 34000 and Rs. 10000 respectively in a business. Out of a profit of Rs. 3500, B's share is :
   - (a) Rs. 1300
   - (b) Rs. 1700
   - (c) Rs. 500
   - (d) Rs. 1500

2. A's capital is equal to twice B's capital and B's capital is three times C's capital. The ratio of the capitals is :
   - (a) 2 : 1 : 3
   - (b) 1 : 2 : 6
   - (c) 6 : 3 : 1
   - (d) 1 : 3 : 6

3. If 6 (A's capital) = 8 (B's capital) = 10 (C's capial), then the ratio of their capitals is :
   - (a) 3 : 4 : 5
   - (b) 12 : 15 : 20
   - (c) 20 : 15 : 12
   - (d) 6 : 8 : 10

4. A, B and C are three partners in a business. If twice the investment of A is equal to thrice the capital of B and the capital of B is four times the capital of C. Out of a total profit of Rs. 5940, the share of C is :
   - (a) Rs. 700
   - (b) Rs. 900
   - (c) Rs. 740
   - (d) Rs. 540

5. Kanti started a business investing Rs. 9000. Five months later Sudhakar joined him by investing Rs. 8000. If they make a profit of Rs. 6970 at the end of year, Sudhakar's share of profit is :
   - (a) Rs. 3690
   - (b) Rs. 1883.78
   - (c) Rs. 2380
   - (d) Rs. 3864

6. Karim invests Rs. 30000 for one year in a shop. How much his partner Raunaq should invest in order that the profit after one year may be in the ratio 2 : 3 ?
   - (a) Rs. 20000
   - (b) Rs. 40000
   - (c) Rs. 45000
   - (d) Rs. 18000

7. A, B, C subscribe Rs. 47000 for a business. A subscribes Rs. 7000 more than B and B Rs. 5000 more than C. Out of a total profit of Rs. 9400, B receives :
   - (a) Rs. 4400
   - (b) Rs. 3000
   - (c) Rs. 2000
   - (d) Rs. 1737.90

8. Jayant started a business, investing Rs. 6000. Six months later Madhu joined him, investing Rs. 4000. If they made a profit of Rs. 5200 at the end of the year, how much must be the share of Madhu ?
   - (a) Rs. 2080
   - (b) Rs. 1300

(c) Rs. 1800 (d) Rs. 2600

(Bank P.O. 1991)

9. A and B entered into a partnership investing Rs. 16000 and Rs. 12000 respectively. After 3 months, A withdrew Rs. 5000 while B invested Rs. 5000 more. After 3 more months C joins the business with a capital of Rs. 21000. The share of B exceeds that of C, out of a total profit of Rs. 26400 after one year, by (Excise & I. Tax 1989)

(a) Rs. 1200 (b) Rs. 2400
(c) Rs. 3600 (d) Rs. 4800

10. Rs. 700 is divided among A, B and C so that A receives half as much as B and B half as much as C. Then C's share is : (C.B.I. 1991)

(a) Rs. 200 (b) Rs. 300
(c) Rs. 400 (d) Rs. 600

11. Manoj got Rs. 6000 as his share out of a total profit of Rs. 9000 which he and Ramesh earned at the end of one year. If Manoj invested Rs. 20000 for 6 months, whereas Ramesh invested his amount for the whole year, what was the amount invested by Ramesh ? (Bank P.O. 1991)

(a) Rs. 30000 (b) Rs. 40000
(c) Rs. 10000 (d) Rs. 5000

12. Dilip, Ram and Amar started a shop by investing Rs. 27000, Rs. 81000 and Rs. 72000 respectively. At the end of one year, the profit was distributed. If Ram's share of profit be Rs. 36000, the total profit was : (Bank Trainee Officers Exam 1988)

(a) Rs. 108000 (b) Rs. 116000
(c) Rs. 80000 (d) none of these

13. A and B enter into partnership, investing Rs. 12000 and Rs. 16000 respectively. After 8 months, C joins them with a capital of Rs. 15000. The share of C in a profit of Rs. 45600 after 2 years will be :

(a) Rs. 21200 (b) Rs. 19200
(c) Rs. 14400 (d) Rs. 12000

(Central Excise & I. Tax 1988)

14. A, B and C invest Rs. 2000, Rs. 3000 and Rs. 4000 in a business. After one year, A removed his money but B and C continued for one more year. If the net profit after 2 years be Rs. 3200, them A's share in the profit is : (Assistant Grade 1987)

(a) Rs. 1000 (b) Rs. 600
(c) Rs. 800 (d) Rs. 400

15. A, B and C enter into partnership. A invests some money at the begin-

Partnership

ning; B invests double the amount after 6 months and C invests thrice the amount after 8 months. If the annual profit be Rs. 18000, C's share is :

(a) Rs. 7500　　　　□　　(b) Rs. 7200　　□
(c) Rs. 6000　　　　□　　(d) Rs. 5750　　□

16. A and B enter into partnership. A invests Rs. 16000 for 8 months and B remains in the business for 4 months. Out of a total profit, B claims $\frac{2}{7}$ of the profit. B contributed :

(a) Rs. 11900　　　□　　(b) Rs. 10500　　□
(c) Rs. 13600　　　□　　(d) Rs. 12800　　□

17. A, B and C enter into partnership by making investments in the ratio 3 : 5 : 7. After a year, C invests another Rs. 337600 while A withdrew Rs. 45600. The ratio of investments then changes to 24 : 59 : 167. How much did A invest initially ?

(a) Rs. 45600　　　□　　(b) Rs. 96000　　□
(c) Rs. 141600　　 □　　(d) none of these　□
　　　　　　　　　　　　　　　　　　(L.I.C. A.A.O. 1988)

18. A and B started a joint firm. A's investment was thrice the investment of B and the period of his investment was two times the period of investment of B. If B got Rs. 4000 as profit, then their total profit is :

(a) Rs. 24000　　　□　　(b) Rs. 16000　　□
(c) Rs. 28000　　　□　　(d) Rs. 20000　　□
　　　　　　　　　　　　　　　　　　(Bank P.O. 1989)

19. A and B start a business with initial investments in the ratio 12 : 11 and their annual profits were in the ratio 4 : 1. If A invested the money for 11 months, B invested the money for :

(a) 3 months　　　　□　　(b) $3\frac{2}{3}$ months　□
(c) 4 months　　　　□　　(d) 6 months　　□

20. A, B, C enter into a partnership and their capitals are in the proportion of $\frac{1}{3} : \frac{1}{4} : \frac{1}{5}$. A withdraws half his capital at the end of 4 months. Out of a total annual profit of Rs. 847, A's share is :

(a) Rs. 252　　　　□　　(b) Rs. 280　　□
(c) Rs. 315　　　　□　　(d) Rs. 412　　□

21. In a partnership, A invests (1/6) of the capital for (1/6) of the time, B invests (1/3) of the capital for (1/3) of the ime and C, the rest of the capital for the whole time. Out of a profit of Rs. 4600, B's share

is :
- (a) Rs. 800
- (b) Rs. 1000
- (c) Rs. 650
- (d) Rs. 960

22. A, B and C start a business. A investes 3 times as much as B invests and B invests two-third of what C invests. Then, the ratio of capitals of A, B and C is :
- (a) 3 : 9 : 2
- (b) 6 : 10 : 15
- (c) 5 : 3 : 2
- (d) 6 : 2 : 3

23. Jagmohan, Rooplal and Pandeyji rented a video cassette for one week at a rent of Rs. 350. If they use it for 6 hours, 10 hours and 12 hours respectively, the rent to be paid by Pandeyji is :
- (a) Rs. 75
- (b) Rs. 125
- (c) Rs. 135
- (d) Rs. 150

24. Four milkmen rented a pasture. A grazed 18 cows for 4 months; B 25 cows for 2 months, C 28 cows for 5 months and D 21 cows for 3 months. If A's share of rent is Rs. 360, the total rent of the field is :
- (a) Rs. 1500
- (b) Rs. 1600
- (c) Rs. 1625
- (d) Rs. 1650

25. A is a working and B, a sleeping partner in a business. A puts in Rs. 12000 and B Rs. 20000. A receives 10% of the profits for managing, the rest being divided in proportion to their capitals. Out of a total profit of Rs. 9600, the money received by A is :
- (a) Rs. 3240
- (b) Rs. 4200
- (c) Rs. 3600
- (d) Rs. 4500

26. A, B, C enter into a partnership with shares in the ratio $\frac{7}{2} : \frac{4}{3} : \frac{6}{5}$. After 4 months, A increases his share by 50%. If the toal profit at the end of one year be Rs. 21600, then B's share in the profit is :
- (a) Rs. 2100
- (b) Rs. 2400
- (c) Rs. 3600
- (d) Rs. 4000

27. A, B and C contract a work for Rs. 550. Together A and B are to do $\frac{7}{11}$ of the work. The share of C should be :
- (a) Rs. $183\frac{1}{3}$
- (b) Rs. 200
- (c) Rs. 300
- (d) Rs. 400

28. A and B invest in a business in the ratio 3 : 2. If 5% of the total profit goes to charity and A's share is Rs. 855, total profit is :

Partnership

(a) Rs. 1576 (b) Rs. 1537.50
(c) Rs. 1500 (d) Rs. 1425

Answers (Exercise 9)

1. (b) 2. (c) 3. (c) 4. (d) 5. (c) 6. (c) 7. (b) 8. (b) 9. (c)
10. (c) 11. (d) 12. (c) 13. (d) 14. (d) 15. (c) 16. (d) 17. (c) 18. (c)
19. (a) 20. (b) 21. (a) 22. (d) 23. (d) 24. (c) 25. (b) 26. (d) 27. (b)
28. (c)

Solution (Exercise 9)

1. Ratio of shares of $A, B, C = 26000 : 34000 : 10000 = 13 : 17 : 5$.

   $\therefore$ B's share = Rs. $\left(3500 \times \dfrac{17}{35}\right)$ = Rs. 1700.

2. Let C's capital = Rs. x. Then, B's capital $3x$.
   and A's capital = Rs. $6x$.
   $\therefore$ Ratio of capitals of A, B and $C = 6x : 3x : x = 6 : 3 : 1$.

3. 6 (A's capital) = 8 (B's capital) = 10 (C's capital) = x.

   Then, A's capital = $\dfrac{x}{6}$, B's capital = $\dfrac{x}{8}$ and C's capital = $\dfrac{x}{10}$.

   $\therefore$ Ratio of capitals of A, B and $C = \dfrac{x}{6} : \dfrac{x}{8} : \dfrac{x}{10} = 20 : 15 : 12$.

4. Let C's capital = Rs. x. Then, B's capital = Rs. $4x$.
   2 (A's capital) = 3 (B's capital) = $12x$.
   So, A's capial = $6x$.
   $\therefore$ $A : B : C = 6x : 4x : x = 6 : 4 : 1$.

   C's share = Rs. $\left(5940 \times \dfrac{1}{11}\right)$ = Rs. 540.

5. Ratio of shares = $9000 \times 12 : 8000 \times 7 = 108 : 56 = 27 : 14$.

   $\therefore$ Sudhakar's share = Rs. $\left(6970 \times \dfrac{14}{41}\right)$ = Rs. 2380.

6. $\dfrac{30000}{x} = \dfrac{2}{3} \Rightarrow 2x = 90000$ or $x = 45000$.

7. Suppose C invests Rs. x.
   Then, B's investment = Rs. $(x + 5000)$.
   And, A's invesment = Rs. $(x + 12000)$.
   $\therefore$ $x + x + 5000 + x + 12000 = 47000$ or $x = 10000$.
   Thus, $A : B : C = 22000 : 15000 : 10000 = 22 : 15 : 10$.

∴ B's share = Rs. $\left(9400 \times \dfrac{15}{47}\right)$ = Rs. 3000.

8. Ratio of their shares = $6000 \times 12 : 4000 \times 6 = 3 : 1$.

   ∴ Madhu's share = Rs. $\left(5200 \times \dfrac{1}{4}\right)$ = Rs. 1300.

9. $A : B : C$ = Rs. $(16000 \times 3 + 11000 \times 9 : 12000 \times 3 + 17000 \times 9$
   $+ 21000 \times 6) = 7 : 9 : 6$

   ∴ (B's share) − (C's share) = Rs. $\left[\left(26400 \times \dfrac{9}{22}\right) - \left(26400 \times \dfrac{6}{22}\right)\right]$
   = Rs. $(10800 - 7200)$ = Rs. 3600.

10. Let C's share = Rs. x. Then, B's share = Rs. $\dfrac{x}{2}$.

    And, A's share = Rs. $\dfrac{x}{4}$.

    ∴ $A : B : C = \dfrac{x}{4} : \dfrac{x}{2} : x = 1 : 2 : 4$.

    Hence, C's share = Rs. $\left(700 \times \dfrac{4}{7}\right)$ = Rs. 400.

11. Let the amount invested by Ramesh = Rs. x.
    Then, $20000 \times 6 : 12x = 6000 : 3000$

    or $\dfrac{120000}{12x} = \dfrac{2}{1}$ or $x = 5000$.

12. Ratio of shares = $27000 : 81000 : 72000 = 3 : 9 : 8$.
    If Ram's share is Rs. 9, total profit = Rs. 20

    If Ram's share is Rs. 36000, total profit = Rs. $\left(\dfrac{20}{9} \times 36000\right)$
    = Rs. 80000.

13. Ratio of shares = $12000 \times 24 : 16000 \times 24 : 15000 \times 16 = 6 : 8 : 5$.

    ∴ C's share = Rs. $\left(45600 \times \dfrac{5}{19}\right)$ = Rs. 12000.

14. $A : B : C = 2000 \times 12 : 3000 \times 24 : 4000 \times 24 = 1 : 3 : 4$.

    A's share = Rs. $\left(3200 \times \dfrac{1}{8}\right)$ = Rs. 400.

15. Suppose A invested Rs. x.
    Then, $A : B : C = 12x : 6 \times (2x) : 4 \times (3x) = 1 : 1 : 1$.

    ∴ C's share = Rs. $\left(18000 \times \dfrac{1}{3}\right)$ = Rs. 6000.

Partnership 171

16. Ratio of profits of A and $B = \dfrac{5}{7} : \dfrac{2}{7} = 5 : 2$.

   $\dfrac{16000 \times 8}{x \times 4} = \dfrac{5}{2}$ or $20x = 256000$ or $x = 12800$.

   So, B contributed Rs. 12800.

17. Let initial investments be $3x, 5x$ and $7x$ rupees.

   $(3x - 45600) : 5x : (7x + 337600) = 24 : 59 : 167$.

   $\therefore \dfrac{3x - 45600}{5x} = \dfrac{24}{59}$ or $x = 47200$.

   $\therefore$ Initial investment of A = Rs. (47200×3) = Rs. 141600.

18. Suppose B invested Rs. x for y months.
   Then, A's investment is Rs. $3x$ for $2y$ months.
   Ratio of investments of A and $B = 6xy : xy = 6 : 1$.
   Now, B's share = Rs. 4000.
   $\therefore$ A's share = Rs. 24000.
   Hence, total profit = Rs. 28000.

19. Suppose B invesed the money for x months.
   Then, the ratio of investments = $(12 \times 11 : 11x) = 12 : x$

   $\therefore \dfrac{12}{x} = \dfrac{4}{1}$ or $x = 3$ months.

20. Ratio of capitals in the beginning = $\dfrac{1}{3} : \dfrac{1}{4} : \dfrac{1}{5} = 20 : 15 : 12$.

   Ratio of investments for the whole year
   $= (20 \times 4 + 10 \times 8) : (15 \times 12) : (12 \times 12) = 40 : 45 : 36$.

   $\therefore$ A's share = Rs. $\left(847 \times \dfrac{40}{121}\right)$ = Rs. 280.

21. Suppose A invests Rs. $\dfrac{x}{6}$ for $\dfrac{y}{6}$ months; B invests Rs. $\dfrac{x}{3}$ for $\dfrac{y}{3}$ months

   and C invests Rs. $\left[x - \left(\dfrac{x}{6} + \dfrac{x}{3}\right)\right]$ for y months.

   Ratio of their investments = $\left(\dfrac{x}{6} \times \dfrac{y}{6}\right) : \left(\dfrac{x}{3} \times \dfrac{y}{3}\right) : \left(\dfrac{x}{2} \times y\right)$.

   $= \dfrac{1}{36} : \dfrac{1}{9} : \dfrac{1}{2} = 1 : 4 : 18$.

   $\therefore$ B's share = Rs. $\left(4600 \times \dfrac{4}{23}\right)$ = Rs. 800.

22. Suppose C invests Rs. x. Then, B invests Rs. $\left(\dfrac{2x}{3}\right)$ and A invests

Rs. (2 x).

∴ Ratio of investments of $A, B, C = 2x : \frac{2}{3}x : 2x$ or $6 : 2 : 3$.

23. Ratio of rents $= 6 : 10 : 12 = 3 : 5 : 6$.

∴ Pandeyji has to pay $=$ Rs. $\left(350 \times \frac{6}{12}\right) =$ Rs. 150.

24. Ratio of rents $= (18 \times 4 : 25 \times 2 : 28 \times 5 : 21 \times 3)$
$= 72 : 50 : 140 : 63$.

Let, total rent $=$ Rs. x.

Then, A's share $=$ Rs. $\left(x \times \frac{72}{325}\right) =$ Rs. $\left(\frac{72x}{325}\right)$.

∴ $\frac{72x}{325} = 360$ or $x = \left(\frac{325 \times 360}{72}\right) = 1625$.

25. For management, A receives $=$ Rs. 960.

Balance $=$ Rs. $(9600 - 960) =$ Rs. 8640.

Ratio of their investments $= 12000 : 20000 = 3 : 5$.

∴ A's share $=$ Rs. $\left(8640 \times \frac{3}{8}\right) =$ Rs. 3240.

So, A receives $=$ Rs. $(3240 + 960) =$ Rs. 4200.

26. Given Ratio $= \frac{7}{2} : \frac{4}{3} : \frac{6}{5} = 105 : 40 : 36$.

Let them initially invest Rs. 105, Rs. 40 and Rs. 36 respectively.

Ratio of investments
$= [105 \times 4 + (150\% \text{ of } 105) \times 8] : (40 \times 12) : (36 \times 12)$
$= 1680 : 480 : 432 = 35 : 10 : 9$.

∴ B's share $=$ Rs. $\left(21600 \times \frac{10}{54}\right) =$ Rs. 4000.

27. C's share $=$ Rs. $\left(550 \times \frac{4}{11}\right) =$ Rs. 200.

28. Let the total profit be Rs. 100.

After paying to charity, A's share $=$ Rs. $\left(95 \times \frac{3}{5}\right) =$ Rs. 57.

If A's share is Rs. 57, total profit $=$ Rs. 100

If A's share is Rs. 855, total profit $=$ Rs. $\left(855 \times \frac{100}{57}\right) =$ Rs. 1500.

10
PROFIT & LOSS

Cost Price (written as C.P.) : *The price at which an article is purchased is called the cost price of the article.*

Selling Price (Written as S.P.) : *The price at which an article is sold is called the selling price of the article.*

Profit or Gain : *If S.P. is greater than the cost price, the seller is said to have a profit or gain.*

Clearly, **Gain** = *(S.P.) − (C.P.)*.

Loss : *If S.P. is less than the cost price, the seller is said to have a loss.*

Clearly, **Loss** = *(C.P.) − (S.P.)*.

Remarks :
   (i) Loss or gain are always reckoned on cost price.
   (ii) Gain on Rs. 100 is **Gain percent**.
   (iii) Loss on Rs. 100 is **Loss percent**.

Formulae :
   (i) Gain = (S.P.) − (C.P.).
   (ii) Loss = (C.P.) − (S.P.).
   (iii) Gain % = $\left(\dfrac{\text{Gain} \times 100}{C.P.}\right)$.
   (iv) Loss % = $\left(\dfrac{\text{Loss} \times 100}{C.P.}\right)$.
   (v) S.P. = $\left(\dfrac{100 + \text{Gain \%}}{100}\right) \times$ (C.P.).
   (vi) S.P. = $\left(\dfrac{100 - \text{Loss \%}}{100}\right) \times$ (C.P.).
   (vii) C.P. = $\left(\dfrac{100}{100 + \text{Gain \%}}\right) \times$ (S.P.).
   (viii) C.P. = $\left(\dfrac{100}{100 - \text{Loss \%}}\right) \times$ (S.P.).
   (ix) If an article is sold at a gain of 20%, then S.P. = (120% of C.P.).
   (x) If an article is sold at a loss of 20%, then S.P. = (80% of C.P.).

SOLVED PROBLEMS

Ex. 1. Find gain or loss percent, when :
(i) C.P. = Rs. 9.50 and S.P. = Rs. 11.40.
(ii) C.P. = Rs. 10.20 and S.P. = Rs. 8.50.

Sol. (i) C.P. = Rs. 9.50, S.P. = Rs. 11.40.

∴ Gain = Rs. (11.40 − 9.50) = Rs. 1.90.

Hence, gain % = $\left(\dfrac{1.90}{9.50} \times 100\right)$ % = 20%.

(ii) C.P. = Rs. 10.20, S.P. = Rs. 8.50.

∴ Loss = Rs. (10.20 − 8.50) = Rs. 1.70.

Hence, Loss % = $\left(\dfrac{1.70}{10.20} \times 100\right)$ % = $16\dfrac{2}{3}$ %.

Ex. 2. Find S.P., when :
(i) C.P. = Rs. 56.25, gain = 20%.
(ii) C.P. = Rs. 40.20, loss = 15%.

Sol. (i) C.P. = 56.25, gain = 20%.

∴ S.P. = 120% of Rs. 56.25 = Rs. $\left(\dfrac{120}{100} \times 56.25\right)$ = Rs. 67.50.

(ii) C.P. = Rs. 40.20, loss = 15%.

∴ S.P. = 85% of Rs. 40.20 = Rs. $\left(\dfrac{85}{100} \times 40.20\right)$ = Rs. 34.17.

Ex. 3. Find C.P., when :
(i) S.P. = Rs. 517, gain = 10%.
(ii) S.P. = Rs. 585, loss = 10%.

Sol. (i) S.P. = Rs. 517, gain = 10%.

∴ C.P. = $\left(\dfrac{100}{100 + \text{gain \%}}\right) \times$ (S.P.)

= Rs. $\left(\dfrac{100}{110} \times 517\right)$

= Rs. 470.

(ii) S.P. = Rs. 585, loss = 10%.

∴ C.P. = $\left(\dfrac{100}{100 - \text{loss \%}}\right) \times$ (S.P.) = Rs. $\left(\dfrac{100}{90} \times 585\right)$

= Rs. 650.

Ex. 4. By selling a watch for Rs. 144, a man loses 10%. At what price should he sell it to gain 10% ?

Sol. Let the new S.P. be Rs. x. Then,

(S.P. with C.P. as Rs. 100) : (Actual S.P.)

Profit & Loss   175

$= $ (New S.P. with C.P. as Rs. 100) : (New S.P.)

$\therefore$ 90 : 144 = 110 : x or $90 \times x = 144 \times 110$.

or $x = \dfrac{144 \times 110}{90} = 176$.

Hence, the S.P. should be Rs. 176.

Ex. 5. Gurdeep lost 20% by selling a bicycle for Rs. 1536. What per cent shall he gain or lose by selling it for Rs. 2000 ?

Sol. S.P. = Rs. 1536, Loss = 20%.

$\therefore$ C.P. = Rs. $\left(\dfrac{100}{80} \times 1536\right)$ = Rs. 1920.

New S.P. = Rs. 2000.

Gain = Rs. (2000 − 1920) = Rs. 80.

$\therefore$ Gain % = $\left(\dfrac{80}{1920} \times 100\right)\% = 4\dfrac{1}{6}\%$.

Ex. 6. A man sold two houses for Rs. 375890 each. On one he gains 15% and on the other he loses 15%. How much does he gain or lose in the whole transaction ?

Sol. *In such a type of questions, there is always a loss. The S. P. is immaterial.*

We use the formula : Loss % = $\left(\dfrac{\text{Common loss and gain \%}}{10}\right)^2$.

$\therefore$ Loss % = $\left(\dfrac{15}{10}\right)^2 = \dfrac{9}{4} = 2.25\%$.

Ex. 7. A man sells an article at a profit of 20%. If he had bought it at 20% less and sold it for Rs. 5 less, he would have gained 25%. Find the cost price of the article.

Sol. Let the original C.P. be Rs. x.

Then, first S.P. = (120% of x) = Rs. $\dfrac{6x}{5}$.

New C.P. = 80% of x = Rs. $\dfrac{4x}{5}$.

New S.P. = 125% of $\dfrac{4x}{5} = x$. $\therefore \dfrac{6x}{5} - x = 5$ or $x = 25$.

Hence, the cost price of the article = Rs. 25.

Ex. 8. A sells an article to B at a gain of 20% and B sells it to C at a gain of 10% and C sells it to D at a gain of $12\frac{1}{2}$%. If D pays Rs. 29.70, what did it cost A ?

Sol. Let C.P. of A be Rs. 100. Then, C.P. of B = Rs. 120.

C.P. of C = (110% of Rs. 120) = Rs. 132.

C.P. of D = ($112\frac{1}{2}$% of Rs. 132) = Rs. $\frac{297}{2}$.

Now, less is the C.P. of D, less is the C.P. of A.

$\therefore \frac{297}{2} : 29.70 = 100 : x$

$\therefore x = \left(\frac{29.70 \times 100}{297} \times 2\right)$ = Rs. 20.

Hence, the article was purchased by A for Rs. 20.

Ex. 9. A reduction of 20% in the price of sugar enables a purchaser to obtain 4 kg more for Rs. 160. What is the reduced price per kg ? Also, find the original rate.

Sol. Let original rate = Rs. x per kg.

Quantity of sugar purchased = Rs. $\left(\frac{160}{x}\right)$.

New rate = 80% of Rs. x = Rs. $\left(\frac{4x}{5}\right)$ per kg.

Quantity purchased = $\left(\frac{160 \times 5}{4x}\right) = \left(\frac{200}{x}\right)$ kg.

$\therefore \frac{200}{x} - \frac{160}{x} = 4$ or $x = 10$.

So, original rate = Rs. 10 per kg.

Reduced rate = Rs. $\left(\frac{4x}{5}\right)$ per kg = Rs. $\left(\frac{4 \times 10}{5}\right)$ per kg = Rs. 8 per kg.

Ex. 10. A dishonest dealer professes to sell his goods at cost price, but uses a weight of 960 gms for a kg weight. Find his gain per cent.

Sol. Formula : $Gain\ \% = \left[\frac{Error}{(True\ value) - (Error)} \times 100\right]\%$

$\therefore Gain\ \% = \left(\frac{40}{960} \times 100\right)\% = 4\frac{1}{6}\%.$

Profit & Loss

Ex. 11. A grocer purchased 80 kg of rice at Rs. 13.50 per kg and mixed it with 120 kg available at Rs. 16 per kg. At what rate per kg should he sell the mixture to have a gain of 20% ?

Sol. C.P. of 200 kg = Rs. $(80 \times 13.50 + 120 \times 16)$ = Rs. 3000

S.P. of 200 kg = 120% of Rs. 3000 = Rs. $\left(\dfrac{120}{100} \times 3000\right)$

= Rs. 3600

$\therefore$ Rate of S.P. of the mix. = Rs. $\left(\dfrac{3600}{200}\right)$ per kg = Rs. 18 per kg.

Ex. 12. A man sold an article for Rs. 161, gaining $\dfrac{1}{6}$th of his outlay; find the cost price of the article.

Sol. Let C.P. = Rs. x. Then, gain = Rs. $\dfrac{x}{6}$.

$\therefore$ S.P. = Rs. $\left(x + \dfrac{x}{6}\right)$ = Rs. $\dfrac{7x}{6}$.

$\therefore \dfrac{7x}{6} = 161 \Rightarrow x = \dfrac{161 \times 6}{7} = 138.$

Hence, C.P. = Rs. 138.

Ex. 13. 2 chairs and 1 table cost Rs. 640, while 1 chair and 2 tables cost Rs. 740. Find the cost of each.

Sol. Let the cost of 1 chair = Rs. x and the cost of 1 table = Rs. y

Then, $2x + y = 640$ .... (i)

$x + 2y = 740$ .... (ii)

Solving (i) and (ii), we get : $x = 180$ and $y = 280$.

$\therefore$ Cost of 1 chair = Rs. 180 and cost of 1 table = Rs. 280.

Ex. 14. If the S.P. of 10 articles is the same as C.P. of 12 articles, find gain per cent.

Sol. Let C.P. of each article = Re. 1.

C.P. of 10 articles = Rs. 10.

S.P. of 10 articles = C.P. of 12 articles = Rs. 12.

$\therefore$ Gain = Rs. $(12 - 10)$ = Rs. 2.

So, gain % = $\left(\dfrac{2}{10} \times 100\right)$ % = 20%.

Ex. 15. By selling 100 pens, a shopkeeper gains the S.P. of 20 pens. Find his gain per cent.

Sol. Gain = (S.P. of 100 pens) − (C.P. of 100 pens).

∴ (S.P. of 20 pens) = (S.P. of 100 pens) − (C.P. of 100 pens)

So, S.P. of 80 pens = C.P. of 100 pens.

Let C.P. of each pen = Re. 1.

C.P. of 80 pens = Rs. 80.

S.P. of 80 pens = C.P. of 100 pens = Rs. 100.

∴ Gain % = $\left(\dfrac{20}{80} \times 100\right)$ % = 25%.

Ex. 16. A vendor sells 5 lemons for a rupee, gaining thereby 40%. How many did he buy for a rupee ?

Sol. S.P. of 5 lemons = Re. 1, gain = 40%.

∴ C.P. of 5 lemons = Re. $\left(1 \times \dfrac{100}{140}\right)$ = Re. $\dfrac{5}{7}$.

Re. $\dfrac{5}{7}$ yield 5 lemons; Re. 1 yields = $\left(5 \times \dfrac{7}{5}\right)$ = 7 lemons.

Thus, he bought 7 lemons for a rupee.

Ex. 17. A vendor bought toffees at 6 for a rupee. How many for a rupee must he sell to gain 20% ?

Sol. C.P. of 6 toffees = Re. 1, Gain = 20%.

∴ S.P. of 6 toffees = Rs. $\left(\dfrac{120}{100} \times 1\right)$ = Rs. $\dfrac{6}{5}$.

Rs. $\dfrac{6}{5}$ is the S.P. of 6 toffees.

Re. 1 is the S.P. of $\left(6 \times \dfrac{5}{6}\right)$ = 5 toffees.

Ex. 18. A vendor bought a number of bananas at 3 for a rupee and sold them at 2 for a rupee. Find his gain per cent.

Sol. Suppose he bought 6 bananas (l.c.m. of 3 and 2).

Then, C.P. of 6 bananas = Rs. $\left(\dfrac{1}{3} \times 6\right)$ = Rs. 2.

S.P. of 6 bananas = Rs. $\left(\dfrac{1}{2} \times 6\right)$ = Rs. 3.

Profit & Loss 179

∴ Gain % = $\left(\dfrac{1}{2} \times 100\right)$ % = 50%.

PROBLEMS ON DISCOUNT

Ex. 19. A radio dealer marks a radio with a price which is 20% more than the cost price and allows a discount of 10% on it. Find the gain per cent.

Sol. Let C.P. = Rs. 100.

Marked price = Rs. 120; Discount = 10%

S.P. = 90% of Rs. 120 = Rs. 108.

∴ Gain = (108 − 100)% = 8%.

Ex. 20. A tradesman allows a discount of 15% on the written price. How much above the C.P. must he mark his goods to gain 19%?

Sol. Let C.P. = Rs. 100. Gain required = 19%.

∴ S.P. must be = Rs. 119.

Now, 85% of marked price = Rs. 119.

∴ $\dfrac{85}{100} \times x = 119$ or $x = \dfrac{119 \times 100}{85} = 140$.

∴ Marked price = Rs. 140.

So, the trader must mark his goods 40% above cost price.

Ex. 21. A tradesman marks his goods at such a price that after allowing a discount of 15%, he makes a profit of 20%. Find the marked price of an article which costs him Rs. 850.

Sol. C.P. = Rs. 850, Gain = 20%.

∴ S.P. = Rs. $\left(\dfrac{120}{100} \times 850\right)$ = Rs. 1020.

Now, 85% of marked price = Rs. 1020.

∴ $\dfrac{85}{100} \times x = 1020$ or $x = \dfrac{1020 \times 100}{85} = 1200$.

Hence, the marked price = Rs. 1200.

Ex. 22. If a commission of 10% is given on the written price of an article, the gain is 20%. Find the gain percent, if the commission is increased to 20%.

Sol. Let marked price = Rs. 100. Then, commission = Rs. 10.

∴ S.P. = Rs. (100 − 10) = Rs. 90.

But, gain = 20%.

$\therefore$ C.P. = $\left(\dfrac{100}{120} \times 90\right)$ = Rs. 75.

New commission = Rs. 20.

S.P. in 2nd case = Rs. (100 − 20) = Rs. 80.

$\therefore$ Gain % = $\left(\dfrac{5}{75} \times 100\right)$ % = $6\dfrac{2}{3}$ %.

Ex. 23. Find the single discount equivalent to a series discount of 20%, 10% and 5%.

Sol. Let marked price = Rs. 100. S.P. after 1st discount = Rs. 80.

S.P. after 2nd discount = 90% of Rs. 80 = Rs. 72.

S.P. after 3rd discount = 95% of Rs. 72 = Rs. 68.40.

$\therefore$ Single Discount = (100 − 68.40) = 31.6%.

EXercise 10

1. By selling an article for Rs. 100, one gains Rs. 10. Then, the gain per cent is :
   - (a) 9%
   - (b) 10%
   - (c) $11\dfrac{1}{9}$%
   - (d) none of these.

2. By selling an article for Rs. 100, one loses Rs. 10. Then, the loss per cent is :
   - (a) $11\dfrac{1}{9}$%
   - (b) $9\dfrac{1}{11}$%
   - (c) 10%
   - (d) none of these

3. A man sold a radio for Rs 1980 and gained 10%. The radio was bought for :
   - (a) Rs. 1782
   - (b) Rs. 1800
   - (c) Rs. 2178
   - (d) none of these

4. By selling an article for Rs 247.50, we get a profit of $12\dfrac{1}{2}$%. The cost of the article is : (Clerical Grade, 1991)
   - (a) Rs. 210
   - (b) Rs. 220
   - (c) Rs. 224
   - (d) Rs. 225

5. What is the cost price of an article which is sold at a loss of 25% for Rs. 150 ? (R.R.B. Exam, 1991)

Profit & Loss 181

    (a) Rs. 125 ☐   (b) Rs. 175 ☐
    (c) Rs. 200 ☐   (d) Rs. 225 ☐

6. A man buys 10 articles for Rs. 8 and sells them at the rate of Rs. 1.25 per article. His gain is :   **(R.R.B. Exam, 1991)**
    (a) 20% ☐   (b) 50% ☐
    (c) $19\frac{1}{2}\%$ ☐   (d) $56\frac{1}{4}\%$ ☐

7. By selling a watch for Rs. 1140, a man loses 5%. In order to gain 5%, the watch must be sold for
    (a) Rs. 1311 ☐   (b) Rs. 1197 ☐
    (c) Rs. 1254 ☐   (d) Rs. 1260 ☐

8. There would be 10% loss if a toy is sold at Rs. 10.80 per piece. At what price should it be sold to earn a profit of 20% ?
    (a) Rs. 12 ☐   (b) Rs. 12.96 ☐
    (c) Rs. 14.40 ☐   (d) none of these ☐
    (Bank P.O., 1991)

9. There would be 10% loss if rice is sold at Rs. 5.40 per kg. At what price per kg should it be sold to earn a profit of 20 %.?
    (a) Rs. 6 ☐   (b) Rs. 6.48 ☐
    (c) Rs. 7.02 ☐   (d) Rs. 7.20 ☐
    (S.B.I. P.O. Exam, 1988)

10. The selling price of 12 articles is equal to the cost price of 15 articles. The gain per cent is :
    (a) $6\frac{2}{3}\%$ ☐   (b) 20% ☐
    (c) 25% ☐   (d) 80% ☐

11. A man sells 320 mangoes at the cost price of 400 mangoes. His gain per cent is :   **(Astt Grade Exam, 1987)**
    (a) 10% ☐   (b) 15% ☐
    (c) 20% ☐   (d) 25% ☐

12. If the cost price of 15 tables be equal to the selling price of 20 tables, the loss per cent is :
    (a) 20% ☐   (b) 30% ☐
    (c) 25% ☐   (d) 37.5% ☐

13. If the selling price of 40 articles is equal to the C.P. of 50 articles, the loss or gain per cent is :
    (a) 25% loss ☐   (b) 20% loss ☐
    (c) 25% gain ☐   (d) 20% gain ☐

14. If books bought at prices ranging from Rs. 200 to Rs. 350 are sold at prices ranging from Rs. 300 to Rs. 425, what is the greatest possible profit that might be made in selling 8 books ? (S.B.I. P.O. Exam, 1988)
    (a) Rs. 400 ☐ (b) Rs. 600 ☐
    (c) cannot be determined ☐ (d) none of these ☐

15. A fruitseller buys lemons at 2 for a rupee and sells them at five for three rupees. His gain per cent is :
    (a) 10% ☐ (b) 15% ☐
    (c) 20% ☐ (d) none of these ☐

16. If I purchased 11 books for Rs. 10 and sold all the books at the rate of 10 books for Rs. 11, the profit per cent is : (R.R.B. Exam, 1989)
    (a) 10% ☐ (b) 11% ☐
    (c) 21% ☐ (d) 100% ☐

17. By selling 8 dozen of pencils, a shopkeeper gains the selling price of 1 dozen pencils. His gain per cent is :
    (a) 12.5% ☐ (b) 87.5% ☐
    (c) $14\frac{2}{7}$ % ☐ (d) none of these ☐

18. By selling 100 bananas, a fruitseller gains the selling price of 20 bananas. His gain per cent is :
    (a) 10% ☐ (b) 15% ☐
    (c) 20% ☐ (d) 25% ☐

19. By selling 36 oranges, a vendor loses the selling price of 4 oranges. His loss per cent is :
    (a) $12\frac{1}{2}$ % ☐ (b) $11\frac{1}{9}$ % ☐
    (c) 10% ☐ (d) none of these ☐

20. A man purchased a watch for Rs. 400 and sold it at a gain of 20% of the selling price. The selling price of the watch is :
    (a) Rs. 300 ☐ (b) Rs. 320 ☐
    (c) Rs. 440 ☐ (d) Rs. 500 ☐
    (Clerk's Grade Exam, 1990)

21. By selling a book for Rs. 10, the publisher loses (1/11) of what it costs him. His cost price is :
    (a) Rs. 9 ☐ (b) Rs. 10 ☐
    (c) Rs. 11 ☐ (d) Rs. 12 ☐

22. The cost of 2 T.V. sets and a radio is Rs. 7000, while 2 radios and one T.V. set together cost Rs. 4250. The cost of a T.V. set is :

Profit & Loss 183

　　(a) Rs. 3000　☐　　(b) Rs. 3160　☐
　　(c) Rs. 3240　☐　　(d) none of these　☐

23. By selling an article for Rs. 144, a man loses $\frac{1}{7}$ of his outlay. By selling it for Rs. 168, his gain or loss per cent is :
　　(a) 20% loss　☐　　(b) 20% gain　☐
　　(c) $4\frac{1}{6}$ % gain　☐　　(d) none of these　☐

24. The C.P. of an article is 40% of the S.P. The per cent that the S.P. is of C.P. is :　　**(C.B.I. Exam, 1990)**
　　(a) 40　☐　　(b) 60　☐
　　(c) 240　☐　　(d) 250　☐

25. A shopkeeper mixes two varieties of tea, one costing Rs. 35 per kg and another at Rs. 45 per kg in the ratio 3 : 2. If he sells the mixed variety at Rs. 41.60 per kg, his gain or loss per cent is :
　　(a) $6\frac{2}{3}$ % gain　☐　　(b) $6\frac{2}{3}$ % loss　☐
　　(c) 4% gain　☐　　(d) 4% loss　☐

26. Aloke bought 25 kg of rice at the rate of Rs. 6 per kg and 35 kg of rice at the rate of Rs. 7 per kg. He mixed the two and sold the mixture at the rate of Rs. 6.75 per kg. What was his gain or loss in the transaction ?　　**(A.O. Exam, 1990)**
　　(a) Rs. 16 gain　☐　　(b) Rs. 16 loss　☐
　　(c) Rs. 20 gain　☐　　(d) none of these　☐

27. A man sold 20 articles for Rs. 60 and gained 20%. How many articles did he buy for Rs. 60 ?　　**(R.R.B. Exam : 1991)**
　　(a) 22　☐　　(b) 24　☐
　　(c) 25　☐　　(d) 26　☐

28. A dealer professing to sell at cost price, uses a 900 gms weight for a kilogram. His gain per cent is :　　**(R.R.B. Exam, 1991)**
　　(a) 9　☐　　(b) 10　☐
　　(c) 11　☐　　(d) $11\frac{1}{9}$　☐

29. A dishonest dealer professes to sell his goods at cost price. But he uses a false weight and thus gains $6\frac{18}{47}$ %. For a kg, he uses a weight of :
　　(a) 953 gms　☐　　(b) 940 gms　☐
　　(c) 960 gms　☐　　(d) 947 gms　☐

30. Toffees are bought at the rate of 8 for a rupee. To gain 60%, they must be sold at :
    (a) 6 for a rupee   (b) 5 for a rupee
    (c) 9 for Rs. 2   (d) 24 for Rs. 5

31. By selling 12 oranges for one rupee, a man loses 20%. How many for a rupee should he sell to get a gain of 20% ? (C.D.S. Exam, 1989)
    (a) 5   (b) 8
    (c) 10   (d) 15

32. By selling toffees at 20 for a rupee, a man loses 4%. To gain 20%, for one rupee he must sell (Clerical Grade, 1991)
    (a) 16 toffees   (b) 20 toffees
    (c) 25 toffees   (d) 24 toffees

33. Jimmy bought paper sheets for Rs. 7200 and spent Rs. 200 on transport. Paying Rs. 600 he had 330 boxes made, which he sold at Rs. 28 each. What is his profit percentage ? (Bank P.O. Exam, 1991)
    (a) 15.5   (b) 40
    (c) 60   (d) none of these

34. Ram bought 4 dozen apples at Rs. 12 per dozen and 2 dozen apples at Rs. 16 per dozen. He sold all of them to earn 20%. At what price per dozen did he sell the apples ? (Bank P.O. Exam, 1991)
    (a) Rs. 14.40   (b) Rs. 16.00
    (c) Rs. 16.80   (d) Rs. 19.20

35. A sold a watch at a gain of 5% to B and B sold it to C at a gain of 4%. If C paid Rs. 91 for it, then the price paid by A is :
    (a) Rs. 82.81   (b) Rs. 83
    (c) Rs. 83.33   (d) none of these

36. A owns a house worth Rs. 10000. He sells it to B at a profit of 10% based on the worth of the house. B sells the house back to A at a loss of 10%. In this transaction A gets (C.B.I. Exam, 1990)
    (a) no profit no loss   (b) profit of Rs. 1000
    (c) profit of Rs. 1100   (d) profit of Rs. 2000

37. When the price of a toy was increased by 30%, the number of toys sold fell by 30%. What is the effect on the sale of the shop ?
    (a) no effect   (b) 9% increase
    (c) 9% decrease   (d) 7% decrease

38. When the price of a toy was increased by 20%, the number of toys sold was decreased by 15% what was the effect on the sales of the shop ? (P.O. Exam, 1990)

Profit & Loss 185

(a) 4% increase (b) 4% decrease
(c) 2% increase (d) 2% decrease

39. When the price of fans was reduced by 20%, the number of fans sold increased by 40%. What was the effect on the sales in rupees ?

(a) 12% increase (b) 12% decrease
(c) 30% increase (d) 40% increase
                                      (Bank P.O. Exam, 1991)

40. An article is sold at a certain price. By selling it at $\frac{2}{3}$ of that price, one loses 10%. The gain per cent at original price is :

(a) 20% (b) $33\frac{1}{3}$%
(c) 35% (d) 40%

41. A dealer sold two T.V. sets for Rs. 3700 each. On one he gained 10% and on the other he lost 10%. The dealer's loss or gain per cent is :

(a) 0% (b) 0.1% loss
(c) 1% gain (d) 1% loss

42. A man sold two houses for Rs. 7.81 lakhs each. On one he gained 5% and on the other he lost 5%. What per cent is the effect of the sale on the whole ? (R.R.B. Exam, 1991)

(a) 0.25% loss (b) 0.25% gain
(c) 25% loss (d) 25% gain

43. A horse and a cow were sold for Rs. 12000 each. The horse was sold at a loss of 20% and the cow at a gain of 20%. The entire transaction resulted in (C.B.I. Exam, 1991)

(a) no loss or gain (b) loss of Rs. 1000
(c) gain of Rs. 1000 (d) gain of Rs. 2000

44. By selling an article for Rs. 144, a man gained such that the percentage gain equals the cost price. The C.P. of the article is :

(a) Rs. 60 (b) Rs. 64
(c) Rs. 72 (d) Rs. 80

45. A merchant sold his goods for Rs. 75 at a profit per cent equal to C.P. The C.P. was : (Clerical Grade, 1991)

(a) Rs. 40 (b) Rs. 50
(c) Rs. 60 (d) Rs. 70

46. Profit after selling a commodity for Rs. 425 is same as loss after selling it for Rs. 355. The cost of the commodity is : (Bank P.O. Exam, 1989)

(a) Rs. 385 (b) Rs. 390

(c) Rs. 395   (d) Rs. 400

47. By selling 45 oranges for Rs. 40, a man loses 20%. How many should he sell for Rs. 24 so as to gain 20% in the transaction ?
    (a) 16   (b) 18
    (c) 20   (d) 22

48. If two mixers and one T.V. cost Rs. 7000, while two T.V.s and one mixer cost Rs. 9800, the value of one T.V. is :
    (a) Rs. 2800   (b) Rs. 2100
    (c) Rs. 4200   (d) Rs. 8400
    (S.B.I. P.O. Exam, 1987)

49. Bhajan Singh purchased 120 reams of paper at Rs. 80 per ream. He spent Rs. 280 on transportation, paid octroi at the rate of 40 paise per ream and paid Rs. 72 to the coolie. If he wants to have a gain of 8%, what must be the selling price per ream ?   (Bank P.O. Exam, 1988)
    (a) Rs. 86   (b) Rs. 87.48
    (c) Rs. 89   (d) Rs. 90

50. A man sells a car to his friend at 10% loss. If the friend sells it for Rs. 54000 and gains 20%, the original C.P. of the car was :
    (a) Rs. 25000   (b) Rs. 37500
    (c) Rs. 50000   (d) Rs. 60000
    (S.S.C. Exam, 1987)

51. A shopkeeper sells (3/4)th of its articles at a gain of 20% and the remaining at C.P. His real gain in the transaction is :
    (a) 10%   (b) 15%
    (c) 20%   (d) 25%

52. A man purchased sugar worth of Rs. 400. He sold (3/4)th at a loss of 10% and the remainder at a gain of 10%. On the whole, he gets :
    (a) a loss of 5%   (b) a gain of $5\frac{1}{2}$ %
    (c) a loss of $5\frac{1}{19}$ %   (d) a loss of $5\frac{5}{19}$ %

53. If an article is sold at a gain of 6% instead of at a loss of 6% then the seller gets Rs. 6 more. The C.P. of the article is :
    (a) Rs. 50   (b) Rs. 94
    (c) Rs. 100   (d) Rs. 106

54. The cost price of an article, which on being sold at a gain of 12% yields Rs. 6 more than when it is sold at a loss of 12%, is :
    (a) Rs. 30   (b) Rs. 25

(c) Rs. 24   (d) Rs. 20

(C.B.I. Exam, 1990)

55. A man gains 10% by selling an article for a certain price. If he sells it at double the price, the profit made is :

(a) 20%   (b) 60%
(c) 100%   (d) 120%

56. A dealer sells a radio at a gain of 10%. If he had bought it at 10% less and sold it for Rs. 132 less, he would have still gained 10%. The C.P. of the radio is :

(a) Rs. 1188   (b) Rs. 1200
(c) Rs. 1320   (d) none of these

57. A person bought an article and sold it at a loss of 10%. If he had bought it for 20% less and sold it for Rs. 55 more, he would have had a profit of 40%. The C.P. of the article is : (Central Excise & I. Tax, 1988)

(a) Rs. 200   (b) Rs. 225
(c) Rs. 250   (d) none of these

58. A man sells two horses for Rs. 4000 each, neither losing nor gaining in the deal. If he sold one horse at a gain of 25%, the other horse is sold at a loss of :

(a) $16\frac{2}{3}$%   (b) $18\frac{2}{9}$%
(c) 25%   (d) none of these

59. A grocer sells rice at a profit of 10% and uses weights which are 20% less than the market weight. The total gain earned by him will be :

(a) 30%   (b) 35%
(c) 37.5%   (d) none of these

60. A man sold an article for Rs. 75 and lost something. Had he sold it for Rs. 96, his gain would have been double the former loss. The C.P. of the article is :

(a) Rs. 81   (b) Rs. 82
(c) Rs. 83   (d) Rs. 85.5

61. A bicycle is sold at a gain of 16%. If it had been sold for Rs. 20 more, 20% would have been gained. The C.P. of the bicycle is :

(a) Rs. 350   (b) Rs. 400
(c) Rs. 500   (d) Rs. 600

62. Due to an increase of 30% in the price of eggs, 3 eggs less are available for Rs. 7.80. The present rate of eggs per dozen is :

(a) Rs. 8.64   (b) Rs. 8.88

(c) Rs. 9.36 (d) none of these

63. Rahim sells a chair at a gain of $7\frac{1}{2}$%. If he had bought it at $12\frac{1}{2}$% less and sold it for Rs. 5 more, would have gained 30%. The C.P. of the chair is :

(a) Rs. 72 (b) Rs. 80
(c) Rs. 88 (d) Rs. 96

64. A man sells an article at a gain of 15%. If he had bought it at 10% less and sold it for Rs. 4 less, he would have gained 25%. The C.P. of the article is :

(a) Rs. 140 (b) Rs. 150
(c) Rs. 160 (d) Rs. 180

65. The per cent profit when an article is sold for Rs. 78 is twice as when it is sold for Rs. 69. The C.P. of the article is :

(a) Rs. 49 (b) Rs. 51
(c) Rs. 57 (d) Rs. 60

66. A radio dealer sold a radio at a loss of 2.5%. Had he sold it for Rs. 100 more, he would have gained $7\frac{1}{2}$%. In order to gain $12\frac{1}{2}$%, he should sell it for :

(a) Rs. 850 (b) Rs. 925
(c) Rs. 1080 (d) Rs. 1125

67. At what price must Kantilal sell a mixture of 80 kg sugar at Rs. 6.75 per kg with 120 kg at Rs. 8 per kg to gain 20% ?

(a) Rs. 7.50 per kg (b) Rs. 8.20 per kg
(c) Rs. 8.85 per kg (d) Rs. 9 per kg

(S.B.I. P.O. Exam, 1987)

68. Subhash purchased a taperecorder at $\frac{9}{10}$ th of its selling price and sold it at 8% more than its S.P. His gain is :   (S.B.I. P.O. Exam, 1987)

(a) 8% (b) 10%
(c) 18% (d) 20%

69. 6% more is gained by selling a radio for Rs. 475 than by selling for Rs. 451. The C.P. of the radio is :

(a) Rs. 400 (b) Rs. 434
(c) Rs. 446.50 (d) none of these

Profit & Loss

70. A tradesman by means of a false balance defrauds to the extent of 8% in buying goods and also defrauds to 8% in selling. His gain per cent is :
(a) 15.48% (b) 16%
(c) 16.64% (d) none of these

71. A discount series of 10%, 20% and 40% is equal to a single discount of : (Central Excise & I. Tax, 1989)
(a) 50% (b) 56.8%
(c) 60% (d) 70.28%

72. The ratio of the prices of three different types of cars is 4 : 5 : 7. If the difference between the costliest and the cheapest cars is Rs. 60000, the price of the car of modest price is : (Bank P.O. 1991)
(a) Rs. 80000 (b) Rs. 100000
(c) Rs. 140000 (d) Rs. 120000

73. Kabir buys an article with 25% discount on its marked price. He makes a profit of 10% by selling it at Rs. 660. The marked price is :
(a) Rs. 600 (b) Rs. 700
(c) Rs. 800 (d) Rs. 685
(Bank P.O. 1991)

74. An umbrella marked at Rs. 80 is sold for Rs. 68. The rate of discount is : (Railway Recruitment 1989)
(a) 15% (b) 12%
(c) $17\frac{11}{17}\%$ (d) 20%

75. A retailer buys a sewing machine at a discount of 15% and sells it for Rs. 1955. Thus, he makes a profit of 15%. The discount is :
(a) Rs. 270 (b) Rs. 290
(c) Rs. 300 (d) none of these
(L.I.C. A.A.O. Exam, 1988)

76. A shopkeeper earns a profit of 12% on selling a book at 10% discount on the printed price. The ratio of the cost price and the printed price of the book is : (G.I.C. A.A.O. Exam, 1988)
(a) 45 : 56 (b) 50 : 61
(c) 99 : 125 (d) none of these

77. While selling a watch, a shopkeeper gives a discount of 5%. If he gives a discount of 7%, he earns Rs. 15 less as profit. The marked price of the watch is : (L.I.C. A.A.O. Exam, 1988)
(a) Rs. 697.50 (b) Rs. 712.50
(c) Rs. 787.50 (d) none of these

78. The marked price of a radio is Rs. 1920. The shopkeeper allows a discount of 10% and gains 8%. If no discount is allowed, his gain per cent would be :

   (a) 18% (b) 20%
   (c) 18.5% (d) 20.5%

79. A tradesman marks his goods 30% more than the cost price. If he allows a discount of $6\frac{1}{4}$ %, then his gain percent is :

   (a) $23\frac{3}{4}$% (b) 22%
   (c) $21\frac{7}{8}$% (d) none of these

80. A trader lists his articles 20% above C.P. and allows a discount of 10% on cash payment. His gain percent is :   (Railway Recruitment 1991)

   (a) 10% (b) 8%
   (c) 6% (d) 5%

81. The marked price is 10% higher than the cost price. A discount of 10% is given on the marked price. In this kind of sale, the seller

   (a) bears no loss, no gain (b) gains
   (c) loses 1% (d) none of these

   (Railway Recruitment 1991)

82. A man purchases an electric heater whose printed price is Rs. 160. If he received two successive discounts of 20% and 10%, he paid :

   (a) Rs. 112 (b) Rs. 129.60
   (c) Rs. 119.60 (d) Rs. 115.20

   (Clerk's Grade 1991)

83. Tarun bought a T.V. with 20% discount on the labelled price. Had he bought it with 25% discount, he would have saved Rs. 500. At what price did he buy the T.V. ?   (Bank P.O. 1990)

   (a) Rs. 5000 (b) Rs. 10000
   (c) Rs. 12000 (d) Rs. 16000

84. The difference between a discount of 40% on Rs. 500 and two successive discounts of 36% and 4% on the same amount is :   (C.B.I. 1990)

   (a) 0 (b) Rs. 2
   (c) Rs. 1.93 (d) Rs. 7.20

85. The price of an article was increased by p%. Later the new price was decreased by p%. If the latest price was Re. 1, the original price was :   (Delhi Police 1990)

   (a) Re. 1

Profit & Loss

(b) Rs. $\left(\dfrac{1-p^2}{100}\right)$

(c) Rs. $\left(\dfrac{10000}{10000-p^2}\right)$

(d) Rs. $\left(\dfrac{\sqrt{1-p^2}}{100}\right)$

86. A cloth merchant has announced 25% rebate in prices. If one needs to have a rebate of Rs. 40, then how many shirts, each costing Rs. 32, he should purchase ?   (Railway Recruitment 1991)

   (a) 6   (b) 5
   (c) 10   (d) 7

87. A dealer marks his goods 20% above cost price. He then allows some discount on it and makes a profit of 8%. The rate of discount is :

   (a) 12%   (b) 10%
   (c) 6%   (d) 4%

   (C.B.I. 1991)

88. A fan is listed at Rs. 150, with a discount of 20%. What additional discount must be offered to the customer to bring the net price to Rs. 108 ?

   (a) 8%   (b) 10%
   (c) 15%   (d) none of these

89. If a commission of 10% is given on the marked price of a book, the publisher gains 20%. If the commission is increased to 15%, the gain is :

   (a) $16\dfrac{2}{3}\%$ (b) $13\dfrac{1}{3}\%$
   (c) $15\dfrac{1}{6}\%$ (d) none of these

Answers

1. (c) 2. (b) 3. (d) 4. (b) 5. (c) 6. (d) 7. (d) 8. (c) 9. (d)
10. (c) 11. (d) 12. (c) 13. (c) 14. (d) 15. (c) 16. (c) 17. (c) 18. (d)
19. (c) 20. (d) 21. (c) 22. (d) 23. (d) 24. (d) 25. (a) 26. (d) 27. (b)
28. (d) 29. (b) 30. (b) 31. (b) 32. (a) 33. (a) 34. (b) 35. (c) 36. (c)
37. (c) 38. (c) 39. (a) 40. (c) 41. (d) 42. (a) 43. (b) 44. (d) 45. (b)
46. (b) 47. (b) 48. (c) 49. (d) 50. (c) 51. (b) 52. (a) 53. (a) 54. (b)
55. (d) 56. (b) 57. (c) 58. (a) 59. (c) 60. (b) 61. (c) 62. (c) 63. (b)
64. (c) 65. (d) 66. (d) 67. (d) 68. (d) 69. (a) 70. (c) 71. (b) 72. (b)
73. (c) 74. (a) 75. (c) 76. (a) 77. (d) 78. (b) 79. (c) 80. (b) 81. (c)
82. (d) 83. (b) 84. (d) 85. (c) 86. (b) 87. (b) 88. (d) 89. (b)

SOLUTION (Exercise 10)

1. S.P. = Rs. 100, gain = Rs. 10.
   ∴ C.P. = (S.P.) − (Gain) = Rs. 90.
   ∴ Gain % = $\left(\dfrac{10}{90} \times 100\right)\% = 11\dfrac{1}{9}\%$.

2. S.P. = Rs. 100, loss = Rs.10.
   ∴ C.P. = (S.P.) + (Loss) = Rs. 110.
   ∴ Loss % = $\left(\dfrac{10}{110} \times 100\right)\% = 9\dfrac{1}{11}\%$.

3. S.P. = Rs. 1980, Gain = 10%.
   ∴ C.P. = Rs. $\left(\dfrac{100}{110} \times 1980\right)$ = Rs. 1800.

4. S.P. = Rs. 247.50, Gain = $\dfrac{25}{2}\%$
   ∴ C.P. = Rs. $\left\{\dfrac{100}{\left(100+\dfrac{25}{2}\right)} \times 247.50\right\}$ = Rs. $\left(\dfrac{100 \times 2}{225} \times 247.50\right)$
   = Rs. 220.

5. S.P. = Rs. 150, Loss = 25%.
   ∴ C.P. = Rs. $\left(\dfrac{100}{75} \times 150\right)$ = Rs. 200.

6. C.P. of 10 articles = Rs. 8.
   S.P. of 10 articles = Rs. (1.25 × 10) = Rs. 12.50.
   ∴ Gain = $\left(\dfrac{4.5}{8} \times 100\right)\% = 56\dfrac{1}{4}\%$.

7. 95 : 1140 :: 105 : x
   ∴ $x = \dfrac{1140 \times 105}{95} = 1260$.
   Hence, the watch must be sold for Rs. 1260.

8. 90 : 10.80 :: 120 : x
   ∴ $x = \dfrac{10.80 \times 120}{90} = 14.40$.
   Hence, the toy must be sold for Rs. 14.40.

9. 90 : 5.40 :: 120 : x
   ∴ $x = \dfrac{5.40 \times 120}{90} = 7.20$.
   So, the rice must be sold at Rs. 7.20 per kg.

Profit & Loss   193

10. Let C.P. of each article = Rs. 1.
    Then, C.P. of 12 articles = Rs. 12.
        S.P. of 12 articles = C.P. of 15 articles = Rs. 15.
    $\therefore$ Gain = $\left(\dfrac{3}{12} \times 100\right)\% = 25\%$.

11. Let C.P. of each mango = Re. 1.
    C.P. of 320 mangoes = Rs. 320.
    S.P. of 320 mangoes = Rs. 400.
    $\therefore$ Gain = $\left(\dfrac{80}{320} \times 100\right)\% = 25\%$.

12. Let C.P. of each table = Re. 1.
    C.P. of 20 tables = Rs. 20.
    S.P. of 20 tables = C.P. of 15 tables = Rs. 15.
    $\therefore$ Loss = $\left(\dfrac{5}{20} \times 100\right)\% = 25\%$.

13. Let C.P. of each article = Re. 1.
    C.P. of 40 articles = Rs. 40.
    S.P. of 40 articles = Rs. 50.
    $\therefore$ Gain = $\left(\dfrac{10}{40} \times 100\right)\% = 25\%$.

14. Profit is maximum when C.P. is minimum and S.P. is maximum.
    Thus, C.P. = Rs. (200×8) = Rs. 1600.
    S.P. = Rs. (425×8) = Rs. 3400
    $\therefore$ Gain = Rs. 1800.

15. Suppose he buys 10 lemons.
    C.P. = Rs. $\left(\dfrac{10}{2}\right)$ = Rs. 5, S.P. = Rs. $\left(\dfrac{3}{5} \times 10\right)$ = Rs. 6.
    Gain % = $\left(\dfrac{1}{5} \times 100\right)\% = 20\%$.

16. Suppose I purchased 110 books.
    C.P. = Rs. $\left(\dfrac{10}{11} \times 110\right)$ = Rs. 100.
    S.P. = Rs. $\left(\dfrac{11}{10} \times 110\right)$ = Rs. 121.
    $\therefore$ Gain % = 21%.

17. Gain = (S.P. of 8 dozen) − (C.P. of 8 dozen)
    (S.P. of 1 dozen) = (S.P. of 8 dozen) − (C.P. of 8 dozen).

∴ (C.P. of 8 dozen) = (S.P. of 7 dozen).
Let C.P. of each dozen be Re. 1.
C.P. of 7 dozen = Rs. 7. S.P. of 7 dozen = Rs. 8.
∴ Gain % = $\left(\dfrac{1}{7} \times 100\right)$ % = $14\dfrac{2}{7}$%.

18. Gain = (S.P. of 100 bananas) − (C.P. of 100 bananas)
(S.P. of 20) = (S.P. of 100) − (C.P. of 100)
∴ S.P. of 80 = C.P. of 100.
Let C.P. of each = Re. 1.
C.P. of 80 = Rs. 80
S.P. of 80 = Rs. 100.
∴ Gain % = $\left(\dfrac{20}{80} \times 100\right)$ % = 25%.

19. Loss = (C.P. of 36 oranges) − (S.P. of 36 oranges)
(S.P. of 4) = (S.P. of 36) − (S.P. of 36).
∴ (S.P. of 40) = (C.P. of 36).
Let C.P. of each = Re. 1.
C.P. of 40 = Rs. 40, S.P. of 40 = Rs. 36.
Loss = $\left(\dfrac{4}{40} \times 100\right)$ % = 10%.

20. Let S.P. = Rs. x.
Then, 400 + 20 % of $x = x$
or $400 + \dfrac{x}{5} = x$ or $\dfrac{4x}{5} = 400$ or $x = \dfrac{400 \times 5}{4} = 500$.
∴ S.P. = Rs. 500.

21. Let C.P. = Rs. x.
Then, $x - \dfrac{x}{11} = 10$ or $\dfrac{10x}{11} = 10$ or $x = 11$.
∴ C.P. = Rs. 11.

22. $2x + y = 7000$ .... (i)
$x + 2y = 4250$ .... (ii)
Solving (i) and (ii), we get $x = 3250$.
∴ Cost of a T.V. set is Rs. 3250.

23. Let C.P. = Rs. x. Then, loss = Rs. $\left(\dfrac{x}{7}\right)$.
S.P. = (C.P.) − (Loss) = $\left(x - \dfrac{x}{7}\right)$ = Rs. $\dfrac{6x}{7}$.

Profit & Loss 195

$\therefore \dfrac{6x}{7} = 144$ or $x = \dfrac{144 \times 7}{6} = 168$.

Thus, C.P. = Rs. 168.
If S.P. is Rs. 168, then gain percent is 0%.

24. Let S.P. = Rs. 100.
Then, C.P. = Rs. 40.
$\therefore$ Required per cent = $\left(\dfrac{100}{40} \times 100\right) \% = 250\%$.

25. Suppose he purchases 3 kg and 2 kg of tea of first and second kind respectively.
C.P. = Rs. $(3 \times 35 + 2 \times 45)$ = Rs. 195.
S.P. = Rs. (5×41.60) = Rs. 208.
Gain % = $\left(\dfrac{13}{195} \times 100\right) \% = 6\dfrac{2}{3} \%$.

26. C.P. of 60 kg mix. = Rs. $(25 \times 6 + 35 \times 7)$ = Rs. 395.
S.P. of 60 kg mix. = Rs. (60×6.75) = Rs. 405.
Gain = Rs. $(405 - 395)$ = Rs. 10.

27. S.P. of 20 articles = Rs. 60, Gain = 20%.
$\therefore$ C.P. of 20 articles = Rs. $\left(\dfrac{100}{120} \times 60\right)$ = Rs. 50.
For Rs. 50, he bought = 20 articles.
For Rs. 60, he bought = $\left(\dfrac{20}{50} \times 60\right)$ = 24 articles.

28. Gain % = $\left\{\dfrac{\text{Error}}{\text{(True value)} - \text{(Error)}} \times 100\right\} \%$
$= \left(\dfrac{100}{900} \times 100\right) \% = 11\dfrac{1}{9} \%$.

29. Let the error be x gms. Then,
$\dfrac{x}{1000 - x} \times 100 = \dfrac{300}{47}$ or $\dfrac{x}{1000 - x} = \dfrac{3}{47}$
$\therefore 47x = 3000 - 3x$ or $x = 60$.
So, he uses a weight = $(1000 - 60)$ gm = 940 gm for a kg.

30. Suppose he buys 8 toffees.
Then, C.P. = Re. 1.
Gain = 60%
$\therefore$ S.P. = Rs. $\left(\dfrac{160}{100} \times 1\right)$ = Rs. $\dfrac{8}{5}$.

For Rs. $\frac{8}{5}$, toffees sold = 8

For Re. 1, toffees sold = $\left(8 \times \frac{5}{8}\right) = 5$.

So, he must sell them at 5 for a rupee.

31. Suppose he buys 12 oranges. Then, S.P. = Re. 1.
Now, 80 : 1 :: 120 : x

$\therefore x = \frac{1 \times 120}{80} = \frac{3}{2}$.

$\therefore$ For Rs. $\frac{3}{2}$, oranges sold = 12

For Re. 1, oranges sold = $\left(12 \times \frac{2}{3}\right) = 8$.

So, he must sell them at 8 for a rupee.

32. Suppose he sells 20 toffees.
Then, S.P. = Re. 1 and Loss = 4%.

$\therefore$ C.P. = $\left(\frac{100}{96} \times 1\right)$ = Rs. $\frac{25}{24}$.

Gain = 20%.

$\therefore$ S.P. = Rs. $\left(\frac{120}{100} \times \frac{25}{24}\right)$ = Rs. $\frac{5}{4}$.

For Rs. $\frac{5}{4}$, toffees sold = 20

For Re. 1, toffees sold = $\left(20 \times \frac{4}{5}\right) = 16$.

So, he must sell at 16 for a rupee.

33. C.P. of 330 boxes = Rs. (7200 + 200 + 600) = Rs. 8000.
S.P. of 330 boxes = Rs. (330 × 28) = Rs. 9240.

$\therefore$ Gain % = $\left(\frac{1240}{8000} \times 100\right)$ % = 15.5%.

34. C.P. of 6 dozen apples = Rs. (12 × 4 + 16 × 2) = Rs. 80.
Gain = 20%.

$\therefore$ S.P. = Rs. $\left(\frac{120}{100} \times 80\right)$ = Rs. 96.

S.P. per dozen = Rs. $\left(\frac{96}{6}\right)$ = Rs. 16.

35. Let A's C.P. = Rs. 100
B's C.P. = Rs. 105

C's C.P. = 104% of Rs. 105 = Rs. 109.20.
109.20 : 91 = 100 : x

$\therefore x = \dfrac{91 \times 100}{109.20}$ = Rs. 83.33.

36. C.P. of B = 110% of Rs. 10000 = Rs. 11000.
    Loss of B = 10%
    S.P. of B = 90% of Rs. 11000 = Rs. 9900.
    Thus, C.P. of A = Rs. 9900.
    So, A gets [(10% of Rs. 10000) + (10000 – 9900)] = Rs. 1100.

37. Let original cost of each toy be Rs. 100 and number sold be 100.
    Then, sale proceed = Rs. (100 × 100) = Rs. 10000
    New sale proceed = Rs. (130 × 70) = Rs. 9100.

    Decrease % = $\left(\dfrac{900}{10000} \times 100\right) \%$ = 9%.

38. Let original cost of each toy be Rs. 100 and number originally sold be 100.
    $\therefore$ Original sale proceed = Rs. (100 × 100) = Rs. 10000.
    New sale proceed = Rs. (120 × 85) = Rs. 10200

    $\therefore$ Increase % = $\left(\dfrac{200}{10000} \times 100\right) \%$ = 2%.

39. Let original cost of each be Rs. 100 and number originally sold be 100.
    Original sale proceed = Rs. (100 × 100) = Rs. 10000.
    New sale proceed = Rs. (80 × 140) = Rs. 11200.

    $\therefore$ Increase % = $\left(\dfrac{1200}{10000} \times 100\right) \%$ = 12%.

40. Let C.P. = Rs. 100. S.P. at 10% loss = Rs. 90.

    $\therefore \dfrac{2}{3}$ of actual S.P. = Rs. 90

    So, actual S.P. = Rs. $\left(90 \times \dfrac{3}{2}\right)$ = Rs. 135. $\therefore$ Gain = 35%.

41. Loss % = $\left(\dfrac{\text{Common gain or loss \%}}{10}\right)^2 = \left(\dfrac{10}{10}\right)^2$ = 1%.

42. Loss % = $\left(\dfrac{5}{10}\right)^2 = \dfrac{1}{4} \%$ = 0.25%.

43. Loss % = $\left(\dfrac{20}{10}\right)^2 = (2)^2$ = 4%.
    Total S.P. = Rs. 24000.

Total C.P. = Rs. $\left(\dfrac{100}{96} \times 24000\right)$ = Rs. 25000.

∴ Loss = Rs. 1000.

44. Let C.P. = Rs. x.

∴ $x + x\%$ of $x = 144$ or $x + \dfrac{x^2}{100} = 144$

or $x^2 + 100x - 14400 = 0$

∴ $(x + 180)(x - 80) = 0$

∴ $x = 80$ (neglecting $x = -180$)

45. Let C.P. = Rs. x.

∴ $x + x\%$ of $x = 75$

or $x + \dfrac{x^2}{100} = 75$ or $x^2 + 100x - 7500 = 0$

or $(x + 150)(x - 50) = 0$.

∴ $x = 50$ (neglecting $x = -150$)

46. Let C.P. = Rs. x. Then,
$425 - x = x - 355$ or $2x = 780$ or $x = 390$.

47. S.P. of 1 orange = Re. $\left(\dfrac{40}{45}\right)$ = Re. $\dfrac{8}{9}$.

80% of C.P. = $\dfrac{8}{9}$ or C.P. = $\left(\dfrac{8}{9} \times \dfrac{100}{80}\right)$ = Rs. $\dfrac{10}{9}$.

S.P. = $\left(120\% \text{ of Rs. } \dfrac{10}{9}\right)$ = Rs. $\dfrac{4}{3}$.

For Rs. $\dfrac{4}{3}$, he sells 1 orange

For Rs. 24, he would sell $\left(\dfrac{3}{4} \times 24\right)$ = 18 oranges.

48. $2x + y = 7000$ .... (i)
$x + 2y = 9800$ .... (ii)

Solving (i) and (ii), we get $y = 4200$.

49. C.P. of 120 reams = Rs. $(120 \times 80 + 280 + 72 + 120 \times 40)$
= Rs. 10000.

C.P. of 1 ream = $\left(\dfrac{10000}{120}\right)$ = Rs. $\left(\dfrac{250}{3}\right)$

∴ S.P. of 1 ream = Rs. $\left(\dfrac{108}{100} \times \dfrac{250}{3}\right)$ = Rs. 90.

50. S.P. = Rs. 54000, Gain earned = 20%.

Profit & Loss

$\therefore$ C.P. = Rs. $\left(\dfrac{100}{120} \times 54000\right)$ = Rs. 45000.

Now, S.P. = Rs. 45000 and loss = 10%.

$\therefore$ C.P. = Rs. $\left(\dfrac{100}{90} \times 45000\right)$ = Rs. 50000.

51. Let total C.P. of all the articles = Rs. 100.

C.P. of $\dfrac{3}{4}$ th part = Rs. $\left(\dfrac{3}{4} \times 100\right)$ = Rs. 75.

S.P. of $\dfrac{3}{4}$ th part = Rs. $\left(\dfrac{120}{100} \times 75\right)$ = Rs. 90.

S.P. of $\dfrac{1}{4}$ th part = Rs. $\left(\dfrac{1}{4} \times 100\right)$ = Rs. 25.

Total S.P. = Rs. (90 + 25) = Rs. 115.

$\therefore$ Gain = 15%.

52. S.P. = 90% of $\left(\dfrac{3}{4}\text{ of Rs. } 400\right)$ + 110% of $\left(\dfrac{1}{4}\text{ of Rs. } 400\right)$

= Rs. $\left(\dfrac{90}{100} \times \dfrac{3}{4} \times 400\right)$ + Rs. $\left(\dfrac{110}{100} \times \dfrac{1}{4} \times 400\right)$

= Rs. (270 + 110) = Rs. 380.

$\therefore$ Loss % = $\left(\dfrac{20}{400} \times 100\right)$ % = 5%.

53. 6% of C.P. + 6% of C.P. = Rs. 6.

$\therefore$ 12% of C.P. = Rs. 6 or $\dfrac{12}{100} \times x = 6$

or $x = \dfrac{100 \times 6}{12} = 50$.

$\therefore$ C.P. = Rs. 50.

54. Let C.P. = Rs. x.

Then, $\dfrac{112}{100} x - \dfrac{88}{100} x = 6$

or $24x = 600$ or $x = \dfrac{600}{24} = 25$.

$\therefore$ C.P. = Rs. 25.

55. Let C.P. = Rs. x.

First S.P. = 110% of x = Rs. $\left(\dfrac{11}{10} x\right)$. Second S.P. = $\dfrac{22}{10} x$

New gain = $\left(\dfrac{22}{10} x - x\right) = \dfrac{12x}{10}$.

$\therefore$ New gain % = $\left(\dfrac{12x}{10 \times x} \times 100\right)$ % = 120%.

56. Let C.P. = Rs. x. Then, S.P. = Rs. $\left(\dfrac{110}{100} \times x\right)$ = Rs. $\dfrac{11x}{10}$.

   New C.P. = Rs. $\left(\dfrac{90}{100} \times x\right)$ = Rs. $\dfrac{9x}{10}$.

   New S.P. = $\left(\dfrac{110}{100} \times \dfrac{9x}{10}\right)$ = Rs. $\dfrac{99x}{100}$.

   $\therefore \dfrac{11x}{10} - \dfrac{99x}{100} = 132$ or $x = 1200$.

   $\therefore$ C.P. = Rs. 1200.

57. Let C.P. = Rs. x.

   Then, S.P. = Rs. $\left(\dfrac{90}{100} \times x\right)$ = Rs. $\left(\dfrac{9}{10}x\right)$.

   New C.P. = Rs. $\left(\dfrac{80}{100} \times x\right)$ = Rs. $\left(\dfrac{4x}{5}\right)$.

   Now, gain = 40%.

   $\therefore$ New S.P. = Rs. $\left(\dfrac{140}{100} \times \dfrac{4x}{5}\right)$ = Rs. $\left(\dfrac{28}{25}x\right)$.

   $\therefore \dfrac{28}{25}x - \dfrac{9}{10}x = 55$ or $x = 250$.

   Hence, C.P. = Rs. 250.

58. C.P. of two horses = Rs. 8000.

   S.P. of one horse = Rs. 4000, gain = 25%.

   $\therefore$ C.P. of this horse = Rs. $\left(\dfrac{100}{125} \times 4000\right)$ = Rs. 3200.

   C.P. of another horse = Rs. (8000 − 3200) = Rs. 4800.

   S.P. of this horse = Rs. 4000.

   $\therefore$ Loss % = $\left(\dfrac{800}{4800} \times 100\right)$ % = $16\dfrac{2}{3}$ %.

59. Let us consider a packet of rice marked 1 kg.

   Then, its actual weight = (80% of 1 kg) = 0.8 kg.

   Let C.P. of 1 kg be Rs. x.

   Then, C.P. of 0.8 kg = Rs. $0.8x$

   Now, S.P. = 110% of C.P. of 1 kg.

   = $\left(\dfrac{110}{100} \times x\right)$ = Rs. $1.1x$

Profit & Loss

$$\text{Gain \%} = \left(\frac{0.3\,x}{0.8\,x} \times 100\right)\% = 37.5\%.$$

60. Let the loss be Rs. x.
Then, $75 = \text{C.P.} - x$ and $96 = \text{C.P.} + 2x$.
On subtracting, we get $3x = 21$ or $x = 7$.
$\therefore$ C.P. $= 75 + x =$ Rs. 82.

61. (20% of C.P.) − (16% of C.P.) = Rs. 20.

or 4% of C.P. = 20 or $\left(\dfrac{4}{100} \times \text{C.P.}\right) = 20.$

or C.P. = Rs. $\left(\dfrac{100 \times 20}{4}\right) =$ Rs. 500.

62. Let the original rate be x paise per egg.
Number of eggs bought for Rs. 7.80 = $(780/x)$
New rate = (130% of x) paise per egg.

$= \dfrac{13x}{10}$ paise per egg.

Number of eggs bought for Rs. 7.80 = $\dfrac{780 \times 10}{13x} = \dfrac{600}{x}$.

$\therefore \dfrac{780}{x} - \dfrac{600}{x} = 3$ or $3x = 180$ or $x = 60.$

So, present rate = $\left(\dfrac{13 \times 60}{10}\right)$ paise per egg

= 78 paise per egg
= Rs. 9.36 per dozen.

63. Let C.P. = Rs. 100. Then, 1st S.P. = Rs. 107.50
New C.P. = Rs. 87.50 and gain on it = 30%

$\therefore$ 2nd S.P. = (130% of 87.50) = $\left(\dfrac{130}{100} \times 87.50\right)$

= Rs. 113.75.
Difference in two S.P.'s = Rs. (113.75 − 107.50) = Rs. 6.25

$\therefore$ Actual C.P. = Rs. $\left(\dfrac{100}{6.25} \times 5\right) =$ Rs. 80.

64. (115% of C.P.) − (125% of 90% of C.P.) = 4.

or $\dfrac{115}{100} x - \dfrac{125}{100} \times \dfrac{90}{100} x = 4$ or $\dfrac{23x}{20} - \dfrac{9x}{8} = 4$ or $x = 160$

$\therefore$ C.P. = Rs. 160.

65. Let the C.P. be Rs. x.

Then, $\dfrac{2(69-x)}{100} = \dfrac{78-x}{100}$

or $138 - 2x = 78 - x$ or $x = 60$

∴ C.P. = Rs. 60.

66. It is clear that

(2.5% of C.P. + 75% of C.P.) = 100.

or 10% of C.P. = 100 or $\dfrac{1}{10}$ of C.P. = 100

∴ C.P. = Rs. 1000.

Now, gain = $12\dfrac{1}{2}$ %

So, S.P. = $112\dfrac{1}{2}$ % of C.P. = Rs. $\left(\dfrac{225}{200} \times 1000\right)$ = Rs. 1125.

67. Total C.P. of 200 kg of sugar

= Rs. (80 × 6.75 + 120 × 8) = Rs. 1500.

C.P. of 1 kg = Rs. $\left(\dfrac{1500}{200}\right)$ = Rs. 7.50.

Gain required = 20%

∴ S.P. of 1 kg = (120% of Rs. 7.50)

= Rs. $\left(\dfrac{120}{100} \times 7.50\right)$ = Rs. 9 per kg.

68. Let the S.P. be Rs. x.

Then, C.P. paid by Subhash = Rs. $\dfrac{9x}{10}$.

S.P. received by Subhash = (108% of Rs. x)

= Rs. $\dfrac{27x}{25}$

∴ Gain = Rs. $\left(\dfrac{27x}{25} - \dfrac{9x}{10}\right)$ = Rs. $\dfrac{9x}{50}$.

Hence, gain % = $\left(\dfrac{9x}{50} \times \dfrac{10}{9x} \times 100\right)$ % = 20%.

69. Difference between two selling prices = Rs. 24.

∴ 6% of C.P. = Rs. 24

Hence, C.P. = Rs. $\left(\dfrac{24 \times 100}{6}\right)$ = Rs. 400.

70. **Rule.** In such questions we adopt the rule :

Gain % = $\dfrac{(100 + \text{common gain \%})^2}{100} - 100$

Profit & Loss

$= \left\{\dfrac{(108)^2}{100} - 100\right\}\% = 16.64\%.$

71. Let original price = Rs. 100.
Price after first discount = Rs. 90.
Price after second discount = Rs. $\left(\dfrac{80}{100} \times 90\right)$ = Rs. 72
Price after third discount = Rs. $\left(\dfrac{60}{100} \times 72\right)$ = Rs. 43.20
∴ Single discount = (100 − 43.20) = 56.8%

72. Let the prices be $4x, 5x$ and $7x$ rupees.
Then, $7x - 4x = 60000 \Rightarrow x = 20000$
∴ Required price = $5x$ = Rs. 100000

73. Let the original price be Rs. x.
C.P. = $(x - 25\% \text{ of } x) = \dfrac{3x}{4}.$
S.P. = $\left(\dfrac{3x}{4} + 10\% \text{ of } \dfrac{3x}{4}\right) = \dfrac{33x}{40}.$
∴ $\dfrac{33x}{40} = 660 \Rightarrow x = 800.$

74. Discount = $\left(\dfrac{12}{80} \times 100\right)\% = 15\%.$

75. Let the marked price be Rs. x.
Discount availed by the retailer = 15% of Rs. x.
∴ C.P. of the machine by the retailer
$= (x - 15\% \text{ of } x) = \text{Rs.} \dfrac{17x}{20}.$
So, 15% of $\dfrac{17x}{20} = 1955 - \dfrac{17x}{20}$
∴ $\dfrac{51x}{400} + \dfrac{17x}{20} = 1955$ or $x = 2000$
Discount received by retailer = (15% of Rs. 2000) = Rs. 300.

76. Let the printed price of the book be Rs. 100.
After a discount of 10%, S.P. = Rs. 90.
Profit earned = 12%
∴ C.P. of the book = Rs. $\left(\dfrac{100}{112} \times 90\right)$ = Rs. $\dfrac{1125}{14}.$
Hence, (C.P.) : (Printed Price) = $\dfrac{1125}{14}$: 100 or 45 : 56.

77. Let the marked price be Rs. x.
Then, (7% of x) – 15 = 5% of x
or $\dfrac{7x}{100} - \dfrac{5x}{100} = 15$ or $x = 750$.

78. S.P. = (90% of Rs. 480) = Rs. $\left(\dfrac{90}{100} \times 480\right)$ = Rs. 432.
Gain earned on it = 8%.
∴ C.P. = Rs $\left(\dfrac{100}{108} \times 432\right)$ = Rs 400
If no discount is allowed, S.P. = Rs 480.
∴ Gain % = $\left(\dfrac{80}{400} \times 100\right)$ % = 20%.

79. Let the C.P. be Rs. 100.
Then, marked price = Rs. 130.
S.P. = $\left(93\dfrac{3}{4}\% \text{ of Rs. } 130\right)$
= Rs. $\left(\dfrac{375}{4 \times 100} \times 130\right)$ = Rs. $121\dfrac{7}{8}$.
∴ Gain % = $21\dfrac{7}{8}$%.

80. Let C.P. = Rs. 100. Then, marked price = Rs. 120.
S.P. = 90% of Rs. 120 = Rs. 108.
∴ Gain = 8%.

81. Let C.P. = Rs. 100.
Marked Price = Rs. 110.
S.P. = 90% of Rs. 110 = Rs. 99.
∴ Loss = 1%.

82. Price after 1st discount = 80% of Rs. 160 = Rs. 128.
Price after 2nd discount = 90% of Rs. 128 = Rs. 115.20.

83. Let the labelled price be Rs. 100.
S.P. in 1st case = Rs. 80, S.P. in 2nd case = Rs. 75.
If saving is Rs. 5, labelled price = Rs. 100.
If saving is Rs. 500, labelled price = Rs. $\left(\dfrac{100}{5} \times 500\right)$ = Rs. 10000.

84. Sale after 40% discount = 60% of Rs. 500 = Rs. 300.
Price after 36% discount = 64% of Rs. 500 = Rs. 320.
Price after next 4% discount = 96% of Rs. 320 = Rs. 307.20.

Profit & Loss 205

∴ Difference in two prices = Rs. 7.20.

85. Let original price = Rs. x

Price after p % increase = $(100 + p)$ % of $x = \dfrac{(100+p)x}{100}$

New price after p % decrease = $(100 - p)$ % of $\dfrac{(100+p)x}{100}$

$= \dfrac{(100-p)}{100} \times \dfrac{(100+p)}{100} \times x$.

∴ $\dfrac{(100-p)(100+p)}{100 \times 100} \times x = 1$

or $x = \dfrac{100 \times 100}{(100-p)(100+p)} = \dfrac{10000}{(10000-p^2)}$.

86. Suppose the number of shirts = x.

Then, rebate = $\left(\dfrac{25}{100} \times 32\,x\right) = 8\,x$.

∴ $8\,x = 40$ or $x = 5$.

87. Let C.P. = Rs. 100.

Marked Price = Rs. 120, S.P. = Rs. 108.

∴ Discount = $\left(\dfrac{12}{120} \times 100\right)\% = 10\%$.

88. List price = Rs. 150.

Price after 20% discount = 80% of Rs. 150 = Rs. 120.

Sale price = Rs. 108.

∴ Additional discount = $\left(\dfrac{12}{108} \times 100\right) = 11\dfrac{1}{9}\%$.

89. Let C.P. = Rs. 100. Then, S.P. = Rs. 120.

If S.P. is Rs. 90, marked price = Rs. 100.

If S.P. is Rs. 120, marked price = Rs. $\left(\dfrac{100}{90} \times 120\right)$ = Rs. $\dfrac{400}{3}$.

S.P. at 15% commission = Rs. $\left(\dfrac{85}{100} \times \dfrac{400}{3}\right)$ = Rs. $\left(\dfrac{340}{3}\right)$.

∴ Gain % = $\left(\dfrac{340}{3} - 100\right)\% = \dfrac{40}{3}\% = 13\dfrac{1}{3}\%$.

11
TIME & WORK

General Rules :

(i) If A can do a piece of work in n days, then :

work done by A in 1 day $= \dfrac{1}{n}$.

(ii) If A's 1 day's work $= \dfrac{1}{n}$, then A can finish the whole work in n days.

Ex. 1. Geeta can weave a sweater in 8 days.

Her 1 day's work $= \dfrac{1}{8}$.

2. Ram's one day's work $= \dfrac{1}{5}$.

Ram can finish the whole work in 5 days.

(iii) If A is twice as good a workman as B, then :
Ratio of work done by A and B = 2 : 1.
Ratio of time taken by A and B = 1 : 2.

(iv) If the number of men to do a certain work be changed in the ratio m : n, then the ratio of time taken to finish the work, changes in the ratio n : m.

SOLVED EXAMPLES

Ex. 1. Dilip can reap a field in 9 days, which Ram alone can reap in 12 days. In how many days, both together, can reap this field ?

Sol. Dilip's 1 day's work $= \dfrac{1}{9}$.

Ram's 1 day's work $= \dfrac{1}{12}$.

(Dilip + Ram)'s 1 day's work $= \left(\dfrac{1}{9} + \dfrac{1}{12}\right) = \dfrac{7}{36}$.

∴ Both together can reap the field in $\dfrac{36}{7}$ days *i.e.* $5\dfrac{1}{7}$ days.

Ex. 2. A and B together can dig a trench in 12 days, which A alone can dig in 30 days. In how many days B alone can dig it ?

Time & Work

Sol. $(A + B)$'s 1 day's work = $\frac{1}{12}$; A's 1 day's work = $\frac{1}{30}$.

$\therefore$ B's 1 day's work = $\left(\frac{1}{12} - \frac{1}{30}\right) = \frac{1}{20}$.

So, B alone can dig the trench in 20 days.

Ex. 3. *A and B can do a piece of work in 12 days; B and C in 15 days; C and A in 20 days. In how many days will they finish it together and separately ?*

Sol. $(A + B)$'s 1 day's work = $\frac{1}{12}$; $(B + C)$'s 1 day's work = $\frac{1}{15}$;

$(C + A)$'s 1 day's work $\frac{1}{20}$.

On adding, we get :

$2(A + B + C)$'s 1 day's work = $\left(\frac{1}{12} + \frac{1}{15} + \frac{1}{20}\right) = \frac{1}{5}$.

$\therefore$ $(A + B + C)$'s 1 day's work = $\frac{1}{10}$.

So, they all together can finish the work in 10 days.

$\therefore$ A's 1 day's work = $[(A + B + C)$'s 1 day's work$]$
$\qquad - [(B + C)$'s 1 day's work$]$

$= \left(\frac{1}{10} - \frac{1}{15}\right) = \frac{1}{30}$.

$\therefore$ A alone can finish the work in 30 days.

Similarly, B's 1 day's work = $\left(\frac{1}{10} - \frac{1}{20}\right) = \frac{1}{20}$.

$\therefore$ B alone can finish the work in 20 days.

And, C's 1 day's work = $\left(\frac{1}{10} - \frac{1}{12}\right) = \frac{1}{60}$.

$\therefore$ C alone can finish the work in 60 days.

Ex. 4. *A can do a piece of work in 25 days, which B alone can finish in 20 days. Both together work for 5 days and then A leaves off. How many days will B take to finish the remaining work ?*

Sol. $(A + B)$'s 5 day's work = $5\left(\frac{1}{25} + \frac{1}{20}\right) = \frac{9}{20}$.

Remaining work = $\left(1 - \dfrac{9}{20}\right) = \dfrac{11}{20}$.

Now, $\dfrac{1}{20}$ work is done by B in 1 day.

$\therefore$ $\dfrac{11}{20}$ work will be done by B in $\left(\dfrac{20 \times 11}{20}\right) = 11$ days.

Ex. 5. *A is thrice as good a workman as B and is therefore able to finish a piece of work in 60 days less than B. Find the time in which they can do it, working together.*

Sol. Ratio of work done by A and B in the same time = 3 : 1.
Ratio of time taken by A and B = 1 : 3.

Suppose B takes x days to finish a work.

Then, A takes $(x - 60)$ days.

$\therefore$ $\dfrac{x - 60}{x} = \dfrac{1}{3}$ or $3(x - 60) = x$ or $x = 90$.

Thus, time taken by B to finish the work = 90 days.

Time taken by A to finish the work = 30 days.

$\therefore$ $(A + B)$'s 1 day's work = $\left(\dfrac{1}{90} + \dfrac{1}{30}\right) = \dfrac{2}{45}$.

So, both together can finish the work in $\left(\dfrac{45}{2}\right)$ days i.e. $22\dfrac{1}{2}$ days.

Ex. 6. *A can build a wall in 30 days, which B alone can build in 40 days. If they build it together and get a payment of Rs. 700, what is B's share?*

Sol. A's 1 day's work = $\dfrac{1}{30}$ and B's 1 day's work = $\dfrac{1}{40}$.

Ratio of shares of A and B = $\dfrac{1}{30} : \dfrac{1}{40} = 4 : 3$.

$\therefore$ B's share = Rs. $\left(700 \times \dfrac{3}{7}\right)$ = Rs. 300.

Ex. 7. *A can do a piece of work in 10 days, while B alone can do it in 15 days. They work together for 5 days and the rest of the work is done by C in 2 days. If they get Rs. 450 for the whole work, how should they divide the money?*

Sol. $(A + B)$'s 5 day's work = $5\left(\dfrac{1}{10} + \dfrac{1}{15}\right) = \dfrac{5}{6}$

Remaining work = $\left(1 - \dfrac{5}{6}\right) = \dfrac{1}{6}$

$\therefore$ C's 2 day's work = $\dfrac{1}{6}$.

Now, A's 5 day's work : B's 5 day's work : C's 2 day's work

$= \dfrac{5}{10} : \dfrac{5}{15} : \dfrac{1}{6} = \dfrac{1}{2} : \dfrac{1}{3} : \dfrac{1}{6} = 3 : 2 : 1.$

$\therefore$ A's share = Rs. $\left(450 \times \dfrac{3}{6}\right)$ = Rs. 225.

B's share = Rs. $\left(450 \times \dfrac{2}{6}\right)$ = Rs. 150.

C's share = Rs. $[450 - (225 + 150)]$ = Rs. 75.

Exercise 11

1. A can do a piece of work in 30 days while B can do it in 40 days. In how many days can A and B working together do it ?

    (a) 70 days ☐   (b) $42\dfrac{3}{4}$ days ☐

    (c) $27\dfrac{1}{7}$ days ☐   (d) $17\dfrac{1}{7}$ days ☐

    (R.R.B. Exam, 1989)

2. A and B can together do a piece of work in 15 days. B alone can do it in 20 days. In how many days can A alone do it ?

    (a) 30 days ☐   (b) 40 days ☐
    (c) 45 days ☐   (d) 60 days ☐

    (R.R.B. Exam, 1991)

3. A and B can do a piece of work in 6 days and A alone can do it in 9 days. The time taken by B alone to do the work is :

    (a) 18 days ☐   (b) 15 days ☐
    (c) 12 days ☐   (d) $7\dfrac{1}{2}$ days ☐

4. A can do (1/3) of a work in 5 days and B can do (2/5) of the work in 10 days. In how many days both A and B together can do the work ? (R.R.B. Exam, 1991)

    (a) $7\dfrac{3}{4}$ ☐   (b) $8\dfrac{4}{5}$ ☐

(c) $9\frac{3}{8}$ (d) 10

5. A and B can do a piece of work in 18 days; B and C in 24 days; A and C in 36 days. In what time can they do it all working together ?
   (a) 12 days (b) 13 days
   (c) 16 days (d) 26 days

6. A and B can do a piece of work in 12 days; B and C in 15 days; C and A in 20 days. A alone can do the work in :
   (a) $15\frac{2}{3}$ days (b) 24 days
   (c) 30 days (d) 40 days

7. A can do a piece of work in 20 days which B can do in 12 days. B worked at it for 9 days. A can finish the remaining work in :
   (a) 3 days (b) 5 days
   (c) 7 days (d) 11 days

8. A, B and C contract a work for Rs. 550. Together A and B are to do $\frac{7}{11}$ of the work. The share of C should be : (Clerical Grade, 1991)
   (a) Rs. $183\frac{1}{3}$ (b) Rs. 200
   (c) Rs. 300 (d) Rs. 400

9. A can do a piece of work in 80 days. He works at it for 10 days and then B alone finishes the work in 42 days. The two together could complete the work in : (Clerical Grade, 1991)
   (a) 24 days (b) 25 days
   (c) 30 days (d) 35 days

10. A can do a piece of work in 24 days while B alone can do it in 16 days. With the help of C, they finish the work in 8 days. C alone can do the work in :
    (a) 32 days (b) 36 days
    (c) 40 days (d) 48 days

11. A can do a certain job in 25 days which B alone can do in 20 days. A started the work and was joined by B after 10 days. The work lasted for :
    (a) $12\frac{1}{2}$ days (b) $14\frac{2}{9}$ days
    (c) 15 days (d) $16\frac{2}{3}$ days

Time & Work

12. Mahesh and Umesh can complete a work in 10 days and 15 days respectively. Umesh starts the work and after 5 days Mahesh also joins him. In all, the work would be completed in : (Clerical Grade, 1991)
    (a) 7 days　　　　　　　　(b) 9 days
    (c) 11 days　　　　　　　 (d) none of these

13. Twelve men can complete a work in 8 days. Three days after they started the work, 3 more men joined them. In how many days will all of them together complete the remaining work ? (A.O. Exam, 1990)
    (a) 2　　　　　　　　　　(b) 4
    (c) 5　　　　　　　　　　(d) 6

14. The rates of working of A and B are in the ratio 3 : 4. The number of days taken by them to finish the work are in the ratio :
    (a) 3 : 4　　　　　　　　 (b) 9 : 16
    (c) 4 : 3　　　　　　　　 (d) none of these

15. Sunil completes a work in 4 days whereas Dinesh completes the work in 6 days. Ramesh works $1\frac{1}{2}$ times as fast as Sunil. How many days it will take for the three together to complete the work ?
    (a) $\frac{7}{12}$　　　　　　　　　(b) $1\frac{5}{12}$
    (c) $1\frac{5}{7}$　　　　　　　　　(d) none of these
    (Bank P.O., 1989)

16. A can do a piece of work in 10 days and B can do the same piece of work in 20 days. They start the work together but after 5 days, A leaves off. B will do the remaining piece of work in :
    (a) 5 days　　　　　　　　(b) 6 days
    (c) 8 days　　　　　　　　(d) 10 days

17. A and B can together finish a work in 30 days. They worked for it for 20 days and then B left. The remaining work was done by A alone in 20 more days. A alone can finish the work in :
    (a) 48 days　　　　　　　 (b) 50 days
    (c) 54 days　　　　　　　 (d) 60 days
    (Central Excise & I. Tax, 1988)

18. A can complete a job in 9 days, B in 10 days and C in 15 days. B and C start the work and are forced to leave after 2 days. The time taken to complete the remaining work is : (N.D.A. Exam, 1987)
    (a) 6 days　　　　　　　　(b) 9 days
    (c) 10 days　　　　　　　 (d) 13 days

19. A, B and C together earn Rs. 150 per day while A and C together earn Rs. 94 and B and C together earn Rs. 76. The daily earning of C is :
    (a) Rs. 75   □   (b) Rs. 56   □
    (c) Rs. 34   □   (d) Rs. 20   □
    (Bank P.O., 1986)

20. A is twice as good a workman as B and together they finish a piece of work in 14 days. A alone can finish the work in :
    (a) 11 days   □   (b) 21 days   □
    (c) 28 days   □   (d) 42 days   □

21. A is thrice as good a workman as B and takes 10 days less to do a piece of work than B takes. B can do the work in :
    (a) 12 days   □   (b) 15 days   □
    (c) 20 days   □   (d) 30 days   □

22. A can do a certain job in 12 days. B is 60% more efficient than A. The number of days, it takes B to do the same piece of work, is :
    (a) 6   □   (b) $6\frac{1}{4}$ □
    (c) $7\frac{1}{2}$ □   (d) 8   □
    (C.B.I. Exam, 1990)

23. A can do a piece of work in 14 days which B can do in 21 days. They begin together but 3 days before the completion of the work, A leaves off. The total number of days to complete the work is :
    (a) $6\frac{3}{5}$ days   □   (b) $8\frac{1}{2}$ days   □
    (c) $10\frac{1}{5}$ days   □   (d) $13\frac{1}{2}$ days   □

24. A alone can finish a work in 10 days and B alone can do it in 15 days. If they work together and finish it, then out of a total wages of Rs. 75, A will get :
    (a) Rs. 30   □   (b) Rs. 37.50   □
    (c) Rs. 45   □   (d) Rs. 50   □

25. A can do a piece of work in 6 days and B alone can do it in 8 days. A and B undertook to do it for Rs. 320. With the help of C, they finished it in 3 days. How much is paid to C ?
    (a) Rs. 37.50   □   (b) Rs. 40   □
    (c) Rs. 60   □   (d) Rs. 80   □

Time & Work

26. A and B working separately can do a piece of work in 9 and 12 days respectively. If they work for a day alternately, A beginning, in how many days the work will be completed?

    (a) $10\frac{1}{2}$ days   (b) $10\frac{1}{4}$ days
    (c) $10\frac{2}{3}$ days   (d) $10\frac{1}{3}$ days

27. A sum of money is sufficient to pay A's wages for 21 days or B's wages for 28 days. The money is sufficient to pay the wages of both for:

    (a) 12 days   (b) $12\frac{1}{4}$ days
    (c) 14 days   (d) none of these

28. A does half as much work as B in three-fourth of the time. If together they take 18 days to complete a work, how much time shall B take to do it? (L.I.C. A.A.O. Exam, 1988)

    (a) 30 days   (b) 35 days
    (c) 40 days   (d) none of these

29. 12 men or 18 women can reap a field in 14 days. The number of days that 8 men and 16 women will take to reap it, is:

    (a) 5   (b) 7
    (c) 8   (d) 9
    (Clerical Grade, 1991)

30. If 3 men or 4 women can construct a wall in 43 days, then the number of days that 7 men and 5 women take to construct it, is:

    (a) 12   (b) 18
    (c) 24   (d) 30
    (Delhi Police, 1990)

31. 10 men can finish a piece of work in 10 days, whereas it takes 12 women to finish it in 10 days. If 15 men and 6 women undertake to complete the work, how many days will they take to complete it?

    (a) 2   (b) 4
    (c) 5   (d) 11
    (Bank P.O., 1991)

32. A and B can do a piece of work in 45 and 40 days respectively. They began the work together, but A leaves after some days and B finished the remaining work in 23 days. After how many days did A leave?

    (a) 6 days   (b) 8 days
    (c) 9 days   (d) 12 days

33. A certain number of men complete a piece of work in 60 days. If there were 8 men more, the work could be finished in 10 days less. How many men were originally there ?
   (a) 30   (b) 40
   (c) 32   (d) 36

34. 8 children and 12 men complete a certain piece of work in 9 days. If each child takes twice the time taken by a man to finish the work, in how many days will 12 men finish the same work ? (Bank P.O. 1988)
   (a) 8   (b) 15
   (c) 9   (d) 12

35. 8 men can dig a pit in 20 days. If a man works half as much again as a boy, then 4 men and 9 boys can dig a similar pit in :
   (a) 10 days   (b) 12 days
   (c) 15 days   (d) 16 days

36. If 5 men or 9 women can finish a piece of work in 19 days, 3 men and 6 women will do the same work in :
   (a) 10 days   (b) 12 days
   (c) 13 days   (d) 15 days

37. 2 men and 3 women can finish a piece of work in 10 days, while 4 men can do it in 10 days. In how many days will 3 men and 3 women finish it ?
   (a) 6 days   (b) $5\frac{2}{3}$ days
   (c) 8 days   (d) $8\frac{1}{3}$ days

38. 3 men and 4 boys do a piece of work in 8 days, while 4 men and 4 boys finish it in 6 days. 2 men and 4 boys will finish it in :
   (a) 9 days   (b) 10 days
   (c) 12 days   (d) 14 days

39. If 1 man or 2 women or 3 boys can do a piece of work in 44 days, then the same piece of work will be done by 1 man, 1 woman and 1 boy in :
   (a) 21 days   (b) 24 days
   (c) 26 days   (d) 33 days

40. 4 men and 6 women finish a job in 8 days, while 3 men and 7 women finish it in 10 days. 10 women working together will finish it in :
   (a) 24 days   (b) 32 days
   (c) 36 days   (d) 40 days

Time & Work

41. Two men undertake to do a piece of work for Rs. 400. One alone can do it in 6 days, the other in 8 days. With the help of a boy, they finish it in 3 days. The boy's share is :
(a) Rs 40 ☐   (b) Rs 50 ☐
(c) Rs 60 ☐   (d) Rs 80 ☐

Answers (Exercise 11)

1. (d)   2. (d)   3. (a)   4. (c)   5. (c)   6. (c)   7. (b)   8. (b)   9. (c)
10. (b) 11. (d) 12. (b) 13. (b) 14. (c) 15. (d) 16. (a) 17. (d) 18. (a)
19. (d) 20. (b) 21. (b) 22. (c) 23. (c) 24. (c) 25. (b) 26. (b) 27. (a)
28. (a) 29. (d) 30. (a) 31. (c) 32. (c) 33. (b) 34. (d) 35. (d) 36. (d)
37. (c) 38. (c) 39. (b) 40. (d) 41. (b)

Solution (Exercise 11)

1. $(A + B)$'s 1 day's work $= \left(\dfrac{1}{30} + \dfrac{1}{40}\right) = \dfrac{7}{120}$.

   Time taken by both to finish the work $= \dfrac{120}{7}$ days

   $= 17\dfrac{1}{7}$ days.

2. A's 1 day's work $= \left(\dfrac{1}{15} - \dfrac{1}{20}\right) = \dfrac{1}{60}$.

   ∴ A alone can finish it in 60 days.

3. B's 1 day's work $= \left(\dfrac{1}{6} - \dfrac{1}{9}\right) = \dfrac{1}{18}$.

   ∴ B alone can finish it in 18 days.

4. $\dfrac{1}{3}$ of work is done by A in 5 days.

   ∴ Whole work will be done by A in 15 days.

   $\dfrac{2}{5}$ of work is done by B in 10 days

   Whole work will be done by B in $\left(10 \times \dfrac{5}{2}\right)$ i.e. 25 days.

   ∴ $(A + B)$'s 1 day's work $= \left(\dfrac{1}{15} + \dfrac{1}{25}\right) = \dfrac{8}{75}$.

   So, both together can finish it in $\dfrac{75}{8}$ days i.e. $9\dfrac{3}{8}$ days.

5. $(A+B)$'s 1 day's work $= \dfrac{1}{18}$;

   $(B+C)$'s 1 day's work $= \dfrac{1}{24}$;

   $(A+C)$'s 1 day's work $= \dfrac{1}{36}$.

   Adding, $2(A+B+C)$'s 1 day's work $= \left(\dfrac{1}{18} + \dfrac{1}{24} + \dfrac{1}{36}\right) = \dfrac{1}{8}$.

   $\therefore$ $(A+B+C)$'s 1 day's work $= \dfrac{1}{16}$.

   Hence, all working together can finish it in 16 days.

6. $[(A+B)+(B+C)+(C+A)]$'s 1 day's work $= \left(\dfrac{1}{12} + \dfrac{1}{15} + \dfrac{1}{20}\right) = \dfrac{1}{5}$.

   $2(A+B+C)$'s 1 day's work $= \dfrac{1}{5}$.

   or $(A+B+C)$'s 1 day's work $= \dfrac{1}{10}$.

   A's 1 day's work $= \left(\dfrac{1}{10} - \dfrac{1}{15}\right) = \dfrac{1}{30}$.

   $\therefore$ A alone can finish it in 30 days.

7. B's 9 day's work $= 9 \times \dfrac{1}{12} = \dfrac{3}{4}$.

   Remaining work $= \left(1 - \dfrac{3}{4}\right) = \dfrac{1}{4}$.

   $\dfrac{1}{4}$ work is done by A in 5 days.

8. Work to be done by $C = \left(1 - \dfrac{7}{11}\right) = \dfrac{4}{11}$.

   $\therefore$ $(A+B):C = \dfrac{7}{11} : \dfrac{4}{11} = 7:4$.

   $\therefore$ C's share $= $ Rs. $\left(550 \times \dfrac{4}{11}\right) = $ Rs. 200.

9. A's 10 day's work $= \left(10 \times \dfrac{1}{80}\right) = \dfrac{1}{8}$.

   Remaining work $= \left(1 - \dfrac{1}{8}\right) = \dfrac{7}{8}$.

   $\therefore$ $\dfrac{7}{8}$ work is done by A in 42 days.

Time & Work

Whole work will be done by A in $\left(42 \times \dfrac{8}{7}\right)$ i.e. 48 days.

$\therefore (A + B)$'s 1 day's work $= \left(\dfrac{1}{80} + \dfrac{1}{48}\right) = \dfrac{8}{240} = \dfrac{1}{30}$.

Hence, A and B together can finish it in 30 days.

10. C's 1 day's work
$= [(A + B + C)$'s 1 day's work$] - [(A + B)$'s 1 day's work$]$
$= \left[\dfrac{1}{8} - \left(\dfrac{1}{24} + \dfrac{1}{16}\right)\right] = \left(\dfrac{1}{8} - \dfrac{5}{48}\right) = \dfrac{1}{48}$.

$\therefore$ C alone can do it in 48 days.

11. A's 10 day's work $= \left(10 \times \dfrac{1}{25}\right) = \dfrac{2}{5}$.

Remaining work $= \left(1 - \dfrac{2}{5}\right) = \dfrac{3}{5}$.

$\left(\dfrac{1}{25} + \dfrac{1}{20}\right)$ work was done by $(A + B)$ in 1 day

$\therefore \dfrac{3}{5}$ work was done by $(A + B)$ in $\left(\dfrac{100}{9} \times \dfrac{3}{5}\right) = \dfrac{20}{3}$ days.

Hence the work lasted for $16\dfrac{2}{3}$ days.

12. Umesh's 5 day's work $= 5 \times \dfrac{1}{15} = \dfrac{1}{3}$.

Remaining work $= \left(1 - \dfrac{1}{3}\right) = \dfrac{2}{3}$.

$\left(\dfrac{1}{10} + \dfrac{1}{15}\right)$ work is done by both in 1 day.

$\therefore \dfrac{2}{3}$ work is done by both in $\left(6 \times \dfrac{2}{3}\right) = 4$ days.

Hence, the work was completed in 9 days.

13. 1 man's one day's work $= \dfrac{1}{96}$.

12 men's 3 day's work $= \left(3 \times \dfrac{1}{8}\right) = \dfrac{3}{8}$.

Remaining work $= \left(1 - \dfrac{3}{8}\right) = \dfrac{5}{8}$.

15 men's 1 day's work $= \dfrac{15}{96}$.

Now, $\dfrac{15}{96}$ work is done by them in 1 day.

$\therefore \dfrac{5}{8}$ work will be done by them in $\left(\dfrac{96}{15} \times \dfrac{5}{8}\right)$ i.e. 4 days.

14. Ratio of times taken $= \dfrac{1}{3} : \dfrac{1}{4} = 4 : 3$.

15. Time taken by Ramesh alone $= \left(\dfrac{2}{3} \times 4\right) = \dfrac{8}{3}$ days.

    $\therefore$ Their 1 day's work $= \left(\dfrac{1}{4} + \dfrac{1}{6} + \dfrac{3}{8}\right) = \dfrac{19}{24}$.

    So, together they can finish the work in $\dfrac{24}{19}$ days i.e. $1\dfrac{5}{19}$ days.

16. $(A + B)$'s 5 day's work $= 5\left(\dfrac{1}{10} + \dfrac{1}{20}\right) = \dfrac{3}{4}$.

    Remaining work $= \left(1 - \dfrac{3}{4}\right) = \dfrac{1}{4}$.

    $\dfrac{1}{20}$ work is done by B in 1 day.

    $\therefore \dfrac{1}{4}$ work is done by B in $\left(20 \times \dfrac{1}{4}\right)$ i.e. 5 days.

17. $(A + B)$'s 20 day's work $= \left(20 \times \dfrac{1}{30}\right) = \dfrac{2}{3}$.

    Remaining work $= \left(1 - \dfrac{2}{3}\right) = \dfrac{1}{3}$.

    $\dfrac{1}{3}$ work is done by A in 20 days.

    Whole work can be done by A in (3×20) days i.e. 60 days.

18. $(B + C)$'s 2 day's work $= 2\left(\dfrac{1}{10} + \dfrac{1}{15}\right) = \dfrac{1}{3}$.

    Remaining work $= \left(1 - \dfrac{1}{3}\right) = \dfrac{2}{3}$.

    $\dfrac{1}{9}$ work is done by A in 1 day.

    $\therefore \dfrac{2}{3}$ work is done by A in $\left(9 \times \dfrac{2}{3}\right) = 6$ days.

19. B's daily earning = Rs. $(150 - 94)$ = Rs. 56.
    A's daily earning = Rs. $(150 - 76)$ = Rs. 74.
    C's daily earning = Rs. $[150 - (56 + 74)]$ = Rs. 20.

20. (A's 1 day's work) : (B's 1 day's work) $= 2 : 1$.

    Now, $(A + B)$'s 1 day's work $= \dfrac{1}{14}$.

    $\therefore A$'s 1 day's work $= \left(\dfrac{1}{14} \times \dfrac{2}{3}\right) = \dfrac{1}{21}$. $\left[\text{Dividing } \dfrac{1}{14} \text{ in the ratio } 2 : 1\right]$

Time & Work

Hence, A can finish the work in 21 days.

21. Ratio of times taken by A and B = 1 : 3.
    If the difference of time is 2 days, B takes 3 days
    If the difference of time is 10 days, B takes $\left(\dfrac{3}{2} \times 10\right)$ = 15 days.

22. Ratio of times taken by A and B = 160 : 100 = 8 : 5.
    If A takes 8 days, B takes 5 days
    If A takes 12 days, B takes = $\left(\dfrac{5}{8} \times 12\right) = 7\dfrac{1}{2}$ days.

23. B's 3 days work = $\dfrac{3}{21} = \dfrac{1}{7}$.

    Remaining work = $\left(1 - \dfrac{1}{7}\right) = \dfrac{6}{7}$.

    Now, $\left(\dfrac{1}{14} + \dfrac{1}{21}\right)$ i.e. $\dfrac{5}{42}$ work is done by A and B in 1 day.

    So, $\dfrac{6}{7}$ work will be done by A and B in $\left(\dfrac{42}{5} \times \dfrac{6}{7}\right) = \dfrac{36}{5}$ days.

    ∴ Total time taken = $\left(3 + 7\dfrac{1}{5}\right) = 10\dfrac{1}{5}$ days.

24. Ratio of time taken by A and B = 10 : 15 = 2 : 3.
    Ratio of work done in the same time = 3 : 2.
    So, the money is to be divided among A and B in the ratio 3 : 2.
    ∴ A's share = Rs. $\left(75 \times \dfrac{3}{5}\right)$ = Rs. 45.

25. Each worked for 3 days.
    A's work for 3 days = $\left(3 \times \dfrac{1}{6}\right) = \dfrac{1}{2}$.

    So, A gets Rs. $\left(\dfrac{1}{2} \times 320\right)$ = Rs. 160.

    B's work for 3 days = $\left(3 \times \dfrac{1}{8}\right) = \dfrac{3}{8}$.

    So, B gets Rs. $\left(\dfrac{3}{8} \times 320\right)$ = Rs. 120.

    Balance goes to C and therefore, C gets Rs. 40.

26. $(A + B)$'s 2 day's work = $\left(\dfrac{1}{9} + \dfrac{1}{12}\right) = \dfrac{7}{36}$.

    Evidently, the work done by A and B during 5 pairs of days
    $$= \left(5 \times \dfrac{7}{36}\right) = \dfrac{35}{36}.$$

Remaining work $= \left(1 - \dfrac{35}{36}\right) = \dfrac{1}{36}$.

Now, on 11th day, it is A's turn.

Now, $\dfrac{1}{9}$ work is done by A in 1 day

$\therefore \dfrac{1}{36}$ work will be done by A in $\left(9 \times \dfrac{1}{36}\right) = \dfrac{1}{4}$ day.

So, total time taken $= 10\dfrac{1}{4}$ days.

27. A's 1 day's wages = (1/21) of the whole money.
B's 1 day's wages = (1/28) of the whole money.
$(A + B)$'s 1 day's wages $= \left(\dfrac{1}{21} + \dfrac{1}{28}\right) = \dfrac{1}{12}$ of whole money.
So, the money is sufficient to pay the wages of both for 12 days.

28. Suppose B takes x days to do the work.
$\therefore A$ takes $\left(2 \times \dfrac{3}{4} x\right)$ i.e. $\dfrac{3x}{2}$ days to do it.
Now, $(A + B)$'s 1 day's work $= \dfrac{1}{18}$.
$\therefore \dfrac{1}{x} + \dfrac{2}{3x} = \dfrac{1}{18}$ or $x = 30$.

29. 12 men = 18 women or 1 man = $\dfrac{3}{2}$ women.

$\therefore$ 8 men + 16 women = $\left(8 \times \dfrac{3}{2} + 16\right)$ women i.e. 28 women.

Now, 18 women can reap the field in 14 days.

$\therefore$ 28 women can reap it in $\left(\dfrac{14 \times 18}{28}\right) = 9$ days.

30. 3 men = 4 women or 1 man = $\dfrac{4}{3}$ women.

$\therefore$ 7 men + 5 women = $\left(7 \times \dfrac{4}{3} + 5\right)$ women i.e. $\dfrac{43}{3}$ women.

Now, 4 women can construct the wall in 43 days.

$\therefore \dfrac{43}{3}$ women can construct it in $\left(\dfrac{43 \times 4 \times 3}{43}\right) = 12$ days.

31. 10 men = 12 women or 1 man = $\dfrac{6}{5}$ women.

$\therefore$ 15 men + 6 women = $\left(15 \times \dfrac{6}{5} + 6\right)$ women i.e. 24 women.

Now, 12 women can do the work in 10 days.

Time & Work

$\therefore$ 24 women can do it in $\left(\dfrac{10 \times 12}{24}\right) = 5$ days.

32. B's 23 day's work $= \dfrac{23}{40}$.

   Remaining work $= \left(1 - \dfrac{23}{40}\right) = \dfrac{17}{40}$.

   Now, $(A + B)$'s 1 day's work $= \left(\dfrac{1}{45} + \dfrac{1}{40}\right) = \dfrac{17}{360}$.

   $\dfrac{17}{360}$ work is done by A and B in 1 day.

   $\therefore \dfrac{17}{40}$ work is done by A and B in $\left(\dfrac{360 \times 17}{17 \times 40}\right) = 9$ days.

   So, A left after 9 days.

33. Let the original number of men be x.

   Now, x men finish the work in 60 days and $(x + 8)$ men can finish it in 50 days.
   More men, less days
   So, $(x + 8) : x :: 60 : 50$
   or $\dfrac{x + 8}{x} = \dfrac{60}{50}$ or $x = 40$ men.

34. 2 children = 1 man.

   $\therefore$ (8 children + 12 men) = 16 men.
   Now, less men, more days.
   $12 : 16 :: 9 : x$
   $\therefore x = \left(\dfrac{16 \times 9}{12}\right) = 12$ days.

35. 1 man $= \dfrac{3}{2}$ boys, So, (4 men + 9 boys) = 15 boys.

   Also, 8 men $= \dfrac{3}{2} \times 8$ i.e. 12 boys.

   Now, 12 boys can dig the pit in 20 days.

   $\therefore$ 15 boys can dig it in $\left(\dfrac{20 \times 12}{15}\right) = 16$ days.

36. 5 men = 9 women or 1 men $= \dfrac{9}{5}$ women.

   $\therefore$ 3 men + 6 women $= \left(3 \times \dfrac{9}{5} + 6\right)$ women i.e. $\dfrac{57}{5}$ women

   Now, 9 women can do the work in 19 days.

   $\therefore \dfrac{57}{5}$ women can do it in $\left(\dfrac{19 \times 9 \times 5}{57}\right) = 15$ days.

37. 4 men = 2 men + 3 women or 2 men = 3 women.

$\therefore$ 1 women = $\frac{2}{3}$ man.

So, 3 men + 3 women = 3 men + $\left(3 \times \frac{2}{3}\right)$ men = 5 men.

Now, 4 men can finish the work in 10 days

$\therefore$ 5 men can do it in $\left(\frac{10 \times 4}{5}\right)$ = 8 days.

38. (3 men + 4 boys)'s 1 day's work = (1/8)
(4 men + 4 boys)'s 1 day's work = (1/6)
Subtracting :–

1 man's 1 day's work = $\left(\frac{1}{6} - \frac{1}{8}\right) = \frac{1}{24}$.

(2 men + 4 boys)'s 1 day's work = $\left(\frac{1}{8} - \frac{1}{24}\right) = \frac{1}{12}$.

Thus, 2 men and 4 boys will finish it in 12 days.

39. 1 man = 2 women = 3 boys.

$\therefore$ 1 women = $\frac{1}{2}$ man and 1 boy = $\frac{1}{3}$ man.

So, (1 man + 1 woman + 1 boy) = $\left(1 + \frac{1}{2} + \frac{1}{3}\right)$ men = $\left(\frac{11}{6}\text{ men}\right)$

Now, 1 man can do the piece of work in 44 days.

$\therefore$ $\frac{11}{6}$ men can do it in $\left(44 \times \frac{6}{11}\right)$ = 24 days.

40. Let 1 man's and 1 woman's one day's work be x and y respectively.
Then,
$4x + 6y = (1/8)$ and $3x + 7y = (1/10)$
Solving these equations we get, $y = (1/400)$.
Thus, 1 woman can finish it in 400 days
$\therefore$ 10 women can finish it in $(400 \div 10) = 40$ days.

41. One man's 1 day's work = $\frac{1}{6}$. Another man's 1 day's work = $\frac{1}{8}$.

Boy's 1 day's work = $\frac{1}{3} - \left(\frac{1}{6} + \frac{1}{8}\right) = \frac{1}{24}$.

Ratio of their shares = $\frac{1}{6} : \frac{1}{8} : \frac{1}{24} = 4 : 3 : 1$.

$\therefore$ Boy's share = Rs $\left(400 \times \frac{1}{8}\right)$ = Rs 50.

12
PIPES & CISTERNS

Inlet : *A pipe connected with a tank (or a cistern or a reservoir) is called an inlet, if it fills it.*

Outlet : *A pipe connected with a tank is called an outlet, if it empties it.*

FORMULAE :

(i) If a pipe can fill a tank in x hours, then

the part filled in 1 hour = $\dfrac{1}{x}$.

(ii) If a pipe can empty a tank in y hours, then

the part of the full tank emptied in 1 hour = $\dfrac{1}{y}$.

(iii) If a pipe can fill a tank in x hours and another pipe can empty the full tank in y hours, then the net part filled in 1 hour, when both the pipes are opened = $\left(\dfrac{1}{x} - \dfrac{1}{y}\right)$.

SOLVED EXAMPLES

Ex. 1. Two pipes *A* and *B* can fill a tank in 36 hours and 45 hours respectively. If both the pipes are opened simultaneously, how much time will be taken to fill the tank ?

Sol. Part filled by *A* alone in 1 hour = $\dfrac{1}{36}$.

Part filled by *B* alone in 1 hour = $\dfrac{1}{45}$.

∴ Part filled by (A + B) in 1 hour = $\left(\dfrac{1}{36} + \dfrac{1}{45}\right) = \dfrac{9}{180} = \dfrac{1}{20}$.

Hence, both the pipes together will fill the tank in 20 hours.

Ex. 2. A pipe can fill a tank in 15 hours. Due to a leak in the bottom, it is filled in 20 hours. If the tank is full, how much time will the leak take to empty it ?

Sol. Work done by the leak in 1 hour = $\left(\dfrac{1}{15} - \dfrac{1}{20}\right) = \dfrac{1}{60}$.

∴ Leak will empty the full tank in 60 hours.

Ex. 3. Pipe A can fill a tank in 20 hours while pipe B alone can fill it in 30 hours and pipe C can empty the full tank in 40 hours. If all the pipes are opened together, how much time will be needed to make the tank full ?

Sol. Net part filled in 1 hour $= \left(\dfrac{1}{20} + \dfrac{1}{30} - \dfrac{1}{40}\right) = \dfrac{7}{120}$.

∴ The tank will be full in $\dfrac{120}{7}$ i.e. $17\dfrac{1}{7}$ hours.

Ex. 4. Two pipes A and B can fill a cistern in 1 hour and 75 minutes respectively. There is also an outlet C. If all the three pipes are opened together, the tank is full in 50 minutes. How much time will be taken by C to empty the full tank ?

Sol. Work done by C in 1 min. $= \left(\dfrac{1}{60} + \dfrac{1}{75} - \dfrac{1}{50}\right) = \dfrac{3}{300} = \dfrac{1}{100}$.

∴ C can empty the full tank in 100 minutes.

Ex. 5. Two pipes A and B can fill a tank in 24 minutes and 32 minutes respectively. If both the pipes are opened simultaneously, after how much time B should be closed so that the tank is full in 18 minutes ?

Sol. Let B be closed after x minutes. Then,
part filled by (A + B) in x min. + part filled by A in $(18 - x)$ min. = 1.

∴ $x\left(\dfrac{1}{24} + \dfrac{1}{32}\right) + (18 - x) \times \dfrac{1}{24} = 1$

or $\dfrac{7x}{96} + \dfrac{18 - x}{24} = 1$ or $7x + 4(18 - x) = 96$

∴ $3x = 24$ or $x = 8$.

So, B should be closed after 8 min.

Ex. 6. Two pipes A and B can fill a tank in 36 min. and 45 min. respectively. A waste pipe C can empty the tank in 30 min. First A and B are opened. After 7 min., C is also opened. In how much time, the tank is full ?

Sol. Part filled in 7 min. $= 7 \times \left(\dfrac{1}{36} + \dfrac{1}{45}\right) = \dfrac{7}{20}$.

Remaining part $= \left(1 - \dfrac{7}{20}\right) = \dfrac{13}{20}$.

Part filled by (A + B + C) in 1 min. $= \left(\dfrac{1}{36} + \dfrac{1}{45} - \dfrac{1}{30}\right) = \dfrac{1}{60}$.

Now, $\frac{1}{60}$ part is filled by $(A + B + C)$ in 1 min.

So, $\frac{13}{20}$ part will be filled by them in $\left(\frac{60 \times 13}{20}\right) = 39$ min.

∴ Total time taken to fill the tank = (39 + 7) min. = 46 min.

EXERCISE 12

1. Pipes A and B can fill a tank in 10 hours and 15 hours respectively. Both together can fill it in :
   - (a) $12\frac{1}{2}$ hours ☐
   - (b) 6 hours ☐
   - (c) 5 hours ☐
   - (d) none of these ☐

2. A tap can fill a cistern in 8 hours and another can empty it in 16 hours. If both the taps are opened simultaneously, the time (in hours) to fill the tank is : **(Clerical Grade, 1991)**
   - (a) 8 ☐
   - (b) 10 ☐
   - (c) 16 ☐
   - (d) 24 ☐

3. A pipe can fill a tank in x hours and another can empty it in y hours. They can together fill it in $(y > x)$:
   - (a) $(x - y)$ hours ☐
   - (b) $(y - x)$ hours ☐
   - (c) $\frac{xy}{(x - y)}$ hours ☐
   - (d) $\frac{xy}{(y - x)}$ hours ☐

4. One tap can fill a cistern in 2 hours and another can empty the cistern in 3 hours. How long will they take to fill the cistern if both the taps are opened ? **(R.R.B. Exam, 1989)**
   - (a) 5 hours ☐
   - (b) 6 hours ☐
   - (c) 7 hours ☐
   - (d) 8 hours ☐

5. A cistern can be filled by two pipes A and B in 4 hours and 6 hours respectively. When full, the tank can be emptied by a third pipe C in 8 hours. If all the taps be turned on at the same time, the cistern will be full in :
   - (a) 3 hours 18 min. ☐
   - (b) 3 hours 26 min. ☐
   - (c) 3 hours 42 min. ☐
   - (d) 3 hours 48 min. ☐

6. A tank is filled by a pipe A in 32 minutes and pipe B in 36 minutes. When full, it can be emptied by a pipe C in 20 minutes. If all the three pipes are opened simultaneously, half of the tank will be filled in :
   - (a) 16 minutes ☐
   - (b) 24 minutes ☐
   - (c) 48 minutes ☐
   - (d) none of these ☐

7. A tap can fill a tank in 16 minutes and another can empty it in 8 minutes. If the tank is already half full, and both the taps are opened together, the tank will be :
   (a) filled in 12 min. ☐   (b) emptied in 12 min. ☐
   (c) filled in 8 min. ☐   (d) emptied in 8 min. ☐

8. Two taps can separately fill a cistern in 10 minutes and 15 minutes respectively and when the waste pipe is open, they can together fill it in 18 minutes. The waste pipe can empty the full cistern in :
   (a) 7 minutes ☐   (b) 9 minutes ☐
   (c) 13 minutes ☐   (d) 23 minutes ☐

9. A cistern has two taps which fill it in 12 min and 15 min. respectively. There is also a waste pipe in the cistern. When all the pipes are opened, the empty cistern is full in 20 min. How long will the waste pipe take to empty a full cistern ?
   (a) 8 min. ☐   (b) 10 min. ☐
   (c) 12 min. ☐   (d) 16 min. ☐

10. A tank can be filled by one tap in 20 min. and by another in 25 min. Both the taps are kept open for 5 min. and then the second is turned off. In how many minutes more is the tank completely filled ?
    (a) $17\frac{1}{2}$ min. ☐   (b) 12 min. ☐
    (c) 11 min. ☐   (d) 6 min. ☐

11. A cistern is normally filled in 8 hours but takes two hours longer to fill because of a leak in its bottom. If the cistern is full, the leak will empty it in : (R.R.B. Exam, 1991)
    (a) 16 hrs. ☐   (b) 20 hrs. ☐
    (c) 25 hrs. ☐   (d) 40 hrs. ☐

12. Two pipes X and Y can fill a cistern in 24 min. and 32 min. respectively. If both the pipes are opened together, then after how much time Y should be closed so that the tank is full in 18 minutes ?
    (a) 6 min. ☐   (b) 8 min. ☐
    (c) 10 min. ☐   (d) 12 min. ☐

13. A leak in the bottom of a tank can empty the full tank in 6 hours. An inlet pipe fills water at the rate of 4 litres per minute. When the tank is full, the inlet is opened and due to the leak the tank is empty in 8 hours. The capacity of the tank is :
    (a) 5260 litres ☐   (b) 5760 litres ☐
    (c) 5846 litres ☐   (d) 6970 litres ☐

14. A pipe can fill a cistern in 12 minutes and another pipe can fill it in 15 minutes, but a third pipe can empty it in 6 minutes. The first two

Pipes & Cisterns

pipes are kept open for 5 minutes in the beginning and then the third pipe is also opened. In what time is the cistern emptied?

(a) 30 min. ☐   (b) 33 min. ☐

(c) $37\frac{1}{2}$ min. ☐   (d) 45 min. ☐

15. There are two taps to fill a tank while a third to empty it. When the third tap is closed, they can fill the tank in 10 minutes and 12 minutes respectively. If all the three taps be opened, the tank is filled in 15 minutes. If the first two taps are closed, in what time can the third tap empty the tank when it is full?

(a) 7 min. ☐   (b) 9 min. and 32 sec. ☐

(c) 8 min. and 34 sec. ☐   (d) 6 min. ☐

16. Two pipes A and B can fill a tank in 15 hours and 20 hours respectively while a third pipe C can empty the full tank in 25 hours. All the three pipes are opened in the beginning. After 10 hours, C is closed. The time taken to fill the tank is :

(a) 12 hours ☐   (b) $13\frac{1}{2}$ hours ☐

(c) 16 hours ☐   (d) 18 hours ☐

17. If two pipes function simultaneously, the reservoir will be filled in 12 hours. One pipe fills the reservoir 10 hours faster than the other. How many hours does the faster pipe take to fill the reservoir?

(a) 25 hours ☐   (b) 28 hours ☐

(c) 30 hours ☐   (d) 35 hours ☐

18. Three pipes A, B and C can fill a cistern in 6 hours. After working at it together for 2 hours, C is closed and A and B can fill it in 7 hours. The time taken by C alone to fill the cistern is :

(a) 10 hours ☐   (b) 12 hours ☐

(c) 14 hours ☐   (d) 16 hours ☐

19. A cistern has a leak which would empty it in 8 hours. A tap is turned on which admits 6 litres a minute into the cistern, and it is now emptied in 12 hours. How many litres does the cistern hold?

(a) 7580 litres ☐   (b) 7960 litres ☐

(c) 8290 litres ☐   (d) 8640 litres ☐

ANSWERS

1. (b)   2. (c)   3. (d)   4. (b)   5. (b)   6. (d)   7. (d)   8. (b)   9. (b)
10. (c)   11. (d)   12. (b)   13. (b)   14. (d)   15. (c)   16. (a)   17. (c)   18. (c)
19. (d)

SOLUTION (Exercise 12)

1. Part filled by A in 1 hour = $\frac{1}{10}$.

   Part filled by B in 1 hour = $\frac{1}{15}$.

   Part filled by (A + B) in 1 hour = $\left(\frac{1}{10}+\frac{1}{15}\right)=\frac{5}{30}=\frac{1}{6}$.

   ∴ Both pipes together can fill the tank in 6 hours.

2. Part filled by inlet in 1 hour = $\frac{1}{8}$.

   Part emptied by outlet in 1 hour = $\frac{1}{16}$

   Net filling in 1 hour = $\left(\frac{1}{8}-\frac{1}{16}\right)=\frac{1}{16}$.

   ∴ Time taken to fill the tank = 16 hours.

3. Net filling in 1 hour = $\left(\frac{1}{x}-\frac{1}{y}\right)=\left(\frac{y-x}{xy}\right)$

   ∴ Time taken to fill the tank = $\left(\frac{xy}{y-x}\right)$ hrs.

4. Net filling in 1 hour = $\left(\frac{1}{2}-\frac{1}{3}\right)=\frac{1}{6}$.

   ∴ Time taken to fill the cistern = 6 hours.

5. Net filling in 1 hour = $\left(\frac{1}{4}+\frac{1}{6}-\frac{1}{8}\right)=\frac{7}{24}$.

   ∴ Time taken to fill the cistern = $\left(\frac{24}{7}\right)$ hrs = 3 hrs 26 min.

6. Net filling in 1 min. = $\left(\frac{1}{32}+\frac{1}{36}-\frac{1}{20}\right)=\frac{13}{1440}$.

   ∴ Time taken to fill the tank = $\left(\frac{1440}{13}\right)$ min.

   Time taken to fill half of the tank = $\left(\frac{1440}{13 \times 2}\right)$ min.

   = $\left(\frac{720}{13}\right)$ min = $55\frac{5}{13}$ min.

7. Part emptied in 1 min. = $\left(\frac{1}{8}-\frac{1}{16}\right)=\frac{1}{16}$.

   ∴ Time taken to empty the full tank = 16 min.
   Hence, the time taken to empty the half tank = 8 min.

8. Work done by waste pipe in 1 min = $\left(\frac{1}{10}+\frac{1}{15}\right)-\frac{1}{18}$

Pipes & Cisterns

$$= \left(\frac{1}{6} - \frac{1}{18}\right) = \frac{1}{9}.$$

∴ Waste pipe can empty the cistern in 9 min.

9. Work done by waste pipe in 1 min. $= \left(\frac{1}{12} + \frac{1}{15}\right) - \frac{1}{20}$

$$= \left(\frac{3}{20} - \frac{1}{20}\right) = \frac{1}{10}.$$

∴ Waste pipe can empty the cistern in 10 min.

10. Work done by both the taps in 5 min.

$$= 5\left(\frac{1}{20} + \frac{1}{25}\right) = \left(5 \times \frac{9}{100}\right) = \frac{9}{20}.$$

Remaining part $= \left(1 - \frac{9}{20}\right) = \frac{11}{20}.$

Now, $\frac{1}{20}$ part is filled in 1 min.

So, $\frac{11}{20}$ part will be filled in 11 min.

Hence, the tank will be full in 11 min. more.

11. Work done by leak in 1 hour $= \left(\frac{1}{8} - \frac{1}{10}\right) = \frac{1}{40}.$

∴ The leak will empty the cistern in 40 hours.

12. Let Y be closed after x min.

Then, $x\left(\frac{1}{24} + \frac{1}{32}\right) + (18 - x) \cdot \frac{1}{24} = 1$

$\Rightarrow \frac{7x}{96} + \frac{18-x}{24} = 1$ or $7x + 72 - 4x = 96.$

∴ $3x = 24$ or $x = 8$ min.

13. Part filled by inlet in 1 hour $= \left(\frac{1}{6} - \frac{1}{8}\right) = \frac{1}{24}.$

So, the inlet can fill the tank in 24 hours.

∴ Capacity of the tank = Water that flows in 24 hours.

$$= (4 \times 24 \times 60) \text{ litres} = 5760 \text{ litres.}$$

14. Part filled in 5 min. $= 5 \times \left(\frac{1}{12} + \frac{1}{15}\right) = 5 \times \frac{9}{60} = \frac{3}{4}.$

Part emptied in 1 min. (when all the pipes are opened)

$$= \frac{1}{6} - \left(\frac{1}{12} + \frac{1}{15}\right) = \left(\frac{1}{6} - \frac{3}{20}\right) = \frac{1}{60}.$$

Now, $\frac{1}{60}$ part is emptied in 1 min.

$\frac{3}{4}$ part will be emptied in $\left(60 \times \frac{3}{4}\right) = 45$ min.

15. Part emptied by the third pipe in 1 min. $= \left(\frac{1}{10} + \frac{1}{12}\right) - \frac{1}{15} = \frac{7}{60}$.

So, the full tank will be emptied by third pipe in $\left(\frac{60}{7}\right)$ min = 8 min. 34 sec.

16. Part filled in 10 hours $= 10 \times \left(\frac{1}{15} + \frac{1}{20} - \frac{1}{25}\right) = \frac{23}{30}$.

Remaining part $= \left(1 - \frac{23}{30}\right) = \frac{7}{30}$.

Now, $\left(\frac{1}{15} + \frac{1}{20}\right)$ part is filled by A and B in 1 hr.

$\frac{7}{30}$ part will be filled by them in $\left(\frac{60}{7} \times \frac{7}{30}\right) = 2$ hrs.

∴ Total time taken to fill the tank = (10 + 2) hrs = 12 hrs.

17. Suppose that one pipe takes x hours to fill the reservoir. Then, another pipe takes $(x - 10)$ hours.

∴ $\frac{1}{x} + \frac{1}{x-10} = \frac{1}{12} \Rightarrow 12(x - 10 + x) = x(x - 10)$

or $x^2 - 34x + 120 = 0$ or $(x - 30)(x - 4) = 0$

∴ $x = 30$ or $x = 4$

So, the faster pipe takes 30 hours to fill the reservoir.

18. Part filled in 2 hours $= 2 \times \frac{1}{6} = \frac{1}{3}$.

Remaining part $= \left(1 - \frac{1}{3}\right) = \frac{2}{3}$

(A + B)'s 7 hours work $= \frac{2}{3}$

∴ (A + B)'s 1 hour's work $= \left(\frac{2}{3} \times \frac{1}{7}\right) = \frac{2}{21}$

(A + B + C)'s 1 hour's work $= \frac{1}{6}$

C's 1 hour's work $= \left(\frac{1}{6} - \frac{2}{21}\right) = \frac{1}{14}$.

Hence, C alone can fill the cistern in 14 hours.

19. Part filled in 1 hour $= \left(\frac{1}{8} - \frac{1}{12}\right) = \frac{1}{24}$.

∴ Time taken to fill the cistern = 24 hours.

Water moved in 24 hours = $(6 \times 24 \times 60)$ litres = 8640 litres.

Hence, the capacity of the cistern is 8640 litres.

13

TIME & DISTANCE

Formulae :

(i) $\text{Speed} = \dfrac{\text{Distance}}{\text{Time}}.$ (ii) $\text{Time} = \dfrac{\text{Distance}}{\text{Speed}}.$

(iii) Distance = (Speed × Time).

(iv) If a certain distance is covered at x km/hr and the same distance is covered at y km/hr, then the average speed during whole journey is
$$\left(\dfrac{2xy}{x+y}\right) \text{km/hr}.$$

(v) If the speed of a body is changed in the ratio $a : b$, then the ratio of the time taken changes in the ratio $b : a$.

(vi) $x \text{ km/hr} = \left(x \times \dfrac{5}{18}\right) \text{m/sec}.$

(vii) $x \text{ metres/sec.} = \left(x \times \dfrac{18}{5}\right) \text{km/hr}.$

SOLVED EXAMPLES

Ex. 1. (i) Convert 45 km/hr into metres/sec.
 (ii) Convert 6 metres/sec. into km/hr.

Sol. (i) $45 \text{ km/hr} = \left(45 \times \dfrac{5}{18}\right) \text{m/sec.} = 12.5 \text{ m/sec.}$

(ii) $6 \text{ m/sec.} = \left(6 \times \dfrac{18}{5}\right) \text{km/hr.} = 21.6 \text{ km/hr.}$

Ex. 2. Harish covers a certain distance by car driving at 70 km/hr and he returns back at the starting point riding on a scooter at 55 km/hr. Find his average speed for the whole journey.

Sol. Average speed $= \left(\dfrac{2 \times 70 \times 55}{70 + 55}\right) \text{km/hr.} = 61.6 \text{ km/hr.}$

Ex. 3. A man covers a certain distance between his house and office on scooter. Having an average speed of 30 km/hr, he is late by 10 min. However, with a speed of 40 km/hr, he reaches his office 5 min. earlier. Find the distance between his house and office.

Sol. Let the required distance be x km.

Time taken to cover x km at 30 km/hr = $\left(\dfrac{x}{30}\right)$ hrs.

Time taken to cover x km at 40 km/hr = $\left(\dfrac{x}{40}\right)$ hrs.

Difference between the times taken = 15 min = $\dfrac{1}{4}$ hr.

$\therefore \dfrac{x}{30} - \dfrac{x}{40} = \dfrac{1}{4} \Rightarrow 4x - 3x = 30 \Rightarrow x = 30.$

Hence, the required distance is 30 km.

Ex. 4. The distance between two stations, Delhi and Amritsar is 450 km. A train starts at 4 p.m. from Delhi and moves towards Amritsar at an average speed of 60 km/hr. Another train starts from Amritsar at 3.20 p.m. and moves towards Delhi at an average speed of 80 km/hr. How far from Delhi will the two trains meet and at what time ?

Sol. Suppose the trains meet at a distance of x km from Delhi. Let the trains from Delhi and Amritsar be A and B respectively. Then,
[Time taken by B to cover $(450 - x)$ km]

$\qquad\qquad$ − [Time taken by A to cover x km] = $\dfrac{40}{60}$.

$\dfrac{450 - x}{80} - \dfrac{x}{60} = \dfrac{40}{60}$

$\therefore 3(450 - x) - 4x = 160 \Rightarrow 7x = 1190 \Rightarrow x = 170.$

Thus, the trains meet at a distance of 170 km from Delhi.

Time taken by A to cover 170 km = $\left(\dfrac{170}{60}\right)$ hrs = 2 hrs 5 min.

So, the trains meet at 6.05 p.m.

Ex. 5. Walking $\dfrac{3}{4}$ of his usual speed, a peon is 10 min. too late to his office. Find his usual time to cover the distance.

Sol. Let the usual time be x min.

Time taken at $\dfrac{3}{4}$ of the usual speed = $\left(\dfrac{4}{3}x\right)$ min.

$\therefore \dfrac{4}{3}x - x = 10$ or $4x - 3x = 30$ or $x = 30.$

Hence, the usual time taken = 30 min.

Time & Distance

Ex. 6. A man cycles from A to B, a distance of 21 km in 1 hour 40 min. The road from A is level for 13 km and then it is uphill to B. The man's average speed on level is 15 km/hr. Find his average uphill speed.

Sol. Let the average uphill speed be x km/hr.

Then, $\dfrac{13}{15} + \dfrac{8}{x} = \dfrac{5}{3} \Rightarrow \dfrac{8}{x} = \dfrac{5}{3} - \dfrac{13}{15} \Rightarrow \dfrac{8}{x} = \dfrac{12}{15}$

$\Rightarrow \dfrac{8}{x} = \dfrac{4}{5} \Rightarrow x = \dfrac{5 \times 8}{4} = 10.$

$\therefore$ Average uphill speed = 10 km/hr.

Exercise 13

1. A speed of 36 km/hr is the same as :
   (a) 10 m/sec □   (b) 7.2 m/sec □
   (c) 2 m/sec □   (d) 129.6 m/sec □

2. A speed of 30.6 km/hr is the same as :
   (a) 5.1 m/sec □   (b) 8.5 m/sec □
   (c) 110.16 m/sec □   (d) 1.7 m/sec □

3. A speed of 55 m/sec is the same as :
   (a) 198 km/hr □   (b) 11 km/hr □
   (c) $15\dfrac{5}{18}$ km/hr □   (d) 275 km/hr □

4. A speed of 22.5 m/sec. is the same as :
   (a) 40.5 km/hr □   (b) 81 km/hr □
   (c) 36.8 km/hr □   (d) 72 km/hr □

5. A and B are two towns. Mr. Faruqui covers the distance from A to B on cycle at 16 km/hr. However, he covers the distance from B to A on foot at 9 km/hr. His average speed during the whole journey is :
   (a) 12.5 km/hr □   (b) 10.25 km/hr □
   (c) 11.52 km/hr □   (d) 12.32 km/hr □

6. A man crosses a street 600 m long in 5 minutes. His speed in km. per hour is : (Clerical Grade, 1991)
   (a) 7.2 □   (b) 3.6 □
   (c) 10 □   (d) 8.4 □

7. If a man covers 10.2 km. in 3 hours, the distance covered by him in 5 hours is : (Astt. Grade 1987)
   (a) 18 km □   (b) 15 km □

(c) 16 km   (d) 17 km

8. A train is moving with a speed of 92.4 km/hr. How many metres will it cover in 10 minutes : (Bank P.O. 1991)
   (a) 1540   (b) 15400
   (c) 154   (d) 15.4

9. If a man takes 4 hours to cover a distance of 15 km, how much time will be needed to cover 63 km at the same speed :
   (a) 12 hrs 36 min.   (b) 16 hrs 48 min.
   (c) 16 hrs 4 min.   (d) 15 hrs 32 min.

10. A distance is covered in 2 hours 45 min. at 4 km/hr. How much time will be taken to cover it at 16.5 km/hr :
    (a) 40 min   (b) 41 min 15 sec
    (c) 45 min   (d) 90 min

11. A boy goes to school with a speed of 3 km/hr and returns to the village with a speed of 2 km/hr. If he takes 5 hours in all, the distance between the village and the school is : (N.D.A. 1990)
    (a) 6 km   (b) 7 km
    (c) 8 km   (d) 9 km

12. Two cyclists A and B start from the same place at the same time, one going towards north at 18 km/hr and other going towards south at 20 km/hr. What time will they take to be 95 km apart ?
    (a) 4 hrs 30 min   (b) 4 hrs 45 min
    (c) 5 hrs 16 min   (d) 2 hrs 30 min

13. Sharad covers two-third of a certain distance at 4 km/hr and the remaining at 5 km/hr. If he takes 42 minutes in all, the distance is :
    (a) 2.5 km   (b) 4.6 km
    (c) 4 km   (d) 3 km

14. A man performs $\frac{2}{15}$ of the total journey by rail, $\frac{9}{20}$ by tonga and the remaining 10 km on foot. His total journey is :
    (a) 15.6 km   (b) 12.8 km
    (c) 16.4 km   (d) 24 km

15. Rahim covers a certain distance in 14 hrs 40 min. He covers one half of the distance by train at 60 km/hr and the rest half by road at 50 km/hr. The distance travelled by him is :
    (a) 960 km   (b) 720 km
    (c) 1000 km   (d) 800 km

16. Suresh travelled 1200 km by air which formed (2/5) of his trip. One

third of the whole trip, he travelled by car and the rest of the journey he performed by train. The distance travelled by train was :

(a) 1600 km   (b) 800 km
(c) 1800 km   (d) 480 km

(Hotel Management 1991)

17. A car completes a certain journey in 8 hours. It covers half the distance at 40 km/hr and the rest at 60 km/hr. The length of the journey is :

(Clerical Grade 1991)

(a) 350 km   (b) 420 km
(c) 384 km   (d) 400 km

18. A and B are two stations. A train goes from A to B at 64 km/hr and returns to A at a slower speed. If its average speed for the whole journey is 56 km/hr, at what speed did it return : (Hotel Management 1991)

(a) 48 km/hr   (b) 49.77 km/hr
(c) 52 km/hr   (d) 47.46 km/hr

19. A car covers four successive three km stretches at speeds of 10 km/hr, 20 km/hr, 30 km/hr and 60 km/hr respectively. Its average speed over this distance is : (Assistant Grade 1986)

(a) 10 km/hr   (b) 20 km/hr
(c) 30 km/hr   (d) 25 km/hr

20. Two men start together to walk to a certain destination, one at 3.75 km an hour and another at 3 km an hour. The former arrives half an hour before the latter. The distance is :

(a) 9.5 km   (b) 8 km
(c) 7.5 km   (d) 6 km

21. Excluding stoppages, the speed of a bus is 54 km/hr and including stoppages, it is 45 km/hr. For how many minutes does the bus stop per hour :

(a) 9   (b) 10
(c) 12   (d) 20

22. A train covers a distance in 50 minutes, if it runs at a speed of 48 km per hour on an average. The speed at which the train must run to reduce the time of journey to 40 minutes, will be :

(a) 50 km/hr   (b) 55 km/hr
(c) 60 km/hr   (d) 70 km/hr

(Central Excise & I. Tax 1988)

23. Laxman has to cover a distance of 6 km in 45 minutes. If he covers one half of the distance in $\frac{2}{3}$ rd time, what should be his speed to cover

the remaining distance in the remaining time : (Bank P.O. 1991)

(a) 12 km/hr ☐ (b) 16 km/hr ☐
(c) 3 km/hr ☐ (d) 8 km/hr ☐

24. A car travels a distance of 840 km at a uniform speed. If the speed of the car is 10 km/hr more, it takes two hours less to cover the same distance. The original speed of the car was :

(a) 45 km/hr ☐ (b) 50 km/hr ☐
(c) 60 km/hr ☐ (d) 75 km/hr ☐

25. X and Y are two stations 500 km apart. A train starts from X and moves towards Y at 20 km/hr. Another train starts from Y at the same time and moves towards X at 30 km/hr. How far from X will they cross each other :

(a) 200 km ☐ (b) 300 km ☐
(c) 120 km ☐ (d) 40 km ☐

26. Two trains start at the same time from Aligarh and Delhi and proceed towards each other at 16 km/hr and 21 km/hr respectively. When they meet, it is found that one train has travelled 60 km more than the other. The distance between the two stations is : (Bank P.O. 1988)

(a) 445 km ☐ (b) 444 km ☐
(c) 440 km ☐ (d) 450 km ☐

27. A train leaves Meerut at 6 a.m. and reaches Delhi at 10 a.m. Another train leaves Delhi at 8 a.m. and reaches Meerut at 11.30 a.m. At what time do the two trains cross one another :

(a) 9.26 a.m. ☐ (b) 9 a.m. ☐
(c) 8.36 a.m. ☐ (d) 8.56 a.m. ☐

28. A thief steals a car at 1.30 p.m. and drives it at 45 km an hour. The theft is discovered at 2 p.m. and the owner sets off in another car at 50 km an hour. He will overtake the thief at :

(a) 3.30 p.m. ☐ (b) 4 p.m. ☐
(c) 4.30 p.m. ☐ (d) 6 p.m. ☐

29. Ram travels a certain distance at 3 km/hr and reaches 15 min. late. If he travels at 4 km/hr, he reaches 15 min. earlier. The distance he has to travel is : (C.D.S. 1989)

(a) 4.5 km ☐ (b) 6 km ☐
(c) 7.2 km ☐ (d) 12 km ☐

30. If a train runs at 40 km/hr, it reaches its destination late by 11 min. but if it runs at 50 km/hr, it is late by 5 min. only. The correct time for the train to cover its journey is :

(a) 13 min. ☐ (b) 15 min. ☐

(c) 21 min. □ (d) 19 min. □

31. By walking at $\frac{3}{4}$ of his usual speed, a man reaches his office 20 minutes later than usual. His usual time is : **(Railways, 1991)**
   (a) 30 minutes □ (b) 60 minutes □
   (c) 75 minutes □ (d) 1 hr 30 min. □

32. A man travels 35 km partly at 4 km/hr and at 5 km/hr. If he covers former distance at 5 km/hr and later distance at 4 km/hr, he could cover 2 km more in the same time. The time taken to cover the whole distance at original rate is :
   (a) 9 hours □ (b) 7 hours □
   (c) $4\frac{1}{2}$ hours □ (d) 8 hours □

33. A man, on tour, travels first 160 km at 64 km/hr and the next 160 km at 80 km/hr. The average speed for the first 320 km of the tour, is :
   (a) 35.55 km/hr □ (b) 71.11 km/hr □
   (c) 36 km/hr □ (d) 72 km/hr □
   (Bank P.O. 1988)

34. The ratio between the rates of walking of A and B is 2 : 3. If the time taken by B to cover a certain distance is 36 minutes, the time taken by A to cover that much distance is :
   (a) 24 min □ (b) 54 min □
   (c) 48 min □ (d) 21.6 min □

35. A is twice as fast as B and B is thrice as fast as C is. The journey covered by C in 42 minutes, will be covered by A in :
   (a) 14 min □ (b) 28 min □
   (c) 63 min □ (d) 7 min □

36. If a boy takes as much time in running 10 m as a car takes in covering 25 m, the distance covered by the boy during the time the car covers 1 km, is : **(Assistant Grade 1987)**
   (a) 400 m □ (b) 40 m □
   (c) 250 m □ (d) 650 m □

37. A certain distance is covered at a certain speed. If half of this distance is covered in double the time, the ratio of the two speeds is :
   (a) 4 : 1 □ (b) 1 : 4 □
   (c) 2 : 1 □ (d) 1 : 2 □
   (Bank P.O. 1986)

38. The ratio between the rates of travelling of A and B is 2 : 3 and therefore A takes 10 min. more than the time taken by B to reach a destination. If A had walked at double the speed, he would have

covered the distance in :
(a) 30 min (b) 25 min
(c) 15 min (d) 20 min

39. A man walking at 3 km/hr crosses a square field diagonally in 2 min. The area of the field is :
(a) 25 ares (b) 30 ares
(c) 50 ares (d) 60 ares

40. A man goes uphill with an average speed of 35 km/hr and comes down with an average speed of 45 km/hr. The distance travelled in both the cases being the same, the average speed for the entire journey is :
(a) $38\frac{3}{8}$ km/hr (b) $39\frac{3}{8}$ km/hr
(c) 40 km/hr (d) none of these
(L.I.C. A.A.O. 1988)

41. Suresh started cycling along the boundaries of a square field from corner point A. After half an hour, he reached the corner point C, diagonally opposite to A. If his speed was 8 km/hr, what is the area of the field in square km : (Bank Trainee Officers 1988)
(a) 64 (b) 8
(c) 4 (d) can not be determined

42. A bullock cart has to cover a distance of 80 km in 10 hours. If it covers half of the journey in (3/5) th time, what should be its speed to cover the remaining distance in the time left ? (Bank P.O. 1988)
(a) 8 km/hr (b) 20 km/hr
(c) 6.4 km/hr (d) 10 km/hr

43. The distance between two stations A and B is 220 km. A train leaves A towards B at an average speed of 80 km/hr. After half an hour, another train leaves B towards A at an average speed of 100 km/hr. The distance of the point where the two trains meet, from A is :
(a) 120 km (b) 130 km
(c) 140 km (d) 150 km
(Clerk's Grade 1991)

Answers

1. (a) 2. (b) 3. (a) 4. (b) 5. (c) 6. (a) 7. (d) 8. (b) 9. (b)
10. (a) 11. (a) 12. (d) 13. (d) 14. (d) 15. (d) 16. (b) 17. (c) 18. (b)
19. (b) 20. (c) 21. (b) 22. (c) 23. (a) 24. (c) 25. (a) 26. (b) 27. (d)
28. (b) 29. (b) 30. (d) 31. (b) 32. (d) 33. (b) 34. (b) 35. (d) 36. (a)
37. (a) 38. (d) 39. (c) 40. (b) 41. (b) 42. (d) 43. (a)

Solution (Exercise 13)

1. 36 km/hr = $\left(36 \times \dfrac{5}{18}\right)$ m/sec = 10 m/sec.

2. 30.6 km/hr = $\left(30.6 \times \dfrac{5}{18}\right)$ m/sec. = 8.5 m/sec.

3. 55 m/sec = $\left(55 \times \dfrac{18}{5}\right)$ km/hr = 198 km/hr.

4. 22.5 m/sec = $\left(22.5 \times \dfrac{18}{5}\right)$ km/hr = 81 km/hr.

5. Average speed = $\left(\dfrac{2 \times 16 \times 9}{16 + 9}\right)$ km/hr = 11.52 km/hr.

6. Speed = $\left(\dfrac{600}{5 \times 60}\right)$ m/sec = $\left(\dfrac{600}{5 \times 60} \times \dfrac{18}{5}\right)$ km/hr = 7.2 km/hr.

7. Speed = $\left(\dfrac{10.2}{3}\right)$ km/hr = 3.4 km/hr.
   Distance covered in 5 hours = (3.4 × 5) km = 17 km.

8. 92.4 km/hr = $\left(92.4 \times \dfrac{5}{18}\right)$ m/sec.
   ∴ Distance covered in (10 × 60) sec = $\left(92.4 \times \dfrac{5}{18} \times 10 \times 60\right)$ m
   = 15400 m.

9. Required time = $\left(\dfrac{4}{15} \times 63\right)$ hrs = 16 hrs 48 min.

10. Distance = $\left(4 \times 2\dfrac{3}{4}\right)$ km = $\left(4 \times \dfrac{11}{4}\right)$ km = 11 km
    Time taken to cover it at 16.5 km/hr = $\left(\dfrac{11}{16.5} \times 60\right)$ min = 40 min.

11. Let the required distance be x km. Then,
    $\dfrac{x}{3} + \dfrac{x}{2} = 5 \Rightarrow 2x + 3x = 30 \Rightarrow x = 6$.

12. They are 38 km apart in 1 hr.
    ∴ They will be 95 km apart in $\left(\dfrac{1}{38} \times 95\right)$ hrs = 2 hrs 30 min.

13. Let total distance be x km.
    Then, $\dfrac{2}{3}x \cdot \dfrac{1}{4} + \dfrac{1}{3}x \cdot \dfrac{1}{5} = \dfrac{42}{60}$

or $\frac{x}{6} + \frac{x}{15} = \frac{7}{10}$ or $5x + 2x = 21$ or $x = 3$.

∴ Required distance = 3 km.

14. Let the total journey be x km. Then,

$\frac{2}{15}x + \frac{9}{20}x + 10 = x \Rightarrow 8x + 27x + 600 = 60x$

$\Rightarrow x = 24$.

∴ Total journey = 24 km.

15. Let the total distance be x km.

Then, $\frac{x}{2} \times \frac{1}{60} + \frac{x}{2} \times \frac{1}{50} = \frac{44}{3}$

or $\frac{x}{120} + \frac{x}{100} = \frac{44}{3}$ or $5x + 6x = 8800$ or $x = 800$.

∴ Required distance = 800 km.

16. Let total distance be x km.

Then, $\frac{2}{5}x = 1200 \Rightarrow x = \frac{1200 \times 5}{2} = 3000$.

Distance travelled by car = $\left(\frac{1}{3} \times 3000\right)$ = 1000 km.

Distance travelled by train = [3000 − (1200 + 1000)] km
= 800 km.

17. Let the total journey be x km.

$\frac{x}{2} \cdot \frac{1}{40} + \frac{x}{2} \cdot \frac{1}{60} = 8 \Rightarrow \frac{x}{80} + \frac{x}{120} = 8$.

∴ $3x + 2x = 1920 \Rightarrow x = 384$ km.

18. Let the required speed be x km/hr.

Then, $\frac{2 \times 64 \times x}{64 + x} = 56 \Rightarrow 128x = 64 \times 56 + 56x$.

∴ $x = \frac{64 \times 56}{72} = 49.77$ km/hr.

19. Total time taken = $\left(\frac{3}{10} + \frac{3}{20} + \frac{3}{30} + \frac{3}{60}\right)$ hrs = $\frac{3}{5}$ hrs.

∴ Average speed = $\left\{\frac{12}{(3/5)}\right\}$ km/hr = $\left(\frac{12 \times 5}{3}\right)$ km/hr = 20 km/hr.

20. Let the distance be x km. Then,

$\frac{x}{3} - \frac{x}{3.75} = \frac{1}{2}$ or $\frac{3.75x - 3x}{3 \times 3.75} = \frac{1}{2}$

or $1.5x = 3 \times 3.75$ or $x = \frac{3 \times 3.75}{1.5} = 7.5$ km

Time & Distance

21. Due to stoppages, it covers 9 km less per hour.
    Time taken to cover 9 km = $\left(\dfrac{9}{54} \times 60\right)$ min. = 10 min.

22. Distance = $\left(48 \times \dfrac{50}{60}\right)$ km = 40 km.
    Required speed = $\left(\dfrac{40}{40/60}\right)$ km/hr = $\left(\dfrac{40 \times 60}{40}\right)$ km/hr. = 60 km/hr.

23. Time left = $\left(\dfrac{1}{3} \times \dfrac{45}{60}\right)$ hr = $\dfrac{1}{4}$ hr.
    Distance left = 3 km.
    $\therefore$ Speed required = $\left(3 \div \dfrac{1}{4}\right)$ km/hr = 12 km/hr.

24. Let the original speed be x km/hr. Then,
    $\dfrac{840}{x} - \dfrac{840}{x+10} = 2 \Rightarrow 840(x+10) - 840x = 2x(x+10)$
    $\therefore x^2 + 10x - 4200 = 0$ or $(x+70)(x-60) = 0$.
    $\therefore x = 60$ km/hr.

25. Suppose they meet x km from X.
    Then, $\dfrac{x}{20} = \dfrac{500-x}{30} \Rightarrow 30x = 10000 - 20x \Rightarrow x = 200$ km.

26. Suppose they meet after x hours. Then,
    $21x - 16x = 60$ or $x = 12$.
    $\therefore$ Required distance = $(16 \times 12 + 21 \times 12)$ km = 444 km.

27. Let the distance between Meerut and Delhi be y km.
    Average speed of the train leaving Meerut = $\left(\dfrac{y}{4}\right)$ km/hr
    Average speed of the train leaving Delhi = $\left(\dfrac{2y}{7}\right)$ km/hr.
    Suppose they meet x hrs after 6 a.m.
    Then, $\dfrac{xy}{4} + \dfrac{2y(x-2)}{7} = y$ or $\dfrac{x}{4} + \dfrac{2x-4}{7} = 1$
    $\therefore 15x = 44$ or $x = \dfrac{44}{15} = 2$ hrs 56 min.
    So, the trains meet at 8.56 a.m.

28. Distance covered by thief in (1/2) hour = 20 km.
    Now, 20 km is compensated by the owner at a relative speed of 10 km/hr in 2 hours.
    So, he overtakes the thief at 4 p.m.

29. Let the distance be x km.

 Then, $\dfrac{x}{3} - \dfrac{x}{4} = \dfrac{30}{60}$ or $\dfrac{4x - 3x}{12} = \dfrac{1}{2}$ or $x = 6$ km

30. Let the required time $= x$ min. Then
 distance covered in $(x + 11)$ min. at 40 km/hr
 $=$ distance covered in $(x + 5)$ min at 50 km/hr.
 $\therefore\ 40 \times \dfrac{x+11}{60} = 50 \times \dfrac{x+5}{60} \Rightarrow x = 19$ min.

31. At a speed of $\dfrac{3}{4}$ of the usual speed, the time taken is $\dfrac{4}{3}$ of the usual time.

 $\therefore\ \left(\dfrac{4}{3} \text{ of usual time}\right) - (\text{usual time}) = 20$ min.

 $\dfrac{4}{3}x - x = 20 \Rightarrow \dfrac{1}{3}x = 20$ or $x = 60$ min.

32. Suppose the man covers first distance in x hrs and second distance in y hrs. Then,
 $\qquad 4x + 5y = 35$ and $5x + 4y = 37$.
 Solving these equations, we get $x = 5$ and $y = 3$.
 $\therefore\ $ Total time taken $= (5 + 3)$ hrs $= 8$ hrs.

33. Average speed $= \left(\dfrac{2 \times 64 \times 80}{64 + 80}\right)$ km/hr $= \left(\dfrac{2 \times 64 \times 80}{144}\right)$ km/hr.
 $\qquad\qquad\qquad\qquad = 71.11$ km/hr.

34. Ratio of times taken $= \dfrac{1}{2} : \dfrac{1}{3}$.

 $\therefore\ \dfrac{1}{2} : \dfrac{1}{3} = x : 36$ or $\dfrac{1}{3} \times x = \dfrac{1}{2} \times 36$ or $x = 54$ min.

35. Let C's speed $= x$ km/hr. Then, B's speed $= 3x$ km/h
 and A's speed $= 6x$ km/hr.
 $\therefore\ $ Ratio of speeds of $A, B, C = 6x : 3x : x = 6 : 3 : 1$.
 Ratio of times taken $= \dfrac{1}{6} : \dfrac{1}{3} : 1$ or $1 : 2 : 6$.
 $\therefore\ 6 : 1 :: 42 : x$ or $6x = 42$ or $x = 7$ min.

36. $25 : 10 :: 1000 : x$ or $x = \dfrac{10 \times 1000}{25} = 400$ m.

37. Let x km be covered in y hrs. Then,
 1st speed $= \left(\dfrac{x}{y}\right)$ km/hr.

Time & Distance

2nd speed $= \left(\dfrac{x}{2} \div 2y\right)$ km/hr $= \left(\dfrac{x}{4y}\right)$ km/hr.

∴ Ratio of speed $= \dfrac{x}{y} : \dfrac{x}{4y} = 1 : \dfrac{1}{4} = 4 : 1$.

38. Ratio of times taken by A and $B = \dfrac{1}{2} : \dfrac{1}{3}$.

    Suppose B takes x min. Then, A takes $(x + 10)$ min.

    ∴ $(x + 10) : x = \dfrac{1}{2} : \dfrac{1}{3}$ or $\dfrac{x + 10}{x} = \dfrac{3}{2}$ or $2x + 20 = 3x$ or $x = 20$.

39. Speed $= \left(3 \times \dfrac{5}{18}\right)$ m/sec. $= \left(\dfrac{5}{6}\right)$ m/sec.

    ∴ Distance covered in (2×60) sec $= \left(\dfrac{5}{6} \times 2 \times 60\right)$ m $= 100$ m.

    ∴ Length of diagonal $= 100$ m.

    So, area $= \dfrac{1}{2} \times$ (diagonal)$^2 = \left(\dfrac{1}{2} \times 100 \times 100\right)$ m^2

    $= 5000$ m$^2 = 50$ ares.

40. Average speed $= \left(\dfrac{2 \times 35 \times 45}{35 + 45}\right)$ km/hr $= 39\dfrac{3}{8}$ km/hr.

41. Length of diagonal $= \left(8 \times \dfrac{1}{2}\right)$ km $= 4$ km.

    ∴ Area of the field $= \left[\dfrac{1}{2} \times (4)^2\right]$ sq. km. $= 8$ sq. km.

42. Distance left $= \left(\dfrac{1}{2} \times 80\right)$ km $= 40$ km.

    Time left $= \left[\left(1 - \dfrac{3}{5}\right) \times 10\right]$ hrs $= 4$ hours.

    Speed required $= (40 \div 4)$ km/hr $= 10$ km/hr.

43. Let the required distance be x km. Then,

    $\dfrac{x}{80} - \dfrac{220 - x}{100} = \dfrac{1}{2} \Rightarrow 5x - 4(220 - x) = 200$

    $\Rightarrow 9x = 1080 \Rightarrow x = 120$ km.

14

TRAINS

Important Points :

(*i*) Time taken by a train *x* metres long in passing *a signal post* or *a pole* or *a standing man* is the same as the time taken by the train to cover *x* metres with its own speed.

(*ii*) Time taken by a train *x* metres long in passing *a stationary object* of length *y* metres (such as *a bridge* or *a tunnel* or *a platform* or *a train at rest*) is the same as the time taken by the train to cover $(x + y)$ metres with its own speed.

(*iii*) Suppose two trains or two bodies are moving in the same direction at *u* km/hr and *v* km/hr respectively such that $u > v$, then

their relative speed = $(u - v)$ km/hr.

If their lengths be *x* km and *y* km respectively, then *time taken by the faster train to cross the slower train (moving in the same direction)*

$$= \left(\frac{x+y}{u-v}\right) \text{ hrs.}$$

(*iv*) Suppose two trains or two bodies are moving *in opposite directions* at *u* km/hr and *v* km/hr, then their relative speed = $(u + v)$ km/hr.

If their lengths be *x* km & *y* km, then :

time taken to cross each other = $\left(\dfrac{x+y}{u+v}\right)$ hrs.

(*v*) If two trains start at the same time from two points *A* and *B* towards each other and after crossing, they take *a* and *b* hours in reaching *B* and *A* respectively. Then,

A's speed : *B*'s speed = $(\sqrt{b} : \sqrt{a})$.

SOLVED EXAMPLES

Ex. 1. Find the time taken by a train 120 m long, running at 54 km/hr, in crossing an electric pole.

Sol. Speed = 54 km/hr = $\left(54 \times \dfrac{5}{18}\right)$ m/sec = 15 m/sec.

Distance moved in passing the pole = 120 m.

Required time taken = $\left(\dfrac{120}{15}\right)$ sec = 8 sec.

… Trains … 245

Ex. 2. A train 160 m long is running at 40 km/hr. In how much time will it pass a platform 140 m long ?

Sol. Speed = $\left(40 \times \dfrac{5}{18}\right)$ m/sec. = $\left(\dfrac{100}{9}\right)$ m/sec.

Distance covered in passing the platform = (160 + 140) m = 300 m.

∴ Required time taken = $\left(300 \times \dfrac{9}{100}\right)$ sec = 27 sec.

Ex. 3. A train passes a standing man in 2 seconds and a platform 50 m long in $4\dfrac{1}{2}$ seconds. Find the length of the train and its speed.

Sol. Let the speed be x km/hr or $\left(\dfrac{5x}{18}\right)$ m/sec.

Let the length of the train be y metres.

∴ $\dfrac{y}{\frac{5x}{18}} = 2 \Rightarrow 10x = 18y \Rightarrow 5x = 9y.$

Also, $\dfrac{y+50}{\frac{5x}{18}} = \dfrac{9}{2} \Rightarrow 36(y+50) = 45x$

$\Rightarrow 5x - 4y = 200$

$\Rightarrow 9y - 4y = 200$ or $y = 40.$

∴ $5x = 9 \times 40$ or $x = \dfrac{9 \times 40}{5} = 72.$

∴ Speed = 72 km/hr and length of train = 40 m.

Ex. 4. A train 125 m long is running at 50 km/hr. In what time will it pass a man, running at 5 km/hr in the same direction in which the train is going ?

Sol. Speed of train relative to man = (50 – 5) km/hr

$= \left(45 \times \dfrac{5}{18}\right)$ m/sec $= \left(\dfrac{25}{2}\right)$ m/sec.

Distance covered in passing the man = 125 m.

∴ Time taken by it in passing the man = $\left(125 \times \dfrac{2}{25}\right)$ sec = 10 sec.

Ex. 5. A train 110 m long is running at 60 km/hr. In what time will it pass a man, running in the direction opposite to that of the train at 6 km/hr ?

Sol. Speed of the train relative to man = $(60 + 6)$ km/hr

$$= \left(66 \times \frac{5}{18}\right) \text{m/sec} = \left(\frac{55}{3}\right) \text{m/sec}.$$

Distance covered by it in passing the man = 110 m.

$\therefore$ Time taken in passing the man = $\left(110 \times \frac{3}{55}\right)$ sec = 6 sec.

Ex. 6. Two trains 128 m and 132 m long are running towards each other on parallel lines at 42 km/hr and 30 km/hr respectively. In what time will they be clear of each other from the moment they meet ?

Sol. Relative speed = $(42 + 30)$ km/hr = $\left(72 \times \frac{5}{18}\right)$ m/sec = 20 m/sec.

Distance covered in passing each other = $(128 + 132)$ m = 260 m.

$\therefore$ Required time = $\left(\frac{260}{20}\right)$ sec = 13 sec.

Ex. 7. Two trains are moving in the same direction at 50 km/hr and 30 km/hr. The faster train crosses a man in the slower train in 18 seconds. Find the length of the faster train.

Sol. Relative speed = $(50 - 30)$ km/hr = $\left(20 \times \frac{5}{18}\right)$ m/sec = $\left(\frac{50}{9}\right)$ m/sec.

Distance covered in 18 sec at this speed = $\left(18 \times \frac{50}{9}\right)$ m = 100 m.

$\therefore$ Length of faster train = 100 m.

Ex. 8. A man sitting in a train which is travelling at 50 km/hr observes that a goods train, travelling in opposite direction, takes 9 seconds to pass him. If the goods train is 150 m long, find its speed.

Sol. Relative speed = $\left(\frac{150}{9}\right)$ m/sec = $\left(\frac{150}{9} \times \frac{18}{5}\right)$ km/hr = 60 km/hr

$\therefore$ Speed of goods train = $(60 - 50)$ km/hr = 10 km/hr.

Ex. 9. A train 100 m long takes 9 seconds to cross a man walking at 5 km/hr in the direction opposite to that of the train. Find the speed of the train.

Sol. Let the speed of the train be x km/hr.

Relative speed = $(x + 5)$ km/hr = $\frac{5(x+5)}{18}$ m/sec.

Distance covered in passing the man = 100 m.

$$\therefore \frac{100}{\frac{5(x+5)}{18}} = 9 \Rightarrow 1800 = 45(x+5) \text{ or } x = 35.$$

∴ Speed of the train = 35 km/hr.

Ex. 10. A train running at 25 km/hr takes 18 seconds to pass a platform. Next, it takes 12 seconds to pass a man walking at 5 km/hr in the same direction. Find the length of the train and that of the platform.

Sol. Let the length of train = x metres and length of platform = y metres.

Speed of train = $\left(25 \times \frac{5}{18}\right)$ m/sec = $\left(\frac{125}{18}\right)$ m/sec.

$$\therefore \frac{x+y}{\frac{125}{18}} = 18 \Rightarrow \frac{18(x+y)}{125} = 18 \Rightarrow x+y = 125 \quad \ldots (i)$$

Speed of train relative to man = (25 + 5) km/hr

$$= \left(30 \times \frac{5}{18}\right) \text{ m/sec} = \left(\frac{25}{3}\right) \text{ m/sec.}$$

$$\therefore x \times \frac{3}{25} = 12 \Rightarrow x = \left(\frac{25 \times 12}{3}\right) = 100 \text{ m.}$$

Putting $x = 100$ in (i), we get $y = 25$.

∴ Length of train = 100 m. Length of platform = 25 m.

Exercise 14

1. A train moves with the speed of 180 km/hr; then its speed in metres per-second is : **(Clerical Grade, 1991)**
   - (a) 5
   - (b) 30
   - (c) 40
   - (d) 50

2. A speed of 16 metres per second is the same as
   - (a) 40.3 km/hr
   - (b) 57.6 km/hr
   - (c) 51.16 km/hr
   - (d) none of these

3. A train 75 metres long is running with a speed of 20 km/hr. It will pass a standing man in :
   - (a) 12 seconds
   - (b) 13.5 seconds
   - (c) 14 seconds
   - (d) 15.5 seconds

4. A train 250 metres long, running with a speed of 50 km/hr will pass an electric pole in :
   - (a) 30 seconds
   - (b) 18 seconds

　　　　(c) 72 seconds　　　　☐　　(d) 60 seconds　　　　☐
5.　A train 280 metres long is moving at speed of 60 km/hr. The time taken by the train to cross a platform 220 metres long is :
　　(a) 20 seconds　　　　☐　　(b) 25 seconds　　　　☐
　　(c) 30 seconds　　　　☐　　(d) 35 seconds　　　　☐
　　　　　　　　　　　　　　　　　　　　(R.R.B. Exam, 1989)
6.　A train 120 metres long is running at a rate of 54 km/hr. Time taken by the train to cross a tunnel 130 metres long, is :
　　(a) $8\frac{1}{3}$ seconds　　☐　　(b) $16\frac{2}{3}$ seconds　　☐
　　(c) 10 seconds　　　　☐　　(d) 15 seconds　　　　☐
7.　A train running at the speed of 45 kmph took 12 seconds in passing a certain point. Then the length of the train must be :
　　(a) 90 metres　　　　☐　　(b) 120 metres　　　　☐
　　(c) 150 metres　　　　☐　　(d) 540 metres　　　　☐
8.　The length of the train that takes 8 seconds to pass a pole when it runs at a speed of 36 km/hr, is :
　　(a) 288 metres　　　　☐　　(b) 45 metres　　　　☐
　　(c) 48 metres　　　　☐　　(d) 80 metres　　　　☐
9.　A train 300 metres long passes a standing man in 15 seconds. The speed of the train is :
　　(a) 40 km/hr　　　　☐　　(b) 50 km/hr　　　　☐
　　(c) 60 km/hr　　　　☐　　(d) 72 km/hr　　　　☐
10.　A train 50 metres long passes a platform 100 metres long in 10 seconds. The speed of the train is :　　　　(R.R.B. Exam, 1989)
　　(a) 10 km/hr　　　　☐　　(b) 15 km/hr　　　　☐
　　(c) 54 km/hr　　　　☐　　(d) 100 km/hr　　　　☐
11.　A person sees a train passing over 1 km long bridge. The length of the train is half that of bridge. If the train clears the bridge in 2 minutes, the speed of the train is :　　(Hotel Management, 1991)
　　(a) 50 km/hr　　　　☐　　(b) 45 km/hr　　　　☐
　　(c) 60 km/hr　　　　☐　　(d) 30 km/hr　　　　☐
12.　A train 100 metres long, running at 36 kmph takes 25 seconds to pass a bridge. The length of the bridge is :
　　(a) 150 metres　　　　☐　　(b) 144 metres　　　　☐
　　(c) 90 metres　　　　☐　　(d) 540 metres　　　　☐
13.　A train 700 m long is running at the speed of 72 km per hour. If it crosses a tunnel in 1 minute, then the length of the tunnel is :
　　(a) 500 m　　　　☐　　(b) 550 m　　　　☐
　　(c) 600 m　　　　☐　　(d) 700 m　　　　☐
　　　　　　　　　　　　　　　　　　　　(N.D.A. Exam, 1990)

Trains 249

14. A train 100 metres long travels at 70 km per hour. A man is running at 10 km per hour in the same direction in which the train is going. The train will pass the man in :
    (a) 6 seconds ☐   (b) $6\frac{2}{3}$ seconds ☐
    (c) 7 seconds ☐   (d) 8 seconds ☐

15. A train 270 metres long is moving at a speed of 25 kmph. It will cross a man coming from the opposite direction at a speed of 2 km per hour in : (R.R.B. Exam, 1989)
    (a) 36 seconds ☐   (b) 32 seconds ☐
    (c) 28 seconds ☐   (d) 24 seconds ☐

16. A train 300 m long crossed a platform 900 m long in 1 minute 12 seconds. The speed of the train in km/hr was : (C.B.I. Exam, 1990)
    (a) 45 ☐   (b) 50 ☐
    (c) 54 ☐   (d) 60 ☐

17. Two trains 132 metres and 108 metres long are running in opposite directions, one at the rate of 32 kmph and another one at the rate of 40 kmph. From the moment they meet they will cross each other in :
    (a) 10 seconds ☐   (b) 11 seconds ☐
    (c) 12 seconds ☐   (d) 13 seconds ☐

18. Two trains A and B start from stations X and Y towards Y and X respectively. After passing each other, they take 4 hours 48 minutes and 3 hours 20 minutes to reach Y and X respectively. If train A is moving at 45 km/hr, then the speed of train B is :
    (a) 60 km/hr ☐   (b) 54 km/hr ☐
    (c) 64.8 km/hr ☐   (d) 37.5 km/hr ☐

19. Two trains are running on parallel lines in the same direction at a speed of 50 km and 30 km per hour respectively. The faster train crosses a man in slower train in 18 seconds. The length of the faster train is :
    (a) 170 metres ☐   (b) 100 metres ☐
    (c) 98 metres ☐   (d) 85 metres ☐

20. Two trains of equal length are running on parallel lines in the same direction at the rate of 46 kmph and 36 kmph. The faster train passes the slower train in 36 seconds. The length of each train is :
    (a) 50 metres ☐   (b) 72 metres ☐
    (c) 80 metres ☐   (d) 82 metres ☐

21. A train crosses a platform 100 metres long in 60 seconds at a speed of 45 km per hour. The time taken by the train to cross an electric pole, is : (Bank P.O. 1990)
    (a) 8 seconds ☐   (b) 1 minute ☐
    (c) 52 seconds ☐   (d) Data inadequate ☐

22. A train moving at the rate of 36 km per hour crosses a standing man in 10 seconds. It will cross a platform 55 metres long, in :

(a) $5\frac{1}{2}$ seconds ☐ (b) 6 seconds ☐

(c) $7\frac{1}{2}$ seconds ☐ (d) $15\frac{1}{2}$ seconds ☐

23. A train takes 5 seconds to pass an electric pole. If the length of the train is 120 metres, the time taken by it to cross a railway platform 180 metres long, is :

(a) $12\frac{1}{2}$ seconds ☐ (b) $7\frac{1}{2}$ seconds ☐

(c) $6\frac{1}{2}$ seconds ☐ (d) $3\frac{1}{3}$ seconds ☑

24. A train of length 150 metres takes 10 seconds to pass over another train 100 metres long coming from the opposite direction. If the speed of the first train be 30 kmph, the speed of the second train is :

(a) 54 kmph ☐ (b) 60 kmph ☐
(c) 72 kmph ☐ (d) 36 kmph ☐

(R.R.B. Exam, 1991)

25. A train is running at the rate of 40 kmph. A man also is going in the same direction parallel to the train at the speed of 25 kmph. If the train crosses the man in 48 seconds, the length of the train is :

(a) 50 metres ☐ (b) 100 metres ☐
(c) 150 metres ☐ (d) 200 metres ☐

26. A 150 metre long train crosses a man walking at the speed of 6 kmph in the opposite direction in 6 seconds. The speed of the train in km/hr is :

(Bank P.O. 1991)

(a) 66 ☐ (b) 84 ☐
(c) 96 ☐ (d) 106 ☐

27. A train speeds past a pole in 15 seconds and speeds past a platform 100 metres long in 25 seconds. Its length in metres is :

(a) 200 ☐ (b) 150 ☐
(c) 50 ☐ (d) Data inadequate ☐

(Bank P.O. Exam, 1989)

28. A train travelling at 36 kmph completely crosses another train having half its length and travelling in the opposite direction at 54 kmph, in 12 seconds. If it also passes a railway platform in $1\frac{1}{2}$ minutes, the length of the platform is :

(a) 560 metres ☐ (b) 620 metres ☐

(c) 700 metres　　　　　　□　　(d) 750 metres　□

29. A train 100 metres in length passes a milestone in 10 seconds and another train of the same length travelling in opposite direction in 8 seconds. The speed of the second train is :
    (a) 36 kmph　　□　　(b) 48 kmph　□
    (c) 54 kmph　　□　　(d) 60 kmph　□

30. Two trains are running in opposite directions with speed of 62 kmph and 40 kmph respectively. If the length of one train is 250 metres and they cross each other in 18 seconds, the length of the other train is :
    (a) 145 metres　　□　　(b) 230 metres　□
    (c) 260 metres　　□　　(d) cannot be determined　□

31. Two trains running in the same direction at 40 kmph and 22 kmph completely pass one another in 1 minute. If the length of the first train is 125 metres, the length of second train is :
    (a) 125 metres　　□　　(b) 150 metres　□
    (c) 200 metres　　□　　(d) 175 metres　□

32. A train 100 metres long moving at a speed of 50 kmph crosses a train 120 metres long coming from opposite direction in 6 seconds. The speed of second train is :　　　　　　(Bank P.O. Exam, 1988)
    (a) 132 kmph　　□　　(b) 82 kmph　□
    (c) 60 kmph　　□　　(d) 50 kmph　□

33. Two stations A and B are 110 kms. apart on a straight line. One train starts from A at 7 a.m. and travels towards B at 20 km per hour speed. Another train starts from B at 8 a.m. and travels towards A at a speed of 25 km per hour. At what time will they meet ?(R.R.B. Exam, 1989)
    (a) 9 a.m.　　□　　(b) 10 a.m.　□
    (c) 11 a.m.　　□　　(d) none of these　□

34. A train overtakes two persons who are walking in the same direction in which the train is going, at the rate of 2 kmph and 4 kmph and passes them completely in 9 and 10 seconds respectively. The length of the train is :
    (a) 72 metres　　□　　(b) 54 metres　□
    (c) 50 metres　　□　　(d) 45 metres　□

35. A train running at certain speed crosses a stationary engine in 20 seconds. To find out the speed of the train, which of the following information is necessary:　　　　　(Bank P.O. 1991)
    (a) Only the length of the train　□
    (b) Only the length of the engine　□
    (c) Either the length of the train or the length of the engine　□
    (d) Both the length of the train and the length of the engine　□

Answers

1. (d)   2. (b)   3. (b)   4. (b)   5. (c)   6. (b)   7. (c)   8. (d)   9. (d)
10. (c) 11. (b) 12. (a) 13. (a) 14. (a) 15. (a) 16. (d) 17. (c) 18. (b)
19. (b) 20. (a) 21. (c) 22. (d) 23. (a) 24. (b) 25. (d) 26. (b) 27. (b)
28. (c) 29. (c) 30. (c) 31. (d) 32. (b) 33. (b) 34. (c) 35. (d)

Solution (Exercise 14)

1. $180 \text{ km/hr} = \left(180 \times \dfrac{5}{18}\right) \text{ m/sec} = 50 \text{ m/sec}$.

2. $16 \text{ m/sec} = \left(16 \times \dfrac{18}{5}\right) \text{ km/hr} = 57.6 \text{ km/hr}$.

3. Speed of the train $= \left(20 \times \dfrac{5}{18}\right) \text{ m/sec} = \left(\dfrac{50}{9}\right) \text{ m/sec}$.

   Time taken by the train to pass the man
   $= \left(75 \times \dfrac{9}{50}\right) \text{ sec} = 13.5 \text{ sec}$.

4. Speed of the train $= \left(50 \times \dfrac{5}{18}\right) \text{ m/sec} = \left(\dfrac{125}{9}\right) \text{ m/sec}$.

   Time taken by the train to pass the pole $= \left(250 \times \dfrac{9}{125}\right) \text{ sec}$.
   $= 18 \text{ sec}$.

5. Speed of the train $= \left(60 \times \dfrac{5}{18}\right) \text{ m/sec} = \left(\dfrac{50}{3}\right) \text{ m/sec}$.

   Time taken by the train to cross the platform
   $= $ Time taken by it to cover $(280 + 220)$ m
   $= \left(500 \times \dfrac{3}{50}\right) \text{ sec} = 30 \text{ sec}$.

6. Speed of the train $= \left(54 \times \dfrac{5}{18}\right) \text{ m/sec} = 15 \text{ m/sec}$.

   Time taken by the train to cross the tunnel
   $= $ Time taken by it to cover $(120 + 130)$ m
   $= \left(\dfrac{250}{15}\right) \text{ sec.} = 16\dfrac{2}{3} \text{ sec}$.

7. Speed $= \left(45 \times \dfrac{5}{18}\right) \text{ m/sec} = \left(\dfrac{25}{2}\right) \text{ m/sec}$.

   Distance $= $ (Time $\times$ Speed) $= \left(12 \times \dfrac{25}{2}\right) \text{ m} = 150 \text{ m}$.

Trains 253

∴ Length of the train = 150 m.

8. Speed = $\left(36 \times \dfrac{5}{18}\right)$ m/sec = 10 m/sec.

Distance = (Time × Speed) = (8 × 10) m = 80 m.

∴ Length of the train = 80 m.

9. Speed = $\dfrac{\text{Distance}}{\text{Time}} = \left(\dfrac{300}{15}\right)$ m/sec = 20 m/sec.

$= \left(20 \times \dfrac{18}{5}\right)$ km/hr = 72 km/hr.

10. Distance covered by train in 10 sec = (50 + 100) m = 150 m.

∴ Speed = $\left(\dfrac{150}{10}\right)$ m/sec = $\left(15 \times \dfrac{18}{5}\right)$ km/hr = 54 km/hr.

11. Distance covered in $\dfrac{2}{60}$ hr = $\left(1 + \dfrac{1}{2}\right)$ km = $\dfrac{3}{2}$ km.

Distance covered in 1 hr = $\left(\dfrac{3}{2} \times \dfrac{60}{2}\right)$ km = 45 km.

So, speed of the train = 45 km/hr.

12. Speed = $\left(36 \times \dfrac{5}{18}\right)$ m/sec = 10 m/sec.

Let the length of the bridge = x m.
Distance covered = (100 + x) m.
Time taken = 25 sec.

∴ $\dfrac{100 + x}{25} = 10 \Rightarrow 100 + x = 250 \Rightarrow x = 150$ m.

13. Speed = $\left(72 \times \dfrac{5}{18}\right)$ m/sec = 20 m/sec.

Let the length of tunnel = x metres.

Then, $\dfrac{700 + x}{60} = 20 \Rightarrow 700 + x = 1200$ or $x = 500$ m.

14. Relative speed = (70 − 10) km/hr = 60 km/hr

$= \left(60 \times \dfrac{5}{18}\right)$ m/sec = $\left(\dfrac{50}{3}\right)$ m/sec.

∴ Time taken by the train to pass the man

$= \left(100 \times \dfrac{3}{50}\right)$ sec = 6 sec.

15. Relative speed = (25 + 2) km/hr = 27 km/hr

$= \left(27 \times \dfrac{5}{18}\right)$ m/sec = $\left(\dfrac{15}{2}\right)$ m/sec.

Time taken by the train to pass the man
$$= \left(270 \times \frac{2}{15}\right) \sec = 36 \sec.$$

16. Distance covered in 72 sec. = (300 + 900) m
$$\therefore \text{ speed} = \left(\frac{1200}{72}\right) \text{m/sec} = \left(\frac{50}{3}\right) \text{m/sec}$$
$$= \left(\frac{50}{3} \times \frac{18}{5}\right) \text{km/hr} = 60 \text{ km/hr.}$$

17. Relative speed = (32 + 40) km/hr = 72 km/hr
$$= \left(72 \times \frac{5}{18}\right) \text{m/sec} = 20 \text{ m/sec.}$$
Distance covered in crossing each other = (132 + 108) m = 240 m
$$\therefore \text{ Required time} = \left(\frac{240}{20}\right) \sec = 12 \sec.$$

18. $\dfrac{A\text{'s rate}}{B\text{'s rate}} = \sqrt{\dfrac{\text{time taken by } B \text{ to reach } X}{\text{time taken by } A \text{ to reach } Y}}$

or $\dfrac{45}{B\text{'s rate}} = \sqrt{\dfrac{10}{3} \times \dfrac{5}{24}} = \dfrac{5}{6}.$

$\therefore B\text{'s rate} = \left(\dfrac{45 \times 6}{5}\right) \text{km/hr} = 54 \text{ km/hr.}$

19. Relative speed = (50 – 30) km/hr = 20 km/hr
$$= \left(20 \times \frac{5}{18}\right) \text{m/sec} = \left(\frac{50}{9}\right) \text{m/sec.}$$
Let the length of faster train be x

Then, $x \times \dfrac{9}{50} = 18 \Rightarrow x = \dfrac{18 \times 50}{9} = 100 \text{ m.}$

20. Let the length of each train = x metres.
Relative speed = (46 – 36) km/hr = 10 km/hr
$$= \left(10 \times \frac{5}{18}\right) \text{m/sec} = \left(\frac{25}{9}\right) \text{m/sec.}$$
Distance covered in crossing = $(x + x)$ m = $2x$ metres.

$\therefore 2x \times \dfrac{9}{25} = 36$ or $x = \dfrac{25 \times 36}{2 \times 9} = 50 \text{ m.}$

21. Let the length of train = x metres.
Speed $= \left(45 \times \dfrac{5}{18}\right)$ m/sec $= \left(\dfrac{25}{2}\right)$ m/sec.
Distance covered in crossing the platform = $(x + 100)$ m

Trains 255

$\therefore (x + 100) \times \dfrac{2}{25} = 60$ or $2x + 200 = 1500$ or $x = 650$.

Now, time taken to cross the pole $= \left(650 \times \dfrac{2}{25}\right)$ sec $= 52$ sec.

22. Speed $= \left(36 \times \dfrac{5}{18}\right)$ m/sec $= 10$ m/sec.

Let the length of the train be x metres.

Then, $\dfrac{x}{10} = 10 \Rightarrow x = 100$ m.

$\therefore$ Time taken to cross the platform $= \left(\dfrac{100 + 55}{10}\right)$ sec $= 15\dfrac{1}{2}$ sec.

23. Speed $= \left(\dfrac{120}{5}\right)$ m/sec $= 24$ m/sec.

Time taken to cross the platform $= \left(\dfrac{120 + 180}{24}\right)$ sec $= 12\dfrac{1}{2}$ sec.

24. Relative Speed $= \left(\dfrac{150 + 100}{10}\right)$ m/sec $= 25$ m/sec.

$\phantom{\therefore\text{Relative Speed}} = \left(25 \times \dfrac{18}{5}\right)$ km/hr $= 90$ km/hr.

$\therefore$ Speed of second train $= (90 - 30)$ km/hr $= 60$ km/hr

25. Relative speed $= (40 - 25)$ km/hr

$\phantom{\text{Relative speed}} = \left(15 \times \dfrac{5}{18}\right)$ m/sec $= \left(\dfrac{25}{6}\right)$ m/sec.

Length of the train $= \left(48 \times \dfrac{25}{6}\right)$ m $= 200$ m.

26. Let the speed of the train be x km/hr.

Relative speed $= (x + 6)$ km/hr $= \left[(x + 6) \times \dfrac{5}{18}\right]$ m/sec.

$\dfrac{150}{6} = \dfrac{(x + 6) \times 5}{18}$ or $5x + 30 = 450$ or $x = 84$ km/hr.

27. Let the length of the train be x metres and its speed be y metres/sec.

Then, $\dfrac{x}{y} = 15 \Rightarrow y = \dfrac{x}{15}$.

Now, $\dfrac{x + 100}{25} = \dfrac{x}{15} \Rightarrow x = 150$ m.

28. Let the length of slower train be x metres and the length of faster train be $\left(\dfrac{x}{2}\right)$ metres.

Relative speed = $(36 + 54)$ km/hr = $\left(90 \times \dfrac{5}{18}\right)$ m/sec = 25 m/sec.

$\therefore \dfrac{3x}{2 \times 25} = 12 \Rightarrow 3x = 600 \Rightarrow x = 200$ m.

$\therefore$ Length of slower train = 200 m

Let the length of platform be y metres.

Then, $\dfrac{200 + y}{36 \times \dfrac{5}{18}} = 90 \Rightarrow 200 + y = 900$ or $y = 700$ m.

$\therefore$ Length of platform = 700 m.

29. Speed of first train = $\left(\dfrac{100}{10}\right)$ m/sec = 10 m/sec.

Let the speed of 2nd train be x m/sec.

Relative speed = $(10 + x)$ m/sec.

$\therefore \dfrac{200}{10 + x} = 8 \Rightarrow 200 = 80 + 8x \Rightarrow x = 15.$

$\therefore$ Speed of 2nd train = 15 m/sec = $\left(15 \times \dfrac{18}{5}\right)$ km/hr. = 54 km/hr.

30. Let the length of another train = x metres.

Their relative speed = $(62 + 40)$ km/hr.

= $\left(102 \times \dfrac{5}{18}\right)$ m/sec = $\left(\dfrac{85}{3}\right)$ m/sec.

$\dfrac{250 + x}{\left(\dfrac{85}{3}\right)} = 18 \Rightarrow \dfrac{3(250 + x)}{85} = 18$

$\Rightarrow 250 + x = 510 \Rightarrow x = 260.$

$\therefore$ Length of another train = 260 m.

31. Relative speed = $(40 - 22)$ km/hr = $\left(18 \times \dfrac{5}{18}\right)$ m/sec = 5 m/sec.

Let the length of 2nd train be x metres.

Then, $\dfrac{125 + x}{5} = 60 \Rightarrow 125 + x = 300 \Rightarrow x = 175.$

$\therefore$ Length of second train = 175 metres.

32. Let the speed of the second train be x km/hr.

Relative speed = $(50 + x)$ km/hr = $\left[(50 + x) \times \dfrac{5}{18}\right]$ m/sec.

$$= \left(\frac{250 + 5x}{18}\right) \text{ m/sec.}$$

$$\therefore \frac{100 + 120}{\frac{250 + 5x}{18}} = 6 \text{ or } 220 \times 18 = 6 (250 + 5x)$$

or $30 x = 3960 - 1500$ or $x = \frac{2460}{30} = 82.$

$\therefore$ Speed of the second train = 82 km/hr.

33. Suppose they meet x hrs after 7 a.m.
    Distance covered by A in x hrs = $(20 \times x)$ km.
    Distance covered by B in $(x - 1)$ hrs = $25 (x - 1)$ km.
    $\therefore$ $20 x + 25 (x - 1) = 110$ or $45 x = 135$ or $x = 3.$
    So, they meet at 10 a.m.

34. Let the length of the train be x km and its speed be y km/hr.
    Then, speed relative to first man = $(y - 2)$ km/hr.
    Speed relative to second man = $(y - 4)$ km/hr.
    $\therefore \frac{x}{y-2} = \frac{9}{60 \times 60}$ and $\frac{x}{y-4} = \frac{10}{60 \times 60}$
    $\therefore 9y - 18 = 3600 x$ & $10 y - 40 = 3600 x.$
    So, $9 y - 18 = 10 y - 40$ or $y = 22.$
    $\therefore \frac{x}{22-2} = \frac{9}{3600}$ or $x = \frac{20 \times 9}{3600} = \frac{1}{20}$ km = $\left(\frac{1}{20} \times 1000\right)$ m = 50 m.

35. Since the sum of the lengths of the train and the length of the engine is needed, so both the lengths must be known.

15
BOATS & STREAMS

Important Points :
(i) Direction along the stream is called **downstream**.
(ii) Direction against the stream is called **upstream**.
(iii) Let, speed of boat in still water be a km/hr and the speed of stream be b km/hr. Then,
Speed downstream = $(a + b)$ km/hr.
Speed upstream = $(a - b)$ km/hr.
(iv) If a man rows in still water at a km/hr and the rate of current or stream is b km/hr., then
Man's rate with the current = $(a + b)$ km/hr.
Man's rate against the current = $(a - b)$ km/hr.
Rate in still water
$$= \frac{1}{2} \text{ [(rate with the current)} + \text{(rate against the current)]}$$
Rate of Current
$$= \frac{1}{2} \text{ [(rate with the current)} - \text{(rate against the current)]}$$

SOLVED EXAMPLES

Ex. 1. A man can row upstream at 11 km/hr and downstream at 16 km/hr. Find man's rate in still water and the rate of current.

Sol. Rate in still water = $\frac{1}{2}$ (11 + 16) km/hr = 13.5 km/hr.

Rate of current = $\frac{1}{2}$ (16 – 11) km/hr = 2.5 km/hr.

Ex. 2. A man rows downstream 30 km and upstream 18 km, taking 5 hours each time. What is the velocity of current ?

Sol. Man's rate downstream = $\left(\frac{30}{5}\right)$ km/hr = 6 km/hr.

Man's rate upstream = $\left(\frac{18}{5}\right)$ km/hr.

Boats & Streams

$\therefore$ Velocity of current $= \frac{1}{2}\left(6 - \frac{18}{5}\right)$ km/hr = 1.2 km/hr.

Ex. 3. A man can row 6 km/hr in still water. It takes him twice as long to row up as to row down the river. Find the rate of stream.

Sol. Let man's rate upstream = x km/hr.

Then, man's rate downstream = $2x$ km/hr.

$\therefore$ Man's rate in still water $= \frac{1}{2}(x + 2x)$ km/hr.

$\therefore \frac{3x}{2} = 6$ or $x = 4$ km/hr.

Thus, man's rate upstream = 4 km/hr.

Man's rate downstream = 8 km/hr.

$\therefore$ Rate of stream $= \frac{1}{2}(8 - 4)$ km/hr = 2 km/hr.

Ex. 4. A man can row 6 km/hr in still water. When the river is running at 1.2 km/hr, it takes him 1 hour to row to a place and back. How far is the place?

Sol. Man's rate downstream = (6 + 1.2) km/hr = 7.2 km/hr.

Man's rate upstream = (6 – 1.2) km/hr = 4.8 km/hr

Let the required distance be x km. Then,

$\frac{x}{7.2} + \frac{x}{4.8} = 1 \Rightarrow 4.8 x + 7.2 x = 7.2 \times 4.8$

$\Rightarrow x = \frac{7.2 \times 4.8}{12} = 2.88$ km.

Ex. 5. In a stream running at 2 km/hr, a motor boat goes 10 km upstream and back again to the starting point in 55 minutes. Find the speed of motorboat in still water.

Sol. Let the speed of motorboat in still water be x km/hr.

Then, speed downstream = $(x + 2)$ km/hr.

And, speed upstream = $(x - 2)$ km/hr.

$\therefore \frac{10}{x+2} + \frac{10}{x-2} = \frac{55}{60}$ or $11 x^2 - 240 x - 44 = 0$

$\therefore (x - 22)(11x + 2) = 0$

So, $x = 22$ km/hr. [*neglecting the –ve value*]

Ex. 6. A man can row 30 km upstream and 44 km downstream in 10 hours. Also, he can row 40 km upstream and 55 km downstream in 13 hours. Find the rate of current and the speed of the man in still water.

Sol. Let, rate upstream = x km/hr and rate downstream = y km/hr.

Then, $\dfrac{30}{x} + \dfrac{44}{y} = 10$ .... (i)

$\dfrac{40}{x} + \dfrac{55}{y} = 13$ .... (ii)

or $\quad 30u + 44v = 10$ .... (iii)

$\quad 40u + 55v = 13$ .... (iv)

where $u = \dfrac{1}{x}$ and $v = \dfrac{1}{y}$.

Solving (iii) and (iv), we get $u = \dfrac{1}{5}$ and $v = \dfrac{1}{11}$.

$\therefore \dfrac{1}{x} = \dfrac{1}{5}$ and $\dfrac{1}{y} = \dfrac{1}{11}$ i.e. $x = 5$ and $y = 11$.

$\therefore$ Rate in still water = $\dfrac{1}{2}(5 + 11)$ km/hr = 8 km/hr.

Rate of current = $\dfrac{1}{2}(11 - 5)$ km/hr = 3 km/hr.

Exercise 15

1. A man can row with the stream at 11 km/hr and against the stream at 8 km/hr. The speed of the stream is :
   - (a) 3 km/hr ☐
   - (b) 9.5 km/hr ☐
   - (c) 1.5 km/hr ☐
   - (d) 6 km/hr ☐

2. A man can row downstream at 14 km/hr and upstream at 9 km/hr. Man's rate in still water is :
   - (a) 5 km/hr ☐
   - (b) 23 km/hr ☐
   - (c) 11.5 km/hr ☐
   - (d) none of these ☐

3. The speed of a boat in still water is 2 km/hr. If its speed upstream be 1 km/hr, then speed of the stream is :   (Astt. Grade 1987)
   - (a) 1.5 km/hr ☐
   - (b) 3 km/hr ☐
   - (c) 1 km/hr ☐
   - (d) none of these ☐

4. The speed of a boat downstream is 15 km/hr and the speed of the stream is 1.5 km/hr. The speed of the boat upstream is :
   - (a) 13.5 km/hr ☐
   - (b) 16.5 km/hr ☐
   - (c) 12 km/hr ☐
   - (d) 8.25 km/hr ☐

5. If a man rows at 5 km/hr in still water and 3.5 km/hr against the current,

Boats & Streams

his rate along the current is :
- (a) 8.5 km/hr
- (b) 6.5 km/hr
- (c) 6 km/hr
- (d) 4.25 km/hr

6. If a man's rate with the current is 12 km/hr and the rate of the current is 1.5 km/hr, then man's rate against the current is :
- (a) 9 km/hr
- (b) 6.75 km/hr
- (c) 5.25 km/hr
- (d) 7.5 km/hr

7. A boat goes 40 km upstream in 8 hours and 36 km downstream in 6 hours. The speed of the boat in standing water is :
- (a) 6.5 km/hr
- (b) 6 km/hr
- (c) 5.5 km/hr
- (d) 5 km/hr

8. A boat travels upstream from B to A and downstream from A to B in 3 hours. If the speed of the boat in still water is 9 km/hr and the speed of the current is 3 km/hr, the distance between A and B is :
- (a) 4 km
- (b) 6 km
- (c) 8 km
- (d) 12 km

(BSRB Exam. 1990)

9. A man can row at 5 km/hr in still water and the velocity of current is 1 km/hr. It takes him 1 hour to row to a place and back. How far is the place :
- (a) 2.5 km
- (b) 2.4 km
- (c) 3 km
- (d) 3.6 km

10. Speed of a boat in standing water is 6 km/hr and the speed of the stream is 1.5 km/hr A man rows to a place at a distance of 22.5 km and comes back to the starting point. The total time taken by him, is :
- (a) 6 hrs 30 min.
- (b) 8 hrs 24 min.
- (c) 8 hrs
- (d) 4 hrs 12 min.

11. A man rows upstream 16 km and downstream 28 km, taking 5 hours each time. The velocity of the current is :
- (a) 2.4 km/hr
- (b) 1.2 km/hr
- (c) 3.6 km/hr
- (d) 1.8 km/hr

12. A boat moves upstream at the rate of 1 km in 10 minutes and downstream at the rate of 1 km in 6 minutes. The speed of the current is :
- (a) 1 km/hr
- (b) 1.5 km/hr
- (c) 2 km/hr
- (d) 2.5 km/hr

13. A man rows to a place 48 km distant and back in 14 hours. He finds that he can row 4 km with the stream in the same time as 3 km against

the stream. The rate of the stream is :
(a) 0.5 km/hr   (b) 1 km/hr
(c) 3.5 km/hr   (d) 1.8 km/hr

14. The current of a stream runs at the rate of 4 km an hour. A boat goes 6 km and back to the starting point in 2 hours. The speed of the boat in still water is :
(a) 6 km/hr   (b) 7.5 km/hr
(c) 8 km/hr   (d) 6.8 km/hr

15. A boat covers 24 km upstream and 36 km downstream in 6 hours, while it covers 36 km upstream and 24 km downstream in $6\frac{1}{2}$ hours. The velocity of the current is :
(a) 1.5 km/hr   (b) 1 km/hr
(c) 2 km/hr   (d) 2.5 km/hr

16. The current of a stream runs at 1 km/hr. A motor boat goes 35 km upstream and back again to the starting point in 12 hours. The speed of motorboat in still water is :
(a) 6 km/hr   (b) 7 km/hr
(c) 8.5 km/hr   (d) 8 km/hr

17. A man can row $9\frac{1}{3}$ km/hr in still water and he finds that it takes him thrice as much time to row up than as to row down the same distance in river. The speed of the current is :   (Central Excise & I. Tax 1991)
(a) $3\frac{1}{3}$ km/hr   (b) $3\frac{1}{9}$ km/hr
(c) $1\frac{1}{4}$ km/hr   (d) $4\frac{2}{3}$ km/hr

18. A man can row three quarters of a kilometre against the stream in $11\frac{1}{4}$ minutes and return in $7\frac{1}{2}$ minutes. The speed of the man in still water is :
(a) 2 km/hr   (b) 3 km/hr
(c) 4 km/hr   (d) 5 km/hr

19. A man can swim 3 km/hr in still water. If the velocity of the stream be 2 km/hr, the time taken by him to swim to a place 10 km upstream and back, is :
(a) $8\frac{1}{3}$ hrs   (b) $9\frac{1}{5}$ hrs

Boats & Streams

(c) 10 hrs (d) 12 hrs

Answers (Exercise 15)

1. (c) 2. (c) 3. (c) 4. (c) 5. (b) 6. (a) 7. (c) 8. (d) 9. (b)
10. (c) 11. (b) 12. (c) 13. (b) 14. (c) 15. (c) 16. (a) 17. (d) 18. (d)
19. (d)

Solution (Exercise 15)

1. Speed of stream = $\frac{1}{2}(11-8)$ km/hr = 1.5 km/hr

2. Man's rate in still water = $\frac{1}{2}(14+9)$ km/hr = 11.5 km/hr

3. Let the speed of stream be x km/hr.
   Then, speed upstream = $(2-x)$ km/hr.
   $2 - x = 1 \Rightarrow x = 1$ km/hr.

4. Let the speed of boat in still water be x km/hr.
   Then, $x + 1.5 = 15 \Rightarrow x = 13.5$.
   ∴ Speed upstream = $(13.5 - 1.5)$ km/hr = 12 km/hr.

5. Let the rate along the current be x km/hr.
   Then, $\frac{x + 3.5}{2} = 5 \Rightarrow x = (10 - 3.5) = 6.5$ km/hr.

6. Let the rate against the current be x km/hr. Then,
   $\frac{12 - x}{2} = 1.5 \Rightarrow 12 - x = 3 \Rightarrow x = 9$ km/hr.

7. Speed upstream = $\left(\frac{40}{8}\right)$ km/hr = 6 km/hr.
   Speed downstream = $\left(\frac{36}{6}\right)$ km/hr = 6 km/hr.
   Speed of boat in still water = $\frac{1}{2}(5 + 6)$ km/hr = 5.5 km/hr

8. Speed downstream = $(9 + 3)$ km/hr = 12 km/hr.
   Speed upstream = $(9 - 3)$ km/hr = 6 km/hr.
   Let the distance $AB = x$ km.
   Then, $\frac{x}{6} + \frac{x}{12} = 3 \Rightarrow 2x + x = 36 \Rightarrow x = 12$.
   ∴ Distance $AB = 12$ km.

9. Speed downstream = $(5 + 1)$ km/hr = 6 km/hr.

Speed upstream = $(5-1)$ km/hr = 4 km/hr.
Let the required distance be x km.
Then, $\dfrac{x}{6} + \dfrac{x}{4} = 1 \Rightarrow 2x + 3x = 12$ or $x = 2.4$ km.

10. Speed upstream = $(6 - 1.5)$ km/hr = 4.5 km/hr.
Speed downstream = $(6 + 1.5)$ km/hr = 7.5 km/hr.
Total time taken = $\left(\dfrac{22.5}{4.5} + \dfrac{22.5}{7.5}\right)$ hrs = 8 hrs.

11. Speed downstream = $\left(\dfrac{28}{5}\right)$ km/hr = 5.6 km/hr.
Speed upstream = $\left(\dfrac{16}{5}\right)$ km/hr = 3.2 km/hr.
Velocity of current = $\dfrac{1}{2}(5.6 - 3.2)$ km/hr = 1.2 km/hr.

12. Speed upstream = 6 km/hr
Speed downstream = 10 km/hr.
$\therefore$ Speed of the current = $\dfrac{1}{2}(10 - 6)$ km/hr = 2 km/hr.

13. Suppose he moves 4 km downstream in x hrs.
Then, speed downstream = $\left(\dfrac{4}{x}\right)$ km/hr.
Speed upstream = $\left(\dfrac{3}{x}\right)$ km/hr.
$\therefore \dfrac{48}{\frac{4}{x}} + \dfrac{48}{\frac{3}{x}} = 14 \Rightarrow 12x + 16x = 14$ or $x = \dfrac{1}{2}$.
$\therefore$ Speed downstream = 8 km/hr.
Speed upstream = 6 km/hr.
$\therefore$ Rate of stream = $\dfrac{1}{2}(8-6)$ km/hr = 1 km/hr.

14. Let the speed in still water be x km/hr.
Then, $\dfrac{6}{x+4} + \dfrac{6}{x-4} = 2 \Rightarrow 6[x-4+x+4] = 2(x^2 - 16)$
or $x^2 - 16 = 6x$ or $x^2 - 6x - 16 = 0$
or $(x-8)(x+2) = 0$. So, $x = 8$ km/hr.

15. Let the speed upstream be x km/hr and the speed downstream be y km/hr. Then,

$\dfrac{24}{x} + \dfrac{36}{y} = 6 \Rightarrow 24u + 36v = 6$, where $u = \dfrac{1}{x}$, $v = \dfrac{1}{y}$

And, $\dfrac{36}{x} + \dfrac{24}{y} = \dfrac{13}{2} \Rightarrow 36u + 24y = \dfrac{13}{2}$

Adding these equations, we get

$60(u+v) = \dfrac{25}{2}$ or $u+v = \dfrac{5}{24}$.

Subtracting, we get $12(u-v) = \dfrac{1}{2}$ or $u-v = \dfrac{1}{24}$.

Solving, $u+v = \dfrac{5}{24}$ and $u-v = \dfrac{1}{24}$, we get

$u = \dfrac{1}{8}$ and $v = \dfrac{1}{12}$.

$\therefore\ x = 8$ km/hr & $y = 12$ km/hr.

$\therefore\ $ Velocity of current $= \dfrac{1}{2}(12-8)$ km/hr $= 2$ km/hr.

16. Let the speed in still water be x km/hr.

$\dfrac{35}{x-1} + \dfrac{35}{x+1} = 12$

or $35(2x) = 12(x^2 - 1)$

or $12x^2 - 70x - 12 = 0$

or $12x^2 - 72x + 2x - 12 = 0$

or $12x(x-6) + 2(x-6) = 0$

or $(x-6)(12x+2) = 0$

$\therefore\ x = 6$.

17. Let speed upstream $= x$ km/hr

Then, speed downstream $= 3x$ km/hr

$\therefore\ $ Speed in still water $= \dfrac{1}{2}(x+3x)$ km/hr $= 2x$ km/hr

Speed of the current $= \dfrac{1}{2}(3x-x)$ km/hr $= x$ km/hr

$\therefore\ 2x = \dfrac{28}{3}$ or $x = \dfrac{14}{3} = 4\dfrac{2}{3}$ km/hr.

18. Speed upstream $= \left(\dfrac{3}{4} \times \dfrac{4}{45} \times 60\right)$ km/hr $= 4$ km/hr.

Speed downstream $= \left(\dfrac{3}{4} \times \dfrac{2}{15} \times 60\right)$ km/hr $= 6$ km/hr.

Speed in still water = $\frac{1}{2}$ (4 + 6) km/hr = 5 km/hr.

19. Speed upstream = (3 − 2) km/hr = 1 km/hr
    Speed downstream = (3 + 2) km/hr = 5 km/hr
    Total time taken = $\left(\frac{10}{1} + \frac{10}{5}\right)$ hr = 12 hrs.

16
PROBLEMS ON NUMBERS

Exercise 16

1. The difference of two numbers is 5 and the difference of their squares is 135. The sum of the numbers is :
   (a) 27
   (b) 25
   (c) 30
   (d) 32

2. The sum of two numbers is 29 and the difference of their squares is 145. The difference between the numbers is :
   (a) 13
   (b) 5
   (c) 8
   (d) 11

3. The difference of two numbers is 8 and $\frac{1}{8}$th of their sum is 35. The numbers are :
   (a) 132, 140
   (b) 128, 136
   (c) 124, 132
   (d) 136, 144

4. The sum of two numbers is 100 and their difference is 37. The difference of their squares is : (Clerk Grade Exam. 1991)
   (a) 37
   (b) 100
   (c) 63
   (d) 3700

5. The ratio between two numbers is 3 : 4 and their sum is 420. The greater of the two numbers is : (Railways, 1991)
   (a) 175
   (b) 200
   (c) 240
   (d) 315

6. The difference between the squares of two consecutive numbers is 35. The numbers are : (Railways, 1991)
   (a) 14, 15
   (b) 15, 16
   (c) 17, 18
   (d) 18, 19

7. Three fourth of one-fifth of a number is 60. The number is :
   (a) 300
   (b) 400
   (c) 450
   (d) 1200
   (Bank P.O. 1990)

8. A number is 25 more than its two-fifth. The number is :

(a) 60   (b) 80
(c) $\frac{125}{3}$ (d) $\frac{125}{7}$

(Clerk's Grade 1991)

9. 24 is divided into two parts such that 7 times the first part added to 5 times the second part makes 146. The first part is : (Railways, 1991)
   (a) 11   (b) 13
   (c) 16   (d) 17

10. If one-fifth of a number decreased by 5 is 5, then the number is :
    (a) 25   (b) 50
    (c) 60   (d) 75

(Clerk's Grade, 1991)

11. $\frac{1}{4}$ of a number subtracted from $\frac{1}{3}$ of the number gives 12. The number is :
    (a) 144   (b) 120
    (c) 72   (d) 63

12. $\frac{3}{4}$ of a number is 19 less than the original number. The number is :
    (a) 84   (b) 64
    (c) 76   (d) 72

13. A number is as much greater than 31 as is less than 55. The number is :
    (a) 47   (b) 52
    (c) 39   (d) 43

14. 11 times a number gives 132. The number is : (Clerk's Grade 1991)
    (a) 11   (b) 12
    (c) 13.2   (d) none of these

15. Three-fourth of a number is more than two-third of the number by 5. The number is :
    (a) 72   (b) 60
    (c) 84   (d) 48

16. $\frac{4}{5}$ of a certain number is 64. Half of that number is : (BSRB, 1991)
    (a) 32   (b) 40
    (c) 80   (d) 16

17. A positive number when decreased by 4, is equal to 21 times the reciprocal of the number. The number is : (N.D.A. 1987)

(a) 3 (b) 5
(c) 7 (d) 9

18. The sum of two numbers is 15 and sum of their squares is 113. The numbers are :
    (a) 4, 11 (b) 5, 10
    (c) 6, 9   (d) 7, 8

19. The sum of two numbers is twice their difference. If one of the numbers is 10, the other number is : **(Railways, 1991)**
    (a) $3\frac{1}{3}$ (b) 30
    (c) $-3\frac{1}{3}$ (d) $4\frac{1}{4}$

20. The sum of squares of two numbers is 80 and the square of their difference is 36. The product of the two numbers is :
    (a) 22 (b) 44
    (c) 58 (d) 116

    (Clerk's Grade, 1991)

21. The product of two numbers is 120. The sum of their squares is 289. The sum of the two numbers is : **(Clerk's Grade 1991)**
    (a) 20 (b) 23
    (c) 169 (d) none of these

22. A number whose fifth part increased by 5 is equal to its fourth part diminished by 5, is :
    (a) 160 (b) 180
    (c) 200 (d) 220

23. If one-fourth of one-third of one-half of a number is 15, the number is :
    (a) 72 (b) 120
    (c) 180 (d) 360

24. $\frac{4}{5}$ of a number exceeds its $\frac{2}{3}$ by 8. The number is : **(R.R.B., 1989)**
    (a) 30 (b) 60
    (c) 90 (d) none of these

25. If 1 is added to the denominator of a fraction, the fraction becomes $\frac{1}{2}$. If 1 is added to the numerator, the fraction becomes 1. The fraction is : **(C.D.S., 1991)**

(a) $\dfrac{4}{7}$ □ (b) $\dfrac{5}{9}$ □

(c) $\dfrac{2}{3}$ □ (d) $\dfrac{10}{11}$ □

26. A fraction becomes 4 when 1 is added to both the numerator and denominator; and it becomes 7 when 1 is subtracted from both the numerator and denominator. The numerator of the given fraction is :

(a) 2 □ (b) 3 □
(c) 7 □ (d) 15 □

(N.D.A. Exam. 1990)

27. If 3 is added to the denominator of a fraction, it becomes $\dfrac{1}{3}$ and if 4 be added to its numerator, it becomes $\dfrac{3}{4}$. The fraction is :

(a) $\dfrac{4}{9}$ □ (b) $\dfrac{3}{20}$ □

(c) $\dfrac{7}{24}$ □ (d) $\dfrac{5}{12}$ □

28. A certain number of two digits is three times the sum of its digits and if 45 be added to it, the digits are reversed. The number is :

(a) 32 □ (b) 72 □
(c) 27 □ (d) 23 □

29. The sum of three consecutive odd numbers is 57. The middle one is :

(a) 19 □ (b) 21 □
(c) 23 □ (d) 17 □

30. Three numbers are in the ratio 3 : 4 : 5. The sum of the largest and the smallest equals the sum of the third and 52. The smallest number is :

(a) 20 □ (b) 27 □
(c) 39 □ (d) 52 □

(Accountant's Exam. 1986)

31. The sum of three numbers is 68. If the ratio between first and second be 2 : 3 and that between second and third be 5 : 3, then the second number is : (S.S.C. Exam. 1986)

(a) 30 □ (b) 20 □
(c) 58 □ (d) 48 □

32. The sum of three numbers is 132. If the first number be twice the second and third number be onethird of the first, then the second number is :

(a) 32 □ (b) 36 □

Problems On Numbers 271

    (c) 48   (d) 60

33. Three numbers are in the ratio 4 : 5 : 6 and their average is 25. The largest number is :
    (a) 42   (b) 36
    (c) 30   (d) 32

34. If the unit digit in the product $75\,?\,\times 49\times 867\times 943$ be 1, then the value of ? is :
    (a) 1   (b) 3
    (c) 7   (d) 9

35. What number must be added to the numerator and denominator of $\frac{3}{4}$ to give $\frac{11}{12}$:
    (a) 5   (b) 6
    (c) 7   (d) 8

36. The number x is exactly divisible by 5 and the remainder obtained on dividing the number y by 5 is 1. What remainder will be obtained when $(x + y)$ is divided by 5 :
    (a) 0   (b) 1
    (c) 2   (d) 3

37. A number exceeds 20% of itself by 40. The number is :
    (a) 50   (b) 60
    (c) 80   (d) 320
    (Assistant Grade, 1990)

38. If 16% of 40% of a number is 8, the number is :
    (a) 200   (b) 225
    (c) 125   (d) 320
    (Assistant Grade, 1990)

39. Of the three numbers, the first is twice the second and is half of the third. If the average of three numbers is 56, the smallest number is :
    (a) 24   (b) 36
    (c) 40   (d) 48
    (Central Excise, 1988)

40. Which of the following numbers is not a square of any natural number :
    (a) 34692   (b) 4096
    (c) 15309   (d) none of these

41. The number $6^{2n}-1$, where n is any positive integer, is always divisible by :

    (a) 11   (b) 5
    (c) 7   (d) both 5 and 7

42. Of the three numbers, the sum of first two is 45; the sum of the second and the third is 55 and the sum of the third and thrice the first is 90. The third number is :
    (a) 20   (b) 25
    (c) 30   (d) 35

43. There are two numbers such that the sum of twice the first and thrice the second is 18, while the sum of thrice the first and twice the second is 17. The larger of the two is :
    (a) 4   (b) 6
    (c) 8   (d) 12

44. If a number is subtracted from the square of its one half, the result is 48. The square root of the number is :
    (a) 4   (b) 5
    (c) 6   (d) 8

45. The ratio between two numbers is 2 : 3. If the consequent is 24, the antecedent is :
    (a) 36   (b) 16
    (c) 48   (d) 72

46. Two numbers are such that the ratio between them is 3 : 5; but if each is increased by 10, the ratio between them becomes 5 : 7. The numbers are :   **(R.R.B. Exam. 1989)**
    (a) 3, 5   (b) 7, 9
    (c) 13, 22   (d) 15, 25

47. Divide 50 into two parts so that the sum of their reciprocals is (1/12) :   **(R.R.B. Exam. 1988)**
    (a) 20, 30   (b) 24, 26
    (c) 28, 22   (d) 36, 14

48. The sum of seven numbers is 235. The average of the first three is 23 and that of the last three is 42. The fourth number is :
    (a) 40   (b) 126
    (c) 69   (d) 195
    (Clerk's Grade Exam. 1991)

49. A number when divided by 6 is diminished by 40. The number is :
    (a) 72   (b) 84
    (c) 60   (d) 48

Problems On Numbers 273

50. The sum of squares of two numbers is 68 and the square of their difference is 36. The product of the two numbers is :

(Clerk's Grade Exam. 1991)

(a) 16 ☐ (b) 32 ☐
(c) 58 ☐ (d) 104 ☐

Answers (Exercise 16)

1. (a) 2. (b) 3. (d) 4. (d) 5. (c) 6. (c) 7. (b) 8. (c) 9. (b)
10. (b) 11. (a) 12. (c) 13. (d) 14. (b) 15. (b) 16. (b) 17. (c) 18. (d)
19. (b) 20. (a) 21. (b) 22. (c) 23. (d) 24. (b) 25. (c) 26. (d) 27. (d)
28. (c) 29. (a) 30. (c) 31. (a) 32. (b) 33. (c) 34. (d) 35. (d) 36. (b)
37. (a) 38. (c) 39. (a) 40. (a) 41. (d) 42. (a) 43. (a) 44. (a) 45. (b)
46. (d) 47. (a) 48. (a) 49. (d) 50. (a)

SOLUTION (Exercise 16)

1. Let the numbers be a and b.

Then, $(a + b) = \dfrac{(a^2 - b^2)}{(a - b)} = \dfrac{135}{5} = 27.$

2. Let the numbers be a and b.

Then, $(a - b) = \dfrac{(a^2 - b^2)}{(a + b)} = \dfrac{145}{29} = 5.$

3. Let the numbers be x and $(x + 8)$.

Then, $\dfrac{1}{8}[x + (x + 8)] = 35$ or $2x + 8 = 280$

or $2x = 272$ or $x = 136$.

So, the numbers are 136 and 144.

4. Let the numbers be a and b.

Then, $a + b = 100$ and $a - b = 37$.

$\therefore a^2 - b^2 = (a + b)(a - b) = 100 \times 37 = 3700.$

5. Let the numbers be $3x$ and $4x$.

Then, $3x + 4x = 420 \Rightarrow 7x = 420 \Rightarrow x = 60.$

$\therefore$ Greater number $= 4 \times 60 = 240$.

6. Let the numbers be x and $(x + 1)$.

Then, $(x + 1)^2 - x^2 = 35 \Rightarrow x^2 + 2x + 1 - x^2 = 35$

$\Rightarrow 2x = 34$ or $x = 17$.

So, the numbers are 17 and 18.

7. Let the number be x. Then,
$\frac{3}{4} \times \frac{1}{5} \times x = 60 \Rightarrow 3x = 1200$ or $x = 400$.

8. Let the number be x. Then,
$x - 25 = \frac{2}{5}x$ or $5x - 125 = 2x$ or $x = \frac{125}{3}$.

9. Let the parts be x and $24 - x$. Then,
$7x + 5(24 - x) = 146 \Rightarrow 7x + 120 - 5x = 146$
$\Rightarrow 2x = 26$ or $x = 13$.
$\therefore$ First part = 13.

10. Let the number be x. Then,
$\frac{x}{5} - 5 = 5 \Rightarrow \frac{x}{5} = 10 \Rightarrow x = 50$.

11. Let the number be x. Then,
$\frac{x}{3} - \frac{x}{4} = 12 \Rightarrow \frac{4x - 3x}{12} = 12 \Rightarrow x = 144$.

12. Let the original number be x. Then,
$\frac{3}{4}x + 19 = x \Rightarrow 3x + 76 = 4x \Rightarrow x = 76$.

13. Let the number be x. Then,
$x - 31 = 55 - x \Rightarrow 2x = 55 + 31 = 86$ or $y = 43$.

14. Let the number be x.
Then, $11x = 132 \Rightarrow x = 12$.

15. Let the number be x. Then,
$\frac{3}{4}x - \frac{2}{3}x = 5 \Rightarrow \frac{9x - 8x}{12} = 5 \Rightarrow x = 60$.

16. Let the number be x. Then,
$\frac{4}{5}x = 64 \Rightarrow x = \frac{64 \times 5}{4} = 80$.
$\therefore$ Half of the number = 40.

17. Let the number be x. Then,
$x - 4 = \frac{21}{x} \Rightarrow x^2 - 4x - 21 = 0$
$\Rightarrow x^2 - 7x + 3x - 21 = 0$
$\Rightarrow x(x - 7) + 3(x - 7) = 0$
$\Rightarrow (x - 7)(x + 3) = 0$
$\Rightarrow x = 7$ (neglecting $x = -3$)

Problems On Numbers   275

18. Let the numbers be x and $(15-x)$.
    Then, $x^2 + (15-x)^2 = 113$ or $x^2 - 15x + 56 = 0$
    ∴ $x = 8$ or $x = 7$.
    So, the numbers are 7, 8.

19. Let the other number be x.
    Then, $10 + x = 2(x - 10) \Rightarrow x = 30$.

20. Let the numbers be a and b. Then,
    $a^2 + b^2 = 80$ and $(a-b)^2 = 36$.
    $(a-b)^2 = 36 \Rightarrow a^2 + b^2 - 2ab = 36$
    $\Rightarrow 2ab = (a^2 + b^2) - 36 = 80 - 36 = 44$
    $\Rightarrow ab = 22$.

21. Let the numbers be a and b. Then,
    $(a+b)^2 = (a^2 + b^2) + 2ab = 289 + 2 \times 120 = 289 + 240 = 529$
    ∴ $a + b = \sqrt{529} = 23$.

22. Let the number be x. Then,
    $\frac{x}{5} + 5 = \frac{x}{4} - 5 \Rightarrow \frac{x}{4} - \frac{x}{5} = 10$ or $\frac{5x - 4x}{20} = 10$
    $\Rightarrow x = 200$.

23. Let the number be x. Then,
    $\frac{1}{4}$ of $\frac{1}{3}$ of $\frac{1}{2}$ of $x = 15 \Rightarrow \frac{1}{24} x = 15 \Rightarrow x = 24 \times 15 = 360$.

24. Let the number be x. Then,
    $\frac{4}{5} x - \frac{2}{3} x = 8 \Rightarrow \frac{12x - 10x}{15} = 8 \Rightarrow 2x = 120$ or $x = 60$.

25. Let the required fraction be $\frac{x}{y}$. Then,
    $\frac{x}{y+1} = \frac{1}{2} \Rightarrow 2x - y = 1$ and $\frac{x+1}{y} = 1 \Rightarrow x - y = -1$.
    Solving $2x - y = 1$ & $x - y = -1$, we get $x = 2, y = 3$.
    ∴ The fraction is $\frac{2}{3}$.

26. Let the required fraction be $\frac{x}{y}$.
    Then, $\frac{x+1}{y+1} = 4 \Rightarrow x - 4y = 3$

And, $\dfrac{x-1}{y-1} = 7 \Rightarrow x - 7y = -6$.

Solving these equations, we get $x = 15, y = 3$.

27. Let the required fraction be $\dfrac{x}{y}$.

    $\dfrac{x}{y+3} = \dfrac{1}{3} \Rightarrow 3x - y = 3$.

    And, $\dfrac{x+4}{y} = \dfrac{3}{4} \Rightarrow 4x - 3y = -16$.

    Solving these equations, we get $x = 5, y = 12$.

    $\therefore$ Required fraction $= \dfrac{5}{12}$.

28. Let unit digit $= x$ & ten's digit $= y$.
    $3(x + y) = 10y + x$, $110y + x + 15 = 10x + y$
    $2x - 7y = 0$, $9x - 9y = 45$ or $x - y = 5$.
    Solving these equations, we get $x = 7, y = 2$.
    $\therefore$ Required number $= 27$.

29. Let the required odd integers be $x, x + 2$ and $x + 4$. Then,
    $x + x + 2 + x + 4 = 57 \Rightarrow 3x = 51 \Rightarrow x = 17$.
    $\therefore$ The integers are 17, 19, 21.

30. Let the numbers be $3x, 4x$ and $5x$.
    Then, $5x + 3x = 4x + 52 \Rightarrow 4x = 52 \Rightarrow x = 13$.
    $\therefore$ The smallest number $= 3x = 3 \times 13 = 39$.

31. Let the numbers be a, b, c. Then,
    $\dfrac{a}{b} = \dfrac{2}{3}, \dfrac{b}{c} = \dfrac{5}{3} \Rightarrow \dfrac{a}{b} = \dfrac{2 \times 5}{3 \times 5} = \dfrac{10}{15}$ and $\dfrac{b}{c} = \dfrac{5 \times 3}{3 \times 3} = \dfrac{15}{9}$
    $\Rightarrow a : b : c = 10 : 15 : 9$.
    Let the numbers be $10x, 15x$ and $9x$.
    Then, $10x + 15x + 9x = 68 \Rightarrow 34x = 68 \Rightarrow x = 2$.
    $\therefore$ Second number $= 15x = 15 \times 2 = 30$.

32. Let second number be $3x$. Then, first one is $6x$ and the third one is $2x$.
    $\therefore$ $3x + 6x + 2x = 132 \Rightarrow 11x = 132 \Rightarrow x = 12$.
    $\therefore$ Second number $= 3x = 3 \times 12 = 36$.

33. Let the numbers be $4x, 5x$ and $6x$.
    Then, $\dfrac{4x + 5x + 6x}{3} = 25$ or $15x = 75$ or $x = 5$.

Problems On Numbers

∴ The largest number $= 6x = 6 \times 5 = 30$.

34. $x \times 9 \times 7 \times 3 =$ a number with unit digit 1.
    Clearly, the minimum value of x is 9.

35. Let $\dfrac{3+x}{4+x} = \dfrac{11}{12}$. Then,
    $12(3+x) = 11(4+x) \Rightarrow x = 44 - 36 = 8$.

36. Let $\dfrac{x}{5} = p$. Let y when divided by 5, give q as quotient and 1 as remainder. Then, $y = 5q + 1$.
    Now, $x = 5p$ and $y = 5q + 1$.
    ∴ $x + y = 5p + 5q + 1 = 5(p+q) + 1$.
    So, required remainder = 1.

37. Let the required number be x.
    Then, $x - \dfrac{20}{100}x = 40$ or $5x - x = 200$ or $x = 50$.

38. Let $\dfrac{16}{100} \times \dfrac{40}{100} \times x = 8$. Then, $x = \dfrac{8 \times 100 \times 100}{16 \times 40} = 125$.

39. Let the second number be x.
    Then, first number = $2x$ and third number = $4x$.
    ∴ $\dfrac{2x + x + 4x}{3} = 56 \Rightarrow 7x = 3 \times 56$ or $x = \dfrac{3 \times 56}{7} = 24$.
    So, the smallest number is 24.

40. The square of a natural number never ends in 2.

41. $6^2 - 1 = 35$, which is divisible by both 5 and 7.

42. Let the numbers be x, y, z. Then,
    $x + y = 45$, $y + z = 55$, $z + 3x = 90$.
    Now, $y = (45 - x)$ and $z = 55 - y = 55 - (45 - x) = 10 + x$.
    ∴ $10 + x + 3x = 90 \Rightarrow x = 20$.
    So, third number = $10 + x = 30$.

43. Let the numbers be x and y. Then,
    $2x + 3y = 18$, $3x + 2y = 17$.
    Solving, we get $x = 3$, $y = 4$.
    ∴ Larger number = 4.

44. Let the number be x. Then,
    $\left(\dfrac{x}{2}\right)^2 - x = 48 \Rightarrow \dfrac{x^2}{4} - x = 48 \Rightarrow x^2 - 4x - 192 = 0 \Rightarrow x = 16$.

∴ The square root of the number is 4.

45. Let the antecedent be x. Then,

$\dfrac{x}{24} = \dfrac{2}{3} \Rightarrow x = \dfrac{24 \times 2}{3} = 16$.

46. Let the numbers be $3x$ and $5x$. Then,

$\dfrac{3x + 10}{5x + 10} = \dfrac{5}{7} \Rightarrow 7(3x + 10) = 5(5x + 10) \Rightarrow x = 5$.

∴ The numbers are 15 and 25.

47. Let the numbers be x and $(50 - x)$. Then,

$\dfrac{1}{x} + \dfrac{1}{50 - x} = \dfrac{1}{12} \Rightarrow \dfrac{50 - x + x}{x(50 - x)} = \dfrac{1}{12}$

$\Rightarrow x^2 - 50x + 600 = 0 \Rightarrow x = 30$ or 20.

∴ The numbers are 20, 30.

48. $(23 \times 3 + x + 42 \times 3) = 235 \Rightarrow x = 40$.

∴ Fourth number = 40.

49. Let the required number be x. Then,

$\dfrac{x}{6} + 40 = x \Rightarrow x + 240 = 6x \Rightarrow x = 48$.

50. Let the numbers be a and b. Then,

$a^2 + b^2 = 68$ and $(a - b)^2 = 36$.

Now, $(a - b)^2 = 36 \Rightarrow a^2 + b^2 - 2ab = 36$

$\Rightarrow 68 - 2ab = 36 \Rightarrow 2ab = 32 \Rightarrow ab = 16$.

17

PROBLEMS ON AGES

Exercise 17

1. The sum of the ages of a mother and a daughter is 50 years. Also, 5 years ago, the mother's age was 7 times the age of the daughter. The present ages of the mother and the daughter respectively are :
   - (a) 35 yrs, 15 yrs ☐
   - (b) 38 yrs, 12 yrs ☐
   - (c) 40 yrs, 10 yrs ☐
   - (d) 42 yrs, 8 yrs ☐

2. The sum of the ages of a son and father is 56 years. After four years, the age of the father will be three times that of the son. Their ages respectively are : **(Railway Recruitment 1989)**
   - (a) 12 years, 44 years ☐
   - (b) 16 years, 42 years ☐
   - (c) 16 years, 48 years ☐
   - (d) 18 years, 36 years ☐

3. Mr. Sohanlal is 4 times as old as his son. Four years hence the sum of their ages will be 43 years. The present age of son is :
   - (a) 5 years ☐
   - (b) 7 years ☐
   - (c) 8 years ☐
   - (d) 10 years ☐

4. In 10 years, A will be twice as old as B was 10 years ago. If A is now 9 years older than B, the present age of B is : **(L.I.C. Exam 1989)**
   - (a) 19 years ☐
   - (b) 29 years ☐
   - (c) 39 years ☐
   - (d) 49 years ☐

5. Rajan's age is 3 times that of Ashok. In 12 years, Rajan's age will be double the age of Ashok. Rajan's present age is :
   - (a) 27 years ☐
   - (b) 32 years ☐
   - (c) 36 years ☐
   - (d) 40 years ☐

6. The sum of the ages of a father and son is 45 years. Five years ago the product of their ages was 4 times the fathers age at that time. The present ages of the father and son, respectively are :
   - (a) 25 yrs, 10 yrs ☐
   - (b) 36 yrs, 9 yrs ☐
   - (c) 39 yrs, 6 yrs ☐
   - (d) none of these ☐

   (Hotel Management 1991)

7. The age of a man is 4 times that of his son. Five years ago, the man was nine times as old as his son was at that time. The present age of the man is :
   (a) 28 years   (b) 32 years
   (c) 40 years   (d) 44 years

8. Five years ago Viney's age was onethird of the age of Vikas and now Viney's age is 17 years. What is the present age of Vikas ?
   (a) 9 years   (b) 36 years
   (c) 41 years   (d) 51 years
   (Railway Recruitment 1991)

9. The difference between the agers of two persons is 10 years. 15 years ago, the elder one was twice as old as the younger one. The present age of the elder person is :
   (a) 25 years   (b) 35 years
   (c) 45 years   (d) 55 years

10. Pushpa is twice as old as Rita was two years ago. If the difference between their ages be 2 years, how old is Pushpa today ?
    (a) 6 years   (b) 8 years
    (c) 10 years   (d) 12 years
    (Railway Recruitment 1991)

11. The age of Arvind's father is 4 times his age. If 5 years ago, father's age was 7 times of the age of his son at that time, what is Arvind's father's present age ?   (S.B.I. P.O. Exam 1987)
    (a) 35 years   (b) 40 years
    (c) 70 years   (d) 84 years

12. After five years the age of a father will be thrice the age of his son, whereas five years ago, he was seven times as old as his son was. What is father's present age ?
    (a) 35 years   (b) 40 years
    (c) 45 years   (d) 50 years

13. 10 years ago, Chandravati's mother was 4 times older than her daughter. After 10 years, the mother will be twice older than the daughter. The present age of Chandravati is :   (Bank P.O. 1988)
    (a) 5 years   (b) 10 years
    (c) 20 years   (d) 30 years

14. The ratio of the father's age to the son's age is 4 : 1. The product of their ages is 196. The ratio of their ages after 5 years will be :
    (a) 3 : 1   (b) 10 : 3
    (c) 11 : 4   (d) 14 : 5

Problems On Ages

15. The ratio of Laxmi's age to the age of her mother is 3 : 11. The difference of their ages is 24 years. The ratio of their ages after 3 years will be :
    (a) 1 : 3   ☐   (b) 2 : 3   ☐
    (c) 3 : 5   ☐   (d) none of these   ☐

16. Kamla got married 6 years ago. Today her age is $1\frac{1}{4}$ times her age at the time of marriage. Her son's age is (1/10) times her age. Her son's age is :   **(Bank P.O. 1988)**
    (a) 2 years   ☐   (b) 3 years   ☐
    (c) 4 years   ☐   (d) 5 years   ☐

17. The age of a father 10 years ago was thrice the age of his son. Ten years hence, the father's age will be twice that of his son. The ratio of their present ages is :
    (a) 8 : 5   ☐   (b) 7 : 3   ☐
    (c) 5 : 2   ☐   (d) 9 : 5   ☐

18. One year ago a father was four times as old as his son. In 6 years time, his age exceeds twice his son's age by 9 years. Ratio of their ages is :
    (a) 13 : 4   ☐   (b) 12 : 5   ☐
    (c) 11 : 3   ☐   (d) 9 : 2   ☐

19. Ratio of Ashok's age to Pradeep's age is equal to 4 : 3. Ashok will be 26 years old after 6 years. How old is Pradeep now ?
    (a) 12 years   ☐   (b) 15 years   ☐
    (c) $19\frac{1}{2}$ years   ☐   (d) 21 years   ☐

    (Railway Recruitment, 1989)

20. The ratio of the ages of father and son at present is 6 : 1. After 5 years the ratio will become 7 : 2. The present age of the son is :
    (a) 5 years   ☐   (b) 6 years   ☐
    (c) 9 years   ☐   (d) 10 years   ☐

    (Bank P.O. 1991)

21. The ratio between the ages of A and B at present is 2 : 3. Five years hence the ratio of their ages will be 3 : 4. What is the present age of A ?
    (a) 10 years   ☐   (b) 15 years   ☐
    (c) 25 years   ☐   (d) data inadequate   ☐

    (S.B.I. P.O. Exam, 1991)

22. The ages of A and B are in the ratio 2 : 5. After 8 years their ages will be in the ratio 1 : 2. The difference of their ages is :
    (a) 20 years (b) 24 years
    (c) 26 years (d) 29 years

23. One year ago the ratio between Samir and Ashok's age was 4 : 3. One year hence the ratio of their age will be 5 : 4. What is the sum of their present ages in years ?
    (a) 12 years (b) 15 years
    (c) 16 years (d) cannot be determined
    (A.O. Exam 1991)

24. Three years ago the average age of A and B was 18 years. With C joining them, the average becomes 22 years. How old is C now ?
    (a) 24 years (b) 27 years
    (c) 28 years (d) 30 years
    (P.N.B. P.O. Exam 1987)

25. Jayesh is as much younger to Anil as he is older to Prashant. If the sum of the ages of Anil and Prashant is 48 years, what is the age of Jayesh ? (P.O. Exam 1991)
    (a) 20 years (b) 24 years
    (c) 30 years (d) cannot be determined

26. The ratio of Vimal's age and Aruna's age is 3 : 5 and sum of their ages is 80 years. The ratio of their ages after 10 years will be :
    (a) 2 : 3 (b) 1 : 2
    (c) 3 : 2 (d) 3 : 5
    (Bank P.O. 1990)

27. Ten years ago A was half of B in age. If the ratio of their present ages is 3 : 4, what will be the total of their present ages ?
    (a) 8 years (b) 20 years
    (c) 35 years (d) 45 years
    (S.B.I. P.O. Exam 1991)

Answers (Exercise 17)

1. (c) 2. (a) 3. (b) 4. (c) 5. (c) 6. (b) 7. (b) 8. (c) 9. (b)
10. (b) 11. (b) 12. (b) 13. (c) 14. (c) 15. (a) 16. (b) 17. (b) 18. (c)
19. (b) 20. (a) 21. (a) 22. (b) 23. (c) 24. (a) 25. (b) 26. (a) 27. (c).

Solution (Exercise 17)

1. Let the daughter's present age be x years.
   Then, mother's present age $= (50 - x)$ years.
   Now, $7(x - 5) = (50 - x - 5)$ or $x = 10$
   So, their present ages are 40 yrs and 10 yrs.

2. Let the present ages of son and father be x years and $(56 - x)$ years respectively. Then,
   $(56 - x + 4) = 3(x + 4)$ or $4x = 48$ or $x = 12$.
   So, their ages are 12 years, 44 years respectively.

3. Let the son's age be x years.
   Then, $(x + 4) + (4x + 4) = 43$ or $5x = 35$ or $x = 7$.

4. Let the present ages of B and A be x yrs and $(x + 9)$ yrs respectively.
   Then, $(x + 9 + 10) = 2(x - 10)$ or $x = 39$.

5. Let Ashok's age be x years. Then, Rajan's age $= 3x$ years
   $\therefore 2(x + 12) = (3x + 12)$ or $x = 12$.
   Hence, Rajan's present age is 36 years.

6. Let the present ages of father and son be x years and $(45 - x)$ years.
   Then, $(x - 5)(45 - x - 5) = 4(x - 5)$
   or $-x^2 + 41x - 180 = 0$ or $x = 36$.
   $\therefore$ The present ages of father and son are 36 years and 9 years respectively.

7. Let the son's age be x years. Then, father's age $= 4x$ years
   $\therefore (4x - 5) = 9(x - 5)$ or $5x = 40$ or $x = 8$.
   $\therefore$ Present age of the man $= 32$ years.

8. Let the present age of Vikas be x years. Then,
   $$17 - 5 = \frac{1}{3}(x - 5) \text{ or } x - 5 = 36 \text{ or } x = 41.$$

9. Let the present age of the elder person be x years.
   Then, the present age of the other person $= (x - 10)$ years
   $(x - 15) = 2(x - 10 - 15)$ or $x = 35$
   $\therefore$ The present age of the elder person is 35 years.

10. Let Rita's age 2 years ago be x years.
    Pushpa's present age $= (2x)$ years
    $2x - (x + 2) = 2 \Rightarrow x = 4$
    $\therefore$ Pushpa's present age $= 8$ years.

11. Let Arvind's age be x years.
    Then, his father's age $= 4x$ years.
    $\therefore (4x - 5) = 7(x - 5)$ or $3x = 30$ or $x = 10$

Hence, Arvind's father's age is 40 years.

12. Let son's age 5 years hence = x years.
Then, father's age 5 years hence = $(3x)$ years.
$7(x - 10) = (3x - 10)$ or $x = 15$.
∴ Father's present age = $(3x - 5) = 40$ years.

13. Let Chandravati's age 10 years ago be x years.
Mother's age 10 years ago = $(4x)$ years.
$2(x + 20) = (4x + 20) \Rightarrow x = 10$.
Present age of Chandravati = $(x + 10) = 20$ years.

14. Let father's age be $4x$ and son's age x years.
∴ $4x \times x = 196$ or $x^2 = 49$ or $x = 7$.
Father's age after 5 years = $(4x + 5) = 33$ years.
Son's age after 5 years = $(x + 5) = 12$ years.
∴ Ratio of their ages after 5 years = $33 : 12 = 11 : 4$.

15. $11x - 3x = 24 \Rightarrow x = 3$.
∴ Ratio of their ages after 3 years
$= (3x + 3 : 11x + 3) = 12 : 36 = 1 : 3$.

16. Let Kamla's age 6 years ago be x years. Then,
Kamla's present age = $(x + 6)$ years.
∴ $x + 6 = \frac{5}{4}x$ or $4x + 24 = 5x$ or $x = 24$.
So, Kamla's present age = 30 years.
Son's present age = $\left(\frac{1}{10} \times 30\right) = 3$ years.

17. Let son's age 10 years ago be x years.
Father's age 10 years ago = $(3x)$ years.
$3x + 20 = 2(x + 20) \Rightarrow x = 20$.
Ratio of their present ages = $(3x + 10 : x + 10)$
$= 70 : 30 = 7 : 3$.

18. Let son's age 1 year ago be x years.
Father's age 1 year ago = $(4x)$ years.
$4x + 7 = 2(x + 7) + 9 \Rightarrow x = 8$.
Ratio of father's and son's present ages
$= (4x + 1 : x + 1) = 33 : 9 = 11 : 3$.

19. Let Ashok's age = $4x$ and Pradeep's age = $3x$ years.
∴ $4x + 6 = 26 \Rightarrow x = 5$.
∴ Pradeep's age = $3x = 15$ years.

Problems On Ages

20. $\dfrac{6x+5}{x+5} = \dfrac{7}{2} \Rightarrow 2(6x+5) = 7(x+5) \Rightarrow x = 5.$

    $\therefore$ Son's present age = 5 years.

21. Let the ages of A and B be $2x$ and $3x$ years.

    $\dfrac{2x+5}{3x+5} = \dfrac{3}{4} \Rightarrow 4(2x+5) = 3(3x+5) \Rightarrow x = 5.$

    $\therefore$ A's present age = $2x$ = 10 years.

22. $\dfrac{2x+8}{5x+8} = \dfrac{1}{2} \Rightarrow 2(2x+8) = (5x+8) \Rightarrow x = 8.$

    Difference of their ages = $(5x - 2x) = 3x = 24$ years.

23. Let their ages one year ago be $4x$ and $3x$ years.

    $\dfrac{4x+2}{3x+2} = \dfrac{5}{4} \Rightarrow 4(4x+2) = 5(3x+2) \Rightarrow x = 2.$

    Sum of their present ages = $(4x+1+3x+1) = 16$ years.

24. Sum of ages of A and B, 3 years ago = $(18 \times 2) = 36$ years.

    Sum of ages of A, B and C, now = $(22 \times 3) = 66$ years.

    Sum of ages of A and B, now = $(36+6)$ years = 42 years.

    $\therefore$ C's age = $(66 - 42)$ years = 24 years.

25. Let Anil's age = x years.

    Then, Prashant's age = $(48 - x)$ years.

    Let the age of Jayesh be p years. Then,

    $p - (48 - x) = x - p \Rightarrow 2p = 48$ or $p = 24.$

26. $3x + 5x = 80 \Rightarrow x = 10.$

    Ratio of their ages after 10 years = $(3x+10 : 5x+10)$
    $= 40 : 60 = 2 : 3.$

27. Let A's age 10 years ago = x years.

    Then, B's age 10 years ago = $2x$ years.

    $\dfrac{x+10}{2x+10} = \dfrac{3}{4} \Rightarrow 4(x+10) = 3(2x+10) \Rightarrow x = 5.$

    Total of their present ages = $(x+10+2x+10) = (3x+20) = 35$ years.

18

SIMPLE INTEREST

The money borrowed or lent out for a certain period is called the **principal**. Extra money paid for using other's money is called **interest**.

If the interest on a certain sum borrowed for a certain period is reckoned uniformly, then it is called **simple interest**.

$$\text{Amount} = \text{Principal} + S.I.$$

Formulae : Let $Principal = P$, $Rate = R\%$ per annum and $Time = T$ years. Then,

(i) $S.I. = \dfrac{P \times R \times T}{100}$

(ii) $P = \dfrac{100 \times S.I.}{R \times T}$; $R = \dfrac{100 \times S.I.}{P \times T}$ & $T = \dfrac{100 \times S.I.}{P \times R}$.

SOLVED EXAMPLES

Ex. 1. Find :

(i) S.I. on Rs. 5664 at $13\dfrac{3}{4}\%$ per annum for 9 months.

(ii) S.I. on Rs. 3125 at 15% per annum for 73 days.

(iii) S.I. on Rs. 1500 at 18% per annum for the period from 5th Feb, 1992 to 18th April, 1992.

Sol. (i) $P = $ Rs. 5664, $R = 13\dfrac{3}{4}\%$, $T = \left(\dfrac{9}{12}\right)$ year $= \left(\dfrac{3}{4}\right)$ year.

$\therefore S.I. = \dfrac{P \times R \times T}{100}$

$= $ Rs. $\left(5664 \times \dfrac{55}{4} \times \dfrac{3}{4} \times \dfrac{1}{100}\right) = $ Rs. 584.10.

(ii) $P = $ Rs. 3125, $R = 15\%$, $T = \left(\dfrac{73}{365}\right)$ year $= \left(\dfrac{1}{5}\right)$ year.

$\therefore S.I. = \dfrac{P \times R \times T}{100} = $ Rs. $\left(3125 \times 15 \times \dfrac{1}{5} \times \dfrac{1}{100}\right) = $ Rs. 93.75.

(iii) $P = $ Rs. 1500 , $R = 18\%$.

Simple Interest 287

Time = (24 + 31 + 18) days = 73 days = $\frac{1}{5}$ year.

∴ S.I. = Rs. $\left(1500 \times 15 \times \frac{1}{5} \times \frac{1}{100}\right)$ = Rs. 45.

Remark : *The day on which money is deposited is not reckoned while the day on which money is withdrawn, is counted.*

Ex. 2. **A sum when reckoned at simple interest at $12\frac{1}{2}$ % per annum amounts to Rs. 2437.50 after 4 years. Find the sum.**

Sol. Let the sum be Rs. x.

Then, S.I. = Rs. $\left(x \times \frac{25}{2} \times 4 \times \frac{1}{100}\right)$ = Rs. $\frac{x}{2}$.

∴ Amount = $\left(x + \frac{x}{2}\right)$ = Rs. $\left(\frac{3x}{2}\right)$.

Thus, $\frac{3x}{2} = 2437.50 \Rightarrow x = \frac{2437.50 \times 2}{3} = 1625$.

Hence, the sum = Rs. 1625.

Ex. 3. **A certain sum of money amounts to Rs. 756 in 2 years and to Rs. 873 in $3\frac{1}{2}$ years. Find the sum and the rate of interest.**

Sol. P + (S.I. for $3\frac{1}{2}$ years) = Rs. 873

P + (S.I. for 2 years) = Rs. 756

On subtraction, S.I. for $\frac{3}{2}$ years = Rs. 117

∴ S.I. for 2 years = Rs. $\left(117 \times \frac{2}{3} \times 2\right)$ = Rs. 156.

∴ P = Rs. (756 – 156) = Rs. 600.

Now, P = Rs. 600, T = 2 years, S.I. = Rs. 156.

∴ Rate = $\frac{100 \times 156}{600 \times 2}$ = 13% per annum.

Ex. 4. **At what rate per cent per annum will a sum of money double in 8 years ?** (Railway Recruitment 1989)

Sol. Let principal = Rs. P, Then, S.I. = Rs. P and Time = 8 years.

∴ Rate = $\frac{100 \times S.I.}{P \times T} = \frac{100 \times P}{P \times 8} = \frac{100}{8} = \left(\frac{25}{2}\right) = 12\frac{1}{2}$ % per annum.

Ex. 5. A shopkeeper borrowed Rs. 25000 from two money-lenders. For one loan he paid 12% per annum and for the other 14% per annum. The total interest paid for one year was Rs. 3260. How much did he borrow at each rate ?

Sol. Suppose money borrowed at 12% = Rs. x.

Then money borrowed at 14% = Rs. $(25000 - x)$.

$$\therefore \frac{x \times 12 \times 1}{100} + \frac{(25000 - x) \times 14 \times 1}{100} = 3260$$

or $12x + 350000 - 14x = 326000$

or $2x = 24000$ or $x = 12000$.

$\therefore$ Money borrowed at 12% = Rs. 12000.

Money borrowed at 14% = Rs. 13000.

Ex. 6. Simple interest on a certain sum is $\frac{16}{25}$ of the sum. Find the rate percent and time, if both are equal.

Sol. Let the sum = Rs. x. Then, S.I. = $\frac{16}{25}x$.

Let rate = $R\%$ and Time = R years.

Now, S.I. = $\frac{P \times R \times T}{100}$.

$$\therefore \frac{16}{25}x = \frac{x \times R \times R}{100} \text{ or } \frac{R^2}{100} = \frac{16}{25} \text{ or } R^2 = \frac{1600}{25}.$$

$\therefore R = \frac{40}{5} = 8$ and $T = 8$.

Hence, rate = 8% and time = 8 years.

Ex. 7. A sum was put at simple interest at a certain rate for 2 years. Had it been put at 3% higher rate, it would have fetched Rs. 300 more. Find the sum.

Sol. Let the sum = Rs. x and let original rate be $y\%$ per annum. Then, new rate = $(y + 3)\%$ per annum.

$$\therefore \frac{x \times (y+3) \times 2}{100} - \frac{x \times y \times 2}{100} = 300.$$

$xy + 3x - xy = 15000$ or $x = 5000$.

Thus, the sum = Rs. 5000.

Ex. 8. What annual instalment will discharge a debt of Rs. 4600 due in 4 years at 10% simple interest?

Sol. Let each instalment = Rs. x.

Clearly, 1st instalment will be paid after 1 year.

This money will remain with the lender for 3 years.

Similarly, he will have Rs. x for 2 years, Rs. x for 1 year and Rs. x at the end.

∴ (Amount of Rs. x for 3 years) + (Amount of Rs. x for 2 years)

+ (Amount of Rs. x for 1 year) + Rs. x = 2210.

So, $\left(x + \dfrac{x \times 10 \times 3}{100}\right) + \left(x + \dfrac{x \times 10 \times 2}{100}\right) + \left(x + \dfrac{x \times 10 \times 1}{100}\right)$

$+ x = 4600$

or $\dfrac{13x}{10} + \dfrac{12x}{10} + \dfrac{11x}{10} + \dfrac{10x}{10} = 4600$

or $46x = 46000$ or $x = 1000$.

∴ Each instalment = Rs. 1000.

Exercise 18

1. The simple interest on a certain sum for 3 years at 14% per annum is Rs. 235.20. The sum is :
   - (a) Rs. 480
   - (b) Rs. 560
   - (c) Rs. 650
   - (d) Rs. 720

2. If Rs. 64 amount to Rs. 83.20 in 2 years, what will Rs. 86 amount to in 4 years at the same rate per cent per annum ?
   - (a) Rs. 137.60
   - (b) Rs. 124.70
   - (c) Rs. 114.80
   - (d) Rs. 127.40

3. A sum of money amouns to Rs. 850 in 3 years and Rs. 925 in 4 years. The sum is :
   - (a) Rs. 600
   - (b) Rs. 575
   - (c) Rs. 625
   - (d) data inadequate

4. A sum of money amounts to Rs. 702 in 2 years and Rs. 783 in 3 years. The rate per cent is :
   - (a) 12% per annum
   - (b) 13% per annum
   - (c) 14% per annum
   - (d) 15% per annum

5. A money lender finds that due to a fall in the rate of interest from 13% to $12\frac{1}{2}$%, his yearly income diminishes by Rs. 104. His capital is :

   (a) Rs. 21400 (b) Rs. 20800
   (c) Rs. 22300 (d) Rs. 24000

6. If the amount of Rs. 360 in 3 years is Rs. 511.20, what will be the amount of Rs. 700 in 5 years ?

   (a) Rs. 1190 (b) Rs. 1230
   (c) Rs. 1060 (d) Rs. 1225

7. A sum of Rs. 2540 is lent out into two parts, one at 12% and another one at $12\frac{1}{2}$%. If the total annual income is Rs. 311.60, he money lent at 12% is :

   (a) Rs. 1180 (b) Rs. 1360
   (c) Rs. 1240 (d) Rs. 1340

8. A sum of Rs. 2600 is lent out in two parts in such a way that the interest on one part at 10% for 5 years is equal to that on another part at 9% for 6 years. The sum lent out at 10% is :

   (a) Rs. 1150 (b) Rs. 1250
   (c) Rs. 1350 (d) Rs. 1450

9. The simple interest on a sum of money is $\frac{1}{9}$ of the principal and the number of years is equal to the rate per cent per annum. The rate percent per annum is : (Clerk's Grade 1991)

   (a) 3 (b) $\frac{1}{3}$
   (c) $3\frac{1}{3}$ (d) $\frac{3}{10}$

10. Simple interest on a certain sum at a certain rate is $\frac{9}{16}$ of the sum. If the number representing rate per cent and time in years be equal, then the time is :

    (a) $5\frac{1}{2}$ years (b) $6\frac{1}{2}$ years
    (c) $6\frac{1}{4}$ years (d) $7\frac{1}{2}$ years

11. A sum of money will double itself in 16 years at simple interest with yearly rate of : (Clerk's Grade 1991)

Simple Interest 291

(a) 10% (b) $6\frac{1}{4}$%
(c) 8% (d) 16%

12. A sum of money, put at simple interest trebles itself in 15 years. The rate per cent per annum is :
(a) $13\frac{1}{3}$% (b) $16\frac{2}{3}$%
(c) $12\frac{2}{3}$% (d) 20%

13. At a certain rate of simple interest, a certain sum doubles itself in 10 years. It will treble itself in :
(a) 15 years (b) 20 years
(c) 30 years (d) 12 years

14. Rs. 800 amounts to Rs. 920 in 3 years at simple interest. If the interest rate is increased by 3%, it would amount to how much ?
(a) Rs. 1056 (b) Rs. 1112
(c) Rs. 1182 (d) Rs. 992
(Bank P.O. 1991)

15. A sum of money at simple interest amounts to Rs. 2240 in 2 years and Rs. 2600 in 5 years. The sum is : (Bank P.O. 1989)
(a) Rs. 1880 (b) Rs. 2000
(c) Rs. 2120 (d) data inadequate

16. A certain sum of money at simple interest amounts to Rs. 1260 in 2 years and to Rs. 1350 in 5 years. The rate per cent per annum is :
(a) 2.5% (b) 3.75%
(c) 5% (d) 7.5%
(Central Excise & I. Tax 1988)

17. A lent Rs. 600 to B for 2 years and Rs. 150 to C for 4 years and received altogether from both Rs. 90 as simple interest. The rate of interest is :
(a) 4% (b) 5%
(c) 10% (d) 12%
(Railway Recruitment 1988)

18. A man invested $\frac{1}{3}$ of his capital at 7%; $\frac{1}{4}$ at 8% and remainder at 10%. If his annual income is Rs. 561, the capital is :
(a) Rs. 5400 (b) Rs. 6000
(c) Rs. 6600 (d) Rs. 7200

19. The simple interest on a sum of money will be Rs. 600 after 10 years. If the principal is trebled after 5 years, what will be the total interest at the end of the tenth year? (Bank P.O. 1987)
    (a) Rs. 600 ☐ (b) Rs. 900 ☐
    (c) Rs. 1200 ☐ (d) data inadequae ☐

20. In how many years will a sum of money double itself at 12% per annum :
    (a) 6 years 9 months ☐ (b) 8 years 3 months ☐
    (c) 7 years 6 months ☐ (d) 8 years 6 months ☐

21. The simple interest at x% for x years will be Rs. x on a sum of :
    (a) Rs. x ☐ (b) Rs. $100\, x$ ☐
    (c) Rs. $\left(\dfrac{100}{x}\right)$ ☐ (d) Rs. $\left(\dfrac{100}{x^2}\right)$ ☐

22. If the interest on Rs. 1200 be more than the interest on Rs. 1000 by Rs. 50 in 3 years, the rate per cent is :
    (a) $10\dfrac{1}{3}$% ☐ (b) $6\dfrac{2}{3}$% ☐
    (c) $8\dfrac{1}{3}$% ☐ (d) $9\dfrac{2}{3}$% ☐

23. A sum was put at simple interest at a certain rate for 2 years. Had it been put at 1% higher rate, it would have fetched Rs. 24 more. The sum is :
    (a) Rs. 600 ☐ (b) Rs. 800 ☐
    (c) Rs. 1200 ☐ (d) Rs. 480 ☐

24. A sum of money becomes (8/5) of itself in 5 years at a certain rate of interest. The rate per cent per annum is :
    (a) 5% ☐ (b) 8% ☐
    (c) 10% ☐ (d) 12% ☐

25. A man lends Rs. 10000 in four parts. If he gets 8% on Rs. 2000; $7\dfrac{1}{2}$% on Rs. 4000 and $8\dfrac{1}{2}$% on Rs. 1400; what per cent must he get for the remainder, if the average interest is 8.13% ?
    (a) 7% ☐ (b) 9% ☐
    (c) $9\dfrac{1}{4}$% ☐ (d) $10\dfrac{1}{2}$% ☐

26. The simple interest on a sum of money at 8% per annum for 6 years is half the sum. The sum is : (C.B.I. 1991)
    (a) Rs. 4800 ☐ (b) Rs. 6000 ☐

Simple Interest 293

    (c) Rs. 8000   (d) data inadequate

27. At simple interest, a sum doubles after 20 years. The rate of interest per annum is :   (Bank P.O. 1990)
    (a) 5%   (b) 10%
    (c) 12%   (d) data inadequate

28. A certain sum of money at simple interest amounts to Rs. 1012 in $2\frac{1}{2}$ years and to Rs. 1067.20 in 4 years. The rate of interest per annum is :   (Central Excise & I. Tax 1989)
    (a) 2.5%   (b) 3%
    (c) 4%   (d) 5%

29. What annual payment will discharge a debt of Rs. 580 due in 5 years, the rate being 8% per annum ?
    (a) Rs. 166.40   (b) Rs. 65.60
    (c) Rs. 100   (d) Rs. 120

30. The difference between the interests received from two different banks on Rs. 500 for 2 years, is Rs. 2.50. The difference between their rates is :
    (a) 1%   (b) 0.5%
    (c) 2.5%   (d) 0.25%

31. Two equal amounts of money are deposited in two banks, each at 15% per annum, for $3\frac{1}{2}$ years and 5 years. If the difference between their interests is Rs. 144, each sum is :
    (a) Rs. 460   (b) Rs. 500
    (c) Rs. 640   (d) Rs. 720

32. The rate of interest on a sum of money is 4% per annum for the first 2 years, 6% per annum for the next 4 years and 8% per annum for the period beyond 6 years. If the simple interest accrued by the sum for a total period of 9 years is Rs. 1120, what is the sum ?
    (a) Rs. 1500   (b) Rs. 2000
    (c) Rs. 2500   (d) Rs. 4000
                                            (Bank P.O. 1991)

Answers (Exercise 18)

1. (b)   **2.** (a)   **3.** (c)   **4.** (d)   **5.** (b)   **6.** (a)   **7.** (a)   **8.** (c)   **9.** (c)
10. (d)   **11.** (b)   **12.** (a)   **13.** (b)   **14.** (d)   **15.** (b)   **16.** (a)   **17.** (b)   **18.** (c)
19. (c)   **20.** (d)   **21.** (c)   **22.** (c)   **23.** (c)   **24.** (d)   **25.** (b)   **26.** (d)   **27.** (a)
28. (c)   **29.** (c)   **30.** (d)   **31.** (c)   **32.** (b)

Solution (Exercise 18)

1. Sum = Rs. $\left(\dfrac{100 \times 235.20}{3 \times 14}\right)$ = Rs. 560.

2. S.I. on Rs. 64 for 2 years = Rs. 19.20

   $\therefore$ Rate = $\left(\dfrac{100 \times 19.20}{64 \times 2}\right)$ = 15%.

   $\therefore$ S.I. on Rs. 86 for 4 years = Rs. $\left(\dfrac{86 \times 4 \times 15}{100}\right)$ = Rs. 51.60.

   $\therefore$ Amount of Rs. 86 = Rs. (86 + 51.60) = Rs. 137.60.

3. S.I. for 1 year = Rs. (925 − 850) = Rs. 75.

   S.I. for 3 years = Rs. (75 × 3) = Rs. 225.

   $\therefore$ Sum = Rs. (850 − 225) = Rs. 625.

4. S.I. for 1 year = Rs. (783 − 702) = Rs. 81.

   S.I. for 2 years = Rs. (81 × 2) = Rs. 162.

   $\therefore$ Sum = Rs. (702 − 162) = Rs. 540.

   $\therefore$ Rate = $\left(\dfrac{100 \times 162}{540 \times 2}\right)$% = 15%.

5. Let, capital = Rs. x.

   Then, $\left(\dfrac{x \times 13 \times 1}{100}\right) - \left(x \times \dfrac{25}{2} \times \dfrac{1}{100}\right) = 104$

   or $\dfrac{13x}{100} - \dfrac{x}{8} = 104$ or $26x - 25x = (104 \times 200)$ or $x = 20800$.

   $\therefore$ Capital = Rs. 20800.

6. S.I. for 3 years = Rs. (511.20 − 360) = Rs. 151.20.

   $\therefore$ Rate = $\dfrac{100 \times 151.20}{360 \times 3}$ = 14%.

   $\therefore$ S.I. on Rs. 700 for 5 years = Rs. $\left(\dfrac{700 \times 5 \times 14}{100}\right)$ = Rs. 490.

   $\therefore$ Its amount = Rs. (700 + 490) = Rs. 1190.

7. Let, money lent at 12% = Rs. x.

   Then, money lent at $12\dfrac{1}{2}$% = Rs. $(2540 - x)$.

   $\therefore$ $\dfrac{x \times 12 \times 1}{100} + (2540 - x) \times \dfrac{25}{2} \times \dfrac{1}{100} = 311.60$

   or $\dfrac{3x}{25} + \dfrac{2540 - x}{8} = 311.60$

   or $24x + 25(2540 - x) = 200 \times 311.60$

Simple Interest

$x = 63500 - 62320 = 1180.$

8. Let the money at 10% be Rs. x.
   Then, the money at 9% is Rs. $(2600 - x)$.
   $\therefore \dfrac{x \times 10 \times 5}{100} = \dfrac{(2600-x) \times 9 \times 6}{100}$
   or $104x = 2600 \times 54$ or $x = \dfrac{2600 \times 54}{104}$

9. Let, Principal $= P$. Then, S.I. $= \dfrac{P}{9}$.
   Let, Rate $= R\%$ per annum and Time $= R$ years.
   Then, $\dfrac{P}{9} = \dfrac{P \times R \times R}{100}$ or $R^2 = \dfrac{100}{9}$ or $R = \dfrac{10}{3} = 3\dfrac{1}{3}\%$ per annum.

10. Let, Principal $= P$. Then, S.I. $= \dfrac{9}{16}P$.
    Let, Rate $= R\%$ per annum and Time $= R$ years.
    Then, $\dfrac{9}{16}P = \dfrac{P \times R \times R}{100}$. So, $R^2 = \dfrac{900}{16}$ or $\dfrac{30}{4} = 7\dfrac{1}{2}$ years.

11. Let, Principal $= P$. Then, S.I. $= P$.
    Then, Rate $= \dfrac{100 \times P}{P \times 16} = \dfrac{100}{16} = 6\dfrac{1}{4}\%$.

12. Let Principal $= P$. Then, S.I. $= 2P$. Also, Time $= 15$ years.
    $\therefore$ Rate $= \dfrac{100 \times 2P}{P \times 15} = \dfrac{200}{15} = 13\dfrac{1}{3}\%$ per annum

13. Let, Principal $= P$. Then, S.I. $= P$ and Time 0 years.
    $\therefore$ Rate $= \dfrac{100 \times P}{P \times 10} = 20$ years.

14. Principal $=$ Rs. 800, S.I. $=$ Rs. $(920 - 800) =$ Rs.120 and Time $= 3$ years.
    $\therefore$ Original rate $= \dfrac{100 \times 120}{800 \times 3} = 5\%..$
    New rate $= 8\%$.
    Now, S.I. $=$ Rs. $\left(\dfrac{800 \times 8 \times 3}{100}\right) =$ Rs. 192.
    $\therefore$ Amount $=$ Rs. 992.

15. S.I. for 3 years $=$ Rs. $(2600 - 2240) =$ Rs. 360.
    S.I. for 2 years $=$ Rs. $\left(\dfrac{360}{3} \times 2\right) =$ Rs. 240.
    $\therefore$ Sum $=$ Rs. $(2240 - 240) =$ Rs. 2000.

16. S.I. for 3 years = Rs. (1350 − 1260) = Rs. 90.

　　S.I. for 2 years = Rs. $\left(\dfrac{90}{3} \times 2\right)$ = Rs. 60.

　　∴ Sum = Rs. (1260 − 60) = Rs. 1200.

　　∴ Rate = $\dfrac{100 \times 60}{1200 \times 2}$ = 2.5%.

17. Let, rate = x% per annum. Then,

　　$\dfrac{600 \times x \times 2}{100} + \dfrac{150 \times x \times 4}{100} = 90$

　　or $18x = 90$ or $x = 5$.

18. Let the capital be Rs. x. Then,

　　$\dfrac{x}{3} \times \dfrac{7}{100} + \dfrac{x}{4} \times \dfrac{8}{100} + \left[x - \left(\dfrac{x}{3} + \dfrac{x}{4}\right)\right] \times \dfrac{10}{100} = 561$

　　or $\dfrac{7x}{300} + \dfrac{x}{50} + \dfrac{x}{24} = 561$

　　or $42x + 36x + 75x = 1009800$ or $x = \dfrac{1009800}{153} = 6600$.

19. Let, sum = Rs. x. Then, S.I. = Rs. 600, Time = 10 years.

　　∴ Rate = $\left(\dfrac{100 \times 600}{x \times 10}\right) = \left(\dfrac{6000}{x}\right)$ % per annum.

　　S.I. on Rs. x for 1st five years = Rs. $\left(x \times \dfrac{6000}{x} \times 5 \times \dfrac{1}{100}\right)$ = Rs. 300.

　　S.I. on Rs. $3x$ for next 5 years = Rs. $\left(3x \times \dfrac{6000}{x} \times 5 \times \dfrac{1}{100}\right)$

　　　　　　　　　　　　　　= Rs. 900.

　　∴ Total interest = Rs. (300 + 900) = Rs. 1200.

20. Let, Principal = Rs. P. Then, S.I. = Rs. P, Rate = 12%.

　　Time = $\left(\dfrac{100 \times P}{P \times 12}\right)$ years = 8 years 4 months.

21. Sum = $\left(\dfrac{100 \times x}{x \times x}\right)$ = Rs. $\left(\dfrac{100}{x}\right)$.

22. Let, rate = x% per annum. Then,

　　$\dfrac{1200 \times x \times 3}{100} - \dfrac{1000 \times x \times 3}{100} = 50$ or $6x = 50$ or $x = 8\dfrac{1}{3}$.

　　∴ Rate = $8\dfrac{1}{3}$ % per annum.

23. Let, sum = Rs. x and original rate = y% per annum.

Simple Interest

Then, $\dfrac{x \times (y+1) \times 2}{100} - \dfrac{x \times y \times 2}{100} = 24$ or $x = 1200$.

24. Let, sum = Rs. x. Then, amount = Rs. $\left(\dfrac{8x}{5}\right)$.

    $\therefore$ S.I. = Rs. $\left(\dfrac{8x}{5} - x\right)$ = Rs. $\left(\dfrac{3x}{5}\right)$.

    $\therefore$ Rate = $\left(\dfrac{100 \times \dfrac{3x}{5}}{x \times 5}\right)$ % = 12%.

25. $\left(\dfrac{2000 \times 8 \times 1}{100}\right) + \left(4000 \times \dfrac{15}{2} \times \dfrac{1}{100}\right) + \left(1400 \times \dfrac{17}{2} \times \dfrac{1}{100}\right)$
    $+ \left(\dfrac{2600 \times x \times 1}{100}\right) = \left(\dfrac{10000 \times 8.13 \times 1}{100}\right)$.

    or $160 + 300 + 119 + 26x = 813$ or $26x = 234$ or $x = 9\%$.

26. Let, sum = P. Then, S.I. = $\dfrac{1}{2} P$, Rate = 8%

    and Time = 6 years.

    $\therefore \dfrac{P}{2} = \dfrac{P \times 8 \times 6}{100}$.

    Thus, data is inadequate.

27. Let, sum = P. Then, S.I. = P and Time = 20 years.

    $\therefore$ Rate = $\dfrac{100 \times P}{P \times 20}$ = 5% per annum.

28. S.I. for $\dfrac{3}{2}$ years = Rs. $(1067.20 - 1012)$ = Rs. 55.20.

    S.I. for $\dfrac{5}{2}$ years = Rs. $\left(55.20 \times \dfrac{2}{3} \times \dfrac{5}{2}\right)$ = Rs. 92.

    $\therefore$ Sum = Rs. $(1012 - 92)$ = Rs. 920.

    Hence, Rate = $\left(\dfrac{100 \times 92 \times 2}{920 \times 5}\right)$ = 4%.

29. Let the annual instalment be Rs. x.

    Then, $\left[x + \left(\dfrac{x \times 4 \times 8}{100}\right)\right] + \left[x + \left(\dfrac{x \times 3 \times 8}{100}\right)\right] + \left[x + \left(\dfrac{x \times 2 \times 8}{100}\right)\right]$
    $+ \left[x + \left(\dfrac{x \times 1 \times 8}{100}\right)\right] + x = 580$

    or $\dfrac{33x}{25} + \dfrac{31x}{25} + \dfrac{29x}{25} + \dfrac{27x}{25} + x = 580$ or $x = 100$.

30. Let the rates be $x\%$ and $y\%$. Then,

$$\frac{500 \times x \times 2}{100} - \frac{500 \times y \times 2}{100} = 2.5$$

$\therefore 10(x-y) = 2.5$ or $x - y = 0.25$.

31. Let each sum be Rs. P. Then,

$$\frac{P \times 15 \times 5}{100} - \frac{P \times 15 \times 7}{100 \times 2} = 144$$

$\therefore \dfrac{3}{4}P - \dfrac{21}{40}P = 144$ or $\dfrac{9P}{40} = 144$.

$\therefore P = \dfrac{144 \times 40}{9} = 640$.

32. Let, sum = Rs. x. Then,

$$\frac{x \times 4 \times 2}{100} + \frac{x \times 6 \times 4}{100} + \frac{x \times 8 \times 3}{100} = 1120$$

$56x = 112000$ or $x = \dfrac{112000}{56} = 2000$.

19
COMPOUND INTEREST

Introduction : Sometimes the borrower and the lender agree to fix up a certain unit of time, say *yearly* or *half-yearly* or *quarterly* to settle the previous account. In such cases, the amount after first unit of time becomes principal for second unit of time, the amount after second unit of time becomes principal for third unit of time and so on.

After a certain period, the difference between the amount and the principal is called *compound interest*.

Formulae

1. Let Principal = Rs P, Time = n years and Rate = $R\%$ p.a.

Case I : When interest is compounded Annually :

$$\text{Amount} = P\left(1 + \frac{R}{100}\right)^n.$$

Case II : When interest is compounded Half-Yearly :

$$\text{Amount} = P\left(1 + \frac{\frac{1}{2}R}{100}\right)^{2n}.$$

Case III : When interest is compounded Quarterly :

$$\text{Amount} = P\left(1 + \frac{\frac{1}{4}R}{100}\right)^{4n}.$$

Case IV : When time is fraction of a year, say $3\frac{1}{5}$ years, then

$$\text{Amount} = P\left(1 + \frac{R}{100}\right)^3 \times \left(1 + \frac{\frac{1}{5}R}{100}\right).$$

Case V : When Rate of interest is $R_1\%$, $R_2\%$ and $R_3\%$ for
1st year, 2nd year and 3rd year respectively, then

$$\text{Amount} = P\left(1 + \frac{R_1}{100}\right) \times \left(1 + \frac{R_2}{100}\right) \times \left(1 + \frac{R_3}{100}\right).$$

2. Present Worth of a sum of Rs. x due n years hence is given by :

$$\text{Present Worth} = \left(\frac{x}{1+\dfrac{R}{100}}\right).$$

SOLVED EXAMPLES

Ex. 1. Find compound interest on Rs. 50000 at 16% per annum for 2 years, compounded annually.

Sol. Amount after 2 years = Rs. $\left[50000 \times \left(1+\dfrac{16}{100}\right)^2\right]$

= Rs. $\left(50000 \times \dfrac{29}{25} \times \dfrac{29}{25}\right)$ = Rs. 67280.

∴ Compound interest = Rs. (67280 − 50000) = Rs. 17280.

Ex. 2. Find compound interest on Rs. 100000 at 20% per annum for 2 years 3 months, compounded annually.

Sol. Here time = $2\dfrac{1}{4}$ years.

∴ Amount = Rs. $\left[100000 \times \left(1+\dfrac{20}{100}\right)^2 \times \left(1+\dfrac{\frac{1}{4} \times 20}{100}\right)\right]$

= Rs. $\left(100000 \times \dfrac{6}{5} \times \dfrac{6}{5} \times \dfrac{21}{20}\right)$ = Rs. 151200.

∴ Compound interest = Rs. (151200 − 100000) = Rs. 51200.

Ex. 3. Find the compound interest on Rs. 6250 at 12% per annum for 1 year, compounded half-yearly.

Sol. Rate = 12% per annum = 6% per half-year.

Time = 1 year = 2 half-years.

∴ Amount = Rs. $\left[6250 \times \left(1+\dfrac{6}{100}\right)^2\right]$

= Rs. $\left(6250 \times \dfrac{53}{50} \times \dfrac{53}{50}\right)$ = Rs. 7022.50.

∴ Compound interest = Rs. (7022.50 − 6250) = Rs. 772.50.

Ex. 4. Find compound interest on Rs. 51200 at 15% per annum for 9 months, compounded quarterly.

Sol. Time = 9 months = 3 quarters.

Rate = 15% per annum = $\left(\dfrac{15}{4}\right)$% quarterly.

Compound Interest

$$\therefore \text{ Amount} = \text{Rs.} \left[51200 \times \left(1 + \frac{15}{4 \times 100}\right)^3\right]$$

$$= \text{Rs.} \left(51200 \times \frac{83}{80} \times \frac{83}{80} \times \frac{83}{80}\right) = \text{Rs. } 57178.70$$

∴ Compound interest = Rs. (57178.70 − 51200) = Rs. 5978.70.

Ex. 5. If the compound interest on a certain sum of money for 3 years at 10% per annum be Rs. 993, what would be the simple interest ?

Sol. Let, principal = Rs. P. Then,

$$P\left(1 + \frac{10}{100}\right)^3 - P = 993$$

$$\Rightarrow \left(\frac{11}{10} \times \frac{11}{10} \times \frac{11}{10} - 1\right) P = 993$$

$$\Rightarrow \left(\frac{1331 - 1000}{1000}\right) P = 993 \text{ or } P = \frac{993 \times 1000}{331} = 3000.$$

$$\therefore \text{ Simple interest} = \text{Rs.} \left(\frac{3000 \times 3 \times 10}{100}\right) = \text{Rs. } 900.$$

Ex. 6. The difference between compound interest and the simple interest on a certain sum at $12\frac{1}{2}$ % per annum for 3 years is Rs. 250. Find the sum.

Sol. Let the sum be Rs. x.

Then, amount = Rs. $\left[x \times \left(1 + \frac{25}{2 \times 100}\right)^3\right]$ = Rs. $\left(\frac{9}{8} \times \frac{9}{8} \times \frac{9}{8} \times x\right)$

$$= \text{Rs.} \left(\frac{729}{512}\right) x.$$

$\therefore$ Compound interest = Rs. $\left[\frac{729}{512} x - x\right]$ = Rs. $\left(\frac{217}{512}\right) x.$

Simple interest = Rs. $\left[x \times \frac{25}{2} \times \frac{3}{100}\right]$ = Rs. $\frac{3x}{8}$.

$\therefore \frac{217}{512} x - 3\frac{x}{8} = 250 \Rightarrow 217 x - 192 x = 250 \times 512.$

or $x = \frac{250 \times 512}{25} = 5120.$

Ex. 7. A certain sum on compound interest amounts to Rs. 2809 in 2 years and Rs. 2977.54 in 3 years. Find the sum and rate per cent.

Sol. S.I. on Rs. 2809 for 1 year = Rs. (2977.54 − 2809) = Rs. 168.54.

$\therefore$ S.I. on Rs. 100 for 1 year = Rs. $\left(\dfrac{168.54}{2809} \times 100\right)$ % = 6%

$\therefore$ Rate = 6% per annum.

Let the sum be Rs. 100.

Amount of Rs. 100 for 2 years = Rs. $\left[100 \times \left(1 + \dfrac{6}{100}\right)^2\right]$

$\qquad\qquad\qquad\qquad\qquad\quad$ = Rs. $\left(\dfrac{2809}{25}\right)$.

$100 : \dfrac{2809}{25} = x : 2809.$

$\therefore x = \dfrac{100 \times 2809 \times 25}{2809} = 2500.$

Hence, the sum = Rs. 2500.

Exercise 19

1. If Rs. 7500 are borrowed at C.I. at the rate of 4% per annum, then after 2 years the amount to be paid is : **(P.O. Exam, 1991)**
   - (a) Rs. 8082 ☐
   - (b) Rs. 7800 ☐
   - (c) Rs. 8100 ☐
   - (d) Rs. 8112 ☐

2. The compound interest on Rs. 2800 for $1\dfrac{1}{2}$ years at 10% per annum, is :
   - (a) Rs. 441.35 ☐
   - (b) Rs. 436.75 ☐
   - (c) Rs. 434 ☐
   - (d) Rs. 420 ☐

3. The compound interest of Rs. 20480 at $6\dfrac{1}{4}$ % per annum for 2 years 73 days is :
   - (a) Rs. 3000 ☐
   - (b) Rs. 3131 ☐
   - (c) Rs. 2929 ☐
   - (d) Rs. 3636 ☐

4. The difference between simple interest and the compound interest on Rs. 600 for 1 year at 10% per annum, reckoned half yearly is :
   - (a) Nil ☐
   - (b) Rs. 6.60 ☐
   - (c) Rs. 4.40 ☐
   - (d) Rs. 1.50 ☐

5. The difference of compound interests on Rs. 800 for 1 year at 20%

per annum when compounded half yearly and quarterly is :

(a) Nil ☐ (b) 2.50 ☐
(c) Rs. 4.40 ☐ (d) Rs. 6.60 ☐

6. Simple interest on a sum at 4% per annum for 2 years is Rs. 80. The compound interest on the same sum for the same period is :

(a) Rs. 81.60 ☐ (b) Rs. 160 ☐
(c) Rs. 1081.60 ☐ (d) none of these ☐

(Astt. Grade 1987)

7. Rs. 800 at 5% per annum compound interest will amount to Rs. 882 in : (Clerical Grade, 1991)

(a) 1 year ☐ (b) 2 years ☐
(c) 3 years ☐ (d) 4 years ☐

8. The compound interest on Rs. 30000 at 7% per annum for a certain time is Rs. 4347. The time is :

(a) 2 years ☐ (b) $2\frac{1}{2}$ years ☐
(c) 3 years ☐ (d) 4 years ☐

9. A sum amounts to Rs. 1352 in 2 years at 4% compound interest. The sum is :

(a) Rs. 1300 ☐ (b) Rs. 1250 ☐
(c) Rs. 1260 ☐ (d) Rs. 1200 ☐

10. At what rate of compound interest per annum will a sum of Rs. 1200 become Rs. 1348.32 in 2 years ?

(a) 7% ☐ (b) 7.5% ☐
(c) 6% ☐ (d) 6.5% ☐

11. What is the principal amount which earns Rs. 132 as compound interest for the second year at 10% per annum ? (Bank P.O. 1989)

(a) Rs. 1000 ☐ (b) Rs. 1200 ☐
(c) Rs. 1320 ☐ (d) none of these ☐

12. The simple interest on a certain sum for 2 years at 10% per annum is Rs. 90. The corresponding compound interest is :

(a) Rs. 99 ☐ (b) Rs. 95.60 ☐
(c) Rs. 94.50 ☐ (d) Rs. 108 ☐

13. If the compound interest on a certain sum for 2 years at 12.5% per annum is Rs. 170, the simple interest is :

(a) Rs. 150 ☐ (b) Rs. 152.50 ☐
(c) Rs. 160 ☐ (d) Rs. 162.50 ☐

14. The difference between the compound interest and the simple in-

terest on a certain sum at 5% per annum for 2 years is Rs. 1.50. The sum is : (Bank P.O. 1987)

(a) Rs. 600 (b) Rs. 500
(c) Rs. 400 (d) Rs. 300

15. The compound interest on a certain sum of money for 2 years at 10% per annum is Rs. 420. The simple interest on the same sum at the same rate and for the same time will be : (Clerical Grade, 1991)

(a) Rs. 350 (b) Rs. 375
(c) Rs. 380 (d) Rs. 400

16. The difference between simple interest and compound interest at the same rate for Rs. 5000 for 2 years is Rs. 72. The rate of interest is :

(a) 10% (b) 12%
(c) 6% (d) 8%
(Astt. Grade, 1990)

17. A sum is invested at compound interest payable annually. The interest in two successive years was Rs. 500 and Rs. 540. The sum is :

(a) Rs. 3750 (b) Rs. 5000
(c) Rs. 5600 (d) Rs. 6250

18. A sum of money placed at C.I. doubles itself in 5 years. It will amount to eight times itself in :

(a) 15 years (b) 20 years
(c) 12 years (d) 10 years

19. A sum of Rs. 12000 deposited at compound interest becomes double after 5 years. After 20 years it will become

(a) 120000 (b) 192000
(c) 124000 (d) 96000

20. A sum of money amounts to Rs. 10648 in 3 years and Rs. 9680 in 2 years. The rate of interest is : (L.I.C., 1986)

(a) 5% (b) 10%
(c) 15% (d) 20%

21. A sum amounts to Rs. 2916 in 2 years and to Rs. 3149.28 in 3 years at compound interest. The sum is : (P.C.S., 1985)

(a) Rs. 1500 (b) Rs. 2000
(c) Rs. 2500 (d) Rs. 3000

22. A loan was repaid in two annual instalments of Rs. 112 each. If the rate of interest be 10% per annum compounded annually, the sum borrowed was :

(a) Rs. 200 (b) Rs. 210

(c) Rs. 217.80 (d) Rs. 280

23. A sum of Rs. 550 was taken as a loan. This is to be repaid in two equal annual instalments. If the rate of interest be 20% compounded annually, then the value of each instalment is :
   (a) Rs. 421 (b) Rs. 396
   (c) Rs. 360 (d) Rs. 350

24. A man borrows Rs. 4000 from a bank at $7\frac{1}{2}$ % compound interest. At the end of every year he pays Rs. 1500 as part repayment of loan and interest. How much does he still owe to the bank after three such instalments :
   (a) Rs. 123.25 (b) Rs. 125
   (c) Rs. 400 (d) Rs. 469.18

25. The least number of complete years in which a sum of money put out at 20% C.I. will be more than doubled is :
   (a) 3 (b) 4
   (c) 5 (d) 6

26. A tree increases annually by $\frac{1}{8}$ th of its height. By how much will it increase after 2 years, if it stands today 64 cm high ?
   (a) 72 cm (b) 74 cm
   (c) 75 cm (d) 81 cm

27. The value of a machine depreciates every year at the rate of 10% on its value at the beginning of that year. If the present value of the machine is Rs. 729, its worth 3 years ago was :
   (a) Rs. 947.10 (b) Rs. 800
   (c) Rs. 1000 (d) Rs. 750.87

28. The difference in C.I. and S.I. for 2 years on a sum of money is Rs. 160. If the S.I. for 2 years be Rs. 2880, the rate percent is :
   (a) $5\frac{5}{9}$ % (b) $12\frac{1}{2}$ %
   (c) $11\frac{1}{9}$ % (d) 9 %

29. The compound interest on a sum for 2 years is Rs. 832 and the simple interest on the same sum for the same period is Rs. 800. The difference between the compound and simple interests for 3 years will be :
   (a) Rs. 48 (b) Rs. 66.56
   (c) Rs. 98.56 (d) none of these

Objective Arithmetic

30. The difference between simple interest and compound interest on a sum for 2 years at 8%, when the interest is compounded annually is Rs. 16. If the interest were compounded half yearly, the difference in two interests would be nearly :

(a) Rs. 16 ☐ (b) Rs. 16.80 ☐
(c) Rs. 21.85 ☐ (d) Rs. 24.64 ☐

31. Rs. 1600 at 10% per annum compound interest compounded half yearly amount to Rs. 1944.81 in

(a) 2 years ☐ (b) 3 years ☐
(c) $1\frac{1}{2}$ years ☐ (d) $2\frac{1}{2}$ years ☐

32. A sum of money becomes Rs. 6690 after three years and Rs. 10,035 after six years on compound interest. The sum is

(a) Rs. 4400 ☐ (b) Rs. 4445 ☐
(c) Rs. 4460 ☐ (d) Rs. 4520 ☐

Answers

1. (d)   2. (c)   3. (c)   4. (d)   5. (c)   6. (a)   7. (b)   8. (a)   9. (b)
10. (c)   11. (b)   12. (c)   13. (c)   14. (a)   15. (d)   16. (b)   17. (d)   18. (a)
19. (b)   20. (b)   21. (c)   22. (b)   23. (c)   24. (a)   25. (b)   26. (d)   27. (c)
28. (c)   29. (c)   30. (d)   31. (a)   32. (c)

Solution (Exercise 19)

1. Amount = Rs. $\left[7500 \left(1 + \frac{4}{100}\right)^2 \right]$

= Rs. $\left[7500 \times \frac{26}{25} \times \frac{26}{25} \right]$ = Rs. 8112.

2. Amount = Rs. $\left[2800 \times \left(1 + \frac{10}{100}\right)\left(1 + \frac{5}{100}\right) \right]$

= Rs. $\left[2800 \times \frac{11}{10} \times \frac{21}{20} \right]$ = Rs. 3234

∴ C.I. = Rs. (3234 − 2800) = Rs. 434.

3. C.I. = Rs. $\left[20480 \times \left(1 + \frac{25}{4 \times 100}\right)^2 \left(1 + \frac{1}{5} \times \frac{25}{4 \times 100}\right) - 20480 \right]$

= Rs. $\left[\left(20480 \times \frac{17}{16} \times \frac{17}{16} \times \frac{81}{80}\right) - 20480 \right]$ = Rs. 2929.

Compound Interest

4. S.I. = Rs. $\left(\dfrac{600 \times 10 \times 1}{100}\right)$ = Rs. 60.

   C.I. = Rs. $\left[600 \times \left(1 + \dfrac{5}{100}\right)^2 - 600\right]$ = Rs. 61.50

   ∴ Difference = Rs. (61.50 – 60) = Rs. 1.50.

5. C.I. when reckoned half yearly

   = Rs. $\left[800 \times \left(1 + \dfrac{10}{100}\right)^4 - 800\right]$ = Rs. 172.40

   ∴ Difference = Rs. (172.40 – 168) = Rs. 4.40.

6. Principal = Rs. $\left(\dfrac{100 \times 80}{4 \times 2}\right)$ = Rs. 1000

   ∴ C.I. = Rs. $\left[\left\{1000 \times \left(1 + \dfrac{4}{100}\right)^2 - 1000\right\}\right]$ = Rs. 81.60.

7. Let time be t years

   $882 = 800 \left(1 + \dfrac{5}{100}\right)^t \Rightarrow \dfrac{882}{800} = \left(\dfrac{21}{20}\right)^t$

   $\Rightarrow \left(\dfrac{21}{20}\right)^2 = \left(\dfrac{21}{20}\right)^t \Rightarrow t = 2$

   ∴ Time = 2 years.

8. $30000 \times \left(1 + \dfrac{7}{100}\right)^t = 30000 + 4347$

   or $\left(\dfrac{107}{100}\right)^t = \dfrac{34347}{30000} = \dfrac{11449}{10000} = \left(\dfrac{107}{100}\right)^2$

   ∴ Time = 2 years.

9. Let the sum be P. Then,

   $1352 = P\left(1 + \dfrac{4}{100}\right)^2 \Rightarrow 1352 = P \times \dfrac{26}{25} \times \dfrac{26}{25}$

   $\Rightarrow P = \dfrac{1352 \times 25 \times 25}{26 \times 26} = 1250$

   ∴ Principal = Rs. 1250.

10. Let the rate be $x\%$ per annum. Then,

    $1200 \times \left(1 + \dfrac{x}{100}\right)^2 = 1348.32$

or $\left(1 + \dfrac{x}{100}\right)^2 = \dfrac{1348.32}{1200} = 1.1236 = (1.06)^2$

or $\left(1 + \dfrac{x}{100}\right) = 1.06$ or $\dfrac{x}{100} = 0.06$ or $x = 6\%$

11. Let x be the principal at the end of first year

  Then, $\dfrac{x \times 10 \times 1}{100} = 132 \Rightarrow x = 1320$.

  Let y be the original principal

  Then, $y + \dfrac{y \times 10 \times 1}{100} = 1320 \Rightarrow y = 1200$.

12. Sum = Rs. $\left(\dfrac{100 \times 90}{2 \times 10}\right)$ = Rs. 450.

  C.I. = Rs. $\left[450 \times \left(1 + \dfrac{10}{100}\right)^2 - 450\right]$ = Rs. 94.50.

13. S.I. on Re. 1 = Rs. $\left(1 \times 2 \times \dfrac{25}{2} \times \dfrac{1}{100}\right)$ = Re. $\dfrac{1}{4}$

  C.I. on Re. 1 = Rs. $\left[1 \times \left(1 + \dfrac{25}{2 \times 100}\right)^2 - 1\right]$ Re. $\dfrac{17}{64}$

  $\dfrac{\text{S.I.}}{\text{C.I.}} = \left(\dfrac{1}{4} \times \dfrac{64}{17}\right) = \dfrac{16}{17}$.

  S.I. = $\dfrac{16}{17} \times$ C.I. = Rs. $\left(\dfrac{16}{17} \times 170\right)$ = Rs. 160.

14. Let the sum be Rs. 100. Then,

  S.I. = Rs. $\left(\dfrac{100 \times 5 \times 2}{100}\right)$ = Rs. 10

  C.I. = Rs. $\left[\left\{100 \times \left(1 + \dfrac{5}{100}\right)^2\right\} - 100\right]$ = Rs. $\dfrac{41}{4}$

  Difference between C.I. and S.I. = Rs. $\left(\dfrac{41}{4} - 10\right)$ = Re. .25

  .25 : 1.50 :: 100 : x

  $\therefore x = \left(\dfrac{1.50 \times 100}{.25}\right)$ = Rs. 600.

.5. Let principal be P. Then,

  $P\left(1 + \dfrac{10}{100}\right)^2 - P = 420 \Rightarrow P =$ Rs. 2000

Compound Interest

$$\text{S.I.} = \text{Rs.} \left(\frac{2000 \times 2 \times 10}{100} \right) = \text{Rs. } 400.$$

16. $5000 \times \left(1 + \frac{R}{100}\right)^2 - 5000 - \frac{5000 \times 2 \times R}{100} = 72$

$\Rightarrow 5000 \left[\left(1 + \frac{R}{100}\right)^2 - 1 - \frac{R}{50} \right] = 72$

$\Rightarrow 1 + \frac{R^2}{10000} + \frac{2R}{100} - 1 - \frac{R}{50} = \frac{72}{5000}$

$\Rightarrow R^2 = \left(\frac{72}{5000} \times 10000 \right) = 144$ or $R = 12\%$.

17. S.I. on Rs. 500 for 1 year = Rs. 40.

$\therefore$ Rate $= \left(\frac{100 \times 40}{500 \times 1} \right) = 8\%$.

And, sum = Rs. $\left(\frac{100 \times 500}{8 \times 1} \right) = $ Rs. 6250.

18. Let the principal be P and rate be $r\%$. Then,

$2P = P \left(1 + \frac{r}{100}\right)^5$ or $\left(1 + \frac{r}{100}\right)^5 = 2$

Let it be 8 times in t years. Then,

$8P = P \left(1 + \frac{r}{100}\right)^t$

or $\left(1 + \frac{r}{100}\right)^t = 8 = (2)^3 = \left(1 + \frac{r}{100}\right)^{15}$

$\therefore$ $t = 15$ years.

19. $2P = P \left(1 + \frac{r}{100}\right)^5$ or $\left(1 + \frac{r}{100}\right)^5 = 2$

$\therefore \left(1 + \frac{r}{100}\right)^{20} = 2^4 = 16$.

Thus, $P \left(1 + \frac{r}{100}\right)^{20} = 16 P = $ Rs. $(12000 \times 16) = $ Rs. 192000.

20. Let P be the principal and $R\%$ per annum be the rate. Then,

$P \left(1 + \frac{R}{100}\right)^3 = 10648$ .... (i)

and $P \left(1 + \frac{R}{100}\right)^2 = 9680$ .... (ii)

on dividing (i) by (ii), we have

$$\left(1 + \frac{R}{100}\right) = \frac{10648}{9680}$$

or $\frac{R}{100} = \frac{968}{9680} = \frac{1}{10}$ or $R = \frac{1}{10} \times 100 = 10\%$.

21. Let P be the principal and $R\%$ per annum be rate

Then, $P\left(1 + \frac{R}{100}\right)^3 = 3149.28$ .... (i)

and $P\left(1 + \frac{R}{100}\right)^2 = 2916$ .... (ii)

On dividing (i) and (ii), we get

$$\left(1 + \frac{R}{100}\right) = \frac{3149.28}{2916}$$

or $\frac{R}{100} = \frac{233.28}{2916}$ or $R = \frac{233.28}{2916} \times 100 = 8\%$.

Now, $P\left(1 + \frac{8}{100}\right)^2 = 2916$ or $P \times \frac{27}{25} \times \frac{27}{25} = 2916$

or $P = \frac{2916 \times 25 \times 25}{27 \times 27} = $ Rs. 2500.

22. Principal = (P.W. of Rs. 121 due 1 year hence)

+ (P.W. of Rs. 121 due 2 years hence)

$$= \text{Rs.} \left[\frac{121}{\left(1 + \frac{10}{100}\right)} + \frac{121}{\left(1 + \frac{10}{100}\right)^2}\right] = \text{Rs. } 210.$$

23. Let the vaue of each instalment be Rs. x.

Then, $\left\{\dfrac{x}{\left(1 + \dfrac{20}{100}\right)} + \dfrac{x}{\left(1 + \dfrac{20}{100}\right)^2}\right\} = 550$

or $\frac{5x}{6} + \frac{25x}{36} = 550$ or $x = 360$.

24. Balance = Rs. $\left[\left\{4000 \times \left(1 + \frac{15}{2 \times 100}\right)^3\right\}\right.$

$\left. - \left\{1500 \times \left(1 + \frac{15}{2 \times 100}\right)^2 + 1500 \times \left(1 + \frac{15}{2 \times 100}\right) + 1500\right\}\right]$

= Rs. 123.25.

25. $x\left(1 + \dfrac{20}{100}\right)^n > 2x$ or $\left(\dfrac{6}{5}\right)^n > 2$.

Now, $\left(\dfrac{6}{5} \times \dfrac{6}{5} \times \dfrac{6}{5} \times \dfrac{6}{5}\right) > 2$

∴ $n = 4$ years.

26. Increase % = $\left(\dfrac{1}{8} \times 100\right)\% = 12.5\%$

Height after 2 years = $64 \times \left(1 + \dfrac{25}{2 \times 100}\right)^2$

$= \left(64 \times \dfrac{9}{8} \times \dfrac{9}{8}\right) = 81$ cm.

27. $P\left(1 - \dfrac{10}{100}\right)^3 = 729$

∴ $P = $ Rs. $\left(\dfrac{729 \times 10 \times 10 \times 10}{9 \times 9 \times 9}\right) = $ Rs. 1000.

28. S.I. for 1 year = Rs. 1440.

∴ S.I. on Rs. 1440 for 1 year = Rs. 160.

Hence, rate per cent = $\left(\dfrac{100 \times 160}{1440 \times 1}\right) = 11\dfrac{1}{9}\%$.

29. S.I. for first year = Rs. 400.

S.I. on Rs. 400 for 1 year = Rs. 32 .

∴ Rate = $\left(\dfrac{100 \times 32}{400 \times 1}\right) = 8\%$.

Hence, the difference for 3rd year is S.I. on Rs. 832.

= Rs. $\left(832 \times \dfrac{8}{100}\right) = $ Rs. 66.56

∴ Total difference = Rs. (32 + 66.56) = Rs. 98.56.

30. For first year, S.I. = C.I.

Thus, Rs. 16 is the S.I. on S.I. for 1 year, which at 8% is thus Rs. 200 *i.e.* S.I. on the principal for 1 year is Rs. 200.

∴ Principal = Rs. $\left(\dfrac{100 \times 200}{8 \times 1}\right) = $ Rs. 2500.

Amount for 2 years, compounded half yearly

= Rs. $\left[2500 \times \left(1 + \dfrac{4}{100}\right)^4\right] = $ Rs. 2924.64.

∴ C.I. = Rs. 424.64.

Also, S.I. = Rs. $\left(\dfrac{2500 \times 8 \times 2}{100}\right)$ = Rs. 400

Hence, [(C.I.) − (S.I.)] = Rs. (424.64 − 400) = Rs. 24.64.

31. $1600\left(1 + \dfrac{5}{100}\right)^T = 1944.81$

$\Rightarrow \left(\dfrac{21}{20}\right)^T = \dfrac{1944.81}{1600.00} = \dfrac{194481}{160000} = \left(\dfrac{441}{400}\right)^2 = \left(\dfrac{21}{20}\right)^4$

∴ $T = 4$ (Half-years) or $T = 2$ years

32. Let the sum be P.

Then, $P\left(1 + \dfrac{R}{100}\right)^3 = 6690$ .... (i)

and $P\left(1 + \dfrac{R}{100}\right)^6 = 10{,}035$ .... (ii)

∴ Dividing (ii) by (i), we get

$\left(1 + \dfrac{R}{100}\right)^3 = \dfrac{10035}{6690} = \dfrac{3}{2}$

∴ $P = \left(6690 \times \dfrac{2}{3}\right)$ = Rs. 4460.

20
AREA

Formulae :

1. (*i*) Area of a rectangle = (Length × Breadth).
   (*ii*) Length = $\left(\dfrac{\text{Area}}{\text{Breadth}}\right)$; Breadth = $\left(\dfrac{\text{Area}}{\text{Length}}\right)$.
   (*iii*) (Diagonal)^2 = (Length)^2 + (Breadth)^2.

2. Area of a square = (side)^2 = $\dfrac{1}{2}$ (Diagonal)^2.

3. Area of 4 walls of a room = 2 × (Length + Breadth) × Height.

4. Area of a parallelogram = (Base × Height).

5. Area of a rhombus = $\dfrac{1}{2}$ × (product of diagonals).

6. Area of an equilateral triangle = $\dfrac{\sqrt{3}}{4}$ × (Side)^2.

7. If a, b, c are the lengths of the sides of a triangle and
   $s = \dfrac{1}{2}(a+b+c)$, then :
   Area of the triangle = $\sqrt{s(s-a)(s-b)(s-c)}$.

8. Area of a triangle = $\left(\dfrac{1}{2} \times \text{Base} \times \text{Height}\right)$.

9. Area of a trapezium
   = $\dfrac{1}{2}$ (sum of parallel sides × distance between them).

10. (*i*) Circumference of a circle = $2\pi r$.
    (*ii*) Area of a circle = πr^2.
    (*iii*) arc $AB = \dfrac{2\pi r \theta}{360}$, where $\angle AOB = \theta$.
    (*iv*) Area of sector $ACBO = \dfrac{\pi r^2 \theta}{360}$.
    (*v*) Area of sector $ACBO = \left(\dfrac{1}{2} \times \text{arc } AB \times r\right)$.

SOLVED EXAMPLES

Ex. 1. Find the area of a rectangle one of whose sides is 3m and diagonal 5 m.

Sol. Another side $= \sqrt{(5)^2 - (3)^2}$ m
$= \sqrt{16}$ m $= 4$ m.
$\therefore$ Area of the plot $= (5 \times 4)$ m$^2 = 20$ m^2.

Ex. 2. Find the area of a square, the length of whose diagonal is 2.4 m.

Sol. Area $= \frac{1}{2} \times$ (diagonal)$^2 = \left[\frac{1}{2} \times (2.4)^2\right]$ m^2
$= \left(\frac{5.76}{2}\right)$ m$^2 = 2.88$ m^2.

Ex. 3. Find the area of an equilateral triangle, each of whose sides is 12 m long.

Sol. Area of the triangle $= \frac{\sqrt{3}}{4} \times$ (Side)^2
$= \left(\frac{1.73}{4} \times 12 \times 12\right)$ m$^2 = 62.28$ m^2.

Ex. 4. Find the area of a right anlged triangle, whose base is 6.5 m and hypotenuse 9 m.

Sol. Height $= \sqrt{(9)^2 - (6.5)^2} = \sqrt{42.25} = 6.5$ m
$\therefore$ Area $= \frac{1}{2} \times$ Base $\times$ Height
$= \left(\frac{1}{2} \times 6.5 \times 6.5\right)$ m$^2 = 21.125$ m^2.

Ex. 5. The base of a triangular field is three times its altitude. If the cost of cultivating the field at Rs. 24 per hectare be Rs. 324, find its base and height.

Sol. Let, altitude $= x$ metres. Then, base $= 3 x$ metres.
$\therefore$ Area $= \left(\frac{1}{2} \times 3 x \times x\right) = \left(\frac{3 x^2}{2}\right)$ m^2.
Now, Area $= \frac{\text{Total Cost}}{\text{Rate}} = \left(\frac{324}{24}\right)$ hectares $= 13.5$ hectatres
$= (13.5 \times 10000)$ m$^2 = 135000$ m^2.
$\therefore \frac{3 x^2}{2} = 135000$ or $x^2 = \left(135000 \times \frac{2}{3}\right) = 90000$.

Area 315

$\therefore x = \sqrt{90000} = 300.$

Hence, altitude = 300 m and base = 900 m.

Ex. 6. Find the area of a triangle whose sides are 9 cm, 12 cm and 7 cm.

Sol. Let $a = 9, b = 12$ and $c = 7$.

Then, $s = \frac{1}{2}(9 + 12 + 7)$ cm = 14 cm.

$\therefore (s-a) = 5, (s-b) = 2$ and $(s-c) = 7$.

$\therefore$ Area $= \sqrt{s(s-a)(s-b)(s-c)}$

$= \sqrt{14 \times 5 \times 2 \times 7}$ cm^2 = $14\sqrt{5}$ cm^2 = (14×2.23) cm^2

$= 31.22$ cm^2.

Ex. 7. Find the area of a rhombus one side of which measures 20 cm and one diagonal 24 cm.

Sol. We know that the diagonals of a rhombus bisect each other at right angles. So, one side and halves of diagonals form a right angled triangle.

Let $AB = 20$ cm and $BD = 24$ cm.

Then, $OB = 12$ cm.

$\therefore AB^2 = OA^2 + OB^2$

$\Rightarrow OA^2 = (AB^2 - OB^2) = [(20)^2 - (12)^2] = 256.$

$\therefore OA = 16$ and so $AC = 32$ cm.

Hence, area of rhombus

$= \frac{1}{2} \times AC \times BD = \left(\frac{1}{2} \times 32 \times 24\right)$ cm^2 = 384 cm^2.

Ex. 8. Find the cost of carpeting a room 13 m long and 9 m broad with a carpet 75 cm broad at the rate of Rs. 20 per metre.

Sol. Area of the floor = (13×9) m^2 = 117 m^2.

$\therefore$ Area of the carpet = 117 m^2

Breadth of the carpet = 75 cm = $\left(\frac{3}{4}\right)$ m.

$\therefore$ Length of the carpet = $\frac{\text{Area}}{\text{Breadth}} = \left(117 \times \frac{4}{3}\right)$ m = 156 m.

Hence, the cost of carpet = Rs. (156×20) = Rs. 3120.

Ex. 9. A rectangular grassy plot is 112 m by 78 m. It has a gravel path 2.5 m wide all round it on the inside. Find the area of the path and the cost of constructing it at Rs. 2 per square metre.

Sol. Area of plot = (112×78) m^2 = 8736 m^2

Area of plot excluding the path

$= [(112 - 5) \times (78 - 5)]$ m^2 = 7811 m^2

∴ Area of the path

$= (8736 - 7811)$ m^2 = 925 m^2.

Cost of constructing the path

= Rs. (925×2) = Rs. 1850.

Ex. 10. A room is 13 m long, 9 m broad and 10 m high. Find the cost of painting the four walls of the room at Rs. 15 per square metre, it being given that the doors and windows occupy 40 sq. metres.

Sol. Area of 4 walls = 2 (length + breadth) × height

$= [2(13 + 9) \times 10]$ m^2 = 440 m^2.

Area to be painted = $(440 - 40)$ m^2 = 400 m^2.

∴ Cost of painting = Rs. (400×15) = Rs. 6000.

Ex. 11. Find the circumference and the area of a circle of radius 3.5 cm.

Sol. Circumference = $2\pi r = \left(2 \times \dfrac{22}{7} \times 3.5\right)$ cm = 22 cm

Area = $\pi r^2 = \left(\dfrac{22}{7} \times 3.5 \times 3.5\right)$ cm^2 = 38.5 cm^2.

Ex. 12. A rope 1 m long has been put in the form of a circle. Find the area of the circle so formed.

Sol. Circumference of the circle = 1 m = 100 cm.

∴ $2\pi r = 100 \Rightarrow r = \dfrac{50}{\pi}$.

So, area = $\pi r^2 = \left(\pi \times \dfrac{50}{\pi} \times \dfrac{50}{\pi}\right)$ cm^2 = $\left(\dfrac{2500}{22} \times 7\right)$ cm^2 = 795.45 cm^2.

Ex. 13. In a circle of radius 35 cm, an arc subtends an angle of 72° at the centre. Find the length of the arc and the area of the sector.

Sol. Length of the arc = $\left(\dfrac{2\pi r \theta}{360}\right) = \left(2 \times \dfrac{22}{7} \times 35 \times \dfrac{72}{360}\right)$ cm^2 = 44 cm^2.

Area of the sector = $\left(\dfrac{\pi r^2 \theta}{360}\right) = \left(\dfrac{22}{7} \times 35 \times 35 \times \dfrac{72}{360}\right)$ cm^2 = 770 cm^2.

Area   317

Ex. 14. A circular grassy plot of land 70 m in diameter has a path 7 m wide running round it on the outside. Find the cost of gravelling the path of Rs. 3 per square metre.

Sol. Radius of plot = 35 m

Radius of outer circle = (35 + 7) m = 42 m

Area of path = $\pi \times (42)^2 - \pi \times (35)^2$

= $\pi \times [(42)^2 - (35)^2] = \left(\dfrac{22}{7} \times 77 \times 7\right) m^2$

= 1694 m².

∴ Cost of gravelling = Rs. (1694 × 3) = Rs. 5082.

Ex. 15. The diameter of the driving wheel of a bus is 140 cm. How many revolutions per minute must the wheel make in order to keep a speed of 66 km. per hour ?

Sol. Distance covered by the wheel in 1 minute

= $\left(\dfrac{66 \times 1000 \times 100}{60}\right)$ cms = 110000 cms.

Circumference of the wheel = $\left(2 \times \dfrac{22}{7} \times 70\right)$ cms = 440 cms.

Number of revolutions in 1 minute = $\left(\dfrac{110000}{440}\right)$ = 250.

Ex. 16. The length of a rectangular park is 50 m and its breadth is 20 m. There is a 7 m wide path all around it on the outside. Find the area of the path.   (Bank P.O. 1991)

Sol. Area of the park = (50 × 20) m² = 1000 m²

Length of park with path = (50 + 14) m = 64 m

Breadth of park with path = (20 + 14) m = 34 m

Area of outer rectangle = (64 × 34) m² = 2176 m²

Area of path = (2176 − 1000) m² = 1176 m²

Exercise 20

1. One side of a rectangular field is 4 metres and its diagonal is 5 metres. The area of the field is :

   (a) 12 m² ☐   (b) 15 m² ☐

   (c) 20 m² ☐   (d) 4√5 m² ☐

2. If the length of diagonal AC of a square ABCD is 5.2 cm, then area of the square ABCD is : (C.D.S. Exam, 1989)
   (a) 15.12 sq. cm
   (b) 13.52 sq. cm.
   (c) 12.62 sq. cm.
   (d) 10 sq. cm.

3. The length of a plot is four times its breadth. A playground measuring 1200 square metres occupies a third of the total area of the plot. What is the length of the plot, in metres ? (Bank P.O. Exam, 1990)
   (a) 20
   (b) 30
   (c) 60
   (d) none of these

4. The length and breadth of a playground are 36 m and 21 m respectively. Flagstaffs are required to be fixed on all along the boundary at a distance of 3 m apart. The number of flagstaffs will be :
   (a) 37
   (b) 38
   (c) 39
   (d) 40
   (I. Tax & Central Excise Exam, 1989)

5. The area of a rectangle 144 m long is the same as that of a square having a side 84 m long. The width of the rectangle is :
   (a) 7 m
   (b) 14 m
   (c) 49 m
   (d) cannot be determined

6. The length of a rectangular plot is twice its width. If the length of a diagonal is $9\sqrt{5}$ metres, the perimeter of the rectangle is :
   (a) 27 m
   (b) 54 m
   (c) 81 m
   (d) none of these

7. The length and breadth of a rectangular piece of land are in ratio of 5 : 3. The owner spent Rs. 3000 for surrounding it from all the sides at Rs. 7.50 per metre. The difference between its length and breadth is :
   (a) 50 m
   (b) 100 m
   (c) 150 m
   (d) 200 m
   (Bank P.O. Exam, 1991)

8. The ratio between the length and breadth of a rectangular field is 5 : 4. If the breadth is 20 metres less than the length, the perimeter of the field is : (Bank P.O. Exam, 1990)
   (a) 260 m
   (b) 280 m
   (c) 360 m
   (d) none of these

9. A verandah 40 metres long, 15 metres broad is to be paved with stones, each measuring 6 dm by 5 dm. The number of stones required is :
   (a) 1000
   (b) 2000
   (c) 3000
   (d) none of these

Area 319

10. Area of a square is $\frac{1}{2}$ hectare. The diagonal of the square is :
   (a) 250 metres
   (b) 100 metres
   (c) $50\sqrt{2}$ metres
   (d) 50 metres

11. If the side of a square be increased by 4 cms, the area increases by 60 sq. cms. The side of the square is :
   (a) 12 cm
   (b) 13 cm
   (c) 14 cm
   (d) none of these

12. A rectangular plot is half as long again as it is broad. The area of the lawn is (2/3) hectares. The length of the plot is :
   (a) 100 metres
   (b) 66.66 metres
   (c) $33\frac{1}{3}$ metres
   (d) $\left(\frac{100}{\sqrt{3}}\right)$ metres

13. If the side of a square is increased by 25%, then how much per cent does its area get increased : (Astt. Grade Exam, 1990)
   (a) 125
   (b) 156.25
   (c) 50
   (d) 56.25

14. If the side of a square is doubled, then the ratio of the resulting square to that of the given square is :
   (a) 1 : 2
   (b) 2 : 1
   (c) 3 : 1
   (d) 4 : 1

15. The length of a hall is (4/3) times its breadth. If the area of the hall be 300 square metres, the difference between the length and the breadth is : (S.B.I. P.O. Exam, 1987)
   (a) 15 metres
   (b) 4 metres
   (c) 3 metres
   (d) none of these

16. The cost of cultivating a square field at the rate of Rs. 160 per hectare is Rs. 1440. The cost of puting a fence around it at 75 paise per metre is :
   (a) Rs. 900
   (b) Rs. 1800
   (c) Rs. 360
   (d) Rs. 810

17. The cost of carpeting a room 15 metres long with a carpet 75 cm wide at 30 paise per metre is Rs. 36. The breadth of the room is :
   (a) 6 metres
   (b) 8 metres
   (c) 9 metres
   (d) 12 metres

18. The length of a rectangle is doubled while its breadth is halved. What is the percentage change in area ?
   (a) 50
   (b) 75
   (c) no change
   (d) none of these

19. The area of a rectangle is thrice that of a square. Length of the rectangle is 40 cm and the breadth of the rectangle is (3/2) times that of the side of the square. The side of the square in cm is :
    (a) 15 (b) 20
    (c) 30 (d) 60
    (Bank P.O. Exam, 1989)

20. The ratio of the areas of two squares, one having double its diagonal than the other is :
    (a) 2 : 1 (b) 3 : 1
    (c) 3 : 2 (d) 4 : 1

21. A park is 10 metres long and 8 metres broad. What is the length of the longest pole that can be placed in the park ?
    (a) 10 metres (b) 12.8 metres
    (c) 13.4 metres (d) 18 metres

22. The length of a rectangle is increased by 60%. By what per cent would the width have to be decreased to maintain the same area ?
    (S.B.I. P.O. Exam. 1988)
    (a) $37\frac{1}{2}\%$ (b) 60%
    (c) 75% (d) 120%

23. If the ratio of the areas of two squares is 9 : 1, the ratio of their perimeters is : (Astt. Grade Exam, 1990)
    (a) 9 : 1 (b) 3 : 1
    (c) 3 : 4 (d) 1 : 3

24. Of the two square fields, the area of the one is 1 hectare, while the another one is broader by 1%. The difference in areas is :
    (a) 101 sq. metres (b) 201 sq. metres
    (c) 100 sq. metres (d) 200 sq. metres

25. A rectangular lawn 60 metres by 40 metres has two roads each 5 metres wide running in the middle of it, one parallel to length and the other parallel to breadth. The cost of gravelling the roads at 60 paise per sq. metre is :
    (a) Rs. 300 (b) Rs. 280
    (c) Rs. 285 (d) Rs. 250

26. A hall 20 m long and 15 m broad is surrounded by a verandah of uniform width of 2.5 m. The cost of flooring the verandah at the rate of Rs. 3.50 per sq. metre is : (R.R.B. Exam, 1991)
    (a) Rs. 500 (b) Rs. 600
    (c) Rs. 700 (d) Rs. 800

Area

27. The length and breadth of a square are increased by 40% and 30% respectively. The area of the resulting rectangle exceeds the area of the square by : **(I. Tax & Central Excise Exam, 1988)**
    - (a) 42%
    - (b) 62%
    - (c) 82%
    - (d) none of these

28. The length of a rectangular room is 4 metres. If it can be partitioned into two equal square rooms, what is the length of each partition in metres ? **(Bank P.O. Exam, 1987)**
    - (a) 1
    - (b) 2
    - (c) 4
    - (d) data inadequate

29. A rectangle has 15 cm as its length and 150 cm^2 as its area. Its area is increased to $1\frac{1}{3}$ times the original area by increasing only its length. Its new perimeter is : **(Bank P.O. Exam, 1989)**
    - (a) 50 cm
    - (b) 60 cm
    - (c) 70 cm
    - (d) 80 cm

30. Area of four walls of a room is 77 square metres. The length and breadth of the room are 7.5 metres and 3.5 metres respectively. The height of the room is :
    - (a) 3.5 metres
    - (b) 5.4 metres
    - (c) 6.77 metres
    - (d) 7.7 metres

31. Area of four walls of a room is 168 sq. metres. The breadth and height of the room are 8 metres and 6 metres respectively. The length of the room is :
    - (a) 14 metres
    - (b) 12 metres
    - (c) 6 metres
    - (d) 3.5 metres

32. The cost of papering the four walls of a room is Rs. 48. Each one of the length, breadth and height of another room is double that of this room. The cost of papering the walls of this new room is :
    - (a) Rs. 384
    - (b) Rs. 288
    - (c) Rs. 192
    - (d) Rs. 96

33. The length of a rectangle is twice its breadth. If its length is decreased by 5 cm and the breadth is increased by 5 cm, the area of the rectangle is increased by 75 cm^2. Therefore, the length of the rectangle is :
    - (a) 20 cm
    - (b) 30 cm
    - (c) 40 cm
    - (d) 50 cm

    (C.D.S. Exam, 1991)

34. If the base of a rectangle is increased by 10% and the area is unchanged, then the corresponding altitude must be decreased by :

(a) $9\frac{1}{11}\%$ (b) 10%

(c) 11% (d) $11\frac{1}{9}\%$

(C.B.I. Exam, 1990)

35. If the diagonal of a square is doubled, how does the area of the square change? (Astt. Grade, 1990)
    (a) becomes four fold (b) becomes three fold
    (c) becomes two fold (d) none of the above

36. The base of a rightangled triangle is 5 metres and hypotenuse is 13 metres. Its area will be :
    (a) 25 m^2 (b) 28 m^2
    (c) 30 m^2 (d) none of these

37. The sides of a triangular board are 13 metres, 14 metres and 15 metres. The cost of painting it at the rate of Rs. 8.75 per m^2 is :
    (a) Rs. 688.80 (b) Rs. 735
    (c) Rs. 730.80 (d) Rs. 722.50

38. The perimeter of an isosceles triangle is equal to 14 cm; the lateral side is to the base in the ratio 5 : 4. The area of the triangle is :
    (a) $\frac{1}{2}\sqrt{21} \text{ cm}^2$ (b) $\frac{3}{2}\sqrt{21} \text{ cm}^2$
    (c) $\sqrt{21} \text{ cm}^2$ (d) $2\sqrt{21} \text{ cm}^2$

(C.D.S. Exam, 1989)

39. The area of an equilateral triangle whose side is 8 cms, is :
    (a) 64 cm^2 (b) $16\sqrt{3} \text{ cm}^2$
    (c) 21.3 cm^2 (d) $4\sqrt{3} \text{ cm}^2$

40. The length of each side of an equilateral triangle having an area of $4\sqrt{3} \text{ cm}^2$, is :
    (a) $\frac{4}{\sqrt{3}} \text{ cm}$ (b) $\frac{\sqrt{3}}{4} \text{ cm}$
    (c) 3 cm (d) 4 cm

41. The altitude of an equilateral triangle of side $2\sqrt{3}$ cm is :
    (a) $\frac{\sqrt{3}}{2} \text{ cm}$ (b) $\frac{1}{2} \text{ cm}$
    (c) $\frac{\sqrt{3}}{4} \text{ cm}$ (d) 3 cm

42. In a triangle ABC; BC = 5 cm, AC = 12 cm and AB = 13 cm. The length of the altitude drawn from B on AC is :

Area 323

    (a) 4 cm   (b) 5 cm
    (c) 6 cm   (d) 7 cm

43. Area of a square with side x is equal to the area of a triangle with base x. The altitude of the triangle is :   (Railway Recruitment, 1991)
    (a) $\frac{x}{2}$ (b) x
    (c) $2x$ (d) $4x$

44. The ratio of the area of a square of side a and and equilateral triangle of side a, is :
    (a) 2 : 1   (b) 2 : $\sqrt{3}$
    (c) 4 : 3   (d) 4 : $\sqrt{3}$

45. If the circumference of a circle is 352 metres, then its area in m^2 is :
  (N.D.A. Exam, 1990)
    (a) 9856   (b) 8956
    (c) 6589   (d) 5986

46. The area of a circle is 38.5 sq. cm. Its circumference is :
    (a) 6.20 cm   (b) 11 cm
    (c) 22 cm   (d) 121 cm

47. The area of a circular field is 13.86 hectares. The cost of fencing it at the rate of 20 paise per metre is :
    (a) Rs. 277.20   (b) Rs. 264
    (c) Rs. 324   (d) Rs. 198

48. The difference between the circumference and the radius of a circle is 37 cms. The area of the circle is :
    (a) 148 sq. cm   (b) 111 sq. cm
    (c) 154 sq. cm   (d) 259 sq. cms

49. The radius of a circle has been reduced from 9 cms to 7 cm. The approximate percentage decrease in area is :
    (a) 31.5%   (b) 39.5%
    (c) 34.5%   (d) 65.5%

50. If the radius of a circle be reduced by 50%, its area is reduced by :
    (a) 25%   (b) 50%
    (c) 75%   (d) 100%
  (Clerical Grade, 1991)

51. If the diameter of a circle is increased by 100%, its area is increased by :   (R.R.B. Exam, 1991)
    (a) 100%   (b) 200%
    (c) 300%   (d) 400%

52. If the circumference of a circle is increased by 50%, then its area will be increased by :
    (a) 50% (b) 100%
    (c) 125% (d) 225%

53. If 88 m of wire is required to fence a circular plot of land, then the area of the plot is :
    (a) 526 m^2 (b) 556 m^2
    (c) 616 m^2 (d) none of these

54. The area of the largest circle that can be drawn inside a square of 14 cm length is :
    (a) 84 cm^2 (b) 154 cm^2
    (c) 204 cm^2 (d) none of these

55. The area of the largest circle that can be drawn inside a rectangle with sides 7 m by 6 m is :
    (a) $28\frac{2}{7}$ m^2 (b) $64\frac{8}{9}$ m^2
    (c) $59\frac{2}{3}$ m^2 (d) none of these

56. A circular wire of radius 42 cm is cut and bent in the form of a rectangle whose sides are in the ratio of 6 : 5. The smaller side of the rectangle is : (I. Tax & Central Excise, 1989)
    (a) 30 cm (b) 60 cm
    (c) 72 cm (d) 132 cm

57. The area of a square is 50 sq. units. Then the area of the circle drawn on its diagonal is :
    (a) 25 π sq. units (b) 100 π sq. units
    (c) 50 π sq. units (d) none of these

58. The ratio of the radii of two circles is 1 : 3. The ratio of their areas is :
    (a) 1 : 3 (b) 1 : 6
    (c) 1 : 9 (d) none of these

59. The inner circumference of a circular race track, 14 m wide, is 440 m. Then the radius of the outer circle is :
    (a) 70 m (b) 56 m
    (c) 77 m (d) 84 m

Area

60. A circular road runs round a circular ground. If the difference between the circumferences of the outer circle and the inner circle is 66 metres, the width of the road is :
  (a) 21 metres ☐   (b) 10.5 metres ☐
  (c) 7 metres ☐   (d) 5.25 metres ☐

61. The diameter of a wheel is 63 cms. Distance travelled by the wheel in 100 revolutions is :
  (a) 99 metres ☐   (b) 198 metres ☐
  (c) 63 metres ☐   (d) 136 metres ☐

62. A wheel makes 1000 revolutions in covering a distance of 88 km. The diameter of the wheel is :
  (a) 24 metres ☐   (b) 40 metres ☐
  (c) 28 metres ☐   (d) 14 metres ☐

63. The number of rounds that a wheel of diameter $\frac{7}{11}$ m will make in going 4 km, is : (C.D.S. Exam, 1991)
  (a) 1000 ☐   (b) 1500 ☐
  (c) 1700 ☐   (d) 2000 ☐

64. A circular disc of area $0.49\,\pi$ square metres rolls down a length of 1.76 km. The number of revolutions it makes is :
  (a) 300 ☐   (b) 400 ☐
  (c) 600 ☐   (d) 4000 ☐

65. The radius of a wheel is 1.4 decimetre. How many times does it revolve during a journey of 0.66 km ?
  (a) 375 ☐   (b) 750 ☐
  (c) 1500 ☐   (d) 3000 ☐

66. The radius of the wheel of a vehicle is 70 cm. The wheel makes 10 revolutions in 5 seconds. The speed of the vehicle is :
  (a) 29.46 km/hr ☐   (b) 31.68 km/hr ☐
  (c) 36.25 km/hr ☐   (d) 32.72 km/hr ☐

67. A circle and a square have same area. The ratio of the side of the square and the radius of the circle is : (C.D.S. Exam, 1991)
  (a) $\sqrt{\pi} : 1$ ☐   (b) $1 : \sqrt{\pi}$ ☐
  (c) $1 : \pi$ ☐   (d) $\pi : 1$ ☐

68. The largest possible square is inscribed in a circle of unit radius. The area of the square in square units is :
  (a) 2 ☐   (b) π ☐
  (c) $(2\sqrt{2})\pi$ ☐   (d) $(4\sqrt{2})\pi$ ☐

69. A park is in the form of a square one of whose sides is 100 m. The area of the park, excluding the circular lawn, in the centre of the park, is 8614 m². The radius of the circular lawn is :
   (a) 21 cm □   (b) 31 cm □
   (c) 41 cm □   (d) none of these □

70. The area of the circle inscribed in an equilateral triangle of side 24 cms is :
   (a) $24\pi\,cm^2$ □   (b) $36\pi\,cm^2$ □
   (c) $48\pi\,cm^2$ □   (d) $18\pi\,cm^2$ □

71. The area of a circle inscribed in an equilateral triangle is 462 cm². The perimeter of the triangle is :
   (a) $42\sqrt{3}$ cms □   (b) 126 cms □
   (c) 72.6 cms □   (d) 168 cms □

72. The perimeter of a square circumscribed about a circle of radius r is :
   (a) $2r$ □   (b) $4r$ □
   (c) $8r$ □   (d) $21\pi r$ □

73. The vertices of a rectangle with sides 8 m and 6 m, lie on a circle. The area of the circle, excluding the area of the rectangle, is :
   (a) 65.3 m² □   (b) 42.4 m² □
   (c) 30.6 m² □   (d) 39 m² □

74. The area of a sector of a circle of radius 5 cm, formed by an arc of length 3.5 cms, is :
   (a) 35 sq. cms □   (b) 17.5 sq. cms □
   (c) 8.75 sq. cms □   (d) 55 sq. cms □

75. In a circle of radius 21 cm, an arc subtends an angle of 72° at the centre. The length of the arc is :
   (a) 13.2 cm □   (b) 19.8 cm □
   (c) 21.6 cm □   (d) 26.4 cm □

76. The length of minute hand on a wall clock is 7 cms. The area swept by the minute hand in 30 minutes is :
   (a) 147 sq. cm □   (b) 210 sq. cm □
   (c) 154 sq. cm □   (d) 77 sq. cm □

77. The area of the sector of a circle, whose radius is 12 metres and whose angle at the centre is 42°, is :
   (a) 26.4 sq. metres □   (b) 39.6 sq. metres □
   (c) 52.8 sq. metres □   (d) 79.2 sq. metres □

Area

78. The diameter of a circle is 105 cm less than the circumference. What is the diameter of the circle ? *(Astt. Grade Exam, 1990)*
  (a) 44 cm ☐ (b) 46 cm ☐
  (c) 48 cm ☐ (d) 49 cm ☐

79. The circumferences of two concentric circles are 176 m and 132 m respectively. What is the difference between their radii ?
  (a) 5 metres ☐ (b) 7 metres ☐
  (c) 8 metres ☐ (d) 44 metres ☐
  (Astt. Grade Exam, 1990)

80. The radius of a circle is increased so that its circumference increases by 5%. The area of the circle will increase by :
  (a) 10% ☐ (b) 10.25% ☐
  (c) 8.75% ☐ (d) 10.5% ☐

81. The length of a rope by which a cow must be tethered in order that she may be able to graze an area of 9856 sq. m is :
  (a) 56 m ☐ (b) 64 m ☐
  (c) 88 m ☐ (d) 168 m ☐
  (I. Tax & Central Excise, 1989)

82. Four circular cardboard pieces, each of radius 7 cm are placed in such a way that each piece touches two other pieces. The area of the space enclosed by the four pieces is :
  (a) 21 cm^2 ☐ (b) 42 cm^2 ☐
  (c) 84 cm^2 ☐ (d) 168 cm^2 ☐

83. Four horses are tethered at four corners of a square plot of side 63 metres, so that they just cannot reach one another. The area left ungrazed is :
  (a) 675.5 ☐ (b) 780.6 m^2 ☐
  (c) 785.8 m^2 ☐ (d) 850.5 m^2 ☐

84. The area of the largest triangle that can be inscribed in a semi circle of radius r cm is :
  (a) $2r$ cm^2 ☐ (b) r^2 cm^2 ☐
  (c) $2r^2$ cm^2 ☐ (d) $\frac{1}{2}r^2$ cm^2 ☐

85. If a regular hexagon is inscribed in a circle of radius r, then its perimeter is :
  (a) $3r$ ☐ (b) $6r$ ☐
  (c) $9r$ ☐ (d) $12r$ ☐

86. One side of a rhombus is 10 cms and one of its diagonals is 12 cms. The area of the rhombus is :
    (a) 120 sq. cm   (b) 96 sq. cm
    (c) 80 sq. cm   (d) 60 sq. cm

87. The perimeter of a rhombus is 52 metres, while its longer diagonal is 24 metres. Its other diagonal is :
    (a) 5 metres   (b) 10 metres
    (c) 20 metres   (d) 28 metres

88. In a rhombus, whose area is 144 sq. cm, one of its diagonals is twice as long as the other. The lengths of its diagonals are :
    (a) 24 cm, 48 cm   (b) 12 cm, 24 cm
    (c) $6\sqrt{2}$ cm, $12\sqrt{2}$ cm   (d) 6 cm, 12 cm
    (C.D.S. Exam, 1989)

89. The length of the diagonal of a rhombus is 80% of the length of the other diagonal. Then, the area of the rhombus is how many times the square of the length of the longer diagonal ?
    (a) $\frac{4}{5}$ (b) $\frac{2}{5}$
    (c) $\frac{3}{4}$ (d) $\frac{1}{4}$

90. If a square and a rhombus stand on the same base, then the ratio of the areas of the square and the rhombus is :   (N.D.A. Exam, 1990)
    (a) greater than 1   (b) equal to 1
    (c) equal to $\frac{1}{2}$ (d) equal to $\frac{1}{4}$

91. One side of a parallelogram is 14 cm. Its distance from the opposite side is 16 cm. The area of the parallelogram is :
    (a) 112 sq. cm   (b) 224 sq. cm
    (c) 56 π sq. cm   (d) 210 sq. cm

92. The adjacent sides of a parallelogram are 6 cm and 4 cm and the angle between them is 30°. The area of the parallelogram is :
    (a) 12 cm^2 (b) 24 cm^2
    (c) 48 cm^2 (d) none of these

93. A parallelogram has sides 60 m and 40 m and one of its diagonals is 80 m long. Then, its area is :   (N.D.A. Exam, 1987)
    (a) 480 sq. m   (b) 320 sq. m
    (c) 600 $\sqrt{15}$ sq. m   (d) 450 $\sqrt{15}$ sq. m

94. The two parallel sides of a trapezium are 1 metre and 2 metres respectively. The perpendicular distance between them is 6 metres. The area of the trapezium is :
   (a) 18 sq. metres (b) 12 sq. metres
   (c) 9 sq. metres (d) 6 sq. metres

95. The area of a trapezium is 384 sq. cm. If its parallel sides are in ratio 3 : 5 and the perpendicular distance between them be 12 cm, the smaller of parallel sides is :
   (a) 16 cm (b) 24 cm
   (c) 32 cm (d) 40 cm

96. The cross section of a canal is a trapezium in shape. If the canal is 10 metres wide at the top and 6 metres wide at bottom and the area of cross section is 640 sq. metres, the length of canal is :
   (a) 40 metres (b) 80 metres
   (c) 160 metres (d) 384 metres

97. ABCD is a trapezuim in which AB || CD and AB = 2CD. If its diagonals intersect each other at O, then ratio of areas of triangles AOB and COD is :
   (a) 1 : 2 (b) 2 : 1
   (c) 1 : 4 (d) 4 : 1

98. In $\triangle$ ABC, side BC = 10 cm and height AD = 4.4 cm. If AC = 11 cm, then altitude BE equals :
   (a) 5 cm (b) 4 cm
   (c) 5.6 cm (d) 5.5 cm

99. If D, E and F are respectively the mid points of the sides BC, CA and AB of a $\triangle$ ABC and the area of $\triangle$ ABC = 36 cm^2, then area of $\triangle$ DEF is :
   (a) 12 cm^2 (b) 9 cm^2
   (c) 18 cm^2 (d) 24 cm^2

100. The ratio of the corresponding sides of two similar triangles is 3 : 4. The ratio of their areas is :
   (a) 4 : 3 (b) 3 : 4
   (c) 9 : 16 (d) $\sqrt{3}$: 2

101. Radhika runs along the boundary of a rectangular park at the rate of 12 km/hr and completes one full round in 15 minutes. If the length of the park is 4 times its breadth, the area of the park is :
   (a) 360000 m^2 (b) 36000 m^2
   (c) 3600 m^2 (d) none of these

102. Area of smallest square that can circumscribe a circle of area 616 cm², is :
   (a) 784 cm² ☐   (b) 824 cm² ☐
   (c) 864 cm² ☐   (d) none of these ☐

103. A room 5.44 m × 3.74 m is to be paved with square tiles. The least number of tiles required to cover the floor is :
   (a) 162 ☐   (b) 176 ☐
   (c) 184 ☐   (d) 192 ☐

104. If x is the length of a median of an equilateral triangle, then its area is :
   (a) x^2 ☐   (b) $\dfrac{x^2 \sqrt{3}}{2}$ ☐
   (c) $\dfrac{x^2 \sqrt{3}}{3}$ ☐   (d) $\dfrac{x^2}{2}$ ☐

105. A rectangular carpet has an area of 120 sq. m and a perimeter of 46 m. The length of its diagonal is :   (Railways, 1991)
   (a) 15 m ☐   (b) 16 m ☐
   (c) 17 m ☐   (d) 20 m ☐

106. A rectangular carpet has an area of 60 sq. m. Its diagonal and longer side together equal 5 times the shorter side. The length of the carpet is :   (Central Excise & I. Tax, 1991)
   (a) 5 m ☐   (b) 12 m ☐
   (c) 13 m ☐   (d) 14.5 m ☐

Answers (Exercise 20)

1. (a)   2. (b)   3. (d)   4. (b)   5. (c)   6. (b)   7. (a)   8. (c)   9. (b)
10. (b)   11. (d)   12. (a)   13. (d)   14. (d)   15. (d)   16. (a)   17. (a)   18. (c)
19. (b)   20. (d)   21. (b)   22. (a)   23. (b)   24. (b)   25. (c)   26. (c)   27. (c)
28. (b)   29. (b)   30. (a)   31. (c)   32. (c)   33. (c)   34. (a)   35. (a)   36. (c)
37. (b)   38. (d)   39. (b)   40. (d)   41. (d)   42. (b)   43. (c)   44. (d)   45. (a)
46. (c)   47. (b)   48. (c)   49. (b)   50. (c)   51. (c)   52. (c)   53. (c)   54. (b)
55. (a)   56. (b)   57. (a)   58. (c)   59. (d)   60. (b)   61. (b)   62. (c)   63. (d)
64. (b)   65. (b)   66. (b)   67. (b)   68. (a)   69. (a)   70. (c)   71. (b)   72. (c)
73. (c)   74. (c)   75. (d)   76. (d)   77. (c)   78. (d)   79. (b)   80. (b)   81. (a)
82. (b)   83. (d)   84. (b)   85. (b)   86. (b)   87. (b)   88. (b)   89. (b)   90. (b)
91. (b)   92. (a)   93. (c)   94. (c)   95. (b)   96. (b)   97. (d)   98. (b)   99. (b)
100. (c)   101. (a)   102. (a)   103. (b)   104. (c)   105. (c)   106. (b)

Area   331

Solutions (Exercise 20)

1. Other side = $\sqrt{5^2 - 4^2} = \sqrt{9} = 3$ m.
    $\therefore$ Area = (4×3) m^2 = 12 m^2.

2. Area = $\frac{1}{2} \times$ (diagonal)^2 = $\left(\frac{1}{2} \times 5.2 \times 5.2\right)$ cm^2 = 13.52 cm^2.

3. Area of the plot = (3×1200) m^2 = 3600 m^2.
    Let breadth = x metres. Then, length = $4x$ metres.
    $\therefore$ $4x \times x = 3600$ or $x^2 = 900$ or $x = 30$.
    $\therefore$ Length of plot = $4x = (4 \times 30)$ m = 120 m.

4. Perimeter = $2 \times (36 + 21)$ m = 114 m.
    $\therefore$ Number of flagstaffs = $\left(\frac{114}{3}\right) = 38$.

5. Area of the square = (84×84) m^2.
    Area of the rectangle = (84×84) m^2.
    $\therefore$ Width = $\left(\frac{84 \times 84}{1.44}\right)$ m = 49 m.

6. Let breadth = x metres. Then, length = $2x$ metres.
    $\therefore$ diagonal = $\sqrt{x^2 + 4x^2} = \sqrt{5x^2} = \sqrt{5}\, x$ metres.
    So, $\sqrt{5}\, x = 9\sqrt{5}$ or $x = 9$.
    Thus, breadth = 9 m and length = 18 m.
    $\therefore$ Perimeter = $2(18 + 9)$ m = 54 m.

7. Let length = $5x$ metres and breadth = $3x$ metres.
    Then, perimeter = $2 \times (5x + 3x)$ m = $16x$ metres.
    But, perimeter = $\frac{\text{Total cost}}{\text{Rate}} = \left(\frac{3000}{7.50}\right)$ m = 400 m.
    $\therefore$ $16x = 400$ or $x = 25$
    $\therefore$ (length) − (breadth) = $(5 \times 25 − 3 \times 25)$ m = (2×25) m = 50 m.

8. $5x − 4x = 20$ or $x = 20$.
    $\therefore$ Length = (5×20) m = 100 m, Breadth = (4×20) m = 80 m.
    $\therefore$ Perimeter = $2(100 + 80)$ m = 360 m.

9. Length = (40×10) dm = 400 dm, Breadth = (15×10) dm = 150 dm.
    Area of verandah = (400×150) dm^2
    Area of one stone = (6×5) dm^2.
    $\therefore$ Number of stones = $\left(\frac{400 \times 150}{6 \times 5}\right) = 2000$.

10. Area = $\left(\frac{1}{2} \times 10000\right)$ m^2 = 5000 m^2.

    $\therefore \frac{1}{2} \times$ (diagonal)^2 = 5000 or (diagonal)^2 = 10000

    or   diagonal = 100 m

11. Let each side = x cm.

    Then, $(x+4)^2 - x^2 = 60$ or $x^2 + 8x + 16 - x^2 = 60$

    $\therefore x = 5.5$ cm.

12. Let breadth = x metres. Then, length = $\frac{3}{2}x$ metres.

    $\therefore x \times \frac{3}{2}x = \frac{2}{3} \times 10000$ or $x^2 = \frac{4}{9} \times 10000$ or $x = \left(\frac{2}{3} \times 100\right)$ m.

    $\therefore$ Length = $\left(\frac{3}{2} \times \frac{2}{3} \times 100\right)$ m = 100 m.

13. Let area = 100 m^2. Then, side = 10 m.

    New side = (125% of 10) m = $\left(\frac{125}{100} \times 10\right)$ m = 12.5 m.

    New area = (12.5 × 12.5) m^2 = (12.5)^2 sq. m.

    $\therefore$ Increase in area = $\left[(12.5)^2 - (10)^2\right]$ m^2

    $= [(12.5 + 10)(12.5 - 10)]$ m^2

    $= (22.5 \times 2.5)$ m^2 = 56.25 m^2.

    $\therefore$ Increase = 56.25%.

14. Let original length = x metres. New length = $(2x)$ metres

    $\therefore$ Ratio of the areas = $\frac{4x^2}{x^2} = \frac{4}{1} = 4:1$.

15. Let breadth = x metres. Then, length = $\left(\frac{4}{3}x\right)$ metres.

    $\therefore x \times \frac{4}{3}x = 300$ or $x^2 = 300 \times \frac{3}{4} = 225$ or $x = 15$.

    Hence, [(length) − (breadth)] = $\left(\frac{4}{3}x - x\right) = \frac{1}{3}x = \left(\frac{1}{3} \times 15\right)$ m = 5 m.

16. Area = $\left(\frac{1440}{160}\right)$ hectares = 90000 m^2.

    $\therefore$ side = $\sqrt{90000}$ m = 300 m.

    So, perimeter = (4×300) m = 1200 m.

    $\therefore$ Cost of fencing = Rs. $\left(1200 \times \frac{75}{100}\right)$ = Rs. 900.

Area

17. Length of carpet = $\dfrac{\text{Total cost}}{\text{Rate}} = \dfrac{3600}{30} = 120$ m.

Area of carpet = $\left(120 \times \dfrac{75}{100}\right)$ m^2 = 90 m^2.

∴ Area of the room = 90 m^2.

Hence, breadth of the room = $\dfrac{\text{Area}}{\text{Length}} = \left(\dfrac{90}{15}\right)$ m = 6 m.

18. Let length = l and breadth = b.
Then, area = lb.

New length = $2\,l$ and new breadth = $\dfrac{b}{2}$.

∴ New area = $\left(2\,l \times \dfrac{b}{2}\right) = l\,b$.

So, there is no change in area.

19. Let the side of the square = x cm.

Then, breadth of the rectangle = $\dfrac{3}{2} x$ cm.

∴ Area of rectangle = $\left(40 \times \dfrac{3}{2} x\right)$ cm^2 = $(60\,x)$ cm^2.

∴ $60\,x = 3\,x^2$ or $x = 20$.

Hence, the side of the square = 20 cm.

20. Let the diagonal of one square be $(2\,x)$ cm.
Then, diagonal of another square = x cm.

∴ Area of first square = $\left[\dfrac{1}{2} \times (2x)^2\right]$ cm^2 = $(2\,x^2)$ cm^2.

Area of second square = $\left(\dfrac{1}{2} x^2\right)$ cm^2.

∴ Ratio of area = $\dfrac{2\,x^2}{\left(\dfrac{1}{2} x^2\right)} = \dfrac{4}{1} = 4 : 1$.

21. Length of the longest pole = $\sqrt{(10)^2 + (8)^2}$ m = $\sqrt{164}$ m = 12.8 m.

22. Initially, let length = x and breadth = y.

Let, new breadth = z. Then, new length = $\left(\dfrac{160}{100} x\right) = \dfrac{8}{5} x$.

∴ $\dfrac{8}{5} x \times z = xy$ or $z = \dfrac{5y}{8}$.

Decrease in breadth = $\left(y - \dfrac{5y}{8}\right) = \dfrac{3}{8} y$.

334　　　　　　　　　　　　　　　　　　　　　　　　　*Objective Arithmetic*

∴ Decrease per cent = $\left(\dfrac{3}{8} y \times \dfrac{1}{y} \times 100\right)\% = 37\dfrac{1}{2}\%$.

23. Let the areas of squares be $(9x^2)$ m^2 and (x^2) m^2.
    Then, their sides are $(3x)$ metres & x metres respectively.
    ∴ Ratio of their perimeters = $\dfrac{12x}{4x} = 3:1$.

24. Area of one square field = 10000 m^2.
    Side of this square = $\sqrt{10000}$ m = 100 m.
    Side of another square = 101 m.
    ∴ Difference of areas = $\left[(101)^2 - (100)^2\right]$ m^2
    　　　　　　　　　　　 = $[(101+100)(101-100)]$ m^2 = 201 m^2.

25. Area of the roads
    = $(60 \times 5 + 40 \times 5 - 5 \times 5)$ m^2 = 475 m^2.
    ∴ Cost of gravelling = Rs. $\left(475 \times \dfrac{60}{100}\right)$
    = Rs. 285.

26. Area of verandah = $[(25 \times 20) - (20 \times 15)]$ m^2 = 200 m^2.
    ∴ Cost of flooring = Rs. (200×3.50) = Rs. 700.

27. Let the side of the square = 100 m.
    New length = 140 m, New breadth = 130 m.
    Increase in area = $[(140 \times 130) - (100 \times 100)]$ m^2 = 8200 m^2.
    ∴ Increase per cent = $\left(\dfrac{8200}{100 \times 100} \times 100\right)\% = 82\%$.

28. Let the width of the room be x metres.
    Then, its area = $(4x)$ m^2.
    Area of each new square room = $(2x)$ m^2.
    Let the side of each new room = y metres.
    Then, $y^2 = 2x$.
    Clearly, $2x$ is a complete square when $x = 2$.
    ∴ $y^2 = 4$ or $y = 2$ m.

29. Breadth of the rectangle = $\left(\dfrac{150}{15}\right)$ cm = 10 cm.
    New area = $\left(\dfrac{4}{3} \times 150\right)$ cm^2 = 200 cm^2.
    New length = $\left(\dfrac{200}{10}\right)$ cm = 20 cm.

Area

New perimeter = 2 (20 + 10) cm = 60 cm.

30. $2 \times (7.5 + 3.5) \times$ height = 77

$\therefore$ Height $= \left(\dfrac{77}{2 \times 11}\right)$ m = 3.5 m.

31. $2 \times$ (length + 8) $\times 6 = 168 \Rightarrow$ (length + 8) = 14.

$\therefore$ Length = (14 – 8) m = 6 m.

32. Let the dimensions of one room be l, b and h metres respectively. Then, the dimensions of the new room are $2l$, $2b$ and $2h$ metres respectively.

$\therefore$ Area of 4 walls of the new room

$= [2 \times (2l + 2b) \times 2h]$ m^2 = $8 \times [(l + b) \times h]$ m^2

$= 4 \times [2\,(l + b) \times h]$ m^2

$= 4 \times$ (area of 4 walls of the 1st room).

$\therefore$ Required cost = Rs. (4×48) = Rs. 192.

33. Let, breadth = x cm and length = $(2x)$ cm.

Then, $(2x - 5)(x + 5) - x \times 2x = 75$

or $2x^2 + 5x - 25 - 2x^2 = 75$ or $5x = 100$ or $x = 20$.

$\therefore$ Length = $(2x)$ cm = 40 cm.

34. Let base = b and altitude = h. Then area = (bh).

New base $= \left(\dfrac{110}{100} b\right) = \left(\dfrac{11}{10} b\right)$. Let, new altitude = H.

Then, $\dfrac{11}{10} b \times H = bh$ or $H = \left(\dfrac{10}{11} h\right)$.

$\therefore$ Decrease $= \left(h - \dfrac{10}{11} h\right) = \dfrac{1}{11} h$.

Decrease per cent $= \left(\dfrac{1}{11} h \times \dfrac{1}{h} \times 100\right)\% = 9\dfrac{1}{11}\%$.

35. Ratio of the areas $= \dfrac{\dfrac{1}{2} \times d^2}{\dfrac{1}{2} \times (2d)^2} = \dfrac{1}{4}$.

$\therefore$ New area becomes 4 fold.

36. Altitude $= \sqrt{(13)^2 - (5)^2} = \sqrt{144}$ = 12 m.

$\therefore$ Area of the triangle $= \left(\dfrac{1}{2} \times 5 \times 12\right)$ m^2 = 30 m^2.

37. $s = \dfrac{1}{2}(13 + 14 + 15) = 21, s - a = 8, s - b = 7, s - c = 6.$

∴ Area to be painted = $\sqrt{s(s-a)(s-b)(s-c)}$
= $\sqrt{21 \times 8 \times 7 \times 6}$ m² = 84 m².
∴ Cost of painting = Rs. (84 × 8.75) = Rs. 735.

38. Let, lateral side = $(5x)$ cm and base = $(4x)$ cm.
∴ $5x + 5x + 4x = 14$ or $x = 1$.
So, the sides are 5 cm, 5 cm and 4 cm.
$s = \frac{1}{2}(5 + 5 + 4)$ cm = 7 cm, $(s-a) = 2$ cm, $(s-b) = 2$ cm
and $(s-c) = 3$ cm.
∴ Area = $\sqrt{7 \times 2 \times 2 \times 3}$ cm² = $2\sqrt{21}$ cm².

39. Area = $\left[\frac{\sqrt{3}}{4} \times (8)^2\right]$ cm² = $16\sqrt{3}$ cm².

40. $\frac{\sqrt{3}}{4} a^2 = 4\sqrt{3}$. So, $a^2 = 16$ or $a = 4$ cm.

41. $\frac{1}{2} \times 2\sqrt{3} \times h = \frac{\sqrt{3}}{4} \times (2\sqrt{3})^2$
or $\sqrt{3} h = 3\sqrt{3}$ or $h = 3$ cm.

42. $s = \frac{1}{2}(13 + 5 + 12)$ cm = 15 cm.
$(s-a) = 2$ cm, $(s-b) = 10$ cm and $(s-c) = 3$ cm.
∴ Area = $\sqrt{15 \times 2 \times 10 \times 3}$ cm² = 30 cm².
∴ $\frac{1}{2} \times 12 \times h = 30$ or $h = 5$ cm.

43. $x^2 = \frac{1}{2} \times x \times h$ or $h = \frac{2x^2}{x} = 2x$.

44. Ratio of areas = $\frac{a^2}{\frac{\sqrt{3}}{4} a^2} = \frac{4}{\sqrt{3}} = 4 : \sqrt{3}$.

45. $2 \times \frac{22}{7} \times r = 352 \Rightarrow r = \left(352 \times \frac{7}{22} \times \frac{1}{2}\right) = 56$ m.
∴ Area = $\left(\frac{22}{7} \times 56 \times 56\right)$ m² = 9856 m².

46. $\frac{22}{7} \times r^2 = 38.5 \Rightarrow r^2 = \left(38.5 \times \frac{7}{22}\right) \Rightarrow r = 3.5$ cm.
∴ Circumference = $\left(2 \times \frac{22}{7} \times 3.5\right)$ cm = 22 cm.

Area

47. $\frac{22}{7} \times r^2 = 13.86 \times 10000 \Rightarrow r^2 = \left(13.86 \times 10000 \times \frac{7}{22}\right)$.

∴ $r = 210$ m.

∴ Circumference = $\left(2 \times \frac{22}{7} \times 210\right)$ m = 1320 m.

Cost of fencing = Rs. $\left(1320 \times \frac{20}{100}\right)$ = Rs. 264.

48. $2\pi r - r = 37 \Rightarrow \left(2 \times \frac{22}{7} - 1\right)r = 37 \Rightarrow \frac{37}{7} r = 37$.

∴ $r = 7$.

So, area of the circle = $\left(\frac{22}{7} \times 7 \times 7\right)$ cm^2 = 154 cm^2.

49. Original area = $\left(\frac{22}{7} \times 9 \times 9\right)$ cm^2

New area = $\left(\frac{22}{7} \times 7 \times 7\right)$ cm^2.

∴ Decrease = $\frac{22}{7} \times \left[(9)^2 - (7)^2\right]$ cm^2 = $\left(\frac{22}{7} \times 16 \times 2\right)$ cm^2.

Decrease per cent = $\left(\frac{22}{7} \times 16 \times 2 \times \frac{7}{22 \times 9 \times 9} \times 100\right)$ %

= 39.5%.

50. Original area = $\pi \times r^2$.

New area = $\pi \times \left(\frac{r}{2}\right)^2 = \frac{\pi r^2}{4}$.

Reduction in area = $\left(\pi r^2 - \frac{\pi r^2}{4}\right) = \frac{3\pi r^2}{4}$.

∴ Reduction per cent = $\left(\frac{3\pi r^2}{4} \times \frac{1}{\pi r^2} \times 100\right)$ % = 75%.

51. Original area = $\pi \times \left(\frac{d}{2}\right)^2 = \frac{\pi d^2}{4}$.

New area = $\pi \times \left(\frac{2d}{2}\right)^2 = \pi d^2$.

Increase in area = $\left(\pi d^2 - \frac{\pi d^2}{4}\right) = \frac{3\pi d^2}{4}$.

∴ Increase per cent = $\left(\frac{3\pi d^2}{4} \times \frac{4}{\pi d^2} \times 100\right)$ % = 300%.

52. Original circumference $= 2\pi r$.

New circumference $= \left(\dfrac{150}{100} \times 2\pi r\right) = 3\pi r$.

$\therefore\ 2\pi R = 3\pi r \Rightarrow R = \dfrac{3r}{2}$.

Original area $= \pi r^2$.

New area $= \pi R^2 = \pi \times \dfrac{9r^2}{4} = \dfrac{9\pi r^2}{4}$.

Increase in area $= \left(\dfrac{9\pi r^2}{4} - \pi r^2\right) = \dfrac{5\pi r^2}{4}$.

Increase per cent $= \left(\dfrac{5\pi r^2}{4} \times \dfrac{1}{\pi r^2} \times 100\right)\% = 125\%$.

53. $2 \times \dfrac{22}{7} \times r = 88 \Rightarrow r = \left(88 \times \dfrac{7}{22} \times \dfrac{1}{2}\right) = 14$ m.

$\therefore$ Area $= \left(\dfrac{22}{7} \times 14 \times 14\right)$ m^2 = 616 m^2.

54. Radius of circle = 7 cm.

$\therefore$ Its area $= \left(\dfrac{22}{7} \times 7 \times 7\right)$ cm^2 = 154 cm^2.

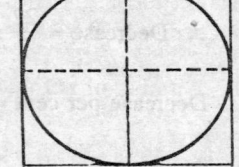

55. Radius of circle = 3 m

Area of circle $= \left(\dfrac{22}{7} \times 3 \times 3\right)$ m^2

$= 28\dfrac{2}{7}$ m^2.

56. Circumference $= \left(2 \times \dfrac{22}{7} \times 42\right)$ cm = 264 cm.

$\therefore\ 2 \times (6x + 5x) = 264$ or $x = 12$.

Smaller side of rectangle $= 5x = 60$ cm.

57. $\dfrac{1}{2} \times$ (diagonal)^2 = 50 $\Rightarrow$ (diagonal) = 10 units.

$\therefore$ Radius of required circle = 5 units

Its area $= \left[\pi \times (5)^2\right]$ cm^2 = (25π) units.

58. Ratio of areas $= \dfrac{\pi r^2}{\pi (3r)^2} = \dfrac{\pi r^2}{9\pi r^2} = \dfrac{1}{9} = 1 : 9$.

59. $2 \times \dfrac{22}{7} \times r = 440 \Rightarrow r = \left(440 \times \dfrac{7}{22} \times \dfrac{1}{2}\right) = 70$ m.

Area 339

Radius of outer circle = (70 + 14) m = 84 m.

60. $2\pi R - 2\pi r = 66 \Rightarrow 2\pi(R-r) = 66$.

$2 \times \dfrac{22}{7} \times (R-r) = 66$ or $(R-r) = \left(66 \times \dfrac{7}{22} \times \dfrac{1}{2}\right) = \dfrac{21}{2} = 10.5$ m.

61. Distance travelled in 100 revolutions = $\left(2 \times \dfrac{22}{7} \times \dfrac{63}{2} \times 100\right)$

$= \left(2 \times \dfrac{22}{7} \times \dfrac{63}{2} \times 100 \times \dfrac{1}{100}\right)$ m = 198 m.

62. Distance covered in 1 revolution = $\left(\dfrac{88 \times 1000}{1000}\right)$ m = 88 m.

$\therefore \pi \times d = 88 \Rightarrow \dfrac{22}{7} \times d = 88$ or $d = \left(88 \times \dfrac{7}{22}\right) = 28$ m.

63. Number of rounds = $\dfrac{4 \times 1000}{\dfrac{22}{7} \times \dfrac{7}{11}} = 2000$.

64. $\pi r^2 = 0.49 \pi \Rightarrow r = 0.7$ m.

Number of revolutions = $\dfrac{1.76 \times 1000}{2 \times \dfrac{22}{7} \times 0.7} = 400$.

65. $r = 0.14$ m.

Number of revolutions = $\left(\dfrac{0.66 \times 1000}{2} \times \dfrac{7}{22} \times \dfrac{1}{0.14}\right) = 750$.

66. Circumference = $\left(2 \times \dfrac{22}{7} \times 70\right)$ cm = 440 cm.

Distance travelled in 10 revolutions = 4400 cm = 44 m.

$\therefore$ Speed = $\dfrac{\text{Distance}}{\text{Time}} = \left(\dfrac{44}{5}\right)$ m/sec = $\left(\dfrac{44}{5} \times \dfrac{18}{5}\right)$ km/hr

= 31.68 km/hr.

67. $x^2 = \pi r^2 \Rightarrow \dfrac{x}{r} = \sqrt{\pi} = \sqrt{\pi} : 1$.

68. Diagonal of the square = 2 units.

$\therefore$ Area = $\left[\dfrac{1}{2} \times (2)^2\right] = 2$ sq. units.

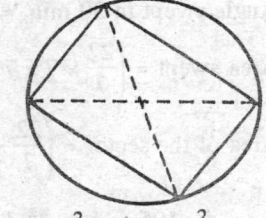

69. Area of circular lawn = $(10000 - 8614)$ m^2 = 1386 m^2

$\therefore \dfrac{22}{7} \times r^2 = 1386 \Rightarrow r^2 = \left(1386 \times \dfrac{7}{22}\right) = (63 \times 7)$ or $r = 21$ cm.

70. $\frac{1}{2} \times 24 \times h = \frac{\sqrt{3}}{4} \times 24 \times 24$ or $h = 12\sqrt{3}$.

$\therefore 3r = 12\sqrt{3} \Rightarrow r = 4\sqrt{3}$ cm.

Area of the circle $= \pi \times (4\sqrt{3})^2$ cm^2
$= 48\pi$ cm^2.

71. $\frac{22}{7} \times r^2 = 462 \Rightarrow r^2 = \left(462 \times \frac{7}{22}\right) \Rightarrow r = 7\sqrt{3}$ cm.

Height of the triangle $= 3r = 21\sqrt{3}$ cm.

Now, $a^2 = \frac{a^2}{4} + (3r)^2$ or $\frac{3a^2}{4} = 9 \times (21\sqrt{3})^2$

or $a^2 = \left(9 \times 1323 \times \frac{4}{3}\right)$ or $a = 63 \times 2 = 126$ cm.

72. Side of the square $= 2r$.

$\therefore$ Perimeter $= (4 \times 2r) = 8r$.

73. Diagonal of the rectangle
$= \sqrt{8^2 + 6^2}$
$= 10$ m.

$\therefore$ Radius $= 5$ m.

(Area of circle) – (Area of rectangle)
$= \left(\frac{22}{7} \times 5 \times 5 - 8 \times 6\right)$ m$^2 = \frac{214}{7}$ m$^2 = 30.6$ m^2.

74. Area of sector $= \left(\frac{1}{2} \times \text{arc length} \times \text{radius}\right)$ cm^2.

$= \left(\frac{1}{2} \times 3.5 \times 5\right)$ cm$^2 = 8.75$ cm^2.

75. Arc length $= \frac{2\pi r \theta}{360} = \left(2 \times \frac{22}{7} \times 21 \times \frac{72}{360}\right)$ cm $= 26.4$ cm.

76. Angle swept in 30 min. $= 180°$.

Area swept $= \left(\frac{22}{7} \times 7 \times 7 \times \frac{180}{360}\right)$ cm$^2 = 77$ cm^2.

77. Area of the sector $= \left(\frac{22}{7} \times 12 \times 12 \times \frac{42}{360}\right)$ m$^2 = 52.8$ m^2.

78. $\pi d - d = 105 \Rightarrow (\pi - 1)d = 105 \Rightarrow \left(\frac{22}{7} - 1\right)d = 105$

$\therefore d = \left(\frac{7}{15} \times 105\right)$ cm $= 49$ cm.

Area

79. $2\pi R - 2\pi r = (176 - 132) \Rightarrow 2\pi(R - r) = 44$
$\Rightarrow (R - r) = \dfrac{44 \times 7}{2 \times 22} = 7$ m.

80. Let circumference = 100 cm. Then, $2\pi r = 100 \Rightarrow r = \dfrac{100}{2\pi} = \dfrac{50}{\pi}$.

   New circumference = 105 cm. Then, $2\pi R = 105 \Rightarrow R = \dfrac{105}{2\pi}$.

   Original area $= \left(\pi \times \dfrac{50}{\pi} \times \dfrac{50}{\pi}\right) = \dfrac{2500}{\pi}$ cm^2.

   New area $= \left(\pi \times \dfrac{105}{2\pi} \times \dfrac{105}{2\pi}\right) = \dfrac{11025}{4\pi}$ cm^2.

   Increase in area $= \left(\dfrac{11025}{4\pi} - \dfrac{2500}{\pi}\right)$ cm$^2 = \dfrac{1025}{4\pi}$ cm^2.

   Increase per cent $= \left(\dfrac{1025}{4\pi} \times \dfrac{\pi}{2500} \times 100\right)\% = \dfrac{41}{4}\% = 10.25\%$.

81. $\dfrac{22}{7} \times r^2 = 9856$.

   Then, $r^2 = \left(9856 \times \dfrac{7}{22}\right)$

   $\therefore r = 56$ m.

82. Required area enclosed
   $= (14 \times 14) - 4 \times$ (area of a quadrant)
   $= \left[196 - 4 \times \dfrac{22}{7} \times 7 \times 7 \times \dfrac{90}{360}\right]$ cm^2
   $= (196 - 154)$ cm$^2 = 42$ cm^2.

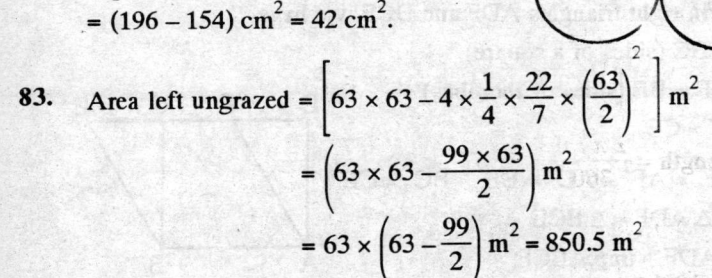

83. Area left ungrazed $= \left[63 \times 63 - 4 \times \dfrac{1}{4} \times \dfrac{22}{7} \times \left(\dfrac{63}{2}\right)^2\right]$ m^2

   $= \left(63 \times 63 - \dfrac{99 \times 63}{2}\right)$ m^2

   $= 63 \times \left(63 - \dfrac{99}{2}\right)$ m$^2 = 850.5$ m^2

84. Area of the triangle
   $= \left(\dfrac{1}{2} \times 2r \times r\right)$ cm^2
   $= r^2$ cm^2

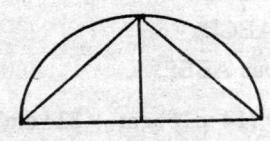

85. Length of each side of hexagon $= r$
   $\therefore$ Its perimeter $= 6r$.

86. AB = 10 cm, OB = 6 cm, $\angle$AOB = 90°

$\therefore$ OA = $\sqrt{(10)^2 - (6)^2}$ = $\sqrt{64}$ = 8 cm.

So, AC = 2 × OA = 16 cm & BD = 12 cm.

$\therefore$ Area of rhombus = $\left(\frac{1}{2} \times 16 \times 12\right)$ cm^2 = 96 cm^2.

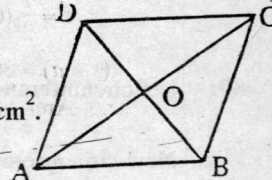

87. Side of the rhombus = $\left(\frac{52}{4}\right)$ m = 13 m.

AB = 13 m, AC = 24 m. So, AO = 12 m.

$\therefore$ OB = $\sqrt{AB^2 - AO^2}$ = $\sqrt{169 - 144}$ = 5 m.

So, BD = 2 × OB = 10 m.

Hence, other diagonal = 10 m.

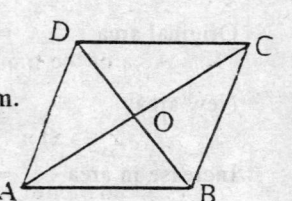

88. $\frac{1}{2} \times x \times 2x = 144 \Rightarrow x^2 = 144$ or $x = 12$.

$\therefore$ Length of diagonals = 12 cm, 24 cm.

89. Let one diagonal = x cm.

Then, another diagonal = $\left(\frac{80}{100} x\right)$ cm = $\left(\frac{4}{5} x\right)$ cm.

Area of rhombus = $\frac{1}{2} x \times \frac{4}{5} x = \frac{2}{5} x^2$.

= $\frac{2}{5} \times$ (square of longer diagonal).

90. Let ABCD be the square and ABEF be the rhombus.

Then, in right triangles ADF and BCE, we have

AD = BC (sides of a square)

and AF = BE (sides of rhombus)

$\therefore$ DF = CE

[$\because$ DF^2 = AF^2 − AD^2 = BE^2 − BC^2 = CE^2]

Thus, $\triangle$ ADF = $\triangle$ BCE.

$\Rightarrow$ $\triangle$ ADF + trap ABCF

= $\triangle$ BCE + trap ABCF

$\Rightarrow$ Area of sq. ABCD

= Area of rhombus ABEF.

91. Area of || gm = (14 × 16) cm^2 = 224 cm^2.

92. AB = 6 cm, AD = 4 cm

and $\angle$ BAD = 30°.

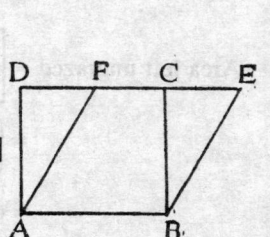

Area 343

93. AB = 60 m, BC = 40 m & AC = 80 m.

$\therefore s = \dfrac{1}{2}(60 + 40 + 80)$ m = 90 m.

$(s - a) = 30$ m, $(s - b) = 50$ m and $(s - c) = 10$ m.

$\therefore$ Area of $\triangle ABC = \sqrt{s(s-a)(s-b)(s-c)}$

$= \sqrt{90 \times 30 \times 50 \times 10}$ m^2 = $300\sqrt{15}$ m^2.

$\therefore$ Area of $\parallel$ gm ABCD = $600\sqrt{15}$ m^2.

94. Area of the trapezium $= \left[\dfrac{1}{2}(1 + 2) \times 6\right]$ m^2 = 9 m^2.

95. $\dfrac{1}{2}(3x + 5x) \times 12 = 384$ or $8x = 64$ or $x = 8$.

$\therefore$ Smaller of the parallel sides = $3x = 24$ cm.

96. $\dfrac{1}{2} \times (10 + 6) \times d = 640$ or $d = \dfrac{640 \times 2}{16} = 80$ m.

97. $\triangle AOB = \dfrac{1}{2} AB \times OE$

$= \dfrac{1}{2} \times 2\, CD \times OE = CD \times OE$.

$\triangle COD = \dfrac{1}{2} \times CD \times OF$.

$\therefore \dfrac{\triangle AOB}{\triangle COD} = \dfrac{CD \times OE}{\dfrac{1}{2} \times CD \times OF} = \dfrac{CD \times 2 \times OF}{\dfrac{1}{2} \times CD \times OF} = \dfrac{4}{1} = 4 : 1$.

[Diagonals of a trapezium intersect at a point which divides the distance between AB and CD in the ratio AB : CD].

98. $\dfrac{1}{2} \times 10 \times 4.4 = \dfrac{1}{2} \times 11 \times h \Rightarrow h = \dfrac{10 \times 4.4}{11} = 4$ cm.

99. Area of a triangle formed by joining the mid points of the sides of the triangle, is $\dfrac{1}{4}$ th of area of the original triangle.

$\therefore$ Area of $\triangle DEF = \dfrac{1}{4} \times$ (area of $\triangle ABC$) = 9 cm^2.

100. Ratio of areas of similar triangles
    = Ratio of the squares of corresponding sides

$= \dfrac{(3x)^2}{(4x)^2} = \dfrac{9x^2}{16x^2} = \dfrac{9}{16} = 9 : 16$.

101. Speed $= \left(12 \times \dfrac{5}{18}\right)$ m/sec $= \left(\dfrac{10}{3}\right)$ m/sec.

∴ Perimeter = $\left(\dfrac{10}{3} \times 15 \times 60\right)$ m = 3000 m.

$2 \times (x + 4x) = 3000$ or $x = 300$.

So, length = 1200 m & breadth = 300 m.

∴ Area = (1200×300) m² = 360000 m².

102. $\dfrac{22}{7} \times r^2 = 616 \Rightarrow r^2 = \left(616 \times \dfrac{7}{22}\right) = 196$.

∴ $r = \sqrt{196} = 14$ cm.

So, diameter = 28 cm

∴ Area of square = (28×28) cm²
= 784 cm².

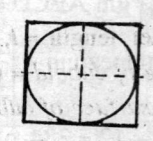

103. Area of the room = (544×374) cm².

Size of largest square tile = H.C.F. of 544 & 374 = 34 cm.

Area of 1 tile = (34×34) cm².

∴ Number of tiles required = $\dfrac{544 \times 374}{34 \times 34} = 176$.

104. $a^2 = \dfrac{a^2}{4} + x^2 \Rightarrow \dfrac{3a^2}{4} = x^2$

∴ $a^2 = \dfrac{4}{3} x^2$.

∴ Area = $\dfrac{\sqrt{3}}{4} a^2 = \dfrac{\sqrt{3}}{4} \times \dfrac{4}{3} x^2$

$= \dfrac{x^2 \sqrt{3}}{3}$.

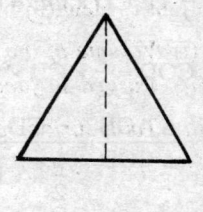

105. Let length = a metres and breadth = b metres.

Then, $2(a + b) = 46$ or $(a + b) = 23$ and $ab = 120$.

∴ Diagonal = $\sqrt{a^2 + b^2} = \sqrt{(a+b)^2 - ab} = \sqrt{(23)^2 - 2 \times 120}$
$= \sqrt{289} = 17$ m.

106. Let longer side = l, shorter side = b and diagonal = d. Then, $lb = 60$ and $d + l = 5b$.

21

VOLUME & SURFACE AREAS

FORMULAE :

1. **Cuboid :** Let, length = l, breadth = b and height = h units.
   - (i) Volume of cuboid = $(l \times b \times h)$ cubic units.
   - (ii) Whole surface of cuboid = $2(lb + bh + lh)$ sq. units.
   - (iii) Diagonal of cuboid = $\sqrt{l^2 + b^2 + h^2}$ units.

2. **Cube :** Let each edge (or side) of a cube be a units. Then :
   - (i) Volume of the cube = a^3 cubic units.
   - (ii) Whole surface of the cube = $(6a^2)$ sq. units.
   - (iii) Diagonal of the cube = $(\sqrt{3}\, a)$ units.

3. **Cylinder :** Let, the radius of the base of a cylinder be r units and its height (or length) be h units. Then :
   - (i) Volume of the cylinder = $(\pi r^2 h)$ cu. units.
   - (ii) Curved surface area of the cylinder = $(2\pi rh)$ sq. units.
   - (iii) Total surface area of the cylinder = $(2\pi rh + 2\pi r^2)$ sq. units.

4. **Sphere :** Let the radius of a sphere be r units. Then :
   - (i) Volume of the sphere = $\left(\dfrac{4}{3}\pi r^3\right)$ cu. units.
   - (ii) Surface area of the sphere = $(4\pi r^2)$ sq. units.
   - (iii) Volume of a hemi sphere = $\left(\dfrac{2}{3}\pi r^3\right)$ cu. units.
   - (iv) Curved surface area of the hemisphere = $(2\pi r^2)$ sq. units.
   - (v) Whole surface area of the hemisphere = $(3\pi r^2)$ sq. units.

5. **Cone :** Let r be the radius of the base, h the height and l the slant height of a cone. Then :
   - (i) Slant height, $l = \sqrt{h^2 + r^2}$.
   - (ii) Volume of the cone = $\left(\dfrac{1}{3}\pi r^2 h\right)$ cu. units.
   - (iii) Curved surface area of the cone :
     = (πrl) sq. units = $(\pi r \sqrt{r^2 + h^2})$ sq. units.

Volume & Surface Areas

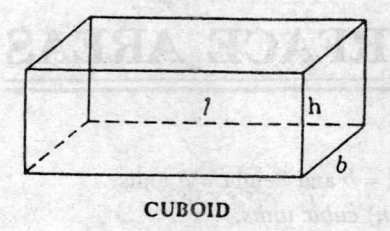

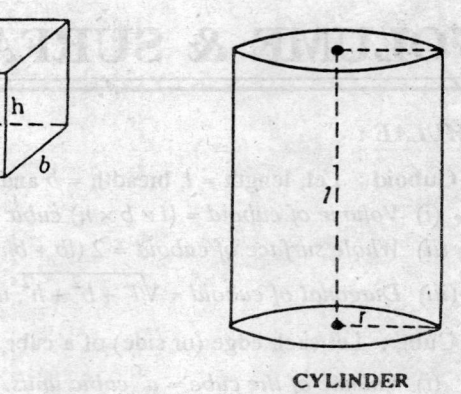

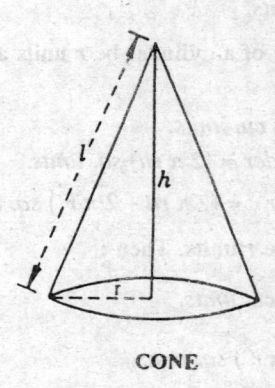

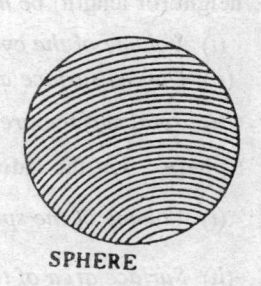

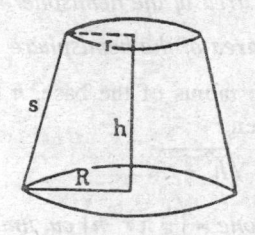

CUBOID

CYLINDER

CONE

SPHERE

FRUSTUM OF A CONE

Volume & Surface Areas 347

(iv) Total surface area of the cone = $(\pi rl + \pi r^2)$ sq. units.

SOLVED EXAMPLES

Ex. 1. Find the volume, surface area and the length of diagonal of a cuboid 12 m long, 9 m broad and 8 m high.

Sol. Volume = $(12 \times 9 \times 8)$ m^3 = 864 m^3.
Surface Area = $2 \times (12 \times 9 + 9 \times 8 + 12 \times 8)$ m^2 = 552 m^2.
Diagonal = $\sqrt{(12)^2 + (9)^2 + (8)^2}$ m = $\sqrt{289}$ m = 17 m.

Ex. 2. Find the length of the longest pole that can be placed in a room 5 m long, 4 m broad and 3 m high.

Sol. Length of longest pole = Length of diagonal = $\sqrt{5^2 + 4^2 + 3^2}$ m
= $\sqrt{50}$ m = $5\sqrt{2}$ m = (5×1.41) m = 7.05 m.

Ex. 3. The diagonal of a cube is $4\sqrt{3}$ m. Find its volume and surface area.

Sol. Let the edge of the cube be a metres.
Then, $\sqrt{3} a = 4\sqrt{3}$ or $a = 4$. ∴ Edge = 4 m.
So, volume = $(4 \times 4 \times 4)$ m^3 = 64 m^3.
Surface area = $6a^2$ = $(6 \times 4 \times 4)$ m^2 = 96 m^2.

Ex. 4. The surface area of a cube is 384 cm^2. Find its volume.

Sol. $6a^2 = 384 \Rightarrow a^2 = 64 \Rightarrow a = 8$.
∴ Volume = $(8 \times 8 \times 8)$ cm^3 = 512 cm^3.

Ex. 5. A wall 8 m long, 6 m high and 22.5 cm thick is made up of bricks each measuring 25 cm × 11.25 cm × 6 cm. Find the number of bricks required to build the wall.

Sol. Number of bricks = $\dfrac{\text{Volume of the wall in cm}^3}{\text{Volume of 1 brick in cm}^3}$
= $\left(\dfrac{800 \times 600 \times 22.5}{25 \times 11.25 \times 6}\right)$ = 6400.

Ex. 6. Three cubes of sides 6 cm, 8 cm and 1 cm are melted to form a new cube. Find the length of the edge of the new cube.

Sol. Volume of new cube = $\left[(6)^3 + (8)^3 + (1)^3\right]$ cm^3 = 729 cm^3.
∴ Edge of new cube = $(9 \times 9 \times 9)^{1/3}$ = 9 cm.

Ex. 7. The capacity of a cylindrical tank is 6160 m^3. If the radius of its base is 14 m, find the depth of the tank.

Sol. $\frac{22}{7} \times 14 \times 14 \times h = 6160$

$\therefore h = \left(6160 \times \frac{7}{22} \times \frac{1}{14 \times 14}\right) = 10$ m.

Ex. 8. A powder tin has a square base with side 8 cm and height 14 cm. Another tin has a circular base with diameter 8 cm and height 14 cm. Find the difference in their capacities.

Sol. Volume of rectangular tin = $(8 \times 8 \times 14)$ cm^3 = 896 cm^3.

Volume of cylindrical tin = $\left(\frac{22}{7} \times 4 \times 4 \times 14\right)$ cm^3 = 704 cm^3.

Difference in their capacities = $(896 - 704)$ cm^3 = 192 cm^3.

Ex. 9. Find the volume and the surface area of a sphere of diameter 42 cm.

Sol. Radius = 21 cm.

$\therefore$ Volume = $\left(\frac{4}{3} \pi r^3\right) = \left(\frac{4}{3} \times \frac{22}{7} \times 21 \times 21 \times 21\right)$ cm^3 = 38808 cm^3.

Surface area = $4 \pi r^2 = \left(4 \times \frac{22}{7} \times 21 \times 21\right)$ cm^2 = 5544 cm^2.

Ex. 10. Find the volume, curved surface area and the total surface area of a hemisphere of radius 21 cm.

Sol. Volume = $\frac{2}{3} \pi r^3$

$= \left(\frac{2}{3} \times \frac{22}{7} \times 21 \times 21 \times 21\right)$ cm^3 = 19404 cm^3.

Curved surface area = $2 \pi r^2$

$= \left(2 \times \frac{22}{7} \times 21 \times 21\right)$ cm^2 = 2772 cm^2.

Total surface area = $3 \pi r^2$

$= \left(3 \times \frac{22}{7} \times 21 \times 21\right)$ cm^2 = 4158 cm^2.

Ex. 11. Find the volume, curved surface area and the total surface area of a right circular cylinder of length 80 cm with diameter of the base 7 cm.

Sol. Here $h = 80$ cm and $r = 3.5$ cm.

Volume = $\pi r^2 h$

$= \left(\frac{22}{7} \times 3.5 \times 3.5 \times 80\right)$ cm^3 = 3080 cm^3.

Curved surface Area = $2 \pi rh$

Volume & Surface Areas

$$= \left(2 \times \frac{22}{7} \times 3.5 \times 80\right) cm^2 = 1760 \ cm^2.$$

Total surface Area $= (2\pi rh + 2\pi r^2) = 2\pi r(h+r)$

$$= \left[2 \times \frac{22}{7} \times 3.5 \times (80 + 3.5)\right] cm^2 = 1837 \ cm^2.$$

Ex. 12. A well with 14 m inside diameter is dug 8 m deep. The earth taken out of it has been evenly spread all around it to a width of 21 m to form an embankment. Find the height of the embankment.

Sol. Volume of earth dug out $= \left(\frac{22}{7} \times 7 \times 7 \times 8\right) m^3 = 1232 \ m^3.$

Area of embankment $= \pi R^2 - \pi r^2 = \pi(R^2 - r^2)$

$$= \frac{22}{7} \times \left[(28)^2 - (7)^2\right] m^2$$

$$= \left(\frac{22}{7} \times 35 \times 21\right) m^2 = 2310 \ m^2.$$

$\therefore$ Height of embankment $= \left(\frac{1232}{2310} \times 100\right) cm = 53.3 \ cm.$

Ex. 13. A copper sphere of diameter 18 cm is drawn into a wire of diameter 4 mm. Find the length of the wire.

Sol. Let the length of wire be h cm. Then,
Volume of sphere = volume of wire.

$\therefore \frac{4}{3} \pi \times 9 \times 9 \times 9 = \pi \times 0.2 \times 0.2 \times h.$

$\therefore h = \frac{4}{3} \times 9 \times 9 \times 9 \times \frac{1}{0.2 \times 0.2} = 24300 \ cm.$

Hence, the length of the wire is 243 m.

Ex. 14. How many bullets can be made out of a lead cylinder 28 cm high and 6 cm radius, each bullet being 1.5 cm in diameter?

Sol. Number of bullets $= \dfrac{\text{Volume of cylinder}}{\text{Volume of 1 bullet}}$

$$= \dfrac{\pi \times 6 \times 6 \times 28}{\frac{4}{3} \times \pi \times 0.75 \times 0.75 \times 0.75} = 1792.$$

Ex. 15. Find the number of lead balls of diameter 1 cm each that can be made from a sphere of diameter 16 cm.

Sol. Number of balls $= \dfrac{\text{Volume of big sphere}}{\text{Volume of 1 small sphere}}$

$$= \frac{\frac{4}{3}\pi \times 8 \times 8 \times 8}{\frac{4}{3}\pi \times 0.5 \times 0.5 \times 0.5} = 4096.$$

Ex. 16. A cone is 8.4 cm high and the radius of its base is 2.1 cm. It is melted and recast into a sphere. Find the radius of the sphere.

Sol. Let the radius of the sphere be r cm.

Then, volume of cone = volume of sphere.

$$\therefore \frac{1}{3}\pi \times 2.1 \times 2.1 \times 8.4 = \frac{4}{3}\pi \times r^3$$

$$\therefore r^3 = (2.1)^3 \text{ and so } r = 2.1 \text{ cm}.$$

Ex. 17. The height of a cone is 28 cm and radius of its base is 21 cm. Find the slant height, volume, curved surface area and whole surface area of the cone.

Sol. Here $h = 28$ and $r = 21$.

$\therefore$ Slant height, $l = \sqrt{h^2 + r^2} = \sqrt{(28)^2 + (21)^2} = \sqrt{1225} = 35$ cm.

Volume $= \frac{1}{3}\pi r^2 h$

$$= \left(\frac{1}{3} \times \frac{22}{7} \times 21 \times 21 \times 28\right) \text{cm}^3 = 12936 \text{ cm}^3.$$

Curved surface Area $= \pi r l$

$$= \left(\frac{22}{7} \times 21 \times 35\right) \text{cm}^2 = 2310 \text{ cm}^2.$$

Total surface Area $= (\pi r l + \pi r^2)$ cm^2

$$= \left(2310 + \frac{22}{7} \times 21 \times 21\right) \text{cm}^2 = 3696 \text{ cm}^2.$$

Ex. 18. Find the area of the iron sheet required to prepare a cone 24 cm high with base radius 7 cm.

Sol. Here $r = 7$ cm, $h = 24$ cm.

$\therefore$ Slant height, $l = \sqrt{h^2 + r^2} = \sqrt{(24)^2 + (7)^2} = \sqrt{625} = 25$ cm

$\therefore$ Area of the sheet $= \pi r l + \pi r^2 = \pi r (l + r)$

$$= \left[\frac{22}{7} \times 7 \times (25 + 7)\right] \text{cm}^2 = 704 \text{ cm}^2.$$

Ex. 19. A closed wooden box with external dimensions 80 cm × 60 cm × 40 cm is made of 2 cm thick wood. If 1 cm^3 of wood weighs 10 gms, find the weight of the empty box.

Sol. Volume of wood $= [(80 \times 60 \times 40) - (76 \times 56 \times 36)]$ cm^3

Volume & Surface Areas

$$= 38784 \text{ cm}^3.$$

∴ Weight of the empty box $= \left(\dfrac{38784 \times 10}{1000}\right)$ kg = 387.84 kg.

Ex. 20. How many iron rods, each of length 7 m and diameter 2 cm can be made out of 0.88 cubic metre of iron ?

Sol. Number of rods $= \dfrac{0.88}{\text{Volume of 1 rod}}$

$= \left(\dfrac{0.88}{\dfrac{22}{7} \times \dfrac{1}{100} \times \dfrac{1}{100} \times 7}\right) = 400.$

EXERCISE 21

1. The surface area of a cube of side 27 cm, is :
   - (a) 2916 cm² □
   - (b) 729 cm² □
   - (c) 4374 cm² □
   - (d) 19683 cm² □

2. The surface area of a cuboid 22 cm by 12 cm by 7.5 cm, is :
   - (a) 1980 cm² □
   - (b) 2076 cm² □
   - (c) 1038 cm² □
   - (d) none of these □

3. The surface area of a cube is 726 m². Its volume is : (N.D.A. 1987)
   - (a) 1300 m³ □
   - (b) 1331 m³ □
   - (c) 1452 m³ □
   - (d) 1542 m³ □

4. The volume of a cube is 512 cm³. Its surface area is :
   - (a) 64 cm² □
   - (b) 256 cm² □
   - (c) 384 cm² □
   - (d) 512 cm² □

5. The length of the diagonal of a cuboid 30 cm long, 24 cm broad and 18 cm high, is :
   - (a) 30 cm □
   - (b) $15\sqrt{2}$ cm □
   - (c) 60 cm □
   - (d) $30\sqrt{2}$ cm □

6. The length of longest rod that can be placed in a room 20 m long, 16 m broad and 12 m high, is :
   - (a) 20 m □
   - (b) 16.4 m □
   - (c) 48 m □
   - (d) 28.2 m □

7. The maximum length of a pencil that can be kept in a rectangular box of dimensions 8 cm × 6 cm × 2 cm, is : (N.D.A. 1990)
   - (a) $2\sqrt{13}$ cm □
   - (b) $2\sqrt{14}$ cm □

(c) $2\sqrt{26}$ cm (d) $10\sqrt{2}$ cm

8. The length of diagonal of a cube is $(14 \times \sqrt{3})$ cm. The volume of the cube is :
   (a) $2744\sqrt{3}$ cm^3 (b) 2744 cm^3
   (c) 588 cm^3 (d) 3528 cm^3

9. The length of longest pole that can be placed on the floor of a room is 10 m and the length of the longest pole that can be placed in the room is $10\sqrt{2}$ m. The height of the room is :
   (a) 6 m (b) 7.5 m
   (c) 8 m (d) 10 m

10. The length of longest rod that can fit in a cubical vessel of side 10 cm, is :
    (a) 10 cm (b) $10\sqrt{2}$ cm
    (c) $10\sqrt{3}$ cm (d) none of these

11. If the length of diagonal of a cube is $8\sqrt{3}$ cm, then its surface area is :
    (a) 512 cm^2 (b) 384 cm^2
    (c) 192 cm^2 (d) 768 cm^2

12. If the length, breadth and the height of a cuboid are in the ratio 6 : 5 : 4 and if the total surface area is 33300 cm^2, then the length, breadth and height in cms, are respectively : (N.D.A. 1990)
    (a) 90, 85, 60 (b) 85, 75, 60
    (c) 90, 75, 70 (d) 90, 75, 60

13. The sum of length, breadth and depth of a cuboid is 19 cm and its diagonal is $5\sqrt{5}$ cm. Its surface area is :
    (a) 361 cm^2 (b) 125 cm^2
    (c) 236 cm^2 (d) 486 cm^2

14. Given that 1 cubic cm of marble weighs 25 gms, the weight of a marble block 28 cm in width and 5 cm thick is 112 kg. The length of the block is :
    (a) 36 cm (b) 37.5 cm
    (c) 32 cm (d) 26.5 cm

15. A wooden box of dimensions 8 m × 7 m × 6 m is to carry rectangular boxes of dimensions 8 cm × 7 cm × 6 cm. The maximum number of boxes that can be carried in 1 wooden box, is : (C.D.S. 1991)
    (a) 1200000 (b) 1000000
    (c) 9800000 (d) 7500000

Volume & Surface Areas

16. The number of small cubes with edges of 10 cm that can be accomodated in a cubical box of 1 metre edge, is :
(a) 10   (b) 100
(c) 1000   (d) 10000

17. The volume of a wall, 5 times as high as it is broad and 8 times as long as it is high, is 12.8 m^3. The breadth of the wall is :
(a) 30 cm   (b) 40 cm
(c) 22.5 cm   (d) 25 cm

18. The area of the base of a rectangular tank is 6500 sq. cm. and the volume of water contained in it is 2.6 cubic metres. The depth of water is :
(a) 3.5 m   (b) 4 m
(c) 5 m   (d) 8 m

19. A metal sheet 27 cm long, 8 cm broad and 1 cm thick is melted into a cube. The difference between the surface areas of two solids, is :
(a) 284 cm^2 (b) 286 cm^2
(c) 296 cm^2 (d) 300 cm^2
(C.D.S. 1991)

20. Bricks are worth Rs. 750 per 1000 and their length, breadth and height 25 cm, 12.5 cm and 7.5 cm respectively. The cost of bricks required to build a wall 200 m long, 1.8 m high and 37.5 cm thick, is :
(a) Rs. 42600   (b) Rs. 43200
(c) Rs. 40750   (d) Rs. 41860

21. A river 2 m deep and 45 m wide is running at the rate of 3 km/hr. The amount of water that runs into the sea per minute, is :
(a) 4500 m^3 (b) 27000 m^3
(c) 3000 m^3 (d) 2700 m^3

22. In a shower, 5 cm of rain falls. The volume of water that falls on 2 hectares of ground, is :
(a) 100 m^3 (b) 1000 m^3
(c) 10 m^3 (d) 10000 m^3

23. Half cubic metre of gold sheet is extended by hammering so as to cover an area of 1 hectare. The thickness of the sheet is :
(a) 0.5 cm   (b) 0.05 cm
(c) 0.005 cm   (d) 0.0005 cm

24. If the volumes of two cubes are in the ratio 8 : 1, the ratio of their edges, is :   (Assistant Grade 1990)
(a) 8 : 1   (b) $2\sqrt{2}$: 1

(c) 2 : 1 ☐   (d) none of these ☐

25. Three metal cubes of sides 5 cm, 4 cm and 3 cm are melted and recast into a new cube. The length of the edge of this cube is :
   (a) 6 cm ☐   (b) 8 cm ☐
   (c) 10 cm ☐   (d) none of these ☐

26. If each side of a cube is doubled, then its volume
   (a) is doubled ☐   (b) becomes 4 times ☐
   (c) becomes 6 times ☐   (d) becomes 8 times ☐

27. The difference in volumes of two cubes is 152 m^3 and the difference in their one face areas is 20 m^2. If the sum of their edges is 10 m, the product of their edges is :
   (a) 21 ☐   (b) 24 ☐
   (c) 36 ☐   (d) 48 ☐

28. If each edge of a cube is increased by 50%, the percentage increase in surface area is :
   (a) 50% ☐   (b) 75% ☐
   (c) 100% ☐   (d) 125% ☐

29. Two cubes have volumes in the ratio 1 : 27. The ratio of their surface areas is :
   (a) 1 : 3 ☐   (b) 1 : 8 ☐
   (c) 1 : 9 ☐   (d) 1 : 18 ☐

30. A tank 3 m long, 2 m wide and 1.5 m deep is dug in a field 22 m long and 14 m wide. If the earth dug out is evenly spread out over the field, the rise in level of the field will be :
   (a) 0.299 cm ☐   (b) 0.29 cm ☐
   (c) 2.98 cm ☐   (d) 4.15 cm ☐

31. The dimensions of an open box are 52 cms, 40 cms and 29 cms. Its thickness is 2 cms. If 1 cm^3 of metal used in the box weighs 0.5 gms, the weight of the box is :
   (a) 8.56 kg ☐   (b) 7.76 kg ☐
   (c) 7.576 kg ☐   (d) 6.832 kg ☐

32. The area of the card board needed to make a box of size 25 cm × 15 cm × 8 cm will be :
   (a) 390 cm^2 ☐   (b) 1000 cm^2 ☐
   (c) 1390 cm^2 ☐   (d) 2780 cm^2 ☐

33. The length of a cylinder is 80 cm and the diameter of its base is 7 cm. The whole surface of the cylinder is :
   (a) 1837 cm^2 ☐   (b) 1760 cm^2 ☐

Volume & Surface Areas 355

    (c) 3080 cm^2 (d) 1942 cm^2

34. The height of a cylinder is 14 cm and its curved surface area is 264 sq. cm. The volume of the cylinder is :
    (a) 308 cm^3 (b) 396 cm^3
    (c) 1848 cm^3 (d) 1232 cm^3

35. The radius of a wire is decreased to one-third. If volume remains the same, length will increase :   (**Railway Recruitment Board 1990**)
    (a) 1 time   (b) 3 times
    (c) 6 times   (d) 9 times

36. The length of the wire of 0.2 mm radius that can be drawn after melting a solid copper sphere of diameter 18 cm, is :
    (a) 24.3 m   (b) 243 m
    (c) 2430 m   (d) 24300 m
                                              (**Central Excise & I. Tax, 1990**)

37. The number of solid spheres, each of diameter 6 cm, that could be moulded to form a solid metal cylinder of height 45 cm and diameter 4 cm, is :   (**N.D.A. 1990**)
    (a) 3   (b) 4
    (c) 5   (d) 6

38. A hollow garden roller 63 cm wide with a girth of 440 cm is made of iron 4 cm thick. The volume of iron used is :
    (a) 56372 cubic m   (b) 58752 cubic cm
    (c) 54982 cubic cm   (d) 57636 cubic cm

39. If 1 cubic cm of cast iron wieghs 21 gms, then the weight of a cast iron pipe of length 1 m with a bore of 3 cm and in which the thickness of the metal is 1 cm, is :
    (a) 21 kg   (b) 24.2 kg
    (c) 26.4 kg   (d) 18.6 kg

40. The radius of a circular cylinder is the same as that of a sphere. Their volumes are equal. The height of the cylinder is :   (**C.D.S. 1989**)
    (a) $\frac{4}{3}$ times its radius   (b) $\frac{2}{3}$ times its radius
    (c) equal to its radius   (d) equal to its diameter

41. A cylindrical vessel of radius 4 cm contains water. A solid sphere of radius 3 cm is lowered into the water until it is completely immersed. The water level in the vessel will rise by :
    (a) 4.5 cm   (b) 2.25 cm

(c) $\frac{4}{9}$ cm □   (d) $\frac{2}{9}$ cm □

42. A right cylinder and a right circular cone have the same radius and the same volume. The ratio of the height of the cylinder to that of the cone, is : (C.D.S. 1991)
    (a) 3 : 5 □   (b) 2 : 5 □
    (c) 3 : 1 □   (d) 1 : 3 □

43. A right cylindrical vessel is full with water. How many right cones having the same diameter and height as those of the right cylinder will be needed to store that water :
    (a) 2 □   (b) 3 □
    (c) 4 □   (d) 5 □

44. The curved surface area of a sphere is 1386 sq. cm. Its volume is :
    (a) 2772 cm^3 □   (b) 4158 cm^3 □
    (c) 4851 cm^3 □   (d) 5544 cm^3 □

45. The volume of a sphere is 38808 cu. cm. The curved surface area of the sphere is :
    (a) 5544 sq. cm □   (b) 1386 sq. cm □
    (c) 8316 sq. cm □   (d) 4158 sq. cm □

46. Volume of a hemisphere is 19404 cubic cm. The total surface area is :
    (a) 2772 sq. cm □   (b) 4158 sq. cm □
    (c) 5544 sq. cm □   (d) 1386 sq. cm □

47. The curved surface areas of two spheres are in the ratio 1 : 4. The ratio of their volumes is :
    (a) 1 : 4 □   (b) 1 : 2$\sqrt{2}$ □
    (c) 1 : 8 □   (d) 1 : 64 □

48. The radii of two spheres are in the ratio 1 : 2. The ratio of their surface areas, is : (N.D.A. 1990)
    (a) 1 : 2 □   (b) 1 : 4 □
    (c) 1 : $\sqrt{2}$ □   (d) 3 : 8 □

49. Two circular cylinders of equal volume have their heights in the ratio 1 : 2. Ratio of their radii is :
    (a) 1 : $\sqrt{2}$ □   (b) $\sqrt{2}$: 1 □
    (c) 1 : 2 □   (d) 1 : 4 □

50. A spherical lead ball of radius 10 cm is melted and small lead balls of radius 5 mm are made. The total number of possible small lead balls is : (N.D.A. 1989)

Volume & Surface Areas

    (a) 800   (b) 125
    (c) 400   (d) 8000

51. How many bullets can be made out of a cube of lead whose edge measures 22 cm, each bullet being 2 cm in diameter ?
    (a) 5324   (b) 2662
    (c) 1347   (d) 2541

52. A spherical ball of lead, 3 cm in diameter is melted and recast into three spherical balls. The diameter of two of these are 1.5 cm and 2 cm respectively. The diameter of the third ball is :
    (a) 2.66 cm   (b) 2.5 cm
    (c) 3 cm   (d) 3.5 cm

53. If the volume and surface area of a sphere are numerically the same, then its radius is :   **(N.D.A. 1990)**
    (a) 1 unit   (b) 2 units
    (c) 3 units   (d) 4 units

54. The ratio of total surface area to lateral surface area of a cylinder whose radius is 80 cm and height 20 cm, is :
    (a) 2 : 1   (b) 3 : 1
    (c) 4 : 1   (d) 5 : 1

55. The radii of two cylinders are in the ratio of 2 : 3 and their heights are in the ratio 5 : 3. The ratio of their volumes is :
    (a) 27 : 20   (b) 20 : 27
    (c) 4 : 9   (d) 9 : 4
                                                (Hotel Management, 1991)

56. A cylindrical vessel 60 cm in diameter is partially filled with water. A sphere, 60 cm in diameter is gently dropped into the vessel. To what further height will water rise in the cylinder :
    (a) 15 cm   (b) 30 cm
    (c) 40 cm   (d) 25 cm
    (e) can not be determined, since the height of the cylinder has not been given

57. A cylindrical piece of metal of radius 2 cm and height 6 cm is shaped into a cone of same radius. The height of the cone is :
    (a) 18 cm   (b) 14 cm
    (c) 12 cm   (d) 8 cm
                                          (Railway Recruitment, 1991)

58. The radius of the base of a right circular cone is 6 cm and its slant height is 28 cm. The curved surface area of the cone is :
    (a) 268 sq. cm   (b) 528 sq. cm

(c) 462 sq. cm   (d) 658 sq. cm

59. If a right circular cone of vertical height 24 cm has a volume of 1232 cm^3, then the area of its curved surface is : **(N.D.A. 1990)**
   (a) 1254 cm^2 (b) 704 cm^2
   (c) 550 cm^2 (d) 154 cm^2

60. If the volumes of two cones are in the ratio 1 : 4 and their diameters are in the ratio 4 : 5, then the ratio of their heights is : **(N.D.A. 1990)**
   (a) 1 : 5   (b) 5 : 4
   (c) 5 : 16   (d) 25 : 64

61. A solid consists of a circular cylinder with an exact fitting right circular cone placed on the top. The height of the cone is h. If the total volume of the solid is three times the volume of the cone, then the height of the cylinder is : **(C.D.S. 1991)**
   (a) $2h$ (b) $4h$
   (c) $\dfrac{2h}{3}$ (d) $\dfrac{3h}{2}$

62. The material of a cone is converted into the shape of a cylinder of equal radius. If the height of the cylinder is 5 cm, the height of the cone is :
   (a) 10 cm   (b) 15 cm
   (c) 18 cm   (d) 24 cm

63. A cone of height 7 cm and base radius 3 cm is carved from a rectangular block of wood 10 cm × 5 cm × 2 cm. The percentage of wood wasted is :
   (a) 34%   (b) 46%
   (c) 54%   (d) 66%

64. The area of the base of a right circular cone is 154 cm^2 and its height is 14 cm. The curved surface of the cone is :
   (a) $(154 \times \sqrt{5})$ cm^2 (b) 11 cm^2
   (c) $(154 \times \sqrt{7})$ cm^2 (d) 5324 cm^2

65. The length of canvas 1.2 m wide required to build a conical tent of height 14 m and the floor area 346.5 m^2, is :
   (a) 665 m   (b) 770 m
   (c) 490 m   (d) 860 m

66. The cost of painting the four walls of a room is Rs. 350. The cost of painting a room three times in length, breadth and height will be :
   (a) Rs. 1050   (b) Rs. 1400

Volume & Surface Areas

(c) Rs. 3150 (d) Rs. 4200

67. The percentage increase in the surface area of a cube when each side is doubled, is :
(a) 25 % (b) 50 %
(c) 150 % (d) 300 %

68. If the height of a cone is doubled, then its volume is increased by :
(a) 100 % (b) 200 %
(c) 300 % (d) 400 %

69. If the radius of a sphere is doubled, then its surface area is increased by :
(a) 100 % (b) 200 %
(c) 300 % (d) 50 %

70. If the radius of a sphere is doubled, then its volume is increased by :
(a) 100 % (b) 200 %
(c) 700 % (d) 800 %

71. A cylinder and a cone have the same height and same radius of the base. The ratio between the volumes of the cylinder and the cone is :
(a) 1 : 3 (b) 3 : 1
(c) 1 : 2 (d) 2 : 1

72. The volume of a sphere is $\frac{88}{21} \times (14)^3$ cm^3. The curved surface of its sphere is :
(a) 2424 cm^2 (b) 2446 cm^2
(c) 2464 cm^2 (d) 2484 cm^2

ANSWERS

1. (c) 2. (c) 3. (b) 4. (c) 5. (d) 6. (d) 7. (c) 8. (b) 9. (d)
10. (c) 11. (b) 12. (d) 13. (c) 14. (c) 15. (b) 16. (c) 17. (b) 18. (b)
19. (b) 20. (b) 21. (a) 22. (b) 23. (c) 24. (c) 25. (a) 26. (d) 27. (b)
28. (d) 29. (c) 30. (c) 31. (d) 32. (c) 33. (a) 34. (b) 35. (d) 36. (d)
37. (c) 38. (b) 39. (c) 40. (a) 41. (b) 42. (d) 43. (b) 44. (c) 45. (a)
46. (b) 47. (c) 48. (b) 49. (b) 50. (d) 51. (d) 52. (b) 53. (c) 54. (d)
55. (b) 56. (c) 57. (a) 58. (b) 59. (c) 60. (d) 61. (c) 62. (b) 63. (a)
64. (a) 65. (b) 66. (c) 67. (d) 68. (a) 69. (c) 70. (c) 71. (b) 72. (c)

SOLUTION (Exercise 21)

1. Surface area = $\left[6 \times (27)^2 \right]$ cm^2 = 4374 cm^2.

2. Surface area = $2(22 \times 12 + 12 \times 7.5 + 22 \times 7.5)$ cm^2 = 1038 cm^2.

3. $6a^2 = 726 \Rightarrow a^2 = 121 \Rightarrow a = 11$ cm.
   $\therefore$ Volume of the cube = $(11 \times 11 \times 11)$ cm^3 = 1331 cm^3.

4. $a^3 = 512 = 8 \times 8 \times 8 \Rightarrow a = 8$ cm.
   $\therefore$ Surface area = $6a^2 = [6 \times (8)^2]$ cm^2 = 384 cm^2.

5. Diagonal = $\sqrt{(30)^2 + (24)^2 + (18)^2} = \sqrt{1800}$ cm = $30\sqrt{2}$ cm.

6. Length of the rod = $\sqrt{(20)^2 + (16)^2 + (12)^2}$ m = $\sqrt{800}$ m.
   = $20\sqrt{2}$ m = (20×1.41) m = 28.2 m.

7. Length of pencil = $\sqrt{(8)^2 + (6)^2 + (2)^2}$ cm = $\sqrt{104}$ cm
   = $2\sqrt{26}$ cm.

8. $\sqrt{3}\, a = 14 \times \sqrt{3} \Rightarrow a = 14$.
   $\therefore$ Volume of the cube = $(14 \times 14 \times 14)$ cm^3 = 2744 cm^3.

9. $l^2 + b^2 = (10)^2 = 100$ and $l^2 + b^2 + h^2 = (10\sqrt{2})^2 = 200$
   $\therefore h^2 = (200 - 100) = 100$ or $h = 10$ m.

10. Longest rod = $\sqrt{(10)^2 + (10)^2 + (10)^2}$ cm = $\sqrt{300}$ cm = $10\sqrt{3}$ cm.

11. $\sqrt{3}\, a = 8\sqrt{3} \Rightarrow a = 8$.
    $\therefore$ Surface area = $6a^2 = (6 \times 8 \times 8)$ cm^2 = 384 cm^2.

12. Let length = $6x$, breadth = $5x$ and height = $4x$ in cm.
    $\therefore 2(6x \times 5x + 5x \times 4x + 6x \times 4x) = 33300$
    $148\, x^2 = 33300 \Rightarrow x^2 = \dfrac{33300}{148} = 225 \Rightarrow x = 15$.
    $\therefore$ Length = 90 cm, Breadth = 75 cm, Height = 60 cm.

13. $l + b + h = 19$ and $l^2 + b^2 + h^2 = (5\sqrt{5})^2 = 125$.
    $\therefore (l + b + h)^2 = (19)^2 \Rightarrow (l^2 + b^2 + h^2) + 2(lb + bh + lh) = 361$
    $\Rightarrow 2(lb + bh + lh) = (361 - 125) = 236$.
    $\therefore$ Surface area = 236 cm^2.

14. Volume = $\left(\dfrac{112 \times 1000}{25}\right)$ cu. cm = 4480 cm^3.
    $\therefore x \times 28 \times 5 = 4480 \Rightarrow x = \left(\dfrac{4480}{28 \times 5}\right)$ cm = 32 cm.

15. Number of boxes = $\dfrac{\text{Volume of wooden box in cm}^3}{\text{Volume of 1 small box}}$

Volume & Surface Areas

$$= \left(\frac{800 \times 700 \times 600}{8 \times 7 \times 6}\right) = 1000000.$$

16. Number of cubes $= \left(\frac{100 \times 100 \times 100}{10 \times 10 \times 10}\right) = 1000.$

17. Let breadth $= x$ metres. Then, height $= 5x$ metres and length $= 40x$ metres.

    $\therefore x \times 5x \times 40x = 12.8$ or $x^3 = \frac{12.8}{200} = \frac{128}{2000} = \frac{64}{1000}$

    $\therefore x = \frac{4}{10}.$

    Thus, breadth $= \left(\frac{4}{10}\right)$ m $= \left(\frac{4 \times 100}{10}\right)$ cm $= 40$ cm.

18. Let depth $= x$ cm. Then,

    $x \times 6500 = 2.6 \times 100 \times 100 \times 100.$

    or $x = \left(\frac{2.6 \times 100 \times 100 \times 100}{6500}\right)$ cm $= 400$ cm $= 4$ m.

19. Volume of sheet $= (27 \times 8 \times 1)$ cm^3 $= 216$ cm^3.

    Volume of cube formed $= 216$ cm^3.

    $\therefore$ Edge of the cube $= (6 \times 6 \times 6)^{1/3} = 6$ cm.

    Surface area of original cuboid $= 2(27 \times 8 + 8 \times 1 + 27 \times 1)$ cm^2

    $= 502$ cm^2

    Surface area of the cube formed $= \left[6 \times (6)^2\right]$ cm^2 $= 216$ cm^2.

    $\therefore$ Difference in areas $= (502 - 216)$ cm^2 $= 286$ cm^2.

20. Number of bricks $= \dfrac{\text{Volume of wall in cm}^3}{\text{Volume of 1 brick}}$

    $= \left(\dfrac{200 \times 100 \times 1.8 \times 100 \times 37.5}{25 \times 12.5 \times 7.5}\right) = 57600.$

    $\therefore$ Cost $=$ Rs. $\left(\dfrac{750 \times 57600}{1000}\right) =$ Rs. $43200.$

21. Speed per min. $= \left(\dfrac{3 \times 1000}{60}\right)$ m $= 50$ m.

    $\therefore$ Volume of water running per min. $= (45 \times 2 \times 50)$ m^3

    $= 4500$ m^3.

22. Volume $= \left(2 \times 10000 \times \dfrac{5}{100}\right)$ m^3 $= 1000$ m^3.

23. Thickness = $\dfrac{\text{Volume}}{\text{area}} = \left(\dfrac{1}{2} \times \dfrac{1}{1000}\right)$ m = $\left(\dfrac{1 \times 100}{2 \times 1000}\right)$ cm = 0.005 cm.

24. Let their volumes be $8x^3$ and x^3 respectively.
    Then, their edges are
    $2x$ and x respectively.
    ∴ Ratio of their edges = 2 : 1.

25. Volume of new cube = $\left[(5)^3 + (4)^3 + (3)^3\right]$ cm^3 = 216 cm^3.
    Edge of this cube = $(6 \times 6 \times 6)^{1/3}$ = 6 cm.

26. Let the edge of original cube = x cm.
    Edge of new cube = $(2x)$ cm.
    Ratio of their volumes = $x^3 : (2x)^3 = x^3 : 8x^3 = 1 : 8$.
    Thus, the volume becomes 8 times.

27. Let the edges of the cubes be x and y metres.
    Then, $x^3 - y^3 = 152$ and $(x^2 - y^2) = 20$.
    Also, $(x + y) = 10$. So, $(x - y) = \left(\dfrac{x^2 - y^2}{x + y}\right) = \dfrac{20}{10} = 2$.
    Now, $\dfrac{x^3 - y^3}{x - y} = \left(\dfrac{152}{2}\right) \Rightarrow x^2 + y^2 + xy = 76$
    $\Rightarrow (x + y)^2 - xy = 76$
    $\Rightarrow xy = (x + y)^2 - 76 = (10)^2 - 76 = 24.$

28. Let, original length of cube = x.
    Then, its surface area = $6x^2$.
    New edge = $\left(\dfrac{150}{100}x\right) = \left(\dfrac{3}{2}x\right)$
    New surface area = $6 \times \left(\dfrac{3}{2}x\right)^2 = \left(6 \times \dfrac{9}{4}x^2\right) = \left(\dfrac{27}{2}\right)x^2$.
    Increase in surface area = $\left(\dfrac{27}{2} - 6\right)x^2 = \dfrac{15}{2}x^2$.
    ∴ Increase per cent = $\left(\dfrac{15}{2}x^2 \times \dfrac{1}{6x^2} \times 100\right)$ % = 125%.

29. Let the volumes be x^3 and $27x^3$.
    ∴ Their edges are x and $3x$.
    Ratio of their surface areas = $6x^2 : 54x^2 = 1 : 9$.

30. Earth dug out = $(3 \times 2 \times 1.5)$ m^3 = 9 m^3.
    Area on which earth has been spread = $(22 \times 14 - 3 \times 2)$ m^2

∴ Rise in level = $\dfrac{\text{Volume}}{\text{area}} = \left(\dfrac{9}{302}\right)$ m = $\left(\dfrac{9 \times 100}{302}\right)$ cm = 2.98 cm.

31. Volume of metal = $(52 \times 40 \times 29 - 48 \times 36 \times 27)$ cm^3
    = 13664 cm^3.
    ∴ Weight of the box = $\left(\dfrac{13664 \times 0.5}{1000}\right)$ kg = 6.832 kg.

32. Area needed = $2(25 \times 15 + 15 \times 8 + 25 \times 8)$ cm^2 = 1390 cm^2.

33. $r = 3.5$ cm and $h = 80$ cm.
    ∴ Whole surface = $2\pi rh + 2\pi r^2 = 2\pi r(h + r)$
    $= \left[2 \times \dfrac{22}{7} \times 3.5 \times (80 + 3.5)\right]$ cm^2 = 1837 cm^2.

34. $2\pi rh = 264$ or $2 \times \dfrac{22}{7} \times r \times 14 = 264$. ∴ $r = 3$.
    So, volume = $\pi r^2 h = \left(\dfrac{22}{7} \times 3 \times 3 \times 14\right)$ cm^3 = 396 cm^3.

35. Let original radius = r and original length = h.
    New radius = $\dfrac{1}{3}r$. Let new length = H.
    Then, $\pi r^2 h = \pi \left(\dfrac{1}{3}r\right)^2 \times H = \dfrac{\pi r^2 H}{9}$ ∴ $H = 9h$.
    Thus, the length becomes 9 times.

36. Radius of sphere = 9 cm.
    Volume of sphere = $\left[\dfrac{4}{3} \times \pi \times (9)^3\right]$ cm^3 = (972π) cm^3.
    Radius of wire = 0.2 mm = $\left(\dfrac{2}{10 \times 10}\right)$ cm = $\left(\dfrac{1}{50}\right)$ cm.
    Let the length be = x cm.
    Then, $972\pi = \pi \times \left(\dfrac{1}{50}\right)^2 \times x \Rightarrow x = (972 \times 50 \times 50)$ cm.
    ∴ Length of wire = $\left(\dfrac{972 \times 50 \times 50}{100}\right)$ m = 24300 m.

37. Let the number of spheres be x.
    Then, $x \times \dfrac{4}{3}\pi \times (3)^3 = \pi \times (2)^2 \times 45$
    or $36x = 180$ or $x = \dfrac{180}{36} = 5$.

38. Circumference of the girth = 440 cm.
    $\therefore$ $2\pi r = 440 \Rightarrow r = \left(\dfrac{440}{2} \times \dfrac{7}{22}\right) = 70$ cm.
    Thus, outer radius = 70 cm, inner radius = (70 − 4) cm = 66 cm.
    Volume of iron = $\pi \left[(70)^2 - (66)^2\right] \times 63$ cm^3
    $= \left(\dfrac{22}{7} \times 136 \times 4 \times 63\right)$ cm^3 = 58752 cm^3.

39. External radius = 2.5 cm, length = 100 cm.
    $\therefore$ External volume = $\left[\pi \times (2.5)^2 \times 100\right]$ cm^3.
    Internal radius = 1.5 cm.
    $\therefore$ Internal volume = $\left[\pi \times (1.5)^2 \times 100\right]$ cm^3.
    Volume of metal = $\left[\pi \times (2.5)^2 \times 100 - \pi \times (1.5)^2 \times 100\right]$ cm^3
    $= \pi \times 100 \times \left[(2.5)^2 - (1.5)^2\right]$ cm^3
    $= \left(\dfrac{22}{7} \times 100 \times 4 \times 1\right)$ cm^3.
    $\therefore$ Weight of metal = $\left(\dfrac{22}{7} \times 100 \times 4 \times 1 \times \dfrac{21}{1000}\right)$ kg = 26.4 kg.

40. $\dfrac{4}{3}\pi r^3 = \pi r^2 h \Rightarrow h = \dfrac{4}{3} r$.
    $\therefore$ Height = $\dfrac{4}{3}$ times its radius.

41. $\pi \times (4)^2 \times h = \dfrac{4}{3}\pi \times (3)^3$ or $h = \dfrac{9}{4}$ cm = 2.25 cm.

42. Let the height of cylinder = h and height of cone = H.
    Then, $\pi r^2 h = \dfrac{1}{3}\pi r^2 H$ or $\dfrac{h}{H} = \dfrac{1}{3} = 1 : 3$.

43. Let x cones be needed.
    Then, $\dfrac{1}{3}\pi r^2 h \times x = \pi r^2 h$ or $x = 3$.

44. $4\pi r^2 = 1386 \Rightarrow r^2 = \left(\dfrac{1386}{4} \times \dfrac{7}{22}\right) = \dfrac{441}{4}$ or $r = \dfrac{21}{2}$.
    $\therefore$ Volume = $\left(\dfrac{4}{3} \times \dfrac{22}{7} \times \dfrac{21}{2} \times \dfrac{21}{2} \times \dfrac{21}{2}\right)$ cm^3 = 4851 cm^3.

45. $\dfrac{4}{3} \times \dfrac{22}{7} \times r^3 = 38808 \Rightarrow r^3 = \left(38808 \times \dfrac{7}{22} \times \dfrac{3}{4}\right) = (21)^3$.
    $\therefore$ $r = 21$ cm.
    So, curved surface area = $4\pi r^2$

$$= \left(4 \times \frac{22}{7} \times 21 \times 21\right) cm^2 = 5544 \ cm^2.$$

46. $\frac{2}{3} \times \frac{22}{7} \times r^3 = 19404 \Rightarrow r^3 = \left(19404 \times \frac{7}{22} \times \frac{3}{2}\right) = (21)^3$

    $\therefore \ r = 21.$

    Surface area $= 3 \pi r^2$

    $= \left(3 \times \frac{22}{7} \times 21 \times 21\right) cm^2 = 4158 \ cm^2.$

47. Let their radii be x and y. Then,

    $\frac{4 \pi x^2}{4 \pi y^2} = \frac{1}{4} \Rightarrow \frac{x^2}{y^2} = \frac{1}{4} \Rightarrow \frac{x}{y} = \frac{1}{2}.$

    $\therefore$ Ratio of volumes $= \dfrac{\frac{4}{3} \pi x^3}{\frac{4}{3} \pi y^3} = \frac{x^3}{y^3} = \left(\frac{x}{y}\right)^3 = \left(\frac{1}{2}\right)^3 = \frac{1}{8}.$

48. Let their radii be x and $2x$.

    Ratio of their surface areas $= \dfrac{4 \pi x^2}{4 \pi (2x)^2} = \frac{1}{4} = 1 : 4.$

49. Let their heights be h and $2h$ and radii be x and y respectively. Then,

    $\pi x^2 h = \pi y^2 (2h)$ or $\dfrac{x^2}{y^2} = \frac{2}{1}$ or $\dfrac{x}{y} = \dfrac{\sqrt{2}}{1}.$

50. Number of balls $= \dfrac{\text{Volume of big ball}}{\text{Volume of 1 small ball}}$

    $= \dfrac{\frac{4}{3} \times \pi \times 10 \times 10 \times 10}{\frac{4}{3} \times \pi \times 0.5 \times 0.5 \times 0.5} = 8000.$

51. Number of bullets $= \dfrac{\text{Volume of cube}}{\text{Volume of 1 bullet}}$

    $= \left(\dfrac{22 \times 22 \times 22}{\frac{4}{3} \times \frac{22}{7} \times 1 \times 1 \times 1}\right) = 2541.$

52. $\frac{4}{3} \pi r^3 = \frac{4}{3} \pi \times \left[\left(\frac{3}{2}\right)^3 - \left\{\left(\frac{3}{4}\right)^3 + 1^3\right\}\right]$

    $\therefore \ r^3 = \frac{125}{64} = \left(\frac{5}{4}\right)^3.$ So, $r = \frac{5}{4}.$

∴ Diameter = $\left(\dfrac{5}{4} \times 2\right)$ cm = 2.5 cm.

53. $\dfrac{4}{3} \pi r^3 = 4 \pi r^2 \Rightarrow r = 3$ units.

54. $\dfrac{\text{Total surface area}}{\text{Lateral surface area}} = \dfrac{2\pi rh + 2\pi r^2}{2\pi rh} = \dfrac{2\pi r(h+r)}{2\pi rh}$

$= \left(\dfrac{h+r}{h}\right) = \left(\dfrac{20+80}{20}\right) = \dfrac{5}{1} = 5:1.$

55. Let their radii be $2r$ and $3r$ and heights $5h$ and $3h$ respectively.

Ratio of their volumes $= \dfrac{\pi(2r)^2 \times 5h}{\pi(3r)^2 \times 3h} = \dfrac{20}{27} = 20:27.$

56. Let h and H be the heights of water level before and after the dropping of the sphere. Then,

$\left[\pi \times (30)^2 \times H\right] - \left[\pi \times (30)^2 \times h\right] = \dfrac{4}{3} \pi \times (30)^3$

or $\pi \times 900 \times (H-h) = \dfrac{4}{3}\pi \times 27000$ or $(H-h) = 40$ cm.

57. $\dfrac{1}{3} \pi \times (2)^2 \times h = \pi \times (2)^2 \times 6 \Rightarrow h = 18$ cm.

58. Curved surface area $= \pi rl = \left(\dfrac{22}{7} \times 6 \times 28\right)$ cm^2 = 528 cm^2.

59. $\dfrac{1}{3} \times \dfrac{22}{7} \times r^2 \times 24 = 1232$ or $r^2 = \left(1232 \times \dfrac{7}{22} \times \dfrac{3}{24}\right) = 49.$

∴ $r = 7$ cm.

Now, $r = 7$ and $h = 24$. So, $l = \sqrt{7^2 + (24)^2} = \sqrt{625} = 25$ cm.

∴ Curved surface area $= \pi rl = \left(\dfrac{22}{7} \times 7 \times 25\right)$ cm^2 = 550 cm^2.

60. Since the diameters are in the ratio 4 : 5, it follows that their radii are in the ratio 4 : 5.

Let them be $4r$ and $5r$. Let the heights be h and H.

Ratio of volumes $= \dfrac{\frac{1}{3}\pi \times (4r)^2 \times h}{\frac{1}{3}\pi \times (5r)^2 \times H} = \dfrac{16h}{25H}.$

∴ $\dfrac{16h}{25H} = \dfrac{1}{4}$ or $\dfrac{h}{H} = \left(\dfrac{1}{4} \times \dfrac{25}{16}\right) = \dfrac{25}{64} = 25:64.$

61. Let the height of the cylinder be H and its radius $= r$.

Volume & Surface Areas

Then, $\pi r^2 H + \frac{1}{3}\pi r^2 h = 3 \times \frac{1}{3}\pi r^2 h$

$\therefore \pi r^2 H = \frac{2}{3}\pi r^2 h$ or $H = \frac{2}{3}h$.

62. $\frac{1}{3}\pi r^2 \times h = \pi r^2 \times 5$ or $h = 15$ cm.

63. Total volume = $(10 \times 5 \times 2)$ cm^3 = 100 cm^3.
    Volume carved = $\left(\frac{1}{3} \times \frac{22}{7} \times 3 \times 3 \times 7\right)$ cm^3 = 66 cm^3.
    Wood wasted = $(100 - 66)\% = 34\%$.

64. $\frac{22}{7} \times r^2 = 154 \Rightarrow r^2 = \left(154 \times \frac{7}{22}\right) = 49$ or $r = 7$ cm.
    Now, $r = 7$ and $h = 14$. So, $l = \sqrt{(7)^2 + (14)^2} = \sqrt{245} = 7\sqrt{5}$ cm.
    $\therefore$ Area of curved surface = $\pi rl = \left(\frac{22}{7} \times 7 \times 7\sqrt{5}\right)$ cm^2 = $154\sqrt{5}$ cm^2.

65. $\frac{22}{7} \times r^2 = 346.5 \Rightarrow r^2 = \left(\frac{346.5 \times 7}{22}\right) = \frac{441}{4} = \left(\frac{21}{2}\right)^2$.
    $\therefore r = \frac{21}{2}$. Also, $h = 14$ m.
    Now, $l = \sqrt{h^2 + r^2} = \sqrt{196 + \frac{441}{4}} = \frac{35}{2}$ m.
    $\therefore$ Area of canvas = $\pi rl = \left(\frac{22}{7} \times \frac{21}{2} \times \frac{35}{2}\right)$ m^2 = 924 m^2.
    Hence, length = $\frac{\text{Area}}{\text{Width}} = \left(\frac{924}{1.2}\right)$ m = 770 m.

66. Area of 4 walls of the room = $[2(l+b) \times h]$ m^2
    Area of 4 walls of new room = $[2(3l+3b) \times 3h]$ m^2
    $\qquad\qquad\qquad\qquad\qquad = 9[2(l+b) \times h]$ m^2.
    $\therefore$ Cost of painting the 4 walls of the new room
    $\qquad\qquad\qquad\qquad = $ Rs. $(9 \times 350) = $ Rs. 3150.

67. Original area = $6a^2$.
    New area = $6(2a)^2 = 24a^2$.
    Increase % = $\left(\frac{18a^2}{6a^2} \times 100\right)\% = 300\%$.

68. Original volume = $\frac{1}{3}\pi r^2 h$; New volume = $\frac{1}{3}\pi r^2(2h) = \frac{2}{3}\pi r^2 h$.

Increase % = $\left(\dfrac{\frac{1}{3}\pi r^2 h}{\frac{1}{3}\pi r^2 h} \times 100\right)$ % = 100% .

69. Original area = $4\pi r^2$; New area = $4\pi(2r)^2 = 16\pi r^2$.

Increase % = $\left(\dfrac{12\pi r^2}{4\pi r^2} \times 100\right)$ % = 300% .

70. Original volume = $\dfrac{4}{3}\pi r^3$.

New volume = $\dfrac{4}{3}\pi (2r)^3 = \dfrac{32}{3}\pi r^3$

Increase % = $\left(\dfrac{28}{3}\pi r^3 \times \dfrac{3}{4\pi r^3}\right)$ % = 700%.

71. Ratio of their volumes = $\dfrac{\pi r^2 h}{\frac{1}{3}\pi r^2 h} = \dfrac{3}{1} = 3 : 1$.

72. $\dfrac{4}{3} \times \dfrac{22}{7} \times r^3 = \dfrac{88}{21} \times (14)^3 \Rightarrow r = 14$.

∴ Curved Surface = $\left(4 \times \dfrac{22}{7} \times 14 \times 14\right)$ cm^2 = 2464 cm^2.

22
CHAIN RULE

The method of finding the fourth proportional when the other three are given is called **Simple proportion** or **Rule of Three**. Repeated use of the rule of three is called **Compound proportion**.

Direct Proportion. *Two quantities are said to be* **directly proportional** *if on the increase or decrease of the one, the other increases or decreases to the same extent.*

Ex. (i) Cost of articles is directly proportional to number of articles. i.e., more articles, more cost & less articles, less cost.

(ii) The work done is directly proportional to the number of men employed to do the work. i.e., more men, more work and less men, less work.

Indirect Proportion. *Two quantities are said to be* **indirectly proportional** *if on the increase of the one, the other decreases to the same extent and vice-versa.*

Ex. (i) Less number of days required to finish a work, more persons are to be employed.

(ii) The time taken to cover a distance is inversely proportional to the speed of the car. i.e., more speed, less is the time taken.

Ex. 1. *If 15 dolls cost Rs. 35 what do 39 dolls cost ?*

Sol. Clearly more dolls, more cost. (Direct Proportion)

So, ratio of dolls is the same as ratio of costs.

Now, let the cost of 39 dolls be Rs. x.

Then $15 : 39 :: 35 : x$

or $\dfrac{15}{39} = \dfrac{35}{x}$ or $x = \dfrac{35 \times 39}{15} = 91$.

Ex. 2. *If 36 men can do a certain piece of work in 25 days, in how many days will 15 men do it ?*

Sol. Clearly, less is the number of men employed, more will be the number of days taken to finish the work.

So, inverse ratio of men is equal to ratio of times taken.

Let the required number of days be x.

Then $15 : 36 :: 25 : x$

or $\dfrac{15}{36} = \dfrac{25}{x}$ or $x = \dfrac{36 \times 25}{15} = 60$.

∴ Required number of days = 60.

Ex. 3. *If 20 men can build a wall 112 metres long in 6 days, what length of a similar wall can be built by 25 men in 3 days ?*

Sol. Since the length is to be found out, we compare each item with the length as shown below :—

More men, more length built (direct proportion)

Less days, less length built (direct proportion)

∴ Men 20 : 25 $\Big\}$: : 112 : x
  Days 6 : 3

or $20 \times 6 \times x = 25 \times 3 \times 112$, or $x = \dfrac{25 \times 3 \times 112}{20 \times 6} = 70$.

Hence, required length of wall built = 70 metres.

Ex. 4. *If 8 men, working 9 hours a day can build a wall 18 metres long, 2 metres broad and 12 metres high in 10 days, how many men will be required to build a wall 32 metres long, 3 metres broad and 9 metres high, by working 6 hours a day, in 8 days ?*

Sol. Since the number of men is to be found out, we compare each item with the number of men, as shown below :—

More length, more men required (direct proportion)

More breadth, more men required (direct proportion)

More height, more men required (direct proportion)

Less daily working hrs., more men required (indirect proportion)

Less days to finish work, more men required (indirect proportion)

Length   18 : 32
Breadth   2 : 3
Height   12 : 9 $\Big\}$: : 8 : x
Daily hrs. 6 : 9
Days   8 : 10

∴ $18 \times 2 \times 12 \times 6 \times 8 \times x = 32 \times 3 \times 9 \times 9 \times 10 \times 8$

or $x = \dfrac{32 \times 3 \times 9 \times 9 \times 10 \times 8}{18 \times 2 \times 12 \times 6 \times 8} = 30.$

∴ Required number of men = 30.

Ex. 5. *A contract is to be completed in 56 days and 104 men were set to work, each working 8 hours a day. After 30 days $\dfrac{2}{5}$ of the work is completed. How many additional men may be employed, so that the work may be completed in time, each man now working 9 hours a day ?*

Sol. Remaining work = $\left(1 - \dfrac{2}{5}\right) = \dfrac{3}{5}$.

Remaining period = (56 − 30) = 26 days.

Chain Rule

$\begin{cases} \text{more work, more men} & \text{(Direct)} \\ \text{more days, less men} & \text{(Indirect)} \\ \text{more hours per day, less men} & \text{(Indirect)} \end{cases}$

$$\therefore \left.\begin{array}{l} \text{Work} \quad \dfrac{2}{5} : \dfrac{3}{5} \\ \text{days} \quad 26 : 30 \\ \text{Hours} \quad 9 : 8 \end{array}\right\} :: 104 : x$$

or $\quad x = \dfrac{3 \times 30 \times 8 \times 104 \times 5}{5 \times 2 \times 26 \times 9} = 160.$

So, $(160 - 104)$ i.e., 56 more men must be employed.

Ex. 6. *2 men and 7 boys together complete a certain work in 16 days, while 3 men and 8 boys together complete the same work in 12 days. Find, in how many days will 8 men and 8 boys together complete a work twice as big as the previous one.*

Sol. (2 men + 7 boys) complete the work in 16 days.

So, $[(2 \times 16) \text{ men} + (7 \times 16) \text{ boys}]$ complete the work in 1 day.

i.e., (32 men + 112 boys) complete the work in 1 day.

Again, (3 men + 8 boys) complete the work in 12 days.

So, $[(3 \times 12) \text{ men} + (8 \times 12) \text{ boys}]$ complete the work in 1 day.

i.e., (36 men + 96 boys) complete the work in 1 day.

$\therefore$ (32 men + 112 boys) ≡ (36 men + 96 boys)

or 4 men ≡ 16 boys or 1 man ≡ 4 boys.

$\therefore$ (2 men + 7 boys) ≡ 15 boys & 8 men + 8 boys ≡ 40 boys.

Thus the problem becomes : 15 boys complete a work in 16 days, in how many days will 40 boys complete twice this work ?

More boys, less days. (indirect)

More work, more boys (direct)

$\left.\begin{array}{l} \text{Boys} \quad 40 : 15 \\ \text{Work} \quad 1 : 2 \end{array}\right\} :: 16 : x$

$\therefore \; 40 \times 1 \times x = 15 \times 2 \times 16 \quad$ or $\quad x = \dfrac{15 \times 2 \times 16}{40 \times 1} = 12.$

So, the required number of days = 12.

Ex. 7. *A garrison of 3300 men had provisions for 32 days, when given at the rate of 850 gms. per head. At the end of 7 days a reinforcement arrives and it was found that now the provisions will last 17 days more, when given at the rate of 825 gm. per head. What is the strength of the reinforcement ?*

Sol. The problem can be put in the form given below :—

3300 men taking 850 gm. per head have provisions for $(32 - 7)$ or 25 days. How many men taking 825 gm. per head have provisions for 17 days ?

Let the number of men be x.

Now Less ration per head, more men (indirect proportion)
Less days, more men (indirect proportion)

Ration 825 : 850
Days   17 : 25 } :: 3300 : x

$\therefore$ 825 × 17 × x = 850 × 25 × 3300 or $x = \dfrac{850 \times 25 \times 3300}{825 \times 17}$

= 5000

So, the strength of new reinforcement = (5000 – 3300) = 1700.

Ex. 8. *If 6 engines consume 15 metric tonnes of coal, when each is running 9 hours a day; how much coal will be required for 8 engines, each running 12 hours a day, it being given that 3 engines of the former type consume as much as 4 engines of latter type ?*

Sol. Since the quantity of coal is to be found out, we compare each item with the coal consumed.

Now, More engines, more coal (direct proportion)
More hours, more coal (direct proportion)
Let 3 engines (former type) consume = 1 unit

$\therefore$ 1 engine (former type) consumes = $\dfrac{1}{3}$ unit

Then, 4 engines (latter type) consume = 1 unit

$\therefore$ 1 engine (latter type) consumes = $\dfrac{1}{4}$ unit

Clearly, less rate of consumption, less coal (direct proportion)
Let the required quantity of coal consumed be x tonnes.

Number of Engines 6 : 8
Hours of working 9 : 12
Rate of consumption $\dfrac{1}{3} : \dfrac{1}{4}$ } :: 15 : x

$\therefore$ 6 × 9 × $\dfrac{1}{3}$ × x = 8 × 12 × $\dfrac{1}{4}$ × 15 or $x = \dfrac{8 \times 12 \times 1 \times 15 \times 3}{6 \times 9 \times 4} = 20$

Hence, the required quantity of coal consumed = 20 tonnes.

EXERCISE 22 (Objective Type Questions)

1. If 22.5 metres of a uniform iron rod weighs 85.5 kg., what will be the weight of 6 metres of the same rod ?
   (a) 22.8 kg.   (b) 25.6 kg.
   (c) 28 kg.   (d) none of these

2. On a scale of a map 0.8 cm. represents 8.8 km. If the distance between two points on the map is 80.5 cm., the distance between these points is approximately
   (a) 9 km.   (b) 70 km.

(c) 90 km. (d) 885 km.
(S.B.I.P.O. Exam. 1987)
3. If 40 persons consume 60 kg. of rice in 15 days, then in how many days will 30 persons consume 12 kg. of rice :
   (a) $3\frac{3}{4}$ days (b) 4 days
   (c) $6\frac{1}{4}$ days (d) 9 days
4. In a hospital there is a consumption of 1350 litres of milk for 70 patients for 30 days. How many patients will consume 1710 litres of milk in 28 days ?
   (a) 59 (b) 85
   (c) 95 (d) 105
5. If the rent for grazing 40 cows for 20 days is Rs. 370, how many cows can graze for 30 days on Rs.111 ?
   (a) 6 (b) 8
   (c) 5 (d) 12
6. If 18 binders bind 900 books in 10 days, how many binders will be required to bind 660 books in 12 days ?
   (a) 55 (b) 14
   (c) 13 (d) 11 (Bank P.O. Exam 1988)
7. If six men working 8 hours a day earn Rs. 840 per week, then 9 men working 6 hours a day will earn per week
   (a) Rs. 840 (b) Rs. 945
   (c) Rs. 1620 (d) Rs. 1680
(Central Excise and I. Tax Exam. 1988)
8. If 3 persons weave 168 shawls in 14 days, how many shawls will 8 persons weave in 5 days ?
   (a) 90 (b) 105
   (c) 126 (d) 160
9. If 20 men can build a wall 112 metres long in 6 days, what length of a similar wall can be built by 25 men in 3 days ?
   (a) 140 metres (b) 44.8 metres
   (c) 105 metres (d) 70 metres
10. If 300 men can do a piece of work in 16 days, how many men would do (1/5) of the work in 15 days ?
    (a) 56 (b) 64
    (c) 60 (d) 72
11. If 20 men working 7 hours a day can do a piece of work in 10 days, in how many days will 15 men working for 8 hours a day do the same piece of work ?

(a) $15\frac{5}{21}$ days (b) $11\frac{2}{3}$ days
(c) $6\frac{9}{16}$ days (d) $4\frac{1}{5}$ days

12. If 4 examiners can examine a certain number of answer books in 8 days by working 5 hours a day; for how many hours a day would 2 examiners have to work in order to examine twice the number of answer books in 20 days ?
    (a) 6 hours (b) 8 hours
    (c) 9 hours (d) $7\frac{1}{2}$ hours

13. If 18 pumps can raise 2170 tonnes of water in 10 days, working 7 hours a day, in how many days will 16 pumps raise 1736 tonnes, working 9 hours a day ?
    (a) 9 days (b) 8 days
    (c) 7 days (d) 6 days

14. 120 men had provisions for 200 days. After 5 days, 30 men died due to an epidemic. The remaining food will last for :
    (a) 150 days (b) $146\frac{1}{4}$ days
    (c) 245 days (d) 260 days

15. A garrison of 500 men had provisions for 24 days. However, a reinforcement of 300 men arrived. The food will now last for
    (a) 18 days (b) $17\frac{1}{2}$ days
    (c) 16 days (d) 15 days

16. A garrison had provisions for a certain number of days. After 10 days (1/5)th of the men desert and it is found that the provisions will now last just as long as before. How long was that :
    (a) 35 days (b) 15 days
    (c) 25 days (d) 50 days

17. 20 men complete one-third of a piece of work in 20 days. How many more men should be employed to finish the rest of the work in 25 more days ?
    (a) 10 (b) 12
    (c) 15 (d) 20

18. If 17 labourers can dig a ditch 26 metres long in 18 days, working 8 hours a day, how many more labourers should be engaged to dig a similar ditch 39 metres long in 6 days, each labourer working 9 hours a day ?
    (a) 51 (b) 68
    (c) 85 (d) 34

Chain Rule

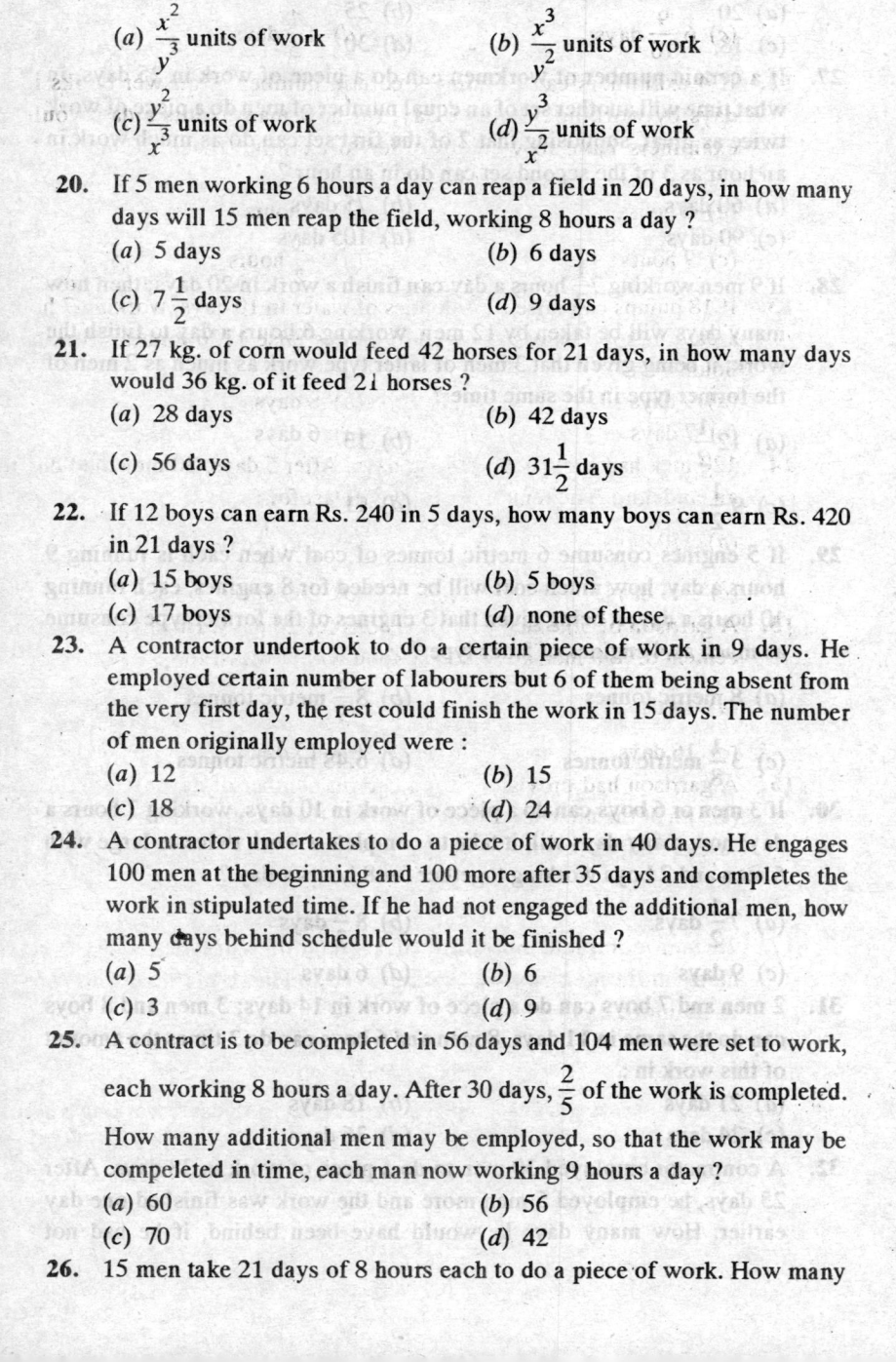

19. If x men working x hours per day can do x units of a work in x days, then y men working y hours per day would be able to complete in y days:
    (a) $\dfrac{x^2}{y^3}$ units of work
    (b) $\dfrac{x^3}{y^2}$ units of work
    (c) $\dfrac{y^2}{x^3}$ units of work
    (d) $\dfrac{y^3}{x^2}$ units of work

20. If 5 men working 6 hours a day can reap a field in 20 days, in how many days will 15 men reap the field, working 8 hours a day?
    (a) 5 days
    (b) 6 days
    (c) $7\dfrac{1}{2}$ days
    (d) 9 days

21. If 27 kg. of corn would feed 42 horses for 21 days, in how many days would 36 kg. of it feed 21 horses?
    (a) 28 days
    (b) 42 days
    (c) 56 days
    (d) $31\dfrac{1}{2}$ days

22. If 12 boys can earn Rs. 240 in 5 days, how many boys can earn Rs. 420 in 21 days?
    (a) 15 boys
    (b) 5 boys
    (c) 17 boys
    (d) none of these

23. A contractor undertook to do a certain piece of work in 9 days. He employed certain number of labourers but 6 of them being absent from the very first day, the rest could finish the work in 15 days. The number of men originally employed were:
    (a) 12
    (b) 15
    (c) 18
    (d) 24

24. A contractor undertakes to do a piece of work in 40 days. He engages 100 men at the beginning and 100 more after 35 days and completes the work in stipulated time. If he had not engaged the additional men, how many days behind schedule would it be finished?
    (a) 5
    (b) 6
    (c) 3
    (d) 9

25. A contract is to be completed in 56 days and 104 men were set to work, each working 8 hours a day. After 30 days, $\dfrac{2}{5}$ of the work is completed. How many additional men may be employed, so that the work may be completed in time, each man now working 9 hours a day?
    (a) 60
    (b) 56
    (c) 70
    (d) 42

26. 15 men take 21 days of 8 hours each to do a piece of work. How many

days of 6 hours each would 21 women take, if 3 women do as much work as 2 men ?
(a) 20 (b) 25
(c) 18 (d) 30

27. If a certain number of workmen can do a piece of work in 25 days, in what time will another set of an equal number of men do a piece of work twice as great, supposing that 2 of the first set can do as much work in an hour as 3 of the second set can do in an hour ?
(a) 60 days (b) 75 days
(c) 90 days (d) 105 days

28. If 9 men working $7\frac{1}{2}$ hours a day can finish a work in 20 days; then how many days will be taken by 12 men, working 6 hours a day to finish the work; it being given that 3 men of latter type work as much as 2 men of the former type in the same time ?
(a) $12\frac{1}{2}$ (b) 13
(c) $9\frac{1}{2}$ (d) 11

29. If 5 engines consume 6 metric tonnes of coal when each is running 9 hours a day, how much coal will be needed for 8 engines, each running 10 hours a day, it being given that 3 engines of the former type consume as much as 4 engines of latter type ?
(a) 8 metric tonnes (b) $8\frac{8}{9}$ metric tonnes
(c) $3\frac{1}{8}$ metric tonnes (d) 6.48 metric tonnes

30. If 3 men or 6 boys can do a piece of work in 10 days, working 7 hours a day; how many days will it take to complete a work twice as large with 6 men and 2 boys working together for 8 hours a day ?
(a) $7\frac{1}{2}$ days (b) $8\frac{1}{2}$ days
(c) 9 days (d) 6 days

31. 2 men and 7 boys can do a piece of work in 14 days; 3 men and 8 boys can do the same in 11 days. 8 men and 6 boys can do 3 times the amount of this work in :
(a) 21 days (b) 18 days
(c) 24 days (d) 36 days

32. A contractor employed 30 men to do a piece of work in 38 days. After 25 days, he employed 5 men more and the work was finished one day earlier. How many days he would have been behind, if he had not

employed additional men ?

(a) 1 day (b) $1\frac{1}{4}$ days

(c) $1\frac{3}{4}$ days (d) $1\frac{1}{2}$ days

33. A rope makes 140 rounds of the circumference of a cylinder whose radius of the base is 14 cms. How many times can it go round a cylinder with radius 20 cms. :

(a) 98 (b) 17
(c) 200 (d) none of these

34. If Raghu can walk a distance of 5 kms. in 20 minutes, how long he can go in 50 minutes :

(a) 10.5 km. (b) 12 km.
(c) 12.5 km. (d) 13.5 km.

35. If (4/5)th of a cistern is filled in 1 minute, how much more time will be required to fill the rest of it :

(a) 20 seconds (b) 15 seconds
(c) 12 seconds (d) 10 seconds

36. Ten pipes through which water flows at the same rate can fill a tank in 24 minutes. If two pipes go out of order, how long will the remaining pipes take to fill the tank ?

(a) 40 minutes (b) 45 minutes
(c) $19\frac{1}{5}$ minutes (d) 30 minutes

37. If 21 cows eat that much as 15 buffaloes, how many cows will eat that much as 35 buffaloes ?

(a) 49 (b) 56
(c) 45 (d) none of these

38. 16 men can reap a field in 30 days. In how many days will 20 men reap the field ?

(a) 25 days (b) 24 days
(c) $10\frac{2}{3}$ days (d) $37\frac{1}{2}$ days

(Railway Board Exam 1989)

ANSWERS (Exercise 22)

1. (a) 2. (d) 3. (b) 4. (c) 5. (b) 6. (d)
7. (b) 8. (d) 9. (d) 10. (b) 11. (b) 12. (b)
13. (c) 14. (d) 15. (d) 16. (d) 17. (b) 18. (a)
19. (d) 20. (a) 21. (c) 22. (b) 23. (b) 24. (a)
25. (b) 26. (d) 27. (b) 28. (a) 29. (a) 30. (a)

31. (a)   32. (a)   33. (a)   34. (c)   35. (b)   36. (d)
37. (a)   38. (b).

SOLUTIONS (Exercise 22)

1. Less length, less weight.
   $\therefore 22.5 : 6 :: 85.5 : x.$
   So, $22.5 \times x = 6 \times 85.5$ or $x = \dfrac{6 \times 85.5}{22.5} = 22.8$ kg.

2. More distance on the map, more actual distance.
   $\therefore 0.8 : 80.5 :: 8.8 : x$
   So, $0.8 \times x = 80.5 \times 8.8$ or $x = \dfrac{80.5 \times 8.8}{0.8} = 885.5$ km.
   $= 885$ km. (approx).

3. Less men, more days (indirect)
   Less kg., less days (direct)
   $\therefore \left.\begin{array}{l}\text{Men } 30:40\\ \text{kgs } 60:12\end{array}\right\} :: 15:x$
   $\therefore 30 \times 60 \times x = 40 \times 12 \times 15$ or $x = \left(\dfrac{40 \times 12 \times 15}{30 \times 60}\right) = 4$ days.

4. More litres, more patients (direct)
   Less days, more patients (indirect)
   $\left.\begin{array}{l}\text{Litres } 1350:1710\\ \text{Days } 28:30\end{array}\right\} :: 70:x$
   $\therefore 1350 \times 28 \times x = 1710 \times 30 \times 70$
   or $x = \left(\dfrac{1710 \times 30 \times 70}{1350 \times 28}\right) = 95$ patients.

5. More days, less cows (indirect)
   Less rent, less cows (direct)
   $\left.\begin{array}{l}\text{Days } 30:20\\ \text{Rent } 370:111\end{array}\right\} :: 18:x$ or $x = \left(\dfrac{20 \times 111 \times 40}{30 \times 370}\right) = 8$ cows.

6. Less books, less number of binders (direct)
   More days, less number of binders (indirect)
   $\left.\begin{array}{l}\text{Books } 900:660\\ \text{Days } 12:10\end{array}\right\} :: 18:x$
   $\therefore x = \left(\dfrac{660 \times 10 \times 18}{900 \times 12}\right) = 11.$

7. More men, more earning (direct)
   Less hours, less earning (direct)
   $\left.\begin{array}{l}\text{Men } 6:9\\ \text{Hours/day } 8:6\end{array}\right\} :: 840:x$

$$\therefore x = \left(\frac{9 \times 6 \times 840}{6 \times 8}\right) = \text{Rs. } 945.$$

8. More persons, more shawls (direct)
   Less days, less shawls (direct)
   $$\left.\begin{array}{l}\text{Persons} \quad 3:8 \\ \text{Days} \quad 14:5\end{array}\right\} :: 168:x$$
   $$\therefore x = \left(\frac{8 \times 5 \times 168}{3 \times 14}\right) = 160 \text{ shawls.}$$

9. More men, more length built (direct)
   Less days, less length built (direct)
   $$\left.\begin{array}{l}\text{Men} \quad 20:25 \\ \text{Days} \quad 6:3\end{array}\right\} :: 112:x$$
   $$\therefore x = \left(\frac{25 \times 3 \times 112}{20 \times 6}\right) = 70 \text{ metres.}$$

10. Less days, more men (indirect)
    Less work, less men (direct)
    $$\left.\begin{array}{l}\text{Days} \quad 15:16 \\ \text{Work} \quad 1:\frac{1}{5}\end{array}\right\} :: 300:x.$$
    $$\therefore x = \left(16 \times \frac{1}{5} \times 300 \times \frac{1}{15 \times 1}\right) = 64 \text{ men.}$$

11. Less men, more days (indirect)
    More working hours, less days (indirect)
    $$\left.\begin{array}{l}\text{Men} \quad 15:20 \\ \text{Working hrs.} \quad 8:7\end{array}\right\} :: 10:x$$
    $$\therefore x = \left(\frac{20 \times 7 \times 10}{15 \times 8}\right) = 11\frac{2}{3} \text{ days.}$$

12. Less examiners, more hours per day (indirect)
    More days, less hours per day (indirect)
    More answer books, more hours per day (direct)
    $$\left.\begin{array}{l}\text{Examiners} \quad 2:4 \\ \text{Days} \quad 20:8 \\ \text{Ans. Books} \quad 1:2\end{array}\right\} :: 5:x$$
    $$\therefore x = \left(\frac{4 \times 8 \times 2 \times 5}{2 \times 20 \times 1}\right) = 8 \text{ hours per day.}$$

13. Less pumps, more days (indirect)
    Less water, less days (direct)
    More working hrs., less days (indirect)
    $$\left.\begin{array}{l}\text{Pumps} \quad 16:18 \\ \text{Water} \quad 2170:1736 \\ \text{Working hours} \quad 9:7\end{array}\right\} :: 10:x$$

$$\therefore x = \left(\frac{18 \times 1736 \times 7 \times 10}{16 \times 2170 \times 9}\right) = 7 \, days.$$

14. The remaining food is sufficient for 120 men for 195 days.
    But, now remaining men = 90.
    Less men, more days (indirect)
    $\therefore 90 : 120 :: 195 : x$
    or $x = \left(\dfrac{120 \times 195}{90}\right) = 260 \, days.$

15. More men, less number of days (indirect)
    $800 : 500 :: 24 : x$
    or $x = \left(\dfrac{500 \times 24}{800}\right) = 15 \, days.$

16. Let, initially there be x men having provisions for y days.
    After 10 days, x men had provisions for $(y - 10)$ days.
    These provisions were for $\left(x - \dfrac{x}{5}\right)$ i.e., $\dfrac{4x}{5}$ men for y days.
    $\therefore \; x(y - 10) = \dfrac{4x}{5} y$ or $xy - 50x = 0$
    or $x(y - 50) = 0$ or $y - 50 = 0$ i.e. $y = 50$.

17. Work done $= \dfrac{1}{3}$, work to be done $= \dfrac{2}{3}$.
    Now, more work, more men (direct)
    More days, less men (indirect)
    Work $\dfrac{1}{3} : \dfrac{2}{3}$ $\bigg\}$ $:: 20 : x$
    Days $25 : 20$
    $\therefore x = \left(\dfrac{2}{3} \times 20 \times 20 \times \dfrac{3}{25}\right) = 32 \, men.$
    So, 12 more men should be employed.

18. More length, more labourers (direct)
    More daily hours, less labourers (indirect)
    Less days, more labourers (indirect)
    Length $\;\; 26 : 39$
    Daily hrs. $\;\; 9 : 8$ $\bigg\}$ $:: 17 : x$
    Days $\;\;\;\;\; 6 : 18$
    or $x = \left(\dfrac{39 \times 8 \times 18 \times 17}{26 \times 9 \times 6}\right) = 68.$
    So, more labourers to be engaged $= (68 - 17) = 51$.

19. More men, more work (direct)
    More working hrs., more work (direct)

Chain Rule

More days, more work (direct)

Men $\quad\quad\quad x:y$
Working hrs. $\; x:y \;\Big\} :: x:z \quad \therefore z = \left(\dfrac{y \times y \times y \times x}{x \times x \times x}\right) = \dfrac{y^3}{x^2}$ units of
Days $\quad\quad\; x:y$
work.

20. More men, less days (indirect)
More working hrs., less days (indirect)

Men $\quad\quad 15:5$
Working hrs. $\;\; 8:6 \Big\} :: 20:x \quad \therefore x = \left(\dfrac{5 \times 6 \times 20}{15 \times 8}\right) = 5$ days.

21. More corn, more days (direct)
Less horses, more days (indirect)

Corn $\quad 27:36$
Horses $\; 21:42 \Big\} :: 21:x \quad \therefore x = \left(\dfrac{36 \times 42 \times 21}{27 \times 21}\right) = 56$ days.

22. More money, more boys (direct)
More days, less boys (indirect)

Money $\; 240:420$
Days $\quad\; 21:5 \quad\Big\} :: 12:x \quad \therefore x = \left(\dfrac{420 \times 5 \times 12}{240 \times 21}\right) = 5$ boys.

23. Let there be x men at the beginning.
Now, less men would take more days.
$\therefore \;\; 15:9 \;::x:(x-6)$
or $\;15 \times (x-6) = 9x \;$ or $\; x = 15$ men.

24. $[(100 \times 35) + (200 \times 5)]$ working for 1 day can finish the work.
Thus, 4500 men can finish it in 1 day.

So, 100 men can finish it in $\left(\dfrac{4500}{100}\right) = 45$ days,

i.e. 5 days behind schedule.

25. Remaining work $= \left(1 - \dfrac{2}{5}\right) = \dfrac{3}{5}$.

Remaining period $= (56 - 30) = 26$ days.

Now, the problem becomes : 104 men working 8 hrs a day can finish (2/5) work in 30 days, how many men working 9 hrs. a day can finish (3/5) work in 26 days ?

More work, more men (direct)
Less days, more men (indirect)
More hours, less men (indirect)

Work $\quad\quad \dfrac{2}{5} : \dfrac{3}{5}$
Days $\quad\quad 26:30 \quad\Big\} :: 104:x$
Hrs./day $\quad 9:8$

$\therefore x = \left(\dfrac{3}{5} \times 30 \times 8 \times 104 \times \dfrac{5}{2} \times \dfrac{1}{26} \times \dfrac{1}{9}\right) = 160$.

So, *more men to be employed* = (160 − 104) = 56.

26. 3 women ≡ 2 men, so 21 women ≡ 14 men.
    Now, Less men, more days (indirect)
    Less hours, more days (indirect)
    $\therefore$ $\left.\begin{array}{l}\text{Men}\qquad 14:15\\ \text{Working hrs.}\quad 6:8\end{array}\right\} :: 21:x \quad \therefore x = \left(\dfrac{15 \times 8 \times 21}{14 \times 6}\right) = 30$ days.

27. Speed of doing work of first and second set of men is $\dfrac{1}{2} : \dfrac{1}{3}$.

    Now, More work, more time (direct)
    Less speed, more time (indirect)
    $\left.\begin{array}{l}\text{Work}\quad 1:2\\ \text{Speed}\quad \dfrac{1}{3}:\dfrac{1}{2}\end{array}\right\} :: 25:x$

    $\therefore x = \left(2 \times \dfrac{1}{2} \times 25 \times \dfrac{3}{1 \times 1}\right) = 75$ days.

28. More men, less days (indirect)
    Less hours a day, more days (indirect)
    More speed, less days (indirect)
    $\left.\begin{array}{l}\text{Men}\qquad 12:9\\ \text{Hrs./day}\quad 6:7\dfrac{1}{2}\\ \text{Speed}\qquad \dfrac{1}{2}:\dfrac{1}{3}\end{array}\right\} :: 20:x$

    $\therefore x = \left(9 \times \dfrac{15}{2} \times \dfrac{1}{3} \times 20 \times \dfrac{2}{12 \times 6 \times 1}\right) = 12\dfrac{1}{2}$ days.

29. More engine, more coal (direct)
    More hrs. a day, more coal (direct)
    More rate of consumption, more coal (direct)
    $\left.\begin{array}{l}\text{Engine}\quad 5:8\\ \text{Hrs./Day}\quad 9:10\\ \text{Rate}\qquad \dfrac{1}{3}:\dfrac{1}{4}\end{array}\right\} :: 6:x$

    $\therefore x = \left(8 \times 10 \times \dfrac{1}{4} \times 6 \times \dfrac{1}{5} \times \dfrac{1}{9} \times 3\right) = 8$ metric tonnes.

30. (6 men + 2 boys) ≡ 14 boys.
    Now, More work, more number of days (direct)
    More boys, less number of days (indirect)
    More hours a day, less number of days (indirect)
    $\left.\begin{array}{l}\text{Work}\quad 1:2\\ \text{Boys}\quad 14:6\\ \text{Hrs./Day}\quad 8:7\end{array}\right\} :: 10:x \quad \therefore x = \dfrac{2 \times 6 \times 7 \times 10}{1 \times 14 \times 8} = 7\dfrac{1}{2}$ days.

Chain Rule 383

31. (2×14) men $+ (7 \times 14)$ boys $\equiv (3 \times 11)$ men $+ (8 \times 11)$ boys
 or 5 men $\equiv$ 10 boys or 1 man $\equiv$ 2 boys.
 $\therefore$ 2 men + 7 boys $\equiv$ 11 boys.
 and 8 men + 6 boys $\equiv$ 22 boys.
 Now, More boys, less days (indirect)
 More work, more days (direct)
 $\left.\begin{array}{ll}\text{Boys} & 22:11 \\ \text{Work} & 1:3\end{array}\right\} :: 14 : x \quad \therefore \quad x = \dfrac{11 \times 3 \times 14}{22 \times 1} = 21\ days.$

32. After 25 days, 35 men complete the work in 12 days.
 Now, 35 men can finish the remaining work in 12 days.
 $\therefore$ 30 men can finish it in $\dfrac{12 \times 35}{30} = 14$ days.
 i.e. 1 day behind.

33. More radius, less rounds (indirect)
 $20 : 14 :: 140 : x$
 or $x = \left(\dfrac{14 \times 140}{20}\right) = 98\ times.$

34. More time, more distance covered (direct)
 $\therefore\ 20 : 50 :: 5 : x$
 or $x = \left(\dfrac{50 \times 5}{20}\right) = 12.5\ km.$

35. Remaining part = (1/5).
 Less part to be filled, less time taken (direct)
 $\therefore \dfrac{4}{5} : \dfrac{1}{5} = 1 : x \quad \text{or} \quad x = \left(\dfrac{1}{5} \times 1 \times \dfrac{5}{4}\right) = \dfrac{1}{4}\ min. \quad = 15\ seconds.$

36. Less pipes, more time (indirect)
 $8 : 10 :: 24 : x$
 or $x = \left(\dfrac{10 \times 24}{8}\right) = 30\ minutes.$
 15 buffaloes $\equiv$ 21 cows
 35 buffaloes $\equiv \left(\dfrac{21}{15} \times 35\right) = 49$ cows.

37. 15 buffaloes $\equiv$ 21 cows
 35 buffaloes $\equiv \left(\dfrac{21}{15} \times 35\right)$ cows = 49 cows.

38. More men; less days (indirect)
 $20 : 16 :: 30 : x \quad \therefore \quad x = \left(\dfrac{16 \times 30}{20}\right) = 24.$

23
ALLIGATION OR MIXTURE

Alligation *is the rule that enables us to find the proportion in which the two or more ingradients at the given price must be mixed to produce a mixture at a given price.*

Cost price of unit quantity of the mixture is called the **Mean Price.**

Rule of Alligation. If two ingradients are mixed in a ratio, then

$$\frac{\text{(Quantity of cheaper)}}{\text{(Quantity of dearer)}} = \frac{\text{(C.P. of dearer)} - \text{(Mean Price)}}{\text{(Mean Price)} - \text{(C.P. of cheaper)}}$$

We represent it as under :

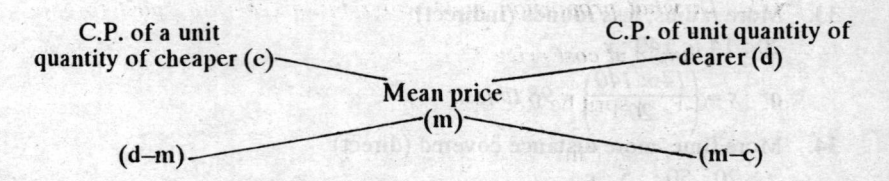

```
    C.P. of a unit                           C.P. of unit quantity of
 quantity of cheaper (c)                        dearer (d)
                         Mean price
                            (m)
         (d–m)                                  (m–c)
```

(Cheaper quantity) : (dearer quantity) = (d – m) : (m – c).

Solved Problems.

Ex. 1. *In what proportion must rice at Rs. 3.10 per kg. be mixed with rice at Rs. 3.60 per kg., so that the mixture be worth Rs. 3.25 a kg. ?*

Sol.

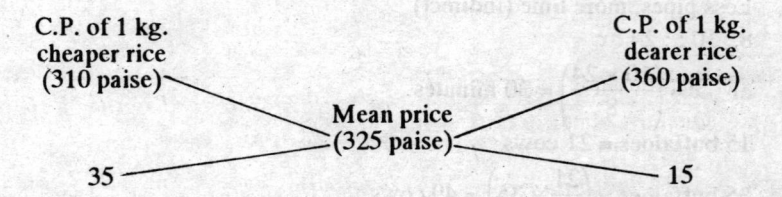

```
   C.P. of 1 kg.                              C.P. of 1 kg.
   cheaper rice                               dearer rice
   (310 paise)                                (360 paise)
                        Mean price
                       (325 paise)
         35                                       15
```

By the alligation rule :

$$\frac{\text{(Quantity of cheaper rice)}}{\text{(Quantity of dearer rice)}} = \frac{35}{15} = \frac{7}{3}.$$

∴ *They must be mixed in the ratio 7 : 3.*

Ex. 2. *How many kilograms of sugar costing Rs. 6.10 per kg. must be mixed with 126 kg. of sugar costing Rs. 2.85 per kg. so that 20% may be gained by selling the mixture at Rs. 4.80 per kg. ?*

Sol. S.P. of 1 kg. of mixture = Rs. 4.80, Gain = 20%.

Alligation Or Mixture

∴ C.P. of kg. of mixture = Rs. $\left(\dfrac{100}{120} \times 4.80\right)$ = Rs. 4.

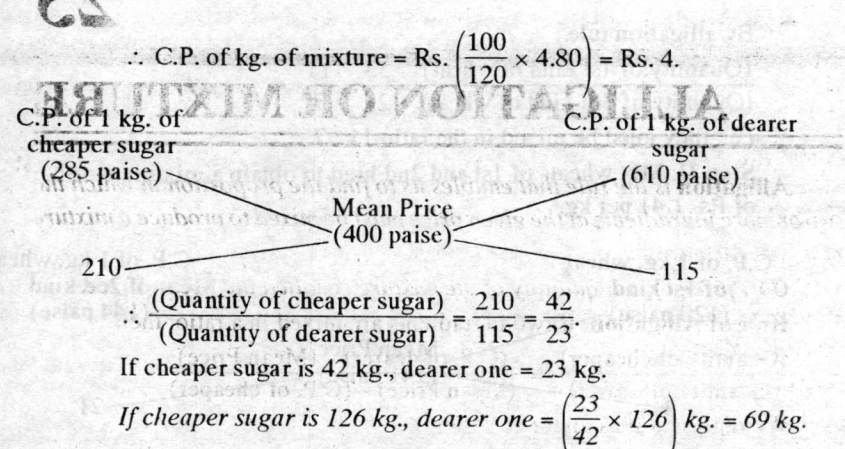

```
C.P. of 1 kg. of                              C.P. of 1 kg. of dearer
  cheaper sugar                                        sugar
   (285 paise)                                      (610 paise)
                        Mean Price
                        (400 paise)
      210                                              115
```

∴ $\dfrac{\text{(Quantity of cheaper sugar)}}{\text{(Quantity of dearer sugar)}} = \dfrac{210}{115} = \dfrac{42}{23}$.

If cheaper sugar is 42 kg., dearer one = 23 kg.

If cheaper sugar is 126 kg., dearer one = $\left(\dfrac{23}{42} \times 126\right)$ kg. = 69 kg.

Ex. 3. *In what proportion must water be mixed with spirit to gain $16\dfrac{2}{3}$ % by selling it at cost price?*

Sol. Let C.P. of sprit be Re. 1 per litre.

Then, S.P. of 1 litre of mixture = Re. 1, Gain = $16\dfrac{2}{3}$ %.

C.P. of 1 litre of mixture = Rs. $\left(\dfrac{100 \times 3 \times 1}{350}\right)$ = Rs. $\left(\dfrac{6}{7}\right)$.

```
C.P. of 1 kg.                                    C.P. of 1 kg.
   water                                           pure spirit
   (Re. 0)                                          (Re. 1)
                        Mean Price
                        (Re. 6/7)
      1/7                                              6/7
```

$\dfrac{\text{(Quantity of water)}}{\text{Quantity of spirit}} = \dfrac{1/7}{6/7} = \dfrac{1}{6}$. or Ratio of water and spirit = 1 : 6.

Ex. 4. *In what ratio must a person mix three kinds of wheat costing him Rs. 1.20, Rs. 1.44 and Rs. 1.74 per kg., so that the mixture may be worth Rs. 1.41 per kg.?*

Sol. Step I. Mix wheats of first and third kind to get a mixture worth Rs. 1.41 per kg.?

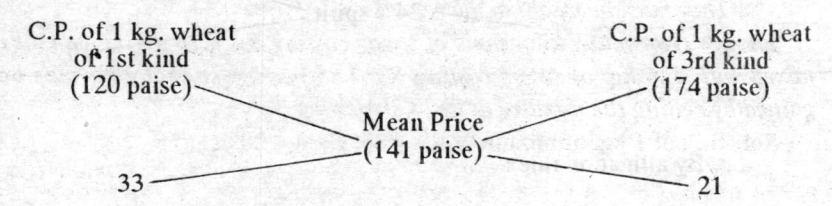

```
C.P. of 1 kg. wheat                          C.P. of 1 kg. wheat
   of 1st kind                                   of 3rd kind
   (120 paise)                                   (174 paise)
                        Mean Price
                        (141 paise)
      33                                               21
```

By alligation rule :

$$\frac{\text{(Quantity of 1st kind of wheat)}}{\text{(Quantity of 3rd kind of wheat)}} = \frac{33}{21} = \frac{11}{7}$$

i.e., they must be mixed in the ratio 11 : 7.

Step II. Mix wheats of 1st and 2nd kind to obtain a mixture worth of Rs. 1.41 per kg.

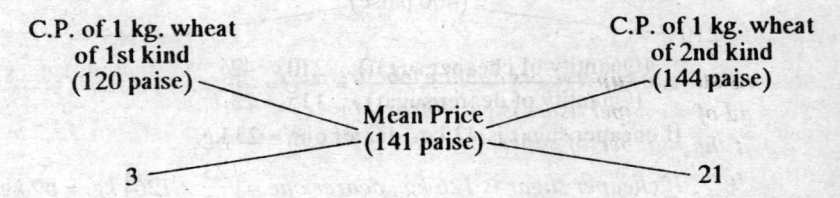

```
C.P. of 1 kg. wheat                                    C.P. of 1 kg. wheat
   of 1st kind                                             of 2nd kind
   (120 paise)                                             (144 paise)
                         Mean Price
                         (141 paise)
         3                                                      21
```

∴ By alligation rule :

$$\frac{\text{(Quantity of 1st kind of wheat)}}{\text{(Quantity of 2nd kind of wheat)}} = \frac{3}{21} = \frac{1}{7}.$$

i.e., they must be mixed in the ratio 1 : 7.

Thus, $\dfrac{\text{(Quantity of 2nd kind of wheat)}}{\text{(Quantity of 3rd kind of wheat)}}$

$= \dfrac{\text{(Quantity of 2nd kind of wheat)}}{\text{(Quantity of 1st kind of wheat)}} \times \dfrac{\text{(Quantity of 1st kind of wheat)}}{\text{(Quantity of 3rd kind of wheat)}}$

$= \left(\dfrac{7}{1} \times \dfrac{11}{7}\right) = \left(\dfrac{11}{1}\right).$

∴ *Quantities of wheat of (1st kind : 2nd kind : 3rd kind)*

$$= \left(1 : 7 : \frac{7}{11}\right) = (11 : 77 : 7).$$

Ex. 5. *A butler stole wine from a butt of sherry which contained 40% of spirit and he replaced, what he had stolen by wine containing only 16% spirit. The butt was then of 24% strength only. How much of the butt did he steal ?*

Sol.

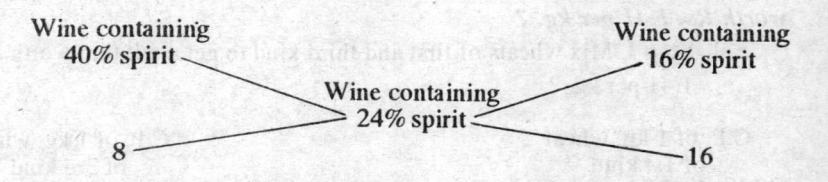

```
Wine containing                                        Wine containing
  40% spirit                                             16% spirit
                       Wine containing
                         24% spirit
         8                                                     16
```

∴ By alligation rule :

Alligation Or Mixture

$$\frac{\text{(Wine with 40\% Spirit)}}{\text{(Wine with 16\% Spirit)}} = \frac{8}{16} = \frac{1}{2}.$$

i.e., they must be mixed in the ratio (1 : 2).

Thus $\frac{1}{3}$ of the butt of sherry was left and hence the butler drew out $\frac{2}{3}$ of the butt.

Ex. 6. *The average weekly salary per head of the entire staff of a factory consisting of supervisors and the labourers is Rs. 60. The average salary per head of the supervisors is Rs. 400 and that of the labourers is Rs. 56. Given that the number of supervisors is 12, find the number of labourers in the factory.*

Sol.

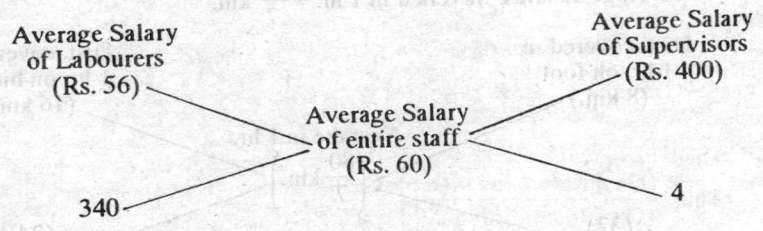

```
Average Salary                              Average Salary
of Labourers                                of Supervisors
(Rs. 56)                                    (Rs. 400)
         \                                 /
          \         Average Salary        /
           \        of entire staff      /
           /          (Rs. 60)           \
          /                               \
       340                                  4
```

By alligation rule:

$$\frac{\text{(Number of labourers)}}{\text{(Number of supervisors)}} = \frac{340}{4} = \frac{85}{1}$$

Thus, if the number of supervisors is 1, number of labourers = 85

∴ If the number of supervisors is 12, number of labourers
= 85 × 12 = 1020.

Ex. 7. *A man possessing Rs. 8400 lent a part of it at 8% simple interest and the remaining at $6\frac{2}{3}$% simple interest. His total income after $1\frac{1}{2}$ years was Rs. 882. Find the sum lent at different rates.*

Sol. Total interest on Rs. 8400 for $1\frac{1}{2}$ years is Rs. 882.

∴ Rate of interest = $\frac{100 \times 882 \times 2}{8400 \times 3}$ = 7%

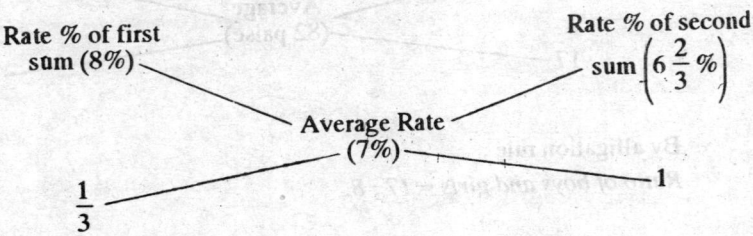

```
Rate % of first                             Rate % of second
sum (8%)                                    sum (6 2/3 %)
         \                                 /
          \         Average Rate          /
           \           (7%)              /
           /                              \
          /                                \
        1/3                                  1
```

Now,

By alligation rule :

$$\frac{\text{Money Given at 8\% S.I.}}{\text{Money Given at } 6\frac{2}{3}\% \text{ S.I.}} = \frac{1}{3} : 1 = 1 : 3$$

$\therefore$ Money lent at 8% = Rs. $\left(8400 \times \frac{1}{4}\right)$ = Rs. 2100

Money lent at $6\frac{2}{3}$ % = Rs. $\left(8400 \times \frac{3}{4}\right)$ = Rs. 6300

Ex. 8. *A man travelled a distance of 80 km. in 7 hours partly on foot at the rate of 8 km. per hour and partly on bicycle at 16 km. per hour. Find the distance travelled on foot.*

Sol. Average distance travelled in 1 hr. = $\frac{80}{7}$ km.

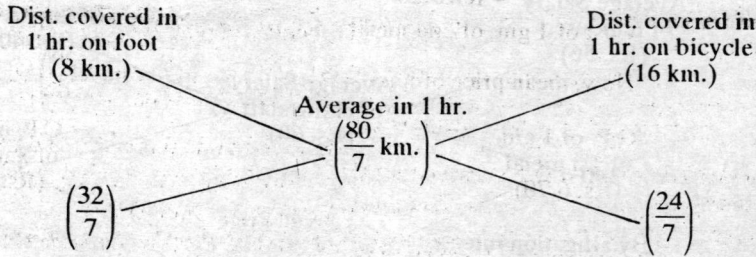

```
Dist. covered in                    Dist. covered in
1 hr. on foot                       1 hr. on bicycle
  (8 km.)                              (16 km.)
            Average in 1 hr.
              ($\frac{80}{7}$ km.)
  ($\frac{32}{7}$)                     ($\frac{24}{7}$)
```

By alligation rule :

$$\frac{\text{Time taken on foot}}{\text{Time taken on bicycle}} = \frac{32}{24} = 4 : 3.$$

Thus out of 7 hours in all, he took 4 hours to travel on foot.

Distance covered on foot in 4 hours = (4×8) km = 32 km.

Ex. 9. *A sum of Rs. 41 was divided among 50 boys and girls. Each boy gets 90 paise and a girl 65 paise. Find the number of boys and girls.*

Sol. Average money received by each = Rs. $\frac{41}{50}$ = 82 P.

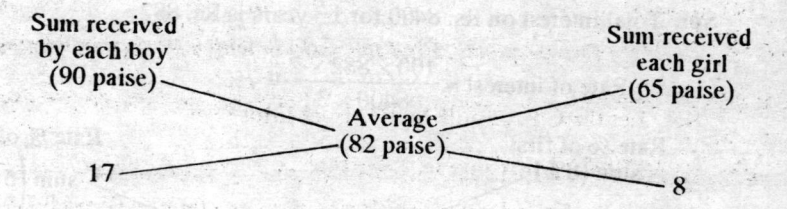

```
Sum received                        Sum received
by each boy                         each girl
(90 paise)                          (65 paise)
              Average
             (82 paise)
  17                                    8
```

By alligation rule :
Ratio of boys and girls = 17 : 8.

Alligation Or Mixture

Ex. 10. *A lump of two metals weighing 18 gms. is worth Rs. 87 but if their weights be interchanged, it would be worth Rs. 78.60. If the price of one metal be Rs. 6.70 per gm., find the weight of the other metal in the mixture.*

Sol. If one lump is mixed with another lump with the quantities of metals interchanged then the mixture of the two lumps would contain 18 gm. of first metal and 18 gm. of second metal and the price of the mixture would be Rs. $(87 + 78.60)$ or Rs. 165.60.

∴ cost of (18 gm. of 1st metal + 18 gm. of 2nd metal)
  $=$ Rs. 165.60

So, cost of (1 gm. of 1st metal + 1 gm. of 2nd metal)
  $=$ Rs. $\dfrac{165.60}{18} =$ Rs. 9.20.

(cost of 1 gm. of 1st metal) + (cost of 1 gm. of 2nd metal)
  $=$ Rs. 9.20

Cost of 1 gm. of 2nd metal $=$ Rs. $(9.20 - 6.70) =$ Rs. 2.50

Now, mean price of lump $=$ Rs. $\left(\dfrac{87}{18}\right)$ per gm. $=$ Rs. $\left(\dfrac{29}{6}\right)$.

C.P. of 1 gm of 1st metal (Rs. 6.70)   C.P. of 1 gm. of 2nd metal (Rs. 2.50)

Mean Price $\left(\text{Rs. } \dfrac{29}{6}\right)$

$\left(\dfrac{14}{6}\right)$ $\left(\dfrac{56}{30}\right)$

∴ By alligation rule :

$\dfrac{\text{Quantity of 1st metal}}{\text{Quantity of 2nd metal}} = \dfrac{14}{6} : \dfrac{56}{30} = 5 : 4.$

In 9 gm. of mix., 2nd metal $= 4$ gm.

In 18 gm. of mix., 2nd metal $= \left(\dfrac{4}{9} \times 18\right)$ gm. $= 8$ gm.

Ex. 11. *Two vessels A and B contain milk and water mixed in the ratio 5 : 2 and 8 : 5 respectively. Find the ratio in which these mixtures are to be mixed to get a new mixture containing milk and water in the ratio 9 : 4.*

Sol. Let the C.P. of milk be Re. 1 per litre.

Milk in 1 litre mix. in $A = \dfrac{5}{7}$ litre.

Milk in 1 litre mix. in $B = \dfrac{8}{13}$ litre.

Milk in 1 litre mix. of this mix. = $\frac{9}{13}$ litre.

C.P. of 1 litre mix. in A = Rs. $\frac{5}{7}$

C.P. of 1 litre mix. in B = Rs. $\frac{8}{13}$.

Mean price = Rs. $\left(\frac{9}{13}\right)$

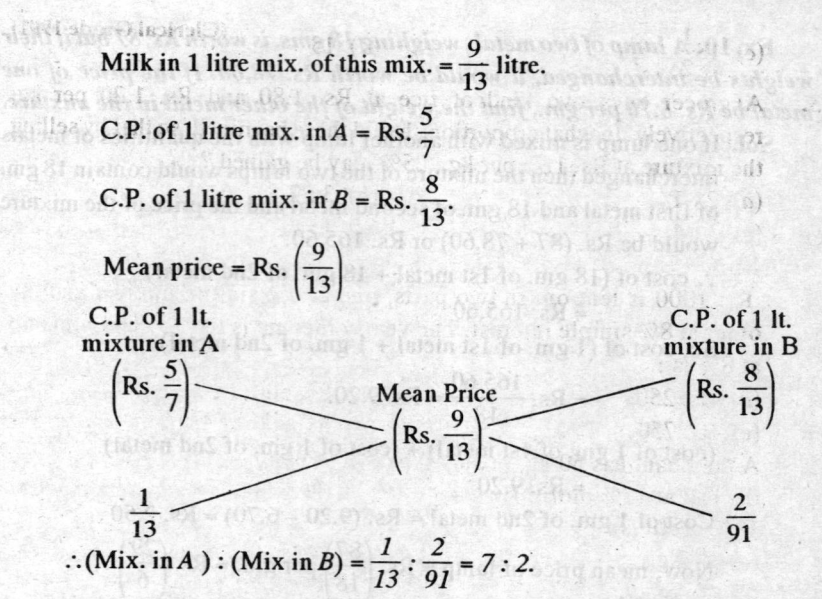

C.P. of 1 lt. mixture in A $\left(\text{Rs. } \frac{5}{7}\right)$ — Mean Price $\left(\text{Rs. } \frac{9}{13}\right)$ — C.P. of 1 lt. mixture in B $\left(\text{Rs. } \frac{8}{13}\right)$

$\frac{1}{13}$ — $\frac{2}{91}$

∴ (Mix. in A) : (Mix in B) = $\frac{1}{13} : \frac{2}{91}$ = 7 : 2.

Ex. 12. *A container contains 80 kg. of milk. From this container, 8 kg. of milk was taken out and replaced by water. This process was further repeated two times. How much milk is now contained by the container?*

Remarks. Amount of liquid left after n operations, when the container originally contains x units of liquid, from which y units is taken out each time is $\left[x\left(1-\frac{y}{x}\right)^n\right]$ units.

Sol. Amount of milk left

$80\left[\left(1-\frac{8}{80}\right)^3\right]$ kg. = 58.34 kg.

EXERCISE 23 (Objective Type Questions)

1. In what proportion must wheat at Rs. 1.60 per kg. be mixed with wheat at Rs. 1.45 per kg., so that the mixture be worth Rs. 1.54 per kg.?
   (a) 2 : 3 (b) 3 : 2
   (c) 3 : 4 (d) 4 : 3

2. 15 litres of a mixture contains 20% alcohol and the rest water. If 3 litres of water be mixed in it, the percentage of alcohol in the new mixture will be :
   (a) 17 (b) $16\frac{2}{3}$

(c) $18\frac{1}{2}$ (d) 15

(Clerical Grade 1991)

3. A grocer buys two kind of rice at Rs. 1.80 and Rs. 1.20 per kg. respectively. In what proportion should these be mixed, so that by selling the mixture at Rs. 1.75 per kg., 25% may be gained ?
   (a) 2 : 1   (b) 3 : 2
   (c) 3 : 4   (d) 1 : 2
   Hint. Mean Price = Rs. 1.40.

4. Rs. 1000 is lent out in two parts, one at 6% simple interest and the other at 8% simple interest. The yearly income is Rs. 75. The sum lent at 8% is :
   (a) Rs. 250   (b) Rs. 500
   (c) Rs. 750   (d) Rs. 600

5. A merchant has 50 kg. of sugar, part of which he sells at 8% profit and the rest at 18% profit. He gains 14% on the whole. The quantity sold at 18% profit is :
   (a) 20 kg.   (b) 30 kg.
   (c) 15 kg.   (d) 35 kg.

6. A mixture of 20 kg. of spirit and water contains 10% water. How much water must be added to this mixture to raise the percentage of water to 25% ?
   (a) 4 kg.   (b) 5 kg.
   (c) 8 kg.   (d) 30 kg.

7. Kantilal mixes 80 kg. of sugar worth of Rs. 6.75 per kg. with 120 kg. worth of Rs. 8 per kg. At what rate shall he sell the mixture to gain 20% ?
   (a) Rs. 7.50   (b) Rs. 9
   (c) Rs. 8.20   (d) Rs. 8.85

(S.B.I. P.O. Exam. 1987)

8. A jar full of whisky contains 40% of alcohol. A part of this whisky is replaced by another containing 19% alcohol and now the percentage of alcohol was found to be 26. The quantity of whisky replaced is :
   (a) $\frac{2}{5}$ (b) $\frac{1}{3}$
   (c) $\frac{2}{3}$ (d) $\frac{3}{5}$

(Hotel Management, 1991)

9. Two vessels A and B contain milk and water mixed in the ratio 5 : 3 and 2 : 3. When these mixtures are mixed to form a new mixture containing half milk and half water, they must be taken in the ratio :
   (a) 2 : 5   (b) 3 : 5
   (c) 4 : 5   (d) 7 : 3

10. The ratio of milk and water in 66 kg of adulterated milk is 5 : 1. Water is added to it to make the ratio 5 : 3. Tho quantity of water added is :
   (a) 22 kg.   (b) 24.750 kg.
   (c) 16.500 kg.   (d) 20 kg.

11. Some amount out of Rs. 7000 was lent at 6% p.a. and the remaining at 4% p.a. If the total simple interest from both the fractions in 5 years was Rs. 1600, the sum lent at 6% p.a. was :
   (a) Rs. 2000   (b) Rs. 5000
   (c) Rs. 3500   (d) none of these
   (Bank P.O. 1988)

12. 729 ml. of a mixture contains milk and water in the ratio 7 : 2. How much more water is to be added to get a new mixture containing milk and water in ratio 7 : 3 ?
   (a) 600 ml.   (b) 710 ml.
   (c) 520 ml.   (d) none of these   (Railways, 1991)

13. A dishonest milkman professes to sell his milk at C.P. but he mixes it with water and thereby gains 25%. The percentage of water in the mixture is :
   (a) 25%   (b) 20%
   (c) 4%   (d) none of these

14. A sum of Rs. 41 was divided among 50 boys and girls. Each boy gets 90 paise and a girl 65 paise. The number of boys is :
   (a) 16   (b) 34
   (c) 14   (d) 36

15. A can contains a mixture of two liquids A and B in proportion 7 : 5. When 9 litres of mixture are drawn off and the can is filled with B, the proportion of A and B becomes 7 : 9. How many litres of liquid A was contained by the can initially ?
   (a) 25   (b) 10
   (c) 20   (d) 21   (Railways, 1991)

16. In a mixture of 60 litres, the ratio of milk and water is 2 : 1. If the ratio of the milk and water is to be 1 : 2, then the amount of water to be further added is :
   (a) 20 litres   (b) 30 litres
   (c) 40 litres   (d) 60 litres   (N.D.A. Exam. 1990)

ANSWERS (Exercise 23)

1. (b)   2. (b)   3. (d)   4. (c)   5. (b)   6. (a)
7. (b)   8. (c)   9. (c)   10. (a)   11. (a)   12. (d)
13. (b)   14. (b)   15. (d)   16. (d).

Alligation Or Mixture 393

HINTS & SOLUTIONS (Exercise 17B)

1.

C.P. of 1 kg. of dearer wheat (160 paise) — Mean Price (154 paise) — C.P. of 1 kg. of cheaper wheat (145 paise)

9 ———— 6

∴ (Dearer wheat) : (cheaper wheat) = 9 : 6 = 3 : 2.

2. Initially, the mixture contains 3 litres of alcohol and 12 litres of water. Afterwards, the mixture contains 3 litres of alcohol and 15 litres of water.

∴ $Percentage\ of\ alcohol = \left(\frac{3}{18} \times 100\right)\% = 16\frac{2}{3}\%$.

3. S.P. of 1 kg. mixture = Rs. 1.75, Gain = 25%.

∴ Mean price = Rs. $\left(\frac{1.75 \times 100}{125}\right)$ = Rs. 1.40.

∴ (Dearer rice) : (cheaper rice) = 20 : 40 = 1 : 2.

4. Total interest = Rs. 75.

Average rate = $\left(\frac{100 \times 75}{1000 \times 1}\right)\% = 7\frac{1}{2}\%$

∴ (Sum at 6%) : (Sum at 8%) = $\frac{1}{2} : \frac{3}{2}$ = 1 : 3.

Hence, sum at 8% = Rs. $\left(1000 \times \frac{3}{4}\right)$ = Rs. 750.

5.

1st part profit (8%) — Mean profit (14%) — 2nd part profit (18%)

4 ———— 6

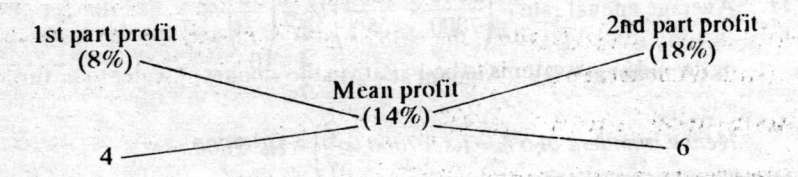

Ratio of 1st and 2nd part = 4 : 6 = 2 : 3.

∴ $Quantity\ sold\ at\ 18\% = \left(50 \times \frac{3}{5}\right)$ kg. = 30 kg.

6. In first mixture :

water = $\left(\dfrac{10}{100} \times 20\right)$ kg. and spirit = 18 kg.

In second mixture :
75 kg. spirit is contained in a mix. of 100 kg.

$\therefore$ 18 kg. spirit is contained in a mix. of $\left(\dfrac{100}{75} \times 18\right)$ = 24 kg.

So, water to be added = (24 – 20) kg. = 4 kg.

7. Total C.P. of 200 kg. of mixture
= Rs. (80 × 6.75 + 120 × 8) = Rs. 1500.
Average rate = Rs. 7.50 per kg.
Required rate = 120% of Rs. 7.50 = Rs. 9 per kg.

8. Using the method of alligation.
Required ratio = 7 : 14 = 1 : 2
$\therefore$ Required quantity = $\dfrac{2}{3}$.

9. Milk in A = $\dfrac{5}{8}$ of whole, Milk in B = $\dfrac{2}{5}$ of whole, Milk in mixture of A and B = $\dfrac{1}{2}$.

$\therefore$ By alligation rule, (Mix. in A) : (Mix in B) = $\dfrac{1}{10} : \dfrac{1}{8}$ = 4 : 5.

10. **In first mixture :**
Milk = $\left(\dfrac{66 \times 5}{6}\right)$ = 55 kg. and water = 11 kg.

In second mixture :
If milk is 55 kg., then water = $\left(\dfrac{3}{5} \times 55\right)$ = 33 kg.

$\therefore$ water to be added = 22 kg.

11. Average annual rate = $\left(\dfrac{1600}{7000} \times \dfrac{1000}{5}\right)\%$ = $\left(\dfrac{32}{7}\right)\%$

$\therefore$ (Amount at 6%) : (Amount at 4%) = $\dfrac{4}{7} : \dfrac{10}{7}$ = 2 : 5.

Hence, sum lent at 6% = Rs. $\left(7000 \times \dfrac{2}{7}\right)$ = Rs. 2000.

12. Milk = $\left(729 \times \dfrac{7}{9}\right)$ = 567 ml.

Water = (729 – 567) = 162 ml.

Now, $\dfrac{567}{162 + x} = \dfrac{7}{3} \Rightarrow x = 81$.

13. Let C.P. of 1 litre of milk be Re. 1.

Alligation Or Mixture

Then, S.P. of 1 litre of mixture = Re.1.
Gain = 25%.

$\therefore$ C.P. of 1 litre of mixture = Re. $\left(\dfrac{100}{125} \times 1\right)$ = Re. $\dfrac{4}{5}$.

$\therefore$ Ratio of milk and water = $\dfrac{4}{5} : \dfrac{1}{5}$ = 4 : 1.

Hence, percentage of water in the mixture = $\left(\dfrac{100 \times 1}{5}\right)$ % = 20%.

14. Average money received by each = Rs. (41/50) = 82 paise.
    Ratio of boys and girls = 17 : 8.
    $\therefore$ Number of boys = $\left(50 \times \dfrac{17}{25}\right)$ = 34.

15. Let the can initially contain $7x$ litres and $5x$ litres of mixtures A and B respectively. Thus, out of $12x$ litres of total mixture, 9 litres were taken out.
    Quantity of A in mix. left
    $= \left(7x - \dfrac{9}{12x} \times 7x\right) = \left(\dfrac{28x - 21}{4}\right)$ litres.
    Quantity of B in mix. left
    $= \left(5x - \dfrac{9}{12x} \times 5x\right) = \left(\dfrac{20x - 15}{4}\right)$ litres
    $\therefore \left(\dfrac{28x-21}{4} : \dfrac{20x-15}{4} + 9\right) :: (7 : 9)$ or $x = 3$.

16. Ratio of milk and water in mixture of 60 litres = 2 : 1.
    $\therefore$ Quantity of milk = 40 litres.
    Quantity of water = 20 litres.
    If ratio of milk and water is to be 1 : 2, then in 40 litres of milk, water should be 80 litres.
    $\therefore$ Quantity of water to be added = 60 litres.

24
RACES & GAMES OF SKILL

Races : *A contest of speed in running, riding, driving, sailing or rowing is called a* **race.** *The ground or path on which contests are made is called a* **race course.** *The point from which a race begins is known as a* **starting point.** *The point set to bound a race is called a* **winning post or a goal.** *The person who first reaches the winning post is called a* **winner.** *If all the persons contesting a race reach the goal exactly at the same time, then the race is said to be a* **dead–heat race.**

Suppose A and B are two contestants in a race. If, before the start of the race, A is at the starting point and B is ahead of A by 15 metres. Then A is said to give B, a start of 15 metres. To cover a race of 200 metres in this case, A will have to cover a distance of 200 metres and B will have to cover (200–15) or 185 metres only.

In a 100 metres race, 'A can give B 15 metres' or 'A can give B, a start of 15 metres' or 'A beats B by 15 metres', means that while A runs 100 metres, B runs (100–15) or 85 metres.

Games. '*A game of 100* means that the person among the contestants who scores 100 points first is the winner.' If A scores 100 points, while B scores only 80 points, then we say that A can give B 20 points.

Solved Examples

Ex. 1. *In a km. race A beats B by 35 metres or 7 seconds. Find A's time over the course.*

Sol. Here B runs 35 metres in 7 seconds.

$\therefore$ B,s time over the course $= \left(\dfrac{7}{35} \times 1000\right)$ sec. $= 200$ seconds

So A's time over the course $= (200 - 7)$ sec $= 193$ seconds
$= 3$ minutes 13 seconds.

Ex. 2. *A runs $1\dfrac{2}{3}$ times as fast as B. If A gives B a start of 80 metres how far must the winning post be so that A and B might reach it at the same time ?*

Sol. The rates of A and B are as $5 : 3$
 i.e., in a race of 5 metres, A gains 2 metres over B.
 2 metres are gained by A in a race of 5 metres.
 80 metres will be gained by A in a race of

$\left(\dfrac{5}{2} \times 80\right)$ metres = 200 metres.

∴ Winning post is 200 metres away from the starting point.

Ex. 3. *A, B and C are the three contestants in a km. race. If A can give B a start of 40 metres and A can give C a start of 64 metres., how many metres start can B give C ?*

Sol. While *A* covers 1000 metres, *B* covers (1000 – 40) or 960 metres and *C* covers (1000 – 64) or 936 metres.

Now when *B* covers 960 metres, *C* covers 936 metres.

∴ When *B* covers 1000 metres, *C* covers

$\left(\dfrac{936}{960} \times 1000\right)$ metres = 975 metres.

So, *B* gives *C* a start of (1000 – 975) or 25 metres.

Ex. 4. *A can run a km. in 3 min. 10 sec. and B in 3 min. 20 sec. By what distance can A beat B ?*

Sol. *A* beats *B* by 10 seconds.

Distance covered by *B* in 200 sec. = 1000 metres.

Distance covered by *B* in 10 sec. = $\dfrac{1000}{200} \times 10 = 50$ metres.

∴ *A* beats *B* by 50 metres.

Ex. 5. *In a 100 metres race, A runs at 6 km. per hour. If A gives B a start of 4 metres and still beats him by 12 seconds, what is the speed of B?*

Sol. Time taken by *A* to cover 100 metres.

$= \left(\dfrac{60 \times 60}{6000} \times 100\right)$ sec. = 60 sec.

∴ *B* covers (100 – 4) or 96 metres in (60 + 12) or 72 sec.

Hence, speed of $B = \left(\dfrac{60 \times 60 \times 60}{72 \times 1000}\right)$ km./hr. = 4.8 km./hr.

Ex. 6. *A can run a kilometre in 4 minutes 50 seconds and B in 5 minutes. How many metre's start can A give B in a km. race so that the race may end in a dead heat ?*

Sol. Time taken by *A* to run 1 km. = 4 mts. 50 sec. = 290 sec.

Time taken by *B* to run 1 km. = 5 mts. = 300 sec.

∴ *A* can give *B*, a start of (300 – 290) or 10 sec.

Now, in 300 Seconds, *B* runs 1000 metres.

∴ In 10 seconds, *B* runs $\left(\dfrac{1000}{300} \times 10\right)$ metres = $33\dfrac{1}{3}$ metres.

So *A* can give *B* a start of $33\dfrac{1}{3}$ metres.

Ex. 7. *In a kilometre race, if A gives B, a start of 40 metres, then A wins by 19 seconds, but if A gives B, a start of 30 seconds, then B wins by 40 metres. Find the time taken by each to run a kilometre.*

Sol. Suppose that the time taken by A and B to run 1 km is x and y seconds respectively.

When A gives B, a start of 40 metres, then A has run 1000 metres, while B has to run only 960 metres.

Time taken by A to run 1000 m $= x$ sec.

Time taken by B to run 960 metres $= \left(\dfrac{y}{1000} \times 960\right)$ sec.

$\qquad\qquad\qquad\qquad\qquad\qquad\quad = \left(\dfrac{24}{25} y\right)$ sec.

Clearly, $\dfrac{24}{25} y - x = 19$ or $24y - 25x = 475$ ...(i)

Again, A gives B, a start of 30 seconds, then B runs for y seconds, while A runs for $(y - 30)$ seconds.

Now, in x seconds, A covers 1000 metres

$\therefore$ In $(y - 30)$ sec., A will cover $\left[\dfrac{1000}{x} \times (y - 30)\right]$ metres.

So, $1000 - \dfrac{1000 \times (y - 30)}{x} = 40$ or $25y - 24x = 750$ ...(ii)

Solving (i) and (ii) we get, $x = 125$ & $y = 150$.

$\therefore$ *Time taken by A to run 1 km. = 125 sec.*

Time taken by B to run 1 km. = 150 sec.

Ex. 8. *A and B run a km. and A wins by 1 minute. A and C run a km and A wins by 375 metres. B and C run a km and B wins by 30 seconds. Find the time taken by each to run a km.*

Sol. Since A beats B by 60 seconds and B beats C by 30 seconds, so A beats C by 90 seconds. But, it being given that A beats C by 375 metres. So, it means that C covers 375 metres in 90 seconds.

$\therefore$ Time taken by C to cover 1 km. $= \left(\dfrac{90}{375} \times 1000\right)$ sec.

$\qquad\qquad\qquad\qquad\qquad\qquad\quad = 240$ seconds.

Time taken by A to cover 1 km.$= (240 - 90)$ sec. $= 150$ *seconds.*

Time taken by B to cover 1 km. $= (240 - 30)$ sec. $= 210$ *seconds.*

Ex. 9. *A and B run a race. A has a start of 50 metres and A sets off 6 minutes before B, at the rate of 10 km an hour. How soon will B overtake A, if his rate of running is 12 km an hour.*

Sol. Distance run by A in 6 minutes $= \left(\dfrac{10}{60} \times 6\right)$ km $= 1$ km

Thus, A has a start of $(1000 + 50)$ or 1050 metres.

Races & Games of Skill

So, in order to overtake A, B has to gain 1050 metres.
Now, 2000 metres is gained by B in 60 minutes.
So, 1050 metres will be gained by B in
$$\left(\frac{60}{2000} \times 1050\right) mts. = 31 \ min. \ 30 \ sec.$$

Ex. 10. *In a race of 600 metres, A can beat B by 60 metres and in a race of 500 metres, B can beat C by 50 metres. By how many metres will A beat C in a race of 400 metres ?*

Sol. Clearly, if A runs 600 metres, B runs = 540 metres.
$\therefore$ If A runs 400 metres, B runs $= \left(\frac{540}{600} \times 400\right) = 360$ metres.
Again, when B runs 500 metres, C runs = 450 metres.
$\therefore$ When B runs 360 metres, C runs $= \left(\frac{450}{500} \times 360\right)$ metres.
$\qquad\qquad\qquad\qquad\qquad\qquad\qquad\quad = 324$ metres.
So, A beats C by $(400 - 324)$ or 76 metres.

Ex. 11. *A can give, B 20 metres and C 25 metres in a 100 metres race, while B can give C one second over the course. How long does each take to run 100 metres ?*

Sol. It is clear that, when A runs 100 metres, then B runs 80 metres and C runs 75 metres.
$\therefore$ When B runs 100 metres, C runs $= \left(\frac{75}{80} \times 100\right)$
$\qquad\qquad\qquad\qquad\qquad\qquad = \left(\frac{375}{4}\right)$ metres.
Thus, B beats C by $\left(100 - \frac{375}{4}\right) = \frac{25}{4}$ metres.
But, it being given that B beats C by 1 second.
$\therefore \frac{25}{4}$ metres are covered by C in 1 second.
So, 100 metres are covered by B in $\left(\frac{4}{25} \times 100\right) = 16$ seconds.
$\therefore$ 100 metres are covered by B in $(16 - 1)$ or 15 seconds.
Now 80 metres are covered by B in $\left(\frac{15}{100} \times 80\right)$ or 12 seconds.
$\therefore$ *100 metres are covered by A in 12 seconds.*

Games of Skill.

Ex. 12. *At a game of billiards, A can give B 10 points in 60 and he can give C 15 in 60. How many can B give C in a game of 90 ?*

Sol. If A scores 60 points, then B scores 50 points.

If A scores 60 points, then C scores 45 point
Now, when B scores 50 points, C scores 45 points.
$\therefore$ When B scores 90 points, C scores $\left(\dfrac{45}{50} \times 90\right) = 81$ points.
Hence, B can give C, 9 points in a game of 90.

Ex. 13. *In a game of billiards, A can give B 12 points in 60 and A can give C 10 in 90. How many can C give B in a game of 70 ?*

Sol. If A scores 60 points, then B scores 48 points.
Also, if A scores 90 points, then C scores 80 points.
$\therefore$ If A scores 60 points, then C scores $\left(\dfrac{80}{90} \times 60\right) = \left(\dfrac{160}{3}\right)$ points.
Now, when C scores $\dfrac{160}{3}$ points, B scores 48 points
$\therefore$ When C scores 70 points, B scores $\left(\dfrac{48 \times 3}{160} \times 70\right) = 63$ points.

Ex. 14. *In a game, A can give B 20 points, A can give C 32 points and B can give C 15 points. How many points make the game ?*

Sol. Suppose x points make the game.
Clearly, when A scores x points, B scores $(x - 20)$ points and C scores $(x - 32)$ points.
Now, when B scores x points, C scores $(x - 15)$ points.
When B scores $(x - 20)$ points, C scores $\left[\dfrac{(x-15)}{x} \times (x - 20)\right]$ points.
$\therefore \dfrac{(x - 15)(x - 20)}{x} = (x - 32)$ or $x = 100$.
Hence, 100 points make the game.

Running Round A Circle.

Ex. 15. *Two men A and B run a 4 km race on a course 250 metres round. If their rates be 5 : 4, how often does the winner pass the other ?*

Sol. Clearly, when A makes 5 rounds, then B makes 4 rounds
Distance covered by A in 5 rounds $\left(\dfrac{5 \times 250}{1000}\right)$ km. $= \left(\dfrac{5}{4}\right)$ km.
Distance covered by B in 4 rounds $= \left(\dfrac{4 \times 250}{1000}\right)$ km. $= 1$ km.
It is clear that A passes B each time, when A makes 5 rounds.
In other words after covering $\dfrac{5}{4}$ km. each time, A passes B.
$\therefore$ In covering $\dfrac{5}{4}$ km., A passes B 1 time.
So, in covering 4 km. A passes B

Races & Games of Skill

$$\left(\frac{1\times 4}{5}\times 4\right)=3\frac{1}{5} \text{ times. i.e., 3 times.}$$

Ex. 16. *Two men, A and B, walk round a circle 1200 metres in circumference. A walks at the rate of 150 metres and B at the rate of 80 metres per minute. If they both start at the same time from the same point and walk in the same direction, when will they be together again for the first time and when will they be together again at the starting point for the first time ?*

Sol. A and B will be together again for the first time when A has gained one complete round on B.

Now, A gains 70 metres on B in 1 min.

∴ A gains 1200 metres on B in $\left(\frac{1}{70}\times 1200\right)=17\frac{1}{7}$ min.

Thus, A and B will be together for the first time in $17\frac{1}{7}$ min.

Again, time taken by A to make 1 round $=\left(\frac{1200}{150}\right)$ min. = 8 min.

Time taken by B to make 1 round $=\left(\frac{1200}{80}\right)=$ min = 115 min.

Thus A will be at the starting point after each interval of 8 min. and B after each interval of 15 minutes. So, they will be together at the starting point after 120 minutes. (L.C.M. of 8 & 15). Thus, A and B will be together at the starting point for the first time after 2 hours.

Ex. 17. *Three men A, B and C walk round a circle 1760 metres in circumference at the rates of 160 metres, 120 metres and 105 metres per minute respectively. If they all start together and walk in the same direction, when will they be first together again ?*

Sol. To gain 40 metres over B, A takes 1 min.

To gain 1760 metres over B, A takes $\left(\frac{1}{40}\times 1760\right)=44$ min.

Again, to gain 55 metres over C, A takes 1 min.

∴ To gain 1760 metres over C, A

takes $\left(\frac{1}{55}\times 1760\right)$ min. = 32 min.

Thus, A and B will be together after 44 minutes, while A and C are together again after 32 minutes.

Now, L.C.M. of 44 & 32 is 352.

So, A, B & C are first together again after 352 minutes or 5 hrs. 32 minutes.

EXERCISE 24 (OBJECTIVE TYPE QUESTIONS)

1. A can run 100 metres in 27 seconds and B in 30 seconds. A will beat B by
   - (a) 9 metres
   - (b) 10 metres
   - (c) $11\frac{1}{8}$ metres
   - (d) 12 metres

2. A can run a kilometer in 4 min. 54 sec. and B in 5 min. How many metres start can A give B in a km. race so that the race may end in a dead heat ?
   - (a) 20 metres
   - (b) 16 metres
   - (c) 18 metres
   - (d) 14.5 metres

3. In a 300 metres race A beats B by 15 metres or 5 seconds. A's time over the course is
   - (a) 100 seconds
   - (b) 95 seconds
   - (c) 105 seconds
   - (d) 90 seconds

4. In a 100 metres race, A can beat B by 25 metres and B can beat C by 4 metres. In the same race, A can beat C by :
   - (a) 29 metres
   - (b) 21 metres
   - (c) 28 metres
   - (d) 26 metres

5. In a 100 metres race A can give B 10 metres and C 28 metres. In the same race, B can give C :
   - (a) 18 metres
   - (b) 20 metres
   - (c) 27 metres
   - (d) 9 metres

6. A can run 20 metres while B runs 25 metres. In a km. race B beats A by :
   - (a) 250 metres
   - (b) 225 metres
   - (c) 200 metres
   - (d) 125 metres

7. A runs $1\frac{3}{4}$ times as fast as B. If A gives B a start of 60 metres, how far must the winning post be in order that A and B reach it at the same time ?
   - (a) 105 metres
   - (b) 80 metres
   - (c) 140 metres
   - (d) 45 metres

8. In a 500 metres race, the ratio of speeds of two contestants A and B is 3 : 4. A has a start of 140 metres. Then, A wins by :
   - (a) 60 metres
   - (b) 40 metres
   - (c) 20 metres
   - (d) 10 metres

9. In a 100 metres race, A beats B by 10 metres and C by 1 metre. In a race of 180 metres, B will beat C by :
   - (a) 5.4 metres
   - (b) 4.5 metres
   - (c) 5 metres
   - (d) 6 metres

10. A can beat B by 31 metres and C by 18 metres in a race of 200 metres. In a race of 350 metres C will beat B by :
    (a) 22.75 metres (b) 25 metres
    (c) $7\frac{4}{7}$ metres (d) 19.5 metres

11. A and B take part in a 100 metres race. A runs at 5 km. per hour. A gives B a start of 8 metres and still beats him by 8 seconds. Speed of B is :
    (a) 5.15 km./hr. (b) 4.14 km./hr.
    (c) 4.25 km./hr. (d) 4.4 km./hr.

12. In a game of 100 points, A can give B 20 points and C 28 points. Then, B can give C :
    (a) 8 points (b) 10 points
    (c) 14 points (d) 40 points

13. At a game of billiards, A can give B 15 points in 60 and A can give C 20 in 60. How many can B give C in a game of 90 ?
    (a) 30 points (b) 20 points
    (c) 10 points (d) 12 points

SOLUTIONS (Exercise 24)

1. Distance covered by B in 3 seconds
$$= \left(\frac{100}{30} \times 3\right) \text{ metres} = 10 \text{ metres}.$$
∴ A beats B by 10 metres.

2. Distance covered by B in 6 seconds
$$= \left(\frac{1000}{300} \times 6\right) \text{ metres} = 20 \text{ metres}.$$
Thus, A beats B by 20 metres.
So, for a dead heat race, A must give B a start of 20 metres.

3. 15 metres are covered by B in 5 seconds
$$300 \text{ metres are covered by B in } \left(\frac{5}{15} \times 300\right) = 100 \text{ seconds}.$$
∴ Time taken by A = (100 − 5) = 95 *seconds*.

4. A : B = 100 : 75 and B : C = 100 : 96.
$$\therefore A : C = \frac{A}{B} \times \frac{B}{C} = \frac{100}{75} \times \frac{100}{96} = \frac{100}{72} = 100 : 72.$$
So, A beats C by (100 − 72) = 28 *metres*.

5. A : B : C = 100 : 90 : 72
$$\therefore B : C = \frac{90}{72} = \frac{\left(90 \times \frac{100}{90}\right)}{\left(72 \times \frac{100}{90}\right)} = \frac{100}{80} = (100 : 80)$$

So, B can give C 20 metres.

6. In a 25 metres race, B beats A by 5 metres

   In a km. race B beats A by $\left(\dfrac{5}{25} \times 1000\right) = 200$ metres.

7. Ratio of rates of A and B = 7 : 4
   i.e., 3 metres are gained by A in a race of 7 metres

   $\therefore$ 60 metres are gained by A in a race of $\left(\dfrac{7}{3} \times 60\right) = 140$ metres.

8. To reach the winning post A will have to cover a distance of (500 − 140) i.e., 360 metres
   While A covers 3 metres, B covers 4 metres
   While, A covers 360 metres, B covers $\left(\dfrac{4}{3} \times 360\right) = 480$ metres.

   So, A reaches the winning post while B remains 20 metres behind.
   $\therefore$ A wins by 20 metres.

9. A : B : C = 100 : 90 : 87

   $\therefore \dfrac{B}{C} = \dfrac{90}{87} = \dfrac{90 \times 2}{87 \times 2} = \dfrac{180}{174}$.

   So, while B covers 180 metres, C covers = 174 metres.
   $\therefore$ B beats C by 6 metres.

10. A : B : C = 200 : 169 : 182.

    $\therefore \dfrac{C}{B} = \dfrac{182}{169} = \dfrac{182 \times \left(\dfrac{350}{182}\right)}{169 \times \left(\dfrac{350}{182}\right)} = \dfrac{350}{325}$.

    So, while C covers 350 metres, B covers 325 metres
    $\therefore$ C beats B by 25 metres.

11. A's speed = $\left(5 \times \dfrac{5}{18}\right)$ metres/sec. = $\dfrac{25}{18}$ metres/sec.

    Time taken by A to cover 100 metres

    = $\left(100 \times \dfrac{18}{25}\right)$ sec. = 72 sec.

    $\therefore$ B covers 92 metres in (72 + 8) or 80 sec.

    B's speed = $\left(\dfrac{92}{80} \times \dfrac{18}{5}\right)$ km./hr. = 4.14 km./hr.

Races & Games of Skill

12. $A : B : C = 100 : 80 : 72$

$\therefore B : C = \dfrac{80}{72} = \dfrac{10}{9} = \dfrac{100}{90}$.

Thus, if B scores 100, C scores 90

$\therefore B$ can give C 10 points.

13. $A : B : C = 60 : 45 : 40$

$\therefore B : C = \dfrac{45}{40} = \dfrac{9}{8} = \dfrac{9 \times 10}{8 \times 10} = \dfrac{90}{80}$.

So, if B scores 90, then C scores 80

$\therefore B$ can give C 10 points in a game of 90.

ANSWERS (Exercise 24)

1. (b) 2. (a)   3. (b)   4. (c)   5. (b)   6. (c)
7. (c) 8. (c)   9. (d)   10. (b) 11. (b) 12. (b)
13. (c)

25
CALENDAR

Under this heading we mainly deal with finding the day of the week on a particular given date. The process of finding it lies in obtaining the number of odd days.

The number of days more than the complete number of weeks in a given period, are called **odd days.**

Leap & Ordinary Year. *Every year which is divisible by 4 such as 1992, is called a leap year. Every 4th century is a leap year but no other century is a leap year viz.* 400, 800, 1200, 1600 are all leap years, but none of 700, 900, 1100 etc. is a leap year.

An ordinary year has 365 days *i.e.* (52 weeks + 1 day).
A leap year has 366 days *i.e.* (52 weeks + 2 days).
An ordinary year has 1 odd day and a leap year has 2 odd days.
A century *i.e.* 100 years has 76 ordinary years and 24 leap years.
∴ 100 years = 76 ordinary years + 24 leap years
  = [(76 × 52) weeks + 76 days]
   + (24 × 52) weeks + 48 days]
  = (5217 weeks + 5 days) = 5 odd days.

i.e., 100 years contain 5 odd days.
200 years contain 10 and therefore 3 odd days.
300 years contain 15 and therefore 1 odd day.
400 years contain (20 + 1) and therefore 0 odd day.
Similarly, the years 800, 1200, 1600 etc. contain no odd day.
We count days according to number of odd days.
Sunday for 0 odd day, Monday for 1 odd day and so on.

Solved Problems.

Ex. 1. *Find the day of the week on*
  (i) 16th July, 1776.
  (ii) 12th January, 1979.
  Sol. (i) 16th July, 1776 means
    (1775 years + 6 months + 16 days)
  Now, 1600 years have 0 odd days.
    100 years have 5 odd days.
75 years contain 18 leap years & 57 ordinary years and therefore

Calendar

(36 + 57) or 93 or 2 odd days.

∴ 1775 years give 0 + 5 + 2 = 7 and so 0 odd day.

Also number of days from 1st Jan., 1776 to 16th July, 1776

Jan. Feb. March April May June July
31 + 29 + 31 + 30 + 31 + 30 + 16
= 198 days = 28 weeks + 2 days = 2 odd days.

∴ Total number of odd days = 0 + 2 = 2.

Hence the day on 16th July, 1776 was *'Tuesday'*.

(ii) 12th January, 1979 means, '(1978 years + 12 days)'

Now 1600 years have   0 odd days

300 years have 15 or   1 odd day

78 years have

$\begin{cases} 19 \text{ leap years} + 59 \text{ ordinary years} \\ = (38 + 59) \text{ or } 97 \text{ odd days } 6 \text{ odd days} \end{cases}$

12 days of January has 5 odd days

Total number of odd days : 0 + 1 + 6 + 5 = 12 *or 5 odd days.*

So, the day was *'Friday'*.

Ex. 2. *On what dates of August 1980 did Monday fall?*

Sol. First find the day on 1st August, 1980.

1st August, 1980 means, '(1979 years + 7 months + 1 day)'.

Now 1600 years contain 0 odd day.

300 years contain 15 or 79 years contain   1 odd day.

$\begin{cases} 19 \text{ leap years} + 60 \text{ ordinary years} \\ = 38 + 60 \text{ or } 98 \text{ or} \end{cases}$ 0 *odd day*

Thus 1979 years contain 0   1 + 0 = 1 *odd day.*

Number of days from Jan., 1980 upto 1st Aug., 1980.

Jan. Feb. March April May June July Aug.
31 + 29 + 31 + 30 + 31 + 30 + 31 + 1
= 214 days = 30 weeks + 4 days = 4 odd days.

Total number of odd days = 1 + 5 = 5.

So, on 1st Aug., 1980, it was 'Friday'.

So, 1st Monday in August, 1980 lies on 4th August.

∴ *Monday falls on 4th, 11th, 18th, & 25th in August, 1980.*

Ex. 3. *Prove that the calendar for 1990 will serve for 2001 also.*

Sol. In order that the calendar for 1934 and 1945 be the same, 1st January of both the years must be on the same day of the week. For this, the total number of odd days between 31st Dec. 1933 and 31st Dec. 1944 must be zero.

Odd days are as under :

Year	1990	1991	1992	1993	1994	1995
odd days	1	1	2	1	1	1

Year	1996	1997	1998	1999	2000 (leap)
odd days	2	1	1	1	2

∴ Total number of odd days = 14 days *i.e.* 0 odd days.
Hence the result follows.

Ex. 4. *Prove that the last day of a century can not be either Tuesday, Thursday or Saturday.*

Sol. Ist Century, *i.e.* 100 years contain 76 ordinary years & 24 leap years and therefore, (76 + 48) or 124 odd days or 5 odd days.
∴ The last day of 1st century is 'Friday'.
Two Centuries, *i.e.* 200 years contain 152 ordinary years & 48 leap years and therefore (152 + 96) or 248 or 3 odd days.
∴ The last day of 2nd century is 'Wednesday'.
Three Centuries, *i.e.* 300 years contain 228 ordinary years & 72 leap years and therefore, (228 + 144) or 372 or 1 odd day.
∴ The last day of third century is 'Monday'.
Four Centuries, *i.e.* 400 years contain 303 ordinary years & 97 leap years and therefore, (303 + 194) or 497 or 0 odd day.
∴ The last day of 4th century is 'Sunday'.
Since the order is continually kept in successive cycles, we see that the last day of a century can not be tuesday, Thursday or Saturday.

Ex. 5. *Prove that any date in March is the same day of the week as the corresponding date in November of that year.*

Sol. In order to prove the required result, we have to show that the total number of odd days between last day of February and last day of October is zero.
Number of days between these dates are :
March April May June July Aug. Sept. Oct.
31 + 30 + 31 + 30 + 31 + 31 + 30 + 31
= 245 days = 35 weeks = 0 odd day.
Hence, the result follows.

Exercise 25 A (Subjective)

1. Find the day of the week on :
   (*i*) 1st January, 1901
   (*ii*) 15th August, 1947
   (*iii*) 28th April, 1973
   (*iv*) 31st October, 1984
   (*v*) 14th March, 1993
   (*vi*) 27th December, 1985
2. On what dates of December, 1984 did Sunday fall ?

Calendar

Hint. *Find the day on 1st December 1984 which was Saturday. So Sunday fell on 2nd and therefore on 9th, 16th, 23rd & 30th.*

3. Prove that the calender for 1993 will serve for 1999 also.
4. Today is 3rd November. The day of the week is sunday. Last year was a leap year. What will be the day of the week on this date after 2 years ?
   Hints. *Clearly, none of the next 2 years is a leap year. Each year gives 1 odd day. So, the required day is 2 days beyond Sunday i.e. it is Tuesday.*
5. If the first day of the year 1979 was Monday, what day of the week must have been on 1st January, 1986 ?
   Hint. *Total number of odd days from 1st January 1979 to 1st January 1986 is 2. So, required day is 2 days beyond Monday.*

ANSWERS (Exercise 25A)

1. (i) Tuesday   (ii) Friday   (iii) Saturday
   (iv) Friday   (v) Wednesday   (vi) Sunday
2. 2nd, 9th, 16th, 23rd & 30th   4. Tuesday   5. Wednesday

EXERCISE 25 B (Objective Type Questions)

1. January 1, 1992 was a Wednesday. What day of the week will it be on January 1, 1993 ?
   (a) Monday   (b) Tuesday
   (c) Sunday   (d) Friday

2. On January 12, 1980, it was Saturday. The day of the week on January 12, 1979 was :
   (a) Saturday   (b) Friday
   (c) Sunday   (d) Thursday

3. On July, 2, 1985, it was Wednesday. The day of the week on July 2, 1984 was :
   (a) Wednesday   (b) Tuesday
   (c) Monday   (d) Thursday

4. Monday falls on 4th April, 1988. What was the day on 3rd November, 1987 ?
   (a) Monday   (b) Sunday
   (c) Tuesday   (d) Wednesday

5. Today is Friday. After 62 days it will be :
   (a) Friday   (b) Thursday
   (c) Saturday   (d) Monday

6. Smt. Indira Gandhi died on 31st October, 1984. The day of the week was:
   (a) Monday   (b) Tuesday
   (c) Wednesday   (d) Friday

7. The number of odd days in a leap year is :
   (a) 1 (b) 2
   (c) 3 (d) 4
8. The year next to 1988 having the same calendar as that of 1988 is :
   (a) 1990 (b) 1992
   (c) 1993 (d) 1995
9. The year next to 1991 having the same calendar as that of 1990 is :
   (a) 1998 (b) 2001
   (c) 2002 (d) 2003
10. Today is 1st August. The day of the week is Monday. this is a leap year. The day of the week on this day after 3 years will be :
    (a) Wednesday (b) Thursday
    (c) Friday (d) Saturday
11. How many days are there from 2nd January 1993 to 15th March 1993 :
    (a) 72 (b) 73
    (c) 74 (d) 71
12. The first republic day of India was celebrated on 26th January, 1950. It was :
    (a) Monday (b) Tuesday
    (c) Thursday (d) Friday
13. P.V. Narsimha Rao was elected party leader on 29th May, 1991. What was the day of the week ?
    (a) Tuesday (b) Friday
    (c) Wednesday (d) Sunday

SOLUTIONS (Exercise 25B)

1. 1992 being a leap year, it has 2 odd days. So, the first day of the year 1993 will be two days beyond Wednesday. *i.e.* it will be Friday.
2. The year 1979 being an ordinary year, it has 1 odd day.
   So, the day on 12th January 1980 is one day beyond the day on 12th January, 1979.
   But, January 12, 1980 being Saturday
   ∴ January 12, 1979 was Friday.
3. The year 1984 being a leap year, it has 2 odd days.
   So, the day on 2nd July, 1985 is two days beyond the day on 2nd July, 1984.
   But, 2nd July 1985 was Wednesday.
   ∴ 2nd July, 1984 was Monday.
4. Counting the number of days after 3rd November, 1987 we have :
   Nov. Dec. Jan. Feb. March April
   days 27 + 31 + 31 + 29 + 31 + 4
   = 153 days containing 6 odd days

Calendar

i.e., (7 − 6) = 1 day beyond the day on 4th April, 1988.
So, the day was Tuesday.

5. Each day of the week is repeated after 7 days.
   ∴ After 63 days, it would be Friday.
   So, after 62 days, it would be Thursday.

6. 1600 years contain 0 odd day; 300 years contain 1 odd day.
   Also, 83 years contain 20 leap years and 63 ordinary years and therefore (40 + 0) odd days i.e., 5 odd days.
   ∴ 1983 years contain (0 + 1 + 5) i.e., 6 odd days.
   Number of days from Jan., 1984 to 31st. Oct. 1984
   = (31 + 29 + 31 + 30 + 31 + 30 + 31 + 31 + 30 + 31) = 305 days
   = 4 odd days
   ∴ Total number of odd days = 6 + 4 = 3 odd days.
   So, 31st Oct., 1984 was Wednesday.

7. A leap year has (52 weeks + 2 days). So, the number of odd days in a leap year is 2.

8. Starting with 1988, we go on counting the number of odd days till the sum is divisible by 7
   Years → 1988 1989 1990 1991 1992
   Odd days → 2 1 1 1 2 = 7 i.e., odd days
   ∴ Calendar for 1993 is the same as that of 1988.

9. We go on counting the odd days from 1991 onwards till the sum is divisible by 7. The number of such days are 14 upto the year 2001.
   So, the calendar for 1991 will be repeated in the year 2002.

10. This being a leap year none of the next 3 years is a leap year. So, the day of the week will be 3 days beyond Monday i.e., it will be Thursday.

11. Jan. Feb. March
    30 + 28 + 15 = 73 days.

12. 1600 years have 0 odd day and 300 years have 1 odd day.
    49 years contain 12 leap years and 37 ordinary years and therefore (24 + 37) odd days i.e., 5 odd days
    i.e., 1949 years contain (0 + 1 + 5) or 6 odd days.
    26 days of January contain 5 odd days.
    Total odd days = (6 + 5) = 11 or 4 odd days.
    So, the day was Thursday.

13. Try youself. It was Wednesday

ANSWERS (Exercise 25 B)

1. (d)	2. (b)	3. (c)	4. (c)	5. (b)	6. (c)
7. (b)	8. (c)	9. (c)	10. (b)	11. (b)	12. (c)
13. (c)					

26

CLOCKS

The face or dial of a clock of watch is a circle whose circumference is divided into 60 equal parts, called *minute spaces*. The clock has two hands, the smaller one, called *hour hand* (or short hand) goes over 5 minute spaces whilst the larger one, called *minute hand* or (long hand) passes over 60 minute spaces.

In 60 minutes, the minute hand gains 55 minutes on the hour hand. It may be noted that :

(i) In every hour, both the hand coincide once.
(ii) When the two hands are at right angle, they are 15 minute spaces apart. This happens twice in every hour.
(iii) When the hands are in opposite directions, they are 30 minute spaces apart. This happens once in every hour.
(iv) The hands are in the same straight line when they are coincident or opposite to each other.

Too Fast & Too Slow : If a clock or watch indicates 9.15, when the correct time is 9, it is said to be 15 minutes too fast. On the other hand, if it indicates 8.45, when the correct time is 9, it is said to be 15 minutes too slow.

Solved Examples.

Ex. 1. *At what time between 3 and 4 O'clock are the hands of a clock together ?*

Sol. At 3 O'clock, the hour hand is at 3 and the minute hand is at 12. i.e., they are 15 min. spaces apart. To be together, the minute hand must gain 15 min. over the hour hand.
Now 55 min. are gained in 60 min.
$\therefore$ 15 min. will be gained in $\left(\dfrac{60}{55} \times 15\right)$ min. $= 16\dfrac{4}{11}$ min.
So, the hands will coincide at $16\dfrac{4}{11}$ min. past 3.

Ex. 2. *At what time between 4 and 5 O'clock will the hand of clock be at right angle ?*

Sol. At 4 O'clock, the minute hand will be 20 min. spaces behind the hour hand. Now, when the two hands are at right angle, they are 15 min. spaces apart. So, there are two cases :

Clocks

Case I. When the min. hand is 15 min. spaces behind the hour hand.
To be in this position, the min. hand will have to gain
$(20 - 15) = 5$ min. spaces.
Now, 55 min. spaces are gained in 60 min.

$\therefore$ 5 min. spaces are gained in $\left(\dfrac{60}{55} \times 5\right)$ min. $= 5\dfrac{5}{11}$ min.

$\therefore$ They are at right angle at $5\dfrac{5}{11}$ min. past 5.

Case II. When the min. hand is 15 min. spaces ahead of the hour hand.
To be in this position, the min. hand will have to gain
$(20 + 15) = 35$ min. spaces.
Now, 55 min. spaces are gained in 60 min.

$\therefore$ 35 min. spaces will be gained in $\left(\dfrac{60}{55} \times 35\right)$ min. $= 38\dfrac{2}{11}$ min.

So, they are at right angle at $38\dfrac{2}{11}$ min. past 4.

Ex. 3. *Find at what time between 8 and 9 O'clock will the hands of a clock be in the same straight line but not together.*

Sol. At 8 O'clock, the hour hand is at 8 and the min. hand is at 12 i.e., the two hands are 20 min. spaces apart. To be in the same straight line but not together they will be 30 min. spaces apart. So, the min. hand will have to gain $(30 - 20) = 10$ min. spaces over the hour hand.
Now, 55 min. are gained in 60 min.

10 min. will be gained in $\left(\dfrac{60}{55} \times 10\right)$ min. $= 10\dfrac{10}{11}$ min.

$\therefore$ The hand will be at right angle but not together at $50\dfrac{10}{11}$ min. past 8.

Ex. 4. *At what time between 5 and 6 are the hands of a clock 3 minutes apart?*

Sol. At 5 O'clock, the minute hand is 25 minute spaces apart.
Case I. *Minute hand is 3 minute spaces behind the hour hand.*
In this case, the minute hand has to gain $(25 - 3)$ i.e., 22 minute spaces.
Now, 55 min. are gained in 60 min.

22 min. are gained in $\left(\dfrac{60}{55} \times 22\right)$ min. $= 24$ min.

$\therefore$ The hands will be 3 minutes apart at 24 min. past 5.

Case II. *Minute hand is 3 minute spaces ahead of the hour hand.*

In this case, the minute hand has to gain (25 + 3) i.e., 28 minute spaces.
Now, 55 min. are gained in 60 min.

28 min. are gained in $\left(\dfrac{60}{55} \times 28\right) = 31\dfrac{5}{11}$ min.

∴ The hands will be 3 minutes apart at $31\dfrac{5}{11}$ min. past 5.

Ex. 5. *The minute hand of a clock overtakes the hour hand at intervals of 65 minutes of correct time. How much a day does the clock gain or lose ?*

Sol. In a correct clock, the minute hand gains 55 minute spaces over the hour hand in 60 minutes. To be together again, the minute hand must gain 60 minutes over the hour hand.

Now, 55 min. are gained in 60 min.

∴ 60 min. are gained in $\left(\dfrac{60}{55} \times 60\right)$ min. $= 65\dfrac{5}{11}$ min.

But, they are together after 65 minutes.

∴ Gain in 65 minutes $= \left(65\dfrac{5}{11} - 65\right) = \dfrac{5}{11}$ min.

Gain in 24 hrs. $= \left(\dfrac{5}{11} \times \dfrac{60 \times 24}{65}\right)$ min. $= 10\dfrac{10}{143}$ min.

Ex. 6. *A watch which gains uniformly, is 5 min. slow at 8 O'clock in the morning on Sunday, and is 5 minutes 48 seconds fast at 8 p.m. on following Sunday. When was it correct ?*

Sol. Time from 8 a.m. on Sunday to 8 p.m. on following Sunday = 7 days 12 hours = 180 hours.

Thus, the watch gains $\left(5 + 5\dfrac{4}{5}\right)$ min. or $\dfrac{54}{5}$ min. in 180 hours

Now, $\dfrac{54}{5}$ min. are gained in 180 hours.

∴ 5 min. are gained in $\left(\dfrac{180 \times 5}{54} \times 5\right)$ hours.

= 83 hrs. 20 min. = 3 days 11 hrs. 20 min.

Thus, the watch is correct 3 days 11 hrs. 20 min. after 8 a.m. on Sunday i.e., *it will be correct at 20 min. past 7 p.m. on Wednesday.*

Ex. 7. *A clock is set right at 8 a.m. The clock gains 10 minutes in 24 hours. What will be the true time when the clock indicates 1 p.m. on the following day ?*

Sol. Time from 8 a.m. on a day to 1 p.m. on the following day is 29 hrs.

Clocks

Now, 24 hrs. 10 min. of this clock are the same as 24 hours of the correct clock.

i.e., $\frac{145}{6}$ hrs. of this clock = 24 hrs. of correct clock.

29 hrs. of this clock = $\left(\frac{24 \times 6}{145} \times 29\right)$ hrs. of correct clock.

= 28 hrs. 48 min. of correct clock.

So, the correct time is 28 hrs. 48 min. after 8 a.m. or 48 min. past 12.

Ex. 8. *A clock is set right at 5 a.m. The clock loses 16 min. in 24 hours. What will be the true time when the clock indicates 10 p.m. on the 4th day?*

Sol. Time from 5 a.m. on a day to 10 p.m. on 4th day is 89 hours.

Now, 23 hrs. 44 min. of this clock are the same as 24 hours of the correct clock.

i.e., $\frac{356}{15}$ hrs. of this clock = 24 hrs. of correct clock.

∴ 89 hrs. of this clock = $\left(\frac{24 \times 15}{356} \times 89\right)$ hrs. of correct clock.

= 90 hrs. of correct clock.

So, the correct time is 11 p.m.

EXERCISE 26 (OBJECTIVE TYPE QUESTIONS)

1. At what time between 5 and 6 are the hands of a clock coincident?
   (a) 22 minutes past 5
   (b) 30 minutes past 5
   (c) $22\frac{8}{11}$ minutes past 5
   (d) $27\frac{3}{11}$ minutes past 5

2. At what time between 9 and 10 will the hands of a watch be together?
   (a) 45 minutes past 9
   (b) 50 minutes past 9
   (c) $49\frac{1}{11}$ minutes past 9
   (d) $48\frac{2}{11}$ minutes past 9

3. At what time between 7 and 8 will the hands of a clock be in the same straight line, but not together?
   (a) 5 minutes past 7
   (b) $5\frac{2}{11}$ minutes past 7
   (c) $5\frac{3}{11}$ minutes past 7
   (d) $5\frac{5}{11}$ minutes past 7

4. At what time between 4 and 5 will the hands of a watch point in opposite directions?
   (a) 45 minutes past 4
   (b) 40 minutes past 4
   (c) $50\frac{4}{11}$ minutes past 4
   (d) $54\frac{6}{11}$ minutes past 4

5. At what time between 5.30 and 6 will the hands of a clock be at right angles?
   (a) $43\frac{5}{11}$ minutes past 5
   (b) $43\frac{7}{11}$ minutes past 5
   (c) 40 minutes past 5
   (d) 45 minutes past 5

6. A watch, which gains uniformly, is 2 min. slow at noon on Monday, and is 4 min. 48 seconds fast at 2 p.m. on the following Monday. When was it correct?
   (a) 2 p.m. on Tuesday
   (b) 2 p.m. on Wednesday
   (c) 3 p.m. on Thursday
   (d) 1 p.m. on Friday

7. A watch which gains 5 seconds in 3 minutes was set right at 7 a.m. In the afternoon of the same day, when the watch indicated quarter past 4 O'clock, the true time is:
   (a) $59\frac{7}{12}$ minutes past 3
   (b) 4 p.m.
   (c) $58\frac{7}{11}$ minutes past 3
   (d) $2\frac{3}{11}$ minutes past 4

8. How much does a watch gain or lose per day, if its hands coincide every 64 minutes?
   (a) loses 96 minutes
   (b) loses 90 minutes
   (c) loses $36\frac{5}{11}$ minutes
   (d) loses $32\frac{8}{11}$ minutes

9. How many times do the hands of a clock coincide in a day?
   (a) 24
   (b) 20
   (c) 21
   (d) 22

10. How many times do the hands of a clock point towards each other in a day?
    (a) 24
    (b) 20
    (c) 12
    (d) 22

11. How many times are the hands of a clock at right angles in a day?
    (a) 24
    (b) 48
    (c) 22
    (d) 44

12. How many times in a day, are the hands of a clock straight?
    (a) 24
    (b) 48
    (c) 22
    (d) 44

13. At what angle the hands of a clock are inclined at 15 minutes past 5?
    (a) $72\frac{1}{2}°$
    (b) $67\frac{1}{2}°$
    (c) $58\frac{1}{2}°$
    (d) $64°$

SOLUTIONS (Exercise 26)

1. At 5 O'clock, the minute hand is 25 minute spaces apart.
   To be coincident, it must gain 25 minute spaces.
   Now, 55 minutes are gained in 60 minutes.

   25 minutes will be gained in $\left(\dfrac{60}{55} \times 25\right)$ min. or $27\dfrac{3}{11}$ min.

   So, the hands are coincident at $27\dfrac{3}{11}$ min. past 5.

2. To be together between 9 and 10, the minute hand has to gain 45 minute spaces.
   Now, 55 min. spaces are gained in 60 minutes.

   ∴ 45 min. spaces are gained in $\left(\dfrac{60}{55} \times 45\right)$ min. or $49\dfrac{1}{11}$ min.

   So, the hands are together at $49\dfrac{1}{11}$ min. past 9.

3. When the hands are in the same straight line, but not together, they are 30 min. spaces apart.
   At 7 O'clock, they are 25 min. spaces apart.
   So, the minute hand has to gain only 5 min. spaces
   Now, 55 min. spaces are gained in 60 min.

   5 min. spaces are gained in $\left(\dfrac{60}{55} \times 5\right)$ min. or $5\dfrac{5}{11}$ min.

   ∴ The hands are in the same straight line, but not together at $5\dfrac{5}{11}$ min. past 7.

4. At 4 O'clock, the hands are 20 min. spaces apart.
   To be in opposite directions, they must be 30 min. spaces apart.
   So, the min. hand has to gain 50 min. spaces.
   Now, 55 min. spaces are gained in 60 min.

   50 min. spaces are gained in $\left(\dfrac{60}{55} \times 50\right)$ min. or $54\dfrac{6}{11}$ min.

   ∴ The hands are in opposite direction at $54\dfrac{6}{11}$ min. past 4.

5. At 5 O'clock, the hands are 25 min. spaces apart. To be at right angles and that too between 5.30 and 6, the min. hand has to gain (25 + 15) or 40 min. spaces.
   Now, 55 min. spaces are gained in 60 min.

   ∴ 40 min. spaces are gained in $\left(\dfrac{60}{55} \times 40\right)$ min. or $43\dfrac{7}{11}$ min.

So, the hands are at right angles at $7\frac{7}{11}$ min. past 5.

6. Time from Monday noon to 2 p.m. on following Monday
$$= 7 \text{ days } 2 \text{ hours} = 170 \text{ hours.}$$
The watch gains $\left(2 + 4\frac{4}{5}\right)$ or $\frac{34}{5}$ min. in 170 hours.

∴ It will gain 2 min. in $\left(\frac{170 \times 5}{34} \times 2\right)$ hrs.= 50 hrs = 2 days 2hrs.

So, the watch is correct 2 days 2 hours after Monday noon. i.e., at 2 p.m. on Wednesday.

7. Time from 7 a.m. to quarter past 4
$$= 9 \text{ hours } 15 \text{ min.} = 555 \text{ min.}$$
Now, $\frac{37}{12}$ min. of this watch = 3 min. of the correct watch.

555 min. of this watch = $\left(\frac{3 \times 12}{37} \times 555\right)$ min.

$= \left(\frac{3 \times 12}{37} \times \frac{555}{60}\right)$ hrs. = 9 hrs. of the correct watch.

Correct time is 9 hours after 7 a.m. i.e., 4 p.m.

8. 55 min. spaces are covered in 60 min.

60 min. spaces are covered in $\left(\frac{60}{55} \times 60\right)$ min. or $65\frac{5}{11}$ min.

∴ Loss in 64 min. = $\left(65\frac{5}{11} - 64\right) = \frac{16}{11}$ min.

Loss in (24×60) min. = $\left(\frac{16}{11 \times 64} \times 24 \times 60\right)$ min. = $32\frac{8}{11}$ min.

9. The hands of a clock coincide 11 times in every 12 hours (because between 11 and 1, they coincide only once, at 12 O'clock). So, the hands coincide 22 times in a day.

10. The hands of a clock point towards each other 11 times in every 12 hours (because between 5 and 7, at 6 O'clock only they point towards each other).
So, in a day the hands point towards each other 22 times.

11. In 12 hours, they are at right angles 22 times (because two positions 3 O'clock and 9 O'clock are common).
So, in a day they are at right angles 44 times.

12. The hands coincide or are in opposite direction (22 + 22) i.e., 44 times in a day.

13. At 15 minutes past 5, the minute hand is at 3 and hour hand slightly advanced from 5. Angle between their 3rd and 5th position

Angle through which hour hand shifts in 15 mts. is $\left(15 \times \frac{1}{2}\right) = 7\frac{1}{2}°$.

∴ Required angle $= \left(60 + 7\frac{1}{2}\right) = 67\frac{1}{2}°$

ANSWERS (Exercise 26)

1. (d)   2. (c)   3. (d)   4. (d)   5. (b)   6. (b)
7. (b)   8. (d)   9. (d)   10. (d)   11. (b)   12. (d)
13. (b)

27
STOCK & SHARES

Stock. In order to meet the expanses of a certain plan, the Government of India sometimes raises a loan from the public at a certain fixed rate of interest. Bonds or Promisery Notes each of a fixed value are issued for sale to the public.

If a man purchases a bond of Rs. 100 at which 5% interest has been fixed by the Government, then the holder of such a bond is said to have, 'a Rs. 100 stock at 5%'. Here Rs. 100 is called the Face value of the stock. Usually, a period is fixed for the repayment of the loan i.e., the stock matures at a fixed date only. Now, if a person holding a stock is in need of the money before the date of maturity of stock, he can sell the bond or bonds to some other person, whereby the claim of interest is transferred to that person.

Stocks are sold and bought in the open market through brokers at stocks exchanges. The broker's charge is usually called 'brokerage'

Remarks
(i) When stock is purchased, brokerage is added to cost price.
(ii) When stock is sold, brokerage is subtracted from selling price.

The selling price of a Rs. 100 stock is said to be at par, above par (or at a premium) and below par (or at a discount), according as the selling price of this stock is Rs. 100 exactly, more than Rs. 100 and less than Rs. 100 respectively.

Remark. 'By a Rs. 700, 6% stock at 97', we mean a stock whose face value is Rs. 700, the market price of a Rs. 100 stock is Rs. 97 and the annual interest on this stock is 5% of the face value.

Solved Problems

Ex. 1. *Find the cost of :*

(i) Rs. 9100, $8\frac{3}{4}$% stock at 92.

(ii) Rs. 8500, $9\frac{1}{2}$% stock at 6 permium.

(iii) Rs. 7200, 10% stock at 7 discount.

(iv) Rs. 6400, 8% stock at par $\left(\text{brokerage } \frac{1}{8}\%\right)$.

Sol. (i) Cost of Rs. 100 stock = Rs. 92

Stock & Shares

Cost of Rs. 9100 stock = Rs. $\left(\dfrac{92}{100} \times 9100\right)$ = Rs. 8372.

(ii) Cost of Rs. 100 stock = Rs. (100 + 6) = Rs. 106.

Cost of Rs. 8500 stock = Rs. $\left(\dfrac{106}{100} \times 8500\right)$ = Rs. 9010.

(iii) Cost of Rs. 100 stock = Rs. (100 − 7) = Rs. 93

Cost of Rs. 7200 stock = Rs. $\left(\dfrac{93}{100} \times 7200\right)$ Rs. = 6696.

(iv) C.P. of Rs. 100 stock = Rs. $\left(100 + \dfrac{1}{8}\right)$ = Rs. $\dfrac{801}{8}$.

C.P. of Rs. 6400 stock = Rs. $\left(\dfrac{801 \times 6400}{8 \times 100}\right)$ = Rs. 6408.

Ex. 2. *Find the cash required to purchase Rs. 1600, $8\dfrac{1}{2}$% stock at 105 (brokerage $\dfrac{1}{2}$%).*

Sol. Cash required for purchasing Rs. 100 stock

$$= Rs. \left(105 + \dfrac{1}{2}\right) = Rs. \left(\dfrac{211}{2}\right).$$

Cash required for purchasing Rs. 1600 stock

$$= Rs. \left(\dfrac{211 \times 1600}{2 \times 100}\right) = Rs. 1688.$$

Ex. 3. *Find the cash realized by selling Rs. 2400, $5\dfrac{1}{2}$% stock at 5 premium (brokerage $\dfrac{1}{4}$%).*

Sol. By selling Rs. 100 stock, cash realized

$$= Rs. \left(105 - \dfrac{1}{4}\right) = Rs. \left(\dfrac{419}{4}\right)$$

By selling Rs. 2400 stock, cash realized

$$= Rs. \left(\dfrac{419 \times 2400}{4 \times 100}\right) = Rs. 2514.$$

Ex. 4. *How much $4\dfrac{1}{2}$% stock at 95 can be pruchased by investing Rs. 1905, (brokerage $\dfrac{1}{4}$%)?*

Sol. By investing Rs. $\left(95 + \dfrac{1}{4}\right)$, stock purchased = Rs. 100.

By investing Rs. 1905, stock purchased

$$= Rs. \left(\dfrac{100 \times 4 \times 1905}{381}\right) = Rs. 2000.$$

Ex. 5. *What is the annual income derived from Rs. 1800, 5% stock at 104?*

Sol. Income from Rs. 100 stock = Rs. 5

$$\text{Income from Rs. 1800 stock} = Rs. \left(\frac{5}{100} \times 1800\right) = Rs.\ 90.$$

Ex. 6. *What is the annual income by investing Rs. 3000 in 6% stock at 120?*

Sol. On investing Rs. 120, income = Rs. 6

$$\text{On investing Rs. 3000, income} = Rs. \left(\frac{6}{120} \times 3000\right) = Rs.\ 150.$$

Ex. 7. *Find the annual income derived by investing Rs. 770 in $4\frac{1}{2}$% stock at 96 (brokerage $\frac{1}{4}$%).*

Sol. On investing Rs. $\left(96 + \frac{1}{4}\right)$, income = Rs. $\frac{11}{2}$.

On investing Rs. 100, income = Rs. $\left(\frac{11 \times 4 \times 100}{2 \times 385}\right) = Rs.\ 5\frac{5}{7}$

∴ Rate = $5\frac{5}{7}$ %

Ex. 9. *Find the market value of a $5\frac{1}{4}$ % stock, in which an income of Rs. 756 is derived by investing Rs. 14976, brokerage being $\frac{1}{4}$%.*

Sol. For an income of Rs. 756, investment = Rs. 14976

For an income of Rs. $\frac{21}{4}$, investment = Rs.

$\left(\frac{14976}{756} \times \frac{21}{4}\right) = Rs.\ 104$

∴ For a Rs. 100 stock, investment = Rs. 104

Hence, market value = Rs. $\left(104 - \frac{1}{4}\right) = Rs.\ 103.75$.

Ex. 10. *Which is the better investment, $5\frac{1}{2}$% stock at 102 or $4\frac{3}{4}$% stock at 96?*

Sol. Let the investment be Rs. (102 × 96) in each case.

Case I. $5\frac{1}{2}$% stock at 102.

Income from this stock = Rs. $\left(\frac{11 \times 102 \times 96}{2 \times 102}\right) = Rs.\ 528.$

Case II. $4\frac{3}{4}$% stock at 96.

Stock & Shares

Income from this stock = Rs. $\left(\dfrac{19 \times 102 \times 96}{4 \times 96}\right)$ = Rs. 484.50

Thus, by investing the same amount, the income from $5\dfrac{1}{2}\%$ stock at 102 is more. So, the investment in this stock is better.

Ex. 11. *How much money must I invest in $6\dfrac{2}{3}\%$ stock at 10 premium to secure an annual income of Rs. 600 ?*

Sol. For an income of Rs. $\left(\dfrac{20}{3}\right)$, investment = Rs. 110

∴ For an income of Rs. 600, investment
$$= Rs. \left(\dfrac{110 \times 3 \times 600}{20}\right) = Rs. 9900.$$

Ex. 12. *A person has Rs. 16500 stock in 3%. He sells it out at $101\dfrac{1}{8}$ and invests the proceeds in 4% railway debentures at $131\dfrac{7}{8}$. Find the change in his income, a brokerage of $\dfrac{1}{8}\%$ being charged on each transaction.*

Sol. Case I. 3% stock at $108\dfrac{1}{8}$ $\left(\text{brokerage } \dfrac{1}{8}\%\right)$.

Income from Rs. 100 stock = Rs. 3.

Income from Rs. 16500 stock = Rs. $\left(\dfrac{3}{100} \times 16500\right)$ = Rs. 495

S.P. of Rs. 100 stock = Rs. $\left(101\dfrac{1}{8} - \dfrac{1}{8}\right)$ = Rs. 101.

S.P. of Rs. 16500 stock = Rs. $\left(\dfrac{101}{100} \times 16500\right)$ = Rs. 16665.

Case II. 4% stock at $131\dfrac{7}{8}$ $\left(\text{brokerage } \dfrac{1}{8}\%\right)$

By investing Rs. $\left(131\dfrac{7}{8} + \dfrac{1}{8}\right)$, income derived = Rs. 4

By investing Rs. 16665, income derived
$$= Rs. \left(\dfrac{4}{132} \times 16665\right) = Rs. 505.$$

∴ Change in income = Rs. (505 – 495) = Rs. 10 increased.

Ex. 13. *A man wishes to invest Rs. 2490. He invests Rs. 900 in $3\dfrac{1}{2}\%$ stock at 75, Rs. 850 in 3% at 68 and the remainder in 6% stock. If the total yield from his investment is 5%, at what price does he buy the 6% stock ?*

Sol. Income from $3\frac{1}{2}\%$ stock at 75 = Rs. $\left(\dfrac{7}{2 \times 75} \times 900\right)$ = Rs. 42.

Income from 3% stock at 68 = Rs. $\left(\dfrac{3}{68} \times 850\right)$ = Rs. 37.50

Total income from these two stocks = Rs. (42 + 37.50) = Rs. (79.50).

But total income from the three stocks = Rs. $\left(\dfrac{5}{100} \times 2490\right)$ = Rs. 124.50

∴ Income from the third stock = Rs. (124.50 − 79.50) = Rs. 45

Investment in this case = Rs. (2490 − {900 + 850}) = Rs. 740.

If income is Rs. 45, investment = Rs. 740.

If income is Rs. 6, investment = Rs. $\left(\dfrac{740}{45} \times 6\right)$ = Rs. $98\dfrac{2}{3}$.

So, he buys 6% stock at $98\dfrac{2}{3}$.

Ex. 14. *A man sells Rs. 5000, $4\dfrac{1}{2}\%$ stock at 144 and invests the proceeds partly in 3% stock at 90 and partly in 4% stock at 108. He, thereby increases his income by Rs. 25. How much of the proceeds were invested in each stock ?*

Sol. Income from Rs. 5000, $4\dfrac{1}{2}\%$ stock at 144

$$= \text{Rs.} \left(\dfrac{9 \times 5000}{2 \times 100}\right) = \text{Rs. } 225.$$

S.P. of this stock = Rs. $\left(\dfrac{144}{100} \times 5000\right)$ = Rs. 7200.

∴ Proceeds = Rs. 7200.

Now, income on an investment of Re. 1 in 3% at 90

$$= \text{Rs.} \left(\dfrac{3}{90} \times 1\right) = \text{Rs.} \left(\dfrac{1}{30}\right).$$

Income on an investment of Re. 1 in 4% at 108

$$= \text{Rs.} \left(\dfrac{4}{108} \times 1\right) = \text{Rs.} \left(\dfrac{1}{27}\right).$$

Total income derived from investment of Rs. 7200 in these stocks

= Rs. (225 + 25) = Rs. 250

Average income = Rs. $\left(\dfrac{250}{7200}\right)$ = Rs. $\left(\dfrac{5}{144}\right)$

By alligation Rule :—

(3% at 90) : (4% at 108) = $\dfrac{1}{432} : \dfrac{1}{720}$ = 5 : 3

∴ Investment in 3% stock = Rs. $\left(\dfrac{7200 \times 5}{8}\right)$ = Rs. 4500

And, investment in 4% stock = Rs. (7200 − 4500) = Rs. 2700.

SHARES. To start a big concern or a business a large amount of money is needed. This is usually beyond the capacity of one or two individuals. However, some persons together associate to form a company. The company issues a prospectus and invites the public to subscribe. The required capital is divided into equal small parts called Shares, each of a particular fixed value. The persons who subscribe in shares are called Shareholders. Sometimes, the company asks its shareholders to pay some money immediately and balance after some period. The total money raised immediately is called the Paid up capital. Parts of the profits divided amongst the shareholders are called dividends. The original value of a share is called its nominal value. The price of a share in the market is called the market value.

Different Kinds of Shares. There are two kinds of shares.

(i) **Preference Shares.** On these shares a fixed rate of dividend is paid to their holders, subject to profits of the company.

(ii) **Ordinary or Equity Shares.** After paying the dividends of the prefence shareholders, the equity shareholders are paid the dividends which depends upon the profit of the company.

Solved problems.

Ex. 1. *Find the cost of 96 shares of Rs. 10 each at $\dfrac{3}{4}$ discount, brokerage being $\dfrac{1}{4}$ per share.*

Sol. Cost of 1 share = Rs. $\left[\left(10 - \dfrac{3}{4}\right) + \dfrac{1}{4}\right]$ = Rs. $\dfrac{19}{2}$

Cost of 96 shares = Rs. $\left(\dfrac{19}{2} \times 96\right)$ = Rs. 912.

Ex. 2. *Find the income derived from 44 shares of Rs. 25 each at 5 premium (brokerage 1/4 per share), the rate of dividend being 5%. Also find the rate of interest on the investment.*

Sol. Cost of 1 share = Rs. $\left(25 + 5 + \dfrac{3}{4}\right)$ = Rs. $\dfrac{171}{4}$

Cost of 44 shares = Rs. $\left(\dfrac{121}{4} \times 44\right)$ = Rs. 1331

∴ Investment made = Rs. 1331.

Now, face value of 1 share = Rs. 25.

∴ Face value of 44 shares = Rs. (44 × 25) = Rs. 1100.

Now, dividend on Rs. 100 = Rs. $\frac{11}{2}$.

∴ Dividend on Rs. 1100 = Rs. $\left(\frac{11}{2 \times 100} \times 1100\right)$ = Rs. 60.50

Also income on investment of Rs. 1331 = Rs. 60.50

∴ income on investment of Rs. 100 = Rs. $\left(\frac{60.50}{1331} \times 100\right)$

   = 4.55%.

Ex. 3. *A man's net income from 5% Government paper is Rs. 1225 after paying an income tax at the rate of 2%. Find the number of shares of Rs. 1000 each owned by him.*

Sol. Face value of 1 share = Rs. 1000.

Gross income on 1 share = Rs. $\left(\frac{5}{100} \times 1000\right)$ = Rs. 50.

Income tax on 1 share's income = Rs. $\left(\frac{2}{100} \times 50\right)$ = Re. 1.

Net income on 1 share = Rs. (45 – 1) = Rs. 49.

If the net income is Rs. 49, number of shares = 1.

If the net income is Rs. 1225, number of shares

$$= \frac{1}{49} \times 1225 = 25.$$

Ex. 4. *A man buys Rs. 25 shares in a company which pays 9% dividend. The money invested by the person is that much as gives 10% on investment. At what price did he buy the shares?*

Sol. Face value of 1 share = Rs. 25.

Dividend on 1 share = Rs. $\left(\frac{9}{100} \times 25\right)$ = Rs. $\frac{9}{4}$

Now, Rs. 10 is an income on an investment of Rs. 100

∴ Rs. $\frac{9}{4}$ is an income on an investment of Rs. $\left(\frac{100}{10} \times \frac{9}{4}\right)$

   = Rs. 22.50.

Hence, cost of share = Rs. 22.50.

EXERCISE 27 (OBJECTIVE TYPE QUESTIONS)

1. The cost price of a Rs. 100 stock at 4 discount, when brokerage is (1/4)%, is :

   (a) Rs. 96
   (b) Rs. $\left(96 + \frac{1}{4}\right)$
   (c) Rs. $\left(96 - \frac{1}{4}\right)$
   (d) Rs. 100

Stock & Shares

2. The income derived from a $5\frac{1}{2}$% stock at 95 is :
   (a) Rs. 5.50   (b) Rs. 5
   (c) Rs. 5.28   (d) none of these

3. The cash realized by selling a $5\frac{1}{2}$% stock at $106\frac{1}{4}$, brokerage being (1/4)%, is :
   (a) Rs. $105\frac{1}{2}$ (b) Rs. $106\frac{1}{2}$
   (c) Rs. 106   (d) none of these

4. By investing in a 6% stock at 96, an income of Rs. 100 is obtained by making an investment of :
   (a) Rs. 1600   (b) Rs. 1504
   (c) Rs. 1666.66   (d) Rs. 5760

5. A 4% stock yields 5%. The market value of the stock is :
   (a) Rs. 125   (b) Rs. 80
   (c) Rs. 99   (d) Rs. 109

6. Rs. 2780 are invested partly in 4% stock at 75 and 5% stock at 80 to have equal amount of incomes. The investment in 5% stock is :
   (a) Rs. 1500   (b) Rs. 1280
   (c) Rs. 1434.84   (d) Rs. 1640

7. To produce an annual income of Rs. 500 in a 4% stock at 90, the amount of stock needed is :
   (a) Rs. 11250   (b) Rs. 12500
   (c) Rs. 18000   (d) Rs. 20000

8. By investing Rs. 1100 in a $5\frac{1}{2}$% stock one earns Rs. 77. The stock is then quoted at :
   (a) Rs. 93   (b) Rs. 107
   (c) Rs. $78\frac{4}{7}$ (d) Rs. $97\frac{3}{4}$

9. A man invests in a $4\frac{1}{2}$% stock at 96. The interest obtained by him is :
   (a) 4%   (b) 4.5%
   (c) 4.69%   (d) $\frac{1}{2}$%

10. A invested some money in 4% stock at 96. Now, B wants to invest in an equally good 5% stock. B must purchase a stock worth of :
    (a) Rs. 120   (b) Rs. 124
    (c) Rs. 76.80   (d) Rs. 80

11. I want to purchase a 6% stock which must yield 5% on my capital. At what price must I buy the stock ?
    (a) Rs. 111

12. Which is the better stock, 5% at 143 or $3\frac{1}{2}$% at 93 ?

    (a) 5% at 143   (b) $3\frac{1}{2}$% at 93

    (c) both are equally good

13. A man invests some money partly in 3% stock at 96 and partly in 4% stock at 120. To get equal dividends from both, he must invest the money in the ratio ?

    (a) 16 : 15   (b) 3 : 4

    (c) 4 : 5   (d) 3 : 5

14. Which is better investment, 4% stock at par with an income tax at the rate of 5 paise per rupee or $4\frac{1}{2}$% stock at 110 free from income tax ?

    (a) 4% at par with income tax

    (b) $4\frac{1}{2}$% at 110 free from income tax

    (c) both are equally good

15. A man invested Rs. 388 in a stock at 97 to obtain an income of Rs. 22. The dividend from the stock is :

    (a) 12%   (b) 3%

    (c) $5\frac{1}{2}$%   (d) 22.68%

16. By investing in $3\frac{3}{4}$% stock at 96, one earns Rs. 100. The investment made is :

    (a) Rs. 36000   (b) Rs. 3600

    (c) Rs. 2560   (d) Rs. 4800

17. A man buys Rs. 20 shares paying 9% dividend. The man wants to have an interest of 12% on his money. The market value of each share must be :

    (a) Rs. 12   (b) Rs. 15

    (c) Rs. 18   (d) Rs. 21

18. A man bought 20 shares of Rs. 50 at 5 discount, the rate of dividend being $4\frac{3}{4}$%. The rate of interest obtained is :

    (a) $4\frac{3}{4}$%   (b) $3\frac{1}{4}$%

    (c) 5.28%   (d) 4.95%

Stock & Shares

19. A man invested Rs. 4455 in Rs. 10 shares quoted at Rs. 8.25. If the rate of dividend be 6%, his annual income is :
    (a) Rs. 267.30
    (b) Rs. 327.80
    (c) Rs. 324
    (d) Rs. 103.70

SOLUTIONS (Exercise 27)

1. C.P. = Rs. $\left(96 + \dfrac{1}{4}\right)$.

2. Income on Rs. 100 stock = Rs. $5\dfrac{1}{2}$ = Rs. 5.50.

3. Cash realized = Rs. $\left(106\dfrac{1}{4} - \dfrac{1}{4}\right)$ = Rs. 106.

4. For an income of Rs. 6, investment = Rs. 96.
   For an income of Rs. 100, investment = Rs. $\left(\dfrac{96}{6} \times 100\right)$ = Rs. 1600.

5. For an income of Rs. 5, investment = Rs. 100.
   For an income of Rs. 4, investment = Rs. $\left(\dfrac{100}{5} \times 4\right)$ = Rs. 80.

6. Let the investment in 4% stock be Rs. x.
   Then, investment in 5% stock = Rs. $(2780 - x)$
   Income from 4% stock = Rs. $\left(\dfrac{4}{75} \times x\right)$
   Income from 5% stock = Rs. $\left[\left(\dfrac{5}{80} \times (2780 - x)\right)\right]$
   $\therefore \dfrac{4x}{75} = \dfrac{2780 - x}{16}$ or $= 1500$.
   So, investment in 5% stock = Rs. $(2780 - 1500)$ = Rs. 1280.

7. For an income of Rs. 4, stock needed = Rs. 100
   For an income of Rs. 500, stock needed = Rs. $\left(\dfrac{100}{4} \times 500\right)$
   $= Rs. 12500$.

8. To earn Rs. 77, investment = Rs. 1100.
   To earn Rs. $\dfrac{11}{2}$, investment = Rs. $\left(\dfrac{1100}{77} \times \dfrac{11}{2}\right)$ = Rs. $78\dfrac{4}{7}$.

9. On Rs. 96, he gets Rs. $\dfrac{9}{2}$.
   On Rs. 100, he gets = Rs. $\left(\dfrac{9 \times 100}{2 \times 96}\right)$ = 4.69%.

10. For an income of Rs. 4, investment = Rs. 96
    For an income of Rs. 5, investment = Rs. $\left(\dfrac{96}{4} \times 5\right)$ = Rs. 120.

11. For an income of Rs. 5, investment = Rs. 100.

For an income of Rs. 6, investment = Rs. $\left(\dfrac{100}{5} \times 6\right)$ = Rs. 120.

12. Let investment in each case be Rs. (143×93).

    Income from 5% stock = Rs. $\left(\dfrac{5}{143} \times 143 \times 93\right)$ = Rs. 465.

    Income from $3\dfrac{1}{2}$% stock = Rs. $\left(\dfrac{7}{2 \times 93} \times 143 \times 93\right)$ = Rs. 500.50.

    ∴ $3\dfrac{1}{2}$ % stock at 93 is better.

13. For an income of Re. 1 in 3% stock, investment
    = Rs. (96/3) = Rs. 32
    For an income of Re. 1 in 4% stock investment
    = Rs. (120/4) = Rs. 30
    ∴ Ratio of investments = 32 : 30 = 16 : 15.

14. Let investment in each case be Rs. (100×110).

    Gross income from 4% stock = Rs. $\left(\dfrac{4}{100} \times 100 \times 100\right)$ = Rs. 440.

    Net income from the stock = Rs. (440 – 22) = Rs. 418.

    Net income from $4\dfrac{1}{2}$ % stock = Rs. $\left(\dfrac{9 \times 100 \times 110}{2 \times 110}\right)$ = Rs. 450.

    ∴ Better stock is $4\dfrac{1}{2}$ % at 110.

15. When investment is Rs. 388, income = Rs. 22.

    When investment is Rs. 97, income = Rs. $\left(\dfrac{22}{388} \times 97\right)$ = Rs. 5.50

    ∴ Dividend on Rs. 100 stock = $5\dfrac{1}{2}$ %.

16. For earning Rs. $\dfrac{15}{4}$, investment = Rs. 96.

    For earning Rs. 100, investment = Rs. $\left(\dfrac{96 \times 4}{15} \times 100\right)$
    = Rs. 2560.

17. Dividend on Rs. 20 = Rs. $\left(\dfrac{9}{100} \times 20\right)$ = Rs. $\dfrac{9}{5}$.

    Rs. 12 is an income on Rs. 100.

    ∴ Rs. $\dfrac{9}{5}$ is an income on Rs. $\left(\dfrac{100}{12} \times \dfrac{9}{5}\right)$ = Rs. 15.

18. Face value = Rs. (50×20) = Rs. 1000.

    Dividend = Rs. $\left(\dfrac{1000 \times 19}{4 \times 100}\right)$ = Rs. $\left(\dfrac{95}{2}\right)$.

    Investment = Rs. (45×20) = Rs. 900.

    Rate = Rs. $\left(\dfrac{95 \times 100}{2 \times 900}\right)$ = 5.28%.

Stock & Shares 431

19. Number of shares $= \dfrac{4455}{8.25} = 540$.

Face value = Rs. (540×10) = Rs. 5400.

Income = Rs. $\left(\dfrac{6}{100} \times 5400\right)$ = Rs. 324.

ANSWERS (Exercise 27)

1. (b)	2. (a)	3. (c)	4. (a)	5. (b)	6. (b)
7. (b)	8. (c)	9. (c)	10. (a)	11. (d)	12. (b)
13. (a)	14. (b)	15. (c)	16. (c)	17. (b)	18. (c)
19. (c)					

28
TRUE DISCOUNT

Suppose a sum say Rs. 136 is due 3 years hence and the borrower wants to clear off the debt right now. Then the question arises as to what money should be paid now. Clearly, the money which amounts to Rs. 136 after 3 years at a standard or agreed rate of interest must be paid now. Let the rate of interest in this case be 12% per annum simple interest. Then clearly, with this rate, Rs. 100 after 3 years will amount to Rs. 136. So clearly, the payment of Rs. 100 now will clear off a debt of Rs. 136 due 3 years hence at 12% per annum. The sum due is called the amount and the money paid now is called the present value or present worth of the sum due and the difference between the amount and the present worth (Rs. 36 in this case) is called the True Discount or Equitable Discount or Mathematical Discount.

Thus, The Present Value or Present Worth (P.W.) of a sum due at the end of a given time is the money which amounts to the sum due in that given time and at a given rate.

The sum due is called the amount.

The difference between the sum due at the end of a given time and its present worth is called True Discount (T.D.).

Thus, T.D. = (interest on P.W.) & Amount = (P.W. + T.D.).

Remark. Interest is reckoned on present worth and discount is reckoned on amount.

Formulae. If rate = R% p.a. & Time = T years, then

(i) $P.W. = \dfrac{100 \times (Amount)}{[100 + (R \times T)]}$

(ii) $T.D. = \dfrac{(P.W.) \times R \times T}{100}$

(iii) $T.D. = \dfrac{(Amount) \times R \times T}{100 + (R \times T)}$

(iv) S.I. on T.D. = (S.I.) – (T.D.)

(v) $Sum = \left[\dfrac{(S.I.) \times (T.D.)}{(S.I.) - (T.D.)} \right]$

(vi) When the sum is put at compound interest, then

$$P.W. = \dfrac{Amount}{\left(1 + \dfrac{R}{100}\right)^T}.$$

Solved Problems.

Ex. 1. *Find the present worth of Rs. 9950 due $3\frac{1}{4}$ years hence at $7\frac{1}{2}\%$ per annum simple interest. Also, find the discount.*

Sol. P.W. $= \dfrac{100 \times (\text{Amount})}{100 + (R \times T)}$

$= \text{Rs.}\left[\dfrac{100 \times 9950}{100 + \left(\dfrac{15}{2} \times \dfrac{13}{4}\right)}\right] = \text{Rs.}\left(\dfrac{100 \times 9950 \times 8}{995}\right)$

$= \text{Rs. } 8000.$

Also, T.D. $= (\text{Amount} - (P.W.))$

$= Rs. (9950 - 8000) = Rs. 1950.$

Ex. 2. *Find the present worth of a bill of Rs. 2916 due 2 years hence at 8% compound interest. Also, calculate the true discount.*

Sol. P.W. $= \dfrac{\text{Amount}}{\left(1 + \dfrac{R}{100}\right)^T}$

$= \text{Rs.}\left\{\dfrac{2916}{\left(1 + \dfrac{8}{100}\right)^2}\right\} = \text{Rs.}\left(\dfrac{2916 \times 25 \times 25}{27 \times 27}\right) = \text{Rs. } 2500.$

Also, T.D. $= Rs. (2916 - 2500) = Rs. 416.$

Ex. 3. *The true discount on a bill due 9 months hence at 6% per annum is Rs. 180. Find the amount of the bill and its present worth.*

Sol. P.W. $= \dfrac{100 \times T.D.}{R \times T} = \text{Rs.}\left(\dfrac{100 \times 180}{6 \times \dfrac{3}{4}}\right) = Rs. 4000.$

Amount $= (P.W. + T.D.)$

$= Rs. (4000 + 180) = Rs. 4180.$

Ex. 4. *The true discount on a certain sum of money due 3 years hence is Rs. 100 and the simple interest on the same sum for the same time and at the same rate is Rs. 120. Find the sum and the rate percent.*

Sol. Sum due $= \dfrac{S.I. \times T.D.}{(S.I.) - (T.D.)} = \text{Rs.}\left(\dfrac{120 \times 100}{20}\right) = Rs. 600.$

Rate $= \dfrac{100 \times 120}{600 \times 3} = 6\dfrac{2}{3}\%.$

Ex. 5. *The difference between the simple interest and the true discount on a certain sum of money for 6 months at 6% is Rs. 27. Find the sum.*

Sol. Let the sum be Rs. 100. Then,

$$\text{S.I.} = \text{Rs.} \left(\frac{100 \times 1 \times 6}{2 \times 100} \right) = \text{Rs. } 3.$$

$$\text{P.W.} = \text{Rs.} \left\{ \frac{100 \times 100}{100 + \left(6 \times \frac{1}{2}\right)} \right\} = \text{Rs.} \frac{10000}{103}.$$

$$\therefore \text{T.D.} = \text{Rs.} \left[100 - \frac{10000}{103} \right] = \text{Rs.} \frac{300}{103}.$$

Now, $(\text{S.I.}) - (\text{T.D.}) = \text{Rs.} \left(3 - \frac{300}{103} \right) = \text{Rs.} \frac{9}{103}.$

If the diff. in S.I. and T.D. is Rs. $\frac{9}{103}$, sum = Rs. 100.

If the diff. in S.I. and T.D. is Rs. 27, sum = Rs. $\left(\frac{100 \times 103}{9} \times 27 \right)$
$$= \text{Rs. } 30900.$$

Ex. 6. *A bill falls due in 9 months. The creditor agrees to accept immediate payment of half and to defer the payment of the other half for 18 months. He finds that by this arrangement he gains Rs. 4.50. What is the amount of the bill, if money be worth 4%?*

Sol. Let the amount of bill be Rs. 200. Then, according to the agreement, the creditor agrees to pay after 9 months, an amount which is the sum of the amount of Rs. 100 for 9 months and P.W. of Rs. 100 due 9 months hence.

Now, S.I. = Rs. $\left(\frac{100 \times 3 \times 4}{4 \times 100} \right) =$ Rs. 3.

$\therefore$ Amount = Rs. $(100 + 3) =$ Rs. 103.

Also, P.W. = Rs. $\left\{ \frac{100 \times 100}{100 + \left(4 \times \frac{3}{4} \right)} \right\} =$ Rs. $\left\{ \frac{10000}{103} \right\}.$

Total amount after 9 months = Rs. $\left\{ 103 + \frac{10000}{103} \right\} =$ Rs. $\frac{20609}{103}.$

Gain = Rs. $\left\{ \frac{20609}{103} - 200 \right\} =$ Rs. $\frac{9}{103}.$

If gain is Rs. $\frac{9}{103}$, sum due = Rs. 200.

If gain is Rs. $\frac{9}{2}$, sum due = Rs. $\left(\frac{200 \times 103}{9} \times \frac{9}{2} \right) =$ Rs. 10300.

Ex. 7. *The true discount on Rs. 1860 due after a certain time at 5% is Rs. 60. Find the time after which it is due.*

True Discount

Sol. P.W. = (sum due) − (T.D.) = Rs. (1860 − 60) = Rs. 1800. Since T.D. is interest on P.W., so Rs. 60 is the simple interest on Rs. 1800 at 5% per annum.

$$\therefore \text{Time} = \left(\frac{100 \times 60}{1800 \times 5}\right) \text{years} = \left(\frac{2}{3} \times 12\right) \text{months} = 8 \text{ months}.$$

Ex. 8. *The true discount on Rs. 2575 due 4 months hence is Rs. 75. Find the rate percent of interest.*

Sol. P.W. = Rs. (2575 − 75) = Rs. 2500.

∴ S.I. on Rs. 2500 for 4 months is Rs. 75.

$$\text{Hence, rate} = \frac{100 \times 75 \times 3}{2500 \times 1} = 9\%.$$

Ex. 9. *The true discount on a bill due 10 months hence at 6% per annum is Rs. 26.25. Find the amount of the bill.*

Sol. S.I. on Rs. 100 for 10 months at 6% per annum

$$= \text{Rs.} \left(100 \times \frac{10}{12} \times \frac{6}{100}\right) = \text{Rs. 5}$$

∴ Amount = Rs. (100 + 5) = Rs. 105.

So, T.D. = Rs. (105 − 100) = Rs. 5

If T.D. is Rs. 5, sum due = Rs. 105

If T.D. is Rs. 26.25, sum due = Rs. $\left(\frac{105}{5} \times 26.25\right)$ = Rs. 551.25.

Ex. 10. *The present worth of a bill due 7 months hence is Rs. 1200, and if the bill were due at the end of $2\frac{1}{2}$ years, its present worth would be Rs. 1016. Find the rate percent and the sum of the bill.*

Sol. Sum due = (P.W.) + (T.D.) = (P.W.) + (S.I. on P.W.)

Now, sum due = (Rs. 1200 + S.I. on Rs. 1200 for 7 months)

Also, sum due = $\left(\text{Rs. } 1016 + \text{S.I. on Rs. } 1016 \text{ for } \frac{5}{2} \text{ years}\right)$

∴ $\left\{\text{Rs } 1200 + \text{S.I. on Rs. } \left(1200 \times \frac{7}{12}\right) \text{for 1 year}\right\}$

$= \left\{\text{Rs } 1016 + \text{S.I. on Rs. } \left(1016 \times \frac{5}{2}\right) \text{for 1 year}\right\}$

or {Rs. 1200 + S.I. on Rs. 700 for 1 year}

= {Rs. 1016 + S.I. on Rs. 2540 for 1 year}

or S.I. on Rs. (2540 − 700) for 1 year = Rs. (1200 − 1016)

or S.I. on Rs. 1840 for 1 year = Rs. 184

$$\therefore \text{Rate} = \frac{100 \times 184}{1840 \times 1} = 10\%.$$

Also, sum due = (Rs. 1200) + (S.I. on Rs. 1200 for 7 months at 10%)

$$= Rs. \left[1200 + \left(1200 \times \frac{7}{12} \times \frac{10}{100} \right) \right] = Rs.\ 1270.$$

EXERCISE 28 (Objective Type Questions)

1. If the true discount on a sum due 2 years hence at 5% per annum be Rs. 75, then the sum due is :
   (a) Rs. 750   (b) Rs. 825
   (c) Rs. 875   (d) Rs. 800

2. I want to sell may scooter. There are two offers, one at cash payment of Rs. 8100 and another at a credit of Rs. 8250 to be paid after 6 months. If money being worth $6\frac{1}{4}\%$ per annum simple interest, which is the better offer :
   (a) Rs. 8100 in cash   (b) Rs. 8250 due 6 months hence
   (c) both are equally good

3. The present worth of Rs. 1404 due in two equal half yearly instalments at 8% per annum simple interest is :
   (a) Rs. 1325   (b) Rs. 1300
   (c) Rs. 1350   (d) Rs. 1500

4. A trader owes a merchant Rs. 901 due 1 year's hence. However, the trader wants to settle the account after 3 months. How much cash should he pay, if rate of interest is 8% per annum :
   (a) Rs. 870   (b) Rs. 850
   (c) Rs. 828.92   (d) Rs. 846.94

5. The interest on Rs. 750 for 2 years is equal to the true discount on Rs. 810 for the same time and at the same rate. The rate percent is :
   (a) $4\frac{1}{3}\%$ (b) $5\frac{1}{6}\%$
   (c) 4%   (d) 5%

6. Goods were bought for Rs. 600 and sold the same day for Rs. 650.25 at a credit of 9 months and still there was a gain of 2%. The rate percent is :
   (a) $6\frac{1}{3}\%$ (b) $8\frac{1}{3}\%$
   (c) 8%   (d) $7\frac{43}{61}\%$

7. The simple interest and the true discount on a certain sum for a given time and at a given rate are Rs. 25 and Rs. 20 respectively. The sum is :
   (a) Rs. 500   (b) Rs. 200
   (c) Rs. 250   (d) Rs. 100

8. If Rs. 10 be allowed as true discount on a bill of Rs. 110 due at the end of a certain time, then the discount allowed on the same sum due at the end of double the time is :
   (a) Rs. 20 (b) Rs. 21.81
   (c) Rs. 22 (d) Rs. 18.33
9. A man buys a watch for Rs. 195 in cash and sells it for Rs. 220 at a credit of 1 year. If the rate of interest is 10%, the man :
   (a) gains Rs. 15 (b) gains Rs. 3
   (c) gains Rs. 5 (d) loses Rs. 5
10. The true discount on Rs. 1860 due after a certain time at 5% is Rs. 60. The time after which it is due is :
    (a) 6 months (b) 8 months
    (c) 9 months (d) 10 months
11. The true discount on Rs. 2575 due 4 months hence is Rs. 75. The rate percent is :
    (a) 6% (b) 8%
    (c) 9% (d) 5%
12. The true discount on a bill due 10 months hence at 6% per annum is Rs. 26.25. The amount of the bill is :
    (a) Rs. 1575 (b) Rs. 500
    (c) Rs. 650.25 (d) Rs. 551.25
13. A man purchased a cow for Rs. 300 and sold it the same day for Rs. 360, allowing the buyer a credit of 9 years. If the rate of interest be $7\frac{1}{2}\%$ per annum, then the man has a gain of :
    (a) $4\frac{1}{2}\%$ (b) $5\frac{3}{7}\%$
    (c) 6% (d) 5%
14. A owes B, Rs. 1120 payable 2 years hence and B owes A, Rs. 1081.50 payable 6 months hence. If they decide to settle their accounts forthwith by payment of ready money and the rate of interest be 6% per annum, then who should pay and how much :
    (a) A, Rs. 50 (b) B, Rs. 50
    (c) A, Rs. 70 (d) B, Rs. 70
15. Rs. 20 is the true discount on Rs. 260 due after a certain time. What will be the true discount on the same sum due after half of the former time, the rate of interest being the same :
    (a) Rs. 10 (b) Rs. 10.40
    (c) Rs. 15.20 (d) Rs. 13

16. *A* has to pay Rs. 220 to *B* after 1 year. *B* asks *A* to pay Rs. 110 in cash and defer the payment of Rs. 110 for 2 years. *A* agrees to it. Counting, the rate of interest at 10% per annum in this new mode of payment :
   (*a*) there is no gain or loss to any one
   (*b*) *A* gains Rs. 7.34
   (*c*) *A* loses Rs. 7.34
   (*d*) *A* gains Rs. 11

SOLUTIONS (Exercise 28)

1. $\text{P.W.} = \dfrac{100 \times T.D.}{R \times T} = \text{Rs.} \left(\dfrac{100 \times 75}{5 \times 2}\right) = \text{Rs.} 750.$

∴ Sum due = Rs. (750 + 75) = Rs. 825.

2. P.W. of Rs. 8250 due 6 months hence

$= \text{Rs.} \left\{ \dfrac{100 \times 8250}{100 + \left(\dfrac{25}{4} \times \dfrac{1}{2}\right)} \right\} = \text{Rs.} 8000.$

∴ *Rs. 8100 in cash is a better offer.*

3. P.W. of Rs. 702 due 6 months hence

$= \text{Rs.} \left\{ \dfrac{100 \times 702}{100 + 8 \times \dfrac{1}{2}} \right\} = \text{Rs.} 675.$

P.W. of Rs. 702 due 1 year hence

$= \text{Rs.} \left\{ \dfrac{100 \times 702}{100 \times (8 \times 1)} \right\} = \text{Rs.} 650.$

∴ Total P.W. = Rs. (675 + 650) = Rs. 1325.

4. P.W. of Rs. 901 due 9 months hence at 8%

$= \text{Rs.} \left\{ \dfrac{100 \times 901}{100 + \left(8 \times \dfrac{3}{4}\right)} \right\} = \text{Rs.} \left(\dfrac{100 \times 901 \times 1}{106}\right) = \text{Rs.} 850.$

5. Since T.D. is S.I. on P.W., we have :
Rs. (810 − 750) or Rs. 60 as S.I. on Rs. 750 for 2 years.

∴ $\text{Rate} = \left(\dfrac{100 \times 60}{750 \times 2}\right) = 4\%.$

6. S.P. = (102% of Rs. 600) = Rs. $\left(\dfrac{102}{100} \times 600\right)$ = Rs. 612.

∴ P.W. of Rs. 650.25 due 9 months hence is Rs. 612.
or Rs. 38.25 is S.I. on Rs. 612 for 9 months.

∴ $\text{Rate} = \left(\dfrac{100 \times 38.25}{612 \times \dfrac{3}{4}}\right)\% = 8\dfrac{1}{3}\%.$

True Discount

7. $\text{Sum} = \dfrac{(S.I.) \times (T.D.)}{(S.I.) - (T.D.)} = \text{Rs.} \left(\dfrac{25 \times 20}{25 - 20} \right) = \text{Rs. } 100.$

8. S.I. on Rs. $(110 - 10)$ for a given time $= \text{Rs. } 10.$
   S.I. on Rs. 100 for double the time $= \text{Rs. } 20.$
   Sum $= \text{Rs. } (100 + 20) = \text{Rs. } 120.$
   T.D. on Rs. $110 = \text{Rs.} \left(\dfrac{20}{120} \times 110 \right) = \text{Rs. } 18.33.$

9. P.W. of Rs. 220 due 1 year hence
   $= \text{Rs.} \left(\dfrac{100 \times 220}{100 + 10} \right) = \text{Rs. } 200.$
   Hence, the man gains Rs. 5.

10. P.W. $=$ (Sum due) $-$ (T.D.) $= \text{Rs. } (1860 - 60) = \text{Rs. } 1800.$
    Thus, Rs. 60 is S.I. on Rs. 1800 at 5% per annum.
    $\therefore \text{Time} = \left(\dfrac{100 \times 60}{1800 \times 5} \right) \text{years} = \dfrac{2}{3} \text{ years} = 8 \text{ months}.$

11. P.W. $= \text{Rs. } (2575 - 75) = \text{Rs. } 2500.$
    $\therefore \text{Rate} = \left(\dfrac{100 \times 75 \times 3}{2500 \times 1} \right)\% = 9\%.$

12. Amount $= (T.D.) \times \left\{ \dfrac{100 + (R \times T)}{R \times T} \right\}$
    $= \text{Rs.} \left(\dfrac{26.25 \times 105}{5} \right) = \text{Rs. } 551.25.$

13. P.W. of Rs. 360 due 2 years hence at $7\dfrac{1}{7}\%$ per annum
    $= \text{Rs.} \left\{ \dfrac{100 \times 360}{100 + \left(\dfrac{50}{7} \times 2 \right)} \right\} = \text{Rs.} \left\{ \dfrac{100 \times 360 \times 7}{800} \right\}$
    $= \text{Rs. } 315.$
    $\therefore \text{S.P.} = \text{Rs. } 315.$
    Hence, gain % $= \left(\dfrac{15 \times 100}{300} \right) = 5\%.$

14. P.W. of Rs. 1120 due 2 years hence at 6%
    $= \text{Rs.} \left[\dfrac{100 \times 1120}{100 + (6 \times 2)} \right] = \text{Rs. } 1000.$
    P.W. of Rs. 1081.50 due 6 months hence at 6%.
    $= \text{Rs.} \left[\dfrac{100 \times 1081.50}{100 + \left(6 \times \dfrac{1}{2} \right)} \right] = \text{Rs.} \left[\dfrac{100 \times 1081.50}{103} \right]$
    $= \text{Rs. } 1050.$
    So, A owes B, Rs. 1000 cash and B owes A Rs. 1050 cash.
    $\therefore$ B must pay Rs. 50 to A.

15. S.I. on Rs. 240 for a given time = Rs. 20
    S.I. on Rs. 240 for half the time = Rs. 10
    ∴ Rs. 10 is T.D. on Rs. 250.
    So, T.D. on Rs. 260 = Rs. $\left(\dfrac{10}{250} \times 260\right)$ = Rs. 10.40.

16. A has to pay the P.W. of Rs. 220 due 1 year hence, which is
    = Rs. $\left[\dfrac{100 \times 220}{100 + (10 \times 1)}\right]$ = Rs. 200.
    A actually pays = Rs. [110 + P.W. of Rs. 110 due 2 years hence]
    = Rs. $\left[110 + \dfrac{100 \times 110}{100 + (8 \times 2)}\right]$ = Rs. 192.66.
    ∴ A gains = Rs. [200 – 192.66] = Rs. 7.34.

ANSWERS (Exercise 28)

1. (b)	2. (a)	3. (a)	4. (b)	5. (c)	6. (b)
7. (d)	8. (d)	9. (c)	10. (b)	11. (c)	12. (d)
13. (d)	14. (b)	15. (b)	16. (b)		

29
BANKER'S DISCOUNT

Suppose a merchant A purchases goods worth of say Rs. 5000 from another merchant B at a credit of a certain period say 4 months. Then B draws up a draft i.e., prepares a special type of a bill, called Hundi or Bill of exchange. On the receipt of the goods, A gives an agreement dually signed on the bill stating that he has accepted the bill and money can be withdrawn from his bank account after 4 months of the date of the bill. On this bill, there is an order from A to his bank asking to pay Rs. 5000 to B after 4 months. More over, 3 more days (known as grace days) are added to the date (called Nominally due date) of expiry of 4 months and on the date so obtained (called the legally due date), the bill can be presented to the bank by B to collect Rs. 5000 from A's account. Suppose the bill is drawn on 5th Jan. at 4 months, then the nominally due date is 5th May and the legally due date is 8th May. The amount given on the draft or bill is called the face value, which is Rs. 5000 in this case.

Now suppose that B needs the money of this bill earlier than 8th may say on 3rd March. In such a case, B can sell the bill to a banker or a broker who pays him the money against the bill but some what less than the face value. Now, the natural questions is, as how much cash the banker should pay to B on 3rd March. Actually, if the banker deducts the true discount on the face value for the period from 3rd March to 8th May, he gains nothing. So in order to make some profit, the banker deducts from the face value, the simple interest on the face value for the unexpired time i.e., from 3rd March to 8th May. This deduction is known as Banker's Discount (B.D.) or Commercial Discount.

Thus, B.D. is the S.I. on face value for the period from the date on which the bill was discounted and the legally due date. The money paid by the banker to the bill holder is called the Discountable value.

Also the difference between the banker's discount and the true discount for the unexpired time is called the Banker's Gain (B.G.). Thus, Banker's Gain
$$B.G. = (B.D.) - (T.D.).$$

Remark. When date of the bill is not given, grace days are not to be added.

Formulae :
(i) B.D. = S.I. on bill for unexpired time.
(ii) **Banker's Gain = (B.D.) – (T.D.)**
(iii) B.G. = S.I. on T.D.

(iv) $T.D. = \sqrt{(P.W.) \times (B.G.)}$; $B.G. = \dfrac{(T.D.)^2}{(P.W.)}$.

(v) $B.D. = \dfrac{\text{Amount} \times \text{Rate} \times \text{Time}}{100}$;

$T.D. = \dfrac{\text{Amount} \times \text{Rate} \times \text{Time}}{100 + (\text{Rate} \times \text{Time})}$

(vi) $\text{Amount} = \dfrac{(B.D.) \times (T.D.)}{(B.D.) - (T.D.)}$, $T.D. = \dfrac{B.G. \times 100}{\text{Rate} \times \text{Time}}$.

Ex. 1. *A bill for Rs. 5656 is drawn on July, 14 at 5 months. It is discounted on October 5th at 5%. Find, the banker's discount; the true discount; the banker's gain and the money that the holder of the bill receives.*

Sol. Face value of the bill = Rs. 5656.
Date on which the bill was drawn = July, 14th at 5 months.
Nominally due date = December, 14th.
Legally due date = December, 17th.
Date on which the bill was discounted = October, 5th.
Period for which the bill has yet to run
Oct. Nov. Dec.
$26 + 30 + 17 = 73$ days or $\dfrac{1}{5}$ year

$\therefore$ B.D. = S.I. on Rs. 5656 for $\dfrac{1}{5}$ years at 5%

$= Rs. \left(\dfrac{5656 \times 1 \times 5}{100 \times 5} \right) = Rs.\ 56.56.$

$T.D. = Rs. \left\{ \dfrac{5656 \times 5 \times \dfrac{1}{5}}{100 + \left(5 \times \dfrac{1}{5}\right)} \right\} = Rs.\ 56$

B.G. = (B.D.) − (T.D.) = 56 paise.
Money received by the holder of the bill
$= Rs.\ (5656 - 56.56) = Rs.\ 5599.44.$

Ex. 2. *A banker paid Rs. 5767.50 for a bill of Rs. 5840, drawn on April 4, at 6 months. On what day was the bill discounted, the rate of interest being 7%?*

Sol. B.D. = Rs. (5840 − 5767.20) = Rs. (72.80)
$\therefore$ Rs. 72.80 is S.I. on Rs. 5840 at 7%.

So, unexpired time $= \dfrac{100 \times 72.80}{7 \times 5840}$ years $= \dfrac{13}{73}$ years = 65 days.

Now, date of draw of bill = April, 4 at 6 months.
Nominally due date = October, 4

Banker's Discount

Legally due date = October, 7.
So, we must go back 65 days from October, 7.
Oct.   Sept.   Aug.
7+   30+   28
i.e., The bill was discounted on 3rd August.

Ex. 3. *If the true discount on a certain sum due 6 months hence at 6% is Rs. 36, what is the banker's discount on the same sum for the same time and at the same rate ?*

Sol. B.G. = S.I. on T.D.

$$= Rs. \left(\frac{36 \times 6 \times 1}{100 \times 2}\right) = Rs. \ 1.08$$

$\therefore$ (B.D.) – (T.D.) = Rs. 1.08
or B.D. = (T.D.) + Rs. 1.08 = Rs. (36 + 1.08) = Rs. 37.08.

Ex. 4. *The banker's discount on Rs. 1800 at 5% is equal to the true discount on Rs. 1830 for the same time and at the same rate. Find the time.*

Sol. $\because$ S.I. on Rs. 1800 = T.D. on Rs. 1830
$\therefore$ P.W. of Rs. 1830 is Rs. 1800.
i.e., Rs. 30 is S.I. on Rs. 1800 at 5%.

$$\therefore Time = \left(\frac{100 \times 30}{1800 \times 5}\right) years = \frac{1}{3} years = 4 \ months.$$

Ex. 5. *The banker's discount and the true discount on a sum of money due 8 months hence are Rs. 52 and Rs. 50, respectively. Find the sum and the rate percent.*

Sol. $Sum = \frac{(B.D.) \times (T.D.)}{(B.D.) - (T.D.)} = Rs. \left(\frac{52 \times 50}{2}\right) = Rs. \ 1300.$

Since B.D. is S.I. on sum due, so S.I. on Rs. 1300 for 8 months is Rs. 52. Consequently,

$$Rate = \left(\frac{100 \times 52}{1300 \times \frac{2}{3}}\right) \% = 6\%.$$

Ex. 6. *The present worth of a bill due sometime hence is Rs. 1100 and the true discount on the bill is Rs. 110. Find the banker's discount and the extra gain the banker would make in the transaction.*

Sol. T.D. = $\sqrt{(P.W.) \times (B.G.)}$

or $B.G. = \frac{(T.D.)^2}{(P.W.)} = Rs. \left(\frac{110 \times 110}{1100}\right) = Rs. \ 11.$

$\therefore$ B.D. = B.G. + T.D. = Rs. (11 + 110) = Rs. 121.

Ex. 7. *The true discount on a bill of Rs. 1860 due after 8 months is Rs. 60. Find the rate, the banker's discount and the banker's gain.*

Sol. Amount = Rs. 1860, T.D. = Rs. 60

∴ P.W. = Rs. (1860 – 60) = Rs. 1800.
S.I. on Rs. 1800 for 8 months = Rs. 60

$$\therefore \text{Rate} = \left[\frac{100 \times 60}{1800 \times \frac{2}{3}}\right]\% = 5\%.$$

$$B.G. = \frac{(T.D.)^2}{(P.W.)} = Rs. \frac{60 \times 60}{1800} = Rs. 2.$$

B.D. = (T.D.) + (B.G.) = Rs. (60 + 2) = Rs. 62.

Ex. 8. *The banker's discount on Rs. 1650 due a certain time hence is Rs. 165. Find the true discount and the banker's gain.*

Sol. $\text{Sum} = \frac{(B.D.) \times (T.D.)}{(B.D.) - (T.D.)} = \frac{(B.D.) \times (T.D.)}{(B.G.)}$

$\therefore \frac{T.D.}{B.G.} = \frac{\text{Sum}}{B.D.} = \frac{1650}{165} = \frac{10}{1}.$

i.e., if B.G. is Re. 1, T.D. = Rs. 10 or B.D. = Rs. 11.
∴ If B.D. is Rs. 11, T.D. = Rs. 10

If B.D. is Rs. 165, T.D. = Rs. $\left[\frac{10}{11} \times 165\right]$ = Rs. 150.

Also, B.G. = Rs. (165 – 150) = Rs. 15.

Ex. 9. *What rate percent does a man get for his money when in discounting a bill due 10 months hence, he deducts 4% of the amount of the bill?*

Sol. Let the amount of bill be Rs. 100.
Money deducted = Rs. 4.
Money received by holder of the bill = Rs. (100 – 4) = Rs. 96.
S.I. on Rs. 96 for 10 months = Rs. 4.

$$\text{Rate} = \left[\frac{100 \times 4 \times 6}{96 \times 5}\right]\% = 5\%.$$

Ex. 10. *A bill was drawn on March 8, at 7 months date and was discounted on May 18, at 5%. If the banker's gain is Rs. 3, find (i) the true discount (ii) the banker's doscount and (iii) the sum of the bill.*

Sol. Date on which the bill was drawn = March 8th, at 7 months.
Nominally due date = Oct. 8th.
Legally due date = Oct., 11th.
Date on which the bill was discounted = May, 18th.
Time for which the bill has yet to run
May June July Aug. Sep. Oct.

13 + 30 + 31 + 31 + 30 + 11 = 146 days = $\frac{2}{5}$ years

Now, (i) Banker's gain = S.I. on T.D.

i.e., Rs. 3 is S.I. on T.D. for $\frac{2}{5}$ years at 5%,

$$\therefore T.D. = Rs. \frac{100 \times 3}{5 \times \frac{2}{5}} = Rs.\ 150.$$

(ii) $B.D. = T.D. + S.I.$ on $T.D.$
 $= Rs.\ 150 + S.I.$ on Rs. 150 for $\frac{2}{5}$ years at 5%
 $= Rs.\ 150 + Rs.\ 150 \times \frac{2}{5} \times \frac{5}{100} = Rs.\ 153.$

(iii) Sum $= \frac{B.D. \times T.D.}{B.D. - T.D.} = Rs. \frac{153 \times 150}{153 - 150} = Rs.\ 7650.$

EXERCISE 29 (Objective Type Questions)

1. The true discount on a bill of Rs. 540 is Rs. 90. The banker's discount is :
   (a) Rs. 60 (b) Rs. 150
   (c) Rs. 180 (d) Rs. 110

2. The present worth of a certain bill due sometime hence is Rs. 800 and the true discount is Rs. 36. Then, the banker's discount is :
   (a) Rs. 37 (b) Rs. 34.38
   (c) Rs. 37.62 (d) Rs. 38.98

3. The banker's discount on a certain sum due 2 years hence is $\frac{11}{10}$ of the true discount. The rate percent is :
   (a) 11% (b) 10%
   (c) 5% (d) $5\frac{1}{3}$%

4. The banker's gain on a certain sum due $2\frac{1}{2}$ years hence is (3/23) of the banker's discount. The rate percent is :
   (a) 5% (b) 6%
   (c) $2\frac{14}{23}$% (d) $6\frac{2}{3}$%

5. The present worth of a certain sum due sometime hence is Rs. 1600 and the true discount is Rs. 160. The banker's gain is :
   (a) Rs. 10 (b) Rs. 16
   (c) Rs. 20 (d) Rs. 24

6. The banker's gain of a certain sum due 2 years hence at 5% per annum is Rs. 8. The present worth is :
   (a) Rs. 800 (b) Rs. 1600
   (c) Rs. 1200 (d) Rs. 880

7. The banker's gain of a certain sum of money is Rs. 36 and the true discount on the same sum for the same time and at the same rate is Rs. 30. The sum is :
   (a) Rs. 1080
   (b) Rs. 180
   (c) Rs. 500
   (d) Rs. 300

8. The banker's discount on a bill due 1 year 8 months hence is Rs. 50 and the true discount on the same sum at the same rate percent is Rs. 45. The rate percent is :
   (a) 6%
   (b) $6\frac{2}{3}\%$
   (c) $6\frac{1}{2}\%$
   (d) $8\frac{44}{59}\%$

9. The banker's discount on Rs. 1600 at 6% is the same as the true discount on Rs. 1624 for the same time and at the same rate. Then, the time is :
   (a) 3 months
   (b) 4 months
   (c) 6 months
   (d) 8 months

10. The banker's discount on a sum of money for $1\frac{1}{2}$ years is Rs. 60 and the true discount on the same sum for 2 years is Rs. 75. The rate percent is :
    (a) 5%
    (b) 6%
    (c) $6\frac{2}{3}\%$
    (d) $3\frac{1}{3}\%$

11. The banker's gain on a bill due 1 year hence at 5% is Re. 1. The true discount is :
    (a) Rs. 15
    (b) Rs. 20
    (c) Rs. 25
    (d) Rs. 5

12. The banker's discount on a bill due 6 months hence at 6% is Rs. 37.08. The true discount is :
    (a) Rs. 6.18
    (b) Rs. 12.36
    (c) Rs. 48
    (d) Rs. 36

13. The present worth of a sum due sometimes hence is Rs. 576 and the banker's gain is Re. 1. The true discount is :
    (a) Rs. 16
    (b) Rs. 18
    (c) Rs. 24
    (d) Rs. 32

14. A bill is discounted at 5% per annum. If banker's discount be allowed, at what rate percent must the proceeds be invested, so that nothing may be lost ?
    (a) 5%
    (b) $4\frac{19}{21}\%$
    (c) $5\frac{5}{19}\%$
    (d) 10%

Banker's Discount   447

15. The banker's gain on a sum due 3 years hence at 5% is Rs. 90. The banker's discount is :
   (a) Rs. 690   (b) Rs. 720
   (c) Rs. 810   (d) Rs. 150

SOLUTIONS (Exercise 29)

1. P.W. = Rs. (540 – 90) = Rs. 450
   S.I. on Rs. 450 = Rs. 90
   B.D. = S.I. on Rs. 540 = Rs. $\left(\dfrac{90}{450} \times 540\right)$ = Rs. 108.

2. B.G. = $\dfrac{(T.D.)^2}{P.W.}$ = Rs. $\left(\dfrac{36 \times 36}{800}\right)$ = Rs. 1.62.
   $\therefore$ B.D. = (T.D.) + (B.G.) = Rs. (36 + 1.62) = Rs. (37.62).

3. Let T.D. be Re. 1. Then, B.D. = Rs. (11/10) = Rs. 1.10.
   $\therefore$ Sum = Rs. $\left(\dfrac{1.10 \times 1}{1.10 - 1}\right)$ = Rs. $\dfrac{1.10}{0.10}$ = Rs. 11.
   So, S.I. on Rs. 11 for 2 years is Rs. 1.10.
   $\therefore$ Rate = $\left(\dfrac{100 \times 1.10}{11 \times 2}\right)\%$ = 5%.

4. Let B.D. be Re. 1. Then, B.G. = Re. (3/23).
   $\therefore$ T.D. = Re. $\left(1 - \dfrac{3}{23}\right)$ = Re. $\left(\dfrac{20}{23}\right)$.
   Sum = Rs. $\left[\left(1 \times \dfrac{20}{23}\right) \Big/ \left(1 - \dfrac{20}{23}\right)\right]$ = Rs. $\left(\dfrac{20}{3}\right)$.
   $\therefore$ S.I. on Rs. $\dfrac{20}{3}$ for $2\dfrac{1}{2}$ years is Re. 1.
   $\therefore$ Rate = $\left(\dfrac{100 \times 1}{\dfrac{20}{3} \times \dfrac{5}{2}}\right)\%$ = 6%.

5. B.G. = $\dfrac{(T.D.)^2}{P.W.}$ = Rs. $\left(\dfrac{160 \times 160}{1600}\right)$ = Rs. 16.

6. T.D. = $\dfrac{B.G. \times 100}{Rate \times Time}$ = Rs. $\left(\dfrac{8 \times 100}{5 \times 2}\right)$ = Rs. 800.

7. Sum = $\dfrac{B.D. \times T.D.}{B.D. - T.D.}$ = Rs. $\left(\dfrac{36 \times 30}{6}\right)$ = Rs. 180.

8. Sum = $\dfrac{B.D. \times T.D.}{B.D. - T.D.}$ = Rs. $\left(\dfrac{50 \times 45}{5}\right)$ = Rs. 450.
   Now, Rs. 50 is S.I. on Rs. 450 for (5/3) years.
   $\therefore$ Rate = $\left(\dfrac{100 \times 50}{450 \times \dfrac{5}{3}}\right)\%$ = $6\dfrac{2}{3}\%$.

9. S.I. on Rs. 1600 = T.D. on Rs. 1624
∴ Rs. 1600 is P.W. of Rs.1624.
i.e., Rs. 24 is the S.I. on Rs. 1600 at 6%.
∴ $Time = \left(\dfrac{100 \times 24}{1600 \times 6}\right) year = \dfrac{1}{4} year = 3\ months.$

10. B.D. for (3/2) years = Rs. 60
B.D. for 2 years = Rs. $\left(\dfrac{60 \times 2}{3} \times 2\right)$ = Rs. 80.
Now, B.D. = Rs. 80 : T.D. = Rs. 75 & Time = 2 years.
∴ Sum = Rs. $\left(\dfrac{80 \times 75}{5}\right)$ = Rs. 1200.
∴ Rs. 80 is S.I. on Rs. 1200 for 2 years.
So, rate = $\left(\dfrac{100 \times 80}{1200 \times 2}\right)\% = 3\dfrac{1}{3}\%.$

11. T.D. = $\dfrac{B.G. \times 100}{R \times T}$ = Rs. $\left(\dfrac{1 \times 100}{5 \times 1}\right)$ = Rs. 20.

12. T.D. = $\dfrac{B.D. \times 100}{100 + (R \times T)}$ = Rs. $\left\{\dfrac{37.08 \times 100}{100 + \left(6 \times \dfrac{1}{2}\right)}\right\}$ = Rs. 36.

13. T.D. = $\sqrt{\{(P.W) \times (B.G.)\}}$ = Rs. $\sqrt{(576 \times 1)}$ = Rs. 24.

14. Let the sum be Rs. 100. Then, B.D. = Rs. 5.
Proceeds = Rs. (100 − 5) = Rs. 95.
∴ Rs. 5 must be the interest on Rs. 95 for 1 year.
So, rate = $\left(\dfrac{100 \times 5}{95 \times 1}\right) = 5\dfrac{5}{19}\%.$

15. T.D. = $\dfrac{B.G. \times 100}{R \times T}$ = Rs. $\left(\dfrac{90 \times 100}{5 \times 3}\right)$ = Rs. 600.
∴ B.D. = Rs. (600 + 90) = Rs. 690.

ANSWERS (Exercise 29)

1. (c) 2. (c) 3. (c) 4. (b) 5. (b) 6. (a)
7. (b) 8. (b) 9. (a) 10. (d) 11. (b) 12. (d)
13. (c) 14. (c) 15. (a)

30
TABULATION

TABULATION

*In studying problems on statistics, the data collected by the investigator are arranged in a systematic form, called the **tabular form**. In order to avoid same heads again, we make tables consisting of horizontal lines (called **rows**) and vertical lines (called **columns**) with distinctive heads, known as **captions**. Units of measurements are given along with the captions.*

Ex. 1. *The following data give year-wise outlay in lakhs of rupees in a certain 5 years plan (1980–1985) of a state, under the heads : Transport and Communication, Education, Health, Housing and Social welfare respectively.*

1st Year : 56219, 75493, 13537, 9596 & 1985.

2nd Year : 71416, 80691, 15902, 10135 & 2073.

3rd Year : 73520, 61218, 16736, 11000 & 3918.

4th Year : 75104, 73117, 17523, 12038 and 4102.

5th Year : 80216, 90376, 19420, 15946 & 10523.

Putting the data in the form of a table, write the total under each head and answer the following questions :

1. During which year the outlay on education was maximum ?
2. How many times, the outlay on education was increased over preceding year ?
3. What is the percentage increase during 1983–84 over 1982–83 in health outlay ?
4. What is total outlay on social welfare during the plan period ?
5. What is the ratio between outlays on (Transport and Communication) and housing during 1984–85.

   SOLUTION : The table may be constructed as shown below :

Outlay (in lakhs of rupees) of a state in a 5 years–plan (1980 to 85):

Year	Transport & Communication	Education	Housing	Health	Social welfare	Total
1980-81	56219	75493	13537	9596	1985	156830
1981-82	71416	80691	15902	10135	2073	180217
1982-83	73520	61218	16736	11000	3918	166392
1983-84	75104	73117	17523	12038	4102	181884
1984-85	80216	90376	19420	15946	10523	21648
Total	356475	380895	83118	58715	22601	901804

As given in the table:
Ans. 1. During 1984–85, the outlay on education was maximum.
Ans. 2. Clearly; the outlay on education was increased in 1981–82 over 1980–81; in 1983–84 over 1982–83 and in 1984–85 over 1983–84.
Thus, it was increased three times during the plan period.
Ans. 3. % increase in 1983–84 over 1982–83 in health
$$= \left(\frac{12038 - 11000}{11000}\right) \times 100\% = 9.43\%.$$
Ans. 4. Total outlay on social welfare during the plan-period is Rs. 22601 lakhs.
Ans. 5. Ratio between outlays on (Transport and communication) and housing during 1984–85 is
= 80216 : 19420 = 4.13 : 1 = (413 : 100).

Ex. 2. *Following table gives the population of a town from 1988 to 1992:*

Year	Men	Women	Children	Total	Increase (+) or Decrease (−) over Preceding Year
1988	65104	60387	......	146947	....
1989	70391	62516	......	......	+(11630)
1990	......	63143	20314	153922	....
1991	69395	......	21560	......	−(5337)
1992	71274	......	23789	160998	....

Complete the table and mark a tick against the correct answer in each question:
1. The number of children in 1988 is:
   (a) 31236 (b) 125491
   (c) 14546 (d) 21456
2. The total population in 1989 is:

Tabulation 451

    (a) 144537   (b) 158577
    (c) 146947   (d) 149637
3. Number of children in 1989 is :
    (a) 25670   (b) 14040
    (c) 13970   (d) 15702
4. Number of men in 1990 is :
    (a) 40645   (b) 60454
    (c) 70465   (d) 58835
5. Number of women in 1991 is :
    (a) 57630   (b) 56740
    (c) 52297   (d) 62957
6. Increase or decrease of population in 1992 over 1991 is :
    (a) –(12413)   (b) +(12413)
    (c) +155661   (d) +7086

Solution

Q. 1.   Number of children in 1988
$$= (146947) - (65104 + 60387) = 21456.$$
∴ Answer (d) is correct.

Q. 2.   Total population in 1988 is 146947 and increase in 1989 is 11630. Therefore, total population in 1989 is
$$= (146947 + 11630) = 158577.$$
∴ Answer (b) is correct.

Q. 3.   Number of children in 1989.
$$= (158577) - (70391 + 62516) = 25670.$$
∴ Answer (a) is correct.

Q. 4.   Number of men in 1990
$$= (153922) - (63143 + 20314) = 70465.$$
∴ Answer (c) is correct.

Q. 5.   Total population in 1990 was 153922 and decrease in next year was 5337. So, the total population in 1991
$$= (153922 - 5337) = 148585.$$
Number of women in 1991
$$= (148585) - (69395 + 21560) = 57630.$$
∴ Answer (a) is correct.

Q. 6.   Total population in 1991 was 148585 and that in 1992 was 160998. So, increase = $(100998 - 148585) = 12415$.
∴ Answer (b) is correct.
Also, number of women in 1992
$$= (160998) - (71274 + 23789) = 65935.$$

Filling all these entries, the complete table is given below:

Year	Men	Women	Children	Total	Increase (+) or Decrease (−) over Preceding Year
1988	65104	60387	21456	146947	....
1989	70391	62516	25670	158577	+ (11630)
1990	70465	63143	20314	153922	− (4655)
1991	69395	57630	21560	148585	− (5337)
1992	71274	65935	23789	160998	+ (12413)

Ex. 3. *The table given below shows the population, litrates and illiterates in thousands and percentage of literacy in three states in a year :*

States	Population	Literates	Illitrates	%age of literacy
Madras	49342	6421	......	....
Bombay	......	4068	16790	....
Bengal	60314	......	......	16.1

After reading the table, mark a tick against the correct answer in each question given below and hence complete the table.

1.   Percentage of literacy in Madras is :
    (a) 14.9%   (b) 13.01%
    (c) 12.61%   (d) 15.04%
2.   Percentage of literacy in Bombay is :
    (a) 19.5%   (β) 16.7%
    (c) 18.3%   (d) 14.6%
3.   Literates in Bengal are :
    (a) 50599   (b) 9715
    (c) 7865   (d) 9475

Solution :

Q. 1.   Percentage of literacy in Madras

$$= \left(\frac{6421}{49342} \times 100\right)\% = 13.01\%.$$

    ∴ Answer (b) is correct.

Q. 2.   Population of Bombay = (4068 + 16790) = 20858 thousands.
    ∴ Percentage of literacy in Bombay

$$= \left(\frac{4068}{20858} \times 100\right)\% = 19.5\%.$$

    ∴ Answer (a) is correct.

Q. 3.   Number of literates in Bengal

$$= \left(\frac{16.1}{100} \times 60314\right) = 9715.$$

    ∴ Answer (b) is correct.

Also, number of illiterates in Bengal
= (60314 – 9715) = 50599 thousands.
Filling these entries, the complete table is given below :

States	Population	Literates	Illiterates	Percentage of Literacy
Madras	49342	6421	42921	13.01%
Bombay	20858	4068	16790	19.5%
Bengal	60314	9715	50599	16.1%

Ex. 4. *The following table shows the production of food grains (in million tonnes) in a state for the period from 1988-89 to 1992-93.*

Year	Production in Million Tonnes				Total
	Wheat	Rice	Maize	Other cereals	
1988–89	580	170	150	350	1350
1989–90	600	220	234	400	1474
1990–91	560	240	228	420	1538
1991–92	680	300	380	460	1660
1992–93	860	260	340	500	1910
Total	3280	1190	1332	2130	7932

Read the above table and mark a tick against the correct answer in each of the following questions :

1. During the period from 1988-89 to 1992-93 what percent of the total production is the wheat ?
   (a) 42.6%   (b) 43.1%
   (c) 41.3%   (d) 40.8%
2. During the year 1992-93 the percentage increase in production of wheat over the previous year was :
   (a) 26.4%   (b) 20.9%
   (c) 23.6%   (d) 18.7%
3. In the year 1991-92, the increase in production was maximum for :
   (a) wheat   (b) rice
   (c) maize   (d) other cereals
4. During the year 1990-91, the percentage of decrease in production of maize was
   (a) 2.63%   (b) 2.56%
   (c) 2.71%   (d) 2.47%
5. The increase in the production of other cereals was minimum during the year :
   (a) 1989-90   (b) 1990-91
   (c) 1991-92   (d) 1992-93

Solution :

Q. 1. Total production during the period = 7932 million tonnes.
Wheat production during the period = 3280 million tonnes.
Percentage of wheat production over total production
$$= \left(\frac{3280}{7932} \times 100\right)\% = 41.3\%.$$
∴ Answer (c) is correct.

Q. 2. Increase in 1992-93 in wheat production over 1991-92
$$= (860 - 680) = 180 \text{ million tonnes.}$$
Increase $\% = \left(\frac{180}{680} \times 100\right)\% = 26.4\%$
∴ Answer (a) is correct.

Q. 3. During 1991-92, as read from the table the increase in the production of wheat, rice, maize and other cereals is 120, 60, 152 and 40 million tonnes respectively. So, increase in maize production is maximum.
So, answer (c) is correct.

Q. 4. Decrease in production of maize in 1990-91
$$= (234 - 228) = 6 \text{ million tonnes.}$$
Decrease $\% = \left(\frac{6}{234} \times 100\right)\% = 2.56\%.$
∴ Answer (b) is correct.

Q. 5. Increase in production of other cereals in 1989-90, 1990-91, 1991-92 and 1992-93 over previous year is 50, 20, 40, 40 million tonnes respectively. So the increase is minimum in 1990-91.
∴ Answer (b) is correct.

Ex. 5. *Study the following table carefully and answer the questions given below :* **(Bank P.O. Exam. 1987)**

LOAN DISBURSED BY 5 BANKS
(Rupees in Crores)

Banks	Years				
	1982	1983	1984	1985	1986
A	18	23	45	30	70
B	27	33	18	41	37
C	29	29	22	17	11
D	31	16	28	32	43
E	13	19	27	34	42
Total	118	120	140	154	203

Tabulation

Q. 1. In which year was the disbursement of loans of all the banks put together least compared to the average disbursement of loans over the years :
(a) 1982
(b) 1983
(c) 1984
(d) 1985
(e) 1986

Q. 2. What was the percentage increase of disbursement of loans of all banks together from 1984 to 1985 :
(a) 110
(b) 14
(c) $90\frac{10}{11}$
(d) 10
(e) none of these

Q. 3. In which year was the total disbursement of loans of banks A & B exactly equal to the total disbursement of banks D and E ?
(a) 1983
(b) 1986
(c) 1984
(d) 1982
(e) none of these

Q. 4. In which of the following banks did the disbursement of loans continuously increase over the years :
(a) A
(b) B
(c) C
(d) D
(e) E

Q. 5. If the minimum target in the preceding years was 20% of the total disbursement of loans, how many banks reached the target in 1983 :
(a) 1
(b) 3
(c) 2
(d) 4
(e) none of these

Q. 6. In which bank was loan disbursement more than 25% of the disbursement of all banks together in 1986 :
(a) A
(b) B
(c) C
(d) D
(e) E

Solutions :

Q. 1. Average disbursement of loans over the years

$$= \frac{1}{5}(118 + 120 + 140 + 154 + 203) = 147.$$

Clearly, it is least in the year 1982.
So, answer (a) is correct.

Q. 2. Increase of loans from 1984 to 1985

$$= \left(\frac{154 - 140}{140}\right) \times 100\% = 10\%.$$

i.e. (d) is correct.

Q. 3. In none of the years is the sum of loans of A & B is equal to sum of loans of D & E. So, answer (e) is correct.

Q. 4. In bank E the disbursement of loans continuously increase over the years. So, answer (e) is correct.

Q. 5. 20% of total loans disbursed in 1982
= (20% of 118) = 23.6 crores.
Clearly, B & C reached the target in 1983.
So, answer (c) is correct.

Q. 6. In 1986, 25% of total disbursement
= (25% of 203) crores = 50.75 crores.
∴ In bank A, the loan disbursed is more than 25% of the total disbursement of all banks in 1986.
Hence, answer (a) is correct.

Ex. 6. *Study the following table carefully and answer the questions given below :* (Bank P.O. Exam. 1989)

FINANCIAL STATEMENT OF A COMPANY OVER THE YEARS
(Rupees in Lakhs)

Year	Gross Turnover Rs.	Profit before interest and depreciation Rs.	Interest Rs.	Depreciation Rs.	Net Profit Rs.
1980–81	1380.00	380.92	300.25	69.90	10.67
1981–82	1401.00	404.98	315.40	71.12	18.46
1982–83	1540.00	520.03	390.85	80.02	49.16
1983–84	2112.00	599.01	444.44	88.88	65.69
1984–85	2520.00	811.00	505.42	91.91	212.78
1985–86	2758.99	920.00	600.20	99.00	220.80

Q. 1. During which year did the 'Net Profit' exceed Rs. 1 crore for the first time ?
(a) 1985-86 (b) 1984-85
(c) 1983-84 (d) 1982-83 (e) none of these

Q. 2. During which year was the "Gross Turnover" closest to thrice the 'Profit before Interest and Depreciation' ?
(a) 1985-86 (b) 1984-85
(c) 1983-84 (d) 1982-83 (e) 1981-82

Q. 3. During which year did the 'Net Profit' form the highest proportion of the 'Profit before Interest and Depreciation' ?
(a) 1984-85 (b) 1983-84
(c) 1982-83 (d) 1981-82 (e) 1980-81

Q. 4. Which of the following registered the lowest increase in terms of rupees from the year 1984-85 to the year 1985-86 ?
(a) Gross Turnover

Tabulation 457

    (b) Profit before Interest and Depreciation
    (c) Depreciation
    (d) Interest
    (e) Net profit

Q. 5. The 'Gross Turnover' for 1982-83 is about what per cent of the 'Gross Turnover' for 1984-85 ?
    (a) 61   (b) 163
    (c) 0.611
    (d) 39   (e) 0.006

Solutions :

Q. 1. Clearly, the net profit exceeded Rs. 1 crore in the year 1984-85.
So, answer (b) is correct.

Q. 2. The ratio of 'Gross turnover' to the 'profit before Interert and Depreciation':

in 1980-81 is $\dfrac{1380}{380.92} = 3.62$;

in 1981-82 is $\dfrac{1401}{404.98} = 3.46$;

in 1982-83 is $\dfrac{1540}{520.03} = 2.96$;

in 1983-84 is $\dfrac{2112}{599.01} = 3.53$;

in 1984-85 is $\dfrac{2520}{810.11} = 3.11$.

in 1985-86 is $\dfrac{2758.99}{920} = 3$.

So, answer (a) is correct.

Q. 3. Let, Net profit= x% of Profit before interest & depreciation.

For 1980-81, we have $x = \dfrac{10.67 \times 100}{380.92} = 2.80$;

For 1981-82, we have $x = \dfrac{18.46 \times 100}{404.98} = 4.56$;

For 1982-83, we have $x = \dfrac{49.16 \times 100}{520.03} = 9.45$;

For 1983-84, we have $x = \dfrac{65.69 \times 100}{599.01} = 10.97$;

For 1984-85, we have $x = \dfrac{212.78 \times 100}{810.11} = 26.26$;

For 1985-86, we have $x = \dfrac{220.80 \times 100}{920} = 24$.

So, in 1984-85, the net profit forms the highest proportion of the 'profit before interest and depreciation'

∴ Answer (a) is correct.

Q. 4. Increase from the year 1984-85 to 1985-86 in
Gross turnover is (2758.99 − 2520) = 238.99 lakhs;
Profit before int. & depreciation is
(920 − 810.11) = 109.89 lakhs;
Interest is (600.20 − 505.42) = (94.78) lakhs;
Depreciation is (99 − 91.91) = (7.09) lakhs;
Net profit is (220.80 − 212.78) = 8.02 lakhs.
Clearly, the increase is lowest in depreciation.
So, answer (c) is correct.

Q. 5. Let $x\%$ of Gross Turnover for 1984-85
= Gross turnover for 1982-83

Then, $\frac{x}{100} \times 2520 = 1540$ or $x = \frac{1540 \times 100}{2520} = 61$ (approx).

So, answer (a) is correct.

Ex. 7. *Study the following table carefully and answer the questions given below :* (Bank P. O. Exam. 1988)

NUMBER OF BOYS OF STANDARD XI PARTICIPATING IN DIFFERENT GAMES

Games ↓ Class →	XI A	XI B	XI C	XI D	XI E	TOTAL
Chess	8	8	8	4	4	32
Badminton	8	12	8	12	12	52
Table Tennis	12	16	12	8	12	60
Hockey	8	4	8	4	8	32
Football	8	8	12	12	12	52
Total no. of boys	44	48	48	48	48	228

Note :
1. Every student (boy or girl) of each class of standard XI participates in a game.
2. In each class, the number of girls participating in each game is 25% of the number of boys participating in each game.
3. Each student (boy or girl) participates in one and only one game.

Q. 1. All the boys of class XI D passed at the annual examination but a few girls failed. If all the boys and girls who passed and entered XII D

Tabulation 459

and if in class XII D, the ratio of boys to girls is 5 : 1, what would be the number of girls who failed in class XI D ?
(a) 8 (b) 5
(c) 2 (d) 1 (e) none of these

Q. 2. Girls playing which of the following games need to be combined to yield a ratio of boys to girls of 4 : 1, if all boys playing Chess and Badminton are combined ?
(a) Table Tennis and Hockey
(b) Badminton and Table Tennis
(c) Chess and Hockey
(d) Hockey and Football
(e) none of these

Q. 3. What should be the total number of students in the school if all the boys of class XI A together with all the girls of class XI B and class XI C were to be equal to 25% of the total number of students ?
(a) 272 (b) 560
(c) 656 (d) 340 (e) none of these

Q. 4. Boys of which of the following classes need to be combined to equal to four times the number of girls in class XI B and class XI C ?
(a) XI D & XI E (b) XI A & XI B
(c) XI A & XI C (d) XI A & XI D
(e) none of these

Q. 5. If boys of class XI E participating in chess together with girls of class XI B and class XI C participating in Table Tennis & hockey respectively are selected for a course at the college of sports; what percent of the students will get this advantage approximately ?
(a) 4.38 (b) 3.51
(c) 10.52 (d) 13.5 (e) none of these

Q. 6. If for social work, every boy of class XI D and class XI C is paired with a girl of the same class, what percentage of the boys of these two classes cannot participate in social work ?
(a) 88 (b) 66
(c) 60 (d) 75 (e) none of these

Solutions :

Q. 1. Total number of boys in XI D = 40
Number of girls in XI D = 25% of 40 = 10.
Since all boys of XI D passed, so the number of boys in XII D = 40.
Ratio of boys & girls in XII D is 5 : 1.

Number of girls in XII D = $\left(\dfrac{1}{5} \times 40\right) = 8$.

So, the number of girls failed in XI D = $(10 - 8) = 2$.

∴ Answer (c) is correct.

Q. 2. Total number of boys playing chess & Badminton
$$= (32 + 52) = 84.$$
Number of girls playing hockey & football
$$= 25\% \text{ of } 84 = \left(\dfrac{1}{4} \times 84\right) = 21.$$

Since $84 : 21$ is $4 : 1$, so the girls playing hockey and football are combined to yield a ratio of boys to girls as $4 : 1$.

So, answer (d) is correct.

Q. 3. Number of boys in XI A = 44;
Number of girls in XI B = 25% of 48 = 12;
Number of girls in XI C = 25% of 48 = 12;
∴ $(44 + 12 + 12) = 68$

Let x be the total number of students.

Then, 25% of $x = 68$ or $x = \dfrac{68 \times 100}{25} = 272$.

Total number of students in the school = 272, i.e. (a) is correct.

Q. 4. 4 times the number of girls in XI B & XI C.
$= 4 (12 + 12) = 96.$

But, none of the pairs of classes given through (A) to (D) has this as the number of boys. So, (e) is correct.

Q. 5. Number of boys of XI E playing chess = 4;
Number of girls of XI B playing table tennis = 25% of 16 = 4;
Number of girls of XI C playing hockey = 25% of 8 = 2
∴ Number of students selected for a course at the college of sports
$$= (4 + 4 + 2) = 10.$$
Total number of students = $(228 + 25\% \text{ of } 228) = 285$.

Let $x\%$ of $285 = 10$ or $x = \left(\dfrac{10 \times 100}{285}\right) = 3.51$.

So, answer (b) is correct.

Q. 6. Since the number of girls = 25% of the number of boys, so only 25% of the boys can participate in social work.

∴ Answer (d) is correct.

31
DATA ANALYSIS

Bar Diagrams

(i) **Multiple Bar Diagrams.** In such bar diagrams two or more adjacent vertical bars are drawn to represent two or more phenomenon for the same place or period.

Ex. 1. *Shown below is the multiple bar diagram depicting the changes in the student's strength of a college in four faculties from 1990-91 to 1992-93. (scale 1 cm. = 100)*

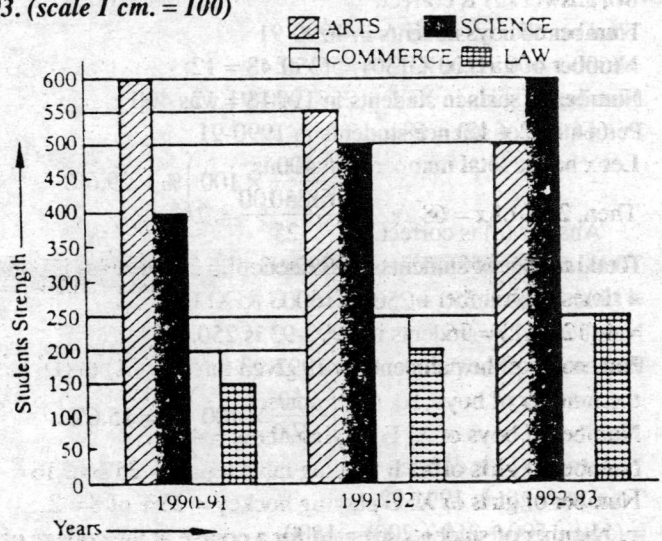

Study the above multiple bar chart and mark a tick against the correct answer in each of the following questions.

Q. 1. The percentage of students in science faculty in 1990-91 was :
 (a) 26.9% (b) 27.8%
 (c) 29.6% (d) 30.2%

Q. 2. The percentage of students in law faculty in 1992-93 was :
 (a) 18.5% (b) 15.6%
 (c) 16.7% (d) 14.8%

Q. 3. How many times was the total strength of the strength of Commerce students in 1991-92 ?
 (a) 3 times (b) 4 times

(c) 5 times (d) 6 times

Q. 4. During which year the strength of arts faculty was minimum ?
(a) 1990-91 (b) 1991-92
(c) 1992-93

Q. 5. How much percent was the increase in science students in 1992-93 over 1990-91 ?
(a) 50% (b) 150%
(c) $66\frac{2}{3}\%$ (d) 75%

Q. 6. A regular decrease in students strength was in the faculty of :
(a) arts (b) Science
(c) Commerce (d) law

Solutions :

Ans. 1. Total number of students in 1990-91
= (600 + 400 + 200 + 150) = 1350.
Number of science students in 1990-91 was 400
Percentage of science students in 1990-91
$$= \left(\frac{400}{1350} \times 100\right)\% = 29.6\%$$
∴ Answer (c) is correct.

Ans. 2. Total number of students in 1992-93
= (500 + 600 + 250 + 250) = 1600.
Number of law students in 1992-93 is 250.
Percentage of law students in 1992-93
$$= \left(\frac{250}{1600} \times 100\right)\% = 15.6\%.$$
∴ Answer (b) is correct.

Ans. 3. Total strength in 1991-92
= (550 + 500 + 250 + 200) = 1500.
∴ $\dfrac{\text{Total strength}}{\text{strength of commerce students}} = \dfrac{1500}{250} = 6.$
So, answer (d) is correct.

Ans. 4. A slight look indicates that the strength in arts faculty in 1990-91, 1991-92 & 1992-93 was 550, 600 and 500 respectively. So, it was minimum in 1992-93.
∴ Answer (c) is correct.

Ans. 5. Number of science students in 1990-91 was 400.
Number of science students in 1992-93 was 600.
Percentage increase $= \left(\dfrac{200}{400} \times 100\right)\% = 50\%.$

∴ Answer (a) is correct.

Ans. 6. As the diagram shows the decrease every year is in arts faculty.
So, answer (a) is correct.

Ex. 2. *Given below is a bar diagram showing the percentage of Hindus, Sikhs and Muslims in a state during the years 1989 to 1992.*

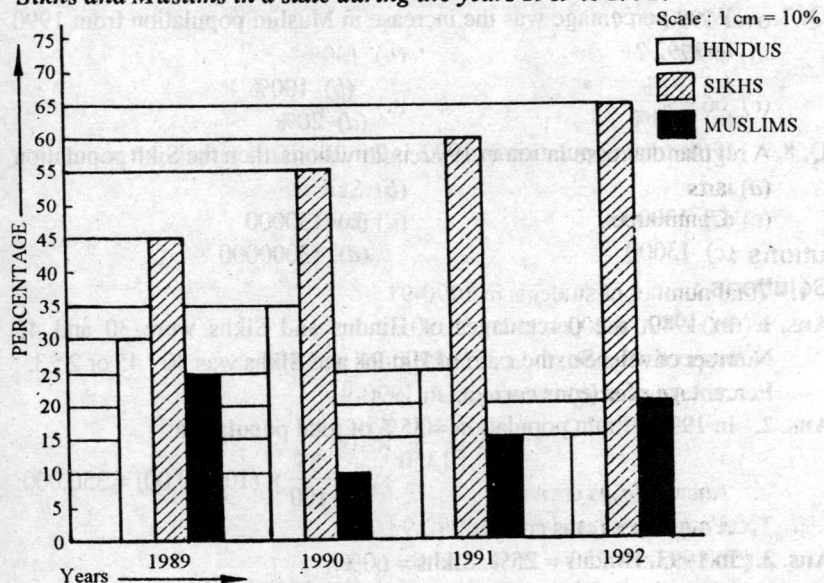

Study the above diagram and mark a tick against the correct answer in each one of the following questions :

Q. 1. The ratio between Hindus & Sikhs in 1989 was :
    (a) 3 : 2   (b) 2 : 3
    (c) can not be calculated

Q. 2. If the total population of the state in 1990 is 1 million, then the Hindus population was :
    (a) 35000000   (b) 3500000
    (c) 350000   (d) 35000

Q. 3. What was the percentage of Sikhs over Hindus in 1991 ?
    (a) 35%   (b) 40%
    (c) 140%   (d) 240%

Q. 4. What percentage was the decrease in Hindus population from 1989 to 1992 ?
    (a) 15%   (b) 45%
    (c) 50%   (d) 25%

Q. 5. If the population of the state in 1989 be 6 lakhs, then what is the total population of Hindus and Muslims in this year ?

(a) 270000 (b) 3300000
(c) 330000 (d) 33000

Q. 6. During which year was the Hindu percentage maximum ?
(a) 1989 (b) 1990
(c) 1991 (d) 1992

Q. 7. What percentage was the increase in Muslim population from 1990 to 1992 ?
(a) 10% (b) 100%
(c) 200% (d) 20%

Q. 8. If the total population in 1992 is 2 millions, then the Sikh population is :
(a) 1300000 (b) 130000
(c) 13000 (d) 13000000

Solutions :

Ans. 1. In 1989, the percentages of Hindus and Sikhs were 30 and 45 respectively. So, the ratio of Hindus and Sikhs was 30 : 45 or 2 : 3.
∴ Answer (b) is correct.

Ans. 2. In 1990, Hindu population = 35% of total population
$$= \frac{35}{100} \times (10,000,00) = 350,000.$$
∴ Answer (c) is correct.

Ans. 3. In 1993, Hindus = 25%, Sikhs = 60%.
∴ Percentage of Sikhs over Hindus = $\left(\frac{60}{25} \times 100\right)$ = 240%.
So, answer (d) is correct.

Ans. 4. Hindus in 1989 = 30%.
Hindus in 1992 = 15%.
Over 30, decrease = 15.
Over 100, decrease = $\left(\frac{15}{30} \times 100\right)$ = 50%.
∴ Answer (c) is correct.

Ans. 5. In 1989, Sikh population = (45% of 600000)
$= \left(\frac{45}{100} \times 600000\right) = 270000.$
∴ (Hindus + Muslims) = 600000 - 270000 = 330000.
So, answer (c) is correct.

Ans. 6. A quick observation of the chart shows that Hindus in 1989, 90, 91 and 92 were 30%, 35%, 25%, 15% respectively.
So, the maximum Hindu percentage was in 1990.
∴ Answer (b) is correct.

Ans. 7. Muslim population in 1990 = 10%.
Muslim population in 1992 = 20%.
Increase on 10 = 10.
Increase on 100 = $\left(\dfrac{10}{10} \times 100\right)\% = 100\%$.
∴ Answer (b) is correct.

Ans. 8. In 1992, Sikh population = (65% of 2000000)
$$= \left(\dfrac{65}{100} \times 2000000\right) = 1300000.$$
∴ Answer (a) is correct.

Ex. 3. *Study the following graph carefully and answer the questions given below it :*

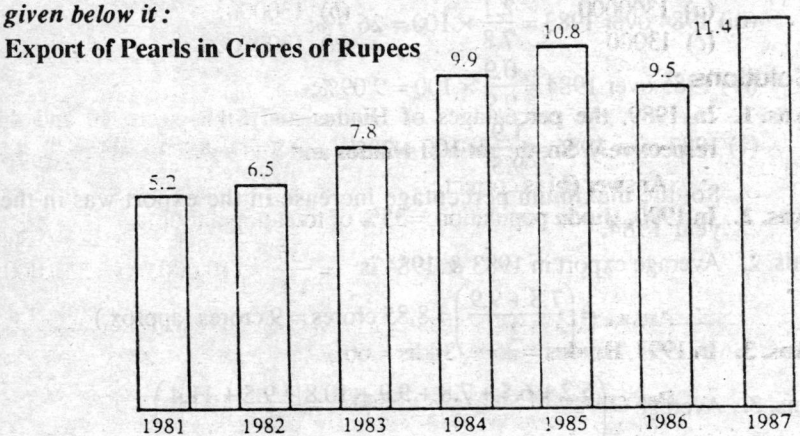

Export of Pearls in Crores of Rupees

(Bar graph values: 1981: 5.2, 1982: 6.5, 1983: 7.8, 1984: 9.9, 1985: 10.8, 1986: 9.5, 1987: 11.4)

Q. 1. In which year there was maximum percentage increase in export of pearls to that in the previous year ?
(a) 1982 (b) 1987
(c) 1985 (d) 1984

Q. 2. In which of the following pairs of years was the average export of pearls around 9 crores ?
(a) 1982 & 1983 (b) 1983 & 1984
(c) 1984 & 1985 (d) 1985 & 1986

Q. 3. In how many years was the export above the average for the given period :
(a) 2 (b) 3
(c) 4 (d) 5

Q. 4. In which year was the export equal to the average export of the preceding and the following year :
(a) 1982 (b) 1983
(c) 1985 (d) 1986

Q. 5. What was the percentage increase in export from 1986 to 1987 ?

(a) $16\frac{2}{3}\%$ (b) 20%

(c) 19% (d) $33\frac{1}{3}\%$

Solutions :

Ans. 1. Percentage increase in export of pearls in :

(i) 1982 over 1981 $= \dfrac{1.3}{5.2} \times 100 = 25\%$;

(ii) 1983 over 1982 $= \dfrac{1.3}{6.5} \times 100 = 20\%$;

(iii) 1984 over 1983 $= \dfrac{2.1}{7.8} \times 100 = 26.9\%$;

(iv) 1985 over 1984 $= \dfrac{0.9}{9.9} \times 100 = 9.09\%$;

(v) 1987 over 1986 $= \dfrac{1.9}{9.5} \times 100 = 20\%$.

So, the maximum percentage increase in the export was in the year 1984.

Ans. 2. Average export in 1983 & 1984 is

$$= \left(\frac{7.8 + 9.9}{2}\right) = 8.85 \text{ crores} = 9 \text{ crores (approx.)}$$

Ans. 3. Average $= \left(\dfrac{5.2 + 6.5 + 7.8 + 9.9 + 10.8 + 9.5 + 11.4}{7}\right)$

$$= \frac{61.1}{7} = 8.73.$$

So, the export above the average was in the years 1984, 1985, 1986 & 1987.

Ans. 4. Average of 1981 & 1983 $= \dfrac{5.2 + 7.8}{2} = 6.5$.

= export in 1982.

Ans. 5. Percentage increase from 1986 to 1987.

$$= \left(\frac{11.4 - 9.5}{9.5}\right) \times 100 = \frac{1.9}{9.5} \times 100 = 20\%.$$

Ex. 4. *Examine the following graph carefully and answer the questions given below it :—*

Production of Cotton bales of 100 kg. each in lacs in states A, B, C, D & E during 1985-86, 1986-87 & 1987-88.

Data Analysis

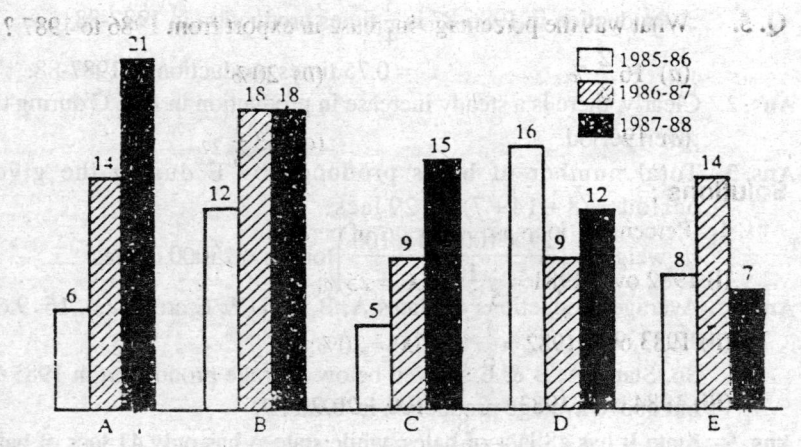

Q. 1. The production of state D in 1986-87 is how many times its production in 1987-88 :
- (a) 1.33
- (b) 0.75
- (c) 0.56
- (d) 1.77

Q. 2. In which states is there a steady increase in the production of cotton during the given period :
- (a) A & B
- (b) A & C
- (c) B only
- (d) D & E

Q. 3. How many tonnes of cotton was produced by state E during the given period :
- (a) 2900
- (b) 29000
- (c) 290000
- (d) 2900000

Q. 4. How many states showing below average production in 1985-86, showed above average production in 1986-87 :
- (a) 4
- (b) 2
- (c) 3
- (d) 1

Q. 5. Which of the following statements is false :
- (a) States A & E showed the same production in 1986-87
- (b) There was no improvement in the production of cotton in state B during 1987-88
- (c) State A has produced maximum cotton during the given period
- (d) Products of states C and D together is equal to that of state B during 1986-87

Solutions :

Ans. 1. $\dfrac{\text{Production in (1986–87)}}{\text{Production in (1987–88)}} = \dfrac{9}{12} = \dfrac{3}{4}$.

∴ Production in 1986-87 is $\frac{3}{4}$ times production in 1987-88

= 0.75 times production in 1987-88.

Ans. 2. Clearly, there is a steady increase in production in A & C during the given period.

Ans. 3. Total number of bales produced by E during the given period = (8 + 14 + 7) *i.e.* 29 lacs.

Its weight = $\left(\dfrac{29 \times 100000 \times 100}{1000}\right)$ tonnes = 29000 tonnes.

Ans. 4. Average productions of states A, B, C, D & E are 13.66, 16, 9.66, 12.33, 9.66.

So, States A, B & E showed below average production in 1985-86 but above average production in 1986-87.

Ans. 5. State B has 48 lacs of bales, while state A has only 41 lacs of bales during the given period.

So, statement (c) is false.

Ex. 5. Study the following graph carefully and answer the following questions : **(Bank P.O. Exam. 1989)**

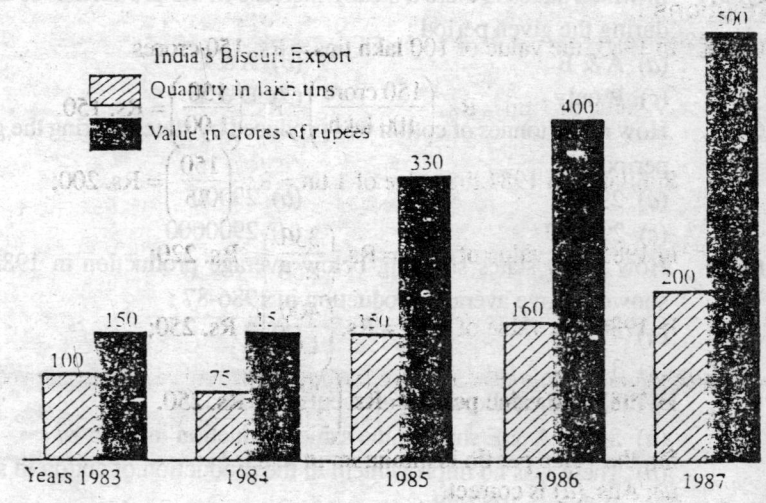

Q. 1. In which year the value per tin was minimum ?
  (a) 1983   (b) 1984
  (c) 1985   (d) 1986
  (e) 1987

Q. 2. What was the difference between the tins exported in 1985 and 1986 ?
  (a) 10   (b) 1000

Data Analysis

      (c) 100000   (d) 1000000
      (e) none of these

Q. 3. What was the approximate percent increase in export value from 1983 to 1987 ?
      (a) 350   (b) 330
      (c) 43   (d) 2.4
      (e) none of these

Q. 4. What was the percentage drop in export quantity from 1983 to 1984 ?
      (a) 75   (b) nil
      (c) 25   (d) 50
      (e) none of these

Q. 5. If in 1986 the tins were exported at the same rate per tin as that in 1985, what would be the value in crores of rupees of export in 1986 ?
      (a) 400   (b) 352
      (c) 375   (d) 330
      (e) none of these

Solutions :

Ans. 1. In 1983, the value of 100 lakh tins = Rs. 150 crores

$\therefore$ Value of 1 tin = Rs. $\left(\dfrac{150 \text{ crore}}{100 \text{ lakh}}\right)$ = Rs. $\left(\dfrac{150}{1.00}\right)$ = Rs. 150.

Similarly, in 1984 the value of 1 tin = Rs. $\left(\dfrac{150}{.75}\right)$ = Rs. 200;

in 1985, the value of 1 tin = Rs. $\left(\dfrac{330}{1.50}\right)$ = Rs. 220;

In 1986, the value of 1 tin = Rs. $\left(\dfrac{400}{1.60}\right)$ = Rs. 250;

In 1987, the value per tin = Rs. $\left(\dfrac{500}{2.00}\right)$ = Rs. 250.

So, the value per tin is minimum in 1983.
i.e. Ans. (a) is correct.

Ans. 2. Difference between the tins exported in 1985 & 1986 is
= [(160 lakhs) − (150 lakhs)] = 10 lakhs = 1000000.
So, answer (d) is correct.

Ans. 3. Percentage increase in export value from 1983 to 1987

$= \left\{\dfrac{(500 \text{ crores} - 150 \text{ crores})}{150 \text{ crores}} \times 100\right\}\%$

$$= \left\{\frac{(500-150)}{150} \times 100\right\}\% = \left(\frac{350}{150} \times 100\right)\% = 233.3\%.$$

So, answer (e) is correct.

Ans. 4. Percentage drop in export quantity from 1983 to 1984

$$= \left\{\frac{(100 \text{ lakh tonnes}) - (75 \text{ lakh tonnes})}{100 \text{ lakh tonnes}} \times 100\right\}$$

$$= \left(\frac{25}{100} \times 100\right)\% = 25\%.$$

∴ Answer (c) is correct.

Ans. 5. In 1985, the cost of 150 lakh tins = Rs. 330 crores.

∴ In 1985, the cost of 1 tin = Rs. $\left(\dfrac{330 \text{ crores}}{150 \text{ lakhs}}\right)$

$$= \text{Rs.} \left(\frac{330}{1.50}\right) \text{Rs. 220.}$$

In 1986, the export value = Rs. (160 lakh × 220)
= Rs. (1.60 × 220) crores
= Rs. 352 crores.

Hence, answer (b) is correct.

Ex. 6. *Study the graph carefully and answer the questions given below it :* (Bank P.O. Exam. 1988)

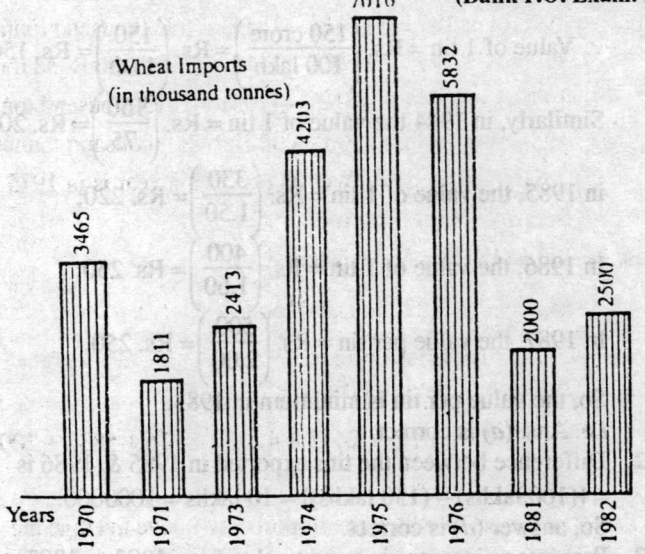

Wheat Imports (in thousand tonnes)

7016, 5832, 4203, 3465, 2500, 2413, 2000, 1811

Years: 1970, 1971, 1973, 1974, 1975, 1976, 1981, 1982

Q. 1. In which year did the imports register highest increase over its preceding year ?
(a) 1973 (b) 1974
(c) 1975 (d) 1982

Data Analysis

Q. 2. The imports in 1976 was approximately how many times that of the year 1971 ?
    (a) 0.31   (b) 1.68
    (c) 2.41   (d) 3.22

Q. 3. What is the ratio of the years which have above average imports to those which have below average imports ?
    (a) 5 : 3   (b) 2 : 6
    (c) 8 : 3   (d) 3 : 8
    (e) none of these

Q. 4. The increase in imports in 1982 was what percent of the imports in 1981 ?
    (a) 25   (b) 5
    (c) 125   (d) 80

Q. 5. The imports in 1974 is approximately what percent of the average imports for the given years ?
    (a) 125   (b) 115
    (c) 190   (d) 85
    (e) 65

Solutions :

Ans. 1. Increase in imports in
1973 over 1971 is (2413 − 1811) = 602 thousand tonnes;
1974 over 1973 is (4203 − 2413) = 1790 thousand tonnes;
1975 over 1974 is (7016 − 4203) = 2813 thousand tonnes;
1981 over 198 is (2500 − 2000) = 500 thousand tonnes.
∴ Highest increase over its preceding year is in 1975.
i.e. Answer (c) is correct.

Ans. 2. Let k (1811) = 5832. Then,
$$k = \frac{5832}{1811} = 3.22 \text{ thousand tonnes.}$$
∴ Answer (d) is correct.

Ans. 3. Average of the imports
$$= \frac{1}{8}(3465 + 1811 + 2413 + 4203 + 7016 + 5832 + 2000 + 2500)$$
$$= 3655.$$
The years in which the imports are above average are 1974, 1975 & 1976. *i.e.* there are 3 such years.
The years in which the imports are below average are 1970, 1971, 1973, 1981 & 1982 *i.e.* there are 5 such years.
∴ Required ratio is 3 : 5.

So, answer (e) is correct.

Ans. 4. Increase in imports in 1982 over 1981

$$= \left(\frac{2500 - 2000}{2000} \times 100\right)\% = 25\%.$$

∴ Answer (a) is correct.

Ans. 5. Average import = 3655 thousand tonnes.
Import in 1974 = 4203 thousand tonnes.
Let $x\%$ of 3655 = 4203.

Then, $x = \left(\dfrac{4203 \times 100}{3655}\right) = 115\%.$

∴ Answer (b) is correct.

Ex. 7. *Study the following graph carefully and answer the following questions.* (Bank P.O. Exam. 1988)

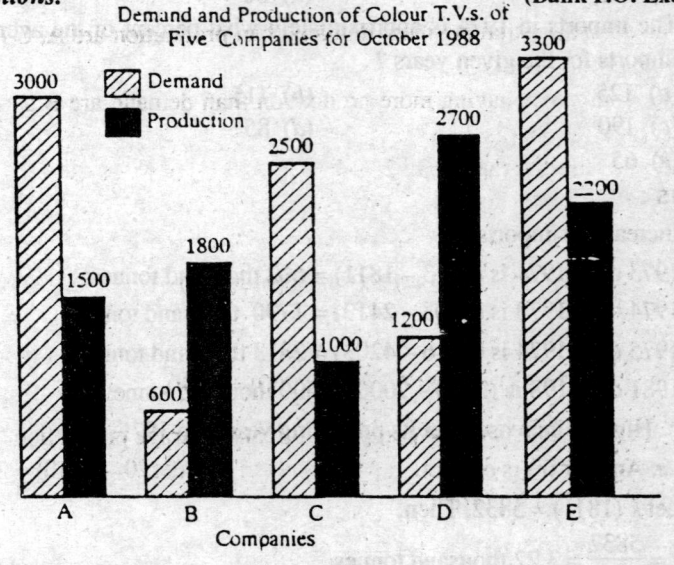

Demand and Production of Colour T.V.s. of Five Companies for October 1988

[Bar graph showing Demand and Production for companies A–E:
A: Demand 3000, Production 1500
B: Demand 600, Production 1800
C: Demand 2500, Production 1000
D: Demand 1200, Production 2700
E: Demand 3300, Production 2200]

Q. 1. What is the ratio of companies having more demand than production to those having more production than demand?
   (a) 2 : 3   (b) 4 : 1
   (c) 2 : 2   (d) 3 : 2

Q. 2. What is the difference between average demand and average production of the five companies taken together?
   (a) 1400   (b) 400
   (c) 280   (d) 138
   (e) none of these

Q. 3. The production of company D is approximately how many times that of the production of the company A?

(a) 1.8 (b) 1.5
(c) 2.5 (d) 1.1
(e) none of these

Q. 4. The demand for company 'B' is approximately what percent of the demand for company 'C' ?
(a) 4 (b) 24
(c) 20 (d) 60

Q. 5. If company 'A' desires to meet the demand by purchasing surplus T.V. sets from a single company, which one of the following companies can meet the need adequately ?
(a) B (b) C
(c) D (d) none of these

Solutions :

Ans. 1. The companies having more demand than production are A, C & E
i.e. their number is 3.
The companies having more production than demand are B and D.
i.e. their number is 2.
So, the required ratio is 3 : 2.
∴ Answer (d) is correct.

Ans. 2. Average demand
$= \frac{1}{5} (3000 + 600 + 2500 + 1200 + 3300) = 2120.$

Average production
$= \frac{1}{5} (1500 + 1800 + 1000 + 2700 + 2200) = 1840.$

∴ Difference between average demand and average production
$= (2120 - 1840) = 280.$
So, answer (c) is correct.

Ans. 3. Let $k (1500) = 2700$ or $k = \frac{2700}{1500} = 1.8.$
So, answer (a) is correct.

Ans. 4. Let x% of (demand for c) = (demand for B).
i.e. $\frac{x}{100} \times 2500 = 600$ or $x = \left(\frac{600 \times 100}{2500}\right) = 24\%.$
∴ Answer (b) is correct.

Ans. 5. Since company D produces highest number of T.V. sets and company A desires to meet the demand by purchasing surplus T.V. sets from a single company. Clearly, D can meet the demand of A.
∴ Answer (c) is correct.

Ex. 8. **Study the following graph and answer the questions given below :** Result of Annual Examination In a High School (P.N.B. P.O. Exam. 1987)

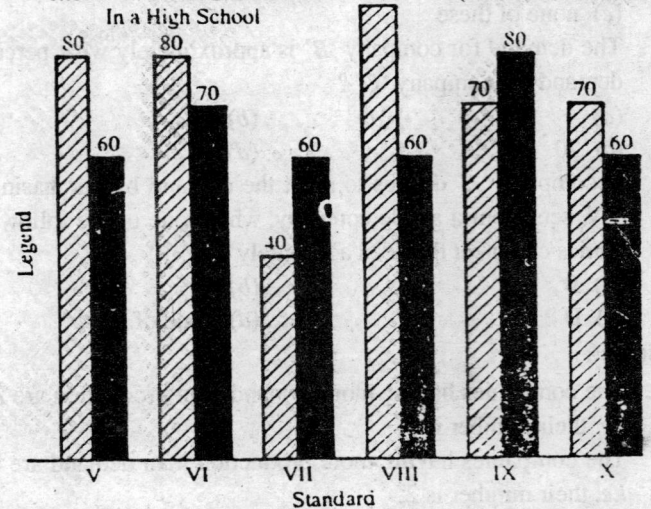

Q. 1. In which standard is the difference between the results of girls and boys maximum ?
(a) V (b) VII
(c) X (d) VIII

Q. 2. In which standard is the result of boys less than the average result of the girls ?
(a) VII (b) IX
(c) VI (d) VIII (e) V

Q. 3. In which pair of standards are the results of girls and boys in inverse proportion ?
(a) V & X (b) V & VI
(c) VI & VIII (d) V & IX (e) VI & IX

Q. 4. In which standard is the result of the girls more than the average result of the boys for the school ?
(a) IX (b) VIII
(c) VI (d) X (e) none of these

Q. 5. In which standard is the failure of girls lowest ?
(a) X (b) VII
(c) VIII (d) V (e) none of these

Solutions :

Ans. 1. The difference between the results of girls and boys
in V standard is 20; in VI standard is 10;
in VII standard is 20; in VIII standard is 30;

Data Analysis

in IX standard is 10 & in X standard is 10.
So, it is maximum in VIII standard, *i.e.* (d) is correct.

Ans. 2. Average result of girls
$$= \frac{1}{6}(60 + 70 + 60 + 60 + 80 + 60) = \frac{390}{6} = 65\%.$$
So, in VII standard the result of boys is less than the average result of the girls. Therefore, (a) is correct.

Ans. 3. In VI standard, the results of boys and girls are in the ratio 8 : 7;
While in IX standard, the results of boys and girls are in the ratio 7 : 8.
So, answer (e) is correct.

Ans. 4. Average result of boys
$$= \frac{1}{6}(80 + 80 + 40 + 90 + 70 + 70) = \frac{430}{6} = 71.7\%.$$
Clearly, in IX standard the result of girls is more than the average result of the boys. So, answer (a) is correct.

Ans. 5. Maximum number of girls passed is in IX standard.
So, the failure of girls is lowest in IX standard.
Hence, answer (e) is correct.

SUB-DIVIDED BAR DIAGRAMS

Sub-divided bar diagrams : In such diagrams every column is divided into certain parts to represent different phenomenon for the same period or place.

Ex. 9. *The sub-divided bar diagram given below depicts the result of B.Sc. students of a college for three years.*

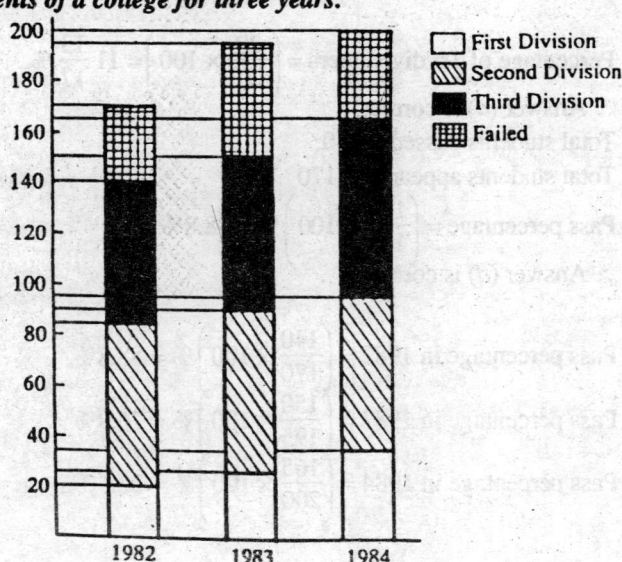

Study the above bar diagram and mark a tick against the correct answer in each question.

Q. 1. How many percent passed in 1st division in 1982 ?
(a) 20% (b) 34%
(c) $14\frac{2}{7}\%$ (d) $11\frac{13}{17}\%$

Q. 2. What was the pass percentage in 1982 ?
(a) 65% (b) 70%
(c) 74.6% (d) 88.8%

Q. 3. In which year the college had the best result for B.Sc. ?
(a) 1982 (b) 1983
(c) 1984

Q. 4. What is the number of third divisioners in 1984 ?
(a) 165 (b) 75
(c) 70 (d) 65

Q. 5. What is the percentage of students in 1984 over 1982 ?
(a) 30% (b) $17\frac{11}{17}\%$
(c) $117\frac{11}{17}\%$ (d) 85%

Q. 6. What is the aggregate pass percentage during three years ?
(a) $51\frac{2}{3}\%$ (b) 82.7%
(c) 80.4% (d) 77.6%

Solutions :

Ans. 1.
Percentage of 1st divisioners $=\left(\frac{20}{170}\times 100\right)=11\frac{13}{17}\%$.
∴ Answer (d) is correct.

Ans. 2. Total students passed = 140.
Total students appeared = 170.
Pass percentage $=\left(\frac{140}{170}\times 100\right)\% = 88.8\%$.
∴ Answer (d) is correct.

Ans. 3.
Pass percentage in 1982 $=\left(\frac{140}{170}\times 100\right)\% = 88.8\%$.
Pass percentage in 1983 $=\left(\frac{150}{195}\times 100\right)\% = 76.9\%$.
Pass percentage in 1984 $=\left(\frac{165}{200}\times 100\right)\% = 82.5\%$.

So, the college recorded best result in 1982.
∴ Answer (a) is correct.

Ans. 4. Third divisioners in 1984 = (165 – 95) = 70.
∴ Answer (c) is correct.

Ans. 5. Students in 1984 = 200.
Students in 1982 = 170.
Required percentage = $\left(\dfrac{200}{170} \times 100\right)\% = 117\dfrac{11}{17}\%$.
∴ Answer (c) is correct.

Ans. 6. Total number of students appeared during 3 years
= (170 + 195 + 200) = 565.
Total number of students passed during 3 years
= (140 + 150 + 165) = 455.
Aggregate pass percentage = $\left(\dfrac{455}{565} \times 100\right)\% = 80.4\%$.
So, answer (c) is correct.

Ex. 10. *Following bar diagram shows the monthly expenditure of two families on food, clothing, education, fuel, house rent and miscellaneous (in percentage).*

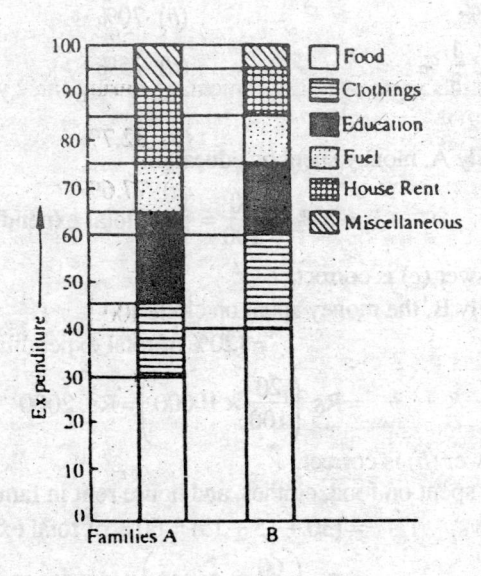

Study the above diagram and mark a tick against the correct answer in each question.

Q. 1. What fraction of the total expenditure is spent on Education in family A ?

(a) $\dfrac{13}{20}$ (b) $\dfrac{2}{3}$

(c) $\dfrac{9}{13}$ (d) none of these

Q. 2. If the total annual expenditure of family B is Rs. 10,000 then money spent on clothes during the year is :
(a) Rs. 200   (b) Rs. 2000
(c) Rs. 600   (d) Rs. 6000

Q. 3. If the total annual expenditure of family A is Rs. 30,000 then money spent on food, clothes and house rent is :
(a) Rs. 18,500   (b) Rs. 18,000
(c) Rs. 21,000   (d) Rs. 15,000

Q. 4. If both the families have the same expenditure, which one spends more on education and miscellaneous together ?
(a) Family A   (b) Family B
(c) none

Q. 5. What percentage is B's expenditure on food over A's expenditure on food ? (Taking equal total expenditure)
(a) 10%   (b) 70%
(c) $133\dfrac{1}{3}$%   (d) 75%

Solutions :

Ans. 1. In family A, money spent on education

$$= 20\% = \dfrac{20}{100} = \dfrac{1}{5} \text{ (of total expenditure)}$$

∴ Answer (c) is correct.

Ans. 2. In family B, the money spent on clothes

$$= (20\% \text{ of total expenditure})$$

$$= \text{Rs.} \left(\dfrac{20}{100} \times 10000\right) = \text{Rs. 2000}.$$

∴ Answer (b) is correct.

Ans. 3. Money spent on food, clothes, and house rent in family A

$$= (30 + 15 + 15) = 60\% \text{ of total expenditure}$$

$$= \text{Rs.} \left(\dfrac{60}{100} \times 30000\right) = \text{Rs. 18000}.$$

∴ Answer (b) is correct.

Ans. 4. Family A spends on Education & Miscellaneous

$$= (20 + 10) = 30\%$$

Family B spends on Education & Miscellaneous

= (15 + 5) = 20%
So, family A spends more on these heads.
∴ Answer (a) is correct.

Ans. 5. B's expenditure on food = 40%
A's expenditure on food = 30%
B's percentage over A's = $\left(\dfrac{40}{30} \times 100\right) = 133\dfrac{1}{3}\%$
∴ Answer (c) is correct.

CIRCLE GRAPH

Ex. 11. *Circle-graph given below shows the expenditure incurred in bringing out a book, by a publisher.*

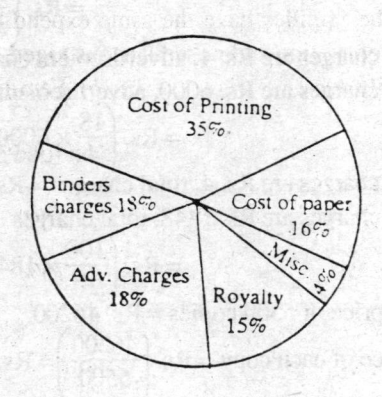

（Pie chart: Cost of Printing 35%, Binders charges 18%, Cost of paper 16%, Misc. 6%, Royalty 15%, Adv. Charges 18%）

Study the graph carefully and answer the questions give below it :

Q. 1. What should be the central angle of the sector for the cost of the paper :
   (a) 22.5°   (b) 16°
   (c) 54.8°   (d) 57.6°

Q. 2. If the cost of printing is Rs. 17500, the rayalty is :
   (a) Rs. 8750   (b) Rs. 7500
   (c) Rs. 3150   (d) Rs. 6300

Q. 3. If the miscellaneous charges are Rs. 6000, the advertisement charges are :
   (a) Rs. 90000   (b) Rs. 1333.33
   (c) Rs. 27000   (d) Rs. 12000

Q. 4. If 5500 copies are published, miscellaneous expenditures amount to Rs. 1848 and publisher's profit is 25%, then marked price of each copy is :
   (a) Rs. 8.40   (b) Rs. 12.50

(c) Rs. 10.50 (d) Rs. 10

Q. 5. Royalty on the book is less than the advertisement charges by :
(a) 3% (b) 20%
(c) $16\frac{2}{3}\%$ (d) none of these

Solutions :

Q. 1.
Requisite angle $= \left(\frac{16}{100} \times 360\right)° = 57.6°$.

Q. 2. If cost of printing is Rs. 35, royalty is Rs. 15
If cost of printing is Rs. 17500, royalty is
$= Rs. \left(\frac{15}{35} \times 17500\right) = Rs. 7500$.

Q. 3. If misc. charges are Rs. 4, advertisement charges = Rs. 18.
If misc. charges are Rs. 6000, advertisement charges
$= Rs. \left(\frac{18}{4} \times 6000\right) = Rs. 27000$.

Q. 4. If misc. charges are Rs. 4, total charges = Rs. 100
If misc. charges are Rs. 1848, total charges
$= Rs. \left(\frac{100}{4} \times 1848\right) = Rs. 46200$.
∴ Cost price of 5500 copies = Rs. 46200.
Cost price of each copy $= Rs. \left(\frac{46200}{5500}\right) = Rs. 8.40$
∴ Marked price of each copy = 125% of Rs. 8.40 = Rs. 10.50.

Q. 5. On Rs. 18, it is less by Rs. 3.
On Rs. 100, it is less by $\left(\frac{3}{18} \times 100\right) = 16\frac{2}{3}\%$.

Ex. 12. *Study the following graphs carefully and answer the questions that follow* **(Bank P.O. Exam. 1988)**

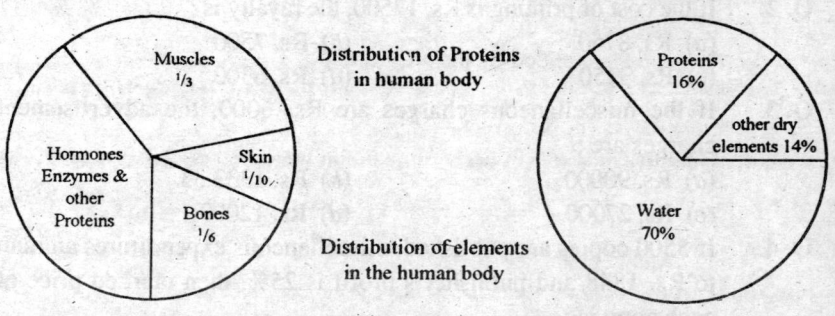

Distribution of Proteins in human body
- Muscles 1/3
- Hormones Enzymes & other Proteins
- Skin 1/10
- Bones 1/6

Distribution of elements in the human body
- Proteins 16%
- other dry elements 14%
- Water 70%

Q. 1. What is the ratio of the distribution of proteins in the muscles to that of the distribution of proteins in the bones ?

(a) 1 : 2   (b) 2 : 1
(c) 18 : 1   (d) 1 : 18

Q. 2. What percent of the total weight of the human body is equivalent to the weight of the skin in the human body ?
(a) .016   (b) 1.6
(c) .16   (d) insufficient information

Q. 3. To show the distribution of proteins and other dry elements in the human body, the arc of the circle should subtend at the centre an angle of
(a) 126°   (b) 54°
(c) 108°   (d) 252°

Q. 4. What will be the quantity of water in the body of a person weighing 50 kg ?
(a) 35 kg   (b) 120 kg
(c) 71.42 kg   (d) 20 kg

Q. 5. In the human body what is made of neither bones nor skin ?
(a) $\dfrac{2}{5}$ (b) $\dfrac{3}{5}$
(c) $\dfrac{1}{40}$ (d) $\dfrac{3}{80}$

Solutions :

Ans. 1. Required ratio $= \dfrac{1}{3} : \dfrac{1}{6} = 6 : 3$ or $2 : 1$.

So, answer (b) is correct.

Ans. 2. Weight of skin $= \dfrac{1}{10}$ parts of 16% of proteins

$$= \dfrac{1}{10} \times 16\% = 1.6\%.$$

So, answer (b) is correct.

Ans. 3. Proteins & other dry elements = 30%.

∴ Angle subtended by the required arc
$$= (30\% \text{ of } 360°) = 108°.$$

So, answer (c) is correct.

Ans. 4. Quantity of water in body of a person weighing 50 kg

$$= 70\% \text{ of } 50 \text{ kg} = \left(\dfrac{70}{100} \times 50\right) \text{kg} = 35 \text{ kg}.$$

∴ Answer (a) is correct.

Ans. 5. Part of the body made of neither bones nor skin

$$= 1 - \left(\dfrac{1}{3} + \dfrac{1}{10} + \dfrac{1}{6}\right) = \left(1 - \dfrac{6}{10}\right) = \dfrac{2}{5}.$$

∴ Answer (a) is correct.

Ex. 13. *The following graph shows the annual premium of an insurance company, charged for an insurance of Rs. 1000 for different ages.*

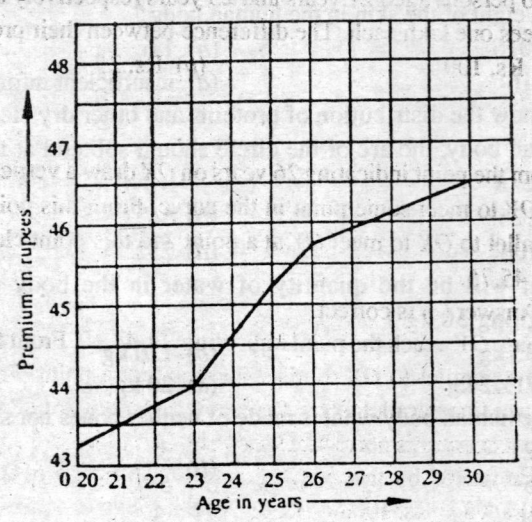

Scale : $\begin{cases} \text{Along } OX \to 10 \text{ small divisions} = 1 \text{ year} \\ \text{Along } OY \to 1 \text{ small division} = 5 \text{ paise.} \end{cases}$

1 big division = 10 small divisions (not shown in the fig.)

Study the graph and mark a tick against the correct answer in each of the following questions.

Q. 1. The premium for a man aged 26 years for an insurance of Rs. 1000 is :
(a) Rs. 46   (b) Rs. 45.75
(c) Rs. 44   (d) Rs. 45

Q. 2. What is the age of a person whose premium is Rs. 44.60 for an insurance of Rs. 1000 ?
(a) 22 years   (b) 23 years
(c) 24 years   (d) 25 years

Q. 3. The premium for a man aged 22 years for an insurance of Rs. 10000 is :
(a) Rs. 435   (b) Rs. 440
(c) Rs. 437.50   (d) Rs. 43.75

Q. 4. How much percent of the premium is increased if a man aged 30 years is insured for Rs. 1000, instead of a man aged 23 years ?
(a) 4.75%   (b) 5.68%
(c) 6.24%   (d) 6%

Data Analysis

Q. 5. Two members of a family aged 20 years and 25 years are to be insured for Rs. 10000 each. The total annual premium to be paid by them is :
(a) Rs. 836.75
(b) Rs. 845.50
(c) Rs. 870.60
(d) Rs. 885

Q. 6. Two persons aged 21 years and 23 years respectively are insured for rupees one lakh each. The difference between their premiums is :
(a) Rs. 100
(b) Rs. 25
(c) Rs. 50
(d) Rs. 20

Solutions :

Ans. 1. From the point indicating 26 years on OX draw a vertical line parallel to OY to meet some point in the curve. From this point draw a line parallel to OX to meet OY at a point and this point clearly indicates Rs. 45.75.
∴ Answer (c) is correct.

Ans. 2. Along, OY, reach the point indicating Rs. 44.60. From this point draw a line parallel to OX to meet the graph at a point. From this point, draw a line parallel to OY to meet OX at a point indicating 24 years.
∴ Answer (c) is correct.

Ans. 3. As indicated by the graph, premium at the age of 22 years for an insurance of Rs. 1000 is Rs. 43.75. So, for an insurance of Rs. 10000, the premium is
Rs. (43.75×10) = Rs. 437.50.
∴ Answer (c) is correct.

Ans. 4. Premium for Rs. 1000 for a man aged 23 years = Rs. 44.
Premium for Rs. 1000 for a man aged 30 years = Rs. 46.50.
Increase % in premium = $\left(\dfrac{2.50}{44} \times 100\right)\% = 5.68\%$.
∴ Answer (b) is correct.

Ans. 5. Premium for Rs. 10000 at 20 years
= Rs. (43.25×10) = Rs. 432.50.
Premium for Rs. 10000 at 25 years
= Rs. (45.25×10) = Rs. 452.50.
Total annual premium for both = Rs. $(432.50 + 452.50)$ = Rs. 885.
∴ Answer (b) is correct.

Ans. 6. Premium for Rs. one lakh at 21 years
= Rs. (100×43.50) = Rs. 4350.
Premium for Rs. one lakh at 23 years
= Rs. (100×44) = Rs. 4400.
Difference in premiums = Rs. 50.
∴ Answer (a) is correct.

Ex. 14. *The following graph shows the temperature of a patient observed in a hospital at a certain interval of time on a certain day, starting at 5 A.M.*

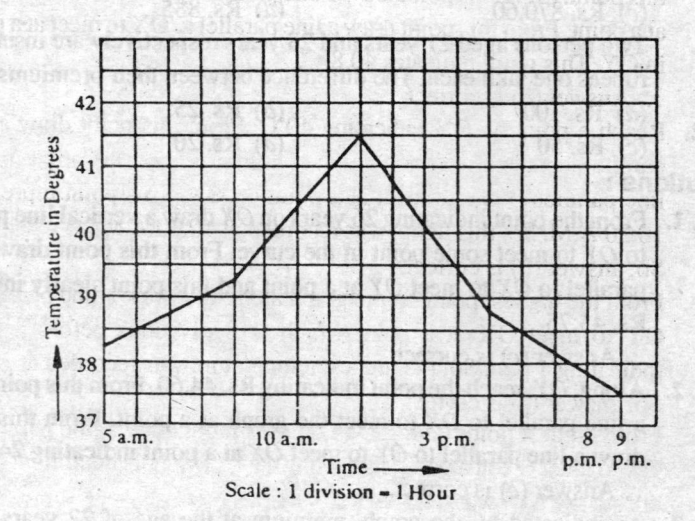

Scale : $\begin{cases} \text{Along } OX \rightarrow 10 \text{ small division} = 15 \text{ minutes} \\ \text{Along } OY \rightarrow 10 \text{ small divisions} = 1°\text{ C.} \end{cases}$

Study the above graph carefully and tick against the correct answer in each of the following questions :

Q. 1. What was the temperature of the patient at 2 p.m. ?
  (a) 40.8° C (b) 41.1° C
  (c) 41.5° C (d) 41.9° C

Q. 2. The time, when the temperature was recorded 40°C, was
  (a) 11 A.M. (b) 10.30 A.M.
  (c) 11.45 A.M. (d) 11.15 A.M.

Q. 3. At what time during the day, the temperature was maximum ?
  (a) 12 P.M. (b) 12.30 P.M.
  (c) 1 P.M. (d) 1.30 P.M.

Q. 4. What was the maximum temperature during the day ?
  (a) 40.7° C (b) 41.5° C
  (c) 40.8° C (d) 41° C

Q. 5. The normal temperature is 37.5°C. At what time was the temperature normal ?
  (a) 5 A.M. (b) 5 P.M.
  (c) 9 P.M. (d) at no time

Data Analysis

Solutions :

Ans. 1. Since we have taken origin at 5 A.M., so 2 P.M. is 9 hours beyond this point. From this point draw a line parallel to OY to meet the graph at a point. From this point draw a line parallel to OX to meet at a point in OY. This point indicates 40.8°C.

∴ Answer (a) is correct.

Ans. 2. Reach a point on OY indicating 40°C. From this point draw a line parallel to OX to meet the graph at a point. From this point draw a line parallel to OY to meet at a point on OX. This point represents 10.30 A.M. So, this temp. was recorded at 10.30 A.M.

So, answer (b) is correct.

Ans. 3. From the highest point on the graph along OY draw a line parallel to OY to meet OX at a point which is 8 divisions before a point indicating 1 p.m. So, the highest temperature was recorded at 1 p.m. So, answer (e) is correct.

Ans. 4. From highest point (along OY) on the graph, draw a line parallel to OX to meet OY at a point, indicating 41.5°C. So, the maximum temp. during the day, was 41.5°C.

∴ Answer (b) is correct.

Ans. 5. We are to find the time when the temperature was 37.5°C. Along OY, take the point indicating 37.5°C. From this point, draw a line parallel to OX to meet the graph at a point. From this point, draw a line parallel to OY, to meet OX at a point. This point indicates 9 p.m.

So, the temperature was normal at 9 p.m.

∴ Answer (c) is correct.

32

Odd Man Out and Series

1. **Turn odd man out.** As the phrase speaks itself, in this type of problems, a set of numbers is given in such a way that each one, except one satisfies a particular definite property. The one which does not satisfy that characteristic is to be taken out.

   Some important properties of numbers are given below:
   - (i) **Prime Numbers.** A counting number greater than 1, which is divisible by itself and 1 only, is called a prime number, e.g. 2, 3, 5, 7, 11, 13, 17, 19, 23, 29, 31, 37, 41, 43, 47, 53, 59, 61, 67, 71, 73, 79, 83, 89, 97 etc.
   - (ii) **Odd numbers.** A number not divisible by 2, is an odd number, e.g. 1, 3, 5, 7, 9, 11, 13, 15 etc.
   - (iii) **Even Numbers.** A number divisible by 2, is an even number e.g. 2, 4, 6, 8, 10 etc.
   - (iv) **Perfect squares.** A counting number whose square root is a counting number, is called a perfect square, e.g. 1, 4, 9, 16, 25, 36, 49, 64 etc.
   - (v) **Perfect Cubes.** A counting number whose cube-root is a counting number is called a perfect cube, e.g. 1, 8, 27, 64, 125 etc.
   - (vi) **Multiples of a number.** A number which is divisible by a given number a, is called the multiple of a e.g. 3, 6, 9, 12 etc. are all multiples of 3.
   - (vii) **Numbers in A.P.** Some given numbers are said to be in A.P. if the difference between two consecutive numbers is same e.g. 13, 11, 9, 7, 5, 3, 1, −1, −3 etc.
   - (viii) **Numbers in G.P.** Some given numbers are in G.P. if the ratio between two consecutive numbers remains the same, e.g. 48, 12, 3 etc.

EXERCISE 32 (Objective Type Questions)

Turn odd man out:

1. 3, 5, 7, 12, 13, 17, 19.
   - (a) 19
   - (b) 17
   - (c) 13
   - (d) 12

Odd Man and Series

2. 10, 14, 16, 18, 21, 24, 26
   - (a) 26
   - (b) 24
   - (c) 21
   - (d) 18
3. 3, 5, 9, 11, 14, 17, 21
   - (a) 21
   - (b) 17
   - (c) 14
   - (d) 9
4. 1, 4, 9, 16, 23, 25, 36
   - (a) 9
   - (b) 23
   - (c) 25
   - (d) 36
5. 6, 9, 15, 21, 24, 28, 30
   - (a) 28
   - (b) 21
   - (c) 24
   - (d) 30
6. 41, 43, 47, 53, 61, 71, 73, 81
   - (a) 61
   - (b) 71
   - (c) 73
   - (d) 81
7. 16, 25, 36, 72, 144, 196, 225
   - (a) 36
   - (b) 72
   - (c) 196
   - (d) 225
8. 10, 25, 45, 54, 60, 75, 80
   - (a) 10
   - (b) 45
   - (c) 54
   - (d) 75
9. 1, 4, 9, 16, 20, 36, 49
   - (a) 1
   - (b) 9
   - (c) 20
   - (d) 49
10. 8, 27, 64, 100, 125, 216, 343
    - (a) 27
    - (b) 100
    - (c) 125
    - (d) 343
11. 1, 5, 14, 30, 50, 55, 91
    - (a) 5
    - (b) 50
    - (c) 55
    - (d) 91
12. 385, 462, 572, 396, 427, 671, 264
    - (a) 385
    - (b) 427
    - (c) 671
    - (d) 264
13. 835, 734, 642, 751, 853, 981, 532
    - (a) 751
    - (b) 853
    - (c) 981
    - (d) 532
14. 331, 482, 551, 263, 383, 242, 111
    - (a) 263
    - (b) 383
    - (c) 242
    - (d) 111
15. 2, 5, 10, 17, 26, 37, 50, 64
    - (a) 50
    - (b) 26
    - (c) 37
    - (d) 64

16. 19, 28, 39, 52, 67, 84, 102
    (a) 52 (b) 102
    (c) 84 (d) 67
17. 253, 136, 352, 460, 324, 631, 244
    (a) 136 (b) 324
    (c) 352 (d) 631
18. 2, 5, 10, 50, 500, 5000
    (a) 0   (b) 5
    (c) 10 (d) 5000
19. 4, 5, 7, 10, 14, 18, 25, 33
    (a) 7   (b) 14
    (c) 18 (d) 33

Find out the wrong number in each sqeuence :

20. 22, 33, 66, 99, 121, 279, 594
    (a) 33   (b) 121
    (c) 279 (d) 594
21. 36, 54, 18, 27, 9, 18.5, 4.5
    (a) 4.5 (b) 18.5
    (c) 54   (d) 18
22. 582, 605, 588, 611, 634, 617, 600
    (a) 634 (b) 611
    (c) 605 (d) 600
23. 46080, 3840, 384, 48, 24, 2, 1
    (a) 1   (b) 2
    (c) 24   (d) 384
24. 1, 8, 27, 64, 124, 216, 343
    (a) 8   (b) 27
    (c) 64   (d) 124
25. 5, 16, 6, 16, 7, 16, 9
    (a) 9   (b) 7
    (c) 6   (d) none
26. 6, 13, 18, 25, 30, 37, 40
    (a) 25   (b) 30
    (c) 37   (d) 40
27. 56, 72, 90, 110, 132, 150
    (a) 72   (b) 110
    (c) 132 (d) 150
28. 8, 13, 21, 32, 47, 63, 83
    (a) 47   (b) 63
    (c) 32   (d) 83
29. 25, 36, 49, 81, 121, 169, 225
    (a) 36   (b) 49
    (c) 121 (d) 169

Odd Man and Series

30. 1, 2, 6, 15, 31, 56, 91
    - (a) 31
    - (b) 91
    - (c) 56
    - (d) 15
31. 52, 51, 48, 43, 34, 27, 16
    - (a) 27
    - (b) 34
    - (c) 43
    - (d) 48
32. 105, 85, 60, 30, 0, –45, –90
    - (a) 0
    - (b) 85
    - (c) –45
    - (d) 60
33. 4, 6, 8, 9, 10, 11, 12
    - (a) 10
    - (b) 11
    - (c) 12
    - (d) 9
34. 125, 127, 130, 135, 142, 153, 165
    - (a) 130
    - (b) 142
    - (c) 153
    - (d) 165
35. 16, 36, 64, 81, 100, 144, 190
    - (a) 81
    - (b) 100
    - (c) 190
    - (d) 36
36. 125, 123, 120, 115, 108, 100, 84
    - (a) 123
    - (b) 115
    - (c) 100
    - (d) 84
37. 3, 10, 21, 36, 55, 70, 105
    - (a) 105
    - (b) 70
    - (c) 36
    - (d) 55
38. 4, 9, 19, 39, 79, 160, 319
    - (a) 319
    - (b) 160
    - (c) 79
    - (d) 39
39. 10, 14, 28, 32, 64, 68, 132
    - (a) 32
    - (b) 68
    - (c) 132
    - (d) 28
40. 8, 27, 125, 343, 1331
    - (a) 1331
    - (b) 343
    - (c) 125
    - (d) none

Insert the missing number :

41. 4, –8, 16, –32, 64, (......)
    - (a) 128
    - (b) –128
    - (c) 192
    - (d) –192
42. 5, 10, 13, 26, 29, 58, 61, (......)
    - (a) 122
    - (b) 64
    - (c) 125
    - (d) 128
43. 1, 4, 9, 16, 25, 36, 49, (......)

(a) 54 (b) 56
(c) 64 (d) 81

44. 1, 8, 27, 64, 125, 216, (......)
    (a) 354 (b) 343
    (c) 392 (d) 245

45. 11, 13, 17, 19, 23, 29, 31, 37, 41, (......)
    (a) 43 (b) 47
    (c) 53 (d) 51

46. 16, 33, 65, 131, 261, (......)
    (a) 523 (b) 521
    (c) 613 (d) 721

47. 3, 7, 6, 5, 9, 3, 12, 1, 15, (......)
    (a) 18 (b) 13
    (c) −1 (d) 3

48. 13, 31, 63, 127, 255, (......)
    (a) 513 (b) 511
    (c) 517 (d) 523

49. 2, 6, 12, 20, 30, 42, 56, (......)
    (a) 60 (b) 64
    (c) 72 (d) 70

50. 8, 24, 12, 36, 18, 54, (......)
    (a) 27 (b) 108
    (c) 68 (d) 72

51. 165, 195, 255, 285, 345, (......)
    (a) 375 (b) 420
    (c) 435 (d) 390

52. 7, 26, 63, 124, 215, 342, (......)
    (a) 481 (b) 511
    (c) 391 (d) 421

53. 2, 4, 12, 48, 240, (......)
    (a) 960 (b) 1440
    (c) 1080 (d) 1920

54. 8, 7, 11, 12, 14, 17, 17, 22, (......)
    (a) 27 (b) 20
    (c) 22 (d) 24

55. 10, 5, 13, 10, 16, 20, 19, (......)
    (a) 22 (b) 40
    (c) 38 (d) 23

56. 1, 2, 4, 8, 16, 32, 64, (......), 256
    (a) 148 (b) 128
    (c) 154 (d) 164

57. 71, 76, 69, 74, 67, 72, (......)
 (a) 77 (b) 65
 (c) 80 (d) 76
58. 9, 12, 11, 14, 13, (......), 15
 (a) 12 (b) 16
 (c) 10 (d) 17
59. Complete the series
 2, 5, 9, 19, 37, ...
 (a) 76 (b) 74
 (c) 75 (d) none of these
 (Railway Recruitment Board Exam. 1989)
60. Find the wrong number in the series :
 3, 8, 15, 24, 34, 48, 63
 (a) 15 (b) 24
 (c) 34 (d) 48
 (e) 63 (Bank P.O. Exam. 1988)
61. Find the wrong number in the series :
 2, 9, 28, 65, 126, 216, 344
 (a) 2 (b) 28
 (c) 65 (d) 126
 (e) 216 (Bank P.O. Exam. 1988)
62. Find out the wrong number in the series :
 5, 15, 30, 135, 405, 1215, 3645
 (a) 3645 (b) 1215
 (c) 405 (d) 30
 (e) 15 (S.B.I.P.O. Exam. 1988)
63. Find out the wrong number in the series :
 125, 106, 88, 76, 65, 58, 53
 (a) 125 (b) 106
 (c) 88 (d) 76
 (e) 65 (S.B.I.P.O. Exam. 1987)

Find out the wrong number in the series :
64. 190, 166, 145, 128, 112, 100, 91
 (a) 100 (b) 166
 (c) 145 (d) 128
 (e) 112 (Bank P.O. 1991)
65. 1, 1, 2, 6, 24, 96, 720
 (a) 720 (b) 96
 (c) 24 (d) 6
 (e) 2 (Bank P.O. 1991)
66. 40960, 10240, 2560, 640 200, 40 10

    (a) 640   (b) 40
    (c) 200   (d) 2560
    (e) 10240   (Bank P.O. 1991)

67. 64, 71, 80, 91, 104, 119, 135, 155
    (a) 71   (b) 80
    (c) 104   (d) 119
    (e) 135   (Bank P.O. 1991)

68. 7, 8, 18, 57, 228, 1165, 6996
    (a) 8   (b) 18
    (c) 57   (d) 228
    (e) 127   (Bank P.O. 1991)

69. 3, 7, 15, 27, 63, 127, 255
    (a) 7   (b) 15
    (c) 27   (d) 63
    (e) 127   (Bank P.O. 1991)

70. 19, 26, 33, 46, 59, 74, 91
    (a) 26   (b) 33
    (c) 46   (d) 59
    (e) 74   (Bank P.O. 1991)

71. 19, 26, 33, 46, 59, 74, 91
    (a) 2880   (b) 480
    (c) 92   (d) 24
    (e) 8   (Bank P.O. 1991)

72. 445, 221, 109, 46, 25, 11, 4
    (a) 221   (b) 109
    (c) 46   (d) 25
    (e) 11   (Bank P.O. 1991)

73. 3, 7, 15, 39, 63, 127, 255, 511
    (a) 7   (b) 15
    (c) 39   (d) 63
    (e) 127   (Bank P.O. 1991)

74. 1, 3, 10, 21, 64, 129, 356, 777
    (a) 10   (b) 21
    (c) 64   (d) 129
    (e) 356   (Bank P.O. 11991)

75. 196, 169, 144, 121, 100, 80, 64
    (a) 169   (b) 144
    (c) 121   (d) 100
    (e) 80   (Bank P.O. 1991)

Odd Man and Series   493

SOLUTIONS (Exercise 32)

1. Each of the numbers except 12, is a prime number.
2. Each of the numbers except 21, is an even number.
3. Each of the numbers except 14, is an odd number.
4. Each of the given numbers except 23, is a perfect square.
5. Each of the numbers except 28, is a multiple of 3.
6. Each of the numbers except 81, is a prime number.
7. Each of the numbers except 72, is a perfect square.
8. Each of the numbers except 54, is a multiple of 5.
9. The pattern is $1^2, 2^2, 3^2, 4^2, 5^2, 6^2, 7^2$. But, instead of 5^2, it is 20, which is to be turned out.
10. The pattern is $2^3, 3^3, 4^3 5^3, 6^3, 7^3$. But 100 is not a perfect cube.
11. The pattern is $1^2, 1^2 + 2^2, 1^2 + 2^2 + 3^2, 1^2 + 2^2 + 3^2 + 4^2, 1^2 + 2^2 + 3^2 + 4^2 + 5^2, 1^2 + 2^2 + 3^2 + 4^2 + 5^2 + 6^2$. But 50 is not of this pattern.
12. In each number except 427, the middle digit is sum of the other two.
13. In each number except 751, the difference of third and first digit is the middle one.
14. In each number except 383, the product of first and third digits is the middle one.
15. The pattern is $x^2 + 1$, where $x = 1, 2, 3, 4, 5, 6, 7, 8$ etc. But, 64 is out of pattern.
16. The pattern is $x^2 + 3$, where $x = 4, 5, 6, 7, 8, 9$ etc. But, 102 is out of pattern.
17. Sum of the digits in each number, except 324 is 10.
18. Pattern is 1st × 2nd = 3rd; 2nd × 3rd = 4th; 3rd × 4th = 5th. But, 4th × 5th = 50 × 500 = 25000 ≠ 5000 = 6th.
19. 2nd = (1st + 1); 3rd = (2nd + 2); 4th = (3rd + 3); 5th = (4th + 4) But, 18 = 6th ≠ 5th + 5 = 14 + 5 = 19.
20. Each number except 279 is a multiple of 11.
21. The terms are alternately multiplied by 1.5 and divided by 3. However 18.5 does not satisfy it.
22. Alternately 23 is added and 17 is subtracted from the terms. So, 634 is wrong.
23. The terms are successively divided by 12, 10, 8, 6, ... etc. So, 24 is wrong.
24. The numbers are $1^3, 2^3, 3^3, 4^3$ etc.
    So, 124 is wrong; it must have been 5^3 i.e. 125.
25. Terms at odd places are 5, 6, 7, 8 etc. and each term at even place is 16.
    So, 9 is wrong.

26. The difference between two successive terms from the beginning are 7, 5, 7, 5, 7, 5.
    So, 36 is wrong.
27. The numbers are $7 \times 8, 8 \times 9, 9 \times 10, 10 \times 11, 11 \times 12, 12 \times 13$.
    So, 150 is wrong.
28. Go on adding 5, 8, 11, 14, 17, 20.
    So, the number 47 is wrong and must be replaced by 46.
29. The numbers are squares of odd natural numbers, starting from 5 upto 15.
    So, 36 is wrong.
30. Add $1^2, 2^2, 3^2, 4^2, 5^2, 6^2$.
    So, 91 is wrong.
31. Subtract 1, 3, 5, 7, 9, 11 from successive numbers.
    So, 34 is wrong.
32. Subtract 20, 25, 30, 35, 40, 45 from successive numbers.
    So, 0 is wrong.
33. Each number is a composite number except 11.
34. Prime numbers 2, 3, 5, 7, 11, 13 are to be added successively.
    So, 165 is wrong.
35. Each number is the square of a composite number except 190.
36. Prime numbers 2, 3, 5, 7, 11, 13 have successively been subtracted.
    So, 100 is wrong. It must be (108 – 11) i.e. 97.
37. The pattern is $1 \times 3, 2 \times 5, 3 \times 7, 4 \times 9, 5 \times 11, 6 \times 13, 7 \times 15$ etc.
38. Double the number and add 1 to it, to get the next number.
    So, 160 is wrong.
39. Alternately, we add 4 and double the next.
    So, 132 is wrong.
    It must be (68×2) i.e. 136.
40. The numbers are cubes of primes i.e. $2^3, 3^3, 5^3, 7^3, 11^3$.
    Clearly, none is wrong.
41. Each number is the preceding number multiplied by –2.
    So, the required number is –128.
42. Numbers are alternately multiplied by 2 and increased by 3.
    So, the missing number = $61 \times 2 = 122$.
43. Numbers are $1^2, 2^2, 3^2, 4^2, 5^2, 6^2, 7^2$.
    So, the next number is $8^2 = 64$.
44. Numbers are $1^3, 2^3, 3^3, 4^3, 5^3, 6^3$. So, the missing number is $7^3 = 343$.
45. Numbers are all primes. The next prime is 43.
46. Each number is twice the preceding one with 1 added or subtracted alternately. So, the next number is $(2 \times 261 + 1) = 523$.

Odd Man and Series

47. There are two series, beginning respectively with 3 and 7. In one 3 is added and in another 2 is subtracted. The next number is $1 - 2 = -1$.
48. Each number is double the preceding one plus 1. So, the next number is $(255 \times 2) + 1 = 511$.
49. The pattern is $1 \times 2, 2 \times 3, 3 \times 4, 4 \times 5, 5 \times 6, 6 \times 7, 7 \times 8$.
    So, the next number is $8 \times 9 = 72$.
50. Numbers are alternately multiplied by 3 and divided by 2.
    So, next number = $54 \div 2 = 27$.
51. Each number is 15 multiplied by a prime number i.e., $15 \times 11, 15 \times 13, 15 \times 17, 15 \times 19, 15 \times 23$. So the next number is $15 \times 29 = 435$.
52. Numbers are $(2^3 - 1), (3^3 - 1), (4^3 - 1), (5^3 - 1), (6^3 - 1), (7^3 - 1)$ etc.
    So, the next number is $(8^3 - 1) = (512 - 1) = 511$.
53. Go on multiplying the given numbers by 2, 3, 4, 5, 6.
    So, the correct next number is 1440.
54. There are two series (8, 11, 14, 17, 20) and (7, 12, 17, 22) increasing by 3 and 5 respectively.
55. There are two series (10, 13, 16, 19) and (5, 10, 20, 40) one increasing by 3 and another multiplied by 2.
56. Each previous number is multiplied by 2.
57. Alternately, we add 5 and subtract 7.
58. Alternately, we add 3 and subtract 1.
59. Second number is one more than twice the first; third number is one less than twice the second; fourth number is one more than twice the third; fifth number is one less than the fourth.
    Therefore, the sixth number is one more than twice the fifth.
    So, the missing number is 75.
60. The difference between consecutive terms are respectively 5, 7, 9, 11 and 13.
    So, 34 is a wrong number.
61. $2 = (1^3 + 1); 9 = (2^3 + 1); 28 = (3^3 + 1); 65 = (4^3 + 1);$
    $126 = (5^3 + 1); 216 \neq (6^3 + 1) \ \& \ 344 = (7^3 + 1)$.
    $\therefore$ 216 is a wrong number.
62. Multiply each term by 3 to obtain the next term.
    Hence, 30 is a wrong number.
63. Go on subtracting prime numbers 19, 17, 13, 11, 7, 5 from the numbers to get the next number. So, 88 is wrong.
64. Go on subtracting 24, 21, 18, 15, 12, 9 from the numbers to get the next number.
    Clearly, 128 is wrong.

65. Go on multiplying with 1, 2, 3, 4, 5, 6 to get the next number.
So, 96 is wrong.
66. Go on dividing by 4 to get the next number.
So, 200 is wrong.
67. Go on adding 7, 9, 11, 13, 15, 17, 19 respectively to obtain the next number.
So, 135 is wrong.
68. Let the given numbers be A, B, C, D, E, F, G. Then,
A, A × 1, B × 2 + 2, C × 3 + 3, D × 4 + 4, E × 5 + 5, F × 6 + 6 are the required numbers.
Clearly, 228 is wrong.
69. Go on multiplying the number by 2 and adding 1 to it to get the next number.
So, 27 is wrong.
70. Go on adding 7, 9, 11, 13, 15, 17 respectively to obtain the next number.
So, 33 is wrong.
71. Go on dividing by 6, 5, 4, 3, 2, 1 respectively to obtain the next number.
Clearly, 92 is wrong.
72. Go on subtracting 3 and dividing the result by 2 to obtain the next number.
Clearly, 46 is wrong.
73. Go on multiplying 2 and adding 1 to get the next number.
So, 39 is wrong.
74. A × 2 + 1, B × 3 + 1, C × 2 + 1, D × 3 + 1 and so on.
∴ 356 is wrong.
75. Numbers must be $(14)^2, (13)^2, (11)^2, (10)^2, (9)^2, (8)^2$.
So, 80 is wrong.

MISCELLANEOUS PROBLEMS
(Test Yourself)

1. $\sqrt{\dfrac{?}{289}} = \dfrac{54}{51}$

   (a) 108 □ (b) 324 □
   (c) 2916 □ (d) 6800 □

2. ?% of 250 + 25% of 68 = 67

   (a) 10 □ (b) 15 □
   (c) 20 □ (d) 25 □

   (Bank P.O. 1990)

3. $12\dfrac{1}{2} \times 3\dfrac{3}{5} \div 1\dfrac{4}{5} = ?$

   (a) 45 □ (b) 81 □
   (c) 405 □ (d) none of these □

   (S.B.I. P.O. Exam 1991)

4. $5.75 - \dfrac{3}{7} \times 15\dfrac{3}{4} + 2\dfrac{2}{35} \div 1.44 = ?$

   (a) $\dfrac{2}{5}$ □ (b) $\dfrac{3}{7}$ □

   (c) $\dfrac{4}{11}$ □ (d) $\dfrac{2}{9}$ □

   (C.B.I. 1991)

5. $\dfrac{1}{7} + \left[\dfrac{7}{9} - \left(\dfrac{3}{9} + \dfrac{2}{9}\right) - \dfrac{2}{9}\right]$ is equal to :

   (a) $\dfrac{1}{7}$ □ (b) $\dfrac{1}{9}$ □

   (c) $\dfrac{2}{9}$ □ (d) $\dfrac{3}{7}$ □

   (Clerical Grade 1991)

6. Which is the biggest of the following fractions ?

   (a) $\dfrac{3}{4}$ □ (b) $\dfrac{4}{5}$ □

   (c) $\dfrac{5}{6}$ □ (d) $\dfrac{6}{7}$ □

   (Railway Recruitment 1991)

7. $1 + \dfrac{1}{1 + \dfrac{1}{1 - \dfrac{1}{6}}} = ?$

   (a) $\dfrac{6}{11}$ (b) $\dfrac{16}{11}$

   (c) $\dfrac{7}{6}$ (d) $\dfrac{1}{6}$

8. The value of $(1502)^2 - (1498)^2$ is

   (a) 12,000   (b) 16,000
   (c) 22,56,004   (d) 22,560

   (Railway Recruitment 1991)

9. $\sqrt[3]{1 - \dfrac{91}{216}}$ is equal to

   (a) $\dfrac{1}{6}$ (b) $\dfrac{5}{6}$

   (c) $1 - \dfrac{\sqrt[3]{91}}{6}$ (d) None of these

   (Clerical Grade 1991)

10. The ratio $\dfrac{1}{2} : \dfrac{1}{3} : \dfrac{1}{5}$ is the same as

    (a) 2 : 3 : 5   (b) 5 : 3 : 2
    (c) 15 : 10 : 6   (d) 6 : 10 : 15

    (C.B.I. 1990)

11. A number exceeds its four seventh by 18. What is the number ?

    (a) 36   (b) 49
    (c) 63   (d) none of these

    (S.B.I. P.O. Exam 1991)

12. $\left(\dfrac{?}{31}\right) \times \left(\dfrac{?}{279}\right) = 1$

    (a) 31   (b) 93
    (c) 217   (d) 8649

    (C.B.I. 1991)

13. The average of the fractions $1\dfrac{1}{2}, 2\dfrac{1}{3}, 3\dfrac{1}{3}, 4\dfrac{5}{6}$ is :

    (a) 2

Miscellaneous Problems

                        (b) $2\frac{1}{2}$ ☐

   (c) 3 ☐   (d) 4 ☐

                                    (Railway Recruitment 1991)

14. The highest common factor of 70 and 245 is :
   (a) 35 ☐   (b) 55 ☐
   (c) 45 ☐   (d) 65 ☐
                                    (Railway Recruitment 1991)

15. Which of the following has the fraction in the ascending order ?
   (a) $\frac{2}{7}, \frac{3}{10}, \frac{4}{13}$ ☐   (b) $\frac{4}{13}, \frac{3}{10}, \frac{2}{7}$ ☐
   (c) $\frac{3}{10}, \frac{2}{7}, \frac{4}{13}$ ☐   (d) $\frac{4}{13}, \frac{2}{7}, \frac{3}{10}$ ☐
                                    (Bank P.O. 1989)

16. If 5 poles are erected at equal distances between two points 20 metres apart, what is the distance between any two poles ?
   (a) 2 metres ☐   (b) 3 metres ☐
   (c) 4 metres ☐   (d) 5 metres ☐
                                    (Hotel Management 1991)

17. One fourth of a two digit number is two less than one third of the same number. What is the sum of the digits of the number ?
   (a) 6 ☐   (b) 8 ☐
   (c) 9 ☐   (d) None of these ☐
                                    (S.B.I. P.O. Exam 1991)

18. A number when divided by 123 leaves remainder 83. If the same number is divided by 41, the remainder will be :
   (a) 0 ☐   (b) 1 ☐
   (c) 40 ☐   (d) 83 ☐
                                    (Clerical Grade 1991)

19. $\frac{1}{4}$ th of Nikhil's money is equal to $\frac{1}{6}$ th of Yogesh's money. If both together have Rs 600, the difference between their amounts is :
   (a) Rs 50 ☐   (b) Rs 120 ☐
   (c) Rs 240 ☐   (d) Rs 360 ☐
                                    (Bank P.O. 1989)

20. Kavita has one quarter more money than Nitin, Nitin has two third money as of Pravin. If Pravin has Rs 876 with him, how much money

Kavita has ?
(a) Rs 365 (b) Rs 467.20
(c) Rs 730 (d) Rs 760

(Bank P.O. 1991)

21. The difference of two numbers is 11 and $\frac{1}{5}$th of their sum is 9. The numbers are :
(a) 31, 20 (b) 30, 19
(c) 29, 18 (d) 28, 17

(Railway Recruitment 1991)

22. The least number, which 715 must be multiplied with in order to get a multiple of 825, is :
(a) 10 (b) 12
(c) 15 (d) 35

(Clerical Grade 1991)

23. The positions of the digits of a two digit number are interchanged. If the sum of the original number and the number obtained by interchanging the digits is 44, what is the sum of digits of that number ?
(a) 2 (b) 4
(c) 11 (d) cannot be determined

(A.O. Exam 1990)

24. Two Consecutive multiples of a certain number add upto 184. The number is
(a) 4 (b) 8
(c) 23 (d) 46

(C.B.I. 1990)

25. The smallest number, which must be added to 1000 to make it a perfect square, is :
(a) 12 (b) 20
(c) 24 (d) 25

(C.B.I. 1990)

26. If the price of some commodity is reduced from Rs 16 to Rs 12.25, then on purchasing four such commodities, how much percentage can one save ?
(a) 15 (b) 49
(c) $23\frac{7}{16}$ (d) $\frac{4900}{64}$

(Bank P.O. 1990)

Miscellaneous Problems

27. The least square number exactly divisible by 8, 2, 15 and 20, is :
    (a) 900
    (b) 1200
    (c) 3600
    (d) 14400
    (Clerical Grade 1991)

28. In an examination, 35% of the total students failed in Hindi, 45% failed in English and 20% in both. Percentage of total students passed in both the subjects is :
    (a) 10
    (b) 20
    (c) 30
    (d) 40
    (C.B.I. 1991)

29. The sum of any seven consecutive whole numbers is always divisible by
    (a) 2
    (b) 3
    (c) 7
    (d) 11
    (C.B.I. 1991)

30. The smallest number which when subtracted from the sum of squares of 11 and 13 gives a perfect square, is
    (a) 1
    (b) 4
    (c) 5
    (d) 9
    (Clerical Grade 1991)

31. A and B finish a job in 12 days, while A, B and C can finish it in 8 days. C alone will finish the job in :
    (a) 14 days
    (b) 16 days
    (c) 20 days
    (d) 24 days
    (Hotal Management 1991)

32. 18 persons can finish a work in 36 days. How much time will 12 persons take to finish the same work ?
    (a) 18 days
    (b) 24 days
    (c) 54 days
    (d) 72 days
    (Bank P.O. 1990)

33. An increase of Rs 60 in the monthly salary of Madan made it 50% of the monthly salary of Kamal. What is Madan's present monthly salary ?
    (a) Rs 180
    (b) Rs 240
    (c) Rs 300
    (d) Data inadequate
    (Bank P.O. 1990)

34. In a garden there are 10 rows and 12 columns of mango trees. The

distance between each tree is of 2 metres and a distance of one metre is left from all sides of the boundary of the garden. The length of the garden is :
(a) 20 metres (b) 22 metres
(c) 24 metres (d) 26 metres
(Bank P.O. 1991)

35. The sum of two numbers is 104 and their difference is 30. The difference of their squares is :
(a) 74 (b) 2160
(c) 2320 (d) 3120

36. For a theatre, the cost of a child ticket is $\frac{1}{3}$ of the cost of an adult ticket. If the cost of tickets for 3 adults and 3 children is Rs 60, the cost of an adult ticket is :
(a) Rs 12 (b) Rs 15
(c) Rs 18 (d) Rs 20
(Clerical Grade 1991)

37. 10% of 24.2 will be how much more than 10% of 24.02 ?
(a) 0.02 (b) 0.18
(c) 0.018 (d) 0.002
(Bank P.O. 1992)

38. A trader lists his articles 20% above C.P. and allows a discount of 10% on cash payment. His gain percent is :
(a) 5% (b) 6%
(c) 8% (d) 10%
(Railway Recruitment 1991)

39. The square root of 824464 is :
(a) 686 (b) 868
(c) 908 (d) none of these
(Railway Recruitment 1991)

40. If the price of one dozen of mangoes is Rs 49.75, what will be the approximate value of 291 mangoes ?
(a) Rs 1000 (b) Rs 1200
(c) Rs 1500 (d) Rs 1800
(A.O. Exam 1990)

41. The difference between the simple interest and the compound interest at the same rate of interest on a sum of money at the end of the second

Miscellaneous Problems 503

year will be Rs 4.00. If the rate of interest is 5% per annum, what is the sum?

(a) Rs 1200 ☐ (b) Rs 1600 ☐
(c) Rs 2000 ☐ (d) none of these ☐

(P.O. Exam 1990)

42. A boy was asked to multiply a certain number by 25. He multiplied it by 52 and got his answer more than the correct one by 324. The number to be multiplied was :

(a) 12 ☐ (b) 15 ☐
(c) 25 ☐ (d) 52 ☐

(C.B.I. 1990)

43. The price of an article was increased by $p\%$. Later the new price was decreased by $p\%$. If the latest price was Re 1, the original price was :

(a) Re 1 ☐ (b) Rs $\dfrac{1-p^2}{100}$ ☐

(c) Rs $\left(\dfrac{10000}{10000-p^2}\right)$ ☐ (d) Rs $\dfrac{\sqrt{1-p^2}}{100}$ ☐

(C.B.I. 1990)

44. Two different natural numbers are such that their product is less than their sum. One of the numbers must oe (C.B.I. 1990)

(a) 1 ☐ (b) 2 ☐
(c) 3 ☐ (d) none of these ☐

45. At an election involving two candidates, only 68 votes are declared as invalid. The winning condidate scores 52% and wins by 98 votes. The total number of votes polled is :

(a) 2382 ☐ (b) 2450 ☐
(c) 2518 ☐ (d) none of these ☐

46. Deepak has Rs 5130 in the form of 1, 2 and 5 rupee notes. If these notes be in the ratio 3: 7: 8, the number of five rupee notes he has is :

(a) 340 ☐ (b) 672 ☐
(c) 720 ☐ (d) 768 ☐

47. Dhawan bought 10 chairs for Rs 500. He got them repaired and sold them at Rs 500 per pair. He got a profit of Rs 100 per chair. How much did he spend on the repair of the chairs ?

(a) Rs 250 ☐ (b) Rs 500 ☐
(c) Rs 1000 ☐ (d) Rs 1500 ☐

(Bank P.O. 1990)

48. The charges of hired car are Rs 4 per km for the first 60 km, Rs 5 km for the next 60 km and Rs 8 for every 5 km for the further journey. If the balance amount left over with Ajit is $\frac{1}{4}$ less than what he paid towards the charges of the hired car for travelling 320 km, how much money did he have initially with him ?
(a) Rs 1032   (b) Rs 1253
(c) Rs 1548   (d) none of these

(Bank P.O. 1990)

49. What number must be added to the numbers 3,7 and 13 so that they are in a continued proportion ?
(a) 5   (b) 6
(c) 8   (d) 9

50. The compound interest on Rs 6000 for $1\frac{1}{2}$ years at 10% per annum, the interest being paid half yearly, will be :
(a) Rs 912.75   (b) Rs 930
(c) Rs 932.50   (d) 945.75

51. Jayant started a business investing Rs 6000. Six months later Madhu joined him investing Rs 4000. If they make a profit of Rs 5200 at the end of the year, how much should be the share of Madhu ?
(a) Rs. 1300   (b) Rs 1732
(c) Rs 3466   (d) Rs 3900

(Bank P.O. 1991)

52. Rs 1200 amounts to Rs 1632 in four years at a certain rate of simple interest. If the rate of interest is increased by 1%, it would amount to how much ?
(a) Rs 1635   (b) Rs 1644
(c) Rs 1670   (d) Rs 1680

(Bank P.O. 1991)

53. 12 buckets of water fill a tank when the capacity of each bucket is 13.5 litres. How many buckets will be needed to fill the same tank if the capacity of each bucket is 9 litres ?
(a) 8   (b) 16
(c) 18   (d) none of these

(Bank P.O.1991)

54. Monika deposits Rs 8000 partly at 10% and partly at 15% interest for one year in a bank. If she gets an interest of Rs 950 at the end of one year, the amount deposited at 15% is :

    (a) Rs 2000 less than deposited at 10%
(b) Rs 1250 less than deposited at 10%
(c) Rs 500 more than deposited at 10%
(d) Rs 1500 less than deposited at 10%

55. A fruit vendor has 24 kg of apples. He sells a part of these at 20% gain and the balance at a loss of 5% . If on the whole he earns a profit of 10%, the amount of apples sold at a loss is

    (a) 6 kg   (b) 4.6 kg
    (c) 9.6 kg   (d) 11.4 kg

56. If the area of an equilateral triangle is $36\sqrt{3}\ cm^2$, the perimeter of the triangle is :

    (a) 18 cm   (b) 24 cm
    (c) 30 cm   (d) 36 cm

57. A sum of Rs 45 is made up of 100 coins of 50 paise and 25 paise. How many of them are 50 paise coins ?

    (a) 40   (b) 50
    (c) 75   (d) 80

                                                                                (Hotel Management 1991)

58. A man donated 5% of his income to a charitable organisation and deposited 20% of the remainder in a bank. If he now has Rs 1919 left, his income is :

    (a) Rs 2300   (b) Rs 2500
    (c) Rs 2525   (d) Rs 2558.60

                                                                                    (Astt. Grade 1990)

59. The L.C.M. of two numbers is 2310 and their H.C.F. is 30. If one number is 210, the other number is :

    (a) 330   (b) 1470
    (c) 2100   (d) 16170

                                                                                    (Clerical Grade 1991)

60. The average of marks obtained by Aakash in seven subjects is 68. His average in six subjects excluding Mathematics is 70. How many marks did he get in Mathematics ?

    (a) 56   (b) 60
    (c) 68   (d) 82

61. B is twice as fast as A and C is three times as fast as A. If B alone can complete a job in 12 days, how long will A, B and C take to complete the same job together?

(a) 3 days   (b) 4 days
(c) 6 days   (d) none of these

62. A person gave Rs 2500 to his eldest son, $\frac{5}{12}$ of the whole property to the second son and to the youngest as much as to the first and the second son together. How much did the youngest son get?

(a) Rs 10000   (b) Rs 15000
(c) Rs 20000   (d) Rs 25000

(Astt. Grade 1990)

63. A train X starts from Meerut at 4 P.M. and reaches Ghaziabad at 5 P.M., while another train Y starts from Ghaziabad at 4 P.M. and reaches Meerut at 5.30 P.M. The two trains will cross each other at

(a) 4.36 P.M.   (b) 4.42 P.M.
(c) 4.48 P.M.   (d) 4.50 P.M.

64. 60% of the length of a pole is painted red, 40% of the rest is painted green and 50% of the balance is painted blue. The remaining unpainted length of the pole is 30 cm. The length of the pole is:

(a) 2.5 m   (b) 3.2 m
(c) 4.8 m   (d) 5.6 m

65. A jar full of whisky contains 40% of alcohol. A part of this whisky is replaced by another containing 19% alcohol and now the percentage of alcohol was found to be 26. The quantity of whisky replaced is:

(a) $\frac{1}{3}$ (b) $\frac{2}{3}$
(c) $\frac{2}{5}$ (d) $\frac{3}{5}$

(Hotel Management 1991)

66. One third of the boys and one half of the girls of a college participate in a social work project. If the number of participating students is 300, out of which 100 are boys, what is the total number of students in the college?

(a) 500   (b) 600
(c) 700   (d) 800

(Bank P.O. 1990)

67. The smallest number which when divided by 10, 15, 20 and 35 leaves 6, 11, 16 and 31 as remainder, is:

Miscellaneous Problems 507

  (a) 416 (b) 424
  (c) 436 (d) none of these

68. There are 20 students with an average height of 125 cm in a class. 5 students with an average height of 116 cm leave the class. What is the average height of the class now ?
  (a) 118 cm (b) 120 cm
  (c) 128 cm (d) 130 cm

69. A third of Vinod's marks in Mathematics exceeds a half of his marks in social studies by 30. If he got 240 marks in the two subjects together, how many marks did he get in social studies ?
  (a) 40 (b) 60
  (c) 80 (d) 90
  (Bank P.O. 1990)

70. The mean proportional of 0.32 and 0.02 is :
  (a) 0.08 (b) 0.16
  (c) 0.30 (d) 0.34
  (Central Excise & I. Tax 1989)

71. The average of first nine multiples of 3 is :
  (a) 12.0 (b) 12.5
  (c) 15.0 (d) 18.5
  (Central Excise & I. Tax 1989)

72. A class starts at 10 A.M. and lasts till 1.27 P.M. Four periods are held during this interval. After every period, 5 minutes are given free to the students. The exact duration of each period is :
  (a) 42 minutes (b) 48 minutes
  (c) 51 minutes (d) 53 minutes

73. A bus goes from A to B at the rate of 30 kmph and from B to A at the rate of 60 kmph. The average speed of the bus is :
  (a) 40 kmph (b) 45 kmph
  (c) 47.5 kmph (d) 52.5 kmph

74. A 63 cm long wire is to be cut into two pieces such that one piece will be $\frac{2}{5}$ as long as the other How many centimetres will the shorter piece be ?
  (a) 9 (b) 18
  (c) 36 (d) 45
  (S.B.I.P.O. Exam, 1991)

75. Pratap bought a radio with 25% discount on the original price. He got Rs 40 more than the original price by selling it at 140% of the price at which he bought. At what price did he buy the radio?
    (a) Rs 600   (b) Rs 700
    (c) Rs 800   (d) Rs 900
    (S.B.I.P.O. Exam 1991)

76. Two numbers are in the ratio 3 : 4 and the product of their L.C.M. and H.C.F. is 10,800. The sum of the numbers is :
    (a) 180   (b) 210
    (c) 225   (d) 240

77. Kasem can do a piece of work in $7\frac{1}{2}$ hours and Sunil can finish it in 10 hours. If Kasem works at it for 3 hours and Sunil for 4 hours the amount of work left unfinished is :
    (a) $\frac{1}{5}$ (b) $\frac{2}{5}$
    (c) $\frac{1}{4}$ (d) $\frac{2}{7}$

78. If the L.C.M. of x and y is z, their H.C.F. is :
    (a) $\frac{xy}{z}$ (b) xyz
    (c) $\frac{(x+y)}{z}$ (d) $\frac{z}{xy}$

79. A student who secures 20% marks in an examination fails by 30 marks. Another student who secures 32% marks, gets 42 marks more than those required to pass. Percent of marks required to pass is :
    (a) 20   (b) 25
    (c) 28   (d) 30
    (Clerical Grade 1991)

80. The average of three numbers is 20. If two of the numbers are 16 and 22, the third is
    (a) 18   (b) 19
    (c) 20   (d) 22
    (Clerical Grade 1991)

81. In a competitive examination, a student scores 4 marks for every correct answer and loses 1 mark for every wrong answer. If he attempts all 75 questions and secures 125 marks, the number of questions he attempts correctly is :

(a) 35 □ (b) 40 □
(c) 42 □ (d) 46 □

82. A sum of money deposited at compound interest amounts to Rs 6690 after 3 years and Rs 10,035 after 6 years. The sum is :
(a) Rs 4400 □ (b) Rs 4445 □
(c) Rs 4460 □ (d) Rs 4520 □

83. A train covers four successive two km stretches at speeds of 10 kmph, 20 kmph, 30 kmph and 60 kmph respectively. Its average speed over this distance is :
(a) 20 kmph □ (b) 24 kmph □
(c) 30 kmph □ (d) 32 kmph □

84. The ratio between a two digit number and the sum of the digits of that number is 7 : 1. If the digit in the tenth place is one more than the digit in the unit place, what is the number ?
(a) 21 □ (b) 32 □
(c) 43 □ (d) none of these □
(S.B.I.P.O. Exam 1991)

85. A car completes a certain journey in 8 hours. It covers half the distance at 40 kmph and the rest at 60 kmph. The length of the journey is :
(a) 350 km □ (b) 384 km □
(c) 400 km □ (d) 420 km □
(Clerical Grade 1991)

86. A man distributed Rs 100 equally among his friends. If there had been five more friends, each would have received one rupee less. How many friends had he ?
(a) 20 □ (b) 25 □
(c) 30 □ (d) 35 □
(C.B.I. 1991)

87. A milkman procures milk at the rate of Rs 4.50 per litre and sells it to his customers at the same rate. If he makes a profit of $12\frac{1}{2}$ %, the quantity of water he mixes for every litre of milk is :
(a) 50 ml □ (b) 100 ml □
(c) 125 ml □ (d) 175 ml □

88. Twenty litres of a mixture contain milk and water in the ratio 5 : 3. If 4 litres of this mixture are replaced by 4 litres of milk, the ratio of milk to water in the new mixture will become :
(a) 2 : 1 □ (b) 6 : 5 □

(c) $7\frac{1}{8} : 3$ (d) $8 : 3$

89. A and B can complete a piece of work in 8 days, B and C in 12 days, while C and A in 16 days. They work together for 3 days when A leaves off. In how many days more will B and C finish the remaining work ?

   (a) $1\frac{1}{2}$ days (b) $2\frac{1}{4}$ days
   (c) $7\frac{1}{8}$ days (d) $4\frac{1}{2}$ days

90. In a division sum, the divisior is twelve times the quotient and five times the remainder. If the remainder be 48, then the dividend is :
   (a) 240 (b) 576
   (c) 4800 (d) 4848
   (C.B.I. 1991)

91. If a man walks at 5 km/hr, he reaches the bus stop 5 minutes too late and if he walks at 6 km/hr, he reaches the stop 5 minutes too early. The bus stop is at a distance of :
   (a) 3 km (b) 5 km
   (c) 6 km (d) 10 km
   (C.B.I. 1991)

92. A's money is to B's money as 4 : 5 and B's money is to C's money as 2 : 3. If A has Rs 800, C has :
   (a) Rs 1000 (b) Rs 1200
   (c) Rs 1500 (d) Rs 2000
   (C.B.I. 1991)

93. Rs 6450 is divided between Rajan and Suresh so that for every Rs 8 that Rajan gets, Suresh gets Rs 7. Their shares differ by :
   (a) Rs 390 (b) Rs 430
   (c) Rs 442 (d) Rs 464

94. A sum of Rs 65000 was divided into 3 parts so that they yielded the same interest when they were lent for 2, 3 and 4 years at 8% simple interest at the end of these periods. The ratio between these parts is :
   (a) 2 : 3 : 4 (b) 4 : 3 : 2
   (c) 6 : 4 : 3 (d) 3 : 4 : 6

95. The difference between the simple interest and the compound interest earned on a sum of money at the end of four years at the rate of 10% p.a. is Rs 256.40. What is the sum ?

Miscellaneous Problems

    (a) Rs 4000   ☐   (b) Rs 4500   ☐
    (c) Rs 5000   ☐   (d) Rs 6000   ☐
                                                          (S.B.I.P.O. Exam 1991)

96. A man drives 4 km distance to go around a rectangular park. If the area of the rectangle is 0.75 sq km., the difference between the length and breadth of the rectangle is :
    (a) 0.5 km   ☐   (b) 1 km   ☐
    (c) 2.75 km   ☐   (d) 10.25 km   ☐

97. 15 persons can fill 35 boxes in 7 days. How many persons can fill 65 boxes in 5 days ?
    (a) 13   ☐   (b) 39   ☐
    (c) 45   ☐   (d) 65   ☐
                                                          (A.O. Exam 1991)

98. If $\frac{a}{3} = \frac{b}{4} = \frac{c}{7}$, the value of $\frac{a+b+c}{c}$ is :
    (a) $\frac{1}{2}$ ☐   (b) $\frac{1}{7}$ ☐
    (c) 2   ☐   (d) 7   ☐
                                                  (Astt. Grade 1990)

99. The average of marks obtained by Sunil in History and Mathematics is 60%. If he got 90 marks out of 150 in Mathematics, how much did he get in History, out of 100 :
    (a) 1   ☐   (b) 6   ☐
    (c) 8   ☐   (d) 12   ☐
                                                  (Bank P.O. 1992)

100. Four different bells ring at intervals of 5, 6, 8 and 10 minutes respectively. If they ring together at 4 p.m. they will ring together again at :
    (a) 5.30 p.m.   ☐   (b) 6.00 p.m.   ☐
    (c) 7.00 p.m.   ☐   (d) 8.10 p.m.   ☐

101. Shankar and Ravi invested Rs 7000 and Rs 10500 in a business. At the end of one year Shankar's share of profit was Rs 2500. The total profit they earned was :
    (a) Rs 3750   ☐   (b) Rs 5200   ☐
    (c) Rs 5750   ☐   (d) Rs 6250   ☐

102. The average of runs scored, by the eleven players of a cricket team is 60. If the runs scored, by the captain are neglected, the average of runs scored by the remaining players increases by 5. How many runs were scored by the captain ?

(a) 0 (b) 10
(c) 55 (d) 120

(P.O. Exam 1991)

103. X and Y invested in a business. They earned some profit which they divided in the ratio of 2 : 3. If X invested Rs 40, The amount invested by Y is :
(a) Rs 50 (b) Rs 60
(c) Rs 80 (d) Rs 1000

(Railway Recruitment 1991)

104. The population of a town increases by $12\frac{1}{2}$ % every year. The population will increase to 121500 after 2 years if the present population is :
(a) 86000 (b) 92000
(c) 96000 (d) 105000

105. 12 grams of an ornament containing gold and copper in the ratio 2 : 1 is melted with 18 grams of another ornament containing them in the ratio 5 : 1 and cast into a new ornament. The new ornament will contain gold and copper in the ratio :
(a) 7 : 2 (b) 10 : 1
(c) 19 : 11 (d) 23 : 7

106. A grocer claims to sell sugar at cost price, but has a concealed weight of 100 gram in the pan in which he keeps sugar. By mistake his son weighs by keeping the weight in this pan and sugar in the other. On sale of 1kg of sugar, he will lose :
(a) $8\frac{1}{3}$ % (b) $9\frac{1}{11}$ %
(c) 10% (d) $11\frac{1}{9}$ %

107. A works twice as fast as B. If B can complete a piece of work independently in 12 days, A and B together can complete the work in :
(a) 4 days (b) 6 days
(c) 8 days (d) 18 days

(Astt. Grade 1990)

108. Bucket P has thrice the capacity as bucket Q. It takes 60 turns for bucket P to fill the empty drum. How many turns it will take for both the buckets P and Q, having each turn together to fill the empty drum ?

	(a) 30		(b) 40	
	(c) 45		(d) 90	

(Bank P.O. 1989)

109. A donkey is tied to a rope 16 m long at the corner of a rectangular field of dimensions 60m×30m. The area over which the donkey can graze is nearly :

 (a) 128 m^2 (b) 201 m^2
 (c) 402 m^2 (d) 805 m^2

110. Two trains 200m and 150m long respectively are running on parallel rails at the rate of 40 km/hr and 45 km/hr respectively. In how much time will they cross each other if they are running in the same direction ?

 (a) 1.2 min   (b) 2.2 min
 (c) 3.2 min   (d) 4.2 min

111. Harish sold a clock at a profit of 15%. Had he sold it for Rs 22.50 less he would have gained only 5%. The C.P. of the clock is :

 (a) Rs 148   (b) Rs 225
 (c) Rs 444   (d) none of these

112. A cloth merchant has announced 25% rebate in prices. If one needs to have a rebate of Rs 40, then how many shirts costing Rs 28 each, should he purchase ?

 (a) 5   (b) 6
 (c) 7   (d) 10

(Railway Recruitment 1991)

113. Sohanlal's wages were first increased by 20%. Again the increased wages were reduced by 20%. His net loss is :

 (a) 0%   (b) 1%
 (c) 4%   (d) $6\frac{1}{4}$%

114. 1854 seats in a theatre form a perfect square except for five seats at the back. The number of seats in each row is :

 (a) 42   (b) 43
 (c) 47   (d) 48

115. The number of students in each section of a school is 24. After admitting the new students, three new sections were started. Now the total number of sections is 16 and there are 21 students in each section. The number of new students admitted is :

(a) 14 □ (b) 24 □
(c) 48 □ (d) none of these □
(A.O. Exam 1991)

116. A's salary is Rs 300 more than B's salary and B's salary is Rs 200 more then C's salary. If the total of B's and C's salary is Rs 1800, then what is the salary of A?
(a) Rs 800 □ (b) Rs 1000 □
(c) Rs 1300 □ (d) Rs 3100 □
(A.O. Exam 1991)

117. The average age of four members of a family is 20 years. If the age of grand father be included, the average is increased by 9 years. What is the age of grand father?
(a) 48 years □ (b) 52 years □
(c) 65 years □ (d) 72 years □

118. A ladder is placed 5 m away from the foot of the wall and it reaches a height of 12 m from the ground. The length of the ladder is :
(a) 11 m □ (b) 12.5 m □
(c) 13 m □ (d) none of these □

119. By selling a pen for Rs 15, a man loses one sixteenth of what it costs him. The cost price of the pen is :
(a) Rs 16 □ (b) Rs 18 □
(c) Rs 20 □ (d) Rs 21 □

120. Vishnu bought 170 kg of sugar at the rate of Rs 5.80 per kg and mixed it in the 130 kg sugar purchased at the rate of Rs 5.30 per kg. He sold the mixture with a profit of Rs 161. The rate of the mixture per kg was :
(a) Rs 5.12 □ (b) Rs 5.68 □
(c) Rs 5.82 □ (d) Rs 6.12 □
(P.O. Exam 1991)

121. Hiralal sold 10 articles for a total profit of Rs 460 and 12 articles for a total profit of Rs 144. At what profit per article should he sell the remainning 20 articles so as to get an average profit of Rs 18 per article?
(a) Rs 7.60 □ (b) Rs 7.40 □
(c) Rs 8 □ (d) Rs 7.80 □

122. A radio dealer gains 15% after allowing a discount of 20% on marked price. The marked price is :
(a) 35% above C.P. □ (b) 15% above C.P. □

(c) 20% above C.P. ☐   (d) none of these ☐

123. In an office, $\frac{3}{4}$th of the staff can neither type nor take shorthand. However, $\frac{1}{5}$th can type and $\frac{1}{3}$rd can take shorthand. What part of the whole staff can do both?
 (a) $\frac{1}{5}$ ☐   (b) $\frac{3}{40}$ ☐
 (c) $\frac{13}{40}$ ☐   (d) $\frac{17}{60}$ ☐

124. Prashant and Vishal contribute $\frac{1}{2}$ and $\frac{1}{3}$ of the capital and Alok contributes the rest. Prashant, Vishal and Alok will share the profit in the proportion:
 (a) 2 : 3 : 1 ☐   (b) 3 : 2 : 1 ☐
 (c) 3 : 2 : 5 ☐   (d) 2 : 3 : 6 ☐

125. The price of an article is reduced by 25% but its daily sale increases by 30%. Thus, the daily sale receipts will:
 (a) increase by $10\frac{1}{2}$% ☐   (b) decrease by $10\frac{1}{2}$% ☐
 (c) decrease by 2.5% ☐   (d) increase by 5% ☐

126. A dealer allows a discount of 10% on the advertised price of a camera, costing him Rs 600. To make a profit of 20%, the marked price of the camera should be
 (a) Rs 660 ☐   (b) Rs 720 ☐
 (c) Rs 750 ☐   (d) Rs 800 ☐

127. A cricketer scored 180 runs in the first test and 258 runs in the second. How many runs should he score in the third test so that his average score in three tests would be 230 runs?
 (a) 230 ☐   (b) 242 ☐
 (c) 252 ☐   (d) 334 ☐

(A.O. Exam 1991)

128. If A is $\frac{1}{3}$ of B and B is $\frac{1}{2}$ of C, then A : B : C is:
 (a) 1 : 3 : 6 ☐   (b) 2 : 3 : 6 ☐
 (c) 3 : 1 : 2 ☐   (d) 3 : 2 : 6 ☐

129. Area of a triangle whose sides are 6, 8 and 10 metres respectively, is:

(a) 24 m² ☐ (b) 30 m² ☐
(c) 40 m² ☐ (d) 48 m² ☐

130. A can do a piece of work in 15 days but with the help of B finishes the work in 10 days. The share of A out of a wage of Rs 120 is :
   (a) Rs 30 ☐ (b) Rs 40 ☐
   (c) Rs 60 ☐ (d) Rs 80 ☐

131. One year ago the ratio of Varun and Veena's age was 4 : 5. One year hence the ratio of their ages will be 5 : 6. The present age of Veena is :
   (a) 9 years ☐ (b) 10 years ☐
   (c) 12 years ☐ (d) none of these ☐

132. Ajay started a business investing Rs 75000. After 3 months Kamal joined him with a capital of Rs 60000. If at the end of the year the total profit is Rs 16000, what will be Kamal's share in it ?
   (a) Rs 4500 ☐ (b) Rs 6000 ☐
   (c) Rs 8000 ☐ (d) Rs 10000 ☐

133. If the diameter of a cone is 14 cm and its height is 9 cm, the area of its curved surface is :
   (a) 198 cm² ☐ (b) 212 cm² ☐
   (c) 222 cm² ☐ (d) 250 cm² ☐

134. A carpet of 16 metres breadth and 20 metres length was purchased for Rs 2496. Its cost per m² is :
   (a) Rs 7.80 ☐ (b) Rs 78 ☐
   (c) Rs 156 ☐ (d) none of these ☐

(A.O. Exam 1991)

135. The average age of 12 children is 20 years. If the age of one more child is added, the average decreases by 1. What is the age of the child added later ?
   (a) 5 years ☐ (b) 7 years ☐
   (c) 19 years ☐ (d) none of these ☐

(P.O. Exam 1991)

Miscellaneous Problems

136. The value of
$$\frac{1}{3-\sqrt{8}} - \frac{1}{\sqrt{8}-\sqrt{7}} + \frac{1}{\sqrt{7}-\sqrt{6}} - \frac{1}{\sqrt{6}-\sqrt{5}} + \frac{1}{\sqrt{5}-\sqrt{4}}$$
  (a) is 0 ☐   (b) lies between 0 and 1 ☐
  (c) is greater than 3 ☐   (d) lies between 2 and 3 ☐

137. A number when divided by 119 leaves a remainder 19. If the same number is divided by 17, the remainder will be :
  (a) 19 ☐   (b) 10 ☐
  (c) 7 ☐   (d) 2 ☐

138. The least number by which 72 must be multiplied in order to produce a multiple of 112, is :
  (a) 16 ☐   (b) 14 ☐
  (c) 12 ☐   (d) 18 ☐

139. A certain number of men could do a piece of work in 60 days. If there were 8 more men, it could be finished in 10 days less. The number of men in the beginning were :
  (a) 30 ☐   (b) 35 ☐
  (c) 40 ☐   (d) 45 ☐

140. A fraction whose denominator is 30 and which lies between $\frac{5}{8}$ and $\frac{7}{11}$ is :
  (a) $\frac{17}{30}$ ☐   (b) $\frac{19}{30}$ ☐
  (c) $\frac{13}{30}$ ☐   (d) $\frac{23}{30}$ ☐

141. The value of $\sqrt{\frac{.081}{.0064} \times \frac{.484}{6.25}}$ is :   (Railway Recruitment Board, 1992)
  (a) 9 ☐   (b) 0.9 ☐
  (c) 99 ☐   (d) 0.99 ☐

142. The profit earned by selling a watch for Rs. 820 is as much as the loss incurred when it is sold for Rs. 650. The cost price of the watch is :
  (a) Rs. 720 ☐   (b) Rs. 750 ☐
  (c) Rs. 690 ☐   (d) Rs. 735 ☐
                                                  (Bank P.O. 1992)

143. Average age of A and B is 24 years and average age of B, C and D is 22 years. The sum of the ages of A, B, C and D is :   (Bank P.O. 1992)

(a) 90 years ☐ (b) 96 years ☐
(c) 114 years ☐ (d) Data inadequate ☐

144. What should be added to 11210 to make it exactly divisible by 11 ?
(a) 1 ☐ (b) 4 ☐
(c) 9 ☐ (d) 10 ☐
(Bank P.O. 1992)

145. If a sum doubles itself in 10 years at simple interest, what must be rate per cent per annum ? (Bank P.O. 1992)
(a) 5 ☐ (b) 10 ☐
(c) 20 ☐ (d) Data inadequate ☐

146. Two numbers are respectively 20% and 50% more than a third number. What percentage is the first of the third ?
(a) 80 ☐ (b) 100 ☐
(c) 120 ☐ (d) 150 ☐

147. Sohan completes (1/10)th of some work everyday. While working with Deepak, he completed the work in 6 days. In how many days will Deepak alone finish the work ? (Bank P.O. 1992)
(a) 10 ☐ (b) 12 ☐
(c) 15 ☐ (d) 30 ☐

148. Sneh's age is (1/6)th of her father's age. Sneh's father's age will be twice of Vimal's age after 10 years. If Vimal's eighth birthday was celebrated two years before, then what is Sneh's present age ?
(a) 24 years ☐ (b) 30 years ☐
(c) $6\frac{2}{3}$ years ☐ (d) None of these ☐
(Bank P.O. 1992)

149. Ashok bought some toys with 20% discount on original price. The original price of each toy is Rs. 40. If he makes a total saving of Rs. 240, how many toys did he buy ? (Bank P.O. 1992)
(a) 8 ☐ (b) 12 ☐
(c) 24 ☐ (d) 30 ☐

150. How many pieces of 3.2 m long can be made out of a 192 m long rod ?
(a) 6 ☐ (b) 60 ☐
(c) 59 ☐ (d) None of these ☐

Miscellaneous Problems

HINTS & SOLUTION

1. Let $\sqrt{\dfrac{x}{289}} = \dfrac{54}{51}$. Then, $\dfrac{x}{289} = \dfrac{54}{51} \times \dfrac{54}{51}$.

   $\therefore x = \left(\dfrac{54}{51} \times \dfrac{54}{51} \times 289\right) = 324.$

2. $\dfrac{x}{100} \times 250 + \dfrac{25}{100} \times 68 = 67 \Rightarrow \dfrac{5x}{2} = (67 - 17) = 50.$

   $\therefore x = \left(50 \times \dfrac{2}{5}\right) = 20.$

3. Given Expression $= \left(\dfrac{25}{2} \times \dfrac{18}{5} \times \dfrac{5}{9}\right) = 25.$

4. Given Expression $= \dfrac{575}{100} - \dfrac{3}{7} \times \dfrac{63}{4} + \dfrac{72}{35} \times \dfrac{100}{144}$

   $= \dfrac{23}{4} - \dfrac{27}{4} + \dfrac{10}{7} = -1 + \dfrac{10}{7} = \dfrac{3}{7}.$

5. Given Expression $= \dfrac{1}{7} + \left[\dfrac{7}{9} - \dfrac{5}{9} - \dfrac{2}{9}\right] = \dfrac{1}{7} + 0 = \dfrac{1}{7}.$

6. $\dfrac{3}{4} = 0.75, \dfrac{4}{5} = 0.8, \dfrac{5}{6} = 0.833$ and $\dfrac{6}{7} = 0.857.$

   $\therefore$ Biggest fraction $= \dfrac{6}{7}.$

7. Given Expression $= 1 + \dfrac{1}{1 + \dfrac{1}{\dfrac{5}{6}}} = 1 + \dfrac{1}{1 + \dfrac{6}{5}} = 1 + \dfrac{5}{11} = \dfrac{16}{11}.$

8. $(1502)^2 - (1498)^2 = (1502 - 1498)(1502 + 1498) = 4 \times 3000 = 12000.$

9. $\sqrt[3]{1 - \dfrac{91}{216}} = \left(\dfrac{216 - 91}{216}\right)^{1/3} = \left(\dfrac{125}{216}\right)^{1/3} = \left(\dfrac{5 \times 5 \times 5}{6 \times 6 \times 6}\right)^{1/3} = \dfrac{5}{6}.$

10. $\dfrac{1}{2} : \dfrac{1}{3} : \dfrac{1}{5} = 15 : 10 : 6.$

11. $x - \dfrac{4}{7}x = 18 \Rightarrow 7x - 4x = 126$ or $x = 42.$

12. Let $\dfrac{x}{31} \times \dfrac{x}{279} = 1.$ Then, $x^2 = 31 \times 279 = (31 \times 31 \times 3 \times 3).$

∴ $x = 31 \times 3 = 93$.

13. Average $= \dfrac{1}{4}\left(\dfrac{3}{2} + \dfrac{7}{3} + \dfrac{10}{3} + \dfrac{29}{6}\right) = \left(\dfrac{9 + 14 + 20 + 29}{24}\right) = \dfrac{72}{24} = 3$.

14.
$$70 \overline{\smash{\big)}\,245\,}\,(3$$
$$\underline{210}$$

$$35 \overline{\smash{\big)}\,70\,}\,(2$$
$$\underline{70}$$
$$\times$$

∴ H. C. F. = 35.

15. $\dfrac{2}{7} = 0.285,\ \dfrac{3}{10} = 0.3$ and $\dfrac{4}{13} = 0.307$.

∴ Fractions in ascending order are $\dfrac{2}{7}, \dfrac{3}{10}$ and $\dfrac{4}{13}$.

16. Distance between two poles $= \dfrac{20}{(5-1)} = 5$ metres.

17. Let unit digit $= x$ and ten's digit $= y$.
$\dfrac{1}{3}(10y + x) - \dfrac{1}{4}(10y + x) = 2$
$\left(\dfrac{1}{3} - \dfrac{1}{4}\right)(10y + x) = 2$ or $10y + x = 24$
∴ Number = 24.
Sum of the digits = 6.

18. $N = 123\,Q + 83 = (41 \times 3)\,Q + (82 + 1) = 41 \times (3Q + 2) + 1$.
∴ Required remainder = 1.

19. $\dfrac{N}{4} = \dfrac{Y}{6} \Rightarrow 6N - 4Y = 0$ or $3N - 2Y = 0$. Also, $N + Y = 600$.
Solving we get, $N = 240$ and $Y = 360$.
∴ Difference $= (360 - 240) = 120$.

20. $N = \dfrac{2}{3}P,\ K = \left(\dfrac{2}{3}P + \dfrac{1}{4} \times \dfrac{2}{3}P\right) = \dfrac{5P}{6}$.
Ratio $= \dfrac{2}{3}P : \dfrac{5}{6}P : P = \dfrac{2}{3} : \dfrac{5}{6} : 1 = 4 : 5 : 6$.
If Pravin has Rs. 6, Kavita has Rs. 5

Miscellaneous Problems

If Pravin has Rs. 876, Kavita has Rs. $\left(\frac{5}{6} \times 876\right)$ = Rs. 730.

21. Let the numbers be x and $x - 11$.

    $\frac{1}{5}(x + x - 11) = 9$ or $2x - 11 = 45$ or $x = 28$.

    $\therefore$ The numbers are 28, 17.

22. $715 = 5 \times 11 \times 13$ and $825 = 5 \times 5 \times 11 \times 3$.

    The least number is 5×3 by which 715 must be multiplied to obtain a multiple of 825.

23. Let ten's digit = x and unit's digit = y.

    Then, $(10x + y) + (10y + x) = 44 \Rightarrow 11(x + y) = 44$ or $x + y = 4$.

24. $184 = 2 \times 2 \times 2 \times 23$.

    $mx + m(x + 1) = 184$. So, $m[2x + 1] = 184$ or $2x + 1 = \frac{184}{m}$

    By hit and trial, $m = 8$ and $x = 11$. So, the number = 8.

25.
    ```
    3 | 10 00 ( 31
      |  9
    ——————————
    61| 100
      |  61
      ——————
      |  39
    ```

    Number to be added = $(32)^2 - 1000 = (1024 - 1000) = 24$.

26. C.P. of 4 commodities = Rs. 64.

    Reduced price of 4 commodities = Rs. 52.

    Saving % = $\left(\frac{12}{64} \times 100\right)\% = 18\frac{3}{4}\%$.

27. l.c.m. of 8, 12, 15, 20 = $2 \times 3 \times 2 \times 5 \times 2$.

    $\therefore$ Least square number divisible by 8, 12, 15, 20
       $= 2 \times 2 \times 3 \times 3 \times 5 \times 5 \times 2 \times 2 = 3600$.

28. Failed in Hindi only = $(35 - 20) = 15\%$

    Failed in English only = $(45 - 20) = 25\%$

    Failed in both = 20%

    Failed in one or both = $(15 + 25 + 20)\% = 60\%$.

    Passed in both = 40%.

29. $1 + 2 + 3 + 4 + 5 + 6 + 7 = 28$, which is divisible by 7.

30. $(13)^2 + (11)^2 = 169 + 121 = 290$.

    $\therefore$ Least number to be subtracted = 1.

31. C's 1 day's work = $\left(\dfrac{1}{8} - \dfrac{1}{12}\right) = \dfrac{1}{24}$.

    $\therefore$ C alone can finish the job in 24 days.

32. Less persons more days

    $12 : 18 : : 36 : x$

    $\therefore$ $x = \dfrac{18 \times 36}{12} = 54$.

33. Data inadequate.

34. Lengthwise there are 12 trees.

    Total distance between them = (11×2) m = 22 m.

    $\therefore$ Length = $(1 + 22 + 1) = 24$ m.

35. $x + y = 104$ and $x - y = 30$.

    $\therefore$ $(x^2 - y^2) = (x + y)(x - y) = 104 \times 30 = 3120$.

36. $3x + 3 \cdot \dfrac{1}{3}x = 60$ or $x = 15$.

    $\therefore$ Cost of an adult ticket = Rs. 15.

37. It is more by $\left(\dfrac{10}{100} \times 24.2 - \dfrac{10}{100} \times 24.02\right)$

    $= 2.42 - 2.402 = 0.018$.

38. Let C.P. = Rs. 100. Then, list price = Rs. 120.

    S.P. = 90% of Rs. 120 = Rs. 108.

    Gain = 8%.

39. Do yourself. It is 908.

40. Cost of 291 mangoes = Rs. $\left(\dfrac{49.75}{12} \times 291\right)$ = Rs. 1200 approx.

41. Let sum = Rs. P.

    Then, S.I. = $\dfrac{P \times 2 \times 5}{100} = \dfrac{P}{10}$.

Miscellaneous Problems

$$\text{C.I.} = \left[P\left(1+\frac{5}{100}\right)^2 - P\right] = \frac{41}{400}P$$

$$\therefore \frac{41}{400}P - \frac{1}{10}P = 4 \text{ or } P\left(\frac{41}{400} - \frac{1}{10}\right) = 4$$

$$\therefore P = (400 \times 4) = \text{Rs. } 1600.$$

42. $52x - 25x = 324 \Rightarrow 27x = 324 \Rightarrow x = 12$.

43. Let original price = Rs. x.

    Increased price = $\left(\dfrac{100+p}{100}\right)x$

    Reduced price = $\dfrac{(100-p)}{100} \times \dfrac{(100+p)}{100} x$

    $\therefore \dfrac{(100)^2 - p^2}{(100)^2} \cdot x = 1$ or $x = \dfrac{10000}{(10000 - p^2)}$

44. Clearly, $1.x < 1 + x$.

    So, one of the numbers must be 1.

45. Let total votes polled = x. Then,

    52% of x + (52% of x – 98) + 68 = x

    $2 \times \dfrac{52}{100}x - x = 30$ or $x = (30 \times 25) = 750$.

46. Let these notes be $3x$, $7x$ and $8x$.

    Ratio of their values = $3x \times 1 : 7x \times 2 : 8x \times 5$
    $= 3x : 14x : 40x = 3 : 14 : 40$.

    Value of 5 rupee notes = Rs. $\left(5130 \times \dfrac{40}{57}\right)$ = Rs. 3600.

    Number of these notes = $\dfrac{3600}{5} = 720$.

47. $2500 - 1000 = 500 + x$ or $x = 1000$.

    So, he spent Rs. 1000 on repairs.

48. Charges for 320 km = $60 \times 4 + 60 \times 5 + 8 \times \left(\dfrac{200}{5}\right)$

    $= \text{Rs. } (240 + 300 + 320) = \text{Rs. } 860.$

    Balance = Rs. $\left(860 - \dfrac{1}{4} \times 860\right)$ = Rs. $(860 - 215)$ = Rs. 645.

    Total amount with Ajit = Rs. $(860 + 645)$ = Rs. 1505.

49. $\dfrac{3+x}{7+x} = \dfrac{7+x}{13+x} \Rightarrow (3+x)(13+x) = (7+x)^2$

or $x^2 + 16x + 39 = x^2 + 14x + 49$ or $x = 5$.

50. C.I. = Rs. $\left[6000 \times \left(1 + \dfrac{5}{100}\right)^3 - 6000 \right]$

    = Rs. $\left[6000 \times \dfrac{21}{20} \times \dfrac{21}{20} \times \dfrac{21}{20} - 6000 \right]$ = Rs. 945.75.

51. Jayant : Madhu = $(6000 \times 12 : 4000 \times 6) = 3 : 1$.

    Madhu's share = Rs. $\left(5200 \times \dfrac{1}{4}\right)$ = Rs. 1300.

52. Rate = $\dfrac{100 \times 432}{1200 \times 4} = 9\%$. New rate = 10%.

    New interest = Rs. $\left(\dfrac{1200 \times 10 \times 4}{100}\right)$ = Rs. 480.

    Amount = Rs. 1680.

53. Capacity of tank = (12×13.5) litres = 162 litres.

    Number of new buckets = $\left(\dfrac{162}{9}\right) = 18$.

54. Let amount at 15% be Rs. x.

    $\dfrac{x \times 15 \times 1}{100} + \dfrac{(8000 - x) \times 10 \times 1}{100} = 950$ or $15x + 8000 - 10x = 95000$

    $5x = 15000$ or $x = 3000$.

    Amount at 15% = Rs. 3000, amount at 10% = Rs. 5000.

55. Let C.P. of apples = Re. 1 per kg.

    C.P. = Rs. 24, S.P. = 110% of Rs. 24 = Rs. 26.40.

    Suppose he sold x kg at a loss of 5%.

    Then, $\dfrac{95}{100} x + \dfrac{120}{100}(24 - x) = 26.40$

    $\therefore 95x + 2880 - 120x = 2640$ or $25x = 240$ or $x = 9.6$ kg.

56. $\dfrac{\sqrt{3}}{4} a^2 = 36\sqrt{3} \Rightarrow a^2 = 144$ or $a = 12$ cm.

    $\therefore$ Perimeter = 36 cm.

57. Let the number of these coins be x and $(100 - x)$.

    $\dfrac{1}{2} x + \dfrac{100 - x}{4} = 45 \Rightarrow 2x + 100 - x = 180$ or $x = 80$.

Miscellaneous Problems

∴ Number of 50-paise coins = 80.

58. Let income = Rs. x. Then,

$$\frac{5}{100}x + \frac{20}{100}\left(x - \frac{5}{100}x\right) + 1919 = x$$

$$\frac{x}{20} + \frac{19x}{100} + 1919 = x \text{ or } 5x + 19x + 191900 = 100x$$

∴ $76x = 191900$ or $x = \frac{191900}{76} = 2525.$

59. Other number = $\frac{2310 \times 30}{210} = 330.$

60. Marks in Mathematics = $(68 \times 7 - 70 \times 6) = (476 - 420) = 56.$

61. B completes in 12 days; A will take 24 days and C will take 8 days.

$(A + B + C)$'s 1 day's work = $\left(\frac{1}{24} + \frac{1}{12} + \frac{1}{8}\right) = \frac{6}{24} = \frac{1}{4}.$

So, all together will complete the job in 4 days.

62. $2\left(2500 + \frac{5}{12}x\right) = x$ or $30000 + 5x = 6x$ or $x = 30000.$

Share of youngest son = $\frac{x}{2}$ = Rs. 15000.

63. Suppose total distance = x km.

Then, X's speed = x km/hr. & Y's speed = $\left(\frac{2x}{3}\right)$ km/hr.

Let them meet after y hours.

Then, $xy + \frac{2xy}{3} = x$

or $y\left(1 + \frac{2}{3}\right) = 1$ or $y = \frac{3}{5}$ hour = $\left(\frac{3}{5} \times 60\right)$ min. = 36 min.

So, they cross each other at 4.36 p.m.

64. Let total length = 100 m.
Then, painted red = 60 m; Balance = 40 m.
Painted green = 16 m, Balance = 24 m.
Painted Blue = 12 m, Balance = 12 m.
If balance is 12 m, total length = 100 m
If balance is $\frac{30}{100}$ m, total length = $\left(\frac{100}{12} \times \frac{30}{100}\right)$ m = 2.5 m.

65. Alcohol in first mix = 40 litres, water in it = 60 litres.

Let x litres be replaced.

Alcohol in $(100-x)$ litres $= \dfrac{40}{100}(100-x)$ litres.

Alcohol in new x litres $= \left(\dfrac{19}{100}x\right)$.

Total Alcohol now $\dfrac{2}{5}(100-x) + \dfrac{19x}{100}$

$\therefore \dfrac{2}{5}(100-x) + \dfrac{19x}{100} = 26$

or $4000 - 40x + 19x = 2600$ or $x = \dfrac{1400}{21} = \dfrac{200}{3}$.

$\therefore$ Part replaced $= \dfrac{x}{100} = \dfrac{200}{3 \times 100} = \dfrac{2}{3}$.

66. Let the number of girls $= x$ & number of boys $= y$.

   Then, $\dfrac{1}{3}y = 100$ or $y = 300$.

   Now, $\dfrac{x}{2} + 100 = 300$ or $x = 400$.

   $\therefore$ Total number of students $= (300 + 400) = 700$.

67. Required number $=$ (l.c.m. of 10, 15, 20, 35) $- 4 = 416$.

68. Average now $= \left(\dfrac{20 \times 125 - 5 \times 116}{15}\right)$ cm $= 128$ cm.

69. $\dfrac{M}{3} - \dfrac{S}{2} = 30 \Rightarrow 2M - 3S = 180$. Also, $M + S = 240$.

   Solving $2M - 3S = 180$ and $M + S = 240$, we get $S = 60$.

70. Mean proportion $= \sqrt{0.32 \times 0.02} = \sqrt{0.0064} = 0.08$.

71. Average $= \dfrac{3(1+2+3+4+5+6+7+8+9)}{9} = 15$.

72. Total time $= (180 + 27)$ min $= 207$ min.
   Free time $= 15$ min.
   Used time $= (207 - 15)$ min. $= 192$ min.
   Duration of each period $= \dfrac{192}{4} = 48$ min.

73. Average speed $= \left(\dfrac{2 \times 30 \times 60}{30 + 60}\right)$ km/hr $= 40$ km/hr.

Miscellaneous Problems

74. $x + \frac{2}{5}x = 63 \Rightarrow 7x = 63 \times 5$ or $x = 45$ cm.

Shorter piece $= \left(\frac{2}{5} \times 45\right)$ cm $= 18$ cm.

75. Suppose he bought the radio for Rs. x.
If C.P. is Rs. 75, original price = Rs. 100
If C.P. is Rs. x, original price = Rs. $\left(\frac{100}{75} \times x\right)$ = Rs. $\left(\frac{4x}{3}\right)$.

$\frac{140}{100}x = \frac{4x}{3} + 40$ or $420x = 400x + 12000$ or $x = 600$.

76. Let the numbers be $3x$ and $4x$.
Then, their H.C.F. = x and their L.C.M. = $12x$.
$\therefore 12x \times x = 10800$ or $x^2 = 900$ or $x = 30$.
So, the numbers are 90 and 120.
The sum of the numbers = 210.

77. Total work done $= \left(3 \times \frac{2}{15} + 4 \times \frac{1}{10}\right) = \left(\frac{2}{5} + \frac{2}{5}\right) = \frac{4}{5}$.

Work unfinished $= \left(1 - \frac{4}{5}\right) = \frac{1}{5}$.

78. H.C.F. $= \frac{\text{Product of numbers}}{\text{Their L.C.M.}} = \frac{xy}{z}$.

79. Let total marks = x. Then,
$\left(\frac{20}{100}x + 30\right) = \left(\frac{32}{100}x - 42\right)$ or $\frac{3x}{25} = 72$.

$\therefore x = \left(\frac{72 \times 25}{3}\right) = 600$.

Pass marks $= \left(\frac{20}{100}x + 30\right) = \left(\frac{20}{100} \times 600 + 30\right) = 150$.

Pass percentage $= \left(\frac{150}{600} \times 100\right)\% = 25\%$.

80. $\frac{16 + 22 + x}{3} = 20 \Rightarrow 38 + x = 60$ or $x = 22$.

81. Suppose the number of correct answers = x.
Wrong answers $= (75 - x)$.
$\therefore 4x - (75 - x) = 125 \Rightarrow 5x = 200$ or $x = 40$.

82. $P\left(1+\dfrac{R}{100}\right)^3 = 6690$ and $P\left(1+\dfrac{R}{100}\right)^6 = 10035$.

On dividing, we get $\left(1+\dfrac{R}{100}\right)^3 = \dfrac{10035}{6690}$.

$\therefore P = \dfrac{6690}{\left(1+\dfrac{R}{100}\right)^3} = \dfrac{6690}{\dfrac{10035}{6690}} = \dfrac{6690 \times 6690}{10035} = 4460$.

83. Total time taken to cover 8 km $= \left(\dfrac{2}{10} + \dfrac{2}{20} + \dfrac{2}{30} + \dfrac{2}{60}\right) = \dfrac{24}{60} = \dfrac{2}{5}$ hours.

$\therefore$ Average speed $= \left(8 \times \dfrac{5}{2}\right)$ km/hr $= 20$ km/hr.

84. Let number $= 7x$ & sum of digits $= x$.
Let unit digit be y. Then, ten's digit $= x - y$
Now $x - y - y = 1$ or $x - 2y = 1$
$10x - 10y + y = 7x$ or $x = 3y$
Solving $x - 2y = 1$ and $x = 3y$, we get $y = 1$ and $x = 3$.
$\therefore$ Number $= 21$.

85. $\dfrac{x}{2(40)} + \dfrac{x}{2(60)} = 8 \Rightarrow \dfrac{x}{80} + \dfrac{x}{120} = 8$.

$\therefore 3x + 2x = 240 \times 8$ or $x = 384$ km.

86. Suppose he had x friends.

$\dfrac{100}{x} - \dfrac{100}{x+5} = 1 \Rightarrow 100(x+5) - 100x = x(x+5)$.

$\therefore x^2 + 5x - 500 = 0$ or $(x+25)(x-20) = 0$.
Hence, $x = 20$.

87. C.P. = Rs. 4.50, S.P. = $112\dfrac{1}{2}$ % of Rs. 4.50

$=$ Rs. $\left(\dfrac{225}{2 \times 100} \times 4.50\right) =$ Rs. $\left(\dfrac{20.25}{4}\right)$

Rs. 4.50 is the cost of 1 litre

Rs. $\dfrac{20.25}{4}$ is the cost of $\left(\dfrac{1}{4.50} \times \dfrac{20.25}{4}\right) = \dfrac{9}{8}$ litres.

$\therefore$ Water added to each litre $= \dfrac{1}{8}$ litre $= \left(\dfrac{1}{8} \times 1000\right)$ ml $= 125$ ml.

Miscellaneous Problems 529

88. Milk in 20 litres = $\left(20 \times \dfrac{5}{8}\right)$ litres = 12.5 litres.

Milk in 4 litres = $\left(4 \times \dfrac{5}{8}\right)$ litres = 2.5 litres.

∴ Milk in new mix. = (12.5 – 2.5 + 4) litres = 14 litres.
Water in it = 6 litres.
∴ Ratio of milk and water in new mix. = 14 : 6 = 7 : 3.

89. $2(A + B + C)$'s 1 day's work = $\left(\dfrac{1}{8} + \dfrac{1}{12} + \dfrac{1}{16}\right) = \dfrac{13}{48}$

$(A + B + C)$'s 3 day's work = $\left(3 \times \dfrac{13}{96}\right) = \dfrac{13}{32}$.

Remaining work = $\left(1 - \dfrac{13}{32}\right) = \dfrac{19}{32}$.

$\dfrac{1}{12}$ work is done by B and C in 1 day.

∴ $\dfrac{19}{32}$ work will be done by them in $\left(\dfrac{19}{32} \times 12\right)$ days = $7\dfrac{1}{8}$ days.

90. Divisor = $12Q = 5R = 5 \times 48 = 240$. So, $Q = 20$.
Dividend = $(240 \times 20 + 48) = 4848$.

91. Let required distance = x km.

$\dfrac{x}{5} - \dfrac{x}{6} = \dfrac{10}{60}$ or $\dfrac{6x - 5x}{30} = \dfrac{1}{6}$ or $6x = 30$ or $x = 5$ km.

92. $A : B = 4 : 5$ and $B : C = 2 : 3$.

∴ $\dfrac{A}{C} = \dfrac{A}{B} \times \dfrac{B}{C} = \dfrac{4}{5} \times \dfrac{2}{3} = \dfrac{8}{15}$. Thus, $A : C = 8 : 15$.

If A has Rs. 8, C has Rs. 15.

If A has Rs. 800, C has Rs. $\left(\dfrac{15}{8} \times 800\right)$ = Rs. 1500.

93. Rajan's share = Rs. $\left(6450 \times \dfrac{8}{15}\right)$ = Rs. 3440.

Suresh's share = Rs. (6450 – 3440) = Rs. 3010.

Difference = Rs. (3440 – 3010) = Rs. 430.

94. $\dfrac{A \times 2 \times 8}{100} = \dfrac{B \times 3 \times 8}{100} = \dfrac{C \times 4 \times 8}{100} = x$

$A = \dfrac{25}{4} x,\ B = \dfrac{25}{6} x$ and $C = \dfrac{25}{8} x$.

$\therefore A : B : C = \dfrac{25}{4} : \dfrac{25}{6} : \dfrac{25}{8} = 6 : 4 : 3.$

95. Let sum = Rs. x.

   S.I. = $\dfrac{x \times 4 \times 10}{100}$ = Rs. $\left(\dfrac{2x}{5}\right)$

   C.I. = $\left[x \left(1 + \dfrac{10}{100}\right)^4 - x\right] = \dfrac{4641}{10000} x.$

   $\therefore \dfrac{4641}{10000} x - \dfrac{2x}{5} = 256.40$ or $641x = 2564000$ or $x = 4000.$

96. $2(x + y) = 4$ or $x + y = 2$. Also, $xy = 0.75$.

   Now, $x - y = \sqrt{(x + y)^2 - 4xy} = \sqrt{4 - 4 \times 0.75} = 1$ km.

97. More boxes, More persons
   Less days, More persons

   $\therefore \left.\begin{array}{c} .35 : 65 \\ 5 : 7 \end{array}\right\} :: 15 : x$ or $x = \dfrac{65 \times 7 \times 15}{35 \times 5} = 39.$

98. Let $\dfrac{a}{3} = \dfrac{b}{4} = \dfrac{c}{7} = x.$ Then, $a = 3x, b = 4x$ and $c = 7x.$

   $\therefore \dfrac{a + b + c}{c} = \dfrac{3x + 4x + 7x}{7x} = \dfrac{14x}{7x} = 2.$

99. Total marks obtained by Sunil = 60% of $(150 + 100) = 150.$

   $\therefore$ Marks obtained in History = $(150 - 90) = 60.$

100. L.C.M. of 5, 6, 8, 10
   = $2 \times 5 \times 3 \times 4 = 120.$
   So, they will ring together again after 2
   hours, i.e. at 6 p.m.

2	5 – 6 – 8 – 10
5	5 – 3 – 4 – 5
	1 – 3 – 4 – 1

101. Shankar : Ravi = 7000 : 10500 = 2 : 3
   If Shankar gets Rs. 2, total profit = Rs. 5.
   If Shankar gets Rs. 2500, total profit = Rs. $\left(\dfrac{5}{2} \times 2500\right)$ = Rs. 6250.

102. Total runs made by 11 players = $(11 \times 60) = 660.$
   Runs of captain = $(660 - 65 \times 10) = 10.$

103. If X invested Rs. 2, Y invested Rs. 3
   If X invested Rs. 40, Y invested Rs. $\left(\dfrac{3}{2} \times 40\right)$ = Rs. 60.

Miscellaneous Problems 531

104. $P\left(1 + \dfrac{25}{2 \times 100}\right)^2 = 121500$ or $P = \left(121500 \times \dfrac{8}{9} \times \dfrac{8}{9}\right) = 96000$.

105. Gold in 1st ornament = $\left(12 \times \dfrac{2}{3}\right)$ gm = 8 gm.
Copper in it = 4 gm.
Gold in 2nd ornament = $\left(18 \times \dfrac{5}{6}\right)$ gm = 15 gm.
Copper in it = 3 gm.
New ornament contains gold = (8 + 15) gm. = 23 gm.
and copper = (4 + 3) gm. = 7 gm.
So, gold and copper are in the ratio 23 : 7.

106. Let cost per kg. = Rs. 100.
C.P. of 1100 gm. sugar = Rs. 110.
S.P. of 1100 gm. sugar = Rs. 100.
Loss = $\left(\dfrac{10}{110} \times 100\right) \% = 9\dfrac{1}{11}\%$.

107. B can finish the work in 6 days.
$(A + B)$'s 1 day's work = $\left(\dfrac{1}{12} + \dfrac{1}{6}\right) = \dfrac{1}{4}$.
∴ Both together can finish the work in 4 days.

108. Let capacity of P be x litres.
Then, capacity of $Q = \dfrac{x}{3}$ litres.
Capacity of drum = $60x$ litres.
∴ Required number of turns = $\dfrac{60x}{\left(x + \dfrac{x}{3}\right)} = \left(60x \times \dfrac{3}{4x}\right) = 45$.

109. Required area = $\left(\dfrac{22}{7} \times 16 \times 16 \times \dfrac{90}{360}\right)$ m^2 = 201 m^2.

110. Relative speed = 5 km/hr = $\left(5 \times \dfrac{5}{18}\right)$ m/sec.
Time taken to cross each other = $\left(350 \times \dfrac{18}{25}\right)$ sec.
= 252 sec. = 4.2 min.

111. Let C.P. = Rs. 100.
Two selling prices are Rs. 115 and Rs. 105.

532   *Objective Arithmetic*

If difference in S.P. is Rs. 10, C.P. = Rs. 100.

If difference in S.P. is Rs. 22.50, C.P. = Rs. $\left(\frac{100}{10} \times 22.50\right)$ = Rs. 225.

112. For a rebate of Rs. 25, cost = Rs. 100.

     For a rebate of Rs. 40, cost = Rs. $\left(\frac{100}{25} \times 40\right)$ = Rs. 160.

     Number of shirts = $\frac{160}{28}$ = 6.

113. Let original wages = Rs. 100.
     Increased wages = Rs. 120.
     Reduced wages = 80% of Rs. 120 = Rs. 96.
     Net loss = 4%.

114. Seats making perfect square = (1854 – 5) = 1849.
     Number of seats in each row = $\sqrt{1849}$ = 43.

115. Number of new students = $(16 \times 21 - 13 \times 24)$ = 24.

116. Let C's salary be Rs. x.
     Then, B's salary = Rs. $(x + 200)$, A's salary = Rs. $(x + 500)$
     $x + x + 200 = 1800 \Rightarrow x = 800.$
     ∴ A's salary = Rs. 1300.

117. Age of grandfather = $(5 \times 29 - 4 \times 20)$ years = 65 years.

118. Length of ladder = $\sqrt{(5)^2 + (12)^2}$ = 13 m.

119. Let C.P. = Rs. x.

     Then, $x - 15 = \frac{1}{16}x$ or $x - \frac{x}{16} = 15$ or $15x = 16 \times 15$ or $x = 16$.

120. Cost of 300 kg sugar = Rs. $(170 \times 5.80 + 130 \times 5.30)$ = Rs. 1675.
     S.P. of 300 kg sugar = Rs. $(1675 + 161)$ = Rs. 1836.

     ∴ Rate per kg = Rs. $\left(\frac{1836}{300}\right)$ = Rs. 6.12.

121. Total profit required = Rs. (42×18) = Rs. 756.
     Profit made by selling 22 articles = Rs. $(460 + 144)$ = Rs. 604.

     ∴ Average profit on rest = Rs. $\left(\frac{152}{20}\right)$ = Rs. 7.60.

122. Let C.P. = Rs. 100. Then, S.P. = Rs. 115.
     If S.P. is Rs. 80, marked price = Rs. 100

Miscellaneous Problems 533

If S.P. is Rs. 115, marked price = Rs. $\left(\frac{100}{80} \times 115\right)$ = Rs. $\frac{575}{4}$

i.e. $\left(\frac{575}{4} - 100\right) = \frac{175}{4}$ % above C.P.

123. Let total strength = x.

Number that can type = $\frac{x}{5}$; Number taking shorthand = $\frac{x}{3}$.

Number doing none = $\frac{3}{4}x$.

Number doing one or the other = $\left(x - \frac{3}{4}x\right) = \frac{x}{4}$.

$\therefore \frac{x}{4} = \frac{x}{5} + \frac{x}{3} - y$ or $y = \left(\frac{x}{5} + \frac{x}{3} - \frac{x}{4}\right) = \frac{17}{60}x$.

124. Parshant : Vishal : Alok = $\frac{1}{2} : \frac{1}{3} : \left[1 - \left(\frac{1}{2} + \frac{1}{3}\right)\right] = \frac{1}{2} : \frac{1}{3} : \frac{1}{6}$
 = 3 : 2 : 1.

125. Let original cost = Rs. 100 and original sale = 100.
Original sale receipt = Rs. (100 × 100) = Rs. 10000.
New sale receipt = Rs. (75 × 130) = Rs. 9750.
Decrease = $\left(\frac{250}{10000} \times 100\right)$ % = 2.5%.

126. S.P. = Rs. $\left(\frac{120}{100} \times 600\right)$ = Rs. 720.

If S.P. is Rs. 90, marked price = Rs. 100.

If S.P. is Rs. 720, marked price = Rs. $\left(\frac{100}{90} \times 720\right)$ = Rs. 800.

127. Runs to be scored = [230 × 3 − (180 + 258)] = 252.

128. $A = \frac{1}{3}B$ and $B = \frac{1}{2}C$

$\therefore 3A = B = \frac{1}{2}C = x$ (say)

$A = \frac{x}{3}, B = x$ and $C = 2x$.

$\therefore A : B : C = \frac{x}{3} : x : 2x = 1 : 3 : 6$.

129. $s = \frac{1}{2}(6 + 8 + 10) = 12$, $(s - a) = 6$; $(s - b) = 4$ and $(s - c) = 2$.

$\therefore$ Area = $\sqrt{12 \times 6 \times 4 \times 2}$ = 24 m^2.

130. $(A + B)$'s 1 day's work = $\frac{1}{10}$; A's 1 day's work = $\frac{1}{15}$.

   B's 1 day's work = $\left(\frac{1}{10} - \frac{1}{15}\right) = \frac{1}{30}$.

   $\therefore A : B = \frac{1}{15} : \frac{1}{30} = 2 : 1$.

   A's share = Rs. $\left(120 \times \frac{2}{3}\right)$ = Rs. 80.

131. Let their ages 1 year ago be $4x$ and $5x$ years.

   Then, $\frac{4x + 2}{5x + 2} = \frac{5}{6} \Rightarrow 24x + 12 = 25x + 10$ or $x = 2$.

   Present age of Veena = $(5x + 1) = 11$ years.

132. Ratio of shares = $(75000 \times 12 : 60000 \times 9) = 5 : 3$.

   Kamal's share = Rs. $\left(16000 \times \frac{3}{8}\right)$ = Rs. 6000.

133. Slant height = $\sqrt{(7)^2 + (9)^2} = \sqrt{130} = 11.4$

   $\therefore$ Area of curved surface = $\pi rl = \left(\frac{22}{7} \times 7 \times 11.4\right) = 250$ cm^2

134. Cost per m^2 = Rs. $\left(\frac{2496}{320}\right)$ = Rs. 7.80.

135. Age of new child = $(13 \times 19 - 12 \times 20)$ years = 7 years.

136. Given Expression
   = $(3 + \sqrt{8}) - (\sqrt{8} + \sqrt{7}) + (\sqrt{7} + \sqrt{6}) - (\sqrt{6} + \sqrt{5}) + (\sqrt{5} + \sqrt{4})$
   = $3 + \sqrt{4} > 3$.

137. Let the number be N and when divided by 119, let the quotient be k.
   Then, $N = (119k \times 19) = (17 \times 7k + 17 + 2) = 17 \times (7k + 1) + 2$.
   $\therefore$ Required remainder = 2.

138. $72 = 2 \times 2 \times 2 \times 3 \times 3$ and $112 = 2 \times 2 \times 2 \times 2 \times 7$.

   $\therefore$ 72 must be multiplied at least by (2×7) i.e. 14 in order that it becomes a multiple of 112.

139. Let x men can finish it in 60 days.

   Then, $(x + 8)$ men can do it in 50 days.

   $\therefore \frac{x}{x+8} = \frac{50}{60}$ or $60x = 50x + 400$ or $x = 40$.

Miscellaneous Problems

140. Let $\frac{5}{8} < \frac{x}{30} < \frac{7}{11}$. Then, $825 < 44x < 840$.

Clearly, $x = 19$.

Hence, required fraction $= \frac{19}{30}$.

141. $\sqrt{\frac{.081}{.0064} \times \frac{.484}{6.25}} = \sqrt{\frac{81 \times 484}{64 \times 625}} = \frac{9 \times 22}{8 \times 25} = \frac{198}{200} = 0.99$.

142. Let C.P. = Rs. x.

Then, $820 - x = x - 650$ or $2x = 1470$ or $x = 735$.

143. Data inadequate.

144. $11 \overline{\smash{\big)}\,11210}$
$\overline{1019 - 1}$

∴ Number to be added $= (11 - 1) = 10$.

145. $P = \frac{100 \times P}{10 \times R}$ or $R = 10\%$ per annum.

146. Let third number $= x$.

Then, first number $= \left(\frac{120}{100} x\right) = \frac{6x}{5}$, second number $= \frac{150}{100} x = \frac{3x}{2}$.

Required percentage $= \left(\frac{\frac{6x}{5}}{\frac{3x}{2}} \times 100\right)\% = \left(\frac{6x}{5} \times \frac{2}{3x} \times 100\right)\% = 80\%$.

147. (Deepak + Sohan)'s 1 day's work $= \frac{1}{6}$

Sohan's 1 day's work $= \frac{1}{10}$.

Deepak's 1 day's work $= \left(\frac{1}{6} - \frac{1}{10}\right) = \frac{1}{15}$.

∴ Deepak alone can finish the work in 15 days.

148. Vimal's age after 10 years $= (8 + 2 + 10)$ years $= 20$ years.

Sneh's father's age after 10 years $= 40$ years.

Sneh's father's present age $= 30$ years.

Sneh's age $= \left(\frac{1}{6} \times 30\right)$ years $= 5$ years.

149. Saving on each toy = Rs. $\left(\dfrac{20}{100} \times 40\right)$ = Rs. 8.

For saving Rs. 8, he buys 1 toy

For saving Rs. 240, he buys $\left(\dfrac{1}{8} \times 240\right)$ = 30 toys.

150. Number of pieces = $\dfrac{192}{3.2} = \dfrac{1920}{32} = 60$.

ANSWERS

1. (b) 2. (c) 3. (d) 4. (b) 5. (a) 6. (d) 7. (b) 8. (a) 9. (b)
10. (c) 11. (d) 12. (b) 13. (c) 14. (a) 15. (a) 16. (d) 17. (a) 18. (b)
19. (b) 20. (c) 21. (d) 22. (c) 23. (b) 24. (b) 25. (c) 26. (d) 27. (c)
28. (d) 29. (c) 30. (a) 31. (d) 32. (c) 33. (d) 34. (c) 35. (d) 36. (b)
37. (c) 38. (c) 39. (c) 40. (b) 41. (b) 42. (a) 43. (c) 44. (a) 45. (d)
46. (c) 47. (c) 48. (d) 49. (a) 50. (d) 51. (a) 52. (d) 53. (c) 54. (a)
55. (c) 56. (d) 57. (d) 58. (c) 59. (a) 60. (a) 61. (b) 62. (b) 63. (a)
64. (a) 65. (b) 66. (c) 67. (a) 68. (c) 69. (b) 70. (a) 71. (c) 72. (b)
73. (a) 74. (b) 75. (a) 76. (b) 77. (a) 78. (a) 79. (b) 80. (d) 81. (b)
82. (c) 83. (a) 84. (a) 85. (b) 86. (a) 87. (c) 88. (c) 89. (c) 90. (d)
91. (b) 92. (c) 93. (b) 94. (c) 95. (a) 96. (b) 97. (b) 98. (c) 99. (a)
100. (b) 101. (d) 102. (b) 103. (b) 104. (c) 105. (d) 106. (b) 107. (a) 108. (c)
109. (b) 110. (d) 111. (b) 112. (b) 113. (c) 114. (b) 115. (b) 116. (c) 117. (c)
118. (c) 119. (a) 120. (d) 121. (a) 122. (d) 123. (d) 124. (b) 125. (c) 126. (d)
127. (c) 128. (a) 129. (a) 130. (d) 131. (d) 132. (b) 133. (d) 134. (a) 135. (b)
136. (c) 137. (d) 138. (b) 139. (c) 140. (b) 141. (d) 142. (d) 143. (d) 144. (d)
145. (b) 146. (a) 147. (c) 148. (d) 149. (d) 150. (b).

Model Test Paper I

Against each of the questions, suggested answers are given. Find out the correct answer and mark it by putting a tick mark in the placeholder :-

1. $\frac{561}{748}$ when reduced to the lowest terms is :

   (a) $\frac{13}{14}$ ☐   (b) $\frac{3}{4}$ ☐

   (c) $\frac{11}{14}$ ☐   (d) $\frac{23}{24}$ ☐

2. The value of $\sqrt{(.121)}$ is :
   (a) .11 ☐   (b) 1.1 ☐
   (c) .347 ☐   (d) None of these ☐

3. The value of 3755 × 9999 is :
   (a) 37556245 ☐   (b) 38297255 ☐
   (c) 37546245 ☐   (d) 34657245 ☐

4. The H.C.F. of $\frac{1}{2}, \frac{3}{4}, \frac{5}{6}, \frac{7}{8}, \frac{9}{10}$ is :

   (a) $\frac{1}{2}$ ☐   (b) $\frac{1}{10}$ ☐

   (c) $\frac{9}{120}$ ☐   (d) $\frac{1}{120}$ ☐

5. The lowest fraction in $\frac{1}{2}, \frac{3}{4}, \frac{5}{6}, \frac{7}{12}, \frac{2}{5}$ is :

   (a) $\frac{1}{2}$ ☐   (b) $\frac{7}{12}$ ☐

   (c) $\frac{5}{6}$ ☐   (d) $\frac{2}{5}$ ☐

6. Five bells begin to toll together and toll respectively at intervals of 6, 7, 8, 9 and 12 seconds. After how many seconds will they toll together again ?
   (a) 72 sec. ☐   (b) 612 sec. ☐
   (c) 504 sec. ☐   (d) 318 sec. ☐

7. What percent of 1 kg is 5 gms?
   (a) .4% ☐   (b) .5% ☐
   (c) .05% ☐   (d) .005% ☐

8. A man travels a certain distance at the rate of 12 km/hr. and returns back to the starting point at the rate of 15 km/hr. His average speed during the whole journey is :

   (a) 13.5 km/hr ☐ (b) $13\frac{1}{3}$ km/hr ☐

   (c) $12\frac{2}{3}$ km/hr ☐ (d) 14 km/hr ☐

9. A candidate needs 35% marks to pass. If he gets 96 marks and fails by 16 marks, then the maximum marks are :

   (a) 250 ☐ (b) 320 ☐
   (c) 300 ☐ (d) 425 ☐

10. In a fort there were provisions for 45 days for 150 men. After 10 days, 25 men left over. The food would now last long for :

    (a) 36 days ☐ (b) 40 days ☐
    (c) 42 days ☐ (d) 50 days ☐

11. 0.144 ÷ 0.012 = ?

    (a) .12 ☐ (b) 1.2 ☐
    (c) 12 ☐ (d) .012 ☐

12. The value of $\dfrac{(2.3)^3 - .027}{(2.3)^2 + .69 + .09}$ is :

    (a) 2 ☐ (b) 2.273 ☐
    (c) 2.327 ☐ (d) None of these ☐

13. 2 of $\dfrac{3}{4} + \dfrac{3}{4} + \dfrac{1}{4}$ = ?

    (a) $\dfrac{3}{2}$ ☐ (b) $\dfrac{9}{4}$ ☐

    (c) $\dfrac{1}{4}$ ☐ (d) None of these ☐

14. In an election one of the two candidates gets 40% votes and loses by 100 votes. Total number of votes is :

    (a) 500 ☐ (b) 400 ☐
    (c) 600 ☐ (d) 1000 ☐

15. A man spends 76% of his income. His income increases by 20% and he increased his expenditure by 15%. His savings are then increased by :

(a) 35% □ (b) $33\frac{1}{3}$% □
(c) 40% □ (d) 33% □

16. If 28 men working 8 hours per day can finish a piece of work in 10 days, how many hours per day 40 men must work to complete the same work in 8 days ?
    (a) 6 hours □ (b) $6\frac{1}{2}$ hours □
    (c) 7 hours □ (d) 9 hours □

17. If $A : B = 2 : 3$ and $B : C = 7 : 8$, then $A : C$ is :
    (a) 9 : 11 □ (b) 7 : 12 □
    (c) 16 : 21 □ (d) None of these □

18. Bananas are bought at 15 for a rupee and sold at the rate of 9 for a rupee. The gain per cent is :
    (a) 30% □ (b) 60% □
    (c) $66\frac{2}{3}$% □ (d) $33\frac{1}{3}$% □

19. A series discount of 20%, 10% is equivalent to a single discount of :
    (a) 30% □ (b) $28\frac{2}{3}$% □
    (c) 28% □ (d) 27% □

20. A mixture contains alcohol and water in the ratio 4 : 3. If 7 litres of water is added to the mixture, the ratio of alcohol and water becomes 3 : 4. The quantity of alcohol in the mixture is :
    (a) 10 litres □ (b) 12 litres □
    (c) 32 litres □ (d) 48 litres □

21. The sum of the digits of a two digit number is 8. If the digits are reversed the number is decreased by 54. The number is :
    (a) 62 □ (b) 71 □
    (c) 53 □ (d) 80 □

22. A 200 metres long train, running at a speed of 60 km/hr. passes a bridge in 1 minute. The length of the bridge is :
    (a) 1200 metres □ (b) 900 metres □
    (c) 800 metres □ (d) 600 metres □

23. The length of a given rectangle is increased by 20% and the breadth of the rectangle is decreased by 20%. Then, the new area :

(a) remains the same   (b) is increased by 4%
(c) is increased by 5% (d) is decreased by 4%

24. If the cost price of 21 copies of a book, are the same as the selling price of 18 copies of the book, then gain percent is :

(a) $14\frac{2}{7}\%$ (b) $16\frac{2}{3}\%$
(c) $33\frac{1}{3}\%$ (d) $23\frac{1}{3}\%$

25. 133% can be written as :

(a) 1.33   (b) .133
(c) .0133   (d) None of these

26. $\sqrt{\{(65)^2 - (16)^2\}} = ?$

(a) 43   (b) 47
(c) 63   (d) 67

27. The price of sugar increased by 12%. To maintain previous budget, the consumption should be reduced by :

(a) 12%   (b) 18%
(c) $11\frac{2}{3}\%$ (d) $10\frac{5}{7}\%$

28. By selling a radio for Rs. 240, I lose 20%. What percent shall I gain by selling it for Rs. 320 ?

(a) $6\frac{2}{3}\%$ (b) $8\frac{1}{3}\%$
(c) $16\frac{2}{3}\%$ (d) 5%

29. If $\frac{13}{15}$ of an estate be worth Rs. 390, then $\frac{3}{5}$ of it is :

(a) Rs. 320   (b) Rs. 270
(c) Rs. 450   (d) Rs. 324

30. The value of $\sqrt{\left(\frac{47}{5}\right)}$ is :

(a) .32   (b) 3.17
(c) 3.06   (d) None of these

31. A and B enter into partnership with capitals as 4 : 5. At the end of 9 months, A withdraws. If the shares of annual profits be in the ratio

9 : 10, then money of B remained invested for :
(a) 10 months (b) 8 months
(c) 6 months (d) 7 months

32. If the numerator of a fraction be increased by 12% and its denominator decreased by 2% the value of the fraction becomes (6/7). The original fraction is :
(a) (3/4) (b) (3/5)
(c) (2/3) (d) (2/5)

33. Insert the missing number :
5, 12, 9, 16, 13, 20, ...
(a) 27 (b) 23
(c) 17 (d) None of these

34. A sum of money at *S.I.* doubles in 7 years. It will become four times in :
(a) 14 years (b) 21 years
(c) 28 years (d) 35 years

35. A monkey ascends a greased pole 36 metres high. He ascends 3 metres in first minute and descends 1 metre in second minute. He again ascends 3 metres in third minute and descends 1 metre in fourth minute and so on. In what time he reaches the top ?
(a) 36 minutes (b) 33 minutes
(c) $33\frac{5}{6}$ minutes (d) $34\frac{2}{3}$ minutes

36. A takes thrice as long to do a piece of work, as B takes. A and B together can finish a piece of work in 15 days. A alone can do it in :
(a) 30 days (b) 45 days
(c) 60 days (d) 120 days

37. The diagonal of a square field is 25 metres. The area of the field is :
(a) 625 sq. metres (b) 312.5 sq. metres
(c) 156.25 sq. metres (d) $\frac{625}{\sqrt{2}}$ sq. metres

38. Circumference of a circle is 132 cm. The area of the circle is :
(a) 792 sq. cm. (b) 1056 sq. cm.
(c) 1386 sq. cm. (d) 924 sq. cm.

39. The length of the longest pole that can be put in a room (25 metres × 12 metres × 8 metres) is :

(a) 25 metres (b) 45 metres
(c) 27.7 metres (d) 28.8 metres

40. The edge of a cube is increased by 100%. The surface area of the cube is increased by :
(a) 100% (b) 200%
(c) 300% (d) 400%

41. The population of a town is decreasing at a uniform rate of 10% per annum for the last 3 years. If the present population of the town is 137700, what it was 2 years ago ?
(a) 152847 (b) 160000
(c) 170000 (d) 163657

42. What is the S.P. of a 7% stock in which an income of Rs. 250 is derived by investing Rs. 3500, brokerage being (1/8)% ?
(a) Rs. $98\frac{1}{8}$ (b) Rs. $97\frac{7}{8}$
(c) Rs. 98 (d) Rs. $107\frac{1}{8}$

43. A watch is bought for Rs. 200 and sold the same day for Rs. 242 at a credit of 2 years. If the rate of interest is 10% compounded annually, then there is :
(a) a gain of 1% (b) a gain of 2%
(c) neither gain nor loss (d) a loss of 1%

44. If the time period of a bill is doubled, then the true discount on the bill is :
(a) doubled (b) halved
(c) becomes (3/2) times (d) None of these

Direction : *The following table gives the plan outlay for 1987-88 for three states A, B and C under the major heads (In lakhs of rupees).*

States	A	B	C	Total
Agriculture	1203.64	916.88	378.54	2499.06
Rural Development	925.46	741.34	217.62	1884.42
Irrigation & Flood control	85.34	72.20	40.36	197.90
Energy	2713.57	1015.65	617.42	4346.64
Industries	1056.28	9000.00	136.46	2092.74
Education	336.86	432.39	186.54	955.79
Social Services	100.97	118.42	31.41	250.80
Communication	81.23	100.20	0.82	182.25
Total	6503.35	4297.08	1609.17	12409.60

Study the table and mark a tick (√) against the correct answer in each of the questions given below :

45. Which area recieved minimum consideration in state *A* ?
    (*a*) Irrigation and flood control ☐
    (*b*) Communication ☐
    (*c*) Social services ☐
    (*d*) Rural Development ☐

46. The total plan outlay for *A* and *C* is in the ratio :
    (*a*) 19 : 50 ☐   (*b*) 101 : 25 ☐
    (*c*) 3 : 2 ☐   (*d*) 65 : 16 ☐

47. Which area received maximum consideration in all the states
    (*a*) Agriculture ☐   (*b*) Rural development ☐
    (*c*) Energy ☐   (*d*) Industries ☐

48. Which is the most appropriate statement ?
    (*a*) outlay for *B* is 6% more than that of *C* ☐
    (*b*) outlay for *B* is 16% more than that of *C* ☐
    (*c*) none of these ☐

A man starting at 6 A.M. walks at the uniform rate of 6 km/hr resting for 10 minutes at the end of every hour. A cyclist, starting from the same place at 7.30 A.M. travels in the same direction at a uniform rate of 12 km/hr. The following graph depicts the distances covered by the man and the cyclist at various intervals of time.

Scale : $\begin{cases} \text{Along OX} \rightarrow 1 \text{ div.} = 30 \text{ mts,} \\ \text{Along OY} \rightarrow 1 \text{ div.} = 2.5 \text{ km.} \end{cases}$

Study the graph and mark a tick (√) against the correct answer in each of the following questions :

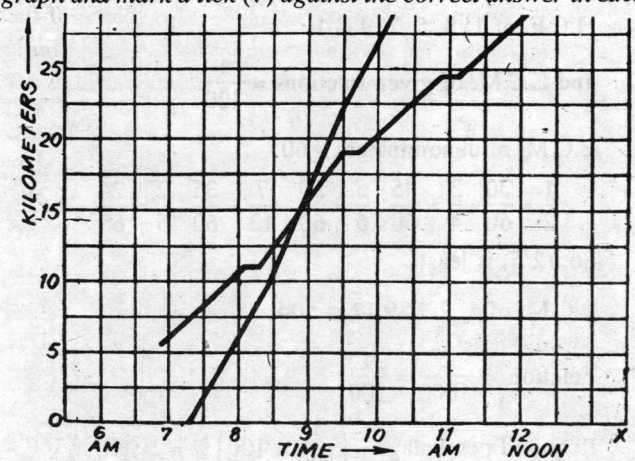

49. At what time will the cyclist pass the man ?
    (a) 9.20 a.m. ☐ (b) 8.50 a.m. ☐
    (c) 7.50 a.m. ☐ (d) 9 a.m. ☐

50. At what distance from the starting point will the cyclist pass the man ?
    (a) 12 km. ☐ (b) 13.5 km. ☐
    (c) 12.6 km. ☐ (d) 15 km. ☐

ANSWERS

1. (b)   2. (c)   3. (c)   4. (d)   5. (d)   6. (c)   7. (b)   8. (b)   9. (b)
10. (c) 11. (c) 12. (a) 13. (b) 14. (a) 15. (a) 16. (c) 17. (b) 18. (c)
19. (c) 20. (b) 21. (b) 22. (c) 23. (d) 24. (b) 25. (a) 26. (c) 27. (d)
28. (a) 29. (b) 30. (c) 31. (b) 32. (a) 33. (c) 34. (b) 35. (d) 36. (c)
37. (b) 38. (c) 39. (d) 40. (c) 41. (c) 42. (b) 43. (c) 44. (d) 45. (b)
46. (b) 47. (c) 48. (b) 49. (b) 50. (d).

SOLUTIONS (Model Test Paper)

1. H.C.F. of 561, 748 is 187.
    Dividing Nr. and Dr. by 187, the fraction is 3/4.

2. $\sqrt{(.121)} = \sqrt{\dfrac{1210}{10000}} = \dfrac{\sqrt{(1210)}}{100} = \dfrac{34.7}{100} = .347$.

3. $3755 \times 9999 = 3755 \times (10^4 - 1)$
    $= 37550000 - 3755 = 37546245$

4. H.C.F. of 1, 3, 5, 7, 9 is 1
    and L.C.M. of given fractions $= \dfrac{1}{120}$.

5. L.C.M. of denominators = 60.
    $\therefore \dfrac{1}{2} = \dfrac{30}{60}, \dfrac{3}{4} = \dfrac{45}{60}, \dfrac{5}{6} = \dfrac{50}{60}, \dfrac{7}{12} = \dfrac{35}{60}, \dfrac{2}{5} = \dfrac{24}{60}$.
    So, (2/5) is least.

6. L.C.M. of 6, 7, 8, 9, 12 is 504.

7. Fraction $= \dfrac{5}{1000} = \dfrac{1}{200}$
    Required percentage $= \left(\dfrac{1}{200} \times 100\right) \% = .5\%$.

Model Test Paper I   545

8. Let that distance be x km.

    Time taken to cover $2x$ km $= \dfrac{x}{12} + \dfrac{x}{15} = \dfrac{9x}{60}$ hrs.

    Average speed $= \dfrac{2x \times 60}{9x}$ km/hr $= 13\dfrac{1}{3}$ km/hr.

9. 35% of $x = 96 + 16 = 112$

    or $\dfrac{35}{100} \times x = 112$ or $x = \dfrac{112 \times 100}{35} = 320$.

10. Remaining days $= 35$, Remaining men $= 125$.
    Now 150 men have provisions for 35 days
    125 men will have it for $\dfrac{35 \times 150}{125} = 42$ days.

11. $\dfrac{0.144}{0.012} = \dfrac{144}{12} = 12$.

12. Given expression $= \dfrac{a^3 - b^3}{a^2 + ab + b^2} = a - b = 2.3 - .3 = 2$.

13. 2 of $\dfrac{3}{4} \div \dfrac{3}{4} + \dfrac{1}{4} = \dfrac{3}{2} \times \dfrac{4}{3} + \dfrac{1}{4} = 2 + \dfrac{1}{4} = \dfrac{9}{4}$.

14. Out of 100, difference in votes $= (60 - 40) = 20$.
    If diff. is 20, total votes $= 100$
    If diff. is 100, total votes $= \left(\dfrac{100}{20} \times 100\right) = 500$.

15. Let income be Rs. 100.
    Then, expenditure $=$ Rs. 75, saving $=$ Rs. 25.
    New income $=$ Rs. 120.
    New expenditure $=$ Rs. $\left(\dfrac{115}{100} \times 75\right) =$ Rs. $\dfrac{345}{4}$.
    Now saving $=$ Rs. $\left(120 - \dfrac{345}{4}\right) =$ Rs. $\dfrac{135}{4}$.
    Increase $\%$ in saving $= \left(\dfrac{35}{4 \times 25} \times 100\right) = 35\%$.

16. More men, less hours per day (indirect)
    Less days, more hours per day (indirect)
    $\left.\begin{matrix}40 : 28\\ 8 : 10\end{matrix}\right\} :: 8 : x$

$$\therefore x = \frac{28 \times 10 \times 8}{8 \times 40} = 7 \text{ hrs.}$$

17. $\dfrac{A}{B} = \dfrac{2}{3}$ and $\dfrac{B}{C} = \dfrac{7}{8}$

    $\therefore \dfrac{A}{C} = \dfrac{A}{B} \times \dfrac{B}{C} = \dfrac{2}{3} \times \dfrac{7}{8} = \dfrac{14}{24} = \dfrac{7}{12}.$

18. Let bananas bought be (15×9).
    Then, C.P. = Rs. 9, S.P. = Rs. 15.
    Gain % = $\left(\dfrac{6}{9} \times 100\right)$ % = $66\dfrac{2}{3}$ %.

19. Let C.P. be Rs. 100.
    S.P. = Rs. $\left(\dfrac{90}{100} \times 80\right)$ = Rs. 72.
    $\therefore$ Discount = Rs. $(100 - 72) = 28\%$.
    So, answer (c) is correct.

20. Let alcohol and water be $4x$ and $3x$ litres respectively. Then
    $\dfrac{4x}{3x + 7} = \dfrac{3}{4}$ or $x = 3$.
    $\therefore$ Alcohol = 12 litres.

21. Let the tens and units places be x and y respectively.
    Then, $x + y = 8$ and $(10x + y) - (10y + x) = 54$
    or $x + y = 8$ and $x - y = 6$
    $\therefore x = 7, y = 1$. So, the number is 71.

22. Distance covered by the train in 1 minute
    $= \dfrac{60 \times 1000}{60} = 1000$ metres
    $\therefore$ 200 + (length of bridge) = 1000
    or length of bridge = 800 metres.

23. Area = $l \times b = A$ (say)
    New area = $\left(\dfrac{120}{100} l \times \dfrac{80}{100} b\right) = \dfrac{24}{25} lb = \dfrac{24}{25} A.$
    Decrease on A = $\left(A - \dfrac{24}{25} A\right) = \dfrac{A}{25}$
    Decrease % = $\left(\dfrac{A}{25A} \times 100\right) = 4\%.$

24. Let C.P. of each book be Re. 1.

Model Test Paper I

C.P. of 21 books = Rs. 21.

∴ S.P. of 18 books = Rs. 21.

S.P. of 1 book = Rs. $\frac{21}{18}$

Gain on re. 1 = Rs. $\left(\frac{21}{18} - 1\right)$ = Re. $\frac{1}{6}$.

Gain% = $\left(\frac{1}{6} \times 100\right)$% = $16\frac{2}{3}$%.

25. $133\% = \frac{133}{100} = 1.33$

26. $\sqrt{[(65)^2 - (16)^2]} = \sqrt{[(65 - 16)(65 + 16)]}$
    $= \sqrt{[(49)(81)]} = 7 \times 9 = 63$.

27. If first expenditure is Rs. 100, then it is increased to Rs. 112. So, consumption of Rs. 12 should be reduced out of Rs. 112.

    ∴ Reduction % = $\left(\frac{12}{112} \times 100\right) = 10\frac{5}{7}$%.

28. 80% of C.P. = Rs. 240 or C.P. = $\frac{240 \times 100}{80}$ = Rs. 300.

    Now, C.P. = Rs. 300, S.P. = Rs. 320.

    Gain % = $\left(\frac{20}{300} \times 100\right)$% = $6\frac{2}{3}$%.

29. $\frac{13}{15} \times x = 390$ or $x = \left(\frac{390 \times 15}{13}\right) = 450$

    $\frac{3}{5}$ of 450 = 270.

30. $\sqrt{\left(\frac{47}{5}\right)} = \frac{\sqrt{(47)}}{\sqrt{(5)}} \times \frac{\sqrt{5}}{\sqrt{5}} = \frac{\sqrt{235}}{5} = \frac{15.32}{5} = 3.06$

31. Ratio of capital = 4 : 5.

    Let B invested his money for x months.

    Ratio of equivalent capital for 1 month = $4 \times 9 : 5 \times x = 36 : 5x$

    ∴ $\frac{36}{5x} = \frac{9}{10}$ or $x = \left(\frac{36 \times 10}{5 \times 9}\right) = 8$ months.

33. Numbers alternately increase by seven and decrease by 3.
    So, missing number is 17.

34. Rs. P is S.I. on Rs. P for 7 years.

Rs. $3P$ is S.I. on Rs. P for $\left(\dfrac{7}{P} \times 3P\right) = 21$ years

35. It is clear that the monkey is capable of covering 2 metres in 2 minutes. So, in 34 minutes, he is able to cover 34 metres. Rest of 2 metres, he covers in (2/3) minutes. So, total time taken by him to reach the top is $34\dfrac{2}{3}$ minutes.

36. The ratio between time taken by A and B to finish work = 3 : 1

    Ratio of the rates of doing work = $\dfrac{1}{3} : 1 = 1 : 3$.

    $(A + B)$'s 1 day's work = $\dfrac{1}{15}$.

    $\therefore$ A's 1 day's work = $\dfrac{1}{15} \times \dfrac{1}{4} = \dfrac{1}{60}$ $\left[\text{divide } \dfrac{1}{15} \text{ in the ratio } 1 : 3\right]$

    So, A can finish the work in 60 days.

37. Area = $\dfrac{(\text{Diagonal})^2}{2} = \dfrac{25 \times 25}{2} = 312.5$ sq. metres.

38. $2\pi r = 132$. So, $r = \dfrac{132 \times 7}{2 \times 22} = 21$ cm.

    Area = $\pi r^2 = \left(\dfrac{22}{7} \times 21 \times 21\right) = 1386$ sq. cms.

39. Length of longest pole = $\sqrt{\{(25)^2 + (12)^2 + (8)^2\}} = 28.8$ metres.

40. Area = $6 \times l^2 = 6A$ (say). New area = $6 \times (2l)^2 = 24A$

    Increase % = $\left(\dfrac{18A}{6a} \times 100\right)\% = 300\%$.

41. $P\left(1 - \dfrac{10}{100}\right)^2 = 137700$

    or $P = \dfrac{137700 \times 10 \times 10}{9 \times 9} = 170000$.

42. To obtain an income of Rs. 7, investment = Rs. $\left(\dfrac{3500}{250} \times 7\right) =$ Rs. 98.

    $\therefore$ S.P. = Rs. $\left(98 - \dfrac{1}{8}\right)$ = Rs. $97\dfrac{7}{8}$.

43. P.W. of Rs. 242 due 2 years hence

Model Test Paper I

$$= \text{Rs.} \left[\frac{242}{\left(1+\frac{10}{100}\right)^2}\right] = \text{Rs.} \left(\frac{242 \times 10 \times 10}{11 \times 11}\right) = \text{Rs. } 200.$$

∴ There is neither gain nor loss.

44. There is no uniform pattern for the true discount and the time of the bill. So, (d) is correct.

45. Least outlay for state A is for communication.

46. Ratio of outlays for A and C = (6503.35) : (1609.17)
$$= (4.04) : (1) = (404 : 100) = (101 : 25).$$

47. The allocation for energy is maximum in each state.

48. (outlay for B) − (outlay for C) = (4297.08 − 1609.17) = 2687.91

∴ Excess of B over A = $\left(\frac{2687.91}{169.017} \times 100\right) \% = 160\%$.

49. At the point of intersection of the graphs, the cyclist passes the man. Drop a line parallel to OY. It meets OX at a point to indicate 8.50 am.

50. From the point of intersection of the graphs, draw a line parallel to OX to meet OY at a point respresenting 15 km.

Model Test Paper II

Directions : *For each of the following questions tick mark the choice that best answers the question :*

1. Which of the following is in descending order ?
   - (a) $\dfrac{3}{8}, \dfrac{8}{15}, \dfrac{11}{23}, \dfrac{25}{81}$ ☐
   - (b) $\dfrac{26}{81}, \dfrac{11}{23}, \dfrac{8}{15}, \dfrac{3}{8}$ ☐
   - (c) $\dfrac{8}{15}, \dfrac{11}{23}, \dfrac{3}{8}, \dfrac{26}{81}$ ☐
   - (d) $\dfrac{3}{8}, \dfrac{11}{23}, \dfrac{8}{15}, \dfrac{26}{81}$ ☐

2. $\sqrt{\left(\dfrac{0.324}{10}\right)} = ?$
   - (a) 1.8 ☐
   - (b) 0.1 ☐
   - (c) .0018 ☐
   - (d) 2.8 ☐

3. $(.98 \times .98 - .98 \times 1.52 + .76 \times .76) = ?$
   - (a) .0484 ☐
   - (b) .2684 ☐
   - (c) .3164 ☐
   - (d) .1562 ☐

4. The value of the expression 1014×986 is:
   - (a) 998924 ☐
   - (b) 999864 ☐
   - (c) 999804 ☐
   - (d) 996724 ☐

5. Which number will replace both the question marks in $\left(\dfrac{361}{?} = \dfrac{?}{81}\right)$?
   - (a) 191 ☐
   - (b) 931 ☐
   - (c) 171 ☐
   - (d) None ☐

6. $37.09 \times ? = (41 - .291)$
   - (a) .11 ☐
   - (b) 1.1 ☐
   - (c) 11.1 ☐
   - (d) 9.1 ☐

7. When the price of a T.V. was increased by 15%, the number of T.V.s sold by a company decreases by 15%. What was the net effect on the sale ?
   - (a) no effect ☐
   - (b) 1.5% increase ☐
   - (c) 2.25% decrease ☐
   - (d) 2.25% increase ☐

8. A, B, C hired a taxi for Rs. 3840 and used it separately for 72 hours, 108 hours and 252 hours respectively. The amount paid by C is :
   - (a) Rs. 960 ☐
   - (b) Rs. 2880 ☐

(c) Rs. 1920 (d) Rs. 2240

9. Four-fifth of a number is 10 more than two-third of the number. The number is:
   (a) 55 (b) 65
   (c) 75 (d) 80

10. The dimensions of an open box are 52 cms, 40 cms, and 26 cms. Its thickness is 1 cm. If 1 Cubic cm. of the metal used in the box weighs 1 gm., then the weight of the box is :
    (a) 8.48 kg (b) 6.58 kg
    (c) 7.28 kg (d) 658 gms.

11. The diameter of a cylindrical tower is 10 metres and its height is 14 metres. The cost of painting the curved surface of the cylinder at 75 paise per square metre is :
    (a) Rs. 105 (b) Rs. 330
    (c) Rs. 220 (d) Rs. 440

12. A is 5 times as old as his son B. Four years hence the sum of their ages will be 50 years. B's age now is :
    (a) 8 years (b) 6 years
    (c) 7 years (d) 5 years

13. Find out the wrong number in the following sequence of numbers 4, 13, 17, 26, 30, 38, 43
    (a) 13 (b) 26
    (c) 38 (d) 43

14. Find out the wrong number in the sequence 1, 8, 27, 84, 125, 216, 343 :
    (a) 1 (b) 27
    (c) 84 (d) 216

15. The length of the diagonal of a square is $4\sqrt{2}$ cms. Its area is :
    (a) 32 cm^2 (b) 16 cm^2
    (c) 8 cm^2 (d) 36 cm^2

16. The average age of the husband and wife at the time of their marriage 6 years ago was 28 years 6 months. Now, the average of the husband, wife and a child is 24 years. How old is the child ?
    (a) $2\frac{1}{2}$ years (b) 3 years

(c) $3\frac{1}{2}$ years ☐ (d) 4 years ☐

17. Deepak is twice as old as Vikas was 3 years ago when Deepak was as old as Vikas is today. If the difference between their ages today be 5 years, what is the present age of Deepak ?
    (a) 12 years ☐ (b) 16 years ☐
    (c) 18 years ☐ (d) 14 years ☐

18. What decimal fraction is 20 mm. of a metre ?
    (a) .02 ☐ (b) .2 ☐
    (c) .05 ☐ (d) .002 ☐

19. The compound interest on Rs. 2800 for $1\frac{1}{2}$ years at 10% per annum, compounded annually is :
    (a) Rs. 441.35 ☐ (b) Rs. 434 ☐
    (c) Rs. 420 ☐ (d) Rs. 436.75 ☐

20. A trader allows two successive discounts of 20% and 10%. If he gets Rs. 108 for an article, then its marked price is :
    (a) Rs. 142.56 ☐ (b) Rs. 140.40 ☐
    (c) Rs. 160 ☐ (d) Rs. 150 ☐

21. If 20 typists can type 480 pages in 6 hours, how many pages will be typed by 25 typists in 4 hours ?
    (a) 256 ☐ (b) 576 ☐
    (c) 900 ☐ (d) 400 ☐

22. Suresh and Jagdish start a business investing Rs. 15000 and 22000 respectively. After 4 months Suresh puts in Rs. 4000 more and Jagdish withdraws Rs. 2000. At the end of year total profit was Rs. 11500. What is the share of Jagdish in it ?
    (a) Rs. 6900 ☐ (b) Rs. 5300 ☐
    (c) Rs. 6200 ☐ (d) Rs. 4600 ☐

23. If twice A is three times B and 5 times B is equal to six times C, then A : C is :
    (a) 4 : 5 ☐ (b) 5 : 9 ☐
    (c) 9 : 5 ☐ (d) 5 : 4 ☐

24. Two taps can separately fill a cistern in 10 minutes and 15 minutes respectively and when the waste pipe is open they can together fill it in 18 minutes. The waste pipe can empty the full cistern in:

(a) 7 minutes (b) 9 minutes
(c) 13 minutes (d) 23 minutes

25. Two towns X and Y are some distance apart. A man cycles from X to Y at a speed of 10 km/hr and then back from Y to X at the rate of 15 km/hr. The average speed during the whole journey is :
   (a) 12.5 km (b) 12 km
   (c) The data is inadequate (d) 13 km/hr

26. A man can row 5 km/hr in still water. If the river is running at 1 km/hr, it takes him 1 hour to row to a place and back. How far is the place ?
   (a) 2.5 km (b) 2.4 km
   (c) 3 km (d) 3.6 km

27. The cost of making an article is divided between materials, labour and overheads in the ratio 3 : 4 : 1. If the materials cost Rs. 11.25, the cost of article is :
   (a) Rs. 33.75 (b) Rs. 45
   (c) Rs. 9.80 (d) Rs. 30

28. $\left(\dfrac{.86 \times .86 \times .86 - .14 \times .14 \times .14}{.86 \times .86 + .86 \times .14 + .14 \times .14}\right) = ?$
   (a) 72 (b) 1
   (c) 32 (d) 26

29. A company declares a dividend of 12% on Rs. 100 shares. A man buys such shares and gets 15% on his investment. At what price he bought the shares ?
   (a) Rs. 125 (b) Rs. 85
   (c) Rs. 80 (d) Rs. 76

30. A lead pipe is 35 cm. long; its external diameter is 2.4 cm. and its thickness is 2 mm. If 1 cubic cm. of lead weighs 5 gms; the weight of the pipe is :
   (a) 220 gms (b) 242 gms
   (c) 420 gms (d) 484 gms

31. A can do a piece of work in 20 days, B can do it in 25 days. They work together for 5 days and then B goes away. In how many days will A finish the work ?
   (a) $17\dfrac{1}{2}$ days (b) 11 days
   (c) $8\dfrac{4}{7}$ days (d) 10 days

32. The greatest number of 4 digits which is a perfect square is :
   (a) 9981
   (b) 9891
   (c) 9902
   (d) 9801

33. $3.\overline{57}$ in fractional form is :
   (a) $\dfrac{357}{99}$
   (b) $\dfrac{354}{99}$
   (c) $\dfrac{357}{90}$
   (d) $\dfrac{354}{90}$

34. $\dfrac{\sqrt{1008}}{\sqrt{7}} = ?$
   (a) 12.75
   (b) 11.68
   (c) 12
   (d) 13.26

35. $\dfrac{1}{\sqrt{3}} = ?$
   (a) 0.632
   (b) .517
   (c) .527
   (d) .577

36. The average score of a cricketer for 10 matches is 38.9 runs. If the average for the first 6 matches is 41, what is the average for last 4 matches ?
   (a) 36.25
   (b) 34.25
   (c) 35.75
   (d) 32.85

37. A can run 1 km. in 3 min. 10 sec. and B in 3 min. 20 sec. By what distance can A beat B ?
   (a) 36 metres
   (b) 50 metres
   (c) 40 metres
   (d) 60 metres

38. Lemons are bought at 5 for a rupee and sold at 8 for three rupees. What is gain or loss percent in the transaction ?
   (a) $37\dfrac{1}{2}\%$
   (b) $57\dfrac{1}{2}\%$
   (c) 6%
   (d) $87\dfrac{1}{2}\%$

39. An article is sold for Rs. 240. If the profit is one-fourth of the cost price, what is the cost price ?
   (a) Rs. 180
   (b) Rs. 164
   (c) Rs. 192
   (d) Rs. 196

40. The sum of two digits of a number is 9. If 9 is subtracted from the

number, then the digits are reversed ? What is the number ?
(a) 36 (b) 45
(c) 54 (d) 72

41. The surface area of a cube is 216 cm^2. What is its volume ?
(a) 1296 cm^3 (b) 648 cm^3
(c) 864 cm^3 (d) 216 cm^3

42. Admission to a course is increased by 15% every year. If the number of students in this course in 1988 is 1600, what is the expected number of students in 1990 ?
(a) 2080 (b) 2116
(c) 2356 (d) 1960

Directions : *Examine the following graph carefully and answer questions 43 to 46 based on the information given in it.*

43. What is the average production (in lakh bales) of these states during 1987-88 ?
(a) 15.6 (b) 24.8
(c) 20.4 (d) 26.5

44. How many states showing below average production in 1985-86 showed above average production in 1986-87 ?
(a) 4 (b) 3
(c) 2 (d) 1

45. Which of the following is a true statement :
   (a) State A has produced maximum cotton during the given period.
   (b) There was no consistent progress shown by C.
   (c) States A and B showed a steady progress in the production of cotton during the given period.
   (d) there is no downfall in the production shown by state B.

46. The production of A during the given period is less than that of B by :
   (a) 6.3% □   (b) 5.9% □
   (c) 7.2% □   (d) 4.8% □

Directions : *The following Pie-diagram shows the expenditure incurred on the preparation of a book by a publisher, under various heads.*

A : Paper 20 %
B : Printing 35%
C : Binding, Canvassing Designing etc 30%
D : Miscellaneous 10%
E : Royalty 15%

Look at the diagram carefully and answer questions 47 to 50.

47. What is the angle of Pie-diagram showing the expenditure incurred on paying the royalty ?
   (a) 24° □   (b) 48° □
   (c) 54° □   (d) 15° □

48. The marked price of a book is 20% more than the C.P. If the marked price of the book be Rs. 30, what is the cost of paper used in a single copy of the book ?
   (a) Rs. 6   □   (b) Rs. 5   □
   (c) Rs. 4.50   □   (d) Rs. 6.50   □

49. Which two expenditures together will form an angle of 108° at the centre of the Pie-diagram ?
   (a) A & E □   (b) B & E □
   (c) A & D □   (d) D & E □

50. If the difference between two expenditures be represented by 18° in the pie-diagram, these expenditures are :
   (a) B & E □   (b) A & C   □
   (c) B & D □   (d) None of these □

Model Test Paper II 557

ANSWERS

1. (c)   2. (b)   3. (a)   4. (c)   5. (c)   6. (b)   7. (c)   8. (d)   9. (c)
10. (b)   11. (b)   12. (c)   13. (c)   14. (c)   15. (b)   16. (b)   17. (b)   18. (a)
19. (b)   20. (d)   21. (d)   22. (c)   23. (c)   24. (b)   25. (b)   26. (b)   27. (d)
28. (a)   29. (c)   30. (b)   31. (b)   32. (d)   33. (b)   34. (c)   35. (d)   36. (b)
37. (b)   38. (d)   39. (c)   40. (c)   41. (d)   42. (b)   43. (b)   44. (d)   45. (d)
46. (b)   47. (c)   48. (b)   49. (c)   50. (d).

SOLUTIONS (Model Test Paper II)

1. $\frac{3}{8} = 0.375; \frac{8}{15} = 0.533; \frac{11}{23} = 0.478; \frac{26}{81} = 0.320.$

   $\therefore 0.533 > 0.478 > 0.375 > 0.320$

   i.e. $\frac{8}{15} > \frac{11}{23} > \frac{3}{8} > \frac{26}{81}.$

2. $\sqrt{\left(\frac{0.324}{10}\right)} = \sqrt{(0.0324)} = .18.$

3. Given expression $= (.98)^2 - 2 \times .98 \times .76 + (.76)^2$
   $= (.98 - .76)^2 = (.22)^2 = .0484.$

4. $1014 \times 986 = (1000 + 14)(1000 - 14)$
   $= (1000)^2 - (14)^2 = (1000000 - 196) = 999804.$

5. Let $\frac{361}{x} = \frac{x}{81}$ or $x^2 = (361 \times 81).$

   $\therefore x = \sqrt{(361 \times 81)} = (19 \times 9) = 171.$

6. $(?) = \frac{40.799}{37.09} = 1.1.$

7. Let the S.P. of a T.V. be Rs. x and number sold be y.
   Then, total sale = Rs. $(x\,y)$.
   Total sale after increase in price
   $= \left(\frac{115}{100} x\right)\left(\frac{85}{100} y\right) = (1.15 \times 0.85)\,xy = 0.9775\,xy.$

   $\therefore$ Decrease in sale $= \left(\frac{.0225}{1} \times 100\right) \% = 2.25\%.$

8. The amounts paid by them are in the ratio 72 : 108 : 252 i.e. 2 : 3 : 7.

   $\therefore$ C's share = Rs. $\left(\frac{3840 \times 7}{12}\right)$ = Rs. 2240.

9. $\frac{4}{5}x - \frac{2}{3}x = 10$ or $\frac{12x - 10x}{15} = 0$ or $2x = 150$ or $x = 75$.

10. Volume of metal
    $= (52 \times 40 \times 26 - 50 \times 38 \times 25)$ cu. cm.
    $= (54080 - 47500)$ cu. cm. $= 6580$ cu. cm.
    $\therefore$ Weight of Metal $= 6.58$ kg.

11. Area of the curved surface $= 2\pi h = 2 \times \frac{22}{7} \times 5 \times 14 = 440$ sq. m.
    $\therefore$ Cost of painting $= $ Rs. $\left(440 \times \frac{3}{4}\right) = $ Rs. 330.

12. Let B's age be x. Then A's age $= 5x$.
    $\therefore (x + 4) + (5x + 4) = 50$ or $x = 7$.

13. The numbers successively increase by 9 and 4 respectively.
    So, 38 is wrong. It must be 39.

14. The number must be $1^3, 2^3, 3^3, 4^3, 5^3, 6^3, 7^3$.
    So, instead of $4^3 = 64$, it is 84.

15. Area $= \frac{1}{2} \times $ (diagonal)$^2 = \frac{1}{2} \times (4\sqrt{2})^2 = 16$ cm^2

16. The total age of husband and wife 6 years ago
    $= \left(28\frac{1}{2} \times 2\right)$ years $= 57$ years.
    The total age of husband and wife now $= (57 + 12)$ years $= 69$ years.
    Total age of husband, wife and the child now
    $= (24 \times 3)$ years $= 72$ years.
    Age of the child $= (72 - 69)$ years $= 3$ years.

17. Let the age of Vikas 3 years ago be x years.
    Deepak's age today $= 2x$ years.
    Vikas's age today $= (x + 3)$ years.
    $\therefore 2x - (x + 3) = 5$ or $x = 8$.
    So, Deepak's age today $= 16$ years.

18. Required fraction $= \left(\frac{20}{1 \times 100 \times 10}\right) = .02$.

19. Amount $= 2800 \times \left(1 + \frac{10}{100}\right)\left(1 + \frac{5}{100}\right) = $ Rs. 3234.

Model Test Paper II   559

20. Let the marked price be Rs. 100.
    Price after 1st discount = Rs. 80.
    Price after 2nd discount = Rs. (80 – 8) = Rs. 72.
    $\therefore$ 72 : 100 = 108 : x or $x = \dfrac{100 \times 108}{72} = 150$.
    So, the marked price = Rs. 150.

21. $\left.\begin{array}{r}20 : 25 \\ 6 : 4\end{array}\right\}$ :: 480 : x.
    $\therefore x = \dfrac{25 \times 4 \times 480}{20 \times 6} = 400$.

21. Ratio of their shares
    = $(15000 \times 4 + 19000 \times 8) : (22000 \times 4 + 20000 \times 8)$
    = 21000 : 24800 = 53 : 62
    $\therefore$ Jagdish's share = Rs. $\left(\dfrac{11500 \times 62}{115}\right)$ = Rs. 6200.

23. $2A = 3B$ and $5B = 6C$ $\therefore \dfrac{A}{B} = \dfrac{3}{2}$ and $\dfrac{B}{C} = \dfrac{6}{5}$
    So, $\dfrac{A}{C} = \dfrac{A}{B} \times \dfrac{B}{C} = \dfrac{3}{2} \times \dfrac{6}{5} = \dfrac{9}{5}$.

24. Work done by waste pipe in 1 minute = $\left(\dfrac{1}{10} + \dfrac{1}{15} - \dfrac{1}{18}\right) = \dfrac{1}{9}$
    $\therefore$ Waste pipe can empty the full cistern in 9 minutes.

25. Average speed = $\dfrac{2 \times 10 \times 15}{(10 + 15)}$ km/hr = 12 km/hr.

26. Man's rate downstream = 6 km/hr.
    Man's rate upstream = 4 km/hr.
    Let the distance be x km.
    Then, $\dfrac{x}{6} + \dfrac{x}{4} = 1$ or $x = 2.4$ km.

27. Ratio of materials and total cost = 3 : 8
    $\therefore$ 3 : 8 :: 11.25 : x or $x = \dfrac{8 \times 11.25}{3}$ = Rs. 30.

28. Given expression = $\dfrac{(a^3 - b^3)}{(a^2 + ab + b^2)} = (a - b)$
    = (0.86 – 0.14) = 0.72.

29. Let the price of Rs. 100 share be Rs. x.

Then, income on Rs. x = Rs. 12

income on an investment of Rs. 100 = $\left(\dfrac{12}{x} \times 100\right)\%$

$\therefore \dfrac{1200}{x} = 15$ or $x = 80$.

30. Volume of lead = $\pi h (R^2 - r^2)$

$= \dfrac{22}{7} \times 35 \times [(1.2)^2 - 1^2] = 48.4$ cu. cm,

$\therefore$ Weight of lead = (48.4×5) gms = 242 gms.

31. Work done in 5 days = $5 \left(\dfrac{1}{20} + \dfrac{1}{25}\right) = \dfrac{9}{20}$.

Remaining work = $\left(1 - \dfrac{9}{20}\right) = \dfrac{11}{20}$.

This work will be finished by A in $\left(\dfrac{11}{20} \times 20\right) = 11$ days.

32. Clearly, $[(99)^2 - 9999] = 198$.
$\therefore$ Required number = $(9999 - 198) = 9801$.

33. $3.\overline{57} = 3\dfrac{57}{99} = \dfrac{354}{99}$.

34. $\dfrac{\sqrt{1008}}{7} = \sqrt{\left(\dfrac{1008}{7}\right)} = \sqrt{144} = 12$.

35. $\dfrac{1}{\sqrt{3}} = \dfrac{1}{\sqrt{3}} \times \dfrac{\sqrt{3}}{\sqrt{3}} = \dfrac{\sqrt{3}}{3} = \dfrac{1.732}{3} = 0.577$.

36. $(6 \times 42) + 4 \times x = (38.9 \times 10)$ or $x = 34.25$.

37. A beats B by 10 sec.

Distance covered by B in 10 sec. = $\left(\dfrac{1000}{200} \times 10\right) = 50$ metres.

38. Suppose (8×5) i.e. 40 lemons be bought.

Then, C.P. = Rs. 8 and S.P. = Rs. $\left(\dfrac{3}{8} \times 40\right)$ = Rs. 15.

$\therefore$ Gain % = $\left(\dfrac{7}{8} \times 100\right)\% = 87\dfrac{1}{2}\%$.

39. Let the C.P. be Rs. x

Then, $x + \dfrac{1}{4}x = 240$ or $x = \left(\dfrac{240 \times 4}{5}\right)$ = Rs. 192.

40. Let the ten's digit be x and the unit digit by y.

Then, $x + y = 9$ and $10x + y - 9 = 10y + x$

Solving, $x + y = 9$ and $x - y = 1$ we get $x = 5$ and $y = 4$.

41. $6a^2 = 226$ or $a^2 = 36$ or $a = 6$.

∴ Volume of the Cube $= (6)^3$ cm^3 = 216 cm^3.

42. Required number of students $= 1600 \times \left(1 + \dfrac{15}{100}\right)^2$

$$= \left(1600 \times \dfrac{23}{20} \times \dfrac{23}{20}\right) = 2116.$$

43. Average production in 1987-88

$$= \left(\dfrac{40 + 32 + 22 + 20 + 10}{5}\right) = 24.8 \text{ lakh bales}$$

44. Average production in 1985-86 is 15.6;

Average production in 1986-87 is 20.4.

States showing below average production in 1986-87 are A, C and E.

States showing above average production in 1986-87 are A and B.

So, the required type of states is A only.

45. Production by A is 79 lakh bales while production by B during this period is 84 lakh bales. So, (a) is false. Statements (b) add (c) are clearly false.

Also, (d) is cleary true.

46. Required percentage $= \left(\dfrac{5}{84} \times 100\right) \% = 5.9\%$.

47. Required angle $= \left(\dfrac{15}{100} \times 360\right)° = 54°$.

48. Let the C.P. of the book be Rs. x.

Then, $120 : 100 = 30 : x$

∴ $x = \dfrac{100 \times 30}{120} =$ Rs. 25.

Thus, C.P. of the book = Rs. 25.

∴ Cost of paper used = (20% of Rs. 25) = Rs. 5.

49. $108° = \left(\dfrac{108}{360} \times 100\right) \% = 30\%$.

So, A and D together will form an angle of 108°.

50. $18° = \left(\dfrac{18}{360} \times 100\right) \% = 5\%$.

LATEST QUESTIONS

1. $(4^{61} + 4^{62} + 4^{63} + 4^{64})$ is divisible by :
   (a) 3   (b) 11   (c) 13   (d) 17   (Astt. Grade, 1996)

2. The unit digit in the sum $(264)^{102} + (264)^{103}$ is :
   (a) 0   (b) 4   (c) 6   (d) 8   (Astt. Grade, 1996)

3. If $p = \frac{3}{5}$, $q = \frac{7}{9}$ and $r = \frac{5}{7}$, then
   (a) $p < q < r$ (b) $q < r < p$ (c) $p < r < q$ (d) $r < q < p$ (S.S.C. 1995)

4. The number of prime factors of $(6)^{10} \times (7)^{17} \times (55)^{27}$ is :
   (a) 54   (b) 64   (c) 81   (d) 91   (S.S.C. 1995)

5. Which of the following numbers is a multiple of 11?
   (a) 978626   (b) 112144   (c) 447355   (d) 869756   (S.S.C. 1995)

6. The number of prime factors in $\left(\frac{1}{6}\right)^{12} \times (8)^{25} \times \left(\frac{3}{4}\right)^{15}$ is :
   (a) 33   (b) 37   (c) 52   (d) None   (Hotel Management, 1995)

7. $(51 + 52 + 53 + \ldots + 100) = ?$
   (a) $\frac{51 \times 52}{2}$ (b) $\frac{52 \times 53}{2}$ (c) $\frac{100 \times 50}{2}$ (d) 3775   (P.C.S. 1995)

8. A number when divided by 32 leaves the remainder 29. This number when divided by 8 will leave the remainder :
   (a) 3   (b) 5   (c) 7   (d) 29   (C.B.I. 1994)

9. If $\frac{a}{b} = \frac{4}{5}$ and $\frac{b}{c} = \frac{15}{16}$, then $\frac{c^2 - a^2}{c^2 + a^2} = ?$
   (a) $\frac{1}{7}$ (b) $\frac{7}{25}$ (c) $\frac{3}{4}$ (d) None   (Hotel Management, 1995)

10. Which one of the following numbers is a multiple of 8?
    (a) 923972   (b) 923962   (c) 923872   (d) 923862   (S.S.C. 1995)

11. What should be added to 18962 to make it exactly divisible by 13?
    (a) 2   (b) 3   (c) 4   (d) 5   (B.S.R.B. 1996)

12. The least number, which when increased by 1 is exactly divisible by 12, 18, 24, 32, 40 is :
    (a) 1439   (b) 1440   (c) 1449   (d) 1459   (S.S.C. 1995)

13. Which of the following numbers is divisible by 25 ?
    (a) 505520   (b) 437950   (c) 124505   (d) 500555   (C.B.I. 1995)

14. A number lying between 1000 and 2000 is such that on division by 2, 3, 4, 5, 6, 7 and 8 leaves remainders 1, 2, 3, 4, 5, 6 and 7 respectively. The number is:
    (a) 1876 (b) 1679 (c) 1778 (d) 1654 (C.B.I. 1995)

15. Four prime numbers are in ascending order of their magnitudes. The product of the first three is 385 and that of last three is 1001. The largest given prime number is :
    (a) 11 (b) 13 (c) 17 (d) 19 (C.B.I. 1995)

16. The nearest integer to 58701 which is exactly divisible by 567 is :
    (a) 58068 (b) 55968 (c) 58968 (d) None (Railway, 1995)

17. The number which when multiplied by 17 increases by 640, is :
    (a) 42 (b) 36 (c) 40 (d) None (Railway, 1996)

18. The square of a number subtracted from its cube gives 100. The number is :
    (a) 25 (b) 16 (c) 6 (d) 5 (Astt. Grade, 1996)

19. If two-third of three-fourth of a number added to three-fourth of the four-fifth of the number is x times the number, the value of x is :
    (a) $\frac{11}{10}$ (b) $1\frac{1}{11}$ (c) $\frac{10}{11}$ (d) $\frac{9}{11}$ (U.D.C. 1995)

20. Which of the following numbers does not lie between $\frac{7}{13}$ and $\frac{4}{5}$?
    $\frac{1}{2}, \frac{2}{3}, \frac{3}{4}, \frac{5}{7}$
    (a) $\frac{1}{2}$ (b) $\frac{2}{3}$ (c) $\frac{3}{4}$ (d) $\frac{5}{7}$ (U.D.C. 1995)

21. The value of $\frac{(625)^{6.25} \times (25)^{2.6}}{(625)^{6.75} \times (5)^{1.2}}$ is :
    (a) 0.25 (b) 6.25 (c) 25 (d) 625 (S.S.C. 1994)

22. $(16)^{1.75} = ?$
    (a) 64 (b) $64\sqrt{2}$ (c) 128 (d) $128\sqrt{2}$ (S.S.C. 1994)

23. Out of the numbers $\sqrt{2}, \sqrt[3]{3}$ and $\sqrt[4]{4}$, we can definitely say that the largest number is :
    (a) $\sqrt{2}$ (b) $\sqrt[3]{3}$ (c) $\sqrt[4]{4}$ (d) all are equal (C.B.I. 1994)

24. If $\frac{5 + 2\sqrt{3}}{7 + 4\sqrt{3}} = a + b\sqrt{3}$, then
    (a) $a = 11, b = -6$ (b) $a = -6, b = 11$
    (c) $a = -11, b = 6$ (d) $a = -11, b = -6$ (S.S.C. 1995)

25. The value of $\sqrt[4]{(625)^3}$ is :
    (a) 25 (b) 125 (c) $\sqrt[3]{1875}$ (d) None of these (I. Tax. 1995)

Latest Questions

26. If $(125)^x = 3125$, then x equals :

    (a) $\frac{3}{5}$ (b) $\frac{5}{3}$ (c) $\frac{1}{4}$ (d) $\frac{1}{5}$ (C.B.I. 1995)

27. The value of $\frac{36 \times 36 \times 36 + 14 \times 14 \times 14}{36 \times 36 + 14 \times 14 - 36 \times 14}$ is :

    (a) 22 (b) 50 (c) 5100 (d) 132   (P.C.S. 1996)

28. The value of $(0.\overline{63} + 0.\overline{37})$ is :

    (a) 1.01 (b) $.\overline{101}$ (c) $1.\overline{01}$ (d) 1.001   (Railway, 1995)

29. If $\frac{1}{3.718} = .2689$, then the value of $\frac{1}{.0003718}$ is :

    (a) 2689 (b) 2.689 (c) 26890 (d) .2689   (Railway, 1995)

30. $(0.333......) \times (0.444......) = ?$

    (a) 0.121212..... (b) 1.333..... (c) 0.777..... (d) 0.148148148......

    (S.S.C. 1995)

31. Which is the largest among the following fractions ?
    $\frac{5}{8}, \frac{2}{3}, \frac{7}{9}, \frac{3}{5}, \frac{4}{7}$

    (a) $\frac{5}{8}$ (b) $\frac{7}{9}$ (c) $\frac{4}{7}$ (d) $\frac{2}{3}$ (L.I.C. 1995)

32. The value of $\frac{(3.06)^3 - (1.98)^3}{(3.06)^2 + (3.06 \times 1.98) + (1.98)^2} = ?$

    (a) 5.04 (b) 1.08 (c) 2.16 (d) 1.92   (Astt. Grade, 1996)

33. $0.04 \times ? = .000016$

    (a) 4 (b) .04 (c) .0004 (d) None

    (Hotel Management, 1995)

34. The value of $\frac{2^{1/2} \cdot 3^{1/3} \cdot 4^{1/4}}{10^{-1/5} \cdot 5^{3/5}} + \frac{3^{4/3} \cdot 5^{-7/5}}{4^{-3/5} \cdot 6}$ is :

    (a) 5 (b) 6 (c) 10 (d) 15   (C.B.I. 1995)

35. $4^7 + 16^4 \times \sqrt{16} = ?$

    (a) $\frac{1}{16}$ (b) $\frac{1}{4}$ (c) 4 (d) 1   (Railway, 1996)

36. H.C.F. of $\frac{7}{90}, \frac{14}{15}$ and $\frac{7}{10}$ is :

    (a) $\frac{7}{90}$ (b) $\frac{7}{45}$ (c) $\frac{7}{675}$ (d) $\frac{14}{45}$ (C.B.I. 1994)

37. Three persons begin to walk around a circular track. They complete their revolutions in $15\frac{1}{6}$ seconds, $16\frac{1}{4}$ seconds and $18\frac{2}{3}$ seconds respectively. After

what time will they be together at the starting point again?

(a) $303\frac{1}{3}$ sec (b) 364 sec (c) 3604 sec (d) 3640 sec   (C.B.I. 1994)

38. $\left(1 + \cfrac{1}{1 + \cfrac{1}{1 + \cfrac{1}{3}}}\right) \div 1\frac{4}{7}$ is equal to :

(a) $1\frac{1}{3}$ (b) $1\frac{1}{4}$ (c) $1\frac{1}{7}$ (d) 1   (S.S.C. 1995)

39. $\dfrac{(0.43)^3 + (1.47)^3 + (1.1)^3 - 3 \times 0.43 \times 1.47 \times 1.1}{(0.43)^2 + (1.47)^2 + (1.1)^2 - 0.43 \times 1.43 - 0.43 \times 1.1 - 1.47 \times 1.1} = ?$

(a) 1.90 (b) 2.87 (c) 3 (d) 3.47   (S.S.C. 1995)

40. If $\dfrac{x}{2y} = \dfrac{3}{2}$, then the value of $\dfrac{2x + y}{x - 2y}$ equals :

(a) $\dfrac{1}{7}$ (b) 7 (c) 7.1 (d) 6.8   (S.S.C. 1995)

41. $\dfrac{1}{4}$th of Nikhil's money is equal to $\dfrac{1}{6}$th of Yogesh's money. If both together have Rs. 600. What is the difference between their amounts ?

(a) 240 (b) 360 (c) 50 (d) 120   (S.S.C. 1995)

42. $\dfrac{(0.05)^2 + (0.41)^2 + (0.073)^2}{(0.005)^2 + (0.041)^2 + (0.0073)^2} = ?$

(a) 100 (b) 10 (c) 1000 (d) None   (Railway, 1995)

43. One litre of water weighs 1 kg. How many cubic millimetres of water will weigh 0.1 gram ?

(a) 10 (b) 100 (c) 0.1 (d) 1   (Railway, 1995)

44. Out of a tank which is $\dfrac{3}{4}$th full, 21 litres of water is drawn out. The tank is now $\dfrac{2}{5}$th full. What is the capacity of the tank in litres?

(a) 200 (b) 120 (c) 40 (d) 60   (Railway, 1995)

45. Talekar is as much heavier than Suresh as he is lighter than Gokhale. If the total weight of Suresh and Gokhale is 140 kg, what is the weight of Talekar?

(a) 55 kg (b) 65 kg (c) 70 kg (d) Data insufficient

(Bank P.O. 1996)

46. A man has Rs. 480 in the denominations of one-rupee notes, five-rupee notes and ten-rupee notes. The number of notes are equal. What is the total number of notes he has ?

(a) 45 (b) 60 (c) 75 (d) 90   (C.B.I. 1995)

47. If $a = 1.2$, $b = 2.1$ and $c = -3.3$, then the value of $(a^3 + b^3 + c^3 - 3abc)$ is :
    (a) 1   (b) 2   (c) 3   (d) 0   (Astt. Grade, 1996)

48. Find out the numbers indicated by x and y in $3\frac{1}{x} \times y\frac{2}{5} = 13\frac{3}{4}$, fractions being in their lowest terms.
    (a) $x = 4, y = 8$ (b) $x = 4, y = 4$
    (c) $x = 2, y = 4$ (d) $x = 8, y = 4$ (Astt. Grade, 1996)

49. $\dfrac{\sqrt{31} - \sqrt{29}}{\sqrt{31} + \sqrt{29}} = ?$

    (a) $60 - 2\sqrt{899}$ (b) $30 - \sqrt{899}$ (c) $30 + \sqrt{899}$ (d) $\dfrac{1}{30 - \sqrt{899}}$
    (S.S.C. 1995)

50. $\left(1 - \dfrac{1}{1 + \sqrt{2}} + \dfrac{1}{1 - \sqrt{2}}\right) = ?$

    (a) $2\sqrt{2} - 1$ (b) $1 - 2\sqrt{2}$ (c) $1 - \sqrt{2}$ (d) $-2\sqrt{2}$ (S.S.C. 1994)

51. If $(676)^2 = 456976$, the value of $\sqrt{45.6976}$ is :
    (a) 0.00676   (b) 0.676   (c) 6.76   (d) 0.0676   (C.B.I. 1994)

52. $\left(\dfrac{3\sqrt{2}}{\sqrt{6} - \sqrt{3}} - \dfrac{4\sqrt{3}}{\sqrt{6} - \sqrt{2}} - \dfrac{6}{\sqrt{8} + \sqrt{12}}\right) = ?$
    (a) 1   (b) $-\sqrt{3}$ (c) $\sqrt{3} + \sqrt{2}$ (d) $\sqrt{3} - \sqrt{2}$ (Astt. Grade, 1996)

53. If $a = \sqrt{6} + \sqrt{5}$ and $b = \sqrt{6} - \sqrt{5}$, then $2a^2 - 5ab + 2b^2 = ?$
    (a) 43   (b) 39   (c) 31   (d) 27   (I. Tax, 1995)

54. The price of cooking oil has increased by 25%. The percentage of reduction that a family should effect in the use of cooking oil so as not to increase the expenditure on this account is :
    (a) 25%   (b) 30%   (c) 20%   (d) 15%   (P.C.S. 1996)

55. 4598 is 95% of ?
    (a) 4800   (b) 4850   (c) 4840   (d) None   (Hotel Management, 1995)

56. In an organisation, 40% of the employees are matriculates 50% of the remaining are graduates and the remaining 180 are post-graduates. How many employees are graduates?
    (a) 360   (b) 240   (c) 300   (d) 180   (L.I.C. 1995)

57. If 40% of the people read newspaper X, 50% read newspaper Y and 10% read both the papers. What percentage of the people read neither newspaper?
    (a) 10%   (b) 15%   (c) 20%   (d) 25%   (U.D.C. 1995)

58. The population of a town increases by 5% annually. If its population in 1995 was 138915, what it was in 1992?
    (a) 110000   (b) 100000   (c) 120000   (d) 90000   (U.D.C. 1995)

59. 25% of a certain number is 15 less than 30% of the same number. What is that number?

    (a) 600 (b) 300 (c) 750 (d) 135 (B.S.R.B., 1996)

60. The population of a village is 4500. $\frac{5}{9}$th of them are males and rest females. If 40% of the males are married, then the percentage of married females is :

    (a) 35 (b) 40 (c) 50 (d) 60 (S.S.C. 1995)

61. A salesman's commission is 5% on all sales upto Rs. 10000 and 4% on all sales exceeding this. He remits Rs. 31100 to his parent company after deducting his commission. His sales was worth:

    (a) Rs. 35000 (b) Rs. 36100 (c) Rs. 35100 (d) Rs. 32500 (I. Tax, 1995)

62. A's income is 10% more than B's. How much percent is B's income less than A's?

    (a) 10% (b) 7% (c) $9\frac{1}{11}\%$ (d) $6\frac{1}{2}\%$ (Railway, 1995)

63. A mixture of 40 litres of milk and water contains 10% water. How much water must be added to make water 20% in the new mixture?

    (a) 10 litres (b) 7 litres (c) 5 litres (d) 3 litres (Railway, 1995)

64. If $z = \frac{x^2}{y}$ and x, y both are increased in value by 10%, then the value of z is :

    (a) unchanged (b) increased by 10%
    (c) increased by 11% (d) increased by 20% (Astt. Grade, 1996)

65. If a exceeds b by $x\%$, then which one of these equations is correct?

    (a) $a - b = \frac{x}{100}$ (b) $b = a + 100x$
    (c) $a = \frac{bx}{100 + x}$ (d) $a = b + \frac{bx}{100}$ (I. Tax, 1995)

66. In an examination, 35% of the examinees failed in G.K. and 25% in English. If 10% of the examinees failed in both, then the percentage of examinees passed will be :

    (a) 40% (b) 45% (c) 48% (d) 50% (U.D.C. 1995)

67. If the price of a television set is increased by 25%, then by what percentage should the new price be reduced to bring the price back to the original level?

    (a) 15% (b) 20% (c) 25% (d) 30% (I.A.S. 1996)

68. The number of grams of water needed to reduce 9 grams of shaving lotion containing 50% alcohol to a lotion containing 30% alcohol, is :

    (a) 4 (b) 5 (c) 6 (d) 7 (Astt. Grade, 1995)

69. A dealer marks his goods 20% above cost price. He then allows some discount on it and makes a profit of 8%. The rate of discount is :

    (a) 4% (b) 6% (c) 10% (d) 12% (P.C.S. 1996)

Latest Questions

70. By selling an umbrella for Rs. 30, a shopkeeper gains 20%. During a clearance sale, the shopkeeper allows a discount of 10% of the marked price. his gain percent during the sale season is :

(a) 7   (b) 7.5   (c) 8   (d) 9   (S.S.C. 1995)

71. A shopkeeper allows a discount of 10% on the marked price of an item but charges a sales tax of 8% on the discounted price. If the customer pays Rs. 680.40 as the price including the sales tax, what is the marked price of the item?

(a) Rs. 630   (b) Rs. 700   (c) Rs. 780   (d) None

(Hotel Management, 1995)

72. The difference between the cost price and sale price of an article is Rs. 240. If the profit percent is 20, at what price was the article sold?   (B.S.R.B. 1995)

(a) Rs. 1240   (b) Rs. 1400   (c) Rs. 1600   (d) None of these.

73. By selling a motor cycle for Rs. 22600 a person gains 13%, what was his gain?

(a) Rs. 600   (b) Rs. 2936   (c) Rs. 2600   (d) Data inadequate

(L.I.C. 1995)

74. A shopkeeper bought locks at the rate of 8 locks for Rs. 34 and sold them at 12 locks for Rs. 57. The number of locks he should sell to have a profit of Rs. 900, is :

(a) 1400   (b) 1600   (c) 1800   (d) 2000   (Railway, 1995)

75. A shopkeepr earns 15% profit on a shirt even after allowing 31% discount on the list price. If the list price is Rs. 125, then the cost price of the shirt is :

(a) Rs. 87   (b) Rs. 80   (c) Rs. 75   (d) Rs. 69   (U.D.C. 1995)

76. Loss incurred by selling a bicycle for Rs. 895 is equal to the profit earned by selling it for Rs. 955. What is the loss/profit in this case?

(a) Rs. 45   (b) Rs. 30   (c) Rs. 75   (d) cannot be determined

(B.S.R.B. 1996)

77. If 2 kg of almonds cost as much as 8 kg of walnuts and the cost of 5 kg of almonds and 16 kg of walnuts is Rs. 1080, the cost of almonds per kg is :

(a) Rs. 160   (b) Rs. 150   (c) Rs. 120   (d) None of these

(Hotel Management, 1995)

78. A manufacturer sells a pair of glasses to a wholesale dealer at a profit of 18%. The wholesaler sells the same to a retailer at a profit of 20%. The retailer in turn sells them to a customer for Rs. 30.09, thereby earning a profit of 25%. The cost price of the manufacturer is :

(a) Rs. 15   (b) Rs. 16   (c) Rs. 17   (d) Rs. 18   (U.D.C. 1995)

79. Chatterjee bought a car and got 15% of its original price as dealer's discount. He then sold it with 20% profit on his purchase price. What percentage profit did he get on the original price of the car ?

(a) 2%   (b) 12%   (c) 5%   (d) 17%   (Bank P.O. 1996)

80. If the difference between selling a shirt at a profit of 10% and 15% is Rs. 10, then the cost price is :

    (a) Rs. 110   (b) Rs. 115   (c) Rs. 150   (d) Rs. 200
    (S.S.C. 1995)

81. The cost of a shirt after 15% discount is Rs. 102. What was the cost of the shirt before the discount ?

    (a) Rs. 117   (b) Rs. 118   (c) Rs. 120   (d) Rs. 121
    (C.B.I. 1995)

82. If a man reduces the selling price of a fan from Rs. 400 to Rs. 380, his loss increases by 20%. The cost price of the fan is :

    (a) Rs. 600   (b) Rs. 500   (c) Rs. 480   (d) None
    (Railway, 1996)

83. By selling a vehicle for Rs. 455000, Samant suffers 25% loss, what was his loss?

    (a) Rs. 115370   (b) Rs. 113570   (c) Rs. 113750   (d) None of these
    (B.S.R.B. 1996)

84. A shopkeeper marks his goods 20% higher than the cost price and allows a discount of 5%. The percentage of his profit is :

    (a) 10%   (b) 14%   (c) 15%   (d) 20%   (Railway, 1995)

85. A dealer offered a machine for sale for Rs. 27500 but even if he had charged 10% less he would have made a profit of 10%. The actual cost of the machine is :

    (a) Rs. 24250   (b) Rs. 22500   (c) Rs. 22275   (d) Rs. 22000
    (Astt. Grade, 1996)

86. A toy car was sold at a loss for Rs. 60. Had it been sold for Rs. 81, the gain would have been $\frac{3}{4}$ of the former loss. The cost of the toy is :

    (a) Rs. 65   (b) Rs. 72   (c) Rs. 80   (d) Rs. 86   (Astt. Grade, 1996)

87. A trader allows a trade discount of 20% and a cash discount of $6\frac{1}{4}$% on the marked price of the goods and gets a net gain of 20% on the cost. By how much above the cost should the goods be marked for sale?

    (a) 40%   (b) 50%   (c) 60%   (d) 70%   (I. Tax. 1995)

88. A merchant has 120 kg of rice. He sells a part of it at a profit of 10% and the rest at a profit of 25%. He gains 15% on the whole. Quanity of rice he sold at 25% gain is :

    (a) 30 kg   (b) 40 kg   (c) 50 kg   (d) 55 kg   (I. Tax, 1995)

89. A wholesaler gains 25% by selling a commodity and a retailer gains 30% by selling it. If the retail value of that commodity is Rs. 325, then the wholesale value is :

    (a) Rs. 200   (b) Rs. 225   (c) Rs. 245   (d) Rs. 255   (U.D.C. 1995)

Latest Questions

90. A shopkeeper decides to give 5% commission on the marked price of an article but also wants to earn 10% profit. If the cost price is Rs. 95, then the marked price is :
    (a) Rs. 100   (b) Rs. 105   (c) Rs. 110   (d) Rs. 115
    (U.D.C. 1995)

91. A bag contains 25-p, 10-p and 5-p coins in the ratio 1 : 2 : 3. If the total value is Rs. 30, the number of 5-p coins is :
    (a) 50   (b) 100   (c) 200   (d) 150   (P.C.S. 1996)

92. If $(x + y) : (x - y) = 4 : 1$, then $(x^2 + y^2) : (x^2 - y^2) = ?$
    (a) 25:9   (b) 16:1   (c) 8:17   (d) 17:8   (C.B.I. 1994)

93. $9^{3.04} : 9^{2.04} = ?$
    (a) 1 : 9   (b) 3 : 2   (c) 76 : 51   (d) None of these   (U.D.C. 1994)

94. If $a : b = b : c$, then $a^4 : b^4 = ?$
    (a) $ac : b^2$ (b) $a^2 : c^2$ (c) $c^2 : a^2$ (d) $b^2 : ac$ (Railway, 1995)

95. If $x : y = 3 : 4$, then $(2x + 3y) : (3y - 2x) = ?$
    (a) 2 : 1   (b) 3 : 2   (c) 3 : 1   (d) 21 : 1   (U.D.C. 1995)

96. Rs. 56250 is to be divided among A, B and C so that A may receive half as much as B and C together and B receives one fourth of what A and C together receive. The share of A is more than that of B by :
    (a) Rs. 7500   (b) Rs. 7750   (c) Rs. 15000   (d) Rs. 16000
    (U.D.C. 1995)

97. A flagstaff 17.5 m high casts a shadow of 40.25 m. The height of the building which casts a shadow 28.75 m long under similar condition, will be :
    (a) 10 m   (b) 12.5 m   (c) 17.5 m   (d) 21.25 m   (S.S.C. 1995)

98. The sum of three numbers is 174. The ratio of second number to the third number is 9 : 16 and the ratio of first number to the third one is 1 : 4. The second number is :
    (a) 24   (b) 54   (c) 96   (d) can not be determined
    (Bank P.O. 1996)

99. 5 mangoes and 4 oranges cost as much as 3 mangoes and 7 oranges. What is the ratio of the cost of one mango to that of one orange?
    (a) 4 : 3   (b) 1 : 3   (c) 3 : 2   (d) 5 : 2   (C.B.I. 1995)

100. If 35% of A's income is equal to 25% of B's income, then the ratio of their incomes is :
    (a) 4 : 3   (b) 5 : 7   (c) 7 : 5   (d) 4 : 7   (Astt. Grade, 1996)

101. Last year the ratio between the salaries of A and B was 3 : 4. But the ratio of their individual salaries between last year and this year were 4 : 5 and 2 : 3 respectively. If the sum of their present salaries is Rs. 4160, then how much is the salary of A now?
    (a) Rs. 1040   (b) Rs. 1600   (c) Rs. 2560   (d) Rs. 3120
    (U.D.C. 1995)

102. A and B have incomes in the ratio 5 : 3. The expenses of A, B and C are in the ratio 8 : 5 : 2. If C spends Rs. 2000 and B saves Rs. 700, A's saving is :
   (a) Rs. 1500   (b) Rs. 1000   (c) Rs. 2500   (d) Rs. 500
   (Astt. Grade, 1996)

103. If $x : 2\frac{1}{3} :: 21 : 50$, then the value of x is :
   (a) $\frac{27}{50}$ (b) $\frac{49}{50}$ (c) $1\frac{1}{50}$ (d) $1\frac{1}{49}$ (Railway, 1996)

104. If 8 women can grind 180 kg. of wheat in 5 days, in how many days will 28 women grind 3780 kg of wheat?
   (a) 32   (b) 45   (c) 60   (d) 30   (Railway, 1995)

105. If 40 men can build a wall 300 m. long in 12 days, working 6 hours a day ; how long will 30 men take to build a similar wall 200 m long, working 8 hours a day?
   (a) $4\frac{1}{2}$ days   (b) 8 days   (c) $10\frac{1}{2}$ days   (d) 11 days   (I. Tax, 1995)

106. If 12 persons can do $\frac{3}{5}$ of a certain work in 10 days, then how many persons are required to finish the whole work in 20 days?
   (a) 10   (b) 9   (c) 8   (d) 7   (C.B.I. 1995)

107. In a fort, ration for 2000 people was sufficient for 54 days. After 15 days, more people came and the ration lasted only for 20 more days. How many people came?
   (a) 2500   (b) 2250   (c) 1900   (d) 1675   (Railway, 1995)

108. One army camp had ration for 560 soldiers for 20 days, 560 soldiers reported for the camp and after 12 days, 112 soldiers were sent to another camp. For how many days, the remaining soldiers can stay in the camp without getting any new ration?
   (a) 12   (b) 16   (c) 10   (d) None   (Railway, 1996)

109. How many men need to be employed to complete a job in 5 days if 10 men can complete half the job in 7 days?
   (a) 7   (b) 14   (c) 28   (d) 35   (Astt. Grade, 1996)

110. A contractor undertook to build a road in 100 days. He employed 110 men. After 45 days, he found that only $\frac{1}{4}$ could be built. In order to complete the work in time, how many more men should be employed?
   (a) 120   (b) 160   (c) 180   (d) 270   (Railway, 1995)

111. 16 men complete one-fourth of a piece of work in 12 days. What is the additional number of men required to complete the work in 12 days?
   (a) 48   (b) 36   (c) 30   (d) 18   (S.S.C. 1995)

112. A, B and C together can do a piece of work in 20 days. After working with B

Latest Questions 573

and C for 8 days, A leaves and then B and C complete the ramaining work in 20 days more. In how many days, A alone could do the work?

(a) 40   (b) 50   (c) 60   (d) 80   (S.S.C. 1995)

113. A, B and C together can complete a piece of work in 10 days. All the three started working at it together and after 4 days, A left. Then, B and C together completed the work in 10 more days. A alone could complete the work in

(a) 15 days   (b) 16 days   (c) 25 days   (d) 50 days   (U.D.C. 1995)

114. 20 men can finish a piece of work in 30 days. After how many days should 5 men leave the work so that it may be finished in 35 days?

(a) 10   (b) 12   (c) 15   (d) 20   (Railway, 1995)

115. A man, a woman or a boy can do a piece of work in 3, 4 and 12 days respectively. How many boys must assist one man and one woman to do the work in one day?

(a) 6   (b) 8   (c) 9   (d) 5   (Astt. Grade, 1996)

116. If 2 men and 3 boys can do a piece of work in 8 days, while 3 men and 2 boys can do it in 7 days, how long will 5 men and 4 boys take to do it?

(a) 3 days   (b) 4 days   (c) 5 days   (d) 6 days   (Astt. Grade, 1996)

117. A and B can do a work in 8 days, B and C can do the same work in 12 days. A, B and C together can finish it in 6 days. A and C together will do it in :

(a) 4 days   (b) 6 days   (c) 8 days   (d) 12 days   (I. Tax, 1995)

118. If I would have been twice as efficient as today, then I would have finished a work in 12 days. If my efficiency is reduced to one-third of what it is at present, then in how many days, I would be able to finish the work?

(a) 8   (b) 18   (c) 52   (d) 72   (U.D.C. 1995)

119. The ratio between the rates of walking of A and B is 2 : 3. If the time taken by B to cover a certain distance is 36 minutes, the time in minutes, taken by A to cover that much distance is :

(a) 24   (b) 38   (c) 48   (d) 54   (S.S.C. 1995)

120. I have to be at a certain place at a certain time and find that I shall be 20 minutes too late if I walk at 3 km/hr and 10 minutes too soon if I walk at 4 km/hr. How far I have to walk?

(a) 6 km.   (b) 10 km   (c) $12\frac{1}{2}$ km   (d) $16\frac{2}{3}$ km   (S.S.C. 1995)

121. Sound travels at 330 metres a second. How many kilometres away is a thunder cloud when its sound follows the flash after 10 seconds?

(a) 3.3   (b) 33   (c) 0.33   (d) 3.33   (U.D.C. 1994)

122. Walking $\frac{6}{7}$ th of his usual speed, a man is 12 minutes too late. The usual time taken by him to cover that distance is :

(a) 1 hour   (b) 1 hour 12 min.   (c) 1 hour 15 min.   (d) 1 hour 20 min.

(U.D.C. 1995)

123. A is twice as fast as B and B is thrice as fast as C. The journey covered by C in 42 minutes will be covered by A in :

(a) 7 min.   (b) 14 min.   (c) 28 min.   (d) 35 min.   (S.S.C. 1995)

124. A car takes 5 hours to cover a distance of 300 km. How much should the speed in km/hr be maintained to cover the same distance in $\frac{4}{5}$th of the previous time?

(a) 48   (b) 60   (c) 75   (d) 120   (Bank P.O. 1996)

125. Two men start together to walk a certain distance at 3.75 km and 3 km per hour respectively. The former arrives 30 minutes before the latter. The distance they walked is :

(a) 7.5 km   (b) 10 km   (c) 12.5 km   (d) 15 km   (Railway, 1995)

126. The wheel of an engine, $7\frac{1}{2}$ metres in circumference makes 7 revolutions in 9 seconds. The speed of the train in km per hour is :

(a) 150   (b) 132   (c) 130   (d) 135   (P.C.S. 1995)

127. A train X starts from a place at the speed of 50 km/hr. After one hour, another train Y starts from the same place at the speed of 70 km/hr. After how much time will Y cross X?

(a) 3 hrs.   (b) $2\frac{3}{4}$ hrs.   (c) $3\frac{1}{2}$ hrs.   (d) $2\frac{1}{4}$ hrs.   (P.C.S. 1995)

128. A person travels equal distances with speeds of 3 km/hr, 4 km/hr and 5 km/hr and takes a total time of 47 minutes. The total distance (in km) is :

(a) 2   (b) 3   (c) 4   (d) 5   (Astt. Grade, 1996)

129. A train covers a distance between station A and station B in 45 minutes. If the speed of the train is reduced by 5 km/hr, then the same distance is covered in 48 minutes. What is the distance between the stations A and B?

(a) 60 km   (b) 64 km   (c) 80 km   (d) 55 km   (U.D.C. 1995)

130. Which of the following trains is the fastest?

(a) 25 m/sec.   (b) 1500 m/min.   (c) 90 km/hr   (d) None   (Hotel Management, 1995)

131. A train passes over a bridge of length 200 m in 40 seconds. If the speed of the train is 81 km per hour, its length is :

(a) 900 m   (b) 1800 m   (c) 700 m   (d) 600 m   (S.S.C. 1995)

132. A 180 m long train crosses a man standing on the platform in 6 seconds. What is the speed of the train?

(a) 90 km/hr   (b) 108 km/hr   (c) 120 km/hr   (d) 88 km/hr   (B.S.R.B. 1995)

133. Two trains are running at 40 km/hr and 20 km/hr respectively in the same direction. Fast train completely passes a man sitting in the slow train in 5 seconds. What is the length of the fast train?

(a) $23\frac{2}{9}$ m (b) 27 m (c) $27\frac{7}{9}$ m (d) 23 m   (*Railway, 1995*)

134. A train passes a 50 m long platform in 14 seconds and a man standing on the platform in 10 seconds. The speed of the train in km/hr is :

    (a) 24 (b) 36 (c) 40 (d) 45   (*I. Tax, 1995*)

135. A train travelling with a constant speed crosses a 96 m long platform in 12 seconds and another 141 m long platform in 15 seconds. The length of the train is :

    (a) 80 m (b) 64 m (c) 84 m (d) 90 m   (*I. Tax, 1995*)

136. A sum of Rs. 2400 amounts to Rs. 3264 in four years at a certain rate of simple interest. If the rate of interest is increased by 1%, the same sum in the same time would amount to:

    (a) Rs. 3288 (b) Rs. 3312 (c) Rs. 3340 (d) Rs 3360   (*I. Tax, 1995*)

137. A sum was put at a certain rate of interest for 3 years. Had it been put at 2% higher rate, it would have fetched Rs. 72 more. The sum is :

    (a) Rs. 1250 (b) Rs. 1400 (c) Rs. 1200 (d) Rs. 1500   (*Railway, 1995*)

138. Rs. 2000 amount to Rs. 2600 in 5 years at simple interest. If the interest rate is increased by 3%, it would amount to how much?

    (a) Rs. 2900 (b) Rs. 3200 (c) Rs. 3600 (d) None of these   (*Bank P.O. 1996*)

139. On a certain sum, the simple interest at the end of $6\frac{1}{4}$ years becomes $\frac{3}{8}$ of the sum. What is the rate percent?

    (a) 7% (b) 6% (c) 5% (d) $5\frac{1}{2}$%   (*U.D.C. 1995*)

140. An amount of Rs. 100000 is invested in two types of shares. The first yields an interest of 9% per annum and the second yields 11% per annum. It the total interest at the end of one year is $9\frac{3}{4}$%, then the amount invested in each share was :

    (a) Rs. 72500, Rs. 27500 (b) Rs. 62500, Rs. 37500
    (c) Rs. 52500, Rs. 47500 (d) Rs. 82500, Rs. 17500   (*Astt. Grade, 1996*)

141. If the compound interest on a certain sum for 2 years at 10% per annum is Rs. 2100, the simple interest on it at the same rate for 2 years will be :

    (a) Rs. 1700 (b) Rs. 1800 (c) Rs. 1900 (d) Rs. 2000   (*I. Tax, 1995*)

142. The length of a rectangle is increased by 10% and its breadth decreased by 10%. The area of new rectangle is :

(a) neither increased nor decreased (b) decreased by 1%
(c) increased by 1% (d) None of these (P.C.S. 1996)

143. A room is 6 m long, 5 m broad and 4 m high. It has one door 2.5 high and 1.2 m broad and has one window 1 m broad and 1 m high. Find the area in sq. metres of the paper required to cover the four walls of the room.
(a) 84 (b) 100 (c) 120 (d) None (Railway, 1995)

144. The length of a rectangular plot of land is $2\frac{1}{2}$ times its breadth. If the area of the plot is 1000 sq. metres, what is the length of the plot in metres?
(a) 20 (b) 25 (c) 30 (d) 50 (e) None (B.S.R.B. 1996)

145. Tiling work of a rectangular hall 60 m long and 40 m broad is to be completed with a square tile of 0.4 m side. If each tile costs Rs. 5, find the total cost of the tiles?
(a) Rs. 60000 (b) Rs. 65000 (c) 75000 (d) 12000 (Bank P.O. 1996)

146. A room is 6 m long, 5 m broad and 4 m high. If all its walls are to be covered with paper 50 cm wide, the length of the paper is
(a) 96 m (b) 176 m (c) 421 m (d) 208 m (Railway, 1995)

147. The perimeters of a circular and another square field are equal. Fine the area in sq. cm of the circular field if the area of the square field is 484 sq. cm.
(a) 888 (b) 770 (c) 616 (d) None of these (R.R.B. 1996)

148. Two cylindrical buckets have their diameters in the ratio 3 : 1 and their heights are as 1 : 3. Their volumes are in the ratio of
(a) 1 : 2 (b) 2 : 3 (c) 3 : 1 (d) 3 : 4 (I. Tax, 1995)

149. If the radius of the base and height of a cylinder and cone are each equal to r, the radius of a hemisphere is also equal to r, then the volumes of cone, cylinder and hemisphere are in the ratio.
(a) 1 : 2 : 3 (b) 1 : 3 : 2 (c) 2 : 1 : 3 (d) 3 : 2 : 1 (C.B.I. 1995)

150. The size of a wooden block is $5 \times 10 \times 20$ cms. How many whole such blocks will be required to construct a solid wooden cube of minimum size?
(a) 6 (b) 8 (c) 12 (d) 16 (P.C.S. 1995)

SOLUTIONS

1. $(d): 4^{61} + 4^{62} + 4^{63} + 4^{64}$
   $= 4^{61}(1 + 4 + 4^2 + 4^3) = 4^{61} \times 85$, which is divisible by 17.

2. $(a): (264)^{102} + (264)^{103} = (264)^{102} \times [1 + 264]$
   $= (264)^{102} \times 265$
   Unit digit in $(264)^4$ is 6
   Unit digit in $[(264)^4]^{25}$ = Unit digit in $6^{25} = 6$

Latest Questions

Unit digit in $(264)^{100} \times (264)^2$ is 6

Unit digit in $(264)^{102} \times 265$ = unit digit in $6 \times 5 = 0$

3. (c): $p = \dfrac{3}{5} = 0.6$, $q = \dfrac{7}{9} = 0.777$, *i.e.* $r = 0.714$

   Clearly, $0.6 < 0.714 < 0.777$ *i.e.* $p < r < q$.

4. (d): $(6)^{10} \times (7)^{17} \times (55)^{27} = 2^{10} \times 3^{10} \times 7^{17} \times 5^{27} \times 11^{27}$

   $\therefore$ Total number of prime factors $= (10 + 10 + 17 + 27 + 27) = 91$.

5. (a): $(6 + 6 + 7) - (2 + 8 + 9) = 0$, so 978626 is divisible by 11.

6. (d): $\left(\dfrac{1}{6}\right)^{12} \times (8)^{25} \times \left(\dfrac{3}{4}\right)^{15} = \dfrac{1}{2^{12} \times 3^{12}} \times (2^3)^{25} \times \dfrac{3^{15}}{2^{15} \times 2^{15}}$

   $= \dfrac{2^{75} \times 3^{15}}{2^{42} \times 3^{12}} = 2^{33} \times 3^3$

   $\therefore$ Total number of prime factors $= (33 + 3) = 36$.

7. (d): $51 + 52 + 53 + \ldots\ldots + 100$

   $= [(1 + 2 + \ldots\ldots + 50) + (51 + 52 + \ldots\ldots + 100)] - (1 + 2 + 3 + \ldots + 50)$

   $= \left(\dfrac{100 \times 101}{2} - \dfrac{50 \times 51}{2}\right) = (5050 - 1275) = 3775$.

8. (b): Let the given number be x. This when divided by 32. suppose gives the quotient K. Then.

   $x = 32 K + 29 = 8 \times (4 K + 3) + 5$

   Thus, when x is divided by 8, it gives $(4 K + 3)$ as quotient and 5 as remainder.

9. (b): $\dfrac{a}{c} = \dfrac{a}{b} \times \dfrac{b}{c} = \dfrac{4}{5} \times \dfrac{15}{16} = \dfrac{3}{4}$.

   $\therefore \dfrac{c^2 - a^2}{c^2 + a^2} = \dfrac{1 - \dfrac{a^2}{c^2}}{1 + \dfrac{a^2}{c^2}} = \dfrac{1 - \dfrac{9}{16}}{1 + \dfrac{9}{16}} = \dfrac{7}{16} \times \dfrac{16}{25} = \dfrac{7}{25}$.

10. (c): From among the given numbers, 923872 is the only number, whose last 3 digits form 872, which is divisible by 8.

11. (d): 18962 when divided by 13 leaves the remainder 8.

    $\therefore$ Number to be added $= (13 - 8) = 5$.

12. (a):

2	12	18	24	32	40	360
2	6	9	12	16	20	4
3	3	9	6	8	10	
2	1	3	2	8	10	
	1	3	1	4	5	

   $\therefore$ L.C.M. of 12, 18, 24, 32, 40 is $(2 \times 2 \times 3 \times 2 \times 3 \times 4 \times 5) = 1440$.

   $\therefore$ Required number $= (1440 - 1) = 1439$.

13. (*b*): 437950 is the only number among given numbers s.t. 437950 = 5 × 87590
    = 5 × 5 × 17518, which has 25 as a factor.
14. (*b*): Note that $(2 - 1) = (3 - 2) = (4 - 3) = \ldots = (8 - 7) = 1$
    L.C.M. of 2, 3, 4, 5, 6, 7, 8 is 840
    ∴ Required number = $(840 K - 1)$
    Since the number lies between 1000 and 2000, so K = 2.
15. (*b*): We note that $5 \times 7 \times 11 = 385$.
    The prime number next to 11 is 13.
    Also, $7 \times 11 \times 13 = 1001$.
    Hence, the required number is 13.
16. (*c*): 567) 5 8 7 0 1 (1 0 3
          5 6 7
          ―――
          2 0 0 1
          1 7 0 1
          ―――
          3 0 0, which is more than half of 567.
    ∴ Required number = $58701 + (567 - 300) = 58968$.
17. (*c*): Let the number be x. Then
    $17x - x = 640 \Rightarrow x = 40$.
18. (*d*): $x^3 - x^2 = 100 \Rightarrow x^3 - x^2 - 100 = 0$.
    Clealy, $x = 5$, satisfies it.
19. (*a*): Let the number be p. Then,
    $\frac{2}{3}$ of $\frac{3}{4}$ of $p + \frac{3}{4}$ of $\frac{4}{5}$ of $p = px$
    $\Rightarrow \frac{1}{2}p + \frac{3}{5}p = xp \Rightarrow x = \left(\frac{1}{2} + \frac{3}{5}\right) = \frac{11}{10}$.
20. (*a*): $\left(\frac{7}{13} = 0.538, \frac{4}{5} = 0.8\right), \left(\frac{1}{2} = 0.5, \frac{2}{3} = 0.666, \frac{3}{4} = 0.75, \frac{5}{7} = 0.714\right)$
    Clearly, 0.5 does not lie between 0.538 and 0.8.
21. (*c*): Given Exp. $= \frac{(5^2)^{2.6}}{(625)^{0.5} \times (5)^{1.2}} = \frac{5^{(5.2 - 1.2)}}{(5^4)^{0.5}} = \frac{5^4}{5^2} = 5^2 = 25$.
22. (*c*): $(16)^{1.75} = (2^4)^{\frac{175}{100}} = (2^4)^{7/4} = 2^{(4 \times \frac{7}{4})} = 2^7 = 128$.
23. (*b*): Given numbers are $2^{1/2}, 3^{1/3}, 4^{1/4}$, L.C.M. of 2, 3, 4 is 12.
    Now, $2^{1/2} = 2^{(6/12)} = \sqrt[12]{2^6} = \sqrt[12]{64}$
             $3^{1/3} = 3^{4/12} = \sqrt[12]{3^4} = \sqrt[12]{81}$
             $4^{1/4} = 4^{3/12} = \sqrt[12]{4^3} = \sqrt[12]{64}$
    Clearly, $\sqrt[12]{81}$ is the largest, *i.e.* $\sqrt[3]{3}$ is the largest.

Latest Questions

24. (a): $\dfrac{5 + 2\sqrt{3}}{7 + 4\sqrt{3}} = \dfrac{(5 + 2\sqrt{3})}{(7 + 4\sqrt{3})} \times \dfrac{(7 - 4\sqrt{3})}{(7 - 4\sqrt{3})} = \dfrac{35 - 24 + 14\sqrt{3} - 20\sqrt{3}}{(49 - 48)}$
 $= 11 - 6\sqrt{3}$
 Thus, $a + b\sqrt{3} = 11 - 6\sqrt{3}$
 Hence, $a = 11, b = -6$.

25. (b): $\sqrt[4]{(625)^3} = (625)^{3/4} = (5^4)^{3/4} = 5^{(4 \times \frac{3}{4})} = 5^3 = 125$.

26. (b): $(125)^x = 3125 \Rightarrow (5^3)^x = 5^5 \Rightarrow 3x = 5 \Rightarrow x = \dfrac{5}{3}$.

27. (b): Given Exp. $= \dfrac{(a^3 + b^3)}{(a^2 + b^2 - ab)} = (a + b) = (36 + 14) = 50$.

28. (c): $0.\overline{63} = \dfrac{63}{99}$ and $0.\overline{37} = \dfrac{37}{99}$.

 $\therefore$ $0.\overline{63} + 0.\overline{37} = \dfrac{63}{99} + \dfrac{37}{99} = \dfrac{100}{99} = 1\dfrac{1}{99} = 1.\overline{01}$.

29. (a): $\dfrac{1}{0.0003718} = \dfrac{10000}{3.718} = 10000 \times .2689 = 2689$.

30. (d): Given Exp. $= 0.\overline{3} \times 0.\overline{4} = \dfrac{3}{9} \times \dfrac{4}{9} = \dfrac{4}{27} = 0.148148148....$

31. (b): $\dfrac{5}{8} = 0.625$, $\dfrac{2}{3} = 0.666$, $\dfrac{7}{9} = 0.777$, $\dfrac{3}{5} = 0.6$, $\dfrac{4}{7} = 0.571$

 Clearly, $\dfrac{7}{9}$ is the largest.

32. (b): Given Exp. $= \dfrac{(a^3 - b^3)}{(a^2 + ab + b^2)} = a - b = (3.06 - 1.98) = 1.08$.

33. (c): Let $.04 \times x = .000016$. Then,

 $x = \dfrac{.000016}{.04} = \dfrac{.0016}{4} = .0004$.

34. (c): Given Exp. $= \dfrac{2^{1/2} \times 3^{1/3} \times (2^2)^{1/4}}{2^{-1/5} \times 5^{-1/5} \times 5^{3/5}} \div \dfrac{3^{4/3} \times 5^{-7/5}}{(2^2)^{-3/5} \times 2 \times 3}$

 $= \dfrac{2^{1/2} \times 3^{1/3} \times 2^{1/2}}{2^{-1/5} \times 5^{-1/5} \times 5^{3/5}} \times \dfrac{2^{-6/5} \times 2 \times 3}{3^{4/3} \times 5^{-7/5}}$

$$= \frac{2^{(\frac{1}{2}+\frac{1}{2}-\frac{6}{5}+\frac{1}{5}+1)} \times 3^{(\frac{1}{3}+1-\frac{4}{3})}}{5^{(-\frac{1}{5}+\frac{3}{5}-\frac{7}{5})}} = \frac{2 \times 3^0}{5^{-1}} = 2 \times 1 \times 5 = 10.$$

35. (d): Given Exp. $= \frac{4^7}{16^4} \times \sqrt{16} = \frac{4^7}{(4^2)^4} \times 4 = \frac{4^8}{4^8} = 4^{(8-8)} = 4^0 = 1.$

36. (a): H.C.F. $= \frac{\text{H.C.F. of } 7, 14, 7}{\text{L.C.M. of } 90, 15, 10} = \frac{7}{90}.$

37. (d): Required time = L.C.M. of $\frac{91}{6}, \frac{65}{4}$ and $\frac{56}{3}$

$$= \frac{\text{L.C.M. of } 91, 65, 56}{\text{H.C.F. of } 6, 4, 3} = \frac{3640}{1} = 3640 \text{ sec.}$$

38. (d): Given Exp. $= \left[1 + \cfrac{1}{1 + \cfrac{1}{(4/3)}}\right] \div \frac{11}{7} = \left[1 + \cfrac{1}{\left(1 + \frac{3}{4}\right)}\right] \div \frac{11}{7}$

$$= \left[1 + \frac{1}{(7/4)}\right] \div \frac{11}{7} = \left(1 + \frac{4}{7}\right) \div \frac{11}{7}$$

$$= \left(\frac{11}{7} \div \frac{11}{7}\right) = 1.$$

39. (c) Given Exp. $= \frac{a^3 + b^3 + c^3 - 3abc}{a^2 + b^2 + c^2 - ab - bc - ca} = (a + b + c)$

$= (0.43 + 1.47 + 1.1) = 3.$

40. (b) $\frac{x}{2y} = \frac{3}{2} \Rightarrow \frac{x}{y} = 3.$

$\therefore \frac{2x + y}{x - 2y} = \frac{2\left(\frac{x}{y}\right) + 1}{\left(\frac{x}{y}\right) - 2} = \frac{2 \times 3 + 1}{3 - 2} = 7.$

41. (d): $\frac{1}{4}N = \frac{1}{6}Y \Rightarrow N = \frac{4}{6}Y = \frac{2}{3}Y.$ $\frac{5}{3}Y = \frac{600 \times 3}{5}$

Now, $N + Y = 600 \Rightarrow \frac{2}{3}Y + Y = 600 \Rightarrow Y = 360$

$\therefore N = (600 - 360) = 240$

Hence, $(Y - N) = (360 - 240) = 120.$

42. (a): Given Exp. $= \frac{a^2 + b^2 + c^2}{\left(\frac{a}{10}\right)^2 + \left(\frac{b}{10}\right)^2 + \left(\frac{c}{10}\right)^2} = \frac{(a^2 + b^2 + c^2) \times 100}{(a^2 + b^2 + c^2)} = 100.$

Latest Questions 581

43. (b): 1000 Cu cm weighs 1000 gms.
   i.e. 1000 gms is the weight of (1000×1000) Cu mm
   0.1 gm is the weight of $\left(\dfrac{1000 \times 1000}{1000} \times 0.1\right)$ Cu mm = 100 Cu mm.

44. (d): Let the capacity of the tank be x litres. Then
   $\dfrac{3}{4}x - 21 = \dfrac{2}{5}x \Rightarrow \dfrac{3x}{4} - \dfrac{2x}{5} = 21 \Rightarrow x = 60.$

45. (c): $T - S = G - T \Rightarrow G + S = 2T$
   $\therefore 2\% = 140 \Rightarrow T = 70.$

46. (d): Let the number of each type of notes be x. Then,
   $x + 5x + 10x = 480 \Rightarrow x = 30.$
   Total number of notes $= 30 + 30 + 30 = 90.$

47. (d): $a + b + c = 1.2 + 2.1 - 3.3 = 0$
   $\Rightarrow a^3 + b^3 + c^3 = 3abc \Rightarrow a^3 + b^3 + c^3 - 3abc = 0.$

48. (d): Take $y = 4$. Then, $3\dfrac{1}{x} \times 4\dfrac{2}{5} = 13\dfrac{3}{4}$
   $\therefore \dfrac{3x+1}{x} = \left(\dfrac{55}{4} \times \dfrac{5}{22}\right) \Rightarrow \dfrac{3x+1}{x} = \dfrac{25}{8}$
   $\Rightarrow 24x + 8 = 25x \Rightarrow x = 8$
   $\therefore x = 8, y = 4.$

49. (b): Given Exp. $= \dfrac{(\sqrt{31} - \sqrt{29})}{(\sqrt{31} + \sqrt{29})} \times \dfrac{(\sqrt{31} - \sqrt{29})}{(\sqrt{31} - \sqrt{29})}$
   $= \dfrac{(\sqrt{31} - \sqrt{29})^2}{(31 - 29)} = \dfrac{31 + 29 - 2\sqrt{31} \times \sqrt{29}}{2} = 30 - \sqrt{899}.$

50. (b): Given Exp. $= 1 - \dfrac{1}{(1+\sqrt{2})} \times \dfrac{(\sqrt{2}-1)}{(\sqrt{2}-1)} - \dfrac{1}{(\sqrt{2}-1)} \times \dfrac{(\sqrt{2}+1)}{(\sqrt{2}+1)}$
   $= 1 - (\sqrt{2}-1) - (\sqrt{2}+1) = 1 - 2\sqrt{2}.$

51. (c): $\sqrt{456976} = 676$
   $\therefore \sqrt{45.6976} = \dfrac{\sqrt{456976}}{\sqrt{10000}} = \dfrac{676}{100} = 6.76.$

52. (b): Given Exp. $= \dfrac{(3\sqrt{2})(\sqrt{6}+\sqrt{3})}{(\sqrt{6}+\sqrt{3})(\sqrt{6}-\sqrt{3})} - \dfrac{(4\sqrt{3})(\sqrt{6}+\sqrt{2})}{(\sqrt{6}-\sqrt{2})(\sqrt{6}+\sqrt{2})}$
   $\qquad - \dfrac{6}{(\sqrt{12}+\sqrt{8})} \times \dfrac{(\sqrt{12}-\sqrt{8})}{(\sqrt{12}-\sqrt{8})}$
   $= \sqrt{2}(\sqrt{6}+\sqrt{3}) - \sqrt{3}(\sqrt{6}+\sqrt{2}) - \dfrac{3}{2}(\sqrt{12}-\sqrt{8})$
   $= \sqrt{12} + \sqrt{6} - 3\sqrt{2} - \sqrt{6} - 3\sqrt{3} + 3\sqrt{2}$
   $= 2\sqrt{3} - 3\sqrt{3} = -\sqrt{3}.$

53. (b): $a + b = 2\sqrt{6}$ and $ab = (6 - 5) = 1$
   $\therefore 2a^2 - 5ab + 2b^2 = 2(a+b)^2 - 9ab = 2(2\sqrt{6})^2 - 9 \times 1 = (48 - 9) = 39$.

54. (c): Required reduction $= \left[\dfrac{r}{(100+r)} \times 100\right]\% = \left(\dfrac{25}{125} \times 100\right) = 20\%$.

55. (c): Let 95% of $x = 4598$
   Then, $x = \left(4598 \times \dfrac{100}{95}\right) = 4840$.

56. (d): Matriculates $= \dfrac{40}{100}x = \dfrac{2x}{5}$.

   Remaining $= \left(x - \dfrac{2x}{5}\right) = \dfrac{3x}{5}$

   Graduates $= \dfrac{50}{100} \times \dfrac{3x}{5} = \dfrac{3x}{10}$

   $\therefore \dfrac{2x}{5} + \dfrac{3x}{10} + 180 = x \Rightarrow x - \dfrac{7x}{10} = 180 \Rightarrow x = 600$.

   $\therefore$ Graduates $= \dfrac{3}{10} \times 600 = 180$.

57. (c): $n(A) = 40$, $n(B) = 50$, $n(A \cap B) = 10$
   $n(A \cup B) = n(A) + n(B) - n(A \cap B) = (40 + 50 - 10) = 80$
   $n(\text{not A and not B}) = n(A^C \cap B^C) = n(A \cup B)'$
   $= 100 - n(A \cup B) = (100 - 80) = 20$.

58. (c): $x \times \left(1 + \dfrac{5}{100}\right)^3 = 138915 \Rightarrow x \times \dfrac{21}{20} \times \dfrac{21}{20} \times \dfrac{21}{20} = 138915$

   $\therefore x = \left(\dfrac{138915 \times 20 \times 20 \times 20}{21 \times 21 \times 21}\right) = 120000$.

59. (b): $\dfrac{30}{100}x - \dfrac{25}{100}x = 15 \Rightarrow x = 300$.

60. (c): Males $= \left(\dfrac{5}{9} \times 4500\right) = 2500$, Females $= 2000$.

   Married males $= \dfrac{40}{100} \times 2500 = 1000$

   Married females $= 1000$

   $\therefore$ Percentage of married females $= \left(\dfrac{1000}{2000} \times 100\right) = 50\%$.

61. (d): Let the total sale be Rs. x.

   Commission $= \dfrac{5}{100} \times 10000 + \dfrac{4}{100} \times (x - 10000) = 100 + \dfrac{4x}{100}$

   $\therefore x - \left(100 + \dfrac{x}{25}\right) = 31100$ or $\dfrac{24x}{25} = 31200$

Latest Questions 583

$\therefore \quad x = \dfrac{31200 \times 25}{25} = 32500.$

62. (c): Required percentage $= \dfrac{10}{(100 + 10)} \times 1000 = 9\dfrac{1}{11}\%.$

63. (c): Milk $= \dfrac{90}{100} \times 40 = 36$ litres, water $= 4$ litre.

   Let x litres of water be added. Then

   $\dfrac{(x + 4)}{41 + x} \times 100 = 20 \Rightarrow \dfrac{x + 4}{40 + x} = \dfrac{1}{5}$

   $\therefore \ 5x + 20 = 40 + x \Rightarrow x = 5.$

64. (b): $z = \dfrac{x^2}{y}$.

   New value of $z = \dfrac{\left(\dfrac{110}{100}x\right)^2}{\left(\dfrac{110}{100}y\right)} = \dfrac{11}{100}\dfrac{x^2}{y} = \dfrac{11}{10}z$

   $\therefore$ Increase % $= \dfrac{\left(\dfrac{11}{10}z - z\right)}{z} \times 10 = 10\%.$

65. (d): $b + \dfrac{bx}{100} = a.$

66. (d): Failed in G.K. only $= (35 - 10) = 25$
   Failed in English only $= (25 - 10) = 15$
   Failed in both $= 10$
   Failed in one or 2 subjects $= (25 + 15 + 10) = 50$
   Number of examinees passed $= (100 - 50) = 50\%.$

67. (b): Let original price be Rs. x.

   New price $= \dfrac{125}{100} \times x = \dfrac{5x}{4}$

   Reduction on $\dfrac{5x}{4} = \left(\dfrac{5x}{4} - x\right) = \dfrac{x}{4}$

   Reduction on 100 $= \left(\dfrac{x}{4} \times \dfrac{4}{5x} \times 100\right) = 20\%$

68. (c): Alcohol in 9 gms $= \left(\dfrac{50}{100} \times 9\right) = 4.5$ gms.

   Let x gm of water be added. Then,

   $\dfrac{4.5}{0 + x} \times 100 = 30 \Rightarrow 270 + 30x = 450 \Rightarrow x = 6$ gms.

69. (c): Let C.P. be Rs. 100. Then, M.P. = Rs. 120
    Also, S.P. = Rs. 108
    Discount on 120 = Rs. (120 − 108) = Rs. 12

    Discount on 100 = $\left(\dfrac{12}{120} \times 100\right)$ = 10%.

70. (c):   C.P. = $\left(\dfrac{100}{120} \times 30\right)$ = 25,   S.P. = 90% of 30 = Rs. 27

    Gain % = $\left(\dfrac{2}{25} \times 100\right)$ = 8%.

71. (b): Let M.P. = x Then,
    $\dfrac{90}{100}x + \dfrac{8}{100} \times \dfrac{90x}{100} = 680.40 \Rightarrow x = 700$.

72. (d): Let S.P. be Rs. x
    Then, C.P. = $(x - 240)$
    $\therefore \dfrac{240}{(x-240)} \times 100 = 20 \Rightarrow x - 240 = 1200 \Rightarrow x = 1440$.

73. (c): S.P. = Rs. 22600, gain = 13%
    C.P. = $\left(\dfrac{100}{113} \times 22600\right)$ = 20000.
    $\therefore$ Gain = Rs. (22600 − 20000) = Rs. 2600.

74. (c): Suppose he purchased 24 locks (l.c.m. of 8 and 12).
    C.P. = $\left(\dfrac{34}{8} \times 24\right)$ = 102,   S.P. = $\left(\dfrac{57}{12} \times 24\right)$ = 114.
    To gain Rs. 12, locks purchased = 24
    To gain Rs. 900, locks purchased = $\left(\dfrac{24}{12} \times 900\right)$ = 1800.

75. (c): Let C.P. be Rs. x Then,
    $\dfrac{115}{100}x = \dfrac{69}{100} \times 125 \Rightarrow x = 75$.

76. (b): Let C.P. be Rs. x. Then,
    $(x - 895) = (955 - x) \Rightarrow x = 925$
    $\therefore$ Loss = Gain = (925 − 895) = 30.

77. (c): Let cost of almond per kg be Rs. x and cost of walnuts per kg be Rs. y. Then, $2x = 8y \Rightarrow y = \dfrac{x}{4}$
    $\therefore 5x + 16y = 1080 \Rightarrow 5x + 16 \times \dfrac{x}{4} = 1080 \Rightarrow x = 120$.

78. (c): $\dfrac{125}{100}$ of $\dfrac{120}{100}$ of $\dfrac{118}{100}x = 30.09$

Latest Questions 585

$$\therefore x = \left(\frac{30.09 \times 100 \times 100 \times 100}{125 \times 120 \times 118}\right) = \left(\frac{3009 \times 4}{6 \times 118}\right) = 17.$$

79. (*a*): Let the original price be Rs. 100
Price after dealer's discount = Rs. 85
$$\text{S.P.} = \frac{120}{100} \times 85 = 102$$
$\therefore$ Profit = 2% on original price.

80. (*d*): Let C.P. be Rs. x. Then,
$$\frac{115}{100}x - \frac{110}{100}x = 10 \Rightarrow 5x = 100 \times 10 \Rightarrow x = 200.$$

81. (*c*): Let the marked price be Rs. x. Then,
$$\frac{85}{100}x = 102 \Rightarrow x = \left(\frac{102 \times 100}{85}\right) = 120.$$

82. (*b*): Let C.P. be Rs. x.
Two losses are $(x - 400)$ and $(x - 380)$
Increase in loss $(x - 380) - (x - 400) = 20$
$$\frac{20}{x - 400} \times 100 = 20 \Rightarrow x - 400 = 100 \Rightarrow x = 500.$$

83. (*d*): $\text{C.P.} = \left(\frac{100}{75} \times 455000\right) = \frac{1820000}{3}$

$\text{Loss} = \left(\frac{1820000}{3} - 455000\right) = \frac{455000}{3}.$

84. (*b*): Let C.P. be Rs. 100. Then, M.P. = Rs. 120.
$$\text{S.P.} = \frac{95}{100} \text{ of Rs. } 120 = \text{Rs. } 114$$
$\therefore$ Profit = 14%.

85. (*b*): Let the cost of the machine be x.
$$\frac{110}{100}x = \frac{90}{100} \times 27500 \Rightarrow x = 22500.$$

86. (*b*): Let the cost of the toy be Rs. x
$$\frac{3}{4}(x - 60) = (81 - x) \Rightarrow 324 - 4x = 3x - 180 \Rightarrow x = 72.$$

87. (*c*): Let the C.P. be Rs. 100 and marked price be $(100 + x)$.
$$\text{S.P.} = \frac{\left(100 - \frac{25}{4}\right)}{100} \text{ of } \frac{80}{100} \times (100 + x)$$
$$= \frac{15}{16} \text{ of } \frac{4}{5}(100 + x) = \frac{3}{4}(100 + x)$$
$\therefore \frac{3}{4}(100 + x) = 120 \Rightarrow x = 60.$

88. (b): Let C.P. of each kg be Re 1. Then, C.P. = Rs. 120
   Suppose he sells x kg at 25% gain. Then,
   $$\frac{125}{100}x + \frac{110}{100}(120 - x) = \frac{115}{100} \times 120$$
   $\Rightarrow$ $125x + 13200 - 110x = 13800 \Rightarrow x = 40.$

89. (a): Retailer's value $= \left(\frac{100}{130} \times 325\right) = 250$
   Wholesaler's value $= \left(\frac{100}{125} \times 250\right) = 200.$

90. (c): S.P. $= \left(\frac{110}{100} \times 95\right) = \left(\frac{209}{2}\right)$, commission = 5%
   $\therefore$ M.P. $= \left(\frac{110}{95} \times \frac{209}{2}\right) = 110.$

91. (d): Let these coins be x, $2x$ and $3x$. Then,
   $$\frac{25}{100}x + \frac{10}{100} \times 2x + \frac{5}{100} \times 3x \Rightarrow 60x = 30 \times 100 \Rightarrow x = 50$$
   Number of 5-p coins = $3x$ = 150.

92. (d): $\frac{x+y}{x-y} = \frac{4}{1} \Rightarrow x + y = 4x - 4y \Rightarrow 3x = 5y \Rightarrow \frac{x}{y} = \frac{5}{3}.$
   $\therefore \frac{x^2 + y^2}{x^2 - y^2} = \frac{\frac{x^2}{y^2} + 1}{\frac{x^2}{y^2} - 1} = \frac{\left(\frac{x}{y}\right)^2 + 1}{\left(\frac{x}{y}\right)^2 - 1} = \frac{34}{16} = \frac{17}{8}.$

93. (d): $\frac{9^{3.04}}{9^{2.04}} = 9^{3.04 - 2.04} = 9^1 = \frac{9}{1}.$

94. (b): Let $\frac{a}{b} = \frac{b}{c} = k.$ Then, $b = ck$ and $a = bk = ck^2$
   $\therefore \frac{a^4}{b^4} = \frac{c^4 k^8}{c^4 k^4} = k^4$ and $\frac{a^2}{c^2} = \frac{c^2 k^4}{c^2} = k^4.$
   Hence, $\frac{a^4}{b^4} = \frac{a^2}{c^2}.$

95. (c): Given, $\frac{x}{y} = \frac{3}{4}$
   $\therefore \frac{2x + 3y}{3y - 2x} = \frac{2\left(\frac{x}{y}\right) + 3}{3 - 2\left(\frac{x}{y}\right)} = \frac{2 \times \frac{3}{4} + 3}{3 - 2 \times \frac{3}{4}} = \frac{18}{6} = \frac{3}{1}.$

96. (a): A $= \frac{1}{2}$(B + C) $\Rightarrow$ B + C = 2A $\Rightarrow$ A + B + C = 3A

Latest Questions

$B = \frac{1}{4}(A + C) \Rightarrow 4B = A + C \Rightarrow A + B + C = 5B$

∴ $3A = 56250$ and $5B = 56250 \Rightarrow A = 18750$ and $B = 11250$

∴ $A - B = (18750 - 11250) = 7500$.

97. (b): $\frac{17.5}{40.25} = \frac{x}{28.75} \Rightarrow x = \frac{17.5 \times 28.75}{40.25} = 12.5$ m.

98. (b): $b : c = 9 : 16$ and $a : c = 1 : 4$

 ∴ $\frac{a}{b} = \frac{a}{c} \times \frac{c}{b} = \frac{1}{4} \times \frac{16}{9} = \frac{4}{9}$.

 ∴ $a : b = 4 : 9$ and $b : c = 9 : 16 \Rightarrow a : b : c = 4 : 9 : 16$.

 ∴ Second number $= \left(\frac{9}{29} \times 174\right) = 54$.

99. (c): Let cost of each mango be x paise and that of each orange be y paise then
 $5x + 4y = 3x + 7y \Rightarrow 2x = 3y \Rightarrow x : y = 3 : 2$.

100. (b): $\frac{35}{100} x = \frac{25}{100} y \Rightarrow \frac{x}{y} = \frac{25}{35} = \frac{5}{7} \Rightarrow x : y = 5 : 7$.

101. (b): Let their last years salaries be $3x$ and $4x$.

 This year's salaries are $\frac{5}{4} \times 3x$ and $\frac{3}{2} \times 4x$ i.e. $\frac{15x}{4}$ and $6x$

 ∴ $\frac{15x}{4} + 6x = 4160 \Rightarrow 39x = 16640 \Rightarrow 3x = 1280$

 ∴ A's salary now $= \frac{5}{4} \times 3x = \frac{5}{4} \times 1280 = 1600$.

102. (a): Let their incomes be $5x$ and $3x$.

 Let their expenses by $8y$, $5y$ and $2y$.

 Then, $2y = 2000 \Rightarrow y = 1000$.

 Also, $3x - 5y = 700 \Rightarrow 3x = 5700 \Rightarrow x = 1900$

 ∴ A's saving $= (5x - 8y) = (5 \times 1900 - 8 \times 1000) = 1500$.

103. (b): $x \times 50 = \frac{7}{3} \times 21 \Rightarrow x = \frac{49}{50}$.

104. (d): More women, less days (indirect)
 More kg, more days (direct)
 women   28 : 8
   kg   180 : 3730   ∴ 5 : x

 ∴ $x = \left(\frac{8 \times 3780 \times 5}{28 \times 180}\right) = 30$.

105. (b): Less men, more days (indirect)
 Less length, less days (direct)
 More working hrs. less days (indirect)
  Men   30 : 40
  Length   300 : 200   ∴ 12 : x

Hrs./day   8 : 6

$$\therefore \quad x = \left(\frac{40 \times 200 \times 6 \times 12}{30 \times 300 \times 8}\right) = 8.$$

106. (a): More work, more persons (direct)
More days, less persons (indirect)

Work $\left.\begin{array}{c}\frac{3}{5} : 1 \\ \text{Days} \quad 20 : 10\end{array}\right\} :: 12 : x$

$$\therefore \quad x = \frac{1 \times 10 \times 12}{\frac{3}{5} \times 20} = 10.$$

107. (c): After 15 days there was ration for 2000 people for 39 days. Suppose x more came
More people, less days

$$\frac{2000}{2000 + x} = \frac{20}{39} \Rightarrow 78000 = 40000 + 20x \Rightarrow x = 1900.$$

108. (c): After 12 days there was ration for 560 soldiers for 8 days.
Remaining persons - (560 – 112) = 448.
Less soldiers, more days

$$\frac{560}{448} = \frac{x}{8} \Rightarrow x = \frac{560 \times 8}{448} = 10.$$

109. (c): 10 men can complete the job in 14 days. Less days, more men

$$\frac{14}{5} = \frac{x}{10} \Rightarrow x = \frac{14 \times 10}{5} = 28.$$

110. (b): Remaining work $= \frac{3}{4}$

Remaining days $= (100 – 45) = 55$

Let x more men may be employed.
More work, more men (direct)
More days, less men (indirect)

Work $\left.\begin{array}{c}\frac{1}{4} : \frac{3}{4} \\ \text{Days} \quad 55 : 45\end{array}\right\} :: 110 : (110 + x)$

$$110 + x = \frac{3}{4} \times 45 \times 110 \times \frac{4}{1} \times \frac{1}{55} = 270.$$

$\therefore \quad x = 160.$

111. (a) More work, more men (direct)

$$\frac{1}{1} : 1 = 16 : 16 + x \Rightarrow \frac{16}{16 + x} = \frac{1}{4}$$

$\therefore \quad 16 + x = 64 \Rightarrow x = 48.$

Latest Questions

112. (b): (A + B + C)'s 8 days' work = $\left(\dfrac{1}{20} \times 8\right) = \dfrac{2}{5}$.

Remaining work = $\left(1 - \dfrac{2}{5}\right) = \dfrac{3}{5}$.

$\dfrac{3}{5}$ work is done by (B + C) in 20 days

Whole work will be done by (B + C) in $\left(20 \times \dfrac{5}{3}\right) = \dfrac{100}{3}$ days.

∴ (B + C)'s 1 day's work = $\dfrac{3}{100}$

∴ A's 1 day's work = $\dfrac{1}{20} - \dfrac{3}{100} = \dfrac{2}{100} = \dfrac{1}{50}$

Hence, A can finish the whole work in 50 days.

113. (c): (A + B + C)'s 4 day's work = $\left(\dfrac{1}{10} \times 4\right) = \dfrac{2}{5}$

Remaining work = $\left(1 - \dfrac{2}{5}\right) = \dfrac{3}{5}$.

$\dfrac{3}{5}$ work is done by (B + C) in 10 days

Whole work can be done by (B + C) in $\left(\dfrac{10 \times 5}{3}\right)$ days.

∴ (B + C)'s 1 day's work = $\dfrac{3}{50}$

A's 1 day's work = $\left(\dfrac{1}{10} - \dfrac{3}{50}\right) = \dfrac{1}{25}$

∴ A alone can finish the work in 25 days.

114. (c): Suppose they leave after x days

Work done in x days = $\dfrac{x}{30}$.

Remaining work = $\left(1 - \dfrac{x}{30}\right) = \left(\dfrac{30 - x}{30}\right)$

Remaining days = $(35 - x)$

15 men's 1 day's work = $\left(\dfrac{1}{20 \times 30} \times 15\right) = \dfrac{1}{40}$

∴ $\dfrac{1}{40}(35 - x) = \dfrac{30 - x}{30}$ ⇒ $1050 - 30x = 1200 - 40x$ ⇒ $x = 15$.

115. (d): 1 man's 1 day's work = $\dfrac{1}{3}$, 1 woman's 1 day's work = $\dfrac{1}{4}$,

1 boy's 1 day's work = $\dfrac{1}{12}$.

Let x boys must be there. Then

$$\frac{1}{3} + \frac{1}{4} + \frac{x}{12} = 1 \Rightarrow x = 5.$$

116. (b): Let 1 man's 1 day work $= x$ and 1 boy's 1 day's work $= y$. Then, $2x + 3y = \frac{1}{8}$, $3x + 2y = \frac{1}{7}$.

Solving, we get : $x = \frac{1}{28}$ and $y = \frac{1}{56}$

$\therefore \quad 5x + 4y = \frac{5}{28} + \frac{4}{56} = \frac{14}{56} = \frac{1}{4}.$

So, 5 men and 4 boys can finish the work in 4 days.

117. (c): $(A + B)$'s 1 day's work $= \frac{1}{8}$.

$(B + C)$'s 1 day's work $= \frac{1}{12}$.

$(A + C)$'s 1 day's work $= \frac{1}{x}$.

$\therefore \quad 2(A + B + C)$'s 1 day's work $= \left(\frac{1}{8} + \frac{1}{12} + \frac{1}{x}\right)$

$\therefore \quad \frac{1}{2}\left(\frac{5}{24} + \frac{1}{x}\right) = \frac{1}{6} \Rightarrow \frac{5}{24} + \frac{1}{x} = \frac{1}{3}$ or $\frac{1}{x} = \frac{1}{3} - \frac{5}{24} = \frac{1}{8} \Rightarrow x = 8.$

118. (d): Suppose, I finish a work now in x days.

With double efficiency, time taken $= \frac{x}{2}$ days.

$\therefore \quad \frac{x}{2} = 12 \Rightarrow x = 24.$

With one third efficiency time taken $= 3x$ days

$= 3 \times 24$ days $= 72$ days.

119. (d): Ratio of rates of walking = inverse ratio of time taken.

$\therefore \quad \frac{2}{3} = \frac{36}{x} \Rightarrow 2x = 108 \Rightarrow x = 54$ min.

120. (a): Let the distance be x km.

$\frac{x}{3} - \frac{x}{4} = \frac{30}{60} \Rightarrow \frac{x}{12} = \frac{1}{2} \Rightarrow x = 6$ km.

121. (a): Distance = (Time × speed) = (330 × 10) m = $\frac{330 \times 10}{1000}$ km = 3.3 km.

122. (b): New speed $= \frac{6}{7}$ of the usual speed.

New time taken $= \frac{7}{6}$ of the usual time

$\left(\frac{7}{6}\text{ of usual time}\right) - (\text{Usual time}) = 12$ min.

Latest Questions

∴ $\frac{1}{6}$ of usual time = 12 min. or usual time = 72 min.

123. (a): A : B = 2 : 1, B : C = 3 : 1 ⇒ A : B : C = 6 : 3 : 1

Ratio of time taken = $\frac{1}{6} : \frac{1}{3} : 1 = 1 : 2 : 6$

If C takes 6 min, A takes 1 min.

If C takes 42 min, A takes = $\left(\frac{1}{6} \times 42\right)$ = 7 min.

124. (c):   Distance = 300 km.

Time required = $\left(\frac{4}{5} \times 5\right)$ = 4 hours.

Speed = $\left(\frac{300}{4}\right)$ = 75 km/hr.

125. (a): Suppose they walked x km. Then,

$\frac{x}{3} - \frac{x}{3.75} = \frac{30}{60} \Rightarrow \frac{0.75\,x}{3 \times 3.75} = \frac{1}{2}$

∴ $x = \frac{3 \times 3.75}{1.5}$ = 7.5 km.

126. (b): Distance covered in 7 revolutions = $\left(7 \times 2 \times \frac{22}{7} \times \frac{15}{2}\right)$ m = 330 m.

Distance covered in 9 sec. = 330 m.

Distance covered in 1 hour = $\left(\frac{330}{9} \times \frac{60 \times 60}{1000}\right)$ m = 132 km.

127. (c): Suppose they cross after x hours.

Distance covered by Y in $(x - 1)$ hours = Distance covered by X in x hours.

$70(x - 1) = 50 x \Rightarrow x = 3\frac{1}{2}$.

128. (b): $\frac{x}{3} + \frac{x}{4} + \frac{x}{5} = \frac{47}{60} \Rightarrow 20x + 15x + 12x = 47 \Rightarrow x = 1$.

∴ Total distance = (1 + 1 + 1) km = 3 km.

129. (a): Let the distance between A and B be x km.

Speed = $\frac{x}{(45/60)} = \frac{4x}{3}$ km/hr.

New speed = $\left(\frac{4x}{3} - 5\right) = \left(\frac{4x - 15}{3}\right)$ km/hr.

∴ $\frac{48}{60} \times \frac{(4x - 15)}{3} = x \Rightarrow 16x - 60 = 15x \Rightarrow x = 60$.

130. (d): 1500 m/min. = $\left(\frac{1500}{60}\right)$ m/sec. = 25 m/sec.

90 km/hr $= \left(90 \times \dfrac{5}{18}\right)$ m/sec. $= 25$ m/sec.

So, all the given speeds are equal.

131. (c): Speed of the train $= \left(81 \times \dfrac{5}{18}\right)$ m/sec. $= \dfrac{45}{2}$ m/sec.

Let the length of the train be x metres.

$\dfrac{x+200}{40} = \dfrac{45}{2} \Rightarrow 2x + 400 = 1800 \Rightarrow x = 700$ m.

132. (b): Speed of the train $= \left(\dfrac{180}{6}\right)$ m/sec. $= 30$ m/sec.

$= \left(30 \times \dfrac{18}{5}\right)$ km/hr $= 108$ km/ph.

133. (c): Relative speed $= (40 - 20) = 20$ km/hr $= \left(20 \times \dfrac{5}{18}\right)$ m/sec.

Length of the train $= \left(20 \times \dfrac{5}{18} \times 5\right)$ m $= 27\dfrac{7}{9}$ m.

134. (d): Let the length of train be x metres. Then

$\dfrac{x}{10} = \dfrac{50+x}{14} \Rightarrow 14x = 500 + 10x \Rightarrow x = 125$.

$\therefore$ Speed $= \left(\dfrac{125}{10}\right)$ m/sec. $= \left(\dfrac{125}{10} \times \dfrac{18}{5}\right)$ km/hr $= 45$ km/hr.

135. (c): Let the length of the train be x metres. Then,

$\dfrac{96+x}{12} = \dfrac{141+x}{15} \Rightarrow 15(96+x) = 12(141+x) \Rightarrow x = 84$ m.

136. (d): Original rate $= \left(\dfrac{864 \times 100}{2400 \times 4}\right) = 9\%$

New rate $= 10\%$

Now, S.I. $= \left(2400 \times 10 \times \dfrac{4}{100}\right) = 960$.

$\therefore$ Amount $= $ Rs. $(2400 + 960) = $ Rs. 3360.

137. (c): Let the sum be x and rate $= R\%$. Then

$\dfrac{x \times (R+2) \times 5}{100} - \dfrac{x \times R \times 5}{100} = 72 \Rightarrow x = 1200$.

138. (a): Rate $= \left(\dfrac{600}{2000} \times \dfrac{100}{5}\right) = 6\%$. New rate $= 9\%$

S.I. $= \left(\dfrac{2000 \times 9 \times 5}{100}\right) = 900$.

$\therefore$ Amount $= $ Rs. $(200 + 900) = 2900$.

139. (b): Let the sum be x. Then, S.I. $= \dfrac{3x}{8}$.

$\therefore$ Rate $= \left(\dfrac{100 \times \dfrac{3x}{8}}{x \times \dfrac{25}{4}}\right) = \dfrac{300x}{8} \times \dfrac{4}{25x} = 6\%$

140. (b): Let the first investment be Rs. x. Then,

$\dfrac{x \times 9 \times 1}{100} + \dfrac{(100000 - x) \times 11 \times 1}{100} = 100000 \times \dfrac{39}{4} \times \dfrac{1}{100}$

$\Rightarrow \dfrac{9x}{100} + \dfrac{1100000 - 11x}{100} = \dfrac{975000}{100}$

$\Rightarrow 1100000 - 2x = 975000 \Rightarrow x = 62500$

$\therefore$ The two amounts are Rs. 62500 and Rs. 37500.

141. (d): $x\left(1 + \dfrac{10}{100}\right)^2 - x = 2100 \Rightarrow x\left[\dfrac{121}{100} - 1\right] = 2100$.

$\therefore x = \left(\dfrac{2100 \times 100}{21}\right) = 10000$.

$\therefore$ S.I. $= $ Rs. $\left(\dfrac{10000 \times 2 \times 10}{100}\right) = $ Rs. 2000.

142. (b): Let original length $= x$ and breadth $= y$.
Then area $= xy$.
New area $= \left(\dfrac{110}{100}x \times \dfrac{90}{100}y\right) = \dfrac{99}{100}xy$

Decrease in area $= \left(xy - \dfrac{99xy}{100}\right) = \dfrac{xy}{100}$

Decrease % $= \left(\dfrac{xy}{100} \times \dfrac{1}{xy} \times 100\right) = 1\%$.

143. (a): Area to be papered
$= 2(6 + 5) \times 4 - [(2.5 \times 1.2) + (1 \times 1)]$ sq.m.
$= (88 - 4) = 84$ m².

144. (d): Let the length of the plot be x metres.

Breadth $= \dfrac{2}{5}x$

$\therefore x \times \dfrac{2}{5}x = 1000 \Rightarrow x^2 = \left(1000 \times \dfrac{5}{2}\right) = 2500 \Rightarrow x = 50$.

$\therefore$ Length $= 50$ m.

145. (c): Number of tiles $= \left(\dfrac{60 \times 40}{0.4 \times 0.4}\right) = 15000$

Total cost $= $ Rs. $(15000 \times 5) = $ Rs. 75000.

146. (*b*): Area of the paper = $2(6 + 5) \times 4 = 88$ m^2.

Length of the paper = $\dfrac{88}{(1/2)}$ m = 176 m.

147. (*c*): Side of square field = $\sqrt{484}$ = 22 cm.

∴ Perimeter = $22 \times 4 = 88$ cm.

$2 \times \dfrac{22}{7} \times R = 88 \Rightarrow R = \left(88 \times \dfrac{7}{44}\right)$ = 14 cm.

Area = $\left(\dfrac{22}{7} \times 14 \times 14\right)$ cm^2 = 616 cm^2.

148. (*c*): Let their diameters be 3R and R and heights be H and 3H. Then,

ratio of their volumes = $\dfrac{\pi \times (3R)^2 \times H}{\pi \times R^2 \times (3H)} = \dfrac{3}{1}$.

149. (*b*): Ratio of their volumes

= $\dfrac{1}{3}\pi r^2 \times r : \pi r^2 \times r : \dfrac{2}{3}\pi r^3$ = 1 : 3 : 2.

150. (*b*): Side of each cube = 5 cm.

∴ Number of blocks = $\left(\dfrac{5 \times 10 \times 20}{5 \times 5 \times 5}\right)$ = 8.

S. CHAND'S BOOKS FOR DIFFERENT COMPETITIVE EXAMINATIONS

S. CHAND'S
GENERAL ENGLISH
FOR COMPETITIONS
A. N. Kapoor

This book is meant to equip students preparing for various competitive examinations. The aim of the book is to help students to master the correct use of English words and phrases on one hand and to develop in him/her a sense of belongingness for the English language.

Code : 06 093   3rd Edn. Rev. 2005   ISBN:-81-219-1762-X

S. CHAND'S CONCISE GENERAL KNOWLEDGE WITH CURRENT AFFAIRS
Prakash & Suman Kant

In this book, the facts are given in a manner which helps in answering objective type questions of various competitive examinations. The students will find ready-made material for questions. Details are given in a concise manner so that the students remember facts without labour and will recall without effort. The chapters have been arranged in a manner so that each chapter has a thematic link with the previous and the following chapter. The book will prove immensely useful for the students appearing in various competitive examinations.

Code : 06 110   4th Rev. Edn. 2005   ISBN:81-219-2186-4

MANIRAM AGGARWAL'S
GENERAL KNOWLEDGE DIGEST
AND GENERAL STUDIES
K. Mohan

This book is for the candidates who are appearing for Union and State Public Service Commissions' Competitive Examinations, L.I.C., G.I.C., A.A.0's, RBI Grade A and B, Bank POS, CDS/NDA/OTA, Delhi Police S.I., Income Tax, Central Excise Inspectors, SSC's Asstt. Grade, L.D.C., Accounts & Auditors, M. BA, Hotel Management, etc., Entrance Examinations. The book is no doubt an appropriate and relevant guide.

Code : 06 001   67th Edn. 2004   ISBN:81-219-0798-5

वस्तुनिष्ठ अंकगणित
(पूर्ण हल सहित)
आर.एस. अग्रवाल

प्रस्तुत पुस्तक प्रतियोगी परीक्षाओं के लिए अंकगणित पर आधारित वस्तुनिष्ठ प्रश्नों से निहित है। सभी प्रश्नों को संक्षिप्त विधि से हल किया गया है। विभिन्न परीक्षाओं में पूछे गए प्रश्नों का विवरण परीक्षार्थियों से पूछ कर उनकी स्मृति के आधार पर दिया गया है। बाजार में उपलब्ध विभिन्न मैगजीनों के प्रश्न भी दिए गए हैं।

Code : 06 033   4th Edn. Rep. 2004   ISBN : 81-219-0426-9

YOUR INTERVIEW
K.L. Kumar

The book will enable the young job seekers to discover his strengths and weaknessesand inspirehimto-prepare and face the interview board with courage and confidence. Sample interviews, caricatures and quickreview inset sheets have increased the utility of the book. It is a valuable book for the young job seekers.

Code : 06 091   2nd Rev. Edn. 2005   ISBN:81-219-1618-6

ARITHMETIC
SUBJECTIVE & OBJECTIVE FOR COMPETITIVE EXAMINATIONS
R.S. Aggarwal

This book is an asset to those who plan to appear in a competitive examination conducted by Banks, LIC, GIC, Excise & Income Tax, Railways, U.P.S.C and other departments for Clerical Grade, Assistant Grade, A.A.O., Inspectors, Probationary Officers, N.D.A. C.D.S., MBA, C.A.T. and other executive posts. The book carries both subjective and objective type of questions.

Code : 14 101   5th Rev. Edn. 2004   ISBN:81-219-0742-X

A MODERN APPROACH TO
VERBAL AND
NON-VERBAL REASONING
R.S. Aggarwal

This book contains all types of questions asked in various competitive examinations; fully solved examples with explanatory answers; and a huge collection of practisable questions. It is a unique book of Reasoning which is meant for competitive examinations like Bank Clerical, Bank P.O., LIC., GIC, M.B.A., Assistant Grade, Excise and Income Tax, IAS, IFS, AAO, Railways, Hotel Management and others. Question papers and references given on memory basis will lead the students to success.

Code : 06 055   3rd Rev. Edn. 2004   ISBN:81-219-0551-6

QUICK ARITHMETIC
Ashish Aggarwal

This book explains the Short-cut methods of solving the problems for L.I.C. & G.I.C. (AAO), Assistant Grade, Auditors, S.O., B.B.A., M.B.A., M.C.A., N.D.A., N.A., C.D.S., Bank Competitions and other Competitive Examinations.

Code : 14 487   1st Edn. Rep. 2004   ISBN:81-219-2387-5

A MODERN APPROACH TO
VERBAL REASONING
R.S. Aggarwal

The book is unique for its coverage of all types of questions asked including those in logical deduction and all the study material available around. It contains a huge collection of practisable questions with fully solved examples and explanatory answers. This book is meant for competitive examinations like Bank Clerical, Bank P.O., LIC, GIC, M.B.A., Assistant Grade, Excise & Income Tax, IAS, IFS, AAO, Railways and others. It is assured that the book will do its deal in making students the masters in this competitive field.

Code : 06 053   2nd Edn. Rep. 2004   ISBN:81-219-0552-4

A MODERN APPROACH TO
NON-VERBAL REASONING
R.S. Aggarwal

The requirements of the candidates have been a major factor kept in mind during the compilation of this book and with this end in view all types of solved questions with a huge collection of practisable questions have been provided. This book also consists of well illustrated examples and fully solved exercises with explanatory answers and clues. This book is highly meant for the competitive examinations like Bank Clerical, Bank P.O., SBI P.O., R.B.I., L.I.C., G.I.C., A.A.O., M.B.A., I.A.S., I.F.S., Railways, V.D.C., Sub-inspectors of Police, Asstt. Grade, Income Tax and Central Excise, etc.

Code : 06 054 **2nd Edn. Rev 2004** **ISBN:81-219-0553-2**

A MODERN APPROACH TO
LOGICAL REASONING
R.S. Aggarwal & Vikas Aggarwal

Nowadays success in every single competitive examinations like Bank Clerical, bank PO, LIC, GIC, MBA, Assistant Grade, Excise & Income Tax, IAS, IFS, AAO, Railway Hotel management and others depend much on the candidate's performance in the Reasoning Paper. So much comprehensive and intelligent approach to it is the need of the day. This book serves the purpose.

Code : 06 104 **2nd Rev. Edn. 2005** **ISBN:81-219-1905-3**

MATHEMATICS FOR C.D.S.
(Fully Solved)
R.S. Aggarwal

Salient features of this book are: (a) Solutions by short-cut methods (b) Large number of challenging problems, fully solved (c) whole lot of solved examples to clarity the facts (d) Latest questions included on memory basis. This book on mathematics is really an asset to those who plan to appear in competitive examination for C.D.S.

Code : 06 066 **3rd Rev. Edn. 2005** **ISBN:81-219-1019-6**

MATHEMATICS FOR M.B.A.
(Fully Solved)
R.S. Aggarwal

This book is an efficient Guide for the candidates preparing for the M.B.A. entrance examination. The book contains a huge accumulation of objective type questions fully solved by short-cut methods and it is hoped that the subject matter will lead candidates to success.

Code : 06 056 **Rev. Edn. 2005** **ISBN:81-219-0845-0**

MATHEMATICS FOR N.D.A. & N.A.
(Fully Solved) (According to New Syllabus)
R.S. Aggarwal

This book provides a comprehensive study of all topics included in N.D.A. syllabus. It contains a large number of challenging problems with solutions; a lot of solved examples to clarify the facts; and latest questions included on memory basis. The subject matter of this book is according to the needs of the students and it is hoped that it will creat a confidence among students to successfully clear N.D.A. examination.

Code : 06 065 **6th Rev. Edn. 2004** **ISBN:81-219-1018-8**

QUANTITATIVE APTITUDE
(Fully Solved)
R.S. Aggarwal

This revised edition of the book will be an asset to the candidates appearing for Bank P.O., Insurance A.A.O., Assistant Grade; Excise & Income Tax Inspectors; C.B.I. Sub-Inspectors; Teachers' Exam.; C. D. S; Railways; Hotel Management; M.B.A. and all other competitive examinations. It contains a huge accumulation of objective type questions with their solutions by short cut methods. Latest questions asked in various examinations have been added. It is hoped that the book will help the students to get through their competitive exams in flying colours.

Code : 06 008   6th Rev. Edn. 2005   ISBN:81-219-0632-6

MATHEMATICS FOR M.C.A.
R.S. Aggarwal & Deepak Aggarwal

The salient features of the book are: (i) Strictly according to the syllabi prescribed by various universities for M.C.A. entrance examinations (ii) Separate exercises for objective and descriptive type questions, fully solved (iii) previous year's questions included. The book is expected to prove a sure shot to success in Mathematics for all aspiring candidates for M.C.A. entrance examination.

Code : 06 084   2nd Edn. Rev. 2004   ISBN:81-219-1482-5

प्रतियोगी परीक्षाओं के लिए
अंकगणित (वस्तुनिष्ठ प्रश्नों सहित)
आर.एस. अग्रवाल

हिन्दी भाषी राज्यों की सिविल सेवा परीक्षा, रेलवे सेवा, जीवन बीमा निगम, साधारण बीमा निगम, पुलिस, आयकर, आबकारी, बैंकिंग सेवा, फारेस्ट रेंजर्स, क्लर्क्स ग्रेड परीक्षा, असिस्टेंट ग्रेड तथा दूसरी प्रतियोगी परीक्षाओं के लिए यह सर्वोत्तम पुस्तक है। सभी परीक्षाओं की आपूर्ति हेतु विषयात्मक तथा वस्तुनिष्ठ प्रश्नों का अपार भंडार इस पुस्तक में निहित हैं। विभिन्न परीक्षाओं में पूछे गए प्रश्नों के विवरण परीक्षार्थियां से पूछ कर उनकी स्मृति के आधार पर एवं विभिन्न प्रकार की बाजार में उपलब्ध मैगजीन आदि से दिए गए हैं।

Code : 14 200   5th Edn. Rev. 2004   ISBN:81-219-0835-3

A COMPREHENSIVE GUIDE FOR MCA ENTRANCE EXAMINATIONS
R.S. Aggarwal & Deepak Aggarwal

This is an unique book for MCA Entrance Examination. It contains two sections comprising of Mathematical Ability and General Aptitude. The book is strictly according to the syllabi prescribed to various universities for MCA entrance examination. Separate exercises for objective and descriptive type questions fully solved are given. Previous years questions are included.

Code : 06 071   2nd Edn. 2005   ISBN:81-219-1481-7

GENERAL SCIENCE FOR COMPETITIVE EXAMINATIONS
C.S. Bedi & R.S. Bedi

CONTENTS : ● Scope of Science ● The Universe ● The Solar System ● The Earth ● Earth Glossary ● Space Science ● Computer Science ● Physics ● Chemistry ● Organisation of life ● The World of Plants ● The Animal Kingdom ● Human Physiology ● Ecology ● Miscellaneous Information ● Science update ● Multiple Choice Questions

Code : 06 119   1st Edn. 2003   ISBN:81-219-2299-2

B.C.A./B.I.T. ENTRANCE GUIDE
Parkash & Suman Kant

CONTENTS : ● Sample Paper ● Review of the Question Baper ● Part-I Proficiency in English ● Practice Papers ● Part-II Reasoning & Intelligence Tests ● Practice Papers ● Part-III Quantitative Aptitude + Numerical Ability ● Practice Papers ● Part-IV General Awareness ● Practice Papers ● Computer Awareness ● Revesion Papers

Code : 06 108   2nd Edn. Rev. 2004   ISPN:81-219-2024-8

प्रतियोगी परीक्षाओं के लिए हिन्दी
(Hindi for Competitive Examinations)
शिवानंद नौटियाल

CONTENTS : ● हिन्दी भाषा का संक्षिप्त परिचय ● वर्ण विचार ● शब्द-विचार ● वाक्य विचार ● रचना विचार ● काव्य खण्ड ● परिशिष्ट

Code : 06 133   1st Edn. 2004   ISBN : 81-219-2422-7

प्रतियोगी परीक्षाओं के लिए गणित
(Mathematics for Competitive Examinations)
प्रमोद कुमार मिश्र

CONTENTS : ● संख्या-अभियोज्यता ● लघुतम समापवर्त्य एवं महत्तम समापवर्तक ● वर्ग एवम् वर्गमूल ● सरलीकरण ● घात, घातांक एवं करणी ● अनुपात एवं समानुपात ● औसत एवं उम्र सम्बन्धी प्रश्न ● प्रतिशत ● लाभ-हानि ● साझेदारी ● द्विआधारी अंकन पद्धति ● मिश्रण ● साधारण ब्याज ● चक्रवृद्धि ब्याज ● शेयर एवं लाभांश ● समय और काम ● समय और दूरी ● क्षेत्रफल एवम् परिमाप ● आयतन ● लघुगणक ● लेखाचित्र ● सारणीकरण ● सांख्यिकी ● संख्या-श्रेणी ● बीजगणित ● समुच्चय सिद्धांत ● त्रिकोणमिति ● ज्यामिति ● कलन ● प्रायिकता ● टेस्ट पेपर्स

Code : 06 126   1st Edn. 2004   ISBN : 81-219-2415-4

वस्तुनिष्ठ सामान्य हिन्दी
(Objective General Hindi)
आर.एस. अग्रवाल एवं मोनिका अग्रवाल

यह पुस्तक उ.प्र. सी.पी.एम.टी., बी.एड., प्रवेश परीक्षा, यू.जी.सी. परीक्षा, असिस्टेंट ग्रेड स्टेनोग्राफर, लेखा-परीक्षक, हिन्दी अनुवादक, पुलिस सब-इन्सपैक्टर, डिप्टी जेलर, सी.बी.आई., बैंक पी.ओ., ग्रामीण बैंक, जीवन बीमा निगम, पी.सी.एस., रेलवे भर्ती बोर्ड परीक्षा, तथा अन्य प्रतियोगी परीक्षाओं के लिए अति-उपयोगी है। इस पुस्तक में विभिन्न प्रतियोगी परीक्षाओं में पूछे गए प्रश्नों के आधार पर पूर्ण सामग्री समाहित की गई है। आशा है कि इस पुस्तक के अध्ययन से सभी प्रतियोगी परीक्षाओं में सामान्य हिन्दी में सफलता प्राप्त करने में प्रतियोगियों को कोई कठिनाई नहीं होगी।

Code : 06 095   Rev. Edn. 2004   ISBN : 81-219-1753-0

SENSATIONAL OFFER

Reach Your True Potential Through
Body Language : Your Success Mantra!
By Dr. Shalini Verma

Buy Today @ Rs 220/-

Free
Postage cost worth Rs. 35/-
Effective Saving worth Rs. 65/-

Grab your copy Now

Read This Book For

- Creating everlasting first Impression
- Building Instant rapport with anyone you meet
- Projecting yourself effectively in job interviews, group discussions & presentation making
- Making the best of Body Language in Sales negotiations & leadership skills
- Making yourself ultimate winner in your professional field

Pages : 192
Code : 01212
Price : Rs 250.00

Please send this page duly filled at below mentioned address as to avail the special discount offer of
Body Language : Your Success Mantra

Please send me one copy of the book "Body Language : Your Success Mantra"

Name_____ Age_____

Address_____

City _____ Pincode _____

Demand Draft Details

DD No. _____ Dated _____ For Rupees 220/-

Note :
* Please send all payments through DD in favour of S. Chand & Co. Ltd. Payable at New Delhi
* Delivery through Registered post / Courier will be free.
* Please send the order in original form, photocopies of this form will not be accepted.
* This Special Offer valid till 31st March 2006.

S. CHAND & COMPANY LTD.
7361, Ram Nagar, New Delhi- 110055
Ph : 23672080-81-82, Fax : 91-1123677446
Shop at : http://www.schandgroup.com; E-mail : schand@vsnl.com

Win Prizes !

Attention: Students

We request you, for your frank assessment, regarding some of the aspects of the book, given as under:

06 029   **Objective Arithmetic**
                R.S. Aggarwal   **Reprint 2007**

Please fill up the given space in neat capital letters. Add additional sheet(s) if the space provided is not sufficient, and if so required.

(i) What topic(s) of your syllabus that are important from your examination point of view are not covered in the book?

....
....
....

(ii) What are the chapters and/or topics, wherein the treatment of the subject-matter is not systematic or organised or updated?

....
....
....

(iii) Have you come across misprints/mistakes/factual inaccuracies in the book? Please specify the chapters, topics and the page numbers.

....
....
....
....

(iv) Name top three books on the same subject (in order of your preference - 1, 2, 3) that you have found/heard better than the present book? Please specify in terms of quality (in all aspects).

1 ....
....
2 ....
....
3 ....
....

(v) Further suggestions and comments for the improvement of the book:

....
....
....
....

Other Details:

(i) Who recommended you the book? (Please tick in the box near the option relevant to you.)
☐ Teacher ☐ Friends ☐ Bookseller

(ii) Name of the recommending teacher, his designation and address:
....
....
....

(iii) Name and address of the bookseller you purchased the book from:
....
....
....

(iv) Name and address of your institution (Please mention the University or Board, as the case may be)
....
....
....

(v) Your name and complete postal address:
....
....
....

(vi) Write your preferences of our publications (1, 2, 3) you would like to have ....
....

The best assessment will be awarded half-yearly. The award will be in the form of our publications, as decided by the Editorial Board, amounting to Rs. 300 (total).

Please mail the filled up coupon at your earliest to:
Editorial Department
S. CHAND & COMPANY LTD.,
Post Box No. 5733, Ram Nagar, New Delhi 110 055